THE OXFORD HISTORY OF ENGLISH

THE OXFORD HISTORY OF

ENGLISH

Edited by

Lynda Mugglestone

OXFORD

UNIVERSITY PRESS

OXFORD
UNIVERSITY PRESS

Great Clarendon Street, Oxford OX2 6DP

Oxford University Press is a department of the University of Oxford.
It furthers the University's objective of excellence in research, scholarship,
and education by publishing worldwide in

Oxford New York

Auckland Cape Town Dar es Salaam Hong Kong Karachi
Kuala Lumpur Madrid Melbourne Mexico City Nairobi
New Delhi Shanghai Taipei Toronto

With offices in

Argentina Austria Brazil Chile Czech Republic France Greece
Guatemala Hungary Italy Japan Poland Portugal Singapore
South Korea Switzerland Thailand Turkey Ukraine Vietnam

Oxford is a registered trade mark of Oxford University Press
in the UK and in certain other countries

Published in the United States
by Oxford University Press Inc., New York

British Library Cataloguing in Publication Data
Library of Congress Cataloging-in-Publication Data
The Oxford history of the English language/edited by Lynda Mugglestone.
P. cm.
Includes bibliographical references and index.
ISBN-13: 978-0-19-924931-2 (alk. paper)
ISBN-10: 0-19-924931-8 (alk. paper)
1. English language–History. I. Mugglestone, Lynda. II. Title: History of the English language.
PE1075. 097 2006
420. 9–dc22 2006013471

Data available

Typeset by SPI Publisher Services, Pondicherry, India
Printed in Great Britain
on acid-free paper by
Biddles Ltd., King's Lynn, Norfolk

ISBN 978-0-19-924931-2

3 5 7 9 10 8 6 4 2

CONTENTS

ILLUSTRATIONS

ABBREVIATIONS

CEEC   Corpus of Early English Correspondence

EDD   J. Wright (ed.), *The English Dialect Dictionary: being the complete vocabulary of all dialect words still in use, or known to have been in use during the last two hundred years.* 6 vols (London: Henry Froude, 1898–1905)

EDS   English Dialect Society

GVS   Great Vowel Shift

HC   Helsinki Corpus of English Texts

HCOS   Helsinki Corpus of Older Scots

IPA   International Phonetic Alphabet

LALME   *A Linguistic Atlas of Late Mediaeval English* eds. A. McIntosh, M. L. Samuels, and M. Benskin (Aberdeen: Aberdeen University Press, 1984)

LSS   Linguistic Survey of Scotland

MED   *Middle English Dictionary*

OED   *Oxford English Dictionary*

RP   Received Pronunciation

SAWD   Survey of Anglo-Welsh Dialects

SED   Survey of English Dialects

SSBE   Standard Southern British English

SSE   Standard Scottish English

KEY TO PHONETIC SYMBOLS

The following gives a guide to the symbols which are most commonly used throughout the volume. Symbols not included here are chapter-specific, and are explained (with keywords) in the chapters in which they appear.

CONSONANTS

/p/	as in *pick, leap*
/b/	as in *break, bark*
/t/	as in *tea, taste*
/d/	as in *dog, wide*
/k/	as in *king, cupboard*
/f/	as in *find, laugh*
/s/	as in *sleep, pass*
/z/	as in *zest, laze*
/θ/	as in *think, teeth*
/ð/	as in *there, breathe*
/ʃ/	as in *ship, fish*
/ʒ/	as in *leisure, pleasure*
/h/	as in *history, hope*
/m/	as in *make, ham*
/n/	as in *noise, pin*
/ŋ/	as in *ring, think*
/r/	as in *rattle, wriggle*
/l/	as in *listen, fall*
/tʃ/	as in *chirp, fetch*
/dʒ/	as in *judge, jam*
/w/	as in *water, wait*
/j/	as in *yellow, young*
/χ/	as in *loch*

VOWELS

/iː/	as in *bead, feet*
/ɪ/	as in *fit, intend*
/ɛ/	as in *set, bend*
/æ/	as in *cat, pattern*

/uː/	as in *true, food*
/ʊ/	as in *book, could*
/ʌ/	as in *sun, enough*
/ɒ/	as in *not, pond*
/ɔː/	as in *law, board*
/ɒː/	as in *father, cart*
/əː/	as in *heard, bird*
/ə/	as in *wanted, father*

DIPHTHONGS

/aɪ/	as in *file, time*
/eɪ/	as in *take, tail*
/oʊ/	as in *note, bowl*
/au/	as in *loud, found*
/ɔɪ/	as in *toil, toy*

IPA Mouth Diagram

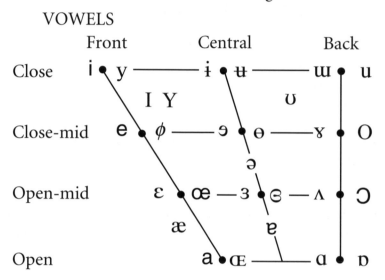

Where symbols appear in pairs, the one to the right represents a rounded vowel.

A HISTORY OF ENGLISH

Lynda Mugglestone

> How can there be a true History, when we see no Man living is able to
> write truly the History of the last Week?
>
> T. Shadwell, *The Squire of Alsatia* (1688)

SIR William Belford's words, spoken in Act II of Thomas Shadwell's late
seventeenth-century play, *The Squire of Alsatia*, articulate the problems of
history with conspicuous ease. As Belford comments to his brother, no history
can be complete. Instead, all historical description is based on acts of interpretation, leading to accounts which may, or may not, conflict with those offered by
other tellers and other tales. In this sense, gaps and absences necessarily beset the
historian; not all can be known, and a change of perspective inevitably brings
new, and different, considerations to the fore. A single true—and all-encompass-
ing—history is an illusion.

These problems are equally pertinent for historians of language for whom
the subject is the many-voiced past. Gaps and absences here may be particularly tantalizing; for the remote past of language—the pre-history of English
(discussed in the opening chapter of this volume)—not a single record remains
and history must be reconstructed, deduced from the patterns of languages
which share the same ancestry. Even later, the historical record may be fragmentary; if the primary form of language is speech, only with the advent of
sound recording (and the invention of the phonograph in 1877) do we begin to

have a record of the actual voices of the past—and even this evidence is necessarily partial and selective. The majority of speakers through the history of English have left not a single trace to document the words they spoke, or the conversations in which they participated. Even for those who had access to the written word, not all has been preserved (and only in the more recent historical past has access to the written word been extended to all, irrespective of class and gender). The passage of historical time has enacted its own selectivities, to which historians have often added others. In many histories of the language, regional voices rarely feature once a standard variety begins to emerge in the fifteenth century. Likewise, the history of the language is often mapped through a progression of canonical landmarks—Chaucer, Shakespeare, Samuel Johnson—that marginalize the range of other voices which co-existed (and which, in a variety of ways, might themselves be seen as more rather than less representative of what 'ordinary' English speakers were doing at a given point in time).

For these and other reasons, the emphasis throughout the following volume is placed on the construction of 'a history' rather than 'the history', recognizing that many other pathways could be navigated through the past—and present—of the English language. The wider emphasis throughout is, however, placed on the twin images of pluralism and diversity, and on the complex patterns of usage which have served to make up English. While the language of Chaucer, Shakespeare, and Johnson does therefore appear (if perhaps more briefly than in other histories of English), then so too does the language of footmen, mining butties, and missionaries, of telegrams and emails, of trade, exploration, and colonization. The language of thieves and the underworld appears in Chapter 8 on Renaissance English; that of, say, eighteenth-century Jamaican English in Chapter 12. The English of ordinary letters, of diaries, and of private testimony—as in Chapters 7, 9, and 10—frequently takes its place in the attempt to engage with what it was like to use English, in a variety of circumstances, in previous centuries. Examples of usage from Scotland, Norfolk, or from Dorset, Spain, Singapore, and America (amongst others) emphasize the diversity of the speakers who make up 'the English language'.

Rather than a seamless synecdoche of the history of English with the history of the standard variety, the image of the past that is explored over the course of this volume is therefore one characterized by its heterogeneity, and by the ebb and flow of a language (and language-varieties) continually on the move. As David Crystal has recently pointed out, 'For every one person who speaks Standard English, there must be a hundred who do not, and another hundred who speak other varieties as well as the standard. Where is their story told?'.[1] The history of the English language in the following pages engages with both domains—documenting the rise of a standard variety, but also continuing to examine the import of regional speech, not only in Middle English ('*par excellence*, the dialectal phase of English', as Barbara Strang has famously stressed),[2] but also through the Renaissance and into the present day. As Chapter 11 affirms, nineteenth-century fears that the demise of dialect—the end of the regional voice—was nigh have resolutely proved unfounded. Instead, as confirmed by the one million plus hits received by the BBC's Voices 2005 website (as at March 2005), diversity is dominant, and interest in language and variation perhaps more compelling than it has ever been.[3]

Any history of the language is, in this respect, enacted through innumerable voices, many of which illustrate that even the history of the standard variety is far more variable than has often been assumed. While Chapters 4 and 5 engage in part with some reassessment of the origins of standard English, a number of other chapters in this volume examine the continuing variability of these non-localized forms of English, especially in contexts unaffected by print. If the eighteenth century is, for example, often characterized by a set of prescriptive stereotypes of correctness which inform popular images of a norm, 'real' English—even within the standard variety—could reveal significant differences within the patterns of usage actually deployed. As a result, just as Johnson's private spellings varied from those publicly commended in his dictionary (as in his usage of *pamflet* for *pamphlet*, or *dutchess* for *duchess*), so too could the grammatical dictates proffered by Robert Lowth in his celebrated grammar fail to coincide with the forms he used in his own letters and correspondence. There is in fact compelling evidence for a set of dual standards of language, with private patterns of usage co-existing alongside those more formally proclaimed (and often adopted in print).[4] Both, however, are part of language history and it is important to recognize that, in this respect, the public image of English does not tell the whole story. As Chapters 9 and 10 examine, printers' readers and correctors habitually normalized the manuscripts which they prepared for public view, concealing the underlying variabilities of ordinary usage. It was a practice which can still lead to a number of prevailing misconceptions about the periods in

[1] D. Crystal, *The Stories of English* (London: Penguin, 2004), 5.

[2] B. M. H. Strang, *A History of English* (London: Methuen, 1970), 224.

[3] See <http:// www.bbc.co.uk/voices/>. Over one million hits had been registered by the end of March 2005.

[4] See especially N. E. Osselton, 'Informal Spelling Systems in Early Modern English: 1500–1800', in N. F. Blake and C. Jones (eds), *English Historical Linguistics: Studies in Development* (Sheffield: CECTAL, 1984), 123–37.

question—and not least in modern editorial (mis)judgements on the spellings or grammatical forms of earlier texts, which, while commonly adjudged awry (and in need of emendation), may instead be entirely typical. Outside the printed text, the realities of informal usage, even in the nineteenth century, could display a variability which is strikingly at odds with many popular images of the language at this time.

Transition—between different language states, between different speakers, and different texts—proves a further enduring theme throughout the volume. While transitions in geographical space inform the diversities analysed in Chapters 2 and 4, for example, with their central focus on Old and Middle English respectively, it is the working-out of change in progress—of transitions in usage—which preoccupies other chapters. The history of English is, in this sense, not a series of static states but, at each and every point in time, patterns of variation reveal the cross-currents of change, whether in the gradual marginalization or loss of older forms, alongside the rise of newer and incoming ones. Susan Irvine examines the strategic intersections of internal and external history in Anglo-Saxon England; Jeremy Smith explores the transitions of the fifteenth century in Chapter 5, a boundary between the conventionally designated 'Middle English' and that of 'early modern English'. Terttu Nevalainen in Chapter 7 uses the evidence of letters and trials to examine a number of significant changes as they took place in the later years of the Renaissance. Factors of age, gender, class, and regional location—just as in the present—influence the patterns of usage which the past also presents. Rather than the familiar (and neat) categorization of discrete periods, changes instead clearly overlap in time; the ebb and flow of the subjunctive is worked out over many centuries while, for instance, shifts of inflexional forms diffuse slowly through time and space. The -s ending of the third person singular (*he walks*, *she runs*) is first found in Old English, as Marilyn Corrie points out in Chapter 4, but it does not become a central part of the standard variety until the later years of the Renaissance (and even later, as Chapter 10 confirms, variability can still be found).

Other transitions are necessarily located in the multilingual past of English, and in the various strands of linguistic conflict and contact which make up its history. Indeed, as Matthew Townend stresses in Chapter 3, 'To write linguistic history by looking only at English would give an entirely false impression of linguistic activity in England; it would be like writing social history by looking at only one class, or only one gender'. Latin, Scandinavian, French, and Dutch all, in various ways, played a part in the earlier history of English; the catalogue of languages which later came to influence it is far wider still. The focus in the final three chapters of the volume is, in various ways, placed on English looking outwards, with reference in particular to the diffusion of English (and English-speakers) outside the British Isles—and to the complex intersection of extra-linguistic forces governing the creation of 'world English'. As Tom McArthur explores in Chapter 13, it is English which is now a world-wide language and the interactions which result from this cannot be forgotten; a whole new set of linguistic identities—such as Singlish or Spanglish—are forged from the contingencies of dissemination and of dominance. Multilingualism is, as Dick Bailey rightly stresses in Chapter 12, perhaps the most important aspect of a history of English—tracing the multilingual history of English from the Renaissance (and before), he adds too the salutary reminder that, for much of this past, it was the skill of the English in assuming new languages which was celebrated (rather than that linguistic incapacity which has come to form a sad part of their modern stereotyping).

'No one man's English is *all* English', wrote the lexicographer James Murray in 1883 as he strove to determine the limits of inclusion of what would become the *Oxford English Dictionary*; diversities of register and region, of style and context, of education and of age, necessarily influence individual linguistic behaviour. A similar awareness of necessary difference has informed the making of this volume. As April McMahon notes in opening Chapter 6, 'there are many different ways of doing linguistic history and of finding out just what the important changes were'. A multi-author volume such as this is, in this respect, particularly appropriate for the diversity of the history of English, enabling a variety of perspectives on the reconstruction of the past to be adopted and applied. The examination of social networks and chains of linguistic influence is explored in Chapter 9; Chapter 7 focuses on the detailed awareness of change in progress enabled by an emphasis on corpus linguistics, and the close-up of variation which this provides; in McMahon's own chapter, there is conversely a move away from the nuances of actual usage in order to examine the wide-scale structural changes which are at work in what is perhaps the most complex of linguistic problems in the history of English—the English Great Vowel Shift. The social texturing of language, in a variety of ways, unites other chapters. Moreover, while the volume maintains a broadly chronological framework, areas of productive intersection and overlap between chapters are also deliberately maintained; historical periods are not neatly confined (even if they may be in the fictions of history which are popularly advanced). Old English does not become Middle English merely with the advent of the Norman Conquest. Indeed, as Susan Irvine explores in Chapter 2, a number of the characteristics which we associate with 'Middle English' (such as the falling together of inflexional endings) are already well established in some areas of Britain by 900. However, to present a different picture yet again, the scribal copying and reproduction of Old English manuscripts continued well into the twelfth and thirteenth centuries. Chapters often span chronological divisions, exploring continuities and the critical debate which this can generate.

As a single-volume history, the *Oxford History of English* is, of course, inevitably selective. It offers, however, the invitation to rethink various aspects of the history for the English language—to engage with the past through private as well as public discourses, to look at the usage of men and women, of standard and non-standard speakers, at English at the borders and margins of time and space, from pre-history to the present-day, and as subject to the changing pressures and contexts which constantly influence usage, as well as to examine some of the motives and explanations which may underpin change as it took place within the past. The aim throughout has been to provide an accessible and discursive text in which primary material is glossed where necessary or (for earlier periods) translated in full. Technical terminology is explained within the chapters, and a guide to phonetic symbols (with keywords) appears on pp. x–xi. Each chapter also incorporates a detailed guide to Further Reading.

As the volume as a whole serves to explore, questions of transmission, of orality, of scribal culture, of manuscript against print, of private usage and public norms, can all complicate notions of what English can be said to be at different points in time. Even within a relatively narrow period of time, speakers will not necessarily agree in usage, depending on facts as diverse as register, gender, or geography, or of age and audience. This diversity—of speakers and the forms they use—is, of course, an essential part of history. Indeed, as the historian John Arnold has eloquently noted, 'the past itself is not a narrative. In its entirety, it is as uncoordinated and complex as life'; history, as a result, is always about 'finding or creating patterns and meaning from the maelstrom'.[5] Histories of the language necessarily share this same complex of origins. And, like historians, their writers too are constantly aware that other patterns also exist, and that many other stories could also—and always—be told.

---

[5] J. Arnold, *History. A Very Short Introduction* (Oxford: Oxford University Press, 2000), 13.

1

PRELIMINARIES: BEFORE ENGLISH

Terry Hoad

LANGUAGES ON THE MOVE

T HE English language is at more than one point in its history a language which is being carried from one part of the world to another. This is true at the beginning of its existence as a recognizably distinct language—the phase which this and later chapters refer to as Old English. Migration of people and the consequent relocation of the languages they speak will therefore be one of the major themes of this chapter, which will focus on the pre-history of English and the various developments which underpin the creation of English as a language in its own right within the British Isles. We can, however, better understand some things about that early period, and what was happening to the language at the time, if we first take a look at certain events in the more recent past which can be seen to offer a number of useful parallels for the much earlier transmission of language varieties through time and space.

Early in the seventeenth century, a period which will be discussed in more detail in Chapters 8 and 12, speakers of English started to migrate from the British Isles to North America. This process of migration, once begun, continued on a significant scale over the best part of three centuries. The forms of English that the migrants took with them varied considerably according to such factors as the part of Britain from which they came, their social class, their age, and the date at which they migrated. Once settled in North America they had contact not only with users of forms of English which were similar to their own, but also with those who spoke different varieties of the language. Furthermore, they encountered and, naturally, had occasion to communicate with speakers of quite different languages, which included those of the Native American inhabitants of the continent as well as the non-English languages of immigrants from other European countries and elsewhere around the globe.

As a result of their geographical separation, the language of the English-speaking migrants began to differ from that of their previous neighbours in Britain. Given what we know of the natural development of languages, we can say with confidence that this would inevitably have happened, even without other factors playing a part. Differently shifting social alignments among English speakers in Britain on the one hand, and in North America on the other, would alone have been sufficient to ensure that. But the multilingual environment which arose in North America helped shape the particular directions of development for the English language as used there. Pronunciation, grammar, and vocabulary were all subject to this interplay of inevitable 'internal' linguistic change with powerful influences from other languages also in use. One of the most obvious results of those influences was the adoption or 'borrowing' into English in North America (and later, in many cases, into English in Britain too) of words from other languages: *skunk* from one of the Native American languages, *cockroach* from Spanish, *prairie* from French. It seems right, though, to think of American English as remaining primarily based on the English of the British Isles. We now, for example, usually consider the forms of English spoken in Britain and in North America as different forms—different 'dialects'—of the 'same' language. We can nevertheless simultaneously be very conscious of how unalike British and North American English are.

The populations of English speakers on each side of the Atlantic were never, of course, completely cut off from contact with one another. There continued to be movement in both directions between Britain and North America; activities such as trade and warfare have alternately led to direct contact of varying degrees of friendliness, while letters, newspapers, books, the telephone, radio, television, and most recently email have successively been some of the main means whereby indirect communication has been maintained on a vast scale.

It is important to remember, too, that English in America did not remain the language solely of the migrants and their descendants. It was also adopted by people whose language, or whose parents' language, was entirely different. These people included other migrant groups from Europe and elsewhere, some of whom retained their ancestral languages (German or Italian, for example) in full and active use alongside the English which they had also acquired. These new speakers of English included many of the previous inhabitants of the continent and their descendants—the Native American peoples—who came to use English alongside or, in many cases, instead of the languages which they and their forebears had previously spoken.

The situation was in many respects very similar at the beginning of the history of what we can call 'English'. In a wave of migrations which extended over a large part of the fifth and sixth centuries AD people from northern continental Europe brought to the British Isles a language of a kind which had previously

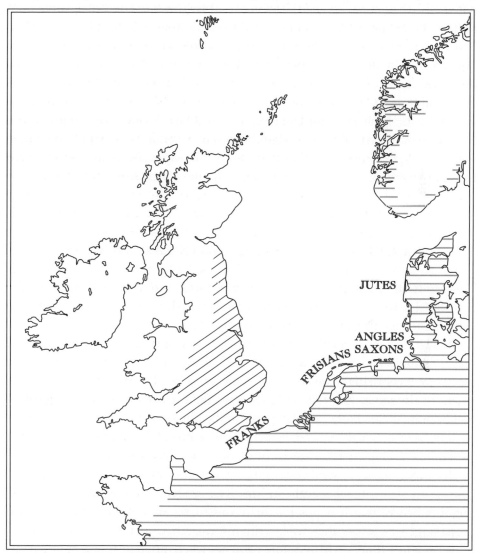

FIG. 1.1. Evidence of English presence in the fifth and sixth centuries from archaeological and historical sources (DIAGONAL SHADING). Germanic areas of cultural and linguistic influence through migration and contact on the continent and in Scandinavia (HORIZONTAL SHADING).

been unknown there. These migrants came, it appears, from a number of different places (see Fig. 1.1) no doubt being distinguishable from one another in the same kinds of ways as the British settlers in North America were to be many centuries later. They spoke a range of dialects and in their new home they each encountered and interacted with speakers of other varieties of their own language, as well as with people speaking quite different languages, namely the Celtic languages of the native British population, and the form of Latin which many of those people seem to have used under the recently ended Roman governance of Britain.

As these migrants (whom we call the Anglo-Saxons) started their new and separate life in the British Isles, their language began to develop in its own distinctive ways and to become different from the language of their previous neighbours on the Continent. It was also exposed to influences from the indigenous Celtic languages and from Latin, as will be discussed in a later chapter. But, again as in the history of modern English in America, the Anglo-Saxons were never completely isolated, and trade and other activities continued to keep them in contact with people across the channel and the North Sea.

LOOKING BACK: INDO-EUROPEAN ORIGINS

The kinds of language which the Anglo-Saxons brought with them to the British Isles had previously been shared with other peoples, who remained behind in their Continental homelands. At that time, with two exceptions—runes and Gothic—which will be discussed below, these peoples (including the Anglo-Saxons) had not yet acquired the skill of writing their language. As a result, we have virtually no recorded evidence of most forms of it. By the time when, in the succeeding few centuries, they did start to write their language it had become divided. The separating off of the 'English' of the Anglo-Saxons has already been touched on, and by very similar processes there developed what we can, for example, recognize as the earliest stages of German and Dutch, and of the Scandinavian languages Danish, Swedish, and Norwegian. These languages are known collectively as the 'Germanic' group of languages, and linguists believe that it is possible to reconstruct a good deal of the history of these languages before they took written form. That history, they also believe, leads back to a time, perhaps before c 200 BC, when different forms of Germanic were as closely similar as were the dialects of English when the later migrations to North America began. In other words, there seems to have been a time when we can reasonably think in terms of a single Germanic language to which linguists have given the name 'Proto-Germanic' or, sometimes in the past, 'Primitive Germanic'.

This Proto-Germanic language is itself recognized by linguists as an offshoot from a still earlier language system which comprises the 'Indo-European' group of languages. Other branchings off from this group (for which see Fig. 1.2) gave rise to the majority of the known languages of Europe and Scandinavia, as well as some in Asia and Asia Minor. In some cases there is evidence, in the form of written texts, of individual languages having separated themselves off and taken distinguishable form at a very early date. Early forms of Greek, for example, survive in written texts from 1500–1200 years BC; in India, the most ancient form of the Indo-European language whose classical representative is Sanskrit can be traced back to 1000–500 years BC; for the Iranian branch of Indo-European, the oldest evidence is for the language known as Avestan, which is of comparable date; and in southern Europe, not much later, come the beginnings of Latin. Earliest of all are the records of Hittite and related languages in Asia Minor, which may start as early as 1700 BC or before.

As Figure 1.2 illustrates, other major branches of Indo-European include the Celtic, Baltic, and Slavonic languages, as well as Armenian and Tocharian (a language of Central Asia). Evidence for these all occurs rather later, in most cases well into the Christian era. The same is true of Germanic, the last major branch of the family to be mentioned, which will be the main concern of the later part of this chapter.

The starting point for the realization that the recorded Indo-European languages had a common source—a 'parent' language, if we use the common image of the family tree—was the recognition that individual words in one of the languages bore systematic resemblances to those in others. Such resemblances are seen, for instance, in many 'basic' words:

	Sanskrit	Greek	Latin	Old Church Slavonic
'house'	*dámah*	*dómos*	*domus*	*domŭ*
'new'	*návah*	*néos*	*novus*	*novŭ*
'three'	*tráyah*	*treîs*	*trēs*	*triye*

In these examples, the consonants have remained to a large extent the same in each language, while the vowels are often different. Having studied not just a few examples such as have been cited here but many thousands of cases which point in the same direction, linguists believe that in the Indo-European from which Sanskrit, Greek, and the other languages later developed, 'house' would have had a form something like **domos/domus*, 'new' would have been something like

Indo-European

	Germanic			Celtic	Italic	Venetic	Albanian	Greek	Baltic	Slavonic	Anatolian	Armenian	Iranian	Indic	Tocharian
	Western group	Northern group	Eastern group												
Recorded pre-1000	Old English, Old Saxon, Old Frisian, Old High German	Old Icelandic, Old Norwegian, Old Swedish, Old Danish	Gothic	Gaulish, Old Irish, Old Welsh, Old Breton	Latin, Faliscan, Oscan, Umbrian	Venetic		Ancient Greek		Old Church Slavonic	Hittite	Classical Armenian	Avestan, Old Persian	Sanskrit	Tocharian
Recorded in modern times	English, Low German, Dutch, German	Icelandic, Norwegian, Swedish, Danish	[None]	Irish, Scots Gaelic, Welsh, Breton	Portuguese, Spanish, Catalan, French, Provençal, Italian, Romanian	[None]	Albanian	Greek	Old Prussian, Lithuanian, Latvian	Czech, Croatian, Serbian, Polish, Slovak, Macedonian, Belorussian, Ukrainian, Bulgarian, Russian	[None]	Armenian	Kurdish, Persian (Farsi), Pashto	Gujarati, Punjabi, Hindi, Bengali	[None]

FIG. 1.2. The Indo-European language group (the listing of individual languages is not comprehensive)

*newos, and 'three' would have been something like *treyes (the asterisks in these and other forms signify their hypothetical and reconstructed status). In Sanskrit the vowels e and o both underwent a change in pronunciation, becoming a, and a vast amount of other evidence confirms that this was a general feature affecting all Indo-European e's and o's in Sanskrit. In the word for 'new', both Latin and Old Church Slavonic have o where there had once been e, and this again can be shown to be a general feature of development in those languages when the vowel was followed by w.

Sometimes the consonants too differ from one 'daughter' language to another, as in the following example:

	Sanskrit	Greek	Latin	Old Church Slavonic
'brother'	bhrātā	phrátēr	frater	bratrŭ

The parent Indo-European form which can be reconstructed in this case is *bhrātēr, and Greek and Latin are believed to have regularly changed the initial bh to ph and f respectively (as in a series of other cases such as Sanskrit bhárāmi, Greek phérō, Latin ferō 'I carry', Old Church Slavonic berǫ 'I gather').

The historical relationship of the Indo-European languages to one another is not, however, seen merely in the fact that in many cases they use words which are demonstrably developed from a common source. The grammar of the various languages also clearly has a common starting point. In its very early stages, Indo-European had a grammar that was heavily dependent on inflections. That is to say, the grammatical relationship between the words in a sentence was—just as it would be in Old English—indicated primarily by the use of appropriate forms of the words (typically, forms with appropriate 'endings'). This kind of grammatical device continued into many of the recorded languages. For example, in the Latin sentences

homō	timorem	superavit
the man	fear	overcame

'the man overcame fear'

and

timor_	hominem	superavit
fear	the man	overcame

'fear overcame the man'

different forms of the words homō ('man') and timor ('fear') are used accord-ing to which word is the subject and which the object of the verb superavit ('overcame'). The order of the words—the sole means of indicating the difference between the equivalent sentences in modern English—is here more susceptible of variation for stylistic effect. In Latin, therefore, provided the forms of the words remain unchanged, the sense too will be unaltered, irrespective of the order in which the individual words are arranged. Inflections were also used in Indo-European to mark such features as plurality and tense:

timor_	hom*ines*	super*abit*
fear	the men	will overcome

'fear will overcome the men'

In the later history of the Indo-European languages, the grammatical systems of some of them (for example, Russian) have continued to rely heavily on inflections, while others have greatly reduced their use of them. English, as later chapters of this book will show, now has very few inflections, although even English continues to mark most noun plurals in this way (*hands* vs *hand*), as well as to indicate tense (*walked* vs *walk*) and the third person singular of the present tense of verbs (*he writes* vs *I write, you write, they write*). The use of different forms to distinguish the subject of a sentence from the object moreover still survives in English with regard to personal pronouns (*He likes the girl* vs *The girl likes him*; *They called to the policeman* vs *The policeman called them*).

The sounds and grammatical forms used by a language, together with the principles according to which sentences are constructed, constitute the system which makes the language what it is and which enables its speakers to communicate with one another. While sounds, forms, and syntactic patterns are all liable to constant change, this necessarily happens in an evolutionary way which preserves the underlying integrity of the system. The vocabulary of the language, on the other hand, is an extremely large and far less tightly bound set of items which speakers are, in some ways, much freer to change. The introduction of a new word into the vocabulary, for example—whether by combining existing words or parts of words or by using a previously foreign word as though it were part of the language—is not likely to seriously disturb the process of communication. This is in part so, no doubt, because, while speakers need to share with one another a knowledge of the sounds and grammar of their language, they will inevitably not share a comparably complete knowledge of vocabulary. Occupation, education, interests, age, reading, experience of travel, and many other factors will affect the range of words which they actively use or which they can passively understand. So too will the dialect of the location in which they live. Furthermore, in any given situation there will frequently be a range of words which a speaker might use more or less interchangeably to express his or her meaning—words which differ in, say, stylistic level (*man* ~ *bloke*) or which overlap in sense (*picture* ~ *photo*). And shifts in the material and other circumstances of the lives of the speakers of a language—technological developments, for example, or changes in social organization—will inevitably mean that corresponding alterations are required in the vocabulary to deal with new concepts. There is likely to be a good amount of continuity in vocabulary, but factors such as those mentioned here nevertheless contribute to making the vocabulary of the language a more fluidly variable entity than its sound or grammatical systems can be said to be.

There is therefore good reason to expect that, in the pre-history of English, Indo-European vocabulary will have undergone significant changes over time, and that it is likely to have differed also from one region to another. That it is helpful to reconstruct 'Indo-European' forms like *domos/*domus*, *newos, and *treyes does not have to imply that there was ever a single Indo-European language community in which those word forms were universally and exclusively used to express the meanings in question, far less that such forms will necessarily have continued (with whatever development of sound or inflection they may have undergone) as part of the vocabulary of any language which subsequently emerged from that 'Indo-European'.

Some items have been, nevertheless, both in very widespread use and extremely durable. For example, the modern English kinship terms *mother, brother, sister* continue words which are represented in all the branches of Indo-European apart from Hittite (the Greek word corresponding to *sister* is recorded only once, as a word needing explanation). They therefore come close, if no more, to being words that we can assume to have been in use throughout a hypothetical Indo-European speech community. The word which appears in modern English as *father*, however, is not only (like *mother*, etc.) unrecorded in Hittite but is also not evidenced in the Baltic languages (such as Lithuanian and Latvian), and only slight traces of it are found in the Slavonic branch of Indo-European. Words corresponding to modern English *son* and *daughter* are missing from what we know of Hittite, but they are also absent from Latin and the Celtic languages.

Rarely can linguists explain such gaps in the evidence for what seem otherwise to be elements of the most ancient Indo-European vocabulary, but they can occasionally see something of what is likely to have happened. For example, the Slavonic word for 'father' represented by Russian *otéts* is generally believed to be in origin a nursery word, like English *daddy*, that has, for reasons we cannot now recover, come to replace the term preserved in more formal use in most of the Indo-European languages.

   To look towards the other end of the spectrum, a word like the modern English verb *mow* has its only close correspondent in Greek *amáō* (one of the few other points of contact elsewhere in Indo-European is through the related word (*after*)*math*, which shares its origins with words of comparable sense in Latin and the Celtic languages). The Old English word *æðm* ('breath') clearly has a closely similar origin to that of Sanskrit *ātmā*, but otherwise the only (uncertain) Indo-European connection seems to be with Old Irish *athach*. It is not possible to know, in examples such as these, whether the words in question were once in use throughout the early Indo-European speech community, or whether they were always less widespread. If the former had been the case we cannot be certain when and why the word fell out of use among particular groups of speakers, although it may sometimes be possible to make an informed guess. For example, the modern English word *arse* corresponds to words in Hittite, Greek, Old Irish, and Armenian, but seems to be unrecorded in any of the other branches of Indo-European. As in other languages, there have at different times been strong restrictions on the circumstances in which it is acceptable to use such words as *arse* in modern English. It seems reasonable to suppose that similar taboos on naming certain parts of the body have at least played a role in the replacement of words like *arse* by other (often euphemistic) terms elsewhere in Indo-European.

THE LESS DISTANT PAST: GERMANIC PRECURSORS

The speakers of the earliest form of a distinct Germanic branch of Indo-European appear to have inhabited an area covering parts of what are now Denmark and southern Sweden, although it is notoriously difficult to match evolving forms of language in pre-literary times with particular population groups in particular regions. Some possibilities do exist for tracing the histories and movements of population groups in the area during the relevant period (the last three centuries or so BC and the first century or two AD), and archaeologists can say much about the material cultures that existed in those regions at different times. But the links between the populations and the material cultures are not necessarily either exclusive or unbreakable, and the same is true of the association of particular languages with particular populations or material cultures. English has, in relatively recent times, been transported to distant places—the Indian subcontinent, for example—where it has become one of the languages used by people who previously spoke only a quite different language, and whose material culture was quite different from that of the people who brought the language to them. Or to take an example in which the language has remained *in situ* but the population has changed, the Scandinavian and Norman French people who took up residence in England during the Old and early Middle English periods eventually (as Chapter 3 discusses) gave up their previous language in favour of English, just as immigrant groups from a range of other countries have done in more recent centuries.

There are several features of Proto-Germanic which mark it out as a language distinct from the other languages of the Indo-European group. Among the most striking are a number of significant changes in the verbs and adjectives which already serve to establish patterns that will later also be features of Old English. In Germanic, for example, verbs had only two different forms to make distinctions of tense, normally referred to as 'present' and 'past' tense forms (some writers use 'preterite' instead of 'past'). Other tenses had to be indicated by the use of another verb (such as 'have') alongside the verb in question. Furthermore, the simple 'present' and 'past' tense forms might themselves convey the sense of more than one tense. The situation can be illustrated with modern English examples, using the verb 'walk'. This verb has just two different tense forms, *walk* and *walked*:

You walk very quickly
He walked into the bank

Beyond that, further tense distinctions (often, in fact, involving other factors than just tense) can be made by the use of one or more 'auxiliary' verbs as in, for example:

I have walked all the way here
They had walked home after having dinner
We were walking side by side
She will walk down to the town
He will have walked there before the bus arrives

Serving even more clearly to mark off Germanic from the other Indo-European languages than this system of two basic tense forms, however, is the shape of the forms themselves. Germanic verbs fall into two groups, according to the way in which their past tense forms are made. (In what follows, modern English forms are used to represent the Germanic patterns.) Most verbs are like *walk*, in that their past tense form is made by adding a suffix including *d* (or sometimes *t*): *heal/ed, love/d, end/ed*, etc. In some cases the formation is less clearly visible, but originally it was essentially the same: *sent, left, bought, said*. But there is another, less numerous, group of verbs in which the past tense form is made not by adding a suffix but by changing the main vowel from that found in the present tense form: *sing ~ sang, take ~ took, rise ~ rose, find ~ found, forgive ~ forgave*, etc. Verbs belonging to the *walk* type are traditionally called 'weak verbs' by linguists, and verbs of the *sing* type are called 'strong verbs'. The weak verbs were, originally, formed from other parts of speech: *drench/ed* from the strong verb *drink ~ drank*, *fill* from the adjective *full*, etc. The strong verbs, on the other hand, were words which had been verbs from the outset and were not built on other words. Generally speaking, the strong verb group has not increased in number but has lost members as time has gone on: modern English *help(ed)* now follows the *walk* pattern, whereas at an earlier stage (and still in Old English) it was a strong verb. The weak verb group has increased enormously in size, since verbs coming into the vocabulary at various times have nearly always been added to that group: English *pray/ed, rejoice/d, discover/ed, tango/ed, televise/d, compute/d*, etc. The same pattern can be seen in the history and development of the other Germanic languages.

The Germanic strong verb system represents a particular development of a way of using alternations of vowels that had existed previously in Indo-European (and that can be seen in Sanskrit, Greek, and the other Indo-European languages). The weak verb system does not have such clear origins, although it no doubt also builds on features already existing in Indo-European. Those origins have been the subject of prolonged—and not yet resolved—debate among linguists.

Another distinctive characteristic of Germanic grammar, and one which remained a conspicuous feature of Old English is that the great majority of adjectives in Germanic may occur in two different forms, depending on the grammar of the sentence in which they appear. Broadly speaking, if an adjective is attached to a noun that is made 'definite' (as, most frequently, by the attachment to it also of a word such as 'this' or 'my' to specify a particular instance of whatever it is the noun signifies), the adjective will appear in one of the forms. In other situations, the other form of the adjective will be used. Somewhat confusingly, in view of the terminology used with regard to verbs, linguists have traditionally often referred to adjective forms of the first kind as 'weak' forms, and to forms of the second kind as 'strong' forms (others prefer 'definite' and 'indefinite' respectively). Thus, using examples from Old English to illustrate what was a pattern in earlier Germanic:

Þær	*wuniaþ*	*þa*	*haligan* (weak)	*menn*		
There	dwell	the	holy	men		

Oft	*halige* (strong)	*menn*	*wunedon*	*on*	*westene*
Often	holy	men	dwelt	in	(the) desert

During the medieval period, as Chapter 4 explores, English gradually lost this formal distinction between adjective forms, along with most other inflections. It continues even today, however, to be reflected in the grammar of modern German and other modern Germanic languages.

Because features such as those just discussed are found in the early stages of all the Germanic languages, it is reasonable to suppose that they were also found in Proto-Germanic, before the individual languages acquired separate identities. Conversely, because these features are not found in the other Indo-European languages, at least with the structural role which they have in the grammar of Germanic, it seems reasonable to suppose that they developed as or after Proto-Germanic became separate from the rest of the Indo-European group.

The same is true of a major contrast between the development of certain sounds in Germanic and in other early Indo-European languages. Pronunciation is very prone to change, even within what we might consider one and the 'same' language. The difference between various regional accents in modern Britain (see further, Chapter 12), or between characteristically British and characteristically American pronunciations, makes this immediately apparent. But there is one extensive, systematic set of differences between pronunciation in Germanic and in Indo-European which can be seen as a further particularly significant part of what made Proto-Germanic a distinct form of language.

This set of differences has been variously labelled the 'Germanic Consonant Shift', the 'First Consonant Shift', and 'Grimm's Law' (from the name of the German scholar Jacob Grimm [1785–1863], who gave one of the first systematic statements of it). In general, where Indo-European had p, t, k, Germanic had f, $þ$, χ respectively ($þ$ stands for the sound represented by th in modern English $thin$, and χ stands for the sound represented by ch in modern German $nach$). Similarly, in place of Indo-European b, d, g Germanic had p, t, k respectively, and in place of Indo-European bh, dh, gh it had b, d, g respectively (bh, etc., stand for sounds supposed to have existed in Indo-European in which the sound b, etc., is accompanied by 'aspiration', i.e. a release of breath similar to that represented by h in modern English $house$).

This leads to such kinds of correspondence as:

	Sanskrit	Greek	Latin	Old English
$(p \sim f)$ 'father'	_p_ita	_p_atēr	_p_ater	_f_æder
$(t \sim þ)$ 'three'	_t_rayas	_t_reîs	_t_rēs	_þ_rīe
$(k \sim \chi)$ 'heart'		_k_ardia	_c_or	_h_eorte

and similarly for the other consonants.

One further feature common to the early Germanic languages (and which can therefore also be assumed to have been present in Proto-Germanic) is the fixing of the stress in most words on the first syllable. In Indo-European the stress fell on different syllables in different words, or in different forms of the same word. Thus Sanskrit has the forms *juhómi* ('I sacrifice'), *juhumás* ('we sacrifice'), *júhvati* ('they sacrifice'). Some modern languages of the Indo-European group show similar variation in the placing of the stress in different words or forms, as in Russian *slóvo* ('word') and *slová* ('words'). Because in Germanic the stress came to be always placed on the first syllable in most words, the prominence of the syllables at the ends of words was reduced. This seems to have played a part in the gradual loss of inflectional endings which came to be characteristic of the various Germanic languages.

ENTERING THE HISTORICAL PERIOD: THE DIVISION OF PROTO-GERMANIC

From their early homeland in the southern parts of Scandinavia, the speakers of Germanic carried it in various directions over succeeding centuries. The process began, perhaps, in the third century BC, and was still active when the Anglo-Saxons came to Britain towards the middle of the first millennium AD. Entirely in keeping with the pattern of linguistic developments which were described at the beginning of this chapter, increasingly differentiated forms of Germanic developed as different groups of speakers became more firmly separated from one another. It has long been common for linguists to speak in terms of a fundamental three-way division of the Germanic speech community, into a North Germanic part, an East Germanic part, and a West Germanic part which, as Figure 1.2 illustrates, includes Old English. For some linguists, the picture has been of three groups of Germanic peoples, each detaching themselves from the previously united Germanic tribal cluster and in the process bringing into being three separate forms of Germanic language. As time progressed, each of the latter would have given rise to the various historically attested Germanic languages: North Germanic would have divided into Danish, Swedish, and Norwegian; East Germanic would have produced the no longer extant Gothic (together with some other now extinct languages of which relatively little is known); and West Germanic would have undergone a separation into the early forms of German, Dutch, Frisian, and English.

The movements of different groups of peoples in northern Europe during this period can be partially reconstructed—at first with considerable difficulty and uncertainty; later, as historical records come into being from the earliest centuries of the Christian era onwards, with somewhat greater confidence—and that reconstruction fits in some broad respects the three-way division outlined above. It is also the case that the historically attested Germanic languages fall rather easily into the three groups mentioned. Nevertheless, opinions on this matter have varied in recent times, with many scholars thinking it more likely that Germanic first split into two languages rather than three: into North West Germanic and East Germanic (or, perhaps, into North East Germanic and West Germanic). The following account, using for convenience a three-fold classification, does not make any claim about the details of the sequence of splits.

Peoples from the East Germanic grouping are believed to have moved eastwards and southwards during the first three or four centuries AD. The people about whom most is known, by far, are the Goths, who over that period and the following three centuries or so (when some of them moved westwards across southern Europe as far as the Iberian peninsula) played a major part in the history of the territories they inhabited. Their language is known mainly from a translation of parts of the Bible believed to have been made in the fourth century AD among a part of the Gothic people living at that time west of the Black Sea, in approximately the same area as modern Romania. That translation, as the first extensive written record of a Germanic language, is of very great importance for linguistic study. Gothic is distinguished from the other Germanic languages by a number of characteristics, some of which preserve features of earlier Proto-Germanic which have not survived into the other historically attested languages, while others are innovations. For example, Gothic has inflectional forms of verbs to indicate the passive voice:

ni	*afdomjaid,*	*jah*	*ni*	*afdomjanda*
not	judge,	and	not	(you) will be judged

'do not judge, and you will not be judged'

In other Germanic languages passive inflections no longer survive in recognizable form, and the passive voice is indicated (as in modern English) by the use of an auxiliary verb. One Old English translation of the gospels has, for the sentence just quoted:

nelle	*ge*	*deman,*	*and*	*ge*	*ne*	*beoð*	*demede*
do not	you	judge	and	you	not	will be	judged

'do not judge, and you will not be judged'

Gothic also makes use, in the past tense forms of a group of strong verbs, of what is known as reduplication; that is, the addition at the beginning of a word of a syllable consisting of the initial consonant of the word and a vowel (sometimes accompanied by a change of the main vowel as in the past tense forms of other strong verbs):

haitan ('call') ~ past tense *haihait*
gretan ('weep') ~ past tense *gaigrot*

In other Germanic languages, only isolated remains of reduplicated forms are to be found and they no longer form a regular grammatical pattern.

These are just two examples from a range of features in which Gothic gives us very valuable information for reconstructing the nature of Proto-Germanic, and hence for the better understanding of what lay distantly behind Old English.

Peoples from the North Germanic grouping, who moved into the areas we now know as Denmark, Sweden, and Norway (and subsequently further afield, to Iceland and other places), left extensive texts dating from *c*1100 AD onwards. They also left a considerable number of much earlier texts (relatively short) carved in 'runes' on metal, wooden, bone, and other objects. The runic 'alphabet' is generally called the 'futhark', after the values of the first six characters of the sequence; this is illustrated in Figure 1.3. It varies in some particulars from one place or time to another and is of disputed origin. The earliest of these runic texts are reckoned no later than the second century AD, and frequently consist of just a name or one or two words. In many cases the identity of the words or the meaning of the texts cannot be confidently made out. In such circumstances it is not surprising that there is uncertainty surrounding the nature of the language in which they are written. Some scholars take it to be an intermediate 'Common Scandinavian' stage

f   u th a r k

FIG. 1.3.   The first six letters of the early *futhark* found on a bracteate [thin gold medallion] from Vadstena in Sweden

between Proto-Germanic and the later separate Scandinavian languages, others that it is a 'North West Germanic' stage that subsequently gave rise not only to the Scandinavian but also to the West Germanic languages (including English).

Runes, with changes over time in their number, shapes, and sound values, continued to be used in Scandinavia into and beyond the Middle Ages, and longer texts came to be written in them. There are also some objects bearing runic inscriptions and possibly of dates between the third and the ninth centuries (although the datings tend to be uncertain) from various parts of continental Europe. Much relating to these objects and texts is very uncertain—from which direction runic writing reached the places in question, for example, or what languages the texts are in, or what the texts mean. The practice of writing in runes is also fairly well evidenced in Anglo-Saxon England, starting very early in the period. It seems likely that an ability to write in runes was simply brought with them by the Anglo-Saxon settlers. Some of the important English runic texts are dealt with in the next chapter.

This lack of clearly interpretable textual evidence until a relatively late date makes it difficult to reconstruct the process by which Danish, Swedish, and Norwegian became separate languages. The Norwegians took their language with them when they began to settle in Iceland in the second half of the ninth century AD. Much of the early literature from the North Germanic group consists of texts preserved (if not always originally composed) in Icelandic after that language had developed its separate identity from the period of settlement onwards, for example, the poems of the *Poetic Edda* and the many prose narratives of the *sagas*. It is a common practice to cite Old Icelandic forms as representative of the early North Germanic languages (which are often referred to collectively as 'Old Norse'), and since this often leads to thirteenth-century Icelandic forms being set alongside, say, fourth-century Gothic ones it can give a misleading impression to the unwary.

Some features of the early North Germanic languages are nevertheless quite clearly different from those found elsewhere in Germanic. Two affect the verb and pronoun systems. In the verbs, a set of 'mediopassive' forms arose in which a suffix in -*mk* (first person) or -*sk* (second and third person), or some variant, was added to the verb form. The suffixes were originally forms of personal pronouns: *mik* ('me', 'myself') and *sik* ('yourself', 'himself', etc.). The 'mediopassive' forms typically expressed a reflexive or passive sense, although this did not always remain transparent:

síðan	*búask*		*boðsmenn*	*í brottu*
then	prepare themselves		guests	away

'then the guests prepare to leave'

Ísland	*bygðisk*	*fyrst*	*ór*	*Norvegi*	*á*	*dǫgum*
Iceland	was settled	first	from	Norway	in	days

Haralds	*ins*	*Hárfagra*
of Harald	the	Fairhaired

'Iceland was first settled from Norway in the days of Harald Fairhair'

munu	*vit*	*báðir*	*í braut*	*komask*
will	we	both	away	manage to go

'we will both get away'

In a further distinctive feature, the North Germanic languages developed a definite article that was suffixed to its noun unless there was also an adjective attached to the noun: *maðrinn* ('the man'), *á grindina* ('to the gate'), *landinu* ('[to] the land'), but *it fyrsta hǫgg* ('the first blow').

The peoples of the West Germanic grouping are those from among whom arose, as has already been mentioned, the forms of language that are eventually identifiable as German, Dutch, Frisian, and English. Before the Germanic peoples began their divergent migrations, the West Germanic group seem to have been located in what is now Denmark and in the more northerly and North Sea coastal territories of modern Germany, the Netherlands, and Belgium. It is difficult to reconstruct the evolving interrelationships between the tribes that constituted this group, or between them and the other Germanic peoples, and harder still to discover the connection between those tribal interrelationships and the gradually emerging different languages which are now generally labelled 'West Germanic'. Another of the issues on which scholars today are divided is whether to posit a more or less unified West Germanic protolanguage at any stage intermediate between Proto-Germanic and the individual West Germanic languages. Some are inclined to believe that 'West Germanic' from the time of its separation from Germanic (or from North Germanic) fell into two parts, one of which was destined to become early German and the other to give rise to English, Frisian, and Dutch. It is at any rate reasonable to think in terms of a prolonged period of fluctuating divergences and convergences, both of peoples and of languages, in complex circumstances which again would have had many similarities to those described at the beginning of this chapter but which are now no longer recoverable in much detail.

The West Germanic languages of which we have early evidence are Old High German, Old Saxon, and Old English. Texts in Old High German and Old English survive from the eighth century AD onwards, whereas the first Old Saxon texts come from the following century. Old Frisian, which is of particular interest because of the number of close similarities which it bears to Old English, is not recorded until considerably later, in thirteenth-century copies of texts which originate in the eleventh century.

Old High German is known in a number of quite markedly different dialectal varieties, broadly classifiable as Alemannic, Bavarian, and Franconian. The two first of these (from the south-west and south-east of the Old High German area respectively) are grouped together as 'Upper German'; the Franconian dialects (further to the north) are referred to as 'Middle German'. A significant number of prose and verse texts survive, together with other records of the language in, for example, glosses in Latin texts and glossaries of Latin words.

Old High German is differentiated from the other West Germanic languages by what is known as the 'Second Consonant Shift'—a systematic set of developments which affected the consonants that had arisen as a consequence of the earlier 'First (or Germanic) Consonant Shift' (described above on p.19). This results in correspondences such as:

	Old English	Old High German
'tooth'	*tōþ*	*zan*
'make'	*macian*	*mahhōn*

The Second Consonant Shift affects a wider range of consonants in some dialects than in others, with the Franconian dialects tending to show less extensive changes than the Upper German dialects.

Old High German is also further distinguished from the other West Germanic languages (including Old English) in retaining from earlier Germanic a distinct form for each of the three 'persons' in the plural of the present and past tenses of verbs, where the other languages have reduced these to just one form, as in the following examples:

	Old High German	Old English
'we carry/carried'	*wir beremēs/bārumēs*	
'you (*pl.*) carry/carried'	*ir beret/bārut*	*wē, gē, hīe beraþ/bǣron*
'they carry/carried'	*sie berent/bārun*	

Old Saxon is the name given to the language represented in two ninth-century scriptural narratives in verse, *Heliand* (nearly 6,000 lines) and *Genesis* (nearly 350 lines). It is not known where these texts were composed, although it may well have been in an area where Franconian Old High German was in use, rather than in what may be thought of as an Old Saxon area. Some shorter texts of various kinds also exist, as do glosses explaining words in Latin texts. Until the beginning of the ninth century the Saxons as a people (or group of peoples) had been politically and militarily very significant in the northern parts of what is now Germany, and had experienced fluctuating fortunes in their dealings with the kings of the Franks, their powerful neighbours to the south. The submission of the Saxon leader Widukind to the Frankish ruler Charlemagne in 785, however, led soon after to the Saxons being finally incorporated into Charlemagne's Empire.

In these circumstances, it is not surprising that the status of the Old Saxon language, especially as represented in *Heliand* and *Genesis*, is uncertain. Scholarly debate has not finally decided on any one of the various possibilities, which include the language of these texts being a more or less direct representation of a local (spoken) dialect but its representing a local dialect but with the introduction by a copyist of written forms which are proper to Old High German, or its not being direct evidence of any spoken dialect at all but being instead a specifically written form of language.

Old Saxon is, however, of particular interest with regard to the origins of Old English, in part because it appears to lie on the supposed path of the earlier Germanic invaders of and migrants to the British Isles, but also since it seems to have been at that earlier time close in a number of respects to the kinds of language that are thought to have developed into Old English. The Saxons are, moreover, named as one of the Germanic peoples who were part of the movement to Britain of the 'Anglo-Saxons' (see further, pp. 34–5). It is nevertheless important to bear in mind that the Anglo-Saxon settlements in Britain took place some centuries before the first surviving evidence for an Old Saxon language. We must therefore be properly cautious about the possibilities of accurately reconstructing what the language of 'Saxons' might have been like at that earlier date.

One feature of Old Saxon which it shares with Old English and Old Frisian, but in which it stands in contrast to Old High German as well as to East Germanic, is that an original *n* or *m* is lost between a vowel and *f, þ,* or *s*:

	Old Saxon	Old English	Old High German	Gothic
'five'	*fīf*	*fīf*	*fimf*	*fimf*
'journey'	*sīð*	*sīþ*	*sind*	*sinþs* ('time')
'us'	*ūs*	*ūs*	*unsih*	*unsis*

Old Frisian, even more than Old Saxon, is a language of which we have no direct knowledge at the period relevant to the Anglo-Saxon migrations to

Britain. The surviving Old Frisian texts, which are mostly legal in nature, may in some cases have their origins in the eleventh century although the earliest manuscript copies are from the late thirteenth century. The territory in which these texts came into being was the coastal region of what is now the Netherlands, together with neighbouring areas in modern Belgium and Germany. The former acceptance by scholars of the probability that Frisians were involved in the Anglo-Saxon migrations to Britain is now questioned, but at any rate the Old Frisian language, although known only from a much later date, appears to have some deep-rooted resemblances to Old English. For some earlier scholars these resemblances were sufficiently strong to justify the postulating of an 'Anglo-Frisian' language as an intermediate stage between West Germanic and the separate Old English and Old Frisian languages, but that view is not favoured these days. The traditional picture of a language undergoing successive splits into discrete parts may well be inadequate, and the similarities between Old English, Old Frisian, and Old Saxon are perhaps better seen as the result of parallel developments in a complex and changing social and linguistic situation.

Old English, finally, is the Germanic language that developed in Britain out of the dialects brought from the continent by the Anglo-Saxons during the period of invasions and settlements (principally the fifth and sixth centuries AD). Historical sources name the Angles and Saxons as two of the peoples who took part in those movements, and archaeological evidence has played a major part in the reconstruction of events (sometimes archaeology yields results not easily reconcilable with all the claims of written historical accounts). There is general agreement on the important role of the Angles and Saxons (the former from a homeland in the southern part of the Jutland peninsula), and also that other peoples involved are likely to have included, for example, Franks. But many details are unclear, including the varieties of language which were spoken by the invaders and settlers. Direct evidence for the continental Germanic languages becomes available only some time after the period of the settlements—for a language like Old Frisian, as we have seen, a long time after—which seriously limits the possibility for reconstructing the earlier linguistic situation. Comparison of the historically attested languages can nevertheless shed some light on the broader issues.

Some of the similarities between Old Frisian and Old English, or between those two languages and Old Saxon, are matters of phonology (the sound system), as in the case of the losses of *n* mentioned above. For example, Old Frisian and Old English have a vowel $\bar{e}$ or $\ae$ (the latter representing a vowel similar to that in modern English *there*) where Old Saxon (usually), Old High German, and Old Norse have $\bar{a}$ and Gothic has $\bar{e}$:

	Old Frisian	Old English	Old Saxon
'were' (*pl.*)	*wēron*	*wǣron*	*wārun*
'deed'	*dēd*	*dǣd*	*dād*

	Old High German	Old Norse	Gothic
'were' (*pl.*)	*wārun*	*váru*	*wēsun*
'deed'	*tāt*	*dáð*	*gadēþs*

There has been disagreement as to whether or not this indicates a particularly close relationship between Old Frisian and Old English. It is known that in Proto-Germanic the vowel in such words was *ǣ*. If, as some scholars think, West Germanic as a whole first changed this vowel to *ā*, and in Old Frisian and Old English it subsequently recovered something like its original sound, that may suggest a close connection between those two languages. Linguists look on 'shared innovations' as having some value for indicating relationships between languages. If, on the other hand, Old Frisian and Old English have merely preserved the Proto-Germanic vowel unchanged, along with Gothic, while the other languages have innovated with *ā*, the similarity between Old Frisian and Old English may be just a matter of coincidence. Linguists do not treat 'shared retentions' as normally of much help in determining relationship.

One important grammatical similarity between Old Frisian, Old English, and Old Saxon is to be found in the system of personal pronouns. For the first and second persons singular ('I' and 'you'), Gothic, Old Norse, and Old High German have different forms for the accusative case (direct object: 'Please help <u>me</u>', 'My friend saw <u>you</u>') and the dative case (indirect object: 'Send <u>me</u> [= to me] a letter', or with a preposition: 'The man gave the book to <u>you</u>'). In contrast, Old Frisian, Old Saxon, and Old English have just one form:

	Old Frisian	Old English	Old Saxon	Old High German		Old Norse		Gothic	
				acc.	dat.	acc.	dat.	acc.	dat.
first person	*mi*	*mē*	*mī*	*mih*	*mir*	*mik*	*mér*	*mik*	*mis*
second person	*thi*	*þē*	*thī*	*dih*	*dir*	*þik*	*þér*	*þuk*	*þus*

However, accusative forms *mec* and *þec* are also found in some dialects of Old English, and the alternation between accusative *mē*, *þē*, and *mec*, *þec* could result either from both forms having been brought to Britain by the Anglo-Saxons, or from *mec*, *þec* having been the only accusative forms brought with them and dative *mē*, *þē* having taken over that function after the settlement. Old Saxon also has, relatively infrequently, accusative *mik*, *thik*.

Once the individual Indo-European languages had begun to take separate form, the possibility arose that words would be borrowed from one language into another, as has happened in much more recent times as English has been carried around the globe. Identifying borrowings at a very early date (as distinct from two languages having each developed the same word from their common source) is usually a very uncertain business, and caution is needed in drawing any conclusions from supposed cases. An example which has been accepted by many scholars is the word which appears in Gothic as the noun *reiks* 'ruler', and both there and in the other Germanic languages as the adjective 'powerful' (Old Norse *ríkr*, Old High German *rīhhi*, Old Saxon *rīki*, Old Frisian *rīke*, Old English *rīce*; the word is the same as modern English *rich*). There exist elsewhere in Indo-European the corresponding forms Latin *rēx* and Old Irish *rí* ('king'). The vowel -*ī*- in Gothic *reiks*, etc. (Gothic *ei* represents *ī*), makes it easier to explain the Germanic word as having been borrowed from an early Celtic form **rīgs* than as its having developed independently in Germanic from the same Indo-European origins as the Celtic and Latin words. Scholars have related this interpretation of the linguistic material to the question of the earliest movements and interrelationships of the peoples speaking Indo-European languages, believing the borrowing to have happened some centuries before the beginning of the Christian era as the Germanic peoples were expanding from their original homeland and encountering the Celts on their way. It has been assumed that it indicates something of the nature of Celtic political organization, relative to that of the Germanic speakers, at the time the borrowing occurred.

Another frequently cited example of what is very probably a borrowing from Celtic is the word that appears in modern English as *iron* (Gothic *eisarn*, etc.). Corresponding forms in Celtic are Old Irish *iarn* and Welsh *haearn*. If the assumption of borrowing from Celtic into Germanic is correct, that may contribute to an understanding of the transmission of iron-working capabilities from one people to another at an early date.

Subsequent contact with Roman traders and armies led to borrowing from that source, too. An early case would be the Latin word *caupō* ('peddler, shopkeeper, innkeeper') having been borrowed as the basis for Germanic words meaning 'merchant' (Old Norse *kaupmaðr*, Old High German *koufo, koufman*, Old English *cȳpa, cēapmann*), 'to trade, buy and/or sell' (Gothic *kaupōn*, Old Norse *kaupa*, Old High German *koufen, coufōn*, Old Saxon *kōpon*, Old Frisian *kāpia*, English *cēapian, cȳpan*), 'act of buying and/or selling' (Old Norse *kaup*,

Old High German *kouf*, Old Saxon *kōp*, Old English *cēap*), and the like. The adoption of this foreign word by early Germanic speakers no doubt reflects the circumstances in which they typically encountered people in the outer reaches of the Roman world.

Much the same can be said of another word that is generally accepted to be one of the early borrowings into Germanic from Latin, the word that in modern English is *wine*. This word, representing Latin *vīnum*, is found across the whole spread of Germanic languages: Gothic *wein*, Old Norse *vín*, Old High German, Old Saxon, Old Frisian, Old English *wīn*. While there is no guarantee that the word was borrowed at a time when the individual Germanic languages were still not fully differentiated from one another, or even that they each owe it directly to Latin rather than in one or more cases having reborrowed it from a neighbouring Germanic language, the pervasiveness of the term may suggest an earlier rather than a later date (for which other arguments have also been put forward). As with the 'iron' word in respect of Celtic, the borrowing of the word for 'wine' reveals something about the early contacts of the Germanic peoples with the more southerly populations and cultures of Europe.

The Anglo-Saxons, on their way to Britain, encountered the Romans and the material and non-material aspects of their way of life in a variety of circumstances, peaceful and less so. As they settled in what would eventually become known as England they would have found much evidence of the civilization of the Roman garrisons and officials who had been leaving as they arrived, and it is likely that a significant part of the Romanized Celtic population that remained spoke a form of Latin. The Anglo-Saxons and their ancestors had by that time had contacts with the Romans over some five hundred years. Those contacts were reflected in a sizable number of borrowings of words from Latin, although it is not possible to reconstruct with great precision the date at or circumstances in which those borrowings occurred. They come from the first phase of an engagement with the Latin culture which in one way or another would be an inescapable and incalculably influential presence in England, as in continental Europe, for centuries to come. The next and subsequent phases will be a major concern of the remainder of this book.

SUGGESTIONS FOR FURTHER READING

For brief descriptions of the various Indo-European languages see Baldi (1983), or with more emphasis on their external histories (with notes on linguistic characteristics and short illustrative texts) Lockwood (1972). Szemerényi (1996) is a fuller, quite technical account of the sounds and inflectional forms of Indo-European. Benveniste (1973) discusses the Indo-European vocabulary related to a number of key areas of social organization.

Accessible and informative accounts of the Germanic language family are Bammes-berger (1992) and Robinson (1992). Bammesberger provides, in particular, a more systematic account of the sounds and forms of Proto-Germanic than has been given here, while Robinson outlines the historical background relevant to the various languages and gives brief descriptions of their linguistic characteristics (with commentary on passages of text illustrative of each language). Useful too, although somewhat technical, are Jasanoff (1997) and Nielsen (1981, 1989, and 1998). Lass (1987) and (1994a) also give some attention to aspects of the Germanic and Indo-European antecedents to Old English.

Runes are dealt with briefly in Page (1987), and more fully in Elliott (1989) and (for English runes) Page (1999). See also pp. 41–4 of this volume.

On the history of the Scandinavian languages, from their Germanic and Indo-European origins to the later twentieth century, see Haugen (1976). For a similar treatment of German see Keller (1978).

Aspects of the vocabulary of the early Germanic languages, with reference to the cultural environment in which they developed, are dealt with in Green (1998).

ACKNOWLEDGEMENTS

The author would like to thank John Hines for his assistance in the preparation of this chapter.

2

BEGINNINGS AND TRANSITIONS: OLD ENGLISH

Susan Irvine

Moððe word fræt. Me þæt þuhte
wrætlicu wyrd, þa ic þæt wundor gefrægn,
þæt se wyrm forswealg wera gied sumes,
þeof in þystro, þrymfæstne cwide
ond þæs strangan staþol. Stælgiest ne wæs   5
wihte þy gleawra, þe he þam wordum swealg.

('A moth devoured the words. That seemed to me a strange happening,
when I heard of that wonder, that the worm, a thief in the darkness,
swallowed up a man's speech, the glorious utterance and its firm
support. The thievish visitor was not at all the wiser for swallowing
those words.')

THIS short but evocative poem from the Exeter Book, one of the four major
extant Old English manuscripts containing poetry, provides a valuable
insight into language from an Anglo-Saxon perspective. The poem, known as
the 'Book-Moth Riddle', explores the transience of language, both spoken
and written. It also acts as a sombre reminder that we rely for our knowledge of
Old English on a relatively small number of manuscripts which have survived
the ravages of time. More importantly perhaps, through its sophisticated word-
play on the insubstantial nature of words it reminds us that these manuscripts reflect a living spoken language which was as familiar to its speakers

as modern English is to us today. In considering both speech and writing, the poem further draws our attention to the transition from orality to literacy in the use of the vernacular in Anglo-Saxon England, a transition which had enormous implications for the development of the Old English language. Although the written form of the language is necessarily the subject of this chapter, the strenuous attempts by Anglo-Saxon scribes to reproduce their spoken language in writing, without the conventions which we now take for granted, can be seen to underlie many of the linguistic features and developments which will be discussed here.

Old English is the term denoting the form of the English language used in England for approximately seven centuries (c450–1150 AD). It is a synthetic language (like Latin) rather than an analytic one (like modern English): it relies on inflections (or endings) on words to denote their function in the sentence. In nouns, pronouns, and adjectives it distinguishes between different cases (nominative, accusative, genitive, dative, and instrumental), genders (masculine, feminine, and neuter), and numbers (singular, plural, and—in some pronouns—dual). Just as in the antecedent stages of the language which have been discussed in the previous chapter, adjectives are not invariable (as they are in modern English) but are inflected strong or weak, depending on the syntactic circumstances in which they find themselves. In verbs, Old English distinguishes between different tenses (present and past), moods (indicative, subjunctive, and imperative), numbers (singular and plural), and persons (first, second, and third). Further discussion of these features, with detailed examples, will be found at pp. 45–6.

The term Old English, although it identifies a distinctive form of the English language, covers in fact a wide range of linguistic usages. In a period marked by enormous changes—political, social, and cultural—it is hardly surprising to find that the language too was far from stable. The theme of this chapter is transitions: the transition in the use of the vernacular from orality to literacy mentioned above was accompanied by a series of other transitions affecting Old English. These transitions can be viewed from both internal and external perspectives: internal in the sense of changes in spelling, grammar, and vocabulary, and external in the sense of the links between these changes and social and political events. This chapter will analyse the Old English language both in terms of its linguistic characteristics and also in relation to the external factors which so indelibly influenced it.

A useful framework within which one might examine the development of the Old English language is provided by five historical watersheds, each of which had significant linguistic implications. First, the invasion of Britain (purportedly in the mid-fifth century) by the Germanic peoples who became the Anglo-Saxons can be linked to the ensuing dialectal diversity which came to be so characteristic of this period of the language. Second, the coming of Christianity to Anglo-Saxon England in 597 AD made available the Roman alphabet for Old English writing, where previously, as Chapter 1 has indicated, only runes had been available. Third, the reign of King Alfred the Great in the West Saxon kingdom (871–99 AD) created a culture in which Old English became recognized as a language of prestige and status in its own right. Fourth, the Benedictine Reform of the second half of the tenth century led indirectly to the establishment of an Old English 'literary language'. Fifth, the Norman Conquest (1066 AD) precipitated developments in the language which would steer it ultimately towards what we now know as Middle English.

Given that the external and the internal histories of the language so clearly interact at these points, this chapter will focus on each of the five watersheds in turn, considering its implications for the forms and development of Old English. This structure is intended to allow flexibility: it is by no means always possible or desirable to link particular features or developments of the language to a specific period, and the discussion of extracts of text, some of which may be relevant historically but written or copied later, provides an opportunity throughout to pick up features of the language, whether orthographical, grammatical, syntactical, or lexical, which are of general interest for the study of Old English.

INVASION AND DIALECTAL DIVERSITY

The Anglo-Saxon monk Bede, in his eighth-century Latin history of the English nation known as the *Ecclesiastical History of the English People*, famously describes the arrival in Britain in 449 AD of a variety of Germanic tribes who had responded to King Vortigern's invitation to settle there. This migration myth, as Nicholas Howe has noted, became canonical in Anglo-Saxon England.[1] It was even incorporated into the Anglo-Saxon Chronicle, an important collection of annals which took shape in King Alfred's reign and then was kept up for over 200 years thereafter. The early part of the Anglo-Saxon Chronicle (the annals up to 890 AD) survives in two distinct forms: in a 'common stock' version and in what is known as the northern recension, a version which includes much material of

---

[1] See N. Howe, *Migration and Mythmaking in Anglo-Saxon England* (New Haven and London: Yale University Press, 1989).

particularly northern interest. The northern recension also incorporated extra material from Bede's *Ecclesiastical History*, including a translation of Bede's account of the migration. This recension is now best represented by the Peterborough Chronicle (also known as the E manuscript of the Chronicle). The following passage (which survives only in this manuscript) is taken from the entry for 449 in the Peterborough Chronicle:

Ða comon þa men of þrim megðum Germanie: of Aldseaxum, of Anglum, of Iotum. Of Iotum comon Cantwara 7 Wihtwara, þet is seo megð þe nu eardaþ on Wiht, 7 þet cyn on Westsexum þe man nu git hæt Iutnacynn. Of Ealdseaxum coman Eastseaxa 7 Suðsexa 7 Westsexa. Of Angle comon, se a syððan stod westig betwix Iutum 7 Seaxum, Eastangla, Middelangla, Mearca and ealla Norþhymbra.   5

('Those people came from three nations of Germany: from the Old Saxons, from the Angles, and from the Jutes. From the Jutes came the inhabitants of Kent and the *Wihtwara*, that is, the race which now dwells in the Isle of Wight, and that race in Wessex which is still called the race of the Jutes. From the Old Saxons came the East Saxons, the South Saxons, and the West Saxons. From the land of the Angles, which has lain waste between the Jutes and the Saxons ever since, came the East Anglians, the Middle Anglians, the Mercians, and all of the Northumbrians.')

The Anglo-Saxon migrations were undoubtedly, as Chapter 1 has suggested, a much more complex process than this account acknowledges. The settlement of the various Germanic peoples in different regions of the country was, however, an important factor in the linguistic diversity which characterized Old English, since dialectal distinctiveness can be linked to geographical areas. The terms Kentish, West Saxon, and Anglian (the latter also divided into Northumbrian and Mercian), which are used to describe the main dialects of Old English, suggest how, for the early stages in the writing of Old English at least, a correspondence can be clearly established between locality and linguistic forms (see Fig. 2.1).

The exact nature of this correspondence in any particular text or manuscript is, however, notoriously difficult to identify. The passage cited above, for example, already illustrates some of the difficulties of attempting to draw conclusions about dates or provenances of Old English texts from dialect evidence. Although it incorporated material composed much earlier, the Peterborough Chronicle was itself copied in about 1122 at Peterborough (and it continued thereafter up to 1154). Its own linguistic forms may well be attributable to a variety of factors: the late West Saxon archetype from which this version of the Chronicle seems ultimately to have derived, Anglian influence at some stage in transmission, the Peterborough scribe's own East Midland dialect (which is, in fact, an early Middle English designation which corresponds in many of its features to Anglian, the antecedent Old English

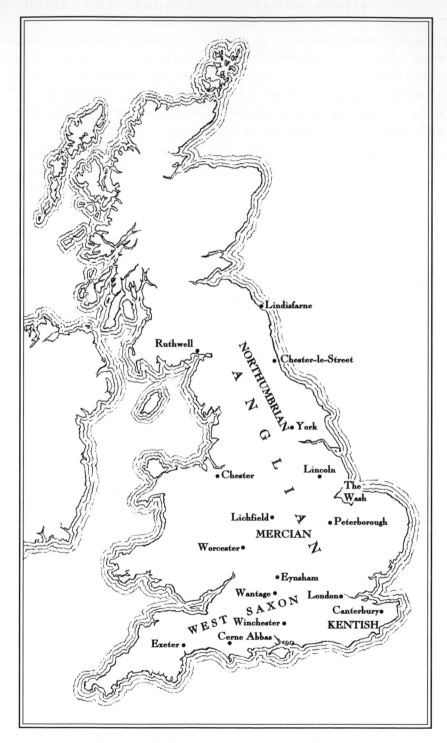

FIG. 2.1. Dialect areas in Anglo-Saxon England

variety; see Fig. 4.1), or the late date of the copy (the language of which shows signs of the transition to early Middle English). Thus, for example, within the passage, the scribe uses two different spellings for the 'Old Saxons', *Aldseaxum* in line 1 and *Ealdseaxum* in line 3. The latter is the normal West Saxon spelling (where *eald-* represents the sound-change known as breaking, by which a front vowel followed by a back consonant or group of consonants is diphthongized; here æ has been broken to *ea* before *ld*). The former spelling, which is non-West Saxon, might be the result of the vestige of an Anglian form introduced in textual transmission (in Anglian æ, rather than being broken to *ea* as in West Saxon, would instead normally be retracted to *a* and hence articulated with the tongue pulled back). Alternatively, it might be the product of the scribe's own East Midland dialect (in which unbroken forms would also be typical) or it might provide evidence of the early Middle English monophthongization of diphthongs by which *ea* was monophthongized to æ which later became *a*.

The link between dialect and geographical area can in some cases, however, be more clearly established, as in the various versions (fourteen in all) of the Old English poem known as Cædmon's *Hymn*. The story behind the composition of this poem—the spontaneous utterance of an illiterate cow-herd who miraculously receives the gift of poetry (see further, pp. 75–6)—is also related by Bede in his *Ecclesiastical History*. Bede himself quotes only a Latin translation of the poem, but several manuscripts contain what is purportedly the vernacular original. The version thought to be the closest to the original is written in a Northumbrian dialect on the last page of the earliest Latin manuscript of Bede's *Ecclesiastical History* (the so-called Moore Manuscript):

> Nu scylun hergan hefænricæs uard,
> metudæs mæcti end his modgidanc,
> uerc uuldurfadur, sue he uundra gihuæs,
> eci dryctin, or astelidæ.
> He ærist scop aelda barnum   5
> heben til hrofe, haleg scepen;
> tha middungeard moncynnæs uard,
> eci dryctin, æfter tiadæ
> firum foldu, frea allmectig.

('Now [we] must praise the Guardian of the heavenly kingdom, the Creator's might and His intention, the glorious Father's work, just as He, eternal Lord, established the beginning of every wonder. He, holy Creator, first shaped heaven as a roof for the children of men, then He, Guardian of mankind, eternal Lord, almighty Ruler, afterwards fashioned the world, the earth, for men.')

Various dialectal features can be used to identify this version as Northumbrian. In *uard* ('Guardian', line 1) and *barnum* ('children', line 5), we can, for example, again see what is known as retraction so that the front vowel æ becomes *a* (with back articulation) before *r* when followed by a consonant (in West Saxon, as we have seen, the expected form would instead have *ea*, the result of the very different process known as breaking by which æ is diphthongized to *ea*). Likewise, in *mæcti* ('might', line 2) and *uerc* ('work', line 3), we can see the results of the process known as Anglian smoothing, by which the diphthongs *ea* and *eo* before certain back consonants or consonant groups (here *c* and *rc*) became respectively the monophthongs æ and *e*. In the form of *scop* ('shaped', line 5) we can furthermore see no sign of a transitional glide vowel between the palatal /ʃ/ (which is articulated at the front of the mouth) and the back vowel represented by *o*—a sound-change which was established at an early stage in West Saxon (giving the comparable form *sceop*) but was more sporadic in Northumbrian. Moreover, in *foldu* ('earth', line 9), we can see early loss of inflectional -*n*, a change which was already typical of Northumbrian.

We can compare this with a later West Saxon version of the same poem in an Old English translation of Bede's *Ecclesiastical History*, made in the second half of the ninth century, perhaps in association with King Alfred's educational programme in Wessex:

> Nu sculon herigean heofonrices weard,
> meotodes meahte and his modgeþanc,
> weorc wuldorfæder, swa he wundra gehwæs,
> ece drihten, or onstealde.
> He ærest sceop eorðan bearnum   5
> heofon to hrofe, halig scyppend;
> þa middangeard monncynnes weard,
> ece drihten, æfter teode
> firum foldan, frea ælmihtig.

Here the Northumbrian forms of the Moore Manuscript version are replaced by West Saxon equivalents: *weard* ('Guardian') and *meahte* ('might'), *weorc* ('work'), *sceop* ('shaped'), *bearnum* ('children'), *scyppend* ('Creator'), *teode* ('fashioned'), *foldan* ('earth'). The distinctive dialectal characteristics of the two versions, instituted in their differences of spelling, are clearly linked to their geographical affiliations.

Cædmon's *Hymn* is, as Katherine O'Brien O'Keeffe notes, the earliest documented oral poem in Old English,[2] and its metrical and alliterative features typify

² See K. O'Brien O'Keeffe, *Visible Song: Transitional Literacy in Old English Verse* (Cambridge: Cambridge University Press, 1990), 24.

those of Old English poetry more generally. In none of its manuscript copies (nor indeed in those of any other Old English poetry—see, for example, the illustration from the *Beowulf* manuscript which appears in Fig. 2.2) is poetic format ever indicated graphically by, for example, lineation, or punctuation. Like all Old English poems, however, Cædmon's *Hymn* is clearly composed in poetic lines, each line being made up of four stresses, dividing into two two-stress half-lines which are linked by alliteration. Each half-line conforms to one of five rhythmical patterns according to its arrangement of stressed syllables and dips (groups of unstressed syllables). The constraints of alliteration and metre have a considerable impact on the language of Old English poetry. Its syntax is often complex: in line 1 of Cædmon's *Hymn*, for example, is the pronoun *we* ('we') missing before *sculon* ('must') (the word appears in some of the manuscripts)? Is *weorc wuldorfæder* ('the glorious Father's work', line 3) part of the object of praise (as in the translation above) or instead part of the subject ('[we], the glorious Father's work, must praise …')? Likewise, exactly what kind of connective is *swa* ('just as', line 3)? And does *firum foldan* mean 'for the men of earth' or '[made] the earth for men'? So too the diction of Old English poetry is characterized by what is known as 'variation' or repetition of sentence elements, as can be illustrated in Cædmon's *Hymn* by the variety of words for God: *heofonrices weard* ('the Guardian of the heavenly kingdom', line 1), *meotodes* ('Creator', line 2), *wuldorfæder*

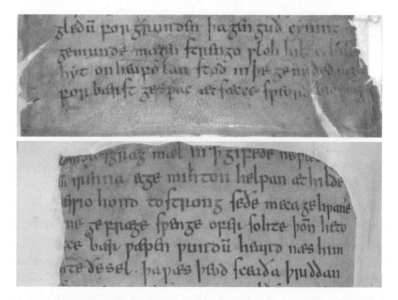

FIG. 2.2.   Lines 2677–87 of the manuscript of *Beowulf*. See p. 53 for the edited text. *Source:* Taken from the *Electronic Beowulf*, K. Kiernan (ed.) (London: The British Library Board, 2004).

('glorious Father', line 3), *ece drihten* ('eternal Lord', lines 4 and 8), *scyppend* ('Creator', line 6), *moncynnes weard* ('Guardian of mankind', line 7), *frea ælmihtig* ('almighty Ruler', line 9). It is also characterized by the use of poetic compounds (that is, words formed by joining together two separate words which already exist) and formulae (or set phrases used in conventional ways). Cædmon's *Hymn* contains both—poetic compounds such as *modgeþanc* ('intention', literally 'mind's purpose', line 2) and *wuldorfæder* ('glorious Father', line 3), and formulae such as *meotodes meahte* ('the Creator's might', line 2), *weorc wuldorfæder* ('the glorious Father's work', line 3), and *ece drihten* ('eternal Lord', lines 4 and 8).

The poem Cædmon's *Hymn* offers, therefore, a useful illustration of the distinctiveness of two Old English dialects, and it also exemplifies the features of Old English verse. For the Old English language, however, it embodies more than dialectal or formal significance. In the poem the most humble of inhabitants, a cow-herd, is shown to have the capacity for divine understanding through communication in the vernacular. The Old English language itself is thus effectively authenticated through its association with the miraculous, both in terms of the creation itself (the subject of the poem), and in terms of the poetic expression of this event by an illiterate cow-herd. England's identity as a Christian nation is presented as being intricately bound up with its language. The significance of Christianity for the development of the English language will be further explored in the next section.

CONVERSION TO CHRISTIANITY: ESTABLISHING A STANDARD SCRIPT

In 597 AD Augustine and his fellow missionaries arrived in Britain and began the gradual process of converting its inhabitants. The event is recorded in Bede's *Ecclesiastical History*, and also in the Anglo-Saxon Chronicle (the Parker Chronicle, the oldest manuscript of the Chronicle which is also known as the A version, attributes it to 601 AD; the Peterborough Chronicle records it twice, once under 596 AD and once under 601 AD). Fascinating from a linguistic perspective is Bede's account, also in his *Ecclesiastical History*, of how this missionary project came to be conceived. According to Bede, an encounter in a Roman market-place with a group of heathen slave-boys from Britain inspired Pope Gregory to send missionaries to convert that country. Bede's account wittily links Old English proper names with Latin terms denoting Christian concepts. The passage cited here is

from the Old English translation of the *Ecclesiastical History*, where the etymological play on words (seen in the linking of *Ongle* with *engla* in lines 2 and 3, *Dere*
with *de ira* in lines 5 and 6, and *Æll* with *Alleluia* in lines 8 and 9) gathers an extra
layer of resonance from its vernacular context:

Eft he [Gregory] frægn, hwæt seo þeod nemned wære, þe heo of cwomon. Ondswarede
him mon þæt heo Ongle nemde wæron. Cwæð he: Wel þæt swa mæg: forðon heo ænlice
onsyne habbað, ond eac swylce gedafonað, þæt heo engla æfenerfeweardas in heofonum
sy. Þa gyt he furðor frægn ond cwæð: Hwæt hatte seo mægð, þe þa cneohtas hider of
lædde wæron. þa ondswarede him mon ond cwæð, þæt heo Dere nemde wæron. Cwæð   5
he: Wel þæt is cweden Dere, *de ira eruti* [removed from anger]; heo sculon of Godes yrre
beon abrogdene, ond to Cristes mildheortnesse gecegde. Ða gyt he ahsode hwæt heora
cyning haten wære: ond him mon ondswarade ond cwæð, þætte he Æll haten wære. Ond
þa plegode he mid his wordum to þæm noman ond cwæð: Alleluia, þæt gedafenað, þætte
Godes lof usses scyppendes in þæm dælum sungen sy.   10

('Again he asked what the race from which they came was called. The reply was that they
were called English. He said: "That is appropriate, because they have a matchless
appearance and likewise it is fitting that they should be joint-heirs with the angels in
heaven." Then he inquired further, saying: "What is the name of the province from which
the boys were brought?" Then the reply came that they were called Deiri. He said: "Deiri
is an appropriate term, *de ira eruiti* [removed from anger]; they shall be removed from
God's anger and called to Christ's mercy." He asked moreover what their king was called;
the reply came that he was called Ælle. And then he punned on the name, saying:
"Alleluia, it is fitting that praise of God our Creator should be sung in those places."')

Here, as with Cædmon's *Hymn*, the nature of the vernacular language itself
becomes testimony to what was seen as the innate Christianity of the inhabitants
of Anglo-Saxon England. The very language that is spoken and written is seen to
bear witness to the nation's Christian identity. The word-play in this passage is of
course enhanced by the way in which Latin and Old English rely on the same
script to represent their language, and it is the origin of this script for English that
will be my focus in this section.

One of the most profound effects of the arrival of Christianity in Britain on the
English language was the development of an Old English script based on the
Roman alphabet. Before the arrival of the Christian missionaries, the only script
available in Anglo-Saxon England had been a different sort of writing altogether, a
runic 'alphabet' developed from the earlier Germanic *futhark* (see p. 22). Because
the fourth character in the sequence had changed, and because it is today
conventional to use 'c' to transliterate the sixth character, the set of runes used
by the Anglo-Saxons is normally referred to as the *futhorc* (and is illustrated in Fig.
2.3). It was used in central Mercia, Kent, and Northumbria from the fourth

continental caroline form *g* for /g/ and /dʒ/, as in *god* ('good') and *secgan* ('say'), and the retention of ȝ for the other sounds including /j/, as in *ȝear* ('year') and *dæȝ* ('day'). Other noteworthy features of the Old English alphabet were the absence of *j* and *v*, and the rarity with which *q*, *x*, and *z* were used. The Old English orthographical system seems in general to have been closely linked to phonemic representation: the exact correlation between the two is of course uncertain (not least given that we no longer have any native speakers of Old English). Nevertheless, as we have already seen, the sound patterns of the different dialects of Old English were clearly reflected in the orthographical usages of scribes.

The introduction of the Roman alphabet which was brought to England with the Christian mission had enormous linguistic implications for Old English, and indeed paved the way for the kind of visionary project to translate Latin works into the vernacular which is the subject of the next section of this chapter.

KING ALFRED AND THE PRODUCTION OF VERNACULAR MANUSCRIPTS

In 871 AD Alfred ascended to the throne of Wessex. Alfred's achievement as a military strategist over the period of his reign (871–99) is matched by his success in championing the vernacular. In his determination to educate as many of his subjects as possible and to make England a centre of intellectual achievement, Alfred set up a scheme by which certain important Latin works were to be translated into English. Alfred was not working in isolation; he seems to have been able to call upon scholars from Mercia as well as from the Continent. In a Preface to his translation of the late sixth-century work by Pope Gregory known as *Pastoral Care*, Alfred outlines his project. The Preface survives in two copies which are contemporary with Alfred: the passage here is cited from the manuscript which Alfred sent to Bishop Wærferth at Worcester:

Forðy me ðyncð betre, gif iow swæ ðyncð, ðæt we eac sumæ bec, ða ðe niedbeðearfosta sien eallum monnum to wiotonne, ðæt we ða on ðæt geðiode wenden ðe we ealle gecnawan mægen, ond gedon swæ we swiðe eaðe magon mid Godes fultume, gif we ða stilnesse habbað, ðætte eall sio gioguð ðe nu is on Angelcynne friora monna, ðara ðe ða speda
5 hæbben ðæt hie ðæm befeolan mægen, sien to liornunga oðfæste, ða hwile ðe hie to nanre oðerre note ne mægen, oð ðone first ðe hie wel cunnen Englisc gewrit arædan: lære mon siððan furður on Lædengeðiode ða ðe mon furðor læran wille ond to hieran hade don wille.

('Therefore it seems better to me, if it seems so to you, that we also translate certain books, those which are most necessary for all men to know, into the language which we can all understand, and bring to pass, as we very easily can with God's help, if we have peace, that all the free-born young people now in England, among those who have the means to apply themselves to it, are set to learning, whilst they are not competent for any other employment, until the time when they know how to read English writing well. Those whom one wishes to teach further and bring to a higher office may then be taught further in the Latin language.')

The passage serves not only to explain the burgeoning in the production of vernacular manuscripts at the end of the ninth century, but also to illustrate the linguistic features which are characteristic of early West Saxon in this period.

In its orthography the passage demonstrates the marked tendency in early West Saxon to use *io* spellings where late West Saxon would use *eo*, as in *iow* ('to you', line 1), *wiotonne* ('know', line 2), *geðiode* ('language', line 2), *sio gioguð* ('the young people', line 4), *liornunga* ('learning', line 5), and *Lædengeðiode* ('Latin language', line 7). In its morphology the passage, again characteristically of early West Saxon, makes full use of the Old English inflectional system. Case, number, and gender are strictly observed in nouns, pronouns, and adjectives, as the following examples (organized according to case) will show.

The nominative case, used to express the subject of the sentence (e.g. '**The boy** dropped the book'), is found in *sio gioguð* ('the young people', line 4), where the demonstrative pronoun *sio* is feminine singular agreeing with the noun; it also appears in the plural pronouns *we* (in lines 1, 2, and 3) and *hie* ('they', in lines 5 and 6).

The accusative case, used to express the direct object of the sentence (e.g. 'The girl found **the book**'), is found in *sumæ bec … niedbeðearfosta* ('certain books … most necessary', lines 1–2), where *sumæ* and *niedbeðearfosta* are feminine plural adjectives (inflected strong since they do not follow a demonstrative pronoun, possessive, or article; see further, pp. 18–19) and agreeing with the plural noun *bec*; we might also note that the feminine plural pronoun form *ða* is used twice in agreement with *bec*, first as part of a relative pronoun in line 1 (*ða ðe*, 'which') and, second, as a demonstrative pronoun in line 2 (meaning 'them'). The accusative case is also used to express the direct object in *ða stilnesse* ('peace', line 3), where the demonstrative pronoun and noun are feminine singular; *ða speda* ('the means', line 4), where the demonstrative pronoun and noun are again feminine plural; *Englisc gewrit* ('English writing', line 6), where the adjective (again inflected strong since it does not follow an article, demonstrative, or possessive pronoun) and noun are neuter singular. The accusative case is also used after some prepositions: *on ðæt geðiode* ('into the language', line 2), where the demonstrative pronoun and noun are neuter singular, *to liornunga* ('to learning', line 5), where the noun is feminine singular, and *oð ðone first* ('until the time', line 6), where the demonstrative pronoun and noun are masculine singular.

The genitive case, used to express a possessive relationship (e.g. 'the **girl's** book'), is found in *Godes* ('God's', line 3), where the noun is masculine singular, *friora monna* ('of free-born men', line 4), where the adjective and noun are masculine plural, and *ðara* ('of those', line 4), a demonstrative pronoun agreeing with *friora monna*.

The dative case, used to express the indirect object (e.g. 'The boy gave the book **to the teacher**'), is found in *eallum monnum* ('for all men', line 2), where the adjective and noun are masculine plural, *me* ('to me', line 1), a first person singular personal pronoun, *iow* ('to you', line 1), a second person plural personal pronoun, and *ðæm* ('to that', line 5), a neuter singular demonstrative pronoun. The dative case is also used after some prepositions: *mid ... fultume* ('with ... help', line 3), where the noun is masculine singular, *on Angelcynne* ('in England', line 4), where the noun is neuter singular, *to nanre oðerre note* ('for no other employment', lines 5–6), where the adjectives and noun are feminine singular, and *to hieran hade* ('to a higher office', line 7), where the comparative adjective (inflected weak as all comparatives are) and noun are masculine singular.

The Old English inflectional system of verb forms is also in evidence in the passage. Hence, for example, in *ðyncð* ('it seems'), which is used twice in line 1, the *-ð* inflection denotes the third person present singular of the verb whose infinitive form is *ðyncan* ('to seem'), and in *habbað* ('we have', line 4) the *-að* denotes the present plural of the verb whose infinitive is *habban* ('to have'). The forms *ðyncð* and *habbað*, which both express statements, are in the indicative mood; Old English also makes frequent use of the subjunctive mood, either to express doubt or unreality or (somewhat arbitrarily) within subordinate clauses. The verb *habban*, for example, also occurs in the present subjunctive plural form *hæbben* ('[they] may have', line 5); the verb *magan* ('to be able') occurs in its present indicative plural form *magon* ('[we] are able') in line 3 and also three times (once in the first person, twice in the third person) in its subjunctive plural form *mægen* ('[we]/[they] may be able'), in lines 3, 5, and 6. Both the infinitive (for example *gecnawan*, *befeolan*, *arædan*, *læran*, and *don*) and the inflected infinitive (*to wiotonne*) occur in the passage.

The freedom in word order which characterizes Old English syntax is equally evident. Although in main clauses Old English commonly used the word order

Subject–Verb–Object—now the basis of modern English word order—the use of inflections also allowed much more flexibility. The word order of the first sentence in the passage is particularly complex: in Old English subordinate clauses it was common for the verb to be placed at the end of the clause, but here the accumulation of subordinate clauses, when combined with the recapitulation of *ðæt we eac sumæ bec* ('that we also certain books', line 1) as *ðæt we ða* ('that we them', line 2), leads to very convoluted syntax indeed. In part at least this may be attributed to the attempt (more prevalent in early West Saxon writings than in late) to apply Latin syntactic constructions to a linguistic structure not suited to them.

That the task of translation which Alfred set himself and his advisers was not always an easy one is suggested by the Old English version of Book I Metre 2 of Boethius's *Consolation of Philosophy*. The translation of Boethius's early sixth-century work, like that of Gregory's *Pastoral Care*, seems to have been undertaken as part of Alfred's educational programme, and possibly by Alfred himself. Two versions of the translation survive, one consisting of prose only, one consisting of alternating prose and verse (as in Boethius's original). It seems that Boethius's metres were first translated into Old English prose, after which they were converted into poetry. It is interesting to compare the prose and poetic versions. Here is part of the prose version of the Old English Metre 2:

Ða lioð þe ic wrecca geo lustbærlice song ic sceal nu heofiende singan, and mid swiþe ungeradum wordum gesettan, þeah ic geo hwilum gecoplice funde; ac ic nu wepende and gisciende ofgeradra worda misfo.

('Those songs which I, an outcast, formerly sang joyfully, I must now sing grieving, and set them down with very discordant words, though I formerly composed as was fitting; but now weeping and sobbing I fail to find appropriate words.')

The Old English poetic version of this passage is more expansive:

> Hwæt, ic lioða fela lustlice geo
> sanc on sælum, nu sceal siofigende,
> wope gewæged, wreccea giomor,
> singan sarcwidas. Me þios siccetung hafað
> agæled, ðes geocsa, þæt ic þa ged ne mæg   5
> gefegean swa fægre, þeah ic fela gio þa
> sette soðcwida, þonne ic on sælum wæs.
> Oft ic nu miscyrre cuðe spræce,
> and þeah uncuðre ær hwilum fond.

('Lo, formerly I sang many songs joyfully in happy times; now, sighing, exhausted by weeping, I, a sad outcast, must sing sorrowful utterances. This sighing and sobbing have hindered me so that I cannot compose those songs so elegantly, although I formerly constructed many true utterances in happy times. Often now I misinterpret known words, and yet previously found unknown ones.')

The poetic passage emphasizes more vehemently than the prose the speaker's difficulty in finding the right words to use; we might perhaps detect in this expansion of the source a rueful admission by the translator of the sometimes tortuous nature of the process of translation into the vernacular. It is hard to imagine that *miscyrre* ('mis-turn', line 8) does not on some level at least apply to the pitfalls of translation.

The comparison of the Old English prose and verse versions of this Latin metre usefully illustrates some of the characteristic features of the language of Old English poetry. The verse contains vocabulary which is distinctively poetic (as in *giomor* 'sad', line 3). It relies on more compound words: *sarcwidas* ('sorrowful utterances', line 4), and *soðcwida* ('true utterances', line 7). Whilst some repetition with variation is found in the prose, as in the sequence of present participle verbs *heofiende ... wepende ... gisciende* ('grieving ... weeping ... sobbing', lines 1, 2 and 3), it is more prevalent in the verse: *siofigende, wope gewæged* ('sighing, exhausted by weeping', lines 2–3); *þios siccetung ... ðes geocsa* ('this sighing ... this sobbing', lines 4–5). Repetition of words or elements of words is found in *on sælum* ('in happy times', lines 2 and 7), *fela* ('many', lines 1 and 6), and *geo/gio* ('formerly', lines 1 and 6), *sarcwidas* and *soðcwidu* ('sorrowful utterances' and 'true utterances', lines 4 and 7), and in *cuðe* and *uncuðre* ('known' and 'unknown', lines 8 and 9). The two-stress half-line structure and alliteration typical of Old English poetry are employed throughout, if rather more loosely than elsewhere.

This section has examined the Old English language in the reign of King Alfred. West Saxon, in keeping with the political dominance of Wessex, was becoming the dialect most commonly used in the writing of the vernacular. The characteristics of early West Saxon in relation to Old English more generally have been analysed with reference to Alfred's Preface to his translation of Gregory's *Pastoral Care*; the characteristics of Old English poetry as distinct from prose have been considered in the light of the Old English prose and verse translation of Boethius's *Consolation of Philosophy*. The vitality of the vernacular in Alfred's reign had a lasting impact on the use and development of the language: its association with the court and with intellectual endeavour gave it an authority and prestige which enabled its acceptance as a literary language in its own right.

THE BENEDICTINE REFORM AND THE REGULARIZING OF OLD ENGLISH

The transition from 'early West Saxon' to 'late West Saxon' was not, of course, as abrupt or as clear-cut as these terms might suggest, although intervening historical circumstances had an important part to play in the development from 'early' to 'late'. In the second half of the tenth century, the English monasteries underwent a sweeping overhaul. Along with this monastic reform came a renewal of interest in the production of texts in the vernacular for didactic purposes. The production of these texts is marked by the considerable attention paid to the form which the vernacular should take. The school of Bishop Æthelwold (d. 984) at Winchester has been identified as the most significant focus of such linguistic scrutiny. Here, the evidence suggests, a concerted effort was made to establish a 'standard' literary language whose conventions were to be observed as consistently as possible. The use of the term 'standard' here denotes not common usage but rather a preferred usage which seems to have been systematically disseminated. The literary language to which it applies apparently developed from the West Saxon dialect (though it did not, as Peter Kitson has noted, necessarily correspond to the speech of the Winchester area),[3] but its influence spread beyond dialectal boundaries, creating an early supra-regional model of usage. A large number of written works which survive from the late tenth and early eleventh centuries can be seen to have been written or revised with the conventions of a standard late West Saxon in mind.

The works of the most prolific writer of the period, Ælfric, epitomize the efforts to achieve the kind of linguistic standardization which originated at Winchester. Ælfric was probably taught by Æthelwold at his Winchester school, before becoming monk and mass-priest at Cerne Abbas in Dorset, and later abbot of Eynsham in Oxfordshire. Ælfric's lexical and grammatical choices, as well as his revisions of his own earlier writings, provide important evidence of the attempts made to 'standardize' written Old English in this period.

Ælfric shows, for example, a number of lexical preferences in his writings. The argument that a regulated vocabulary can be found in several Old English texts or groups of texts associated with the Winchester school was first put forward by Helmut Gneuss and has been further substantiated by, amongst others, Walter

---

[3] Kitson argues, for example, that standard literary Old English reflects the spoken dialect of Wiltshire rather than Hampshire. See his article, 'Geographical Variation in Old English Prepositions and the Location of Ælfric's and Other Literary Dialects', *English Studies* 74 (1993), 1–50.

Hofstetter and Mechthild Gretsch.[4] The works of Ælfric stand out for the number of 'Winchester' words that they include and the consistency with which they are used: *ælfremed* (meaning 'foreign'), for instance, is preferred to *fremde* (a word with the same meaning) as, in precisely the same way, is *gelaðung* ('Christian community') to *cirice*.

Ælfric was also well aware of the importance of a consistent grammatical system. He wrote his own grammar, designed to facilitate the learning of Latin by English people: in a Preface to this work he states unequivocally that *stæfcræft is seo cæg ðe ðæra boca andgit unlicð* ('grammar is the key which unlocks the meaning of the books'). In a Preface to another of his works, his translation of *Genesis*, Ælfric addresses the pitfalls of translating from Latin into English. His attention to grammatical detail is demonstrated in this Preface (quoted here from a copy made in the second half of the eleventh century):

Oft ys seo halige þrinnys geswutelod on þisre bec, swa swa ys on þam worde þe God cwæþ: 'Uton wyrcean mannan to ure anlicnisse'. Mid þam þe he cwæð 'Uton wyrcean' ys seo þrinnis gebicnod; mid þam þe he cwæð 'to ure anlicnisse' ys seo soðe annis geswutelod: he ne cwæð na menifealdlice, 'to urum anlicnissum', ac anfealdlice, 'to ure
5 anlicnisse'.

('Often the holy trinity is revealed in this book, just as it is in the words which God said: "Let us make man in our image". When he said "Let us make", the trinity is betokened; when he said "in our likeness" the true unity is revealed: he did not say in the plural "in our likenesses", but in the singular "in our likeness".')

Here Ælfric focuses on the significance of the distinction between *anlicnisse* ('likeness', lines 2, 3, and 5), with its dative singular inflection -*e*, and *anlicnissum* ('likenesses', line 4), with its dative plural inflection -*um*. Precise grammatical usage, Ælfric insists, can affect meaning in crucial ways. It is ironic that in a twelfth-century copy of this Preface, which was made at a time when the inflectional system was breaking down (see further, pp. 55–8), the reading *anlicnesse* for *anlicnissum* blurs the grammatical distinction that Ælfric had so carefully delineated.

The process of grammatical revision in the work of Ælfric (and other authors) is visible in the manuscripts themselves. In many of the manuscripts containing

---

[4] See Gneuss's seminal article, 'The Origin of Standard Old English and Aethelwold's School at Winchester', *Anglo-Saxon England* 1 (1972), 63–83. Hofstetter's 'Winchester and the Standardization of Old English Vocabulary', *Anglo-Saxon England* 17 (1988), 139–61, and Gretsch's *The Intellectual Foundations of the English Benedictine Reform* (Cambridge: Cambridge University Press, 1999) provide further important contributions.

Ælfric's works, there are signs of corrections and alterations which may be in Ælfric's own hand.[5] One of the manuscripts which shows such corrections is the earliest extant copy of Ælfric's First Series of *Catholic Homilies*, British Library, Royal 7 C.xii, as exemplified by the following passage from Homily Dominica in Quinquagessima:

Ac hwæðre he cwyð on oðre stowe? Eower heofonlica fæder wat hwæs ge behofiað. ær þan þe ge hine æniges þinges biddon; þeahhwæðere wile se gooda god þ we hine georne biddon? for ðan þurh þa gebedu. bið ure heorte onbryrd? 7 gewend to gode; Ða cwæð se blinda? la leof. do þ ic mæge geseon; Ne bæd se blinda. naðor ne goldes ne seolfres? ne nane woruldlice þing? ac bæd his gesihðe.

5

('And yet he said elsewhere: "Your heavenly Father knows what is fitting before you pray to him for anything; however the good God wishes us to pray eagerly to him because through those prayers our hearts are fired up and turned to God". Then the blind man said: "Beloved, make me able to see". The blind man did not pray for gold or silver or any worldly thing, but prayed for his sight.')

Here the form *biddon* ('[you] ask for', line 2) represents an alteration in the manuscript from the original reading *biddað*: the indicative form has been altered to subjunctive after the conjunction *ær þan þe* ('before', lines 1–2). The nouns *goldes* ('gold', line 4) and *seolfres* ('silver', line 4) also represent manuscript alterations from *gold* and *seolfor*, so that the objects sought (or rather not sought) are placed in the genitive rather than the accusative case; curiously the alterations here (and elsewhere in the manuscript) are not consistently made, since *þing* ('thing', line 5) remains in the accusative case. In his revisions Ælfric characteristically alters any dative case inflections on words which follow the preposition *þurh* into the accusative case; the prepositional phrase *þurh þa gebedu* ('through those prayers', line 3) here represents his preferred usage. The types of alterations made by Ælfric and his contemporaries are presumably designed to bring the manuscript copies in line with a recognized literary style. It has to be said, however, that the extent to which these can be linked to the Winchester school's attempt to establish a 'standard' written linguistic usage

---

[5] For detailed discussion of this, see K. Sisam, *Studies in the History of Old English Literature* (Oxford: Oxford University Press, 1953), 172–85, N. Eliason and P. Clemoes (eds), *Ælfric's First Series of Catholic Homilies* (Early English Manuscripts in Facsimile, Copenhagen: Rosenkilde and Bagger, 1966), 33 and, most recently, M. R. Godden, 'Ælfric as Grammarian: the evidence of his Catholic Homilies', in E. Treharne and S. Rosser (eds), *Early Medieval Texts and Interpretations: Studies Presented to Donald C. Scragg* (Tempe, AZ, 2002), 13–29.

rather than to the preferences of individual scribes or monastic houses is, as Donald Scragg has argued, still far from clear.[6]

The excerpt above, taken from the 1997 edition of Ælfric's *Catholic Homilies* by Peter Clemoes, also exemplifies differences between Old English and modern punctuation since its editor has chosen to retain manuscript punctuation. These differences are often obscured in editions which use modern English punctuation, a practice which potentially leads to distortion of meaning. The punctuation in this manuscript is used in a well organized way, if not always entirely evenly. In this passage, three punctuation marks are used: the simple *punctus* (.), a *punctus elevatus* (?), and a *punctus versus* (;), the first two being used within sentences and the last at the close of sentences. A fourth punctuation mark, the *punctus interrogativus*, is used elsewhere but not in the passage. Capitals are mostly, but not always, used at the beginning of a sentence. There is some use of abbreviation: the crossed thorn þ is used for *þæt* (see lines 2 and 4) and the symbol 7 is used for *and*. Although the punctuation practices of Old English scribes from manuscript to manuscript are far from consistent, they have been shown all to derive in one way or another from attempts to facilitate the reading aloud of texts from manuscripts.

Whilst the Benedictine Reform does not seem to have stimulated the composition of poetry in the same way as it did that of prose, the interest in the vernacular which it fostered presumably explains why the majority of Old English poetry survives from manuscripts which were copied in the second half of the tenth or early eleventh centuries. The poetry too seems to have been subject to the regularizing process which characterizes linguistic usage at this time. The language of the texts in the four main extant poetic codices (the Exeter Book, the Vercelli Book, the Cædmon Manuscript, and the Beowulf Manuscript) is largely late West Saxon, albeit with some non-West Saxon elements. The non-West Saxon elements, which are both grammatical and lexical, may have been considered particularly appropriate to poetry.

Excerpts from two poems, one composed in the early eleventh century and one copied in the same period but composed much earlier are here juxtaposed to show their linguistic similarities and differences. The first is lines 2677–87 of *Beowulf* (see Fig. 2.2):

---

[6] See D. G. Scragg, 'Spelling variations in eleventh-century English', in C. Hicks (ed.), *England in the Eleventh Century: Proceedings of the 1990 Harlaxton Symposium* (Stamford: Paul Watkins, 1992), 347–54.

Þa gen guðcyning
mærða gemunde, mægenstrengo sloh
hildebille þæt hyt on heafolan stod
niþe genyded; Nægling forbærst,   2680
geswac æt sæcce sweord Biowulfes
gomol ond grægmæl. Him þæt gifeðe ne wæs
þæt him irenna ecge mihton
helpan æt hilde; wæs sio hond to strong
se ðe meca gehwane mine gefræge   2685
swenge ofersohte; þonne he to sæcce bær
wæpen wundum heard, næs him wihte ðe sel.

('Then once more the war-prince was mindful of glorious deeds; he struck with his battle-sword with great strength so that it stuck in the head, driven by hostility. Nægling snapped, Beowulf's sword, ancient and grey-coloured, failed him in battle. It was not granted him that iron blades could help him in fighting; the hand was too strong which, so I have heard, overtaxed every sword with its stroke; when he carried to battle a wondrously hard weapon, it was not at all the better for him.')

The other is lines 162–8 of *The Battle of Maldon*, a poem which is thought to have been composed a decade or so after the battle of 991 which it describes. It now survives only in a transcript made shortly before the manuscript containing it was destroyed in the Cotton fire of 1731:

Þa Byrhtnoð bræd bill of sceðe
brad and bruneccg, and on þa byrnan sloh.
To raþe hine gelette lidmanna sum,
þa he þæs eorles earm amyrde.   165
Feoll þa to foldan fealohilte swurd:
ne mihte he gehealdan heardne mece,
wæpnes wealdan.

('Then Byrhtnoth drew a broad and shiny-edged sword from its sheath and struck at the coat of mail. Too quickly one of the sailors hindered him, when he injured the earl's arm. Then the golden-hilted sword fell to the ground: he could not hold the hard sword or wield the weapon.')

Both excerpts show their poets exploiting poetic diction. Hence both employ a considerable amount of variation, particularly in their words for 'sword': the distinctively poetic word for 'sword', *mece*, appears in both (*Beowulf*, line 2685, and *Maldon*, line 167), *Beowulf* also includes *hildebille* ('battle-sword', line 2679), *sweord* ('sword', line 2681), *irenna ecge* ('iron blades', line 2683), and *wæpen* ('weapon', line 2687), and *Maldon* includes *bill* ('sword', line 162), *swurd* ('sword', line 166), and *wæpnes* ('weapon', line 168). Likewise both make use of the compound words which are so frequent in Old English poetry: *Beowulf* has, for example, *guðcyning* ('war-prince', line 2677), *mægenstrengo* ('great strength', line 2678), and *grægmæl* ('grey-coloured', line 2682); *Maldon* has, for example, *bruneccg* ('shiny-edged', line 163) and *fealohilte* ('golden-hilted', line 166).

Both passages are written mainly in late West Saxon. The language in *The Battle of Maldon* is, as Scragg has remarked, notable for its uniformity and for the consistency with which it conforms to the late Old English standard. In this passage, for example, *-wur-* for earlier *-weor-* in *swurd* ('sword', line 166), the verb form *mihte* ('could', line 167), and the *-ea-* spellings in *gehealdan* ('hold', line 167) and *wealdan* ('wield', line 168) (which both reveal the operation of breaking; see p. 37) are all characteristic of late West Saxon. The language of *Beowulf* is less consistent, supporting the view of Frederick Klaeber that 'the text was copied a number of times, and that scribes of heterogeneous dialectal habits and different individual peculiarities had a share in that work'.[7] In the passage cited above there are a number of usages which do not seem to conform to late West Saxon: *gen* ('once more', line 2677) is a mainly Anglian word (though it may, like *mece*, have been considered poetic), the *-weor-* in *sweord* ('sword', line 2681) is early rather than late, and the *-io-* in *Biowulfes* ('Beowulf's', line 2681) and in *sio* ('the', line 2684) is characteristically early West Saxon rather than late.

As can be seen, a range of shared orthographical and phonological practices characterizes the 'late West Saxon' language of these two poems, one composed in the early eleventh century and one copied at that time from a much earlier original. There seems no doubt that the interest in linguistic consistency fostered by the Benedictine Reform movement led to a concerted attempt by Æthelwold and other writers associated with his school at Winchester to regularize Old English grammatical and lexical usage. It is also clear, however, that there was still considerable variation in Old English linguistic usage and that any notion of a 'standard' written language in the late tenth century and early eleventh century is to be understood as very different from the notion of a 'standard' when applied to the emergence of standard English in the first half of the fifteenth century onwards, as we shall see in Chapter 5.

---

[7] See F. Klaeber (ed.), *Beowulf and the Fight at Finnsburg* (3rd edn.). (Boston: D. C. Heath, 1950), lxxxviii–lxxxix.

THE CONQUEST: A LANGUAGE IN TRANSITION

Cultural, social, and political upheavals rocked Anglo-Saxon England in the wake of the Norman Conquest. The spoken language too was indubitably undergoing enormous changes as the impact of the invaders' language infiltrated Old English usage, and such changes would eventually be reflected in the development of Middle English (see further Chapters 3 and 4). The written language, however, remained for some time remarkably close to pre-Conquest late West Saxon. In part the conservatism here is due to the fact that the majority of the texts which were written down in the late eleventh and twelfth centuries were copies of earlier Old English works; there is little evidence of much new composition in English taking place in this period. Even those works which do seem to have been composed after the Conquest largely conform to the written conventions familiar from earlier Old English. It is possible, nevertheless, to identify a number of linguistic developments in works copied or composed after the Conquest which do reflect more general changes in the language, and it is these developments which this final section of the chapter will address.

The Norman Conquest itself is recorded briefly in the Parker Chronicle entry for 1066, and in more detail in other versions of the Chronicle including the Peterborough Chronicle version which is cited here:

7 þa hwile com Willelm eorl upp æt Hestingan on Sancte Michaeles mæssedæg, 7 Harold com norðan 7 him wið feaht ear þan þe his here come eall, 7 þær he feoll 7 his twægen gebroðra Gyrð 7 Leofwine. And Willelm þis land geeode 7 com to Westmynstre, 7 Ealdred arcebiscop hine to cynge gehalgode, 7 menn guldon him gyld 7 gislas sealdon 7 syðð̵an heora land bohtan.

5

('And meanwhile the earl William landed at Hastings on St Michael's Day, and Harold came from the north and fought against him before all his army arrived. And he and his two brothers Gurth and Leofwine died there. And William conquered this land and came to Westminster. And Archbishop Ealdred consecrated him as king. And men paid him tribute and gave him hostages, and afterwards redeemed their lands.')

Given that this is part of an annal copied in around 1121, more than half a century after the Conquest, the language is remarkably close to late West Saxon. This was almost certainly the dialect in which the scribe's exemplar (or original) was written. Occasional orthographical inconsistencies do nevertheless give some indication of ongoing linguistic changes. The falling together of unstressed vowels, for instance, which in fact seems to have begun before 900 and gathered momentum thereafter, is reflected in the inflection -*an* (for -*on*) in the past plural verb form *bohtan* ('redeemed', line 5), whereas both *guldon* ('paid', line 4) and *sealdon* ('gave', line 4) have the more usual inflection -*on*. The spelling *ear* ('before', line 2) for *ær* may reflect the late Old English falling together of the sounds represented by *æ*, *e*, and *ea*. On the whole there is, in fact, little to distinguish this language, orthographically, grammatically, or syntactically, from the language as it had been written a century or more earlier.

The Peterborough Chronicle is of interest not only because it offers a twelfth-century copy of earlier annals but also because it offers an example of new composition in English at this time when very little else survives. The language of the annals after 1121 apparently reflects more closely the form of English spoken by their scribes. The First Continuation (covering the years 1122–31) was written by the same scribe who was responsible for copying the earlier entries; the Second or Final Continuation (covering 1132–54) was written by a different scribe. The passage quoted here is from the annal for 1140, where the conflict between King Stephen and the Empress Matilda is recounted thus:

Þa was Engleland suythe todeled: sume helden mid te king 7 sume mid þemperice, for þa þe king was in prisun, þa wenden þe eorles 7 te rice men þat he neure mare sculde cumen ut, 7 sahtleden wyd þemperice 7 brohten hire into Oxenford 7 iauen hire þe burch. Þa þe king was ute, þa herde ðat sægen 7 toc his feord 7 besæt hire in þe tur. 7 me læt hire dun
5   on niht of þe tur mid rapes 7 stal ut, 7 scæ fleh 7 iæde on fote to Walingford.

('Then England was greatly divided: some supported the king and some the empress. When the king was in prison, the eorls and the powerful men thought that he would never get out and made an agreement with the empress and brought her to Oxford and gave her the town. When the king was free, he heard about it and took his army and besieged her in the tower, and she was let down from the tower at night with ropes, and stole away, and walked to Wallingford.')

Here it is word order rather than inflections which points to the grammatical function of words. Hence the marking of cases has become largely superfluous: after prepositions, for example, there is no indication of case (as in *mid te king* in line 1 and *of þe tur* in line 5). The nominative masculine singular pronoun is *þe*, or *te* when it occurs after *d* or *t*; the nominative feminine singular is now *scæ* (line 5), close to its modern English equivalent 'she'. In personal pronouns, the falling together of the accusative and dative forms, which is characteristic of Middle English, is also evident. In, for example, *brohten hire* ('brought her', line 3), whereas in Old English we would have expected to find the direct object of *brohten* expressed by the accusative singular feminine form *hie*, here the Old English dative form is found. The form *me* (line 4) replaces the impersonal pronoun *man* ('one'). The word *king* is regularly spelt with initial *k* rather than *c*, in line with the Middle English usage of *k* rather than *c* before *e*, *i*, and *y*. Nouns show no inflection in the singular (except in the phrase *on fote* in line 5) where the *-e* on *fote* is presumably a vestigial dative). Moreover, in the plural the inflection *-es* is now common: in *mid rapes* ('with ropes', line 5), for example, the *-es* gives no indication of case. On verbs, the *-en* inflection denotes the past tense indicative plural as in *helden* ('supported') in line 1, and *wenden* ('thought') in line 2, as well as the infinitive, as in *cumen* ('come') in line 2 and *sægen* ('say') in line 4. The diction shows the influence of foreign loan-words, as in the French word *prisun* (for more on this subject, see Chapter 3 of this volume).

Much more common than new composition in English in the twelfth century was the copying of earlier texts. Oxford, Bodleian Library, Bodley 343, for example, a manuscript copied in the second half of the twelfth century, contains a substantial collection of works by Ælfric and his contemporaries. Although the language of Bodley 343 is remarkably conservative considering the late date of the manuscript, a number of linguistic changes can be observed when its text is compared with earlier versions. In the following extracts, Passage A comes from the Vercelli Book (from the second half of the tenth century) and Passage B from Bodley 343, copied up to two centuries later. The earlier version in Vercelli Homily X (Passage A) reads:

Hwær syndon þa rican caseras 7 cyningas þa þe gio wæron, oððe þa cyningas þe we io cuðon? Hwær syndon þa ealdormen þa þe bebodu setton? Hwær is demera domstow? Hwær is hira ofermetto, butan mid moldan beþeahte 7 in witu gecyrred? Wa is worulde-scriftum, butan hie mid rihte reccen.

The later version in Bodley 343 (Passage B) reads:

Hwær beoð þæ rice caseres, and þa kyngæs, þe we iu cuþæn? Hwær beoð þa ealdormen þe boden setten? Hwær is domeræ domselt? Hwær beoð heoræ ofermedo, buton mid molde beþeaht, and on wite wræce[n]? Wa byð weorldscryftum buton heo mid rihte ræden and tæcæn.

('Where are the wealthy emperors [and kings of former days (A only)], or [B. and] the kings we previously knew? Where are the noblemen who established laws? Where is the judgment seat of judges? Where is their pride, except covered with dust and turned [B. driven] to torment? Woe is it for earthly judges unless they direct [B. advise and teach] with justice.')

Although the two passages clearly derive (at least ultimately) from the same source, the linguistic distinctions further indicate and confirm some of the changes which characterize the English language in this transitional stage between Old and Middle English. The inflections of the later version show less consistency than the earlier one: in Passage A, for example, the nominative plural nouns *caseras* ('emperors', line 1) and *cyningas* ('kings', twice in line 1) all end in -*as*; in Passage B the corresponding nouns differ from each other in their inflections (*caseres* and *kyngæs*, both in line 1). The vowels used in unstressed syllables (including inflections) are confined in Passage B almost entirely to *æ* and *e*, where Passage A still regularly uses the back vowels *a*, *o*, and *u*: hence, for example, the past plural indicative of verbs is systematically denoted by -*on* in Passage A's *cuðon* ('knew', line 2) and *setton* ('established', line 2), but by -*æn* and -*en* in Passage B's *cuþæn* (line 1) and *setten* (line 2). The scribe of Passage B may be more inclined, as Peter Kitson has argued,[8] to represent the Old English back vowels *a*, *o*, and *u* by *æ*, as in *þæ* ('the', line 1), *kyngæs* ('kings', line 1), *cuþæn* ('knew', line 1), *domeræ* ('of judges', line 2), *heoræ* ('their', line 2), and *tæcæn* ('teach', line 4), and the unaccented front vowel *e* by *e*, but this is by no means a consistent practice. In contrast with Passage A where, as is common in Old English, *c* is used rather than *k*, in Passage B the normal Middle English spellings of *c* before *a*, *o*, and *u*, and *k* before *e*, *i*, and *y*, are used, as in *caseres* ('emperors') and *kyngæs* ('kings') in line 1. Again in accordance with the development towards Middle English, there is a tendency for the earlier more complex inflection of adjectives to be reduced to -*e*, as in Passage B's *rice* ('wealthy', line 1) (beside *rican*, inflected weak since it follows the article, in line 1 of Passage A).

Old English works continued to be used in the late twelfth and even early thirteenth centuries, but fairly extensive rewriting and adaptation into Early Middle English was clearly necessary in the compilation of collections such as the Lambeth and Trinity Homilies, which drew on Old English works. By the time glossators such as the Worcester scribe known as the 'Tremulous Hand' (because of his distinctive shaky handwriting) were at work in the thirteenth century, it is evident that the increasing unfamiliarity with the Old English language had made it virtually incomprehensible without the provision of glosses or explanatory translations accompanying the text.

CONCLUSION

The transition from Old to Middle English is only the last in a series of transitions which the Old English language underwent over its seven centuries of existence. Interrelation between external and internal history, as the structure of this chapter attests, can be used to illuminate and characterize the development of the Old English language.

---

[8] See P. Kitson, 'Old English Dialects and the Stages of Transition to Middle English', *Folia Linguistica Historica* 11 (1992), 27–87.

This chapter began with the 'Book-Moth Riddle' where the image of a moth or worm eating through parchment is used percipiently by the poet to explore the transient nature of both written and spoken words. The Anglo-Saxons were, as that short poem indicates, only too well aware of the precariousness of language. But this is a language which survives, albeit in a very different form from that in which the Anglo-Saxons knew it. The ability of the language to adapt, to change in accordance with the historical circumstances which were so inextricably linked with its fortunes, led ultimately to the English language with which we are familiar today.

REFERENCES AND SUGGESTIONS FOR FURTHER READING

The poem with which I begin is quoted from Krapp and Dobbie (1936). General introductions to Old English can be found in Mitchell and Robinson (2001) and Baker (2003), as well as in Mitchell (1995).

Invasion and dialectal diversity

For Bede's *Ecclesiastical History of the English People*, see Colgrave and Mynors (1969); the passage alluded to here is in Book I, chapter 15. The migration myth is discussed by Howe (1989). The passage from the Peterborough Chronicle is quoted from Irvine (2004). For further information on Old English sound changes, see Campbell (1959) and Hogg (1992b); for further information on Early Middle English sound changes, see Jordan (1974). The Northumbrian version of Cædmon's *Hymn* is from the manuscript Cambridge University Library, Kk.5.16, and is quoted from Dobbie (1942); the West Saxon version is also quoted from Dobbie. On the manuscript lay-out of the poem, see O'Brien O'Keeffe (1990).

Conversion to Christianity: establishing a standard script

For Bede's *Ecclesiastical History*, see Colgrave and Mynors (1969); for Augustine's arrival see Book I, chapter 25, for Gregory and the slave-boys see Book II, chapter 1. For the Parker Chronicle, see Bately (1986); for the Peterborough Chronicle, see Irvine (2004). The passage from the Old English translation of Bede's *Ecclesiastical History* is quoted from Miller (1890–8). The passage from *The Dream of the Rood* is quoted from Swanton (1987), as is also the transliteration of the runic inscription. The runic inscription itself can be found in full in Dickins and Ross (1954). For a useful discussion of Old English runes, see Page (1999).

History of the English People (completed in 731), the Anglo-Saxon monk Bede talks about the five languages of Britain:

Haec in praesenti iuxta numerum librorum quibus lex diuina scripta est, quinque gentium linguis unam eandemque summae ueritatis et uerae sublimitatis scientiam scrutatur et confitetur, Anglorum uidelicet Brettonum Scottorum Pictorum et Latinorum, quae meditatione scripturarum ceteris omnibus est facta communis.

('At the present time, there are five languages in Britain, just as the divine law is written in five books, all devoted to seeking out and setting forth one and the same kind of wisdom, namely the knowledge of sublime truth and of true sublimity. These are the English, British, Irish, Pictish, as well as the Latin languages; through the study of the scriptures, Latin is in general use among them all.')

Bede is talking about Britain here (*Britannia*), not simply England, but one would only need to take away Pictish—spoken in northern Scotland—to represent the situation in England, leaving some four languages at any rate. (By British, Bede means what we would call Welsh, and the language of the *Scotti* is what we would now call Irish.)

For a second snapshot, let us consider a 946 grant of land by King Eadred (who reigned 946–55) to his subject Wulfric. The charter is written in a form of Latin verse, and in it Eadred is said to hold the government *Angulsaxna cum Norþhymbris / paganorum cum Brettonibus* ('of the Anglo-Saxons with the Northumbrians, and of the pagans with the Britons'), while his predecessor Edmund (who reigned 940–46) is described as king *Angulsaxna & Norþhymbra / paganorum Brettonumque* ('of the Anglo-Saxons and Northumbrians, of the pagans and the Britons'). In these texts, 'pagans' means Scandinavians, and so peoples speaking three different languages are recognized here: the Scandinavians speak Norse, the Britons speak Celtic, and the Anglo-Saxons (of whom the Northumbrians had come to form a part) speak Old English. The text itself, being in Latin, adds a fourth language.

And for a third snapshot we may turn to the monk (and historian) Jocelin of Brakelond's early thirteenth-century *Chronicle of the Abbey of Bury St Edmunds*. Jocelin tells us the following about the hero of his work, Abbot Samson:

Homo erat eloquens, Gallice et Latine, magis rationi dicendorum quam ornatui uerborum innitens. Scripturam Anglice scriptam legere nouit elegantissime, et Anglice sermocinare solebat populo, et secundum linguam Norfolchie, ubi natus et nutritus erat, unde et pulpitum iussit fieri in ecclesia et ad utilitatem audiencium et ad decorem
5   ecclesie.

('He was eloquent both in French and Latin, having regard rather to the sense of what he had to say than to ornaments of speech. He read English perfectly, and used to preach in English to the people, but in the speech of Norfolk, where he was born and bred, and to this end he ordered a pulpit to be set up in the church for the benefit of his hearers and as an ornament to the church.')

Here we can observe a trilingual culture exemplified within a single person. Samson's native language is English—and a dialectally marked English at that—and it is English which he uses to preach to the laity; but his eloquence in Latin and French makes him a microcosm of learned and cultured society in the late twelfth and early thirteenth centuries, where two learned languages tended to take precedence over the majority's mother tongue.

It is no coincidence that all three introductory snapshots are taken from texts in Latin; in the written mode (as opposed to the spoken), it is Latin, and not English, which forms the one constant in the linguistic history of medieval England. And it should also be noted how my three snapshots are chronologically distributed over the Old English and early Middle English periods—one from the eighth century, one from the tenth, and one from the early thirteenth. It is sometimes claimed that post-Conquest England was the most multilingual and multicultural place to be found anywhere in medieval Europe at any time; but in fact there was nothing in, say, 1125 which could not have been matched in 1025 or 925, so long as one substitutes the Norse of the Scandinavian settlements for the French of the Norman. The Norman Conquest makes no great difference in terms of the linguistic complexity of medieval England; it merely changes the languages involved.

THE LANGUAGES OF MEDIEVAL ENGLAND

The basic timelines of the non-English languages of medieval England can be stated quickly; a more nuanced account will follow shortly. Celtic (or strictly speaking, Brittonic Celtic or British) was, as Chapter 1 has already noted, the language of those peoples who occupied the country before the arrival of the Anglo-Saxons, and is likely to have remained a spoken language in parts of England through much of the Anglo-Saxon period, before it became confined to those areas which are (from an Anglocentric perspective) peripheral: Cornwall, Wales, Cumbria, and Scotland. Latin was spoken and read right through the medieval period, beginning with the arrival of the missionaries from Rome in

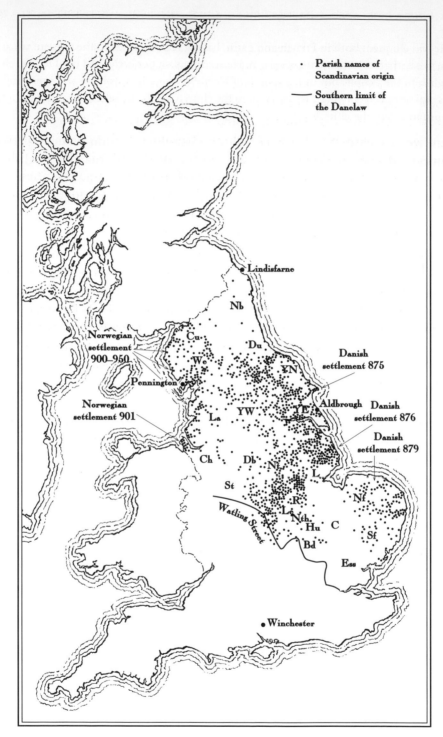

FIG. 3.1. Scandinavian settlement in Anglo-Saxon England
Source: Based on A. H. Smith, *English Place-Name Elements*, 2 vols. (Cambridge: Cambridge University Press, 1956), Map 10.

597. Old Norse was the language of the Scandinavian settlers who entered the country in the Viking Age, and settled especially in the north and east of England (see Fig. 3.1). French was the language of the Norman conquerors who arrived in 1066, although in time it came to be spoken more widely by the upper and middle classes. In the study of language contact and the history of English, these languages—in particular, Latin, French, and Norse—are what would be termed 'source languages' or 'donor languages'. But of course to describe Latin, Norse, and French in such terms, while accurate enough for the study of English, is deeply misleading, as it leads us to think of them only insofar as they exist to contribute to English, like satellites revolving round a sun. But to repeat the point made in the introduction to this chapter, these languages are just as much a part of the linguistic history of England as English is (and their literatures, as will be noted below, are just as much a part of the literary history of England as literature in English is).

Before proceeding to review these three languages as they existed in England, it is worth saying a few words about Celtic. Celtic appears to have had little impact on English; for this reason it is likely to be the most overlooked language of medieval England, and for this reason too it features little in the present chapter. It appears that fewer than a dozen words were borrowed from Celtic into English in the Anglo-Saxon period, such as *brocc* ('badger') and *torr* ('rock'), even though Celtic was widely spoken in Anglo-Saxon England, especially in the early period. The standard explanation for this, which there seems little reason to doubt, is that since the Britons were the subordinate people in Anglo-Saxon England, they are likely to have been the ones who learned the language of their conquerors (Old English) and who gave up their own language: it cannot be a coincidence that the Old English word for 'Briton', *wealh*, also came to mean 'slave' (it survives in modern English as the first element of *walnut*, as the surname Waugh, and, in the plural, as the place-name Wales). However, Celtic would assume a much more central place if one were writing a history of language in England rather than a history of the English language; the most eloquent monument to this is the great quantity of place-names in England which are of Celtic origin, especially river-names (such as Derwent, Ouse, and Lune).

In the languages of medieval England it is Latin, alongside English itself, which is, as has been said, the one constant—a surprising situation for a language which was not, after all, ever a mother tongue. Though its use in Anglo-Saxon England is normally dated to the Roman mission of 597 (and certainly its unbroken history in England begins at this point), it is, as Chapter 1 has pointed out, also possible that the newly settled Anglo-Saxons may have encountered spoken Latin (in addition to Celtic) among the Romano-British peoples whom they conquered in the fifth and sixth centuries. Nevertheless, leaving aside this one exception, the history of Latin in England is of course the history of a primarily written language. This is not to say that Latin was not spoken, for it was—endlessly and exclusively in some environments—but simply that it was always a learned second language. Furthermore, Latin was the language of learning, and for most of the time this meant that it was the language of the church. Church services were conducted in Latin throughout the Middle Ages; Latin was spoken in the monasteries and minsters; Latin was the language of the Bible. But there was almost no one speaking or reading Latin in England who did not also possess English (or sometimes French) as their first language.

Old Norse in England could not have been more different. With the exception of a handful of inscriptions in the runic alphabet, Norse was never written down in England, only spoken. However, spoken Norse appears to have been both geographically widespread and surprisingly long-lived, no doubt because it formed the first language of a substantial immigrant community. Settled Norse speakers were to be found in England from the 870s onwards, following the Viking wars of the time of King Alfred (who reigned over Wessex 871–99) and the establishment of the so-called Danelaw; that is, the area to the north and east of the old Roman road known as Watling Street (although the actual term 'Danelaw' dates from the eleventh century). It is clear that England was settled by both Danes and Norwegians—and perhaps even a few Swedes—although as the Scandinavian languages at this point were hardly differentiated from one another it is not much of a misrepresentation to speak of a unitary language, here called Norse (though some other writers employ the term 'Scandinavian'). Norse continued to be spoken in the north of England certainly into the eleventh century, and quite possibly into the twelfth in some places. In the early eleventh century the status of Norse in England received a high-level fillip through the accession of the Danish King Cnut and his sons (who ruled over England 1016–42).

Finally, we may consider French. As is well known, one of the consequences of the Norman Conquest was that the new rulers of the country spoke a different language from their subjects. Originally the Normans had been Scandinavians—the term 'Norman' comes from 'Northman'—who had been granted a territory in northern France in the early tenth century. These early Normans spoke Old Norse, just like the Scandinavians who settled in England at about the same time. By the early eleventh century, however, the Normans had given up Old Norse and had adopted the French spoken by their subjects and neighbours; it is an irony that this formidable people gave up their own language, and adopted that of their conquered subjects, not once but twice in their history. French, of course, descended from Latin; it was a Romance language, not a Germanic one like Old English and Old Norse. French as it came to be spoken in England is often termed Anglo-Norman, though it should be noted that this designation is based as much on political factors as it is on linguistic ones.

The history of the French or Anglo-Norman language in England falls into a number of episodes, but at the outset it is important to stress that there is little value in older accounts which depict two distinct speech-communities, English and French, running on non-convergent parallel lines for a number of centuries. Nor are direct comparisons between the French and Norse episodes in England's linguistic history necessarily helpful, as the circumstances were significantly different: French speakers in England probably formed a considerably smaller percentage of the population in the eleventh and twelfth centuries than had Norse speakers in the ninth and tenth, and they were also of a higher social status. In the first decades after 1066, of course, those who spoke French were the Norman invaders, but not many generations were required before the situation had become very different; parallels with the languages of other immigrant minorities suggest that this is not surprising. From the middle of the twelfth century at the latest, most members of the aristocracy were bilingual, and what is more their mother tongue is likely to have been English; there can have been very few, if any, monolingual French speakers by that point. A hundred years later, in the thirteenth century, one begins to find educational treatises which provide instruction in French, and it seems from the target audiences of such treatises that not only was French having to be learned by the aristocracy, it was also coming to be learned by members of the middle classes. One consequence of this opening-up of French to those outside the aristocracy is that the language began to be used in increasingly varied contexts. In other words, French became less restricted in usage precisely as it ceased to be anyone's mother tongue in England and instead became a generalized language of culture. And the cause of this was not the Norman Conquest of England—an event that was by now some two centuries in the past—but rather the contemporary currency of French as an international language outside England. In time, however, the pendulum swung back, and English took over more and more of the functions developed by French (as is explored in the next chapter); by the mid- to late-fourteenth century, the 'triumph of English' was assured.

It should also be stressed that, at different times, there was a thriving literary culture in England in all three of these languages. Latin and French are the most obvious. Latin works were composed in England right through the medieval period, from beginning to end and then beyond. Bede and Anglo-Saxon hagiographers, for example, were active in the seventh and eighth centuries, Asser, the biographer of Alfred the Great, in the ninth, Benedictine churchmen like Ælfric in the tenth and eleventh, and Cistercians like Ailred of Rievaulx in the twelfth. Scholastics like Roger Bacon in the thirteenth century and the courtly John Gower in the fourteenth continued this practice, as did the humanist authors of the early Renaissance. As for French, Ian Short has pointed out just how remarkable a body of work was produced in England in the twelfth century: the first romance in French composed anywhere was produced in England, not France, as were the first historical, scientific, and scholastic works in French. Even the *Song of Roland*, a celebrated landmark in medieval French culture, is found first of all in an English manuscript.[1] Indeed, it is little exaggeration to claim that the evolution of French as a written literary language was largely due to the Norman Conquest; while in the eleventh and twelfth centuries French in England may have advanced slowly in its role as 'a language of record' (in Michael Clanchy's phrase),[2] it made exceptionally rapid progress as a language of literature and culture. Even when English was beginning to re-establish itself as a medium for written literature in the thirteenth and fourteenth centuries the composition of French works continued unabated, and it is quite possible that the earliest poems of Geoffrey Chaucer were in French. The English literatures of Latin and French are perhaps familiar enough, but there were also times in the history of England when literature in Old Norse was composed and enjoyed in England, most importantly during the reign of Cnut, king of England, Denmark, and—briefly—of Norway as well. Oral Norse praise-poetry, of the type known as skaldic verse, was a popular genre at Cnut's court at Winchester and elsewhere, and Norse poetry in England exerted an influence over both English and Latin compositions of the period. For all three of these languages, then, it is not just that works circulated and were read in England; many original works were composed in this country, a testimony to the vitality of England's multilingual literary culture, and another reminder of how misleading it is to take a monolingual view of the past.

The phenomenon known as language death occurs when no one speaks or uses a language any more, either on account of the death of its users or (less radically and more commonly) on account of their shift to using a different language. Reviewing the three main 'source languages' in medieval England, one can first see that, since Latin in England was, as already indicated, not a mother tongue, the notion of language death is not really applicable. The death of the Norse

---

[1] I. Short, 'Patrons and Polyglots: French Literature in Twelfth-Century England', *Anglo-Norman Studies* 14 (1992), 229.

[2] M. T. Clanchy, *From Memory to Written Record: England 1066–1307* (2nd edn.). (Oxford: Blackwell, 1993), 220.

language in England is likely to have occurred in the eleventh century in most places, as that is when the Norse speech community seems to have shifted to using English. As for French, one could argue that the standard form of language death occurred in the twelfth century, with the demise of French as the mother tongue of the aristocracy; after the twelfth century, French was in much the same position as Latin in its status as a learned language, although the constituencies and functions of the two languages were different (see further, pp. 70–1). Language death is an important phenomenon, not just for the languages and speech communities involved, but for their neighbours and co-residents. As we shall see in the rest of the chapter, it was in their deaths, just as much as in their lives, that the non-English languages of medieval England exerted an enormous influence on English itself.

CONTACT SITUATIONS

The historical sociolinguist James Milroy insists: 'Linguistic change is initiated by speakers, not by languages'. What is traditionally termed 'language contact', or 'languages in contact', is in reality contact between speakers (or users) of different languages, and an emphasis on speaker-activity has far-reaching implications for the writing of linguistic history. As Milroy observes, 'the histories of languages such as English ... become in this perspective—to a much greater extent than previously—histories of contact between speakers, including speakers of different dialects and languages'.[3] This is one reason why the previous section paid due attention to the non-English speech communities, and to the uses of languages other than English, that were such a defining feature of medieval England. Languages do not exist apart from their users, and any study of language contact must be emphatically social in approach. In this section the actual processes of contact will be examined, before moving on to look at their linguistic consequences.

The nature of the social contact, together with the configurations of the speech communities, has a governing effect on the type of linguistic impact that will occur. Clearly, contact between languages—or rather, between users of languages—involves bilingualism of some sort. This bilingualism can either be individual or societal; that is, one may have a society which is at least partly made up of bilingual speakers, or conversely a bilingual society which is made up

---

[3] J. Milroy, 'Internal vs external motivations for linguistic change', *Multilingua* 16 (1997), 311, 312.

of monolingual speakers. So, for the contact between Norse and English speakers in Viking Age England, it is likely that, at least for pragmatic purposes, speakers of the two languages were mutually intelligible to a sufficient extent to preclude the need for bilingualism on either a major or minor scale (in the form of a society which was made up of bilingual individuals, or else one which relied on a small number of skilled interpreters). Viking Age England was thus a bilingual society dominantly made up of monolingual speakers of different languages; as an analogy it may be helpful to think of contemporary contact between speakers of different dialects of English.

The situation with French was clearly very different, as English and French—being respectively a Germanic language and a Romance one—were so dissimilar as to permit no form of mutual intelligibility. In such circumstances one must therefore think in terms of individual bilingualism. But of course exactly who those individuals were, and what form their bilingualism took, changed over time. Once their early monolingual period had come to an end, initially it was the Norman aristocracy who spoke French as their first language and who learned English as their second. But soon these linguistic roles had been reversed and French, as we have seen, became the learned second language, after which it also began to be learned by those below the level of the aristocracy. However, it is important to stress that French speakers in England always formed a minority; the majority of the population were monolingual, and the language they spoke was English.

The situation for Latin was different again. All those who knew Latin also spoke at least one other language, and in the post-Conquest period sometimes two (French and English). Being the language of books, Latin also introduces another form of language contact: that between an individual and a written text in a foreign language. One might think of the contact between users and books as a sort of second-order contact—clearly it does not represent the same form of societal bilingualism as that between individuals—but at the same time it is important not to overplay this difference. In the medieval period even written texts had a dominantly oral life: literature was social, texts were read out loud, and private silent reading had barely begun. In any case, Latin was the language of conversation and debate in many ecclesiastical and scholarly environments: it was spoken as a learned language in just the same way as French was in the later medieval period, so one should not dismissively characterize Latin as a 'dead' language in contradistinction to French, Norse, and English.

How do these various circumstances of bilingual contact (whether individual and/or societal) work out in terms of their effect on English? That is, the question to be asked is: how exactly do elements from one language come to be transferred into another language, whether those elements are words, sounds, or even syntactical constructions? As stated above, languages in contact do not exist apart from their users, so there must be specific, observable means by which linguistic transfer occurs. Words do not simply float through the air like pollen; as James Milroy insists, what we are dealing with here is the history of people, not of disembodied languages.

In understanding and analysing the processes of linguistic influence a crucial distinction made by modern linguists is that between 'borrowing' on the one hand and 'imposition' or 'interference' on the other (and it should be noted that 'borrowing' has a more precise meaning here than in older treatments of the subject). This distinction turns on the status of the person or persons who act as the bridge between languages, and may best be appreciated through modern examples. Suppose a speaker of British English learns a new word from a speaker of American English, and subsequently uses that American-derived word in their own speech: that would be an example of borrowing, and the primary agent of transfer would be a speaker of the recipient language. Suppose, on the other hand, that a bilingual French speaker uses a word or a pronunciation from their mother tongue when speaking English. A new word or pronunciation, derived from French, would thereby be introduced into a passage of spoken English; that would be an example of imposition or interference, and the primary agent of transfer would be a speaker of the source language. Of course, for either of these processes to lead to a change in the English language more broadly, as opposed to simply in the language of one individual at one time, the word or pronunciation would have to be generalized, by being adopted and used by other speakers of the recipient language. In considering this process of generalization one can see again how a study of language contact must really be part of a wider study of social networks.

This distinction between borrowing and imposition (as I shall henceforth call it) is also very helpful in understanding the phonological form which is taken by transferred elements. The linguist Frans van Coetsem, who has elucidated this distinction, writes as follows:

Of direct relevance here is that language has a constitutional property of *stability*; certain components or *domains* of language are more stable and more resistant to change (e.g. phonology), while other such domains are less stable and less resistant to change (e.g. vocabulary). Given the nature of this property of stability, a language in contact with another tends to maintain its more stable domains. Thus, if the recipient language speaker is the agent, his natural tendency will be to preserve the more stable domains of his language, e.g., his phonology, while accepting vocabulary items from the source language. If the source language speaker is the agent, his natural tendency will again be to preserve the more stable domains of his language, e.g., his phonology and specifically his articulatory habits, which means that he will impose them upon the recipient language.[4]

That is to say, a word that is transferred through borrowing is likely to be nativized to the recipient language in terms of its phonological shape or pronunciation, whereas a word that is transferred through imposition is likely to preserve the phonology of the source language, and introduce that to the recipient language. We shall meet both of these phenomena in the examples analysed below.

Lexical transfer—the transfer of words from the source language to the recipient language—is not, of course, the only form of linguistic influence that may occur when users of two languages come into contact, although it is certainly the most common. So-called bound morphemes (parts of words like prefixes or suffixes) may also be transferred, as may individual sounds, or word-orders and sentence structures, or (at the written level) letter forms and spelling conventions. In other words, while its most common form is lexical, linguistic influence can also be morphological, or phonological, or syntactic, or orthographic. All the so-called subsystems of language can be affected through contact, and in the history of English's contact with other languages in the medieval period, all of them were.

CONSEQUENCES FOR ENGLISH

As we turn to consider the consequences of language contact for the English language, it is inevitable that our point of view should become more Anglocentric, and less able to hold all the languages of medieval England within one balanced, multilingual vision. Nonetheless, a reminder is in order before we go on, that the history of the English language forms only a part of the linguistic history of England in the medieval period, and in the course of what follows I shall also indicate briefly some of the ways in which English influenced the other languages as well; the results of language contact were not in one direction only.

When one considers the consequences for English of contact with other languages, it is vocabulary that inevitably looms largest. It is well known that the size of the English lexicon as a whole has grown steadily over the course of time: estimates place the size of the Old English lexicon at c 50–60,000 words, and

---

[4] F. van Coetsem, *Loan Phonology and the Two Transfer Types in Language Contact* (Dordrecht: Foris, 1988), 3.

that of Middle English at 100–125,000 (that of modern English is placed at over half a million). This expansion has occurred overwhelmingly through the transfer of words from source languages, rather than through the formation of new words out of native resources, as has happened much more, for example, in German. However, it should be noted that Old English was much more similar to German than modern English is in its fondness for word-formation out of native elements; it has been estimated than while as much as 70 per cent of the modern English lexicon is comprised of loanwords, the comparable figure for the Old English lexicon is probably less than 5 per cent.

As a preliminary categorization, prior to looking at some actual passages, it is worth distinguishing between, on the one hand, loanwords proper and, on the other, loan-translations and semantic loans (though the term *loan* or *loanword* is conventionally used to cover the whole range). A loanword, as strictly defined, may arise either through borrowing or imposition, but it involves the incorporation of a lexical item from the source language into the lexicon of the recipient language; and the item may undergo phonological and morphological adaptation in the process, depending on the mode of transfer. Representative loanwords in Old English are *munuc* ('monk', from Latin *monachus*), *lið* ('fleet', from Old Norse *lið*), and *prut* ('proud', from Old French *prud*). In a loan-translation (sometimes known as a calque), the elements of the lexical item in the source language are translated into corresponding elements in the recipient language; the form of the source item is not actually transferred. Old English examples are *wellwillende* (literally 'well-wishing, benevolent', from Latin *benevolens*), *anhorn* (literally 'one-horn, unicorn', from Latin *unicornis*), and (as a partial loan-translation) *liðsmann* ('fleet-man, sailor', 'follower', from Old Norse *liðsmaðr*). Finally, in a semantic loan the form of a lexical item in the recipient language remains the same, but its meaning is replaced by the meaning of an item from the source language; in Saussurean terms, that is, the signifier (i.e. the sequence of sounds, the physical element of the sign) stays the same but the signified (i.e. the meaning) changes. Examples are Old English *synn* (where the original meaning 'crime, fault' has been replaced by the meaning 'religious transgression' from Latin *peccatum*) or modern English *dream* where the present meaning derives from Old Norse *draumr*, but the form derives from the cognate Old English *dream* ('(sounds of) joy'); the Old English word for 'dream' was *swefn*, which has since disappeared from the lexicon. Clearly the category of semantic loan merges into that of semantic change more generally.

With regards to the chronological stratification of the loanwords in English (that is, when the items entered the English lexicon), clearly the broad strata will correlate with the times when the source languages were spoken, or had recently

nine lines: *uard* ('Guardian', line 1), *metud* ('Ordainer', line 2), *uuldurfadur* ('Father of glory', line 3), *dryctin* ('Lord', lines 4 and 8), *scepen* ('Maker', line 6), and *frea* ('Lord', line 9). A hundred years earlier, none of these words meant 'God', for the simple reason that the Anglo-Saxons were as yet an un-Christianized, polytheistic people; contact with missionaries and the church has created a demand for new vocabulary which has been met by native words changing their meaning, rather than new words being introduced from Latin. Other words show a comparable shift: *heben* or *hefæn* ('heaven') seems to be in the process of changing its reference from the literal (line 6) to the spiritual (line 1), while *middungeard* ('middle-earth', line 7) may now allude to this world being positioned between heaven and hell as much as to the land being surrounded by sea. *Allmectig* ('almighty', line 9) appears to be a loan-translation of the Latin *omnipotens* (a word of identical meaning). The opening sentiment of *Nu scylun hergan* ('Now we must praise', line 1) may be modelled on the Psalms. There are other features which might also betray Latin ecclesiastical influence, but the overall character should by now be clear enough, and the moral of this analysis can be spelt out in simple terms. The changes in the Old English language which *Cædmon's Hymn* reveals to us have all arisen through contact with new people and new ways of doing things; language contact is always part of culture contact.

The second text for analysis is the inscription on an early eleventh-century grave-marker from the Old Minster, Winchester, which apparently commemorates a Scandinavian of the time of Cnut. Inscriptions are an excellent resource for linguistic history, even though they feature less regularly in histories of the language than do texts which are found in manuscripts or printed books. For one thing, inscriptions are often datable; more importantly, they tend to be texts which are socially embedded, active, and performative in the public sphere. The text on the Winchester grave-marker reads HER LIÐ GVNNI : EORLES FEOLAGA, which means either 'Here lies Gunni, Eorl's Companion' or 'Here lies Gunni, the earl's companion', and since Eorl is recorded only once as a personal name in England, the strong likelihood is that 'the earl's companion' is the correct reading. Though only five words long, this short inscription is full of interest in terms of language contact, and there are four points to note. First, Gunni is an Old Norse personal name, reminding us that language contact often results in expansion of the onomasticon (or repertoire of names) as well as the lexicon. Second, FEOLAGA is a loanword from Old Norse, where *félagi* means 'companion, comrade, trading partner'; it survives in modern English as *fellow*. Third, EORL is likely to show influence from Old Norse in its meaning; that is, it is a semantic loan. There was a native Old English word *eorl*, which tended to be used in poetry with a general meaning of 'man, warrior, hero'. However, the cognate Old Norse word *jarl* came be a term of rank ('earl'), and in the reign of Cnut this Norse meaning was grafted onto the English form, so that the English word came to mean 'earl', and thereby ousted the earlier English term of rank *ealdormann* (which survives in modern English as *alderman*). Fourth and last, and moving on from vocabulary to syntax, the phrase HER LIÐ ('Here lies') is not found anywhere else in Anglo-Saxon inscriptions, and it is possible that it shows the influence of Latin on Old English. *Hic iacet* ('here lies') is the standard Latin memorial formula, and although it is not found in Anglo-Saxon inscriptions, one does find the comparable *hic requiescit* ('here rests'). This five-word inscription, then, is written in the Old English language using the Roman alphabet; it shows one loanword from Old Norse, one semantic loan, and one personal name; and it probably reveals Latin influence on its syntax and phrasing. Such an inscription seems an entirely fitting product of the Winchester of King Cnut, when Norse and English culture co-existed and interacted at the highest levels of society, and the whole city also partook of a Latinate, ecclesiastical air through the influence of its three royal minsters.

The third passage is from the Peterborough Chronicle, also known as manuscript 'E' of the Anglo-Saxon Chronicle or (in older works) the Laud Chronicle. As Irvine has already discussed in Chapter 2, the annals known collectively as the Anglo-Saxon Chronicle took shape in the reign of Alfred the Great, and thereafter were kept up for some two hundred years. However, following the Norman Conquest the various recensions all fell silent, except one: the Peterborough Chronicle. This, remarkably, was maintained up to the middle of the twelfth century, thereby supplying an all-too-rare example of English composition from a time when most other writing was being done in either Latin or French (although earlier Old English texts continued to be copied in the twelfth century). The twelfth-century parts of the Peterborough Chronicle divide into the so-called First Continuation (covering the years 1122 to 1131) and the Second or Final Continuation (1132–54); the passage quoted here comes from the entry for 1135, reflecting on the death of Henry I and the accession of Stephen:

God man he was and micel æie wes of him: durste nan man misdon wið oðer on his time. Pais he makede men and dær. Wua sua bare his byrthen gold and sylure, durste nan man sei to him naht bute god. Enmang þis was his nefe cumen to Engleland, Stephne de Blais; and com to Lundene; and te lundenisce folc him underfeng and senden æfter þe ærce-biscop Willelm Curbuil; and halechede him to kinge on Midewintre Dæi. On þis kinges time wes al unfrið and yfel and ræflac, for agenes him risen sona þa rice men þe wæron swikes, alre fyrst Balduin de Reduers; and held Execestre agenes him and te king it besæt, and siððan Balduin acordede. Þa tocan þa oðre and helden her castles agenes him.   5

('He [i.e. Henry] was a good man and there was great fear of him; no-one dared act wrongly against another in his time. He made peace for both men and animals. Whoever carried a gold and silver burden, no-one dared say to him anything but good. At this time his nephew, Stephen de Blois, had come to England, and he came to London, and the people of London received him and sent for the archbishop, William Curbeil; and he consecrated him as king on Midwinter Day. In this king's time everything was unpeace and evil and plunder, for those powerful men who were traitors immediately rose against him, first of all Baldwin de Redvers; and he held Exeter against him and the king besieged it, and afterwards Baldwin submitted. Then the others occupied and held their castles against him.')

Although it is a somewhat hackneyed convention for histories of the English language to take in the Peterborough Chronicle as one of the must-see sights, the text is so rich in interest that to uphold such a tradition is more than justified: almost every sentence could provide material for an entire chapter, and would illuminate all the subsystems of the language. The work is usually exhibited, as in Chapter 2, to demonstrate the demise of the Old English inflexional system and the transition to the relatively uninflected state of Middle English. Here, with an eye initially to the lexical consequences of language contact, we should begin by noting the loanwords from both Norse and French. It is not surprising to find Norse influence in a text written in Peterborough, as that place was within the Scandinavian-settled region of the Danelaw, although in fact the only Norse loan in the passage above is *tocan* ('(they) occupied, (they) took', line 8). This is, however, an important and significant word as it is a central item of vocabulary, and in due course came to oust the native Old English term *niman* (of identical meaning) from the lexicon. (In other respects, the language of the passage shows some English words holding their own against the Norse loans which we know had entered the language by this time: for instance, the third person plural possessive personal pronoun here is still the Old English-derived *her*, rather than the Norse-derived *their*). But the passage also shows a sprinkling of French loanwords, most obviously the iconic *castles* in line 9, but also *pais* ('peace', line 2) and *acordede* ('submitted', line 8). One might also note the construction of personal names such as *Stephne de Blais* and *Balduin de Reduers*, using French *de* rather than English *of*. Moreover, French influence in this passage goes beyond the merely lexical. *Pais* is interesting for phonological reasons: following the Germanic Consonant Shift (see further p. 19), only a tiny number of words in Old English began with [p], and so the introduction of Romance (French or Latin) words beginning thus marked a clear development. Orthographically, too, this passage shows a language in conspicuous transition. Anglo-Saxon spelling conventions are still present—for example *sc* has not yet been replaced by *sh* in *ærcebiscop* ('archbishop')—but they are now accompanied by Romance (and specifically French) conventions: *u* is used for medial [v] in *sylure* ('silver'), and the digraph *th* is used in *byrthen* ('burden') alongside the older Anglo-Saxon letters þ and ð in *þis* ('this') and *unfrið* ('unpeace').

These three examples—Cædmon's *Hymn*, the Winchester inscription, and the Peterborough Chronicle—give a representative sample of the kinds of influence (especially lexical) that were exerted on English through contact with Latin, Norse, and French. Further kinds of influence will be discussed shortly, but at this point it is important to stress that not every loanword recorded in a medieval text succeeded in establishing itself and became in any way a continuing (let alone a permanent) part of the language. Instead there were many one-offs and dead ends and, as in other aspects of the history of English, one must not tell a teleological narrative, implying that there is anything inevitable about the forms taken by linguistic change. On the contrary, linguistic change occurs through thousands (or millions) of individual human choices, and so it is in this sense pre-eminently 'evitable'. Similarly, there were many developments which were only local or regional, and never became established more generally across the country. Such local developments and local histories have tended to be occluded or concealed in the post-standardization, post-print era, but in the present context it is essential that we think in terms not of a single nationwide situation of language contact, but rather of countless local situations all over the country.

A text that exemplifies both of these qualities (of dead ends and local developments) is the eleventh-century inscription on the sundial at Aldbrough church in the East Riding of Yorkshire (see Fig. 3.2). Commemorating the act of a benefactor, the inscription reads: VLF [HE]T ARCERAN CYRICE FOR H[A]NUM 7 FOR GVNWARA SAVLA ('Ulf ordered the church to be erected for himself and for Gunnwaru's soul'). The language of the inscription is perfectly normal late Old English, except for the one word HANUM, which appears to be (and surely is) the Old Norse word *honum*, the masculine singular dative form of the third-person personal pronoun (i.e. 'him'). As has already been said, other personal pronouns were transferred from Norse to English (*they*, *them*, and *their*, while *she* may also show Norse influence; see further pp. 100–1), but this is the only extant text that records the importation of *honum* as well. There is nothing very surprising about such a loan, even though the transfer of pronouns between languages is rare: in the late Old English and early Middle English period the personal pronoun system in English (especially in the third person) underwent extensive changes, with the loss of distinctive accusative forms, and the function of the accusative being taken over by the dative forms. The entry of *they*, *them*, and *their* into English is just one sign of this process of change and renovation. But what the Aldbrough inscription shows is that, in this part of late Anglo-Saxon Yorkshire, the

FIG. 3.2.   The inscribed sundial at Aldbrough, East Riding of Yorkshire
Source: © Corpus of Anglo-Saxon Stone Sculpture: Photographer T. Middlemass.

Norse pronoun *honum* was also borrowed and incorporated into the local language. However, this particular innovation did not prove to be productive: it failed to be generalized through the language as a whole, and is not found again in any other source, whereas English-derived *him* has survived to this day. The Aldbrough inscription exemplifies clearly how the consequences of language contact are local and multifarious; it may be that most individual changes fail to catch on.

One might wonder whether speakers of Old English in late Anglo-Saxon Yorkshire were conscious of HANUM as a distinctively Norse item in the language of the Aldbrough inscription, or whether it had come to appear to them as a perfectly unremarkable English word (as would have been the case with CYRICE, even though that too was a loanword, ultimately from Greek but probably via Latin). In other words, how far are loanwords nativized and integrated into the recipient language, or how far do they remain a discernibly 'foreign' element? After a while, does the origin of words matter? Of course, there is no single answer to these questions—as attested by the well-known example of the variant pronunciations of the French loanword *garage* in modern English. It is certainly important to stress that the contemporary connotations of a word are no more based on etymological origin than its denotative meaning is; after a while, most loanwords are indeed nativized and their origins become irrelevant. But what about at an early stage: did late Old English and early Middle English writers deliberately exclude (or indeed include) Norse and French loans precisely because they were conscious that they were loans?

One example that might suggest this possibility is the fascinating text known as the *Ormulum*. Composed in the late twelfth century by a certain Orm (who named the work after himself), the *Ormulum* is an extraordinarily ambitious sequence of metrical homilies, all written out using an equally ambitious spelling system that is Orm's own invention (see further pp. 87–8). The sole manuscript appears to be in the author's own hand, and the work is sadly incomplete. The *Ormulum* was probably composed somewhere in southern Lincolnshire, not far in time and space from the Continuations of the Peterborough Chronicle, and the language of the text is marked by very heavy Norse influence: many Norse loanwords are found recorded there for the first time, and Orm's third-person plural personal pronouns are the new, Norse-derived ones. However, and in this regard strikingly unlike the Peterborough Chronicle, the *Ormulum* contains very few loanwords from French—quite possibly fewer than a dozen. The reason for this cannot be lack of exposure to French influence more generally, as French orthographic practices are prominent in Orm's spelling system: indeed, the *Ormulum* may well be the first extant English manuscript to use French-derived *sh* for earlier *sc*, and *wh* for earlier *hw*. Orm's non-use of French-derived vocabulary therefore looks deliberate, and implies that French-derived terms were sufficiently recognizable to be excluded. The likely reasons for exclusion may be stylistic and/or audience-related: Orm may have felt that French-derived terms were inappropriate in associations or register, or else unfamiliar to his audience. As Orm himself tells us in the extensive Dedication of his work to his brother Walter, the *Ormulum* was conceived as a preaching tool, intended to be read out loud to lay audiences. In his inclusion of French-derived orthography but exclusion of French-derived vocabulary, Orm may permit us to glimpse a sociolinguistic situation in which literate readers were familiar with French spelling, but illiterate listeners were ignorant of French words.

It is also important to stress that the consequences of language contact were not in one direction only. The other languages of medieval England also changed as a result of contact with English, and they thereby came to differ from the variety of language spoken in the homelands from which they had come—as is the manner of 'colonial' languages throughout history. Again, Latin is the exception here, as it was never a mother tongue, whereas the Norse spoken in England came to differ from that spoken in Scandinavia, and the French of England similarly diverged from the French of France (whether as a mother tongue or, later, as a learned language). So, for example, Old Norse poetry composed and recited in England often contains loanwords from Old English: as Roberta Frank has observed, all three of the alliterating words in the tenth stanza of Sigvatr Þórðarson's praise-poem for Cnut (*Knútsdrápa*) are in fact loanwords (Cnut is said to be *kærr keisara, klúss Pétrúsi* 'dear to the Emperor, close to Peter'), the first coming probably from French and the second and third from Latin via Old English, and together they exemplify both Cnut's European ambitions and the new cultural influences exerted upon Norse poetry—and the Norse language—in England.[5]

As has been seen, then, while lexical expansion is the most prominent consequence of language contact, contact-induced change can also occur in the other subsystems of orthography, phonology, morphology, and syntax. If space permitted, much more could be said about all of these areas, but one larger question that cannot remain without discussion is the possible role language contact may have played in the English language's loss of inflexions. As is discussed elsewhere in this volume, in evolving from Old English to Middle English the English language moved from being a dominantly synthetic language (that is, where grammatical relationships are expressed morphologically through the addition of inflexions) to a dominantly analytic one (where grammatical relationships are expressed syntactically). However, did language contact play a part in this process? In this regard, it is contact between speakers of English and speakers of Norse that has often been suggested as having been crucial. As was noted earlier, English and Norse (unlike English and Latin, or English and French) were probably mutually intelligible languages, on account of their close relationship within the family of Germanic languages. However, while cognate English and Norse words were generally similar, or even identical, in their basic form the one aspect in which they often differed was their inflexional endings: compare, for instance, Old English *giest* and Old Norse *gestr* ('guest'), or *guma* and *gumi* ('man'), or *scipu* and *skip* ('ships'). In a situation in which speakers of the two languages were repeatedly in contact with one another, on a daily or even a domestic basis, it is quite possible that these inflexional differences became eroded or ignored, as they played no role (or were even a hindrance) in effective communication between speakers of the two languages. In other words, most

---

[5] R. Frank, 'King Cnut in the verse of his skalds', in A. Rumble (ed.), *The Reign of Cnut: King of England, Denmark and Norway* (London: Leicester University Press, 1994), 118.

inflexions were probably non-functional in Norse–English communication; hence they decayed, and alternative methods of expressing grammatical relationships came to be more prominent—above all, the method of a relatively fixed word-order.

Two points in support of this hypothesis might be mentioned, and also two points of qualification. The first point in support is that English inflexions appear to have decayed earlier in the north and east of England than in the south and west—that is, precisely in those parts of the country where Scandinavian settlement led to contact situations between speakers of Norse and English. The second is that a similar inflexional decay appears to have occurred in the Norse language in England as well as in the English language, as can be seen, for example, in the Pennington inscription in Cumbria, a twelfth-century text in Norse runes which shows both loss of inflexions and (possibly) confusion of grammatical gender. The first point of qualification is that the gradual decay of inflexions and the tendency towards analysis (that is, towards a relatively fixed word-order) were already present in Old English, largely—as Chapter 1 has already discussed—as a result of the fixing of stress on the first syllable in the Germanic period (so that the final syllable became gradually weakened, and less capable of bearing information content); the whole process was certainly not initiated by contact with Norse speakers, only encouraged or accelerated. The second point of qualification is that it is probably misleading to label this contact-induced loss of inflexions as 'creolization'—or the development of a new mother tongue out of a pragmatic contact language—as some linguists have wished to do; pidgins and creoles arise as simplified languages of communication between speakers of two mutually unintelligible languages, whereas mutually intelligible speakers of Norse and English did not find themselves in such a situation.

The Norse inscription from Pennington is unusually late in date, and it is highly likely that by the twelfth century Norse speakers had shifted to English in most other parts of the country. One possible result of a widespread shift on the part of an entire speech community is that the language shifted to may show 'substratum influence' from the earlier language of the shifting speakers. In other words, in this case speakers of Norse may have imported into English various features of Norse in the process of language shift. This is the phenomenon labelled (in van Coetsem's (1988) term) as 'source language agentivity', and it will be recalled (see pp. 71–2) that the most likely consequence of such a shift is phonological influence from the substratum language; that is, Norse speakers may have carried over features of Norse pronunciation and articulation when they shifted to speaking English. This hypothesis may well be the best way of explaining the very common phenomenon in Middle English of Norse-derived variants existing alongside English cognates, and differing only in phonology: so, for example, in Middle English Norse-derived *bleik* ('white, pale') exists beside English-derived *bloc*, while *coupe* ('buy') exists beside *chepe*, and *fisk* ('fish') beside *fish*, and so on (usually with identical meaning). It is hard to explain these Norse-derived variants in terms of borrowings made on account of either need or prestige; to see them as impositions arising through substratum influence is much more persuasive.

Since Latin was not a mother tongue as Norse was, the issue of language death and language shift, as noted earlier, does not arise in the same way. As for French, the process of shift occurred in the twelfth century, when French ceased to be the mother tongue for the Anglo-Norman aristocracy; after that point, the giving up of French as a learned language (like Latin) was not so much a case of language death as simply the abandonment of a curriculum. However, the one other language of medieval England that must have undergone a Norse-style language death, with possible substratum influence on English, was Celtic; but sadly the possible influence of Celtic on English (besides the handful of loanwords mentioned earlier) remains obscure and disputed. Nonetheless it is clear that at least one of the languages of medieval England continued to influence the development of English even after it ceased to be spoken (Norse); and two more, of course, exerted a longstanding influence on English even when they were no longer anyone's mother tongue (Latin and French).

CONCLUSION

I began this chapter with three snapshots that encapsulated the multilingual nature of medieval England, and the role language contact has played in the evolution of English. I will conclude by explicitly stating (or re-stating) three axioms, all of which have been exemplified in the intervening discussion. The first is that, as I said at the beginning, the history of the English language is not at all the same thing as the history of language in England, and to consider only the former is to misrepresent and misunderstand the linguistic history of the country. The second is that language contact is all about people: language contact does not occur apart from human contact, and contact-induced change is always the result of human activity. And the third, consequent on this, is that language contact is part of cultural contact more generally: if one embarks on a study of language contact in medieval England, one is carried irresistibly onwards into the broader history and culture of that inexhaustibly interesting society.

References and Suggestions for Further Reading

My three introductory snapshots are quoted from Colgrave and Mynors (1969), Birch (1885–93), and Butler (1949).

The languages of medieval England

On Latin language and literature in England see Rigg (1992), Lapidge (1993, 1996), and Sharpe (1997). On Old Norse language and literature in England see Townend (2000, 2001, 2002), and also Jesch (2001). On French language and literature in England see Wilson (1943), Rothwell (1968, 1976), Short (1979–80, 1992), Kibbee (1991), and Crane (1997, 1999). On the interplay of Latin, French, and English see Clanchy (1993) and Trotter (2000).

Contact situations

For general accounts of language contact see Weinreich (1953), Thomason and Kauffman (1988), and Thomason (2001); Trudgill (1986) supplies a complementary study of dialect contact.

Consequences for English

General accounts of loanwords in English, which include sections on each of the languages discussed here, can be found in Serjeantson (1935), Jespersen (1956), Strang (1970), Burnley (1992b), Kastovsky (1992), Baugh and Cable (2002), Blake (1996), and Hughes (2000). On Latin loanwords see Campbell (1959), Wollmann (1993), and Gneuss (1996). On Norse loanwords see Björkman (1900–02), Wollmann (1996), and Dance (2003). On French loanwords see Rothwell (1991, 1998) and Cannon (1998). The text of *Cædmon's Hymn* is from the manuscript of Cambridge University Library, Kk.5.16, and is published in Dobbie (1942). The Winchester grave-marker is published in Okasha (1971) and Tweddle *et al.* (1995). The Peterborough Chronicle is quoted from Clark (1970), with abbreviations expanded. The Aldbrough sundial is also published in Okasha (1971). The standard edition of the *Ormulum* is Holt and White (1878). On language contact and the loss of inflexions in English see Mitchell (1991) and Townend (2002); on the 'creole' debate see Görlach (1986) and Allen (1997). For the Pennington inscription, see Page (1971) and Holman (1996).

4

MIDDLE ENGLISH—
DIALECTS AND DIVERSITY

Marilyn Corrie

Annd whase wilenn shall þiss boc efft oþerr siþe writenn,
Himm bidde icc þatt hêt wríte rihht, swa summ þiss boc himm tæcheþþ.

('And whoever may wish to write this book out again on another occasion, I ask him that he write it correctly, just as this book teaches him.')

MIDDLE English, in the words of Barbara Strang, is '*par excellence*, the dialectal phase of English'.[1] This is because it is the period in which dialectal variation was represented in writing and, significantly, in which it was represented without the ideological issues which have underscored the writing of dialects in subsequent times. It is important, however, to recognize developments within the period, and to recognize also that some typical features of Middle English have been manifested in other periods as well. For example, Chapter 2 has shown that dialectal variation in the written medium was more common in the Old English period than was once thought to be the case. And this chapter will suggest that there are other ways in which both the treatment of the language in the Middle English period and attitudes towards it have parallels in other times. One of these is anxiety about how the language should be represented in the written medium: an anxiety which is encapsulated in the lines quoted above.

---

[1] See Strang (1970: 224).

The lines which open this chapter are taken from the late twelfth-century text known as the *Ormulum*, which was mentioned briefly in Chapter 3. They convey, on the one hand, the fear of their author, Orm, that the orthography of his work may be altered when it is copied—an unnecessary fear, ironically, as the single surviving version of the *Ormulum*, written by Orm himself, appears to be the only one that was ever made. A different kind of anxiety, however, is implicit in these lines as well, because the ingenious, and unique, orthography which they exemplify reflects Orm's concern that his writing should reflect the phonological features of his English. In the second line of the cited extract, for example, accents appear above the vowels in *hêt* and *wríte* because Orm wanted to indicate to his readers that these vowels are long (different accents are used because the *e* in *hêt* is in a 'closed' syllable, that is, one ending in a consonant, whereas the *i* in *wríte*, pronounced /wri:tə/, is in an 'open' syllable, that is, one ending in a vowel: the *t* forms part of the second syllable of the word). Conversely, when a vowel in a closed syllable is short, Orm systematically doubles the consonant which follows it, as in *annd* and *þiss* in the first line of the quotation. In the dedication to the text, Orm prays 'forr lufe off Crist' that his work will be of benefit to others. But he describes his dedicatee, Walter (or rather 'Wallterr'), as 'broþerr min i Crisstenndom' ('my brother in Christendom'); the differences in the spelling patterns which Orm deploys suggests that whereas the *i* in *Crist* is long, in the polysyllabic *Crisstenndom* it has been shortened. The orthography of the *Ormulum* thus reveals (among many other things) that our modern distinction between a long and a short vowel in *Christ* and *Christendom* existed already by Orm's day, although—as Chapter 6 will show—the precise realization of the former was to change significantly through the effects of the 'Great Vowel Shift'.

The anxiety which is implicit in Orm's work will be a recurring feature of this chapter, as it will be also of subsequent chapters. The chapter will discuss the issue of dialectal variation in written Middle English by considering, first of all, the causes of this variation. It will then explore some of the principal features which distinguish the dialects of Middle English from one another, before discussing developments in the 'later' Middle English period (after the rough boundary of the mid-fourteenth century) which distance this era from 'earlier' Middle English. The most important later Middle English development, standardization, will be considered in a separate, and final, section. Standardization is a counter-tendency to the diversity which characterizes written Middle English, and can itself be regarded as the manifestation of an unease with the instability of the written language in the centuries covered in this chapter.

DIALECTAL VARIATION IN WRITTEN MIDDLE ENGLISH

Orm's mission to create an orthographic system which appears to reflect his (East Midland) pronunciation of English may be compared with the work of spelling reformers such as John Hart or John Cheke in the sixteenth century. But whereas Hart and Cheke were attempting to reform a substantially standardized written form of the language from which pronunciation had diverged, in the twelfth century there was no non-localized or supra-regional written standard variety of English for Orm to react against. Chapter 3 has discussed the fact that Latin became the language of record following the Norman Conquest, and French the language of much of the 'literary' material which was written down. This meant that those who were trained to write did not have to be trained to write English, and so—unless scribes were merely reproducing existing material—when the language was written, it appears not to have been written according to inculcated rules. Orm's orthography is therefore just one example of various *ad hoc* spelling systems which were devised in response to this linguistic situation; the *Ormulum* is exceptional only in its commitment to the indication of vocalic length, and in its resulting usefulness to modern philologists. In the early Middle English period (up to around the middle of the fourteenth century), there is very little evidence of any scriptorium producing an identifiable 'house style' of English comparable to the variety which, as Chapter 2 has noted, developed at Winchester in the Old English period (although see further, below). There was therefore no variety of written English which might have seemed worthy of imitation by others. The connection between the function of English and the development of its form in the fifteenth and sixteenth centuries will be the subject of the next chapter. Here it is sufficient to say that the diminution of the functions which English had formerly served resulted, in Middle English, in the diversification of its written form.

Local variation

The consequences of the obliteration of standardization in the written language are striking in the following two extracts, which are taken from different versions of the same work. The first extract (Text A) is from MS Cotton Nero A.xiv in the British Library, a copy of the guide for female recluses known as *Ancrene Riwle* ('The Rule for Anchoresses'). The manuscript was written in the second quarter of the thirteenth century, probably in Worcestershire. The second passage (Text B) is from a revised 'edition' of the work in

MS 402 in Corpus Christi College, Cambridge, where it is given the title *Ancrene Wisse* ('The Guide for Anchoresses'). This was copied around the year 1230, almost certainly in north-west Herefordshire. The small time gap between the texts may account for some of the divergences which the extracts display, but most seem rather to be the result of the different geographical provenances of the scribes.

Text A:

Uikelares beoð þreo kunnes. þe uorme beoð vuele inouh, þe oðre þauh beoð wurse, þe þridde ʒet beoð alrewurste. Þe uorme, ʒif a mon is god, preiseð hine biuoren himself, and makeð hine, inouh reðe, ʒet betere þen he beo, and ʒif he seið wel oðer deð wel he hit heueð to heie up mid ouerpreisunge and herunge.

Text B:

Fikeleres beoð þreo cunnes. Þe forme beoð uuele inoh, þe oþre þah beoð wurse, þe þridde þah beoð wurst. Þe forme, ʒef a mon is god, preiseð him biuoren himseolf and makeð him, inoh reaðe, ʒet betere þen he beo, and ʒef he seið wel oðer deð wel heueð hit to hehe up wið ouerherunge.

('Flatterers are three in kind. The first are bad enough; the second, however, are worse; the third are yet worst of all (Text B: 'the third, however, are worst'). The first, if a man is good, praises him to his face and, eagerly enough, makes him out to be even better than he is, and if he says well or does well he makes too much of it [lit. 'raises it up too high'] with excessive praise and glorification' (Text B: 'with excessive glorification').)

Perhaps the most prominent difference between the passages is the fact that words which begin with *u* in Text A begin with *f* in Text B, hence *uikelares* ('flatterers') and *uorme* ('first') against *fikeleres* and *forme* in the first line of each extract. Scribes of English in this period usually use *u* at the beginning of words to represent the voiced fricative /v/ (as Chapter 3 has already noted, it was a new development in Middle English to distinguish /v/ from /f/ ortho-graphically, a reflection of the fact that certain recent loanwords into the language would have fallen together with other words if the distinction had not been made: compare, for example, *vine* with *fine*). The *u* in *uikelares* and *uorme* in Text A hence indicates that this text has been affected by a sound-change called 'initial voicing', which affected an area that included Worcester-shire. But initial voicing does not seem to have spread as far as north-west Herefordshire, which is why Text B has the corresponding voiceless fricative /f/ in *fikeleres* and *forme*. Although the copyists of the texts seem to have been working in relatively close proximity in geographical terms, the extracts reveal that they do not write English according to an agreed orthography. Their guiding principle in writing was instead probably local pronunciations, which were not precisely the same in the two places. Scribes read aloud to themselves when they were transcribing material, and this may sometimes have helped to drive a representation of their own sound systems into the work which they produced. The case of *Ancrene Wisse*, though, is complicated and will be discussed further below.

Further variations between the passages can be seen: for instance, in the first two lines of Text A, the words *inouh* ('enough') and *þauh* ('however') contain diphthongs (caused by the development of a glide before the velar fricative [χ], a sound similar to modern Scottish enunciations of the *ch* in *loch*). Conversely, the corresponding forms in Text B, *inoh* and *þah*, represent the same vowels as monophthongs or simple vowels (*inoh* is from Old English *genog*, *þah* is from *þæh*, which was the form for West Saxon *þeah* in Anglian dialects of Old English). The phonology (or sound system) of Text A, on the whole, shows more changes since the Old English period than does the phonology of Text B. But in other respects, it is Text B which seems more distanced from Old English. Thus Text A uses the Old English preposition *mid* for 'with' in its final line, but Text B has *wið*. The latter had signified 'against' in Old English but in some dialects, it seems, it had already come to assume its modern meaning by the early Middle English period. This example illustrates how dialects were changing at different rates and in different ways, and the absence of a non-localized written standard at this time means that their evolution can often be traced in writing.

Another interesting point is that whereas Text B uses the single word *ouerherunge* ('excessive glorification') in line 4, Text A has the phrase *ouerpreisunge and herunge* (line 4), in which the two nouns have more or less the same meaning ('excessive praise' and 'glorification'). This indicates the tendency of some scribes to rewrite the substance of what they were copying as well as its linguistic traits. But the linked synonyms of Text A are significant from a lexical perspective as well. *Ouerpreisunge* seems to be a neologism: it combines a morpheme derived from French (*preis*) with affixes (*ouer-* and *-ung(e)*) which were present in the language in Old English. The word shows that Middle English did not increase its vocabulary only by incorporating loanwords (compare Chapter 3): it did so also by preserving the habits of word-formation which had been so productive before the Conquest, and which would yield many new words again in the early modern period (see Chapters 2 and 8 respectively). The more established form *herunge* may have been included to ensure that the meaning of *ouerpreisunge* was understood, much as Renaissance prose writers sometimes explain words new to the language by pairing them with synonyms (compare, for example, the intention of the scholar and statesman Sir Thomas Elyot to 'devulgate or sette fourth some part of my studie' in his educational treatise *The Governour*, published in 1531; *devulgate* (or, in its modern form, *divulgate*) is traced back to 1530 in the *OED*, and some glossing or explanation was clearly necessary in order to render it transparent to Elyot's wider audience). The linguistic exuberance that is characteristic of these later writers is clearly foretold in prose which dates from over 300 years earlier.

The major dialect areas: Old English to Middle English

Some of the dialectal differences between the two passages discussed above may derive from the territorial divisions between the original Anglo-Saxon kingdoms which have been described in Chapter 2 (see also Fig. 2.1). Worcestershire, where Text A seems to have been copied, was inside the boundary of the old West Saxon kingdom, whereas north-west Herefordshire, the linguistic home of the scribe of Text B, was in Anglian territory. It is often pointed out that dialects exist in a continuum, but it is true also that territorial boundaries can affect networks of contact, potentially impeding the spread of innovative linguistic features and entrenching any linguistic differences which may already have been present when the boundaries were established.

The Anglian dialect area in the Old English period fell, as has been mentioned, into two distinct regions: Northumbrian to the north of the River Humber (as its name suggests) and Mercian to the south. In the Middle English period, as Figure 4.1 indicates, the old Mercian area itself shows considerable dialectal differentiation, especially between its western and eastern parts. This differentiation seems largely to derive from developments long before the Norman Conquest: the east had been part of the area of Scandinavian settlement which has been described in Chapter 3, the western area of Mercia not. It is only in Middle English, however, that the consequences of the divergent histories of the two regions manifest themselves, with the eastern dialects displaying the impact of intense contact with Norse, as the previous chapter has shown in its discussion of the Continuations of the Peterborough Chronicle and of the *Ormulum*.

The easternmost part of the East Midland area—which is still called East Anglia after the Angles who settled in it in the fifth century—had been made an autonomous kingdom when Britain was carved up among the Angles, Saxons, and Jutes. This, together with its geographical isolation, may have helped to ensure that its dialect diverged from the language of other parts of the East Midlands in certain distinctive ways. Some of the features of East Anglian Middle

And therwithal hire arm over hym she leyde,
And al foryaf, and ofte tyme hym keste.   *forgave; kissed*
He thonked hire, and to hire spak, and seyde
As fil to purpos for his herte reste;   *was pertinent*
And she to that answerde hym as hire leste, 5   *she wished*
And with hire goodly wordes hym disporte
She gan, and ofte his sorwes to comforte.   *she began to cheer him up*

Chaucer, as is well-known, indicates the 'foreignness' of northern speech in his portrayal of the students Aleyn and John in *The Reeve's Tale* (see further p. 123); but in his early poetry, somewhat conspicuously, he occasionally exploits northern morphology too. The most frequently quoted instance of this phenomenon is in these lines from *The Book of the Duchess*, which describe what the narrator will do if the god of sleep will put an end to his insomnia. The northern *-es* ending for the third person singular of the present tense of the verb appears in rhyming position (*falles*) in the first line, a departure from Chaucer's usual *-eþ* ending:

... I wol yive hym al that falles   *give*
To a chamber, and al hys halles   *is appropriate to*
I wol do peynte with pure gold.   *have painted*

The diversity of English may have jeopardized the exact preservation of what Chaucer wrote but, as this example shows, it facilitated much of his writing in the first place.

These excerpts from Chaucer illustrate also how much the language had changed since the Old English period. In morphology, one might note the spread of the plural noun ending derived from Old English *-as* (which had been used only with strong masculine nouns in the nominative and accusative plural in Old English) to nouns which originally would have had other inflections in the plural. Thus the form *sorwes* appears in line 7 of the extract from *Troilus* above: in Old English, the corresponding form would have been *sorga* or *sorge*, since the word was a strong feminine noun (such nouns could take either an *-a* or an *-e* in the nominative and accusative plural in Old English). *Wordes* in line 6 shows how the *-es* ending has spread to cases, as well as genders, in which it was not used originally: following the preposition 'with', the noun would have been in the dative case in Old English and would therefore have had the form *wordum*. Another point of interest is that the old genitive singular ending of a weak feminine noun, *-an*, has been whittled down to *-e* in *herte* ('heart's') in line 4 of the passage from *Troilus* (our *-'s* ending, which comes from the genitive singular ending of strong masculine and neuter nouns in Old English, *-es*, has not yet been adopted in this word). And prepositional phrases appear where Old English would generally have used inflectional endings to express the relationship of nouns or pronouns to the rest of the clause: examples include *to hire*, *to that*, and *with hire goodly wordes* (lines 3, 5, and 6).

Forms derived from the old dative of the personal pronouns (i.e. the form for the indirect object) are now also being used where the accusative (i.e. direct object) forms would have been used in Old English: hence, for instance, *hym keste*, *hym disporte* in lines 2 and 6 of the *Troilus* extract. (Old English would have had accusative *hine* in such contexts.) In the other passages, one might note the contexts in which the old singular forms of the second person pronoun are used: when Chaucer addresses his own literary creation ('So prey I God that non myswrite *the*'), and when Absolon asks Alison to kiss him ('This wol I yeve *thee*, if *thou* me kisse'). These examples (both using the accusative *thee* in accordance with the syntax; the corresponding subject form is *thou*) should be compared with pronoun usage in the following stanza from *Troilus*, in which Troilus expresses his reluctance to part from Criseyde after he has slept with her for the first time:

> Therwith ful soore he <u>syghte</u>, and thus he seyde: *sighed*
> 'My lady right, and of my wele or wo
> The welle and roote, O goodly myn Criseyde,
> And shal I rise, allas, and shal I so?
> Now fele I that myn herte <u>moot a-two</u>, 5   *must (break) in two*
> For how sholde I my lif an houre save,
> Syn that with yow is al the lif ich have?'

Although a single person is being addressed, as in the other passages, Troilus here uses the form derived from what was, in Old English, the plural second person object pronoun (*yow*, line 7, from Old English *ēow*). The corresponding subject form would be *ye*, as in Troilus's earlier observation to Criseyde that God 'wol ye be my steere,/ To do me lyve' ('wishes that you be my guide, to make me live'). This shows that, as in modern French (and some modern English dialects; see further Chapter 11), the selection of the second person pronominal form depended, by Chaucer's day, not just on how *many* people were being addressed, but also on considerations of respectfulness, politeness, and social standing (Troilus and Criseyde are of noble rank, Absolon and Alison in The miller's Tale anything but). Etiquette now determines which form is used if one person is being spoken to, complicating considerably the 'rules' which governed the use of the pronouns in Old English.

Lexically, the passage from *Troilus* on p. 106 is distanced from Old English through the amount of French influence which it displays: the words *purpos*, *disporte,* and *comforte* (lines 4, 6, and 7) are all derived from French. So too are *chamber, peynte,* and *pure* in the extract from *The Book of the Duchess,* although the lines from *The Miller's Tale* quoted on p. 105 contain a higher proportion of 'Anglo-Saxon' vocabulary, complementing the earthiness of the events related. Syntactically, Chaucer's verse can use a word order different from that typical of Old English. In Old English, the words in the first line of the passage from *The Book of the Duchess* would have been arranged 'I wol al that falles hym yive', with the infinitive dependent on the modal *wol* appearing at the end of the clause; Chaucer's word order in the line is the same as in modern English. But Chaucer can also use a word order inherited from Old English which is alien to modern readers, as in the subject–object–verb structure following a subordinating con-junction in 'if thou me kisse'. And Chaucer's sentence construction can be as sinuous, even tortuous, as in the most complex Old English verse, as the stanza from *Troilus* on p. 106 shows. What differentiates it from poetry of the Old English period is the fact that its guiding principle is the need to find rhyming words, not alliterating syllables, at appropriate points in the lines. Chaucer's English clearly represents a different phase of the language from Old English, but at least some of the distinguishing features of Old English can still be detected in his writing.

The permissiveness of the written medium may have been useful to Chaucer, but it caused others some difficulty. Towards the end of the fourteenth century, the New Testament had been translated into English twice, after the Oxford theologian John Wyclif called for Scripture to be made accessible to all. In the early fifteenth century, a concordance to the translations, which are collectively known as the 'Wycliffite Bible', was produced, so that:

> If a man haue mynde oonly of oo word or two of sum long text of þe Newe Lawe and haþ <u>forȝetyn</u> al þe remenaunt, or ellis if he can seie bi herte such an hool text but he haþ forȝeten in what <u>stede</u> it is writen, þis concordaunce wole lede him bi þe fewe wordis þat ben <u>cofrid</u> in his mynde vnto þe ful text, and shewe him in what book and in what
> 5 <u>chapitre</u> he shal fynde þo textis which <u>him list</u> to haue.

> (*forȝetyn:* forgotten; *stede:* place; *cofrid:* contained; *chapitre:* chapter; *him list:* he wishes)

The trouble was that the 'same' word could have different phonological mani-festations (as in *kirke* and *chirche*). It could also vary orthographically (*thyng* and *theef,* for example, could be spelt with an initial *th* or an initial *þ*); or it could appear under an alternative lexical guise (hence the author points out that the Latin borrowing *accesse* might be represented elsewhere by the English loan-translation *nyȝcomynge,* literally 'near-coming'). 'If þou þanne seke a text in ony of suche synonemus, and if þou fynde it not in oon of hem,' the author suggests (*synonemus* is his term for a range of alternative word forms, not just words of similar meaning):

loke in a noþir of hem; ȝhe, loke in alle suche synonemus, þouȝ þer be þre or mo of hem, til þou fynde þe text wiþ which þe liste mete.

(ȝhe: 'yea'; þouȝ: 'though'; *wiþ which þe liste mete*: 'which you want to find')

The diversity of Middle English could be beneficial to an author, but it could also undermine the very viability of what other writers were trying to do.

STANDARDIZATION

There is an exception to what we can see as the centrifugal tendency of written Middle English from the early part of the period. This is the phenomenon known as 'AB language', a variety of English found in the Corpus manuscript containing *Ancrene Wisse* (whence 'A') and MS Bodley 34 in the Bodleian Library in Oxford (whence 'B'). The Bodley manuscript includes copies of such texts as *Sawles Warde* ('The Guardian of the Soul') and *Hali Meiðhad* ('Holy Virginity'), which share many of the stylistic features of *Ancrene Wisse* and appear, like it, to have been composed for a female audience. The two manuscripts are written in different hands but, to a marked and remarkable degree, they share phonological, grammatical, and orthographical systems. Unless one is to assume that the texts were all written by the same individual and then copied *literatim* by different scribes, it seems that the copyists who used AB language had been trained to write in a particular way—thus, as suggested above, the dialect of *Ancrene Wisse* does not necessarily correlate with the speech habits of its scribe. It has often been pointed out that the south-west Midland area in which the manuscripts seem to have been produced was the 'stronghold' of English literary tradition in the early Middle English period. Old English material was still being copied here, and it was systematically studied by the fascinating scribe known as the 'Tremulous Hand' of Worcester, who glossed Old English texts and compiled word lists of their vocabulary (see further p. 58). The works copied in AB language sporadically display a literary texture comparable to the 'alliterative prose' developed in the Old English period by Ælfric (discussed in Chapter 2); it has been claimed that the very idea of writing in a standardized form of English may have come from an awareness of the dialectal and orthographical regularity of much Old English literature. Whether this is the case or not, AB language suggests that at one scriptorium at least, the transcription of English texts was an 'official' activity, and that it was considered important enough to be methodized.

Evidence for standardization in the copying of English increases greatly after the middle of the fourteenth century, an indication of the rising value attached to English literature among those who trained scribes, and among those for whom scribes copied texts. The changing conditions of book production may also have had an impact: manuscripts containing English material were now being produced outside monastic scriptoria, in commercial bookshops, and the copyists who contributed to these books may have been more specialized in the writing of English than their monastic counterparts and predecessors. Two of the hands in the Auchinleck manuscript, which was mentioned previously, share a number of features, and these are replicated in seven other fourteenth-century manuscripts copied in the greater London area. In addition to the East Midland forms already described, these manuscripts contain *þat ich(e)* for 'the same', coexisting with *þat ilch(e)* (which appears to have been the more ancient London form: it is found in Henry III's 1258 proclamation); also the rare southern *oʒain(s)*, along with *aʒen*, for 'again, back', and *ich* for 'each' (another form, it seems, which was contributed to the London dialect by immigrants from the Midlands). The central Midland features in Chaucerian manuscripts, which were noted above, are found also in a number of London documents from the end of the fourteenth and the beginning of the fifteenth centuries, in a manuscript of Langland's *Piers Plowman* (Trinity College Cambridge B.15.17), and in copies of the work of the London poet Thomas Hoccleve. In these, *ilk* has become the form for 'same' and *eche* for 'each', the present participle of verbs ends in *-yng* (in the earlier standardized variety it had been *-ande, -ende,* or *-inde*), and the nominative form of the third person plural pronoun is *they,* replacing earlier *þai* and *hij* (the *h*-form is a vestige of Old English *hie*; the forms with initial *th-* or *þ,* as Chapter 3 has shown, are originally from Old Norse. As in the passage on p. 103, our modern forms for 'them' and 'their' have not yet entered this dialect).

The most widely attested example of a standardized variety of English from the fourteenth century, however, does not seem to have been formulated or written in London, but in the central Midland region which was providing the English of London with so many features at around the same time. This variety is usually called 'Central Midlands Standard', and its diagnostic features include such forms as *sich(e)* for 'such', *ony* for 'any', *silf* for 'self', and *ʒouen* or *ʒouun* for 'given'. The dialect is used in most of the large number of writings which were produced to defend and propagate the teachings of Wyclif and his followers, partly because the central Midland area, the great hotbed of Wycliffite belief, appears to have been where many Wycliffite tracts were copied. But the central Midland dialect may also have become the vehicle of Wycliffite doctrine for strategic reasons, since it lacked the barrier of incomprehensibility to many with which northern and southern dialects were charged (compare pp. 97–8 above). The dialect appears as well in individual manuscripts of non-Wycliffite religious writings, including a number of 'mystical' texts, and in copies of medical treatises and other secular works. Interestingly, it was used over half a century after it first emerged, in writings by the Welsh bishop Reginald Pecock, who was one of the most vehement opponents of the Wycliffites' arguments. Pecock's works thus connect with Wycliffite discourse not just in their subject matter but in their language too.

Greater dissemination and imitation of Central Midlands Standard may have been impeded by the proscription of the material for which it was chiefly used: Wyclif's beliefs were condemned by the Church as heretical, and the Wycliffites were persecuted especially viciously in the reign of Henry V (1414–22). The fate of the dialect—ultimate obsolescence—may be contrasted with that of the fifteenth-century variety of English which evolved in the offices of royal administration which were located at Westminster. Up to 1417, the Signet Office, which produced the personal correspondence of the king, issued its documents in French; but after 1417 the language of the king's missives changed to English. After a hiatus caused by the minority of Henry's heir, Henry VI (r. 1422–61, 1470–71), the Signet Office retained the practice of issuing its letters in English. These documents (as well as ones issued by the Office of the Privy Seal, which also began to use English for certain purposes in Henry VI's reign) were copied in the Chancery—the office of the chancellor—where pleas and other administrative items sent from all over the kingdom were also enrolled. Traditionally, it has been claimed that the English which was written in this office displays certain distinctive usages: the forms *not*, *but*, *gaf*, and *such(e)*, for example (Chaucer's equivalents are, respectively, *nat*, *bot*, *yaf*, and *swich(e)*), together with forms beginning with *th-* (or *þ-*) for 'their' and 'them'. The language of Chancery documents has been labelled 'Chancery Standard', and it was, it has been asserted, familiarized throughout the country because material from the Chancery was disseminated to every region. Gradually, according to the traditional view, this language came to be emulated, apparently because of the authority with which the Chancery was regarded: Chancery was responsible for the 'rise' of a standardized form of English to which people in all parts of England increasingly conformed.

A number of problems with this neat picture have been highlighted by Michael Benskin, who has pointed out that there is no evidence that 'Chancery' language was either unique to the Chancery, or first emanated from it: rather, the Chancery seems to have replicated the English of Signet and Privy Seal documents. Benskin has also argued that the homogeneity which has been claimed for the English of the Chancery is, in fact, a myth; also, it was not the business of the Chancery to produce the writs, summonses, and other documents which were sent to the different parts of the country. It is clear that many of the forms which appear in Chancery material, including those listed above, are, or are close to, those used in modern standard written English. It is equally clear, however, that the relationship between the modern standard and 'Chancery' English is not a simple one—that, as Benskin says, 'the development of a written standard ... was more complex and less determined than it has sometimes been made to appear'.[5] To complicate the issue further, recent research has shown that in the fifteenth century, the spread of 'Chancery' usages depended on the kind of writing which was being undertaken. The writers and copyists of verse, for example, often chose to imitate not the language of administrative documents, but the phonological (as well as the stylistic) characteristics of the individuals who were considered authoritative within the 'literary' sphere, especially Chaucer and his contemporary John Gower. Those who wrote English in the fifteenth century were, it seems, often eager to follow a model, but the model which they selected varied.

The extent to which fifteenth-century English can resemble the modern standard variety may be illustrated by the following royal warrant, which was written in 1438:

The king commandeth the keper of his priue seal to make suffisant warrant to þe Chaunceller of England that he by letters patentȝ yeue licence vnto such lordes as shal be atte tretee of peas at Caleys &c to haue stuff with þeim of gold siluer coyned & in plate & al oþer þinges such as is behoueful to euch of þeim after þair estat: & þat þe same keper of
5   our priue seal make hervpon such seueralx warrentes As þe clerc of þe counseil can declare him after þe kinges entent/ And also þat þe said keper of our priue seal/ make a warrant to þe Tresorer of England & to þe Chamberlains to paie Robert whitingham such wages for þe viage of Caleys abouesaid for a quarter of a yere as so apperteineþ to a Squier to take.

(*yeue*: may give; *tretee of peas*: peace treaty)

Orthographically, this passage shows considerable variation, in the spelling of the same word (compare, for example, the different representations of the

[5] M. Benskin, '"Chancery Standard"', in C. Kay, C. Hough, and I. Wotherspoon (eds), *New Perspectives on English Historical Linguistics: Selected Papers from 12 ICEHL, Glasgow, 21–26 August 2002. Vol. II: Lexis and Transmission.* Amsterdam Studies in The Theory and History of Linguistic Science, 252 (Amsterdam: John Benjamins, 2004), 1–40.

unstressed vowel in the second syllable of *warrant* and *warrentes* in lines 1 and 5) and in the symbols used for certain sounds (thus *th* in *commandeth* in line 1 but *þ* in *apperteineþ* in line 8, and both *the* and *þe* in line 1). Capitalization is not as in modern English: *Squier*, for instance, has an initial capital but the proper name *whitingham* in line 7 does not. Marks of punctuation are different from those with which we are familiar, and they distinguish rhetorical, not grammatical, sense units. The form of the adjective *seueralx* (line 5), which has been given an *-x* because it is modifying a plural noun, follows French usage (as, it seems, does the phrase *þe said* in line 6, which appears to be modelled on the specifying adjective *ledit* with which French legal prose is peppered). The old form for the third person singular of the present tense, as in *commandeth*, remains (and would do, at least in formal registers, into the seventeenth century); so does the 'assimilated' form *atte* (combining *at* and *the*) in line 3. But the language, if sometimes archaic to us, is comprehensible throughout, despite the fact that it dates from a time nearer to the Old English period than to our own. This suggests the relative stability of written English between the fifteenth and the twenty-first centuries—and the great pace of its development between Old English and the end of Middle English.

At the other end of the spectrum is this extract from a postscript to one of the letters of the Paston family which was written in north-east Norfolk (their surviving correspondence provides an extremely important linguistic as well as historical resource). The letter below was sent by Margaret Paston to her husband John in 1448 (although it was written for, not by, her). Gloys is the name of the family's chaplain, who wrote some of Margaret Paston's other letters:

As touchyng Roger Foke Gloys shall telle yow all &c <u>Qwhan</u> Wymdham seyd þat Jamys <u>xuld</u> dy I seyd to hym þat I soposyd þat he xuld repent hym jf he <u>schlow</u> hym or dede to hym any bodyly harm and he seyd nay he xuld never repent hym ner have a <u>ferdyng</u> wurth of harm <u>þow</u> he kelyd <u>3w</u> and hym bothe.

(*Qwhan*: when; *xuld*: should; *schlow*: slew, killed; *ferdyng*: farthing; *þow*: though; *3w*: you)

The word order here may be more or less as in modern English, but a great deal else—including the peculiarly East Anglian spelling *xuld* in line 2—is not. As this illustrates, the similarity of fifteenth-century writing to our typical standard written English clearly depends on whether its scribe (or author) has been exposed to the language of the Chancery; whether he has decided to emulate its forms; which forms he has decided to emulate (since not all features of Chancery language passed into the modern standard variety); if none of these, what his own dialect was (since a scribe writing a London variety of English will use forms close to the language of Chancery whereas a scribe writing a dialect typical of an area far from London will not); and whether his dialect is of restricted currency or diluted by more widely acceptable, 'regional' features (see the next chapter, which discusses the 'Colourless Regional Writing' which is used in many fifteenth-century texts). The projected audience of a text and its genre are important variables too—a piece of writing aimed at a wide readership may avoid forms known to be parochial, whereas a personal letter may not; at the same time, a self-consciously 'literary' piece may aspire to the complex syntax and ornate vocabulary which are features of 'high style' in the period, as Chapter 5 will show. It is far from the case that written English had become dialectally homogenized by the end of the Middle English period: this would not happen until a standard variety of the language was fully regularized and then spread through education, and that is a development of the 'modern' era, not the medieval.

Poets of the fifteenth century initiated a tradition of identifying Chaucer as what Hoccleve calls the 'first fyndere of our faire langage'. But to their contemporaries, it was to Henry V that the development of English, and the expansion of its functions, were to be attributed, as an often-cited entry in the Abstract Book of the Brewers' Guild of London makes clear. The note, which is here given in modern spelling and with modern punctuation, is a translation of a Latin memorandum recording the Brewers' 1422 decision to adopt English as the language of their accounts and proceedings:

… our mother-tongue, to wit the English tongue, hath in modern days begun to be honourably enlarged and adorned, for that our most excellent lord, King Henry V, hath in his letters missive and divers affairs touching his own person, more willingly chosen to declare the secrets of his will, and for the better understanding of his people, hath with a diligent mind procured the common idiom (setting aside others) to be commended by the exercise of writing.

5

Henry's decision (it probably *was* his) to use English in his correspondence seems to have been dictated by a perception that French was a mark of the people who were his military and political enemies. English could be a symbol of the independence of Henry's people: at the Council of Constance in 1417, the official English notary Thomas Polton seemed to speak for his king when he asserted that the autonomy of England was manifest in its language, 'the chief and surest proof of being a nation'. Henry's recognition that the English language could be viewed as a defining feature of the English people was a long-delayed endorsement of what some of the English themselves had noticed long before. One of the texts in the Auchinleck manuscript, *Of Arthour and Merlin*, notes that:

> Freynsche vse þis gentil man
> Ac euerich Inglische Inglische can.

('These high-born people use French, but every English person knows English'.)

One source of anxiety about the linguistic situation of England was removed when Henry, the greatest of all 'gentil' men, embraced the writing of English.

Other concerns, however, remained. When the first English printer, William Caxton, lamented the diachronic instability of the language of his country in his prologue to the *Eneydos* (1490)—'certaynly our langage now vsed varyeth ferre from that whiche was vsed and spoken whan I was borne/ For we englysshe men/ ben borne vnder the domynacyon of the mone, whiche is neuer stedfaste/ but euer wauerynge'—he echoed, probably not merely out of deference, Chaucer's wistful observation about linguistic change in *Troilus and Criseyde* a century before:

> Ye knowe ek that in forme of speche is chaunge
> Withinne a thousand yeer, and wordes tho
> That hadden pris, now wonder nyce and straunge
> <u>Us thinketh hem</u>, and yet thei spake hem so.   *they seem to us*

Caxton's concern about the 'brode and rude' nature of his own English, expressed in the prologue to his *Recuyell of the Historyes of Troye* (1475: see further Chapter 5), likewise reiterates a long-standing authorial topos: towards the end of the fourteenth century, Chaucer's contemporary Thomas Usk can be found apologizing for his 'rude wordes and boystous' (*boystous* means 'rough') in his prose treatise on free will and grace, *The Testament of Love*. And there were new worries to add to the traditional canon. In the prologue to the *Eneydos*, Caxton frets about the opacity of what he calls the 'curyous termes' which were newly fashionable in English (these are discussed further in Chapter 5). His identification of the language of Kent as especially unpolished (again, see Chapter 5) suggests an incipient hierarchy of dialects, with the concomitant stigmatization of those varieties which deviate from the most prestigious forms. But when Caxton in the *Eneydos* expresses his bewilderment at the phonological variation which underpins a range of variant forms in written language—'Loo what sholde a man in thyse dayes now wryte, egges or eyren?'—he stands at the end of an era, not the beginning of a new one.[6] The

---

[6] The passage is discussed in detail on 122–3.

period of Middle English was one of exceptional change in the history of the language, which saw the establishment of new trends together with the demise of old—both in the development of the language itself and in what people were saying about it. In that sense the term 'Middle English' does not adequately capture its importance.

REFERENCES AND SUGGESTIONS FOR FURTHER READING

Accessible discussions of the period covered in this chapter can be found in Baugh and Cable (2002) and Crystal (2004*a*). The account in Blake (1996) focuses especially on the issue of standardization. Strang (1970) is for more advanced students of the language, and treats later Middle English before the earlier part of the period, the two phases being divided at 1370. The most comprehensive examination of the whole period is Blake (1992).

Useful sourcebooks of Middle English texts include Bennett and Smithers (1968), Burnley (1992*a*), Burrow and Turville-Petre (2005), Dickins and Wilson (1956), Freeborn (1998), and Sisam (1921). All of these also contain information about the language in the period.

The lines from the *Ormulum* are quoted from Dickins and Wilson (1956: 84 (ll. 48–9)). For a useful discussion of the text, see, in particular, Burnley (1992*a*: 78–87). My emphasis on the anxiety implicit in Orm's linguistic project queries David Crystal's recent claim that 'metalinguistic awareness' about English is a development of the late fourteenth century (see Crystal 2004*a*: 169).

Dialectal variation in written Middle English

The classic study of the use of Latin and French after the Conquest (and the newly restricted use of English) is Clanchy (1993).

Local variation

The extract from *Ancrene Riwle* ('Text A') is quoted from Dickins and Wilson (1956: 91). The extract from *Ancrene Wisse* ('Text B') is from Tolkien (1962: 46). Shepherd (1991) gives a concise account of the different versions of the text; on its origins, see Dobson (1976). The dates of the Nero and Corpus manuscripts are taken from Laing (1993: 77 and 24 respectively). Carruthers (1990) includes a fascinating account of the processes involved in scribal reading and copying. On compound words in *Ancrene Wisse* which combine English with French elements, compare Crystal (2004*a*: 149). The quotation from Elyot's *The Governour* is taken from Baugh and Cable (2002: 214).

The major dialect areas: Old English to Middle English

Good, basic accounts of the major dialect 'divisions' of Middle English can be found in Burnley (1992*a*) and the introduction to Burrow and Turville-Petre (2005); compare also the more detailed material introducing the notes to the texts in Bennett and Smithers (1968) and Sisam (1921). Samples of the dialects, with concise discussion of their features, are included in Baugh and Cable (2002: 409–21, Appendix A). The passage from the East Anglian bestiary is quoted from Dickins and Wilson (1956: 59 (ll. 1–8)). The extract from Trevisa's translation of Higden's *Polychronicon* is taken from Babington, vol. 2 (1869: 159).

North and south

The lines from *Cursor Mundi* are quoted from Freeborn (1998), who prints the corresponding passage in the later southern manuscript in parallel. The most comprehensive guide to phonological developments in the Old English period is Campbell (1959); on vowel lengthening before certain groups of consonants, see p. 120. Blake (1996) discusses the time delay in the representation of linguistic change which had taken place in the Old English period (see especially chapters 5 and 6). On phonological and morphological developments in early Middle English, and the ways in which these vary between dialects, Strang (1970) is especially helpful. On the origins of the -*s* ending in the present tense of verbs in northern Middle English, see Samuels (1985). Crystal (2004: 218–21) offers an alternative explanation.

The passage from Trevisa in this section is taken from Babington, vol. 2 (1869: 163); Higden's reliance on William of Malmesbury is discussed in Machan (2003: 96). The comments of the author of *Cursor Mundi* regarding his source material are quoted from Turville-Petre (1996: 20), where the claim that regional dialects were thought of as variations of the same language is also made.

Middle English before and after 1350

The copying of texts

The citations from the holograph manuscript of the *Ayenbite of Inwyt* are quoted from Sisam (1921: 32). On the suggestion that *Sir Gawain and the Green Knight* and the other texts in its manuscript might have been written in London, see Bennett (1983) and Putter (1995: 191). The passage from *The Owl and the Nightingale* is taken from Wells (1907: 74 (ll. 897–902)); on the two spelling systems reflected in the Caligula manuscript of the text, see also Cartlidge (2001: xli) and Stanley (1960, esp. pp. 6–9). On *literatim* copying in early Middle English, see Laing (1991) and Smith (1991: 54); on scribal translation in later Middle English, see also Benskin and Laing (1981), who discuss the varying thoroughness with which copyists changed the language of their exemplars. The language of the Thornton manuscript is examined in McIntosh (1967).

The extract from *The Prick of Conscience* is quoted from Wogan-Browne *et al.* (1999: 242–3 (ll. 9–22)).

London English

On the language of twelfth-century London, see Reaney (1925); on its evolution through immigration, see especially Samuels (1963). The excerpts from Henry III's proclamation of 1258 are quoted from Dickins and Wilson (1956: 8). The passages from Chaucer are cited from Benson (1988): see pp. 584, 528, 533, and 531 for the lines from *Troilus and Criseyde* (V. 1793–6, III. 1128–34, III. 1471–77 and III. 1291–2 respectively); see p. 76 for the couplet from *The Miller's Tale* (Fragment I(A). 3797–8); and p. 333 for the extract from *The Book of the Duchess* (ll. 257–9). Burnley (1983) discusses various aspects of Chaucer's (1983) language, including his exploitation of the different dialectal forms familiar in London.

The quotations from the concordance to the Wycliffite Bible, which are found in the preface to the work, are taken from Burnley (1992*a*: 166–7).

Standardization

Shepherd (1991) contains a useful discussion of AB language. The suggestion that AB language may have been influenced by the standardization of English before the Conquest is made by Blake (1996: 129).

Samuels (1963) is the classic account of the appearance of standardized varieties of English in the fourteenth and fifteenth centuries. The standardized language exemplified by the Auchinleck manuscript is called 'Type II' here, that of Chaucerian manuscripts 'Type III', and that of the Chancery 'Type IV'; 'Central Midlands Standard' is 'Type I'. For important qualifications of Samuels' findings, however, see Benskin (1992, 2004), and also Horobin (2003), who emphasizes the perpetuation of Samuels' Type III language after the emergence of Type IV. On the spread of forms typical of Gower's language, see also Smith (1988*a*). On the commercial production of books in fourteenth- and fifteenth-century London, see Christianson (1989).

The royal warrant of 1438 is quoted from Fisher *et al.* (1984: 178); the postscript from Margaret Paston's 1448 letter to her husband is taken from Burnley (1992*a*), but with the modern punctuation inserted there removed. The often-cited Brewers' memorandum is taken from Chambers and Daunt (1931: 139). Thomas Polton's claims regarding the connection between the English language and English autonomy are discussed in Allmand (1992: 417). On Chaucer's importance for fifteenth-century English poets, see especially Lerer (1993); but compare Cannon (1998), who argues that the image of Chaucer created in the fifteenth century misrepresents the truth about his contribution to the development of the English language.

The couplet from *Of Arthour and Merlin* is quoted from Turville-Petre (1996: 21). The passage from Chaucer's *Troilus and Criseyde* which is echoed by Caxton is taken from Benson (1988: 489 (II.22–5)); Usk's apology is quoted from Wogan-Browne *et al.* (1999: 30 (l. 9)). For the sources of Caxton's comments which I quote in this section, see the bibliographical details in the following chapter.

5

FROM MIDDLE TO EARLY
MODERN ENGLISH

Jeremy J. Smith

ANY histories of languages differentiate between 'external' and 'internal' approaches to the subject. Internal history may be defined as the study of evolving systems of lexicon, grammar, and transmission (speech- and writing-systems); external history is to do with the ways in which a language is employed over time, for example the shift from script to print, or how particular languages are associated with particular social functions at particular moments in their history.

Such a distinction is in many ways useful and is, for example, adopted in the chapter which follows this one. However, it is important to realize that this strict separation of internal and external history is a matter of operational scholarly convenience rather than actual fact. Just as living creatures evolve through natural selection, whereby form interacts over time in complex ways with environmental function, so do languages evolve: thus the changing forms of a particular language through time are the result of their interaction with that language's functions. From this point of view, therefore, internal and external histories are intimately connected.

The relationship between form and function clearly underpins many of the comments on their native language which are made by English writers in the late medieval and early modern periods. Thus, for example, William Caxton (England's first printer), in the prologue to his translation of *Eneydos* (1490), makes the point very effectively; his discussion has a local point of reference, but it has wider implications in that he explicitly draws connections between linguistic forms and their social/stylistic functions:

And for as moche as this present booke is not for a rude vplondyssh man to laboure therin/ ne rede it/ but onely for a clerke & a noble gentylman that feleth and vnderstondeth in faytes of armes in loue & in noble chyualrye/ Therfor in a meane bytwene bothe I haue reduced & translated this sayd booke in to our englysshe not ouer rude ne curyous but in suche termes as shal be vnderstanden by goddys grace accordynge to my copye.   5

(*faytes*: deeds)

Almost a century later, in his *The First Part of the Elementarie* (1582), the Elizabethan schoolteacher Richard Mulcaster also points directly to how language change derives from functional considerations:

... our tung doth serue to so manie vses, bycause it is conuersant with so manie peple, and so well acquainted with so manie matters, in so sundrie kindes of dealing. Now all this varietie of matter, and diuersitie of trade, make both matter for our speche, & mean to enlarge it. For he that is so practised, will vtter that, which he practiseth in his naturall tung, and if the strangenesse of the matter do so require, he that is to vtter, rather then he   5 will stik in his vtterance, will vse the foren term, by waie of premunition, that the cuntrie peple do call it so, and by that mean make a foren word, an English denison.

(*premunition*: premonition *denison*: denizen, naturalized inhabitant)

In the terminology of modern sociolinguistics, Mulcaster's description of the *manie vses* of *our tung* could be described as 'elaboration'. In many societies, particular languages—or varieties of the same language—are used with particular functions. As has been discussed earlier in this volume (see Chapter 3), Latin, English, and French all performed distinct functions in England during the Middle Ages. But if a particular language or language-variety has a number of functions, we may consider it to be elaborated.

Elaboration of usage is one of four stages in the process of standardization, the others being selection, codification, and acceptance. It is by means of this process that a particular variety or language is selected for overtly prestigious use, either consciously or unconsciously; it is codified through the enforcement of norms (e.g. by an Academy, or through education); it is elaborated in function; and it is accepted by the community as an elite usage.

It is, however, important to realize that standard varieties of language tend to relate to other varieties clinally rather than discretely: in other words, there is no clear cut-off point between a standard variety and other varieties of the same language. Moreover, as later chapters in this volume illustrate, standardization itself seems to be an ongoing process; the distinction between standard and non-standard forms tends to change over time, and no single stage in the process of standardization of any living language is ever complete (such fixity is of course possible for dead languages, such as Latin). During the transition from Middle to modern English, a 'standardized' variety, based on usages current in London, can nevertheless be discerned. However, since London English itself was changing as a result of the dynamic processes of immigration into the capital which took place at this time, it is hard to pin down any precise set of forms which characterizes it.

The notion of elaboration has usefulness in any context where the multi-functionality of languages or language-varieties is being discussed. The theme of this chapter is that the transition from Middle to early modern English is above all the period of the elaboration of the English language. Between the late fourteenth and sixteenth centuries, the English language began increasingly to take on more functions. These changes in function had, it is argued here, a major effect on the form of English: so major, indeed, that the old distinction between 'Middle' and 'modern' retains considerable validity, although the boundary between these two linguistic epochs was obviously a fuzzy one.

The remainder of this chapter falls into four major sections, dealing with the lexicon, grammar, spelling, and pronunciation respectively. The chapter concludes with some remarks on the linguistic implications of a key cultural event during the period: the arrival of printing in the British Isles in 1476.

LEXICON

As discussed in the previous chapter, the Middle English period is above all the period when linguistic variation is reflected in the written mode. One of the most famous descriptions of such variation may be taken as a starting-point for our discussion of the lexicon during the transition from Middle to early modern English. It is again taken from Caxton's prologue to the *Eneydos*:

And certaynly our langage now vsed varyeth ferre from that. whiche was vsed and spoken whan I was borne/ For we englysshe men/ ben borne vnder the domynacyon of the mone. whiche is neuer stedfaste/ but euer wauerynge/ wexynge one season/ and waneth & dyscreaseth another season/ And that comyn englysshe that is spoken in one shyre varyeth from a nother. In so moche that in my dayes happened that certayn marchauntes were in a shippe in <u>tamyse</u> for to haue sayled ouer the see into ȝelande/ and for lacke of wynde thei taryed atte <u>forlond</u> and wente to lande for to refreshe them And one of theym named sheffelde a mercer cam in to an hows and <u>axed</u> for <u>mete</u>. and specyally he axyd after eggys And the good wyf answerde. That she coude speke no frenshe. And the

marchaunt was angry. for he also coude speke no frenshe. but wold haue hadde egges/   10
and she vnderstode hym not/ And thenne at laste a nother sayd that he wolde haue eyren/
then the good wyf sayd that she vnderstod hym wel/ Loo what sholde a man in thyse
dayes now wryte. egges or eyren/ certaynly it is harde to playse euery man/ by cause of
dyuersite & chaunge of langage. For in these dayes euery man that is in ony reputacyon in
his countre. wyll vtter his commynycacyon and maters in suche maners & termes/ that   15
fewe men shall vnderstonde theym/ And som honest and grete clerkes haue ben wyth me
and desired me to wryte the moste curyous termes that I coude fynde/ And thus bytwene
playn rude/ & curyous I stande abasshed.

(*tamyse*: the River Thames; *ʒelande*: Zealand, in the Low Countries; *forlond*: the North Foreland, the westernmost point on the coast of modern Kent; *axed*: asked; *mete*: food)

This passage, even if Caxton were (as seems likely) exaggerating to strengthen his argument, is interesting for several reasons. Most obviously, in the communicative problems caused by *egges* and *eyren* in lines 9–13, it illustrates what is known as diatopic ('through-space') variation in the lexicon, and thus may be taken as an early comment on Middle English word geography—a somewhat neglected sub-discipline still. Different forms have a different distribution in Middle English. Thus, *kirk* ('church') and *stern* ('star') appear in Northern Middle English but not in the south; and *bigouth* ('began') appears in Older Scots but not in Middle English, where the forms *gan* and *can* were preferred.

Moreover, it is clear that the vocabulary of English varied diatopically during the late Middle Ages not only in forms but also in the meaning of forms. At the end of the fourteenth century, Geoffrey Chaucer observed something of this variation in his representation of Northern dialect in the *Canterbury Tales* when, in *The Reeve's Tale* (l. A.4029) he made his young Northern students Aleyn and John use the word *hope* with its Northern meaning 'think', rather than with its Southern meaning 'hope, wish for'. Thus the line 'Oure maunciple, I hope he wil be deed' is a dialectal joke, depending on the conflict between the Northern meaning 'I think our manciple will die' and the Southern meaning 'I hope our manciple will die'.

But other points made in the passage from Caxton's prologue are also of interest for the arguments of this chapter. For instance, he clearly understands one of the principal axioms which underpin modern theories of language change: the relationship between linguistic variation and linguistic change. Furthermore, he draws attention to the connection between language and social standing; the lines (14–17) referring to the usage of 'euery man that is in ony reputacyon' make this point explicitly. Caxton indicates that for many contemporaries such 'reputacyon' or status correlates with a particular form of 'commynycacyon' which valued heightened expression above clarity. And Caxton distinguishes 'playn', 'rude', and 'curyous [termes]'; to use present-day linguistic terminology, he

an illustration, here is part of a passage from Berners's translation describing an incident in the Hundred Years' War, the death of Sir John Chandos (1369–1370):

And anone it was fayre light day, for in the begynnyng of January the mornynges be soone light. And whan the Frenchmen and Bretons were within a <u>leage</u> of the bridge, they perceyved on the other syde of the bridge Sir Thomas Percy and his company; and he lykewise perceyved the Frenchmen, and rode as fast as he might to get the advantage of
5   the bridge ...

(*leage*: league)

Although Berners does use some subordinated clauses, the dominant syntactic mode in this passage is co-ordination, indicated by the presence of the co-ordinating conjunction 'and'.

Conversely, something more 'rude' (i.e. 'low-style') can be found in the colloquial *Vulgaria* or 'school books' which were designed as sources for translation from English into Latin. These consisted of collections of everyday sentences and the example below comes from such a collection from Magdalen College School, Oxford, *c*1500:

Yesterdaye, I departyde asyde prively oute of the feldys from my felows and went be myselfe into a <u>manys</u> orcherde wher I dyde not only ete rype apples my bely full, but I toke away as many as I coulde bere.

(*manys*: man's)

Of course, even such 'rude' writings are conventionalized and literary. Probably the nearest approximations to the colloquial registers of the period, other than in the dramatic texts cited in the previous section, are to be found in the great collections of private letters and memoranda in English which begin to appear in the fifteenth and sixteenth centuries. Of these pieces of 'everyday English', by far the best known and largest are the archived letters and papers associated with the Paston family (mentioned already in Chapter 4)—an aspirant late-medieval family from Norfolk that rose from humble origins to the nobility. Other collections are also important: the letters of the wealthy Stonor family in Ox-fordshire, of the Cely family (a merchant family with business in London, Flanders, and Calais, some of whose letters will be discussed in Chapter 7), and of John Shillingford (Mayor of Exeter 1447–50), or the sixteenth- and seventeenth-century private documents collected by Bridget Cusack (see pp. 137–8 and the Further Reading to this chapter).

A flavour of this sort of material may be had from some of the letters of John Paston III to his brother John Paston II. In October 1472, John III was living (rather unhappily) with his formidable mother Margaret in Norwich, and the following passage from a frank letter of that date to his brother gives an idea of the kind of language used informally by a member of the 'rising' classes of the late fifteenth century. *Syr Jamys*, about whom John III is complaining, is James Gloys, a family chaplain and retainer already referred to in the previous chapter (see p. 113).

I send yow herwyth the endenture betwyx yow and Townesend. My modyr hathe herd of that mater by the reporte of old Wayte, whyche rennyth on it wyth opyn mowthe in hys werst wyse. My modyr wepyth and takyth on meruaylously, for she seythe she <u>wotyth</u> well it shall neuer be pledgyd ought; wherfor she seythe that she wyll puruey for hyr lond þat ye shall non selle of it, for she thynkys ye wold and [i.e. if] it cam to yowr hand. As for   5 hyr wyll, and all syche maters as wer in hand at your last being here, they thynk that it shall not lye in all oure <u>porys</u> to let it in on poynt.

   Syr Jamys is euyr choppyng at me when my modyr is present, wyth syche wordys as he thynkys wrathe me and also cause my modyr to be dyspleaseid wyth me, evyn as who seyth he wold I wyst that he settyth not by the best of vs. And when he hathe most   10 <u>vnsyttyng</u> woordys to me, I <u>smylle</u> a lytyll and tell hym it is good heryng of thes old talys. Syr Jamys is parson of Stokysby by J. Bernays gyft. I trowe he beryth hym the hyeer.

(*wotyth*: knows; *porys*: powers; *vnsyttyng*: inappropriate; *smylle*: smile)

The simple syntax and uncomplicated vocabulary of the passage, accompanied by what seem (from comparison with modern usage) to be 'natural' expressions (e.g. 'My modyr ... takyth on ... , I smylle a lytyll and tell hym it is good heryng of thes old talys'), are good indications of the main characteristics of the 'playn' style.

TRANSMISSION: WRITING AND SPEECH

It should be clear from the preceding sections that the elaboration of English meant that it was possible to use the language for a very wide set of functions, from ceremonious address to colloquial complaint, and that this elaboration manifested itself in distinct lexical and grammatical usages. This elaboration has implications for the transmission of English, and it is to questions of transmission—writing-system and phonology—that we must now turn.

   It is usual to describe the fifteenth century as the period of spelling standardization and, as discussed in the previous chapter, since Michael Samuels's seminal article of 1963 scholars have generally emphasized the role of 'Chancery English' (sometimes renamed 'Chancery Standard') in this process. Samuels modelled the expression 'Chancery English'—his Type IV of 'incipient standard'—on 'Chancery

German' or *Kanzleideutsch* which emerged in several German states during the later Middle Ages, for example *Das Gemeine Deutsch* used in Austria, Bavaria, Swabia, Alsace, parts of the Rhineland, and some parts of what is modern Switzerland. Chancery English was not envisaged by Samuels as located in any particular English office of state, and more recent work—notably by Michael Benskin, who is currently working on a complete reassessment of the issue (see pp. 111–12 of this volume)—has, as we have seen, tended to downplay any special and explicit intervention by government in the evolution of standard spelling practices.

What is undeniable is that the fifteenth century saw a gradual shift from the richly diverse spellings of the Middle English period to a more muted set of variations where more exotic forms of rarer currency were purged in favour of those more commonly used. The outcome was that late fifteenth-century spelling in England tends to be more various in character than present-day English usage, but nevertheless lacks precise dialectal 'colouring'. For example: there are one hundred and forty-three distinct spellings for the item *such* recorded in the authoritative *Linguistic Atlas of Late Mediaeval English* (LALME), ranging from *schch* recorded in Norfolk through such forms as *swich, seche,* and *soche* to Kentish *zuyche* and Northern *swilk, slik*. But during the course of the fifteenth century, such exotics tend to be replaced by more commonly occurring forms such as *such(e)* and *sich(e)*.

This purging of what have been termed 'grosser provincialisms' seems to derive from communicative pressures relating to the elaboration of English. During the earlier Middle English period, as Chapter 4 has already discussed, written English had a local function—when writing had a national function, Latin and French were used, as (for instance) in the copying of Magna Carta— and therefore it made sense to develop a spelling-system which mapped fairly closely in phonic terms to the varying phonologies of individual localities. An efflorescence of distinct spelling-systems resulted. But as English began, through elaboration, to take on national functions, such variation impeded communi- cation. As a result, a kind of 'lowest common denominator' of usage emerged: colourless written English. Colourless usage emerged at different speeds in different parts of the country; it appeared first in the southern half of the country, later in the north, and it seems to have competed and interacted variously with well-established local usages in (e.g.) the South-West Midlands and East Anglia. These local variations fairly clearly relate to the state of vernacular literacy in these areas.

However, standardization in this context was not a straightforward matter— indeed, as Samuels stressed in 1981, interpreting the process 'bristles with problems'[7]—and the problematic character of the process is well illustrated by the evidence of the Paston letters. Two short quotations might be used to demonstrate the issue. In 1479, John Paston II and his brother Walter both wrote to their mother Margaret. Here is a passage from John's letter:

But on Tywesdaye I was wyth þe Bysshop of Hely [i.e. Ely], whyche shewyth hymselffe goode and worshypfull, and he seyde þat he sholde sende to myn oncle William þat he sholde nott procede in no suche mater till þat he speke wyth hym; and mooreouyre þat he scholde cawse hym to be heer hastelye.

And here is a passage from Walter's:

I marvel soore that yow sent me noo word of the letter wych I sent to yow by Master Wylliam Brown at Ester. I sent yow word that tym that I <u>xold</u> send yow myn exspenses partyculerely, but as at thys tym the <u>berare</u> hereof had a letter sodenly that he xold com hom, and therefore I kowd have noo leysure to send them yow on that wys; and therefore I <u>xall</u> wryt to yow in thys letter the hool som of my exspenses sythyns I was wyth yow tyll   5 Ester last paste, and also the resytys, rekenyng the xx s. that I had of yow to Oxon. Wardys, wyth the Buschopys fyndyng.

(*xold*: should; *berare*: bearer; *xall*: shall)

What is interesting about these two passages is that these two men, from the same family (and social group) and writing to the same person, have distinct spelling systems. John's usage is more dialectally 'colourless' than Walter's; his forms include *whyche* and *sholde/scholde*, both of which have a fairly widespread distribution dialectally. But Walter's *wych* in the passage has been commented on, as has his use of *x-* in *xold*, *xall* ('should', 'shall'); the latter in particular is a distinctively East Anglian usage. The reason for the difference between the brothers seems to be that John was a much-travelled man, part of the entourage of Edward IV, whereas Walter, a decade younger than his sibling, died soon after this letter was written; he was a student at Oxford, but otherwise seems to have lived at home and thus has closer social ties to the Norfolk region. John, more exposed to written English of different kinds, adopts forms of wider currency. Nevertheless, both sons expect to be understood by the person who is to read their letters.

Alongside colourless English, there is evidence for other kinds of usage restricted to particular genres or even particular authors; and in the early modern English period there is evidence that spelling took on an ideological significance. Samuels's Type I ('Central Midlands Standard') seems, as mentioned

[7] See M. L. Samuels, 'Spelling and Dialect in the Late and Post-Middle English Periods', in M. Benskin and M. L. Samuels (eds), *So meny people, longages and tonges: philological essays in Scots and mediaeval English presented to Angus McIntosh* (Edinburgh: Middle English Dialect Project, 1981), 43–54.

in Chapter 4, to have emerged in the mid-fourteenth century as a means of transmitting university learning (particularly theological) to a wider audience who could read the vernacular. At the other end of the period under review, during the sixteenth century in Scotland, it became usual for Catholics to use Older Scots but for Protestants, modelling their usage on the English vernacular bible, to adopt Anglicized forms. It is no coincidence that one of the earliest English spelling reformers, Sir John Cheke, devised a special usage—with (e.g.) long vowels flagged by the doubling of letters, as in *eest* ('East'), *fruut* ('fruit')—for the translation of the Bible that he undertook at the request of the reformer Archbishop Cranmer. Moreover, special spelling systems seem to have been adopted for the copying of particular writers: it seems to have been usual to transcribe the *Confessio Amantis* of John Gower and the *Mirror of the Blessed Life of Jesus Christ* of Nicholas Love, both texts which survive in many copies, using spelling systems peculiar to both textual traditions. Thus a 'typical' Gower will contain slightly odd spellings such as *o(u)ghne* for the adjective 'own', *-ende* inflexions for the present participle, for example *walkende* rather than *walking*, and syncopated forms of the third person present singular verb, for example *brekth* ('breaks') rather than *breketh*, and these spelling systems continued to be used when these works came to be printed.

These last examples indicate that there was a perceived developing need to adopt a particular spelling system, but as yet no particular model had been selected for adoption. Indeed, authoritative norms for spelling in English only appear in the practices of printers in the sixteenth century, alongside the writings of the orthoepists and spelling reformers such as Hart and Cheke. Even then spelling variation in private writings lasted for many years subsequently (see further Chapters 9 and 10). The evolution of standardized spelling, therefore, relates closely to—and depends upon—the elaboration of English during the fifteenth century, and the evidence suggests that standardization was not a straightforward process.

When we turn to the evolution of prestigious and/or standardized accents, the evidence becomes much more indirect and hard to interpret, but it is possible to make some broad observations.

The evidence for accents during the Middle English period derives from a mixture of things such as the analysis of rhyming and alliterating verse and including—for stress patterns—the study of metre, or by means of comparative and internal reconstruction. Particularly important is the study of the relationship between written symbol and what may be presumed to be the corresponding sound; although LALME, the great resource for the study of Middle English dialects, claims only to map the writing systems of the medieval period, it is nevertheless possible, provided that important qualifications are understood, to draw certain conclusions about the sound system relating to the writing systems which LALME records, since the relationship between written symbol and corresponding sound seems to have been closer during the Middle English period than ever since.

No detailed (as opposed to general) discussion of accents by a contemporary writer survives; until the spelling reformers and phoneticians of the sixteenth and seventeenth centuries, there is no English equivalent to the twelfth-century *First Grammatical Treatise* which provides us with a sophisticated phonological analysis of the medieval vernacular of Old Icelandic. However, as Chapter 4 has already revealed, interpretation of this kind of spelling evidence does enable a good deal of the phonological map of the Middle English period to be reconstructed.

It is usual for scholars to argue that, as symbol and sound began to diverge under the impact of standardization during the course of the fifteenth and sixteenth centuries—'silent *k*', for instance, seems to have appeared in English in *knife, knight* during the course of the early seventeenth century—the evidence for speech becomes harder to interpret, or is indeed uninformative (a problem which is addressed in Chapter 6). Nevertheless, this argument has perhaps been overstated, for there are many writings from the fifteenth and sixteenth centuries which, taken alongside the discussion of contemporary writers on language, enable something of the accentual map of the period to be reconstructed.

Some of the most interesting material relevant for this purpose has been collected by Bridget Cusack. The following passage is taken from a letter written by Alice Radcliffe, probably a resident of Winmarleigh in Lancashire. The letter is dated by Cusack to 1524.

Ryght Wryscheppefull Syr in my moste <u>hwmly</u> Wyse I recommande me vnto you Dyssyrynge to here of youre well fare the Wyche I pray iesu <u>in cresse</u> to <u>is plusure</u> & to youre moste herttys Dyssyre Syr <u>has</u> tochynge youre laste letter qwere in I <u>persawe</u> ȝe Dyssyryt me to be gud moder to my <u>swnne</u> & yourys yt there be no <u>predysciall</u> nar hwrtte vnto my swnnys <u>Anarretans</u> Syr has ferre has lys in my pore power I wyll be lotthe to Se yt   5 <u>swlde hwr</u> it And yff yer be ony mon <u>A bowth</u> to do hym Any Wronge youre masterscheppe <u>sall hawe</u> knawlyge trystynge yt ȝe Wylle se remedy for hym for he nor I has <u>no noder socare both</u> you

(*hwmly*: humble; *in cresse*: increase; *is plusure*: his pleasure; *has*: as (also in l. 6); *in*: wherein; *persawe*: perceive; *swnne*: son; *predysciall*: prejudicial; *hwrtte*: hurt; *Anarretans*: inheritance; *swlde hwr*: should hurt; *A bowth*: about; *sall hawe*: shall have; *no noder socare both*: no other succour but)

Alice's usage is of interest for a number of reasons, not least because her spelling—while bearing in mind the oft-cited complexity of the relationship between written and spoken modes—seems to relate fairly closely to what we can reconstruct of contemporary pronunciation. Thus the stressed vowels in *gud* ('good') in line 5 and *knawlyge* ('knowledge') in line 8 seem to reflect the fronted reflexes of the Old English long vowels *ō* and *ā* which are characteristic of Northern English accents both during the Middle English period and in the present day. Similarly typical of Northern speech would be a voiceless alveolar fricative consonant [s] in place of the palato-alveolar [ʃ] in *shall*, represented in the spelling *sall* ('shall', 'must') in line 8. Analysis of Cusack's collection not only shows that a dialect map of the early modern period along the lines of the LALME would not be impossible; it also shows that it is possible to reconstruct something of the informal and dialectal speech which mapped onto this writing.

Nevertheless, such an enterprise would depend much more on such 'everyday English' as Cusack has collected than on the major literary texts which form the core of LALME's analyses. Public writing during the period is comparatively more homogeneous, for the reasons flagged above, and there is good evidence that the elaboration of English during the period correlated with the emergence of prestigious forms of pronunciation.

The clearest statement to this effect is in the famous chapter 'Of Language' in *The Arte of English Poesie* (1589) by the Tudor courtier-critic George Puttenham (*c*1520–90). The poet, advises Puttenham, should avoid the usages of 'marches and frontiers, or in port townes, where straungers haunt for traffike sake'; also to be avoided are the 'peeuish affectation of words out of the primatiue languages' used by scholars in the universities, or the usage of 'poore rusticall or vnciuill people', or

the speach of a craftes man or carter, or other of the inferiour sort, though he be inhabitant or bred in the best towne and Citie in this Realme, for such persons doe abuse good speaches by strange accents or ill shapen soundes, and false ortographie. But he shall follow generally the better brought vp sort, such as the Greekes call [charientes] men
5 ciuill and graciously behauoured and bred. Our maker [i.e. poet] therfore at these dayes shall not follow *Piers plowman* nor *Gower* nor *Lydgate* nor yet *Chaucer*, for their language is now out of vse with vs: neither shall he take the termes of Northern-men, such as they vse in dayly talke, whether they be noble men or gentlemen, or of their best clarkes all is a matter: nor in effect any speech vsed beyond the riuer of Trent, though no man can deny
10 that theirs is the purer English Saxon at this day, yet it is not so Courtly nor so currant as our Southerne English is, no more is the far Westerne mans speech: ye shall therfore take the vsuall speach of the Court, and that of London and the shires lying about London within lx. Myles, and not much aboue. I say not this but that in euery shyre of England there be gentlemen and others that speake but specially write as good Southerne as we of
15 Middlesex or Surrey do, but not the common people of euery shire, to whom the

gentlemen, and also their learned clarkes do for the most part condescend, but herein we are already ruled by th'English Dictionaries and other bookes written by learned men, and therefore it needeth none other direction in that behalfe.

The passage is of considerable interest for a number of reasons. It indicates a codifying stage in the standardization of English (the 'bookes written by learned men' of line 17), an awareness of linguistic change (see lines 5–7), and a sense that non-standard varieties have certain archaic features (see lines 10–14). It also suggests that a 'standard' usage has yet to penetrate beyond the River Trent even among 'noble men and gentlemen'. But most importantly for our purposes, it signals the existence in towns of a class structure correlating with speech—including matters of accent (we might note the reference in the opening lines to the 'ill shapen sounds' of the 'craftes man or carter'). It is therefore permissible to apply, if not all the methods, at least the insights of modern sociolinguistics to the major conurbations of Tudor England—most obviously, to London.

The question arises, though, as to the possibility of detecting class-based accentual distinctions at any earlier date. Puttenham's account is the most explicit of a number of sixteenth-century comments. John Palsgrave, an early sixteenth-century student of French, refers in 1532 to a pronunciation 'where the best englysshe is spoken'; the scholar-diplomat Sir Thomas Elyot, in *The Boke called the Governour* (1531) refers to how a nobleman's son must 'speke none englisshe but that which is cleane, polite, perfectly and articulately pronounced'; and Henry Dowes, tutor to Thomas Cromwell's son, states his charge is learning 'the natural and true kynde of pronunciation'.[8]

But there are very few if any such comments from before the beginning of the sixteenth century. Dialect-awareness is used comically in Geoffrey Chaucer's *The Reeve's Tale*, but the comedy in that poem does not depend on social class; if anything, the Northern students belong to a higher social class than the Cambridgeshire miller they fool. In the first half of the fifteenth century, the Northern shepherds of the *Wakefield Second Shepherds' Play* mock the 'Sothren tothe' of the sheep-stealer Mak in his pose as 'a yoman ... of the kyng', but Mak's 'tothe' seems to be characterized by southern English grammar rather than pronunciation, with *ich be* for *I am* and *ye doth* for *ye do*.

We are therefore forced back on hypotheses based on probabilities and the analysis of historical correspondences; and there are at least indications that a

[8] These (and other comments) are discussed in Eric Dobson's 1955 article, 'Early Modern Standard English', *Transactions of the Philological Society*, 25–54. Reprinted in R. Lass (ed.), *Approaches to English Historical Linguistics* (New York: Holt, Rinehart and Winston, 1969), 419–39.

class-based system was beginning to appear in London English. Indeed, the existence of such a system offers the best hypothesis for the origins of the major phonological distinction between Middle and early modern English: the Great Vowel Shift, which saw a whole series of raisings and diphthongizations of the long vowels of late Middle English in an apparently ordered way. The Shift will be further examined in Chapter 6, so there is no need to examine the detail of its geometry here. But its origins—described as 'mysterious' by Stephen Pinker in 1994—lie, it might be argued, in the interaction of usages in late medieval London. ('Origins' are here seen as the triggering of the process, as distinct from 'inception' as described in the following chapter.)

We know that London underwent a surge in its population during the fourteenth century, and this seems to correspond to the development of 'Types' of London English in the latter half of the century which were formulated by Samuels in 1963. Most immigrants into London came from the Midlands; on arrival, they encountered an elite whose usage had a more southerly basis.

From the analysis of rhymes it is possible to reconstruct the various sound systems existing in late medieval London. It is clear that writers such as Chaucer—an important government official and a member of the royal court—had a distinct sound system from those of Midland writers, most notably in the reflexes of lengthened Middle English short *e*, *o*. For Chaucer, as his rhyming practice confirms, the lengthened forms of these vowels—as in the verb *beren* ('to bear') and *forlore* ('abandoned') respectively—were distinct from the reflexes (i.e. the corresponding forms) of the Old English long vowels *ēa*, *æ*, as in *leren* ('to teach') which derives from Old English *læran*), and *ā* (which was rounded to /ɔː/ in accents south of the Humber, as in Chaucer's *loore* ('teaching') which derives from Old English *lār*). Chaucer can therefore rhyme *loore* with *moore* (from Old English *māra*, but not with, for example, *before* (from Old English *beforan*). However, Midland texts regularly rhyme lengthened *e* with the reflexes of the Old English long vowels *ēa*, *æ*, and lengthened *o* with the reflex of Old English *ā*, giving rhymes such as *reade* ('red'): *iureden* ('injure'), and of *ore* ('mercy', from Old English *ār*): *uorlore* ('abandoned').

When two phonological systems come into contact, it is usual to expect adjustment to take place. We know from the evidence of present-day sound-changes in progress that very slight differences in articulation can have a major systemic effect as these differences are monitored and hyperadaptation—what we can see as 'overshooting the mark'—follows. If Chaucerian-type usage were accommodating itself to Midland usage, then we would predict a hyperadapted lowering. If, on the other hand, Midland usage were accommodating itself to

Chaucerian-type usage, then we would predict a hyperadapted raising; and it is of considerable interest that a raising would correlate with the first stage of the Shift.

That the accommodation had a social basis is indicated by what we know of the social structure of late medieval London. London, like other cities, was dominated socially by an oligarchy: a group of richer citizens, of which Chaucer was one. The tale of Dick Whittington, which dates from this period, is essentially a capitalist success story in which the poor hero joins an elite; it is not a revolutionary attack on the existing order. Although the pantomime story is considerably embellished, it does encapsulate an essential truth: successful incomers to London accommodated themselves to the elites who were in power.

Whatever the origins of the Shift, it seems fairly clear that accents had social implications by the late fifteenth century. Caxton, perhaps, already indicates this, in his prologue to *The Recuyell of the Historyes of Troye* (1475). This prologue seems to be the first he wrote; it was the first book to be printed in English, in Bruges, before Caxton moved to Westminster in 1476.

... I remembryd my self of my symplenes and vnperfightnes that I had in bothe langages/ that is to wete in frenshe & in englissh for in france was I neuer/ and was born & lerned myn englissh in kente in the weeld [i.e. Kent in the Weald] where I doubte not is spoken as brode and rude englissh as is in ony place of englond ....

(*vnperfightnes*: faultiness, imperfection; *wete*: be ascribed to)

The passage indicates that the Kentish of the Weald was, for Caxton, a 'rude', or 'low-status' usage, and it seems likely that this notion of 'rudeness' could be applied to pronunciation as to other levels of language. However, the passage does not necessarily indicate that there was a specific 'correct' usage for him to adopt; he knew what was 'rude', but not yet for certain what was polite. The problem was that, just as with the evolution of standard spelling, a particular model of pronunciation had yet to be clearly distinguished at the end of the fifteenth century.

THE ARRIVAL OF PRINTING

This chapter began with a discussion of the relationship between internal and external approaches to the history of the language; and in this final section we might return to the key 'external' event during the fifteenth century: Caxton's introduction of printing to England in 1476.

Fig. 5.1.   Caxton's English: a passage from Caxton's *The Myrrour of the World* (Westminster: *c* 1490; A4v, Sp Coll Hunterian Bv.2.30)

It is of interest that Caxton worries repeatedly in his own prose, from his very first prologue, about the role of the vernacular; it would seem that technological and linguistic innovation go together, and this is significant for the argument of this chapter. It has often been pointed out that Caxton's success as a printer depended on his linking of supply to demand: if there had been no demand for the books he printed, then Caxton, a shrewd businessman, would not have produced them.

From the discussion above, it is possible to reconstruct where this demand came from: rising folk, aspiring to elite status, who were most at home in the vernacular. The Pastons were such people. Their enemies could think of no more cutting insult than to describe them as 'churles', for their origins seem to have been humble. In a lost document dating from the fifteenth century, the family was founded by 'one Clement Paston dwellyng in Paston, and he was a good pleyn husbond, and lyvyd upon hys lond yt he has in Paston, and kept yron a

Plow alle tymes in ye yer'. But as the Pastons rose—they were regularly MPs and courtiers from the 1460s onwards—they developed the courtly tastes for which Caxton was to cater. Caxton flatters his audience—his books are for 'noble lordes and ladyes'—but he also claims that the act of translation is so that his work 'myght be had and vsed emonge the people for thamendement of their maners'; and in his edition of *The Royal Book* (1488) he tells us that he 'reduced into englisshe' the book 'at the request & specyal desyre of a synguler frende of myn a mercer of london'. Such socially-aspirant mercers—merchant traders, like Caxton himself—were evidently an important part of his clientele. Indeed, they had shown they were eager to engage with courtly culture, even before Caxton provided them with the wherewithal; their 'mercers' marks' are frequently found in major literary manuscripts from the late fourteenth century onwards, for example in MS Oxford, Corpus Christi College B.67, an important early fifteenth-century manuscript of John Gower's *Confessio Amantis*. These folk were conscious that manners—perhaps their manners—needed amendment.

Perhaps the best instance of this aspiration towards the courtly is offered by the career and tastes of Sir John Paston II, an important member of the Paston family whose language has already been discussed on p. 135. John not only took part in 1467 in a famous royal tournament at Eltham—always an occasion for the egregious display of courtly virtues—but he also developed an interest in aristocratic literature. He employed the scribe William Ebesham to compile his 'Great Book' of chivalric texts, and he wrote out for his own use a famous 'List of Books', which included a number of works Caxton was to print, such as Cicero's *Of Old Age* and *Of Friendship*, and Chaucer's *Troilus and Criseyde* and *The Parliament of Foules*, and also what appears to be Caxton's *Game and Play of the Chess*, printed in Bruges in 1475: 'a boke jn preente off ye Pleye of ye < . . . >'. John must have acquired this book soon after it appeared, because he died in 1479; he was clearly part of Caxton's social network (even though Caxton does not refer to him), for Caxton does refer, in his printing of Cicero's *Of Old Age* (1481), to the Pastons' great patron, Sir John Fastolf. Significantly, John Paston II also owned 'myn olde boke off blasonyngys' and 'my boke of knyghthod'.

In miniature, the Pastons encapsulate the processes involved in the elaboration of English during the fifteenth century. For them, and for people like them, English had achieved—or, perhaps more accurately, was achieving—a dignity which made it available for almost every kind of use, both literary and non-literary; and this functional change had clear implications for the formal development of English in terms of written standardization and lexical augmentation. Moreover, it is worth pointing out that there is a profound connection between this development and the historical and social developments of the sixteenth century in which vernacular literacy played so important a role: the English Reformation, and the rise of Elizabethan and Jacobean vernacular culture.

REFERENCES AND SUGGESTIONS FOR FURTHER READING

Useful overviews of the transition between Middle and early modern English appear in all the standard histories of the language (e.g. Barber (1993), Baugh and Cable (2002), Strang (1970)), although the tendency to split Middle and early modern English between chapters can cause problems of continuity. The relevant volumes of the *Cambridge History of the English Language*—specifically Blake (1992) and Lass (1999*a*, 1999*b*)—are crucial resources for all levels of language, though stronger on 'internal' than on 'external' history. An older book which still contains much of value is Wyld (1936); Wyld was almost alone in his generation in seeing the history of English as not simply a process of standardization. Explicit connections, at an introductory level, between Middle and early modern English are made in Smith (1999, second edition forthcoming). On questions of form and function in relation to the history of English, see Samuels (1972), Smith (1996*a*), both of which contain sections on the main levels of language (lexicon, grammar, transmission). For the typology of standardization (elaboration, selection, codification, acceptance), see Haugen (1966), Hudson (1980: 32–4).

A useful resource of texts, with good annotation, is Burnley (1992*a*). Vernacular documents from the Middle/early modern English transition are printed in Chambers and Daunt (1931), Görlach (1991), and Cusack (1998). These editions (especially the latter two) are particularly useful for students of the history of English since there has been minimal editorial intervention. Modern practice—even, unhappily, in scholarly editions—is to make numerous silent decisions in the editing of Middle and early modern English texts; such decisions can disguise important linguistic features such as punctuation, marks of abbreviation, and even spelling. For contemporary comments on the English language, see Bolton (1966). Important texts by Caxton appear in Blake (1973). Crotch (1928: 109–10) is, with minor modification and annotations, the source of the quotations from Caxton's *Eneydos* which appear on pp. 121 and 122–3 of this chapter. The citation from Mulcaster (1582) on p. 121 is taken from Bolton (1966: 10).

Introductions which include relevant material for the transition between Middle and early modern English include Horobin and Smith (2002) and Nevalainen (forthcoming), both part of the *Edinburgh Textbooks on the English Language* series; full references and suggestions for further reading are given in both. The best introduction to Middle English from a literary perspective is Burrow and Turville-Petre (1996); for early modern English, see Barber (1997) and Görlach (1991).

Lexicon

For word geography, see McIntosh (1973); for some possible approaches, see the articles by Hoad, Lewis, and Fellows Jensen in Laing and Williamson (1994). For the examples of diatopic variation discussed at this point in the chapter, see further Smith (1996*a*: 180–5). The citation from Chaucer's *Reeve's Tale* is taken from Benson (1988: 80). For discussion of stylistic choice, see the important chapters on 'literary language' by Burnley and Adamson which appear respectively in Blake (1992) and Lass (1999*b*). A special study of Chaucerian usage, with wider implications, appears in Burnley (1983).

For aureate diction, see Norton-Smith (1966: 192–5); the quotation from Lydgate is taken from Norton-Smith (1966: 26), and a discussion of *nebule* appears on p. 194. *The Boke of St. Albans* was edited by Hands (1975). Eccles (1969) is the source of the extract from *Mankind*. For the quotations from Skelton, see Kinsman (1969: 4 and 62). Further examples of French loanwords from this period can be found in Strang (1970: 184). The quotation from line 247 of *Sir Orfeo* can be found in Burrow and Turville-Petre (1996: 121). On questions of meaning and changes in meaning, see still Waldron (1979); also important are Burnley (1983) and Samuels (1972). The main resources for the study of the lexicon (as well as much else) during the period are of course the historical dictionaries: the *Oxford English Dictionary* (*OED*) and the *Middle English Dictionary* (*MED*). Both these resources are now accessible online by subscription, and can be accessed in most university libraries; electronic publication has massively enhanced their functionality. The *MED* (alongside other resources) may be found at <**http://ets.umdl.umich.edu/m/mec/**>. The *OED* appears at <**http://dictionary.oed.com/**>.

Grammar

On the evolution of grammar during the Middle English/early modern English transition, see Denison (1993) and references there cited. Important discussion is also provided in Samuels (1972). For transmission during this period of transition, see Horobin and Smith (2002, especially chapter 4 and references there cited), for a basic account. Important detailed discussions appear in Barber (1997) and Görlach (1991). The quotation on p. ** from Barbour's *Brus* is from Book 1, 487–8, and is cited from Duncan (1997). Wright (1905: 296, §435) provides evidence of the continuance of the Northern Personal Pronoun Rule into the late nineteenth century. Gray (1985: 327) is the source of the quotation on p. 130 from Douglas (line 145). The Guildhall Letter also cited here derives (with minor modifications) from Chambers and Daunt (1931: 72–3). For Caxton's edition of Malory, see Blake (1973); the cited extract can be found on pp. 7–8. The quotation on p. 132 from Lord Berners' translation of Froissart is taken from Gray (1985: 394), as is the extract from the Magdalen College schoolbook (see pp. 276–7). John Paston's letter to his brother is taken (with minor modifications) from Davis (1971: 582, text 355).

Transmission: writing and speech

On written standardization, the best recent published discussion is Benskin (1992), which prefigures a large-scale reassessment of the problem; an extended discussion appears in Benskin (2004). Benskin's discussion of the spread of colourless usage through the various geographical areas can be found in Benskin (1992: 82–5). However, the most accessible account remains that given in the introduction to LALME. John Fisher's extensive writings on this issue, for example (1977), should be seen in the light of Benskin's comments; the anthology of 'Chancery Standard' texts by Fisher *et al.* (1984) should therefore be consulted with care. On the different usages of the Paston brothers, see Davis (1983). The cited extracts from the letters of John Paston II and his brother Walter are, with minor modifications, taken from Davis (1971: 516, 644). See also Gomez Solino (1984), the preliminary findings for which were reported in Samuels (1981: 43, 52). For an examination of Cheke's principles of reformed spelling, see Dobson (1968: 43–6). On the spelling systems used in copies of Gower and Nicholas Love, see further Smith (1988*b*) and Hellinga (1997).

On the standardization of speech, the best account (with full references) remains Dobson (1955), supplemented by materials in Dobson (1968). Wyld (1936) is also important. On applying the insights of sociolinguistics to past states of the language, see Smith (1996*a*), and also Mugglestone (2003*a*, especially chapter 1). The *First Grammatical Treatise* is discussed by Haugen (1972). The extract from Alice Radcliffe's letter is cited (with minor modifications) from Cusack (1988: 232). That from Puttenham is taken (with some minor changes) from Görlach (1991: 237–8).

On the northernisms in *The Reeve's Tale*, see Tolkien (1934) and Smith (1995); for the *Second Shepherds' Play*, see Cawley (1958: 48, 131). On the origins of the Great Vowel Shift, see Smith (1996*a*, especially chapter 5). For a discussion of rhyming practice in Middle English, see Smith (1996*a*: 98) and references there cited. The extract on p. 141 from Caxton's prologue to *The Recuyell of the Historyes of Troye* is taken (with minor modifications) from Crotch (1928: 4).

The arrival of printing

See Febvre and Martin (1976) for a good account of the impact of printing between 1450–1800. For an overview of a range of early printed books, with illustrations, see <http://special.lib.gla.ac.uk/exhibns/printing/index.html>. The origins of the Paston family are discussed by Davis (1971: p.xli); their designation as 'churles' can be found in Davis (1971, text 129). The quotations from Caxton's *The Royal Book*, which appears on p. 143 are taken from Crotch (1928).

6

RESTRUCTURING RENAISSANCE ENGLISH

April McMahon

EARLY modern English (a convenient if slightly amorphous term which covers at least 1500–1700, the two centuries focused on in this chapter) is a period of paradox. It is during early modern English that many features of present-day English were developed and consolidated: caricaturing slightly, this period is a bridge between the dialectal diversity which, as Chapter 4 has indicated, is widely apparent in Middle English, and the striving for order and regularity which, as Chapter 9 will explore, is often seen to be characteristic of the eighteenth-century grammarians and codifiers. However, this same period involves very considerable structural and systemic change.

In this chapter, I shall concentrate on just these structural changes and specifically on phonology—the sound system of English, where we see some of the most significant developments of the period. Of course, as earlier chapters in this volume have illustrated, there are many different ways of doing linguistic history, and of finding out just what the important changes were. As in Chapter 5, we can look at the practice of individuals which, for this period, will mean examining written documents to see what 'speakers' were doing from generation to generation. We can, as the next chapter will show, bring together documents written by a larger number of individuals for the same period into corpora or, in other words, into substantial collections of electronically available and searchable materials. These can then be examined, for example, to assess whether there were linguistic differences within a period depending on whether the 'speaker' was male or female, was writing for a personal or a public audience, or was communicating about a particular topic. However, in this chapter I shall, for the most part, be working at a rather more abstract level, thinking about the language systems which it seems reasonable for us to posit for the early modern period of English on the basis of all these different kinds of evidence, and comparing those systems with those of English today. I shall also be introducing different perspectives from phonological theory, to see whether we can explain why developments in Renaissance English took the particular course they did.

Working in this way, comparing systems and considering rather abstract changes in those systems, might seem to take our focus away from the individual speakers through whose usage and knowledge the linguistic changes under discussion were percolating at this time. However, we shall see as we go along that this is not necessarily the case. To understand language change as well as we can, we have to deal with two different levels all the time, that of the speaker, and that of the linguistic system: both are useful and necessary. We shall (as the previous chapter has indicated) see that English may have been gradually standardizing but that this does not equate to complete uniformity and does not reduce the importance or utility of dialect variation. A speaker-focused historical linguistics must also, as other chapters have already stressed, allow different speakers to have different systems. On the other hand, as historical linguists, we can use those more abstract notions of systems to make generalizations above the level of the speaker when those seem productive; here, we can also benefit from adopting a pluralistic rather than a monolithic model of English.

A FOCUS ON PHONOLOGY

The main focus of this chapter will be on the sound system of English and, in particular, on the dramatic changes which take place in its long vowels during this period. However, this is not to suggest that nothing was happening in other areas of the language. On the contrary, as Chapters 7 and 8 will confirm, there was in fact considerable contemporaneous grammatical and lexical change. To give an overview at this point in the volume there is, perhaps most obviously, great lexical expansion in early modern English, as English becomes increasingly outward-looking, leading to the borrowing of words such as *cargo* from Spanish, *sheikh* and *sherbet* from Arabic, and *coffee* from Turkish. At the end of our period, the scene is set for the building of the Empire, the development of extraterritorial Englishes in North America, Australia, and beyond (see further Chapter 12), and a consequent quantum leap in borrowed vocabulary.

In morphology, our period sees a gradual but comprehensive decline in the use of the second person singular pronoun *thou* (in subject position) and *thee* (in object position) although, as the linguist Roger Lass has noted, the history of this form remains 'intricate and not well understood (alternatively, not entirely coherent)'.[1] What is clear is that the opposition of *thou/ thee* and *ye/ you* which was a staple feature of Middle English is almost gone by the eighteenth century, except in certain specialist registers and in some parts of the north. As *thou* slips away moreover, it takes along the matching verb ending *-(e)st* of forms such as *thou goest, thou thinkest, thou seest*, which in turn contributes to that general reduction of overt inflectional morphology which, as we have seen, had been under way since the Old English period. In the same vein, the earlier *-(e)th/ -(e)þ* verbal marker for the third person singular present tense first comes to alternate with the originally northern *-(e)s*, and is gradually displaced by it. As the following chapter will examine in detail, forms such as *he goeth, she telleth* are therefore gradually replaced by *he goes, she tells*, via a stage of coexistence when the same writer can use both in the same passage, and sometimes with the same verb. Although here an inflectional marker is retained (*he goes, she tells*), the overall inventory of English inflectional morphological strategies is again reduced during this period.

In syntax, the furthest-reaching development in early modern English involves the use of *do*. At the start of our period this is used quite routinely in declarative, affirmative sentences (e.g. *I do send a letter*) but is not required in questions or negatives such as *I send not a letter; Send I a letter?* Moreover, at this time any verb can appear directly before the negative marker, or can invert with the subject to make a question. This is, in a sense, the converse of the present-day situation where we do not typically find what is termed 'periphrastic *do*', although *do* may still appear in emphatic affirmatives—*I definitely (do) like it*. On the other hand, *do* is now an essential supporting verb in negatives and in questions which lack an auxiliary verb: in modern English, it is now only *have, be*, and *do* which can invert with the subject or precede the negative marker in these constructions, as in the examples below:

I am a terrible singer.	I hear a terrible singer.
Am I a terrible singer?	**Do** I hear a terrible singer?
I am not a terrible singer.	I **do** not hear a terrible singer.

[1] See R. Lass, 'Phonology and morphology', in R. Lass (ed.), *The Cambridge History of the English Language*, Vol. III: *1476–1776* (Cambridge: Cambridge University Press, 1999), 148.

It seems that, around the middle of our period, English might well have been developing into a language which required *do* in every sentence though this possible change was never completed. Instead, *do* found a niche in particular constructions. Periphrastic *do* had by no means disappeared by 1700, but it was clearly on the decline.

Finally, throughout the early modern period, English is becoming more familiar to the modern eye, as spelling (especially in public domains of usage) becomes more regular, encouraged by the commercial pressures accompanying the introduction and spread of printing. Nevertheless, the increasing stabilization does not mean that orthographic practice became completely uniform: much in fact depended on whether the intended audience for a document was more public or more private and intimate.

The following extract, which is also discussed in the next chapter, is, for example, from a letter of Queen Elizabeth I to King James VI of Scotland written in 1591:

My deare brother, As ther is naught that bredes more for-thinking repentance and agrived thoughtes than good turnes to harme the giuers ayde, so hathe no bonde euer tied more honorable mynds, than the shewes of any acquittal by grateful acknwelegement in plain actions; for wordes be leues and dides the fruites.

This reveals a number of typical features of Renaissance orthography such as the continued use of *u* and *v* as positional variants (as in *euer* in line 2, *leves* in line 4) rather than, as in modern English, their deployment as vowel and consonant respectively. It also shows considerable variation in the use of single final -*e*, which was no longer pronounced at this time (see *deare* in line 1, *good* in line 2), as well as in the use of *i* and *y* (as in *ayde* in line 2, and *plain* in line 4). Moreover, in terms of morphology, it also shows that Elizabeth is using the novel third person singular -(*e*)*s* ending, at least in personal correspondence, in contrast to her father King Henry VIII (1491–1547) who had used the older -(*e*)*th* even in personal letters (see further p. 188). In the last line (and in contrast to *bredes* in line 1), we can also see the form *dides* ('deeds') for earlier (and co-existing) *dedes*. Variation here may also provide evidence for the progress of the Great Vowel Shift which, as we shall see, raised /e:/ to /i:/ in words of exactly this kind.

In view of all this action in the lexis and morphosyntax, we might therefore ask why a focus on the phonology of early modern English is either desirable or necessary. First, there is arguably at least as much change in early modern English phonology as in any other area of the grammar: in particular, and as the previous chapter has already indicated, the whole long vowel system is radically reshaped between about 1450 and 1750 in what has come to be known as the Great Vowel

Shift. These shifts of long vowels, and the other changes that lead up to these or that follow in their wake, are probably the major phonological factor which distinguishes Middle English from modern English. As such, their significance cannot be overestimated nor—in reality—discussed in just a few paragraphs. This is especially true given that these changes are also (perhaps understandably, given their magnitude) particularly controversial, and there is a very considerable literature on the so-called 'Great Vowel Shift' and the changes surrounding it. This is itself, therefore, justifies a much closer look at phonological change in the period.

Second, the development of historical corpus linguistics (which will be discussed in more detail in Chapter 7) has led to a great leap forward in our approach to—and understanding of—changes in lexis, morphology, and syntax. For various reasons, however, the effect of this methodological revolution cannot be so significant for phonology. As the next chapter points out, corpora are, for instance, most useful for morphosyntactic change since they may not be sufficiently extensive for an accurate picture of lexical developments, while, in terms of pronunciation, the increasing standardization of spelling can impede systematic evidence of on-going change. Naturally, even in morphosyntax, the collection and analysis of corpus data is not the end of the story. Finding a trend which seems to indicate the introduction, increase, decrease, or loss of a feature is in itself interesting, and is able to take us much further than the painstaking accumulation of small amounts of data which our predecessors had to settle for as they strove to document the linguistic changes of the past. However, the hypothesized changes which underlie any perceived trend then require explanation and this, in itself, the corpus cannot provide. For instance, the decrease in the use of negative *do* in London after 1600 could be explained as a by-product of the influence of the Scots speakers who accompanied King James to the English court (after the death of Queen Elizabeth in 1603 and the Union of the Crowns).[2] Further corpus work establishes that *do* was indeed rarer in Older Scots. Nevertheless, this cannot in itself constitute a proven explanation: as Terttu Nevalainen confirms in the following chapter (see p. 205), 'more work is of course called for to support or reject this contact hypothesis'.

Careful analysis of corpora can, however, sometimes provide phonological evidence too, simply by providing sufficient data for us to observe patterns which might not emerge from isolated examples. Again using Terttu Nevalainen's example in this volume (see pp. 190–3), we know that the originally northern

---

[2] See further A. Nurmi, *A Social History of Periphrastic DO*. (Helsinki: Société Néophilologique, 1999).

third person singular verb ending -(*e*)*s* spread conclusively to the south during the early modern English period to give *she walks, he writes*. Nevertheless, there is an ostensibly odd, opposing development whereby some Scots writers at this time adopted the otherwise declining southern -(*e*)*th* (e.g. *she helpeth*), retaining it right into the seventeenth century. A closer examination of the corpus data shows that many of the verbs with -(*e*)*th* in fact have a stem ending in a sibilant sound, like *ariseth, causeth, increaseth, produceth*. If we examine the evidence more closely, it seems that both -(*e*)*s* and -(*e*)*th* were earlier available not only as simple consonants (being pronounced [s] or [θ] respectively), but also as syllabic forms with a vowel before the consonant—probably as [əs] and [əθ]. These syllabic forms would be more appropriate after a sibilant sound like [s] or [z]: if you added a simple [s] ending after a verb ending in [s] anyway, it would be both difficult to pronounce, and hard to hear whether the extra [s] was there or not. As it happens, the [s] ending had earlier lost its alternative syllabic -*es* form, while -(*e*)*th* remained available in both full and contracted forms, that is as both [əθ] and [θ]. This might therefore be used to explain the otherwise unaccountable preference of Scots writers in our period for -(*e*)*th* on verbs which possess these stem-final sibilants.

Corpus data, then, can indeed put us on the track of phonological generalizations and explanations, and can certainly provide a wealth of data for phonological analysis. As the examples already discussed have indicated, it is this further analysis which is, however, crucial: and in addition, although it is relatively straightforward to search a corpus for a particular ending, it can be very difficult and time-consuming to search for the many different variant spellings for a particular vowel. Orthographic practice during this period was moving towards standardization, but it was, as I have indicated, by no means static; and departures from typical spellings—just as in Queen Elizabeth's *dides* for *dedes*—may also alert historical phonologists to ongoing change. For example, occasional spellings from the fifteenth to seventeenth centuries indicate the progressive loss or at least reduction and instability of /r/ before a consonant, so that in the letters contained in the fifteenth-century Cely Papers, as discussed by Lass in 1993, we find forms such as *monyng* ('morning'), *passel* ('parcel'), and the inverse spelling *marster* ('master') which shows *r* where it would never have been pronounced. These therefore suggest that /r/ in such contexts was becoming so weak or prone to loss that spellers no longer quite knew where to put it.

We also need to interpret carefully our valuable contemporary evidence from the so-called orthoepists, early grammarians and commentators on language. Importantly, this period is the first to possess evidence from writers who, from a variety of perspectives (and levels of aptitude), sought to describe and record the language of the time. Writers such as John Hart and William Bullokar hence engaged with the potential for spelling reform, often providing insights into contemporary pronunciation as they did so. Common sixteenth-century spelling practice operated, as Hart complained, 'Without any regard vnto the seuerall parts of the voice which the writing ought to represent'. Orthoepists such as Richard Hodges engaged more directly with the spoken language, especially in their attempted classification of the sound system, and the systems of transcription which could be implemented in its representation (see Fig. 6.1). Nevertheless, even when we have first-hand descriptions of the English of the period, we still have to interpret this carefully. For example, an orthoepist may be trying very hard to give an objective account of the phonological situation. Nevertheless, in the absence of agreed phonetic symbols (the International Phonetic Alphabet would not be developed until the late nineteenth century) and in the similar absence of an agreed phonetic terminology for the place and manner of articulation, he may be using inherently ambiguous, everyday

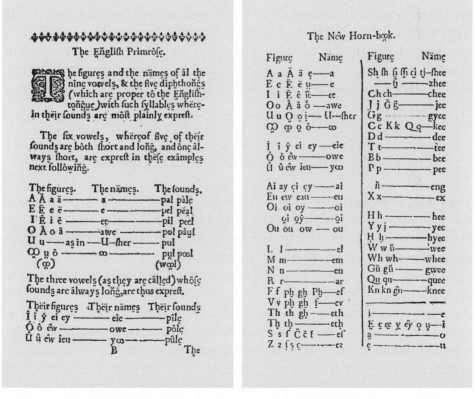

FIG. 6.1.   The opening pages of Richard Hodges, *The English Primrose* (1644), showing his system of transcription and his initial discussion of the vowel sounds of English

vocabulary to do so. In such cases, we might need to bring in external evidence from other sources to confirm a particular reading.

On the other hand, we may be pretty confident from spelling evidence or other descriptions that a particular pronunciation was emerging or increasing in the period, but an orthoepist may not mention it because he does not approve of this new development and is ignoring it in the hope that it will go away. A good example here can be found in Alexander Gil's conservative insistence in his *Logonomia Anglica* of 1619 on the continued use of the palatal and velar fricatives [ç] and [x] in words such as *fight, ought,* even though, as Chapter 5 has incidentally illustrated on p. 141, fifteenth-century back-spellings or scribal 'slips'—as of *unperfightness* for *imperfectness* where *gh* can have carried no sound value—already signalled their loss. It follows from all this that historical phonologists have to introduce their own interpretations in many cases when diagnosing and accounting for changes. For that reason, it is essential to combine careful collection and analysis of examples with hypotheses from phonetics and sociolinguistics, along with application of whichever theoretical phonological model seems useful in casting light on the developments in question. Some might suggest that, although this is what makes historical phonology so particularly satisfying—like historical detective work—it is also what makes it particularly prone to competing interpretations and controversy. There is no better example of both tendencies than the putative Great Vowel Shift of Renaissance English.

TEXTBOOK VIEWS OF THE GREAT VOWEL SHIFT

The Great Vowel Shift (henceforth GVS) is not, of course, the only phonological change to take place between 1500 and 1700. Admittedly, there is not much action in the consonant system at the time, although /r/, except before a vowel, is (as the spelling evidence already discussed suggests) becoming more vulnerable, with considerable consequences for neighbouring vowels. For example, John Hart in his *Orthographie* of 1569 gives transcriptions like [feiër] *fire*, [piuër] *pure*, and [hier] *here*, indicating that 'breaking' or diphthongization before /r/ is already an option by the mid-sixteenth century. /h/ is also progressively dropping in some varieties; but apart from that, the consonant system, even at the start of our period, is very much as it is today. There are more developments in the short vowel system (readers unfamiliar with phonetic notation might find it useful to consult the Key to Phonetic Symbols, and accompanying diagrams, on pp. x–xi for the following discussion). For instance, Middle English short /e o/ in *bed, lot* lowered to /ɛ ɒ/ by the end of the seventeenth century, while short /ʊ/ split to give /ʊ/ in *put*, as opposed to /ʌ/ in *cut*. Not all these changes operated identically in all dialects: many Northern English varieties share the lowering and centraliza- tion of Middle English short /u/ to /ʊ/ (and of Middle English short /i/ to /ɪ/), but do not show the split to /ʊ/ and /ʌ/, so that Yorkshire varieties still have /ʊ/ in both *put* and *cut* (a pattern discussed in Chapter 11 in this volume). There are also changes in diphthongs: early in our period, some of the Middle English diphthongs, such as the /ɔu/ of *grow*, *sow* and the /ai/ of *rain* were monophthon- gizing, while a new subtype of diphthong was created shortly after the end of our period, when the progressive loss of postvocalic /r/ led to the innovation of the centring diphthongs in *here*, *there*, *sure* (now, in turn, often monophthongized again). However, the most significant change, or changes, in early modern English involve the long vowels.

In most accents of English today, the great majority of words with short vowels had identical, or at least strongly similar, short vowels in late Middle English. There has been a general lowering of the high and mid short vowels, with a degree of centralization for the high ones, but the short vowel *system* has scarcely changed, apart from the innovation of /ʊ/ versus /ʌ/ (for a diagrammatic representation of vowel positioning, and illustration of terms such as 'high', 'mid' etc., see p. xi). The case of the long vowels, however, is much more complex, and the classic, textbook statement of the facts is that virtually all words in present-day English which have a long vowel, and which existed in the language in late Middle English, now have a *different* long vowel. Some examples of these correspondences are given below:

	Middle English	Modern English
time	/tiːm/	/taɪm/
green	/greːn/	/griːn/
break	/brɛːk/	/breɪk/
name	/naːmə/	/neɪm/
day	/dai/	/deɪ/
loud	/luːd/	/laud/
boot	/boːt/	/buːt/
boat	/bɔːt/	/boʊt/
law	/lau/	/lɔː/

Some modern English long vowels also existed in Middle English: /aɪ/, /iː/, /uː/, /ɔː/, and /au/, for example, fall into this category. Other vowels in today's English clearly fill the same systemic slot as particular Middle English vowels, although they are not identical: so, Standard Southern British English (SSBE) lacks the

Middle English long high-mid front and back monophthongs /e:/ and /o:/, substituting instead the /eɪ/, /oʊ/ diphthongs in words like *day, grow*. These monophthongs and diphthongs are, however, strikingly phonetically similar; and indeed some accents of English with smaller diphthong systems still use precisely these long, high-mid monophthongs. For instance, *grey, day*, and *rain* for a Standard Southern British English speaker would have /eɪ/, where a Standard Scottish English (SSE) speaker would have /e:/; and likewise, SSBE /oʊ/ in *go, boat, hope* corresponds to the /o:/ monophthong for an SSE speaker. The only vowels in the Middle English system which seem to have disappeared altogether, merging with the reflexes of /e:/, are /ɛ:/ and /a:/ as in Middle English *beat* and *face* (although a long low unrounded vowel, usually now back /ɑ:/, has subsequently re-emerged in words such as *father, bra, calm, part* in many varieties).

However, finding affinities between individual long vowels and diphthongs in this way conceals the vital fact that the Middle English vowels and their closest articulatory equivalents in modern English appear in almost entirely different sets of lexical items. There have been wholesale distributional changes so that, although the same vowels may persist, they can now be found in entirely different sets of words. While words like *time, eye, five* had /i:/ in Middle English, this same high front long monophthong is now found in *green, serene, queen*, while the *time, eye, five* cases now have the diphthong /ai/, earlier found in Middle English *day, plain*. Similarly, whereas Middle English /o:/ is found in *boot, food, root* and /u:/ in *loud, out, down*, the *boot, food, root* cases now have /u:/, and the *loud, out, down* ones, the diphthong /au/. This is not, however, a random and unpredictable series of substitutions. Instead it can be summarized in a diagram of the sort which typically accompanies textbook accounts of the GVS in many histories of the language, as shown in Figures 6.2 and 6.3.

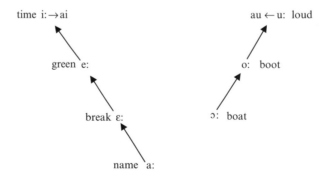

FIG. 6.2.   The Great Vowel Shift
Source: Based on Baugh and Cable (2002: 238), although with some changes in symbols to reflect IPA usage).

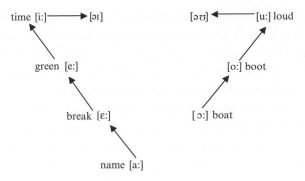

FIG. 6.3. The Great Vowel Shift
Source: Redrawn after Fennell (2001: 159).

These diagrams give slightly different outlines of the Vowel Shift in one respect: Baugh and Cable in Figure 6.2 show the high monophthongs as in Middle English *time* and *loud* diphthongizing directly to their modern values /ai/ and /au/ (although they do note that 'Such a diagram must be taken as only a very rough indication of what happened'). On the other hand, Barbara Fennell in Figure 6.3 shows the high vowels as diphthongizing but does not give the final values, with low first elements, which they have achieved today. As we shall see later, Fennell's view is more accurate historically. It is quite true that these new diphthongs *did* lower later, and that the Middle English /ai/, /au/ diphthongs (in *day* and *law* respectively) also raised and monophthongized: but these changes are usually seen as separate developments which followed after the GVS. Likewise, the impression in both diagrams is of each vowel progressively shifting up one step, from low to low-mid, low-mid to high-mid, high-mid to high. However, the majority of originally low-mid front vowels eventually shifted two steps, to high—hence modern English has /i:/ deriving from two different sets of Middle English words, namely *sea*, *leave* (which had Middle English /ɛ:/ and which raised by two steps) as well as in *green*, *queen* (which had Middle English /e:/, and only raised by a single step). Likewise, Middle English /a:/ in *name* underwent a double raising, to /ɛ:/ and then /e:/. All these second-step raisings are typically regarded as later developments which took place after the Great Vowel Shift 'proper'.

There can be no question that these developments have been instrumental in shaping the modern English vowel system, hence the importance of a detailed investigation of exactly what happened in the phonology of early modern English. The GVS has also had a strong impact on the English orthography, since through this set of changes, each vowel graph comes to be equipped with at least two distinct values. Whereas in Chaucer's time an *a* spelling could only be pronounced as long or short /a/ (as in *name* or *cat*), and an *i* only long or short /i/ (as in *time* or *bit*), today's novice spellers have to face a choice in every case, so that *a*, for example, can be /æ/ in *apple*, /eɪ/ in *name*, or /ɑː/ in *father*, and *i* can be /ɪ/ in *ill*, *bit* or /aɪ/ in *time*, *fine*. Long and short values for the same vowel graph, in other words, no longer match in terms of vowel quality.

Furthermore, the GVS and the various lengthening and shortening changes which preceded or followed it have also contributed to the development of complex morphophonological patterns in modern English, as illustrated below.

various ~ *variety*	*divine* ~ *divinity*
comedy ~ *comedian*	*serene* ~ *serenity*
study ~ *studious*	*sane* ~ *sanity*
harmony ~ *harmonious*	(*fool* ~ *folly*)
	(*profound* ~ *profundity*)

Some of these alternations are more productive than others in the current system, with those in brackets arguably being fossilized. Nevertheless, interactions between morphology and phonology of this kind are particularly challenging for phonological theories, and these Vowel Shift alternations have been the focus of a great deal of phonological attention since they played a central part in Chomsky and Halle's ground-breaking *The Sound Pattern of English* of 1968. Alternations between different vowels in *divine* and *divinity*, for instance, can help us understand more about what native speakers know about their language, which many linguists would see as the real goal of linguistics. If speakers know that *divine* and *divinity* are related, and see them as forms of the same word, they may store only a single form in their mental dictionary, and apply a rule to produce the different pronunciations we find in surface representations of the language. On the other hand, if speakers do not perceive a real and generalizable relationship between the stem vowels in *divine* and *divinity*, their mental dictionaries might contain both forms, and they may simply perceive that the two independent items are similar in meaning. For a phonologist working on modern English, finding out whether the Vowel Shift patterns are real and meaningful to speakers today is therefore a fundamental part of understanding how abstract our mental representations of words might be, as well as in formulating the more abstract phonological systems which underlie different dialects.

Returning to the historical picture, the attraction of diagrams like those given in Figures 6.2 and 6.3 is that they provide an apparently elegant, symmetrical picture of a series of shifts which seem to affect the whole early modern English system in a regular, parallel, and step-wise way. Chain shifts, or circular developments of this kind, are also particularly fascinating for phonologists, partly because such far-reaching changes are challenging to explain. Given their dramatic effects on the English spelling system, and their part in the development of new, complex synchronic morphophonological alternations like those illustrated above, it is perhaps natural, as so many histories of the language have done, to see these changes as large-scale, orderly, momentous shifts. Sometimes this might make us prone to neatening up the overall pattern by deciding what we call part of the Great Vowel Shift, and what we might conversely choose to factor out into other, independent developments. So, the monophthongization of /ai/ and /au/ in *day* and *law*, and the lowering of the new diphthongs—which Fennell in Figure 6.3 gives as /ɔɪ/ and /əʊ/—to eventual /aɪ/ and /au/ (as in *time* and *loud*), are often portrayed as part of the GVS (as in Fig. 6.2 above). Typically, however, the second-step raisings for some front vowels are excluded, so both diagrams show Middle English /ɛ:/ shifting only one step to /e:/, although we know that historically the raising continued for most words, so that *sea*, *speak*, *clean* now have /i:/, and only the leftover cases *great*, *break*, *steak* retain /eɪ/ (or /e:/ for Scots speakers). Similarly, the diagrammatic representations of the GVS depicted in both Figures 6.2 and 6.3 show /ai/ (as in *day*) raising by the regulation single step to /a:/, although it in fact continued to the /eɪ/ or /e:/ that we now find in *day, plain*.

These textbook diagrams, then, bring together what Roger Lass in 1976 called 'THE GVS proper', with some later changes. Other later changes are, however, commonly excluded because they do not fit the pattern. The neat diagrams of Renaissance English phonology might be justified on the grounds that they are excellent teaching aids; but in this sense, therefore, they do not reflect direct historical fact. It is clear, for example, that not all the individual changes in the orderly, composite diagrams happened at the same time, or even took place particularly close together in chronological terms: the whole lot may well have taken upwards of three hundred years, beginning perhaps between 1400 and 1450. Furthermore, some of the changes that are included in some versions of the GVS (like those monophthongizations of /ai/ and /au/ in *day, law*), seem to have been contemporaneous with others that are usually excluded (like the second-step raising of Middle English /ɛ:/ from /e:/ to eventual /i:/ in *sea*).

As a result, neat diagrams of the kind given in Figures 6.2 and 6.3 cannot validly be sold as a composite picture of changes in the long vowel system over a particular time period either. This raises an important question for our under-standing of the GVS and the phonology of early modern English. Are we therefore including or excluding certain changes purely because the overall outline then looks more uniform and easier to handle than the sum of its more realistic parts? As historians of the language, we might also be guilty of setting up a highly idealized 'change' which never really happened, simply because the idealized version resembles a circular chain shift, a phenomenon which is sufficiently mysterious and challenging to make phonological theorists and historical linguists sit up and take notice.

Considering this question might therefore make us wonder whether there really was a Great Vowel Shift in Renaissance English, and if so, which of these elements really counted as part of it. It may then come as no surprise to find that there is indeed a diversity of views in the technical literature about the validity of the 'GVS' concept, and its reality as a single historical phenomenon. We turn in the next section to an outline of the alternative views put forward by the best-known current defender of the GVS, Roger Lass, and the opposing views of the linguists Robert P. Stockwell and Donka Minkova: a range of relevant references is included in the Further Reading at the end of this chapter. Finally, we shall return to the thoroughly problematic question of whether phonologists create diagrams like those in Figures 6.2 and 6.3 because we are particularly easily seduced by patterns, seeing them where they do not really exist; or whether such overarching changes are indeed in any sense 'real' for the period under discussion.

'WHAT, IF ANYTHING, WAS THE GREAT VOWEL SHIFT?'

The subheading above is the title of an article which Lass published in 1992, and it recurs as a section header in 1999, within Lass's chapter on phonology and morphology in the third volume of the *Cambridge History of the English Language*. It neatly expresses a difference of opinion which has been fought out over almost thirty years between Lass on the one hand, and Stockwell and Minkova on the other. There has been a certain degree of rapprochement between their positions, as we shall see later, but a central difference remains, summed up aptly in the quotations below which derive respectively from Lass, and from Stockwell and Minkova:

whatever else has been and still is going on in the history of English vowels—there was one particular set of late mediaeval shiftings that was more coherent and more potent in effect on the system as a whole than others.[3]

the traditional summary of the putative structure of the vowels at some earlier date, abstracted from a range of manuscripts which were certainly not representatives of a type

---

[3] R. Lass, 'Vowel Shifts, Great and Otherwise: Remarks on Stockwell and Minkova', in D. Kastovsky and G. Bauer (eds), *Luick Revisited* (Tübingen: Gunter Narr Verlag, 1988), 407.

of speech from which Modern English is derived, followed by a summary of Modern English vowel contrasts in a single normalized 'standard' dialect, ... creates an appearance of neat regularity that is misleading in a very serious way. It also creates a set of pseudo-problems for structuralism to 'solve' with neatly symmetrical charts and theories that seem to us to have very little to do with what was actually taking place.[4]

In other words, Lass argues that seeing the GVS as a real, single, and unitary phenomenon is both justified and helpful in interpreting the history of English: it is, as he argues in 1999, also the norm, since 'Most recent historians, whether through unaided intuition or brain-washing by teachers and tradition, have been convinced of the reality and unity of the GVS'.[5] Conversely, Stockwell and Minkova consider it counter-productive to reify a series of independent changes as a single object, since this focuses the minds of linguists on accounting for an idealized change which, they contend, never really happened.

The core of the disagreement, then, is partly what we might see as a metatheoretical one: can a series of changes which took place over a considerable period of time, and which might have individual (and therefore arguably independent) motivations, meaningfully be grouped together into a superordinate or over-arching change like the putative GVS of Renaissance English? Furthermore, if that *can* be done, *should* it? There are also different interpretations of the individual changes, though Lass, and Stockwell and Minkova, generally agree that these developments did take place: nobody is arguing that the individual elements of the GVS are phantasms, though in some interpretations the diagrammatic representations connecting them might well be.

To find the source of these views, and take any steps towards evaluating them, we must first identify the similarities and differences between the Lass and Stockwell–Minkova accounts of the development of long vowels during early modern English.

Stockwell and Minkova raise the following five unresolved questions or problems,[6] tracing these back to the work of the philologist Karl Luick (1865–1935):

1 The *inception problem*: what, if anything, started the whole change off?
2 The *merger problem*: is it feasible to think of a chain shift of this kind at all, where a shift of one vowel causes another to move too, to prevent merger and loss of distinctiveness?

---

[4] R. P. Stockwell and D. Minkova (1988*a*), 'The English Vowel Shift: Problems of Coherence and Explanation', in D. Kastovsky and G. Bauer (eds), *Luick Revisited* (Tübingen: Gunter Narr Verlag, 1988), 379.

[5] Lass (1999), 74.   [6] See Stockwell and Minkova (1988*a*), 355–6.

3 The *order problem*: did the shift happen in stages, and if so, what was the chronology for each stage?

4 The *dialect problem*: how can we account for the fact that the supposedly coherent vowel shift seems to have happened differently in different dialects?

5 The *structural coherence problem*: did the GVS really happen as a unitary change, or do linguists want to believe in it because we are attracted to neat patterns?

I shall focus below on problems 1 (inception), 2 (merger), and 5 (structural coherence). I assume that problem 3 (order) is more apparent than real, reflecting as it does a somewhat outmoded view that a particular subshift must be over and done with (or alternatively, in synchronic terms, that a particular phonological rule applies and stops) before the next begins its work. Stockwell and Minkova were absolutely right in 1988 to stress the need for historical linguistics to learn from sociolinguistics, but it can perhaps be regarded as accepted now. As for problem 4 (dialects), many of the issues arising from dialect variation also relate to the inception and structural coherence problems, and will therefore be discussed in connection with those. Otherwise, I set this apparent problem aside in what follows, since it seems axiomatic that we should be able to recognize that 'the same' process, or phonological unit or phenomenon, occurs with relatively minor differences cross-dialectally. For example, it seems reasonable to see Scots [e:] and Standard Southern British English [eɪ], phonetically different though they undoubtedly are, as filling the same notionally high-mid front slot in the respective vowel inventories of these dialects. Indeed, recognizing and using such dialect differences is vital, as we shall see in the next section, to our understanding of sound change.

THE INCEPTION PROBLEM

The inception problem remains one of the most deeply entrenched differences of opinion on the GVS and the phonology of early modern English. Lass, and Stockwell and Minkova base elements of their arguments and ideas on earlier historical scholarship, referring crucially to the work of the Danish linguist Otto Jespersen in the first volume of his *Modern English Grammar on Historical Principles* (1909) and to Luick's two-volume *Historische Grammatik der englischen Sprache* (1920–40). Both Jespersen and Luick saw the GVS as involving largely step-wise lengthening, with diphthongization of the long high vowels. However, they made different suggestions about the first step in the overall change, with Jespersen arguing for high-vowel diphthongization, while Luick instead favours mid-vowel raising.

Jespersen, then, suggests that the high vowels /iː/ (as in *time*) and /uː/ (as in *loud*) moved first, towards some intermediate diphthongal value (Lass in 1999 suggests /ei/: Stockwell in 1961 put forward an alternative suggestion, discussed below). This would have left the high positions vacant, and Jespersen proposes what is now known as a 'drag chain', following terminology later introduced by the French linguist André Martinet. This assumes that linguistic systems follow principles, wherever possible, of economy, symmetry, and good margins of safety between units, so that the shift of the high vowels would have left a gap into which the next highest vowels would have been 'dragged', to preserve the shape of the overall system. This would have had a knock-on effect on the next highest vowels; and as the new diphthongs lowered, they would in turn put pressure on pre-existing /ai au/ (as in Middle English *day* and *law*), which would have risen in early modern English into the vacant low or low-mid monophthong slots, hence avoiding merger (see below). Today, we might support these arguments with the additional typological point (i.e. one based on the structural similarities we can perceive between languages, regardless of their histories) that it is most unusual for a language to lack high vowels, so that the initial diphthongization of the originally long vowels in *time* and *loud* would also have produced an unbalanced system.

Luick, on the other hand, proposes what we would now call a 'push chain'. Here, the vowels that begin the overall process are assumed to be the high-mid ones, /eː/ and /oː/ (as in *green* and *boot*), which start to shift upwards towards the high monophthongs /iː/ and /uː/. If we cast this in functional terms, and think of the vowel system as a set of slots, each occupied by a single vowel unit, one priority for speakers might be to ensure that not too many contrasts fall together or merge, lest lexical items become indistinguishable *en masse*. If the raising vowels had simply collapsed with the vowels one step higher, we should find mergers, for example, rather than a chain shift; hence *feel* would have become identical in pronunciation with *file*, and *boot* with *bout*. Since the facts indicate that wholesale mergers of this kind did not take place, we must hypothesize instead that a gradual change in the articulation of the lower vowels caused them to encroach gradually on the higher ones, which responded by diphthongizing— there would have been little option, since lowering would simply speed the apparently undesirable merger, and high vowels cannot, by definition, raise any further. This might all sound rather anthropomorphic: we can recast it in more sociolinguistically informed, speaker-centred terms by suggesting that a raising

in *house*. Moreover, **all** of them have front rather than back vowels for Middle English /o:/ in *boot*. Lass argues that these facts are not unrelated: the former follows from the latter.

Paul Johnston has observed that, by a sound change known as Northern /o:/-Fronting in the late thirteenth century, /o:/ (as in *boot*) was fronted to /ø:/. It was this development, he argues, which 'soon became a defining characteristic of the whole northern English and Scots groups'.[10] This fronting, depicted below, sets the reflex of Middle English /o:/ as an atypical front rounded vowel in northern English, which lay outside both the back and front monophthong systems.

/o:/-Fronting

i:	*time*			u:	*loud*
e:	*green*	ø: ←	(o:)		*boot*
ɛ:	*break*		ɔ:		*boat*
a:	*name*				

As the bracket indicates, by the onset of the GVS, the northern varieties had developed a gap in the system which was still filled in the southern ones. All varieties did have the high front and back long monophthongs /i:/ and /u:/ (as in *time*, *loud*). As a result, if Jespersen, and Stockwell and Minkova are right in their assumption that the first step in the GVS was indeed high vowel diphthongization, there is no reason why those high vowels should not have been affected in exactly the same way in the north and the south. But this is not what we find. Instead, although the high front vowel diphthongizes in all varieties in *bite*, the northern varieties instead maintain *hoose*, with undiphthongized /u/ (which will be long in the Northern English varieties, and positionally long or short in Scottish ones, following what is known as the Scottish Vowel Length Rule. This therefore suggests that the initial step in the GVS (and the subsequent restructuring of Renaissance phonology) was in fact the raising of lower vowels— although probably not the high-mid /e: o:/, as Luick suggested (given that, as we have seen, /o:/ in the north is absent and yet the rest of the Shift proceeds as normal). A more likely scenario therefore was that it was the low-mid /ɛ:/ and /ɔ:/ which were initially involved. As the low-mid front /ɛ:/ raised, it would therefore begin to displace /e:/ on a push-chain model, which in turn would enforce diphthongization of /i:/. However, the gap left by the departing /ɛ:/ might have attracted low /a:/, suggesting that the 'bottom half' of the Shift was perhaps a

---

[10] P. Johnston, 'Older Scots phonology and its regional variation', in C. Jones (ed.), *The Edinburgh History of the Scots Language* (Edinburgh: Edinburgh University Press, 1997), 69.

drag chain, while the 'top half' must have been a push chain. In the south, matters would proceed in parallel in the back vowel subsystem, with /ɔ:/ raising and in turn encouraging /o:/ to move up, and then /u:/ to diphthongize. In the north, as Johnston suggests, /ɔ:/ alone would have raised, while /u:/ 'apparently stays put because there is no /o:/ to move it, after /o:/-Fronting has occurred'.[11]

In short, if we adopt the view that diphthongization of high vowels (or, to reflect Stockwell and Minkova's view more accurately, the lowering and centralization of pre-existing diphthongs) came first, we lose this very persuasive connection between /o:/-Fronting in the north, and the absence of diphthongization of /u:/ in the same areas. Stockwell and Minkova in their 1988 chapter on 'The English Vowel Shift' suggest that there may be dialects where Middle English /e:/ did not raise, but where /i:/ nonetheless diphthongized; and also that raising Middle English /o:/ in some dialects merged with /u:/ rather than provoking diphthongization. However, they also accept that these dialect data are not robust. The most plausible conclusion, therefore, is that the fronting of /o:/ in the north is connected with the failure of /u:/ to diphthongize in the same areas, hence arguing for long mid-vowel raising as the first step in the GVS.

This comparison and evaluation of the Luick/ Lass and Jespersen/ Stockwell and Minkova views on the starting point for the GVS illustrates very clearly the relevance and, indeed, the necessity of working with detailed present-day dialect data in assessing the shape and chronology of historical sound changes. It may also, therefore, go some way towards answering Stockwell and Minkova's justifiable criticisms that proposing over-idealized, monolithic Middle English and modern English vowel systems can create a wholly misleading picture of the regularity of the shift which supposedly converted one into the other. On the contrary, as the evidence considered so far confirms, we are finding that no responsible consideration of the GVS (or any other change) can afford to ignore variation either then or now. However, Stockwell and Minkova are not only concerned about the evidence used to argue for the GVS. They also dispute other aspects of the allegedly unified change, and we will turn now to the second of these. The next section, however, is particularly detailed in its treatment of phonological issues and problems, and readers of a nervous disposition may be better advised to skip it and move on to the structural coherence problem instead.

[11] See Johnston (1997), 69.

THE MERGER PROBLEM

If we accept the Luick/ Lass view of the inception of the GVS, almost the whole change was a push chain, saving only the raising of the low-mid vowels, which are 'dragged' to high-mid. Clearly, any push chain mechanism must have avoidance of merger as part of its rationale. It seems intuitively obvious that shifting two vowels upwards and merging them with two others, end of story, is likely to be 'simpler', all other things being equal, than the trajectory of the actual change(s), which instead led, during the early modern English period, to wholesale displacement of long vowels and diphthongs from their earlier lexical classes as illustrated on p. 155. Since the knock-on effects of the GVS, in the shape of further monophthongizations, raisings, and lexical resettlements, were still going on in the eighteenth century, this suggests that all other things were, however, not equal. The obvious reason would therefore seem to involve disfavourment of merger.

Stockwell and Minkova do accept that mergers must under some circumstances be avoided, or at least that they do not always take place:

Arguments against mergers would have to show that they are statistically rarer than splits. One's experience with language change, and therefore one's intuition about what is in general likely to be true, to some slight extent supports the position that contrasts are more often preserved than collapsed. And it **has** to be true that these alternatives at least turn out to offset each other fairly evenly, on balance over a period of time. Otherwise it becomes logically impossible to explain why languages have more than one vowel, if mergers win; or why languages don't continue to proliferate vowels beyond measure, if splits win.[12]

However, they also argue that much of the traditionally-described GVS in fact did involve mergers, rather than raisings. For instance, Stockwell and Minkova suggest that both [ɛ:] and [ei], and [ɔ:] and [ou], existed either as variants in the same idiolects, or as dialectal alternatives, so that the gradual dominance of the higher of the available realizations in each case does not necessitate raising. Instead, it could be seen as rather a shift of preference, or perhaps dialect borrowing. Similarly, the later second-step raisings of Middle English /ɛ:/ and /a:/ to /i:/ and /e:/ respectively (as in *read* and *face*) must involve merger on any interpretation. Arguing for avoidance of merger as a major motive for the whole GVS is quite clearly incoherent, if there were in fact mergers involved in that overarching change.

---

[12] Stockwell and Minkova (1988*a*), 358–9.

Stockwell and Minkova do suggest that the Old English mid-high long mono-phthongs in words like *green, boot* were already 'very close vowels indeed' by the time of Middle English.[13] The fact that these did not merge with the pre-existing high vowels might of course support an anti-merger condition in some circum-stances. But this in turn might argue in Stockwell and Minkova's favour: if we do find mergers in some parts of the traditional GVS complex, but high vowel diphthongization and mid vowel raising (or the equivalents in Stockwell and Minkova's system) are partially motivated by avoidance of merger, this may suggest these changes are necessarily independent of the rest of the GVS. The GVS itself is then less well supported as a single, unitary change.

Alternatively, we might use exactly this criterion of merger/ non-merger to help us delimit what we might term 'the Vowel Shift proper' from subsequent changes. Lass in 1999, for example, argues that Phase II of the GVS (Phase I being the push chain combination of mid-vowel raising and high-vowel diphthong-ization) involves progressive raisings, first of /a:/ to /æ:/ in words like *name*, 'giving a somewhat crowded but plausible system', and then of /æ:/ to /ɛ:/, which has the effect of pushing earlier /ɛ:/ into the vacant slot /e:/.[14] Consequently, as Lass had pointed out eleven years earlier, 'The term GVS denotes only that particular no-collapse shift that ends up with the Middle English long monoph-thong system intact, if phonetically displaced'. Further raisings and concomitant mergers can then be seen as later and independent developments, both within and after early modern English. They cannot, therefore, compromise the GVS itself or be counterexamples to its causes or tendencies.

Certainly, avoidance of merger cannot provide a rationale for all the changes which are involved in or which follow the GVS as proposed here. However, this is only a serious problem if we require the motivation for all parts of a composite change to be the same. If we recognize an overall shift because of its shape, its effect on the system, or its results, why should each contributory shift not have its own individual shape and explanation? For readers with an interest in phonological theory, Minkova and Stockwell (2003) return to some of these issues in an Optimality Theoretic account of sound change, and specifically of the different historical outcomes produced by the various possible rankings of four specific constraints. It may be that the difficulties they are clearly wrestling with in 1988, on the obvious opposition between the avoidance of merger in some cases and the apparently antithetical mergers in others, may simply dissipate given an Optimality Theoretic account,

---

[13] Stockwell and Minkova (1988*a*), 376.   [14] Lass (1999), 83.

where universal motivations do not always have to be instantiated in surface linguistic fact.

THE STRUCTURAL COHERENCE PROBLEM

Finally, then, we turn to the crux of the whole issue: was there a Great Vowel Shift in early modern English, or wasn't there? And if we say there was, what do we mean? All parties accept that there were particular changes, whatever their precise nature, involving shifts, diphthongizations, raisings, or preferences of pre-existing structural alternatives. The question is whether all the contributory changes add up to anything: are they independent developments which follow one Germanic type; or did a particular set of changes dating between approximately 1450 and 1750 share something which sanctions us to regard them as a unified change, regardless of any factors of motivation, shape, or outcome which they might share with other changes at other times, or might not share with each other?

It might initially seem that the prospects for reaching any accommodation between, say, Lass in his *English Phonology and Phonological Theory* of 1976 and Stockwell and Minkova in their 1988 essay on 'The English Vowel Shift' are slim to non-existent. Lass seems to regard what we have here been calling the GVS (plus the various later monophthongizations, raisings, and mergers), as part of a single 'system-wide chain: the long nonhigh vowels raise, the high vowels diphthongize, and some of the diphthongs raise their first elements like the corresponding long vowels, while others monophthongize and fill the slots vacated by the raised mid vowels. ... The earlier stages seem to have involved no mergers; but some categories merged later on'.[15] On the other hand, Stockwell and Minkova seem implacably opposed to seeing any of these individual changes as related, remarking that 'It is a hard thing to take to task a long and venerable tradition on the charge that it has erected a notable monument of scholarship that is in a real sense fraudulent, even though of course we do not suggest that there was ever any **intentional** or **knowing** fraud'.[16]

However, a closer consideration of the evidence suggests that there is room for hope. Lass, for example, does regularly distinguish what he calls 'THE GVS

---

[15] R. Lass, *English Phonology and Phonological Theory* (Cambridge: Cambridge University Press, 1976), 87.

[16] Stockwell and Minkova (1988a), 376.

proper' from the later monophthongizations, raisings, and mergers—this core change involves essentially the stepwise raisings of long monophthongs, and the diphthongization of high vowels to an intermediate value. In 1992 he goes further, suggesting a differentiation between the 'top half' of the Great Vowel Shift (the mid vowel raising and high vowel diphthongization) and everything else, which he refers to as 'pseudo-GVS' or 'post-GVS Raising'. Admittedly, he returns to an extent to earlier terminology in 1999, referring to 'Phase I' (mid vowel raising and high vowel diphthongization) and 'Phase II the later raising of the lower vowels', but he still apparently excludes the subsequent mergers. In turn, Stockwell and Minkova in 1997 concede that at least part of Lass's Phase I may constitute a minimal chain shift: 'It is clear that [iː] and [uː] got out of the way, whether pushed or dragged … and whether by our suggestion of merger … or by some even more mysterious process of bouncing off the hard palate and diphthonging their way southward'.[17]

Perhaps, then, we can look forward to a generally agreed strategy of labelling Lass's Phase I, shown in Figure 6.4, as the GVS of Renaissance English. There will still be minor disagreements (the differing realizations for the diphthongs show this; and recall also the different proposals on the inception problem already discussed). This might, however, provide an acceptable compromise.

The question is, of course, whether this does indeed represent the best way forward for an understanding of this aspect of Renaissance phonology. Is it a good, sensible compromise, or is it the lowest common denominator? If we accept that the two subshifts in the diagram fit together, and if they lead on to other things, what is the objection to putting this set of changes and those other things together into a single overarching category, and calling that the GVS? How do we know which components do fit together, and when we have overshot and included elements erroneously? What does it mean (and what does it not mean) in our understanding of the history of the language and of phonology more generally, when we propose a systemic change composed of other more minor changes?

FIG. 6.4.   The Great Vowel Shift

---

[17] Stockwell and Minkova (1997), 287.

What, then, are Stockwell and Minkova's objections to the GVS as a unit? The key issue seems to be their view (stated in their 1988 'rejoinder to Lass') that the subchanges which make up any larger-scale development must share some essential property: 'The crucial property that Lass assigns to the Great Vowel Shift that puts it into a certain category is, **no-mergers** during the relevant time frame'. They argue, however, that this 'no-merger property holds only if quite arbitrary restrictions are placed on the chronology and scope of what is normally called the Great Vowel Shift'.[18] In particular, the two-step raisings of /a:/ to /e:/ in *name*, *late* and of /ɛ:/ to /i:/ in *sea*, *mean* must be excluded. As Stockwell and Minkova therefore continue, this is intrinsically unsatisfactory: 'characterizing the Great Vowel Shift as belonging to one or another category of chain-shifts on the basis of arbitrarily time-delimited properties is of no interest to us … unless such a characterization entails some suggestion about its causation'. On this view, maintaining the traditional GVS militates against recognizing the affinities which individual subchanges bear to other changes at other times; and a focus on types of change throughout English and indeed Germanic would be more productive and enlightening.

But can unity only follow from uniformity of causation? It is certainly valid to group changes together if they have the same motivation. We can, for example, recognize different instances of epenthesis throughout the history of English, and cross-linguistically: thus, we find Latin *facilis* from earlier *faclis* ('easy') with an epenthetic vowel, and in English, *bramble* with epenthetic [b], mirroring the present-day epenthetic [p] in fast or casual speech pronunciations of *hamster* [hampstə]. But would we be prevented from recognizing the affinities between one case of epenthesis and another simply because one of those cases was generally seen as forming part of a trajectory along with a range of other, differently-motivated changes? If common motivation is the only real connection between changes, we may be unable to produce classifications at all, since causation is often the least clear aspect of language change, whether in early modern English or any other period (including our own). Indeed, there may well be more than one motivation for any given change, and sometimes we cannot be sure what the motivation is at all. Even the top half of the GVS, which seems the least controversial part, is problematic in this sense, because it is unclear what started the first step in the first place. Stockwell and Minkova suggest that their first step, dissimilation of the two elements of the high diphthongs, followed from a general condition on diphthong optimality: in other words, diphthongs

---

[18]   R. P. Stockwell and D. Minkova (1988*b*), 'A rejoinder to Lass', in D. Kastovsky and G. Bauer (eds), *Luick Revisited* (Tübingen: Gunter Narr Verlag, 1988), 411–12.

are better if their two subparts are more different from one another, presumably so that the transition between them is easier to hear, and it is therefore easier to perceive the vowel as a diphthong. Since their hypothesis is that the high diphthongs in *time, loud* were rather poor diphthongs, with the two elements of each very close together in quality, there would naturally be pressure for change. However, this is not a condition against mergers, meaning that this change presumably cannot be linked with the mid vowel developments, if causation is the only connection between changes we are allowed to make. If the mid vowels started to shift first, why did that raising happen? In any case, these mid vowels cannot be shifting into the territory of the high ones to satisfy a no-merger condition.

There are still at least two other possibilities for grouping changes together apart from common causation. Perhaps the GVS has an essential unity, not because the contributory changes happen for the same reason, but because one part leads to, or creates the necessary conditions for, the next. This would argue for a GVS which does exclude the subsequent mergers—not because the whole shift is motivated by the avoidance of mergers, but because the changes that show a degree of interdependence stop at the point where all the systemic slots are filled again and the cycle is complete.

This is partly an aesthetic argument (we include the 'circular' aspects of the GVS because they form a neat pattern, and exclude the later mergers because they mess the pattern up, even though we know that language change is really at least as often messy as neat). It is, on the other hand, supported by results. Both the top and bottom halves of the GVS have contributed to the mismatches of orthography and phonology which are such a trial to today's learner spellers. Furthermore, both halves provide the same kinds of outcomes in terms of the modern English morphophonemic alternations they create, with *divine–divinity* created by the top half, and *sane–sanity* by the bottom half. Stockwell and Minkova suggest that such classification by results is possible, though ultimately uninteresting:

The Great Vowel Shift has reality as the historical explanation of phonetic differences among cognates within the Modern English lexicon. … As a 'summation' … it has such reality. There is no basis for disputing anyone's choice of convenient summation labels, only for disputing the reification of them.[19]

In other words, the GVS itself is, on this view, not something that happened, but merely a convenient summary term for a series of independent processes which combine to cause a particular set of effects on early modern English phonology.

[19] Stockwell and Minkova (1988*b*), 411.

Labelling these individual changes as a single unit is both meaningless (because the only rationale for doing so would involve an identification of a single common motivation, which is lacking), and pernicious (because creating a category like the GVS makes us believe in it).

In what sense, then, is the GVS not real? Lass in 1992 provided an entertaining and enlightening view of Stockwell and Minkova's problems with the GVS concept by discussing the affinities of the proposed GVS with zebras and constellations. As he explained, while we know what we think we mean by a zebra (it's a stripy horse), some zebras will in fact turn out to be biologically closer to other horses than they are to other zebras. 'S&M argue in effect that the GVS is like the zebra: its sub-changes have more powerful and compelling affinities with processes outside the package (both earlier and later), and the package is therefore a fake'.[20] Even worse, the elements conventionally included in the GVS have only been grouped together because humans tend to see patterns, just as we group stars into constellations, even though of course there is no Great Bear or Orion's Belt (or Orion, come to that) in the night sky. Nonetheless, we easily fall prey to what Lass here calls 'The constellation fallacy: ... Because a set of points in some space can be joined into an "object" of a definite shape, the *object* exists.'

To continue Lass's metaphor, Stockwell and Minkova seem, therefore, to suggest that we should do away with both zebras and constellations for both early modern English and the GVS. In these terms, then, although humans are naturally good at seeing patterns, we ought to be more disciplined and disallow many of those we think we see. In particular, we should, they warn, be extremely wary of patterns which are 'the product of hindsight'.[21] Historical patterns, however, may not be entirely like either zebras or constellations, as this and other chapters within the volume serve to illustrate. In fact, it is hard to see how we can discuss historical patterns at all except insofar as they are the product of hindsight on the part of linguists.

First, even a change that only takes a generation or two is quite unlikely to be seen as such by the people participating in it. All changes therefore go beyond the individual native speaker's competence, and none can be truly linguistically or conceptually 'real'. Either no change is real, however minor; or we cannot rule out groupings of changes simply because of the time factor involved. Stockwell and Minkova argue that 'Changes that are separated by 300 years surely cannot partake of the same "inner coherence" '[22]—but we have

---

[20] See Lass (1992), 147.   [21] Stockwell and Minkova (1988*a*), 386.   [22] Ibid., 370.

already seen that there are other modes of classification which need not assume common motivation. In fact, when it comes to language change, linguists need to stand outside what is going on to understand it. That is what historians are for. We can see patterns which are partly mysterious, the causation of which we do not fully know, and we can still learn from them. In that sense, as Lass noted in 1999, 'The GVS is problematical in the same way as other "events" with great temporal spans like "the Industrial Revolution" or "the Romantic Period".'[23] Historians propose such labels partly because of that human tendency to see patterns, but those labels catch on because they are helpful—they allow us to classify certain events and ideas together which we might not otherwise do on other grounds. It seems absurd to suggest that we should disregard 'the long eighteenth century' because it took too long, or 'the Enlightenment' because not everyone was enlightened at the same time, or for the same reason.

Perhaps, in the end, the real argument comes down to what different scholars are willing to accept, and how high or low they set their thresholds for realism as opposed to idealism and abstraction. As Lass puts it, 'obviously cognitive preferences differ, and there are personal limits to what anybody can swallow. S & M appear to choke on some I find quite palatable, and vice versa; but in most cases there aren't real empirical issues involved.'[24] We see here a very clear match for another current argument in historical linguistics, this time focusing on grammaticalization, which has been discussed at length by the linguists Paul Hopper and Elizabeth Traugott in their 1993 book of the same name. Grammaticalization is the term for what happens when a lexical word, like a noun or verb or adjective, becomes something more grammatical, like a particle or suffix; and there seems to be general agreement about what a core case of grammaticalization might be. We can see a good English example in the case of *be going to*, which can be used in a lexical way to mean 'I am physically on my way to do something'; if I meet you at the bus stop, and ask where you are going, you may say *I'm going to town*. However, now *be going to* also has a much more grammatical use, which express futurity. So, you may say *I'm going to tell Jane tomorrow*. These grammaticalized usages can be recognized because they no longer necessarily involve motion: in our example, you and Jane may be flatmates and there is no question of travelling in order to do the telling. This loss of some earlier component of meaning is known as

[23] Lass (1999), 396.   [24] Lass (1988), 405–6.

semantic bleaching. In addition, phonological reduction is common in the grammaticalized cases, where we often find *gonna* rather than *going to*: note that *I'm gonna tell Jane tomorrow* is fine, whereas **I'm gonna town* is not.

Historical linguists recognize that these changes of semantic bleaching and phonological reduction are 'real', and that they work together, perhaps overlapping in their chronology, in the development of particular forms from lexical to grammatical. However, battle has been joined over grammaticalization itself, the composite of these individual changes. The issue, which should seem rather familiar by now, is whether grammaticalization is simply a convenient label for a whole set of independent changes, in which case we would be better served by looking for affinities of one kind of semantic bleaching (i.e. the process by which one linguistic element, in becoming more and more functional, loses most of its lexical meaning) with another, for example; or whether we can talk meaningfully about grammaticalization theory, thereby according the overall trajectory of changes a reality and meaning which is greater than the sum of its parts.

Lass argues (and this prefigures some of the arguments about grammaticalization too) that 'the traditional GVS ... can be salvaged to some extent on aesthetic and historiographical grounds; not as an empirical "event", but as a pattern of significance and a focus for story-telling too valuable to discard'.[25] What is absolutely clear is that something did profoundly restructure Renaissance English, at least as far as the long vowel system was concerned. Calling that something the GVS is not in itself a solution, and could be downright obfuscatory if we took that to be the end of the story. Nevertheless, it is a step in the right direction if we accept that one relatively minor change could lead to another, until the whole system had altered, and then try to find out more about the rationale for those individual steps and for their aftermath.

References and Suggestions for Further Reading

There are many textbooks available on the history of English and on historical linguistics more generally, and all include some information on sound change and attempts to explain it: try Fennell (2001), Aitchison (1981), or McMahon (1994). If you need help with basic phonetics and phonology, and with the symbols used throughout this chapter, some introductions which focus specifically on English are Carr (1999) and McMahon (2001). A guide to phonetic symbols can be found in this volume on pp. x–xi.

---

[25] Lass (1992), 148.

A focus on phonology

Turning to change in the relevant period, there are excellent overviews of each area of the grammar in Lass (1999*b*), with a particularly detailed chapter on developments in phonology and morphology from 1476–1776 by Lass himself (1999*a*). This chapter goes into far more depth on far more changes than I can hope to cover here. On syntax, there is a full treatment of historical developments in Denison (1993), while Tieken-Boon van Ostade (1987) gives a very clear and detailed account of the variability in usage of DO in the eighteenth century. Nurmi (1999*a*) is also useful in this context. Barber (1997) and Görlach (1991) both provide good overviews of change during this period.

Textbook views of the Great Vowel Shift

The Great Vowel Shift itself, whatever exactly it was or wasn't, figures at least in passing in all surveys of the history of English, and tends to make an appearance in many textbooks on language change. It is discussed in much more detail in Lass (1976, 1988, 1992, 1999*b*), and by Stockwell (1975) and Stockwell and Minkova (1988*a*, 1988*b*, 1990, 1999).

The inception problem

Orthoepical evidence for this period is presented in detail in the second volume of Dobson (1968); many texts—including those by Hart, Robinson, and Hodges—have been printed in facsimile by The Scolar Press. Nöjd (1978) presents a full analysis of Hodges' work.

Lass discusses the importance of regional evidence for the interpretation of the GVS in both 1976 and 1999. Further information on the Scottish Vowel Length Rule can be found in Aitken (1981), Johnston (1997), and McMahon (2000), and more information on Scots in general in Jones (1997) and in Corbett *et al.* (2003).

The merger problem

Readers interested in Optimality Theory might consult Kager (1999); for papers applying the model specifically to historical problems and data, see Holt (2003).

The structural coherence problem

Grammaticalization is treated in detail in Hopper and Traugott (1993); the controversy over 'grammaticalization theory' in particular is highlighted in Newmeyer (2001), Janda (2001), and Campbell (2001).

7

MAPPING CHANGE IN TUDOR ENGLISH

Terttu Nevalainen

Davphine.	Why? whom do you account for authors, sir Iohn Daw?
Daw.	Syntagma Iuris ciuilis, Corpus Iuris ciuilis, Corpus Iuris canonici, the King of Spaines bible.
Davphine.	Is the King of Spaines bible an author?
Clerimont.	Yes, and Syntagma.
Davphine.	What was that Syntagma, sir?
Daw.	A ciuill lawer, a Spaniard.
Davphine.	Sure, Corpus was a Dutch-man.
Clerimont.	I, both the Corpusses, I knew 'hem: they were very corpulent authors.

Ben Jonson, *Epicoene, or The Silent Woman* (1616), II.iii.

NOW, four hundred years on, Clerimont in Jonson's *Epicoene* is not too far off the mark when he thinks *Corpusses* are authors. Modern corpora (or corpuses) are structured collections of texts, both written and spoken. Different kinds are available for language studies. A *multigenre* corpus contains a variety of genres, and a *single-genre* corpus consists of only one, such as personal letters, pamphlets, or newspapers. Both types usually have multiple authors. Single-author corpora also exist, with the Shakespeare canon as a case in point. As corpora are usually digitized, it is easy to run searches for words and constructions in the texts they contain.

Over the last couple of decades, electronic corpora have greatly enriched the study of the history of the English language. Giving quick and easy access to a wide selection of data, they have made it possible to explore how the language was used not only in successive time periods such as Middle and Early Modern English, but also in various genres, and by diverse groups of people. Apart from the Corpus of Old English, which contains all extant texts from that period, most historical corpora consist of text selections. They aim, in essence, to provide a window on different kinds of writing from administrative documents to early science, handbooks, sermons, fiction, drama, and personal letters, to name but a few. The number of extant genres grows with time as literacy improves and new genres come into being, such as the private diary in the sixteenth century, the newspaper in the seventeenth, and the novel in the eighteenth.

In this chapter, historical corpora will be used to shed light on some of the details of how the English language changed during the Tudor era, roughly, in the sixteenth century (although seventeenth-century English will also be considered at various points). As other chapters in this volume have already stressed, period divisions of this kind are arbitrary in that language change rarely if ever coincides with royal dynasties—or indeed with any of the other landmarks commonly found in history books. The time span adopted in this chapter will therefore be introduced not in terms of absolute boundaries but as a core period for the linguistic processes which will be discussed. As these processes partly extend beyond the sixteenth century, the time span could equally well have been labelled 'the Tudor-Stuart period'. This would have accounted for the fact that what was the Tudor period in England was already part of the Stuart period in Scotland, the linguistic characteristics of which will also be included in our discussion.

As noted in Chapter 5, by the sixteenth century English spelling no longer contained much information that could help us identify a writer's dialectal background. This is obviously the case in Jonson's *Epicoene*, printed in 1616. But the Tudor era also represents the time before prescriptive grammars, and so enables us to see how grammatical changes spread quite unmonitored in the language community, often replacing other, earlier, or more local features as they did so. The use of corpora as a means of investigation importantly enables a close-up of such change, enabling us to map the details of shift and variation in ways which are otherwise impossible. Although often neglected in traditional histories of the language, corpus evidence of this kind is, therefore, extremely valuable, a means of taking us much closer to the 'real English' of the day, and the complexities of language history as it was enacted through the usage of a wide range of writers.

In this context, private writings—such as personal letters and diaries—offer considerable insight into how Tudor English was used by individuals, by women and men, northerners and southerners, and by a range of people from different walks of life. All of these necessarily drew on the English of their time but, in doing so, they often made different linguistic choices where choice was available. Different people and groups of people could hence become leaders of linguistic change, promoting new forms, picking up on-going changes, or avoiding traditional forms such as the second-person pronoun *thou* (an important shift in Tudor English which we will examine in detail later in this chapter). Such speakers can thereby be seen as instrumental in changing the language of their day as many of the changes they implemented eventually diffused throughout the language community. Many features promoted in Tudor English have also become part of modern English—of both mainstream regional varieties and the standard variety alike.

The majority of this chapter will deal with two important processes of change in Tudor English: one that affected the third-person singular verbal ending (e.g. *he knoweth*, which was gradually displaced by *he knows*), and one that introduced the auxiliary *do* into English (so that structures such as *they know not* were gradually displaced by *they do not know*). Both are critical aspects of change in the English of this time, and they have attracted a good deal of scholarly interest. The evidence provided by electronic corpora is nevertheless able to give us a more rounded picture of both of them, but it has also raised some new questions for further studies. Some of these questions are related to other processes of change as, for instance, in the Early Modern English pronoun system (including the disappearance of the pronoun *thou*). This process will also be traced in the light of corpus data, and the evidence of change and variation which it can illuminatingly provide.

SOME HISTORICAL CORPORA

The Tudor period from the late fifteenth to the early seventeenth century (1485–1603) provides us with a rich array of public and private writings, a selection of which has been sampled for the multigenre Helsinki Corpus of English Texts (henceforth referred to as HC). The corpus spans Old, Middle, and Early Modern English, paying attention to both genre continuity and innovation across time. It is organized into shorter sub-periods, two of which—1500–1570 and 1570–1640—are of particular interest for our study of Tudor English.

Both consist of a matching set of fifteen genres ranging from the typical formal kinds of writing such as the *Statutes of the Realm* to more informal kinds such as comedy.[1]

Most of the genres included in the HC were publicly distributed or appeared in print (autobiographies, handbooks, philosophical and educational treatises, histories, and plays) but, where possible, private writings were also included (such as diaries and personal correspondence). Language composed for oral delivery (such as sermons or plays) was similarly sampled, as were texts originally produced in the spoken medium (such as trial proceedings). Using a selection of materials like this we can, for example, trace back processes of change in the grammar of Tudor English which emanate from the more official written end of the genre spectrum as opposed to those that were first manifested in informal, colloquial texts.

The distinction between official and informal colloquial genres is relevant in that official genres were often modelled on French and Latin which, as Chapters 3 and 4 have noted, had much longer histories in England as languages of the law and administration than was true of fifteenth- or sixteenth-century English. It is clear that many formal features such as complex subordinating conjunctions came into English through these channels. The passage below, for instance, illustrates an early case of *provided that* ('on condition that', 'if') in the *Statutes of the Realm* for 1489–91 as sampled for the HC:

Except and **provided that** yt be ordyned by the seid auctorite, that the le*tt*res patentes late made by the Kyng to Thomas Lorde Dacre of Maister Foster of the seid forest, stand and be goode and effectuell to the same Thomas after the teno*r* and effecte of the same le*tt*res patentes, the seid Acte not withstondyng. ([STAT2 II] 532)[2]

Since all the fifteenth-century instances of this conjunction in the HC come from statutory texts, as do nearly all sixteenth-century cases, a convincing case can be made, based on corpus evidence of this kind, that *provided* (*that*) entered the English language through legal and administrative use in the fifteenth century.

---

[1] Each genre in the HC is typically represented by two texts, and each longer text by two samples, so as to make up the minimum of 10,000 words per genre per sub-period. Letters, trials, and the Bible have been sampled up to 20,000 words per sub-period. The HC is large enough for the study of grammar change, but it may not give a reliable picture of lexical changes, especially with less common words, where a larger corpus is needed. As English spelling was becoming standardized in the course of the Tudor period, only private writings by less educated people and imitation of speech in drama can provide some information on the pronunciation of the time.

[2] The corpus examples cited are identified by the year of writing/publication, the name of the writer and the text and, in square brackets, the short title of the text in the corpus (HC, HCOS), or the name of the letter collection (CEEC), followed by a page reference. Any emendations such as expansions of abbreviations have been italicized.

Provided that is also found in a 1554 trial for high treason, in which Sir Nicholas Throckmorton was accused of conspiring to prevent Queen Mary's marriage to Philip of Spain, but there, too, it appears in a passage that quotes from an earlier statute:

> ... yet there is another cause to restraine these your strange and extraordinarie Constructions; that is to say, a Prouiso in the latter ende of the Statute of *Edwarde* the Thirde, hauyng these Wordes: **Provided** always, if any other Case of supposed Treason shall chaunce hereafter to come in Question or Trial before any Justice, other than is in the said Statute expressed, **that** then the Justice shall forbear to adjudge the sayd case, untill it be shewed to the Parliament to trie, whether it should be Treason or Felonie. (1554, *State Trials* [THROCKM I] 75.C1)

If we trace this change further, we can see that although the conjunction continues to be favoured in legal language, it also finds its way into less formal contexts of use towards the end of the sixteenth century and at the beginning of the next. It can be found, for instance, in Gervase Markham's *Countrey Contentments* of 1615, a book on husbandry which gives instructions on farming and housekeeping. The excerpt below comes from a section on exercising horses:

> As for the quantity of his exercise it must be according to his foulenes or cleannes; for if he be very foule you must then exercise moderatelie to breake his grease, if halfe foule, halfe cleane, then somewhat more to melt his grease, if altogether cleane; then you may take what you please of him (**prouided that** you doe nothing to discourage his sprits). ([MARKHAM] 77)

Nevertheless, there are fewer than ten instances of the conjunction in the entire corpus of William Shakespeare's plays (and none in the *The Merry Wives of Windsor* which was sampled for the HC). The following example comes from Act IV of *The Two Gentlemen of Verona*:

> I take your offer, and will liue with you,
> **Prouided that** you do no outrages
> On silly women, or poore passengers.
> (IV. i. 69–71)

Using a range of corpora is particularly useful for establishing the processes of change which may be at work, especially when we consider the variety of usages which may concurrently exist within a given period. The Helsinki Corpus of Older Scots (HCOS), for example, follows the period division of the HC in the sixteenth and seventeenth centuries and with a similar spread of genres. Importantly, however, it gives us an opportunity to compare the pathways of change in Scots and southern British (i.e. English) English. So the new conditional conjunction found in Scottish legal texts in the sixteenth century is, in fact, not the past participle form *provided that* but the present participle *providing* (*always*) *that*, as can be seen in the following example taken from the HCOS evidence of the 1555 *Peebles Records*: 'The inquest ordanis to ansuer Robert Atzin, and ilk ane of the officaris, of ane ferlot of meill in this storme to help thair wiffis and barnis, **providing** allwayis **that** thai clame na possessioun thairof in tyme cuming' ([PEEBLES 1] 225). The past participle form is only generalized in Scottish texts in the seventeenth century, presumably under southern influence after the Union of the Crowns of Scotland and England in 1603.

The Tudor era is also covered by the Corpus of Early English Correspondence (CEEC), which is specifically designed to facilitate the study of social variation in language use. It consists of personal correspondence, private letters written by one person to another. The way this corpus is structured allows great flexibility in analysing periods as short as twenty years (or even shorter), while its range of female as well as male writers facilitates the investigation of the impact of gender on language change and variation (a feature which is clearly important in language history but one which, as previous chapters have shown, is often hampered by lack of evidence). The CEEC also contains letters deriving from writers of various social and regional backgrounds. When data were sampled for the CEEC, particular attention was paid to letter writers from London, East Anglia (Norfolk and Suffolk), and the North. London writers proper were, in addition, separated from those attached to the Royal Court in Westminster in order to make it possible to compare their language use.

It is a sign of the less formal nature of the CEEC letter corpus that there are no more than half a dozen instances of *provided that* in the sixteenth-century data (which amounts to almost a million words). One of these comes from a letter written by the Norfolk lawyer Stephen Drury to Nathaniel Bacon, a local JP and future sheriff of Norfolk, in 1583. The first instance of *provided*, reproduced here in curly brackets, was deleted by Drury himself:

I, thinking yt would come thus to passe {provided} and supposing (as inded yt followed) that Hast would be this day at Aylesham church, **provided that** Mr Neave who had no notyce of the countermaund should be there to arrest him, who came accordingly to Aylesham churche. ([BACON II] 270)

In this chapter the CEEC will be used to examine changes which spread from less formal language use across the language community, as well as the fundamental role of language users (both men and women) from different parts of the country in shaping Tudor English.

at the national level in the period 1500–1570; it occurs in a mere 3 per cent of the cases. It was instead the southern -(e)*th* which was the dominant form in most kinds of writing from the Tyndale Bible to sermons and trial records. Nevertheless, -(e)*s* continued to spread, and in 1570–1640 it had already achieved a mean frequency of 20 per cent of all the third-person singular present-tense endings over a selection of HC genres (diaries, histories, official and private letters, sermons, and trials).

Average figures such as these, however, can only describe a change in progress in very general terms. In order to find out in more detail the kinds of texts (and genres) in which the incoming form first appeared, we need to dig deeper. Here again, corpus evidence proves its value. The HC data, for example, confirms that there were notable differences between genres in the use of third-person endings. A comparison of diaries, histories, and private and official letters reveals that it was in fact only private letters that had any instances of -(e)*s* to speak of between 1500 and 1570. Typically, it occurred in the letters of northern writers, as in an extract from the following letter which was written *c*1506 by Dame Isabel Plumpton to her husband Sir Robert (the Plumptons were a Yorkshire gentry family):

Sir, I have sent to Wright of Idell for the money that he promyst you, and he **saith** he **hath** it not to len, and **makes** choses [\excuses\] and so I can get none nowhere. ([PLUMPTON] 198)

But even Isabel Plumpton alternates between -(e)*s* and -(e)*th*, as in her use of -*s* with *make* and -*th* with *say* and *have* in the second line of this extract. This is, in fact, a general pattern in the data. There are a few verbs, notably *do*, *have*, and *say*, which take the incoming -*s* ending later than others. As a result when, in the latter half of the seventeenth century, most other verbs have more than 90 per cent of -(e)*s* according to the evidence of the corpus, *do* still takes it in only half of the cases, and *have* in merely one third. Such patterns are common in language change. A change usually spreads gradually to all relevant contexts, but it can also have word-specific restrictions and can thereby proceed, just as in the case of -(e)*s*, by means of a process known as *lexical diffusion*.

In the next HC period, 1570–1640, the overall use of -(e)*s* with verbs other than *do* and *have* soars to some 80 per cent in private letters, and comes to about one third of the instances in trials and official letters. This pattern of spread from the private, informal end of the genre spectrum is, of course, precisely the reverse of that which we found with the conjunction *provided* (*that*) which, as we have seen, first gained ground in formal genres, and only afterwards spread to informal ones in the course of time. Meanwhile, to return to the indicative endings, it was the southern -(e)*th* form which, becoming associated with more formal registers, soon gained a distinctly 'literary' status in general use. This passage from a sermon against 'usurie' (or excessive gains made by lending money) by the 'silver-tongued' preacher Henry Smith illustrates a typical context for -(*e*)*th* around 1600:

Now, al the Commandements of God are fulfilled by loue, which Christ **noteth** when hee **draweth** all the Commandements to one Commandement, which is, *Loue God aboue all things, and thy neighbour as thy selfe*: as if hee should say, hee which **loueth** GOD, will keepe all the Commaundements which respect God, and he which **loueth** his neighbour will keepe all the Commaundements which respect his neighbour. (1591, H. Smith, *Of Vsurie* [SMITH] B4R)

The approximate date for this wider generalization of -(*e*)*s* based on the HC gains direct support from the Shakespeare corpus. In Shakespeare's early plays, that is those written between 1591–99, the dominant ending with verbs other than *have* and *do* is -(*e*)*th*, and -(*e*)*s* appears in only one fifth of the cases. In his later plays, however, those written between 1600–13, the situation is reversed, and it is instead -(*e*)*s* which is used in the vast majority of cases.

We can follow the process of change even more closely by referring to some of the other corpora which have been discussed above. In the Corpus of Early English Correspondence, for example, the change can be traced within shorter periods and with more data. The CEEC confirms that -(*e*)*s* was infrequent well into the second half of the sixteenth century, occurring on average in less than 10 per cent of all possible cases. Figure 7.1 presents the increasing frequency of -(*e*)*s* towards the end of the century and in the first half of the next. It reaches 50 per cent around 1600, when -(*e*)*th* and -(*e*)*s* are almost equally frequent in personal correspondence:

Yet even these figures hide a great deal of variation. If we make a comparison between male and female writers, a systematic difference can be seen to emerge between the two sexes and their patterns of indicative usage. Throughout the

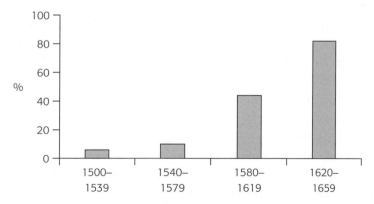

FIG. 7.1. Increasing use of the third-person singular -(*e*)*s* in personal letters between 1500 and 1660
Source: Based on Nevalainen and Raumolin-Brunberg (2003: 215).

sixteenth century, women are shown to be consistently more frequent users of the incoming -(e)s form in the south than men, suggesting perhaps that women were more apt to adopt forms that were in the process of being generalized throughout Tudor England. In fact women turned out to be the leaders in seven out of ten Early Modern English changes which were studied by means of the CEEC corpus. We also know from present-day English that women are usually in the vanguard of linguistic change, especially of those changes that are in the process of spreading to supra-local usage. At the same time, we should not forget that, due to basic differences in education, a much smaller section of the female than the male population could write in Tudor England, which leaves women's language less well represented than that of men. But there were also women—such indeed as Queen Elizabeth herself—who possessed an extensive classical education. The passage below comes from a letter written by her in 1591 to King James VI of Scotland, the man who, twelve years later, would be her successor to the English throne:

My deare brother, As ther is naught that **bredes** more for-thinking repentance and agrived thoughtes than good turnes to harme the giuers ayde, so **hathe** no bonde euer tied more honorable mynds, than the shewes of any acquital by grateful acknowelegement in plain actions; for wordes be leues and dides the fruites. ([ROYAL 1] 65)

In her personal correspondence, Queen Elizabeth chose -(e)s over -(e)th about half of the time with verbs other than *have* and *do*. In this, she clearly belonged to another generation than her father King Henry VIII (1491–1547) who, as in the following extract from a letter of 1528, had not employed the incoming -(e)s form even in the intimacy of his love letters to Anne Boleyn, Elizabeth's mother:

And thus opon trust off your short repaire to London I make an ende off my letter, myne awne swettehart. Wryttyn with the hand off hym whyche **desyryth** as muche to be yours as yow do to have hym—H Rx ([HENRY 8] 112)

The CEEC material can also be used to give us an idea how the change progressed geographically at this time. Figure 7.2 presents the relative frequency of the third-person singular -(e)s from the late fifteenth to the early seventeenth centuries. As -(e)s originates from the north it is only natural that it should be more frequent in the northern texts than it is elsewhere in the early part of the period. It is therefore somewhat surprising to find that, for the better part of the sixteenth century, this higher frequency is no longer in evidence. We can assume, therefore, that the pressure of the southern -eth norm must have had an effect on the general usage among the literate section of the people in the north; we will explore this in more detail in the next section.

As Figure 7.2 also indicates, with the exception of the late fifteenth century, -(e)s is not much used in the capital, either at Court or in the City of London, until the

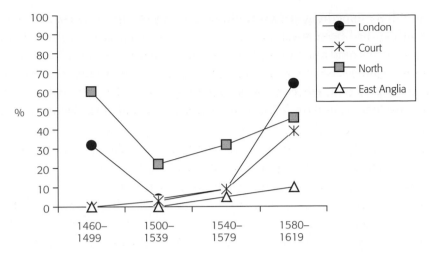

FIG. 7.2.   Regional spread of -(*e*)*s* in verbs other than *have* and *do*
Source: Based on Nevalainen and Raumolin-Brunberg (2003: 178).

last few decades of the sixteenth century. This is the point when the -(*e*)*s* ending made its breakthrough in the City, and also gained ground at Court. We saw above that the Queen herself regularly used -(*e*)*s* in her personal correspondence.

But it nevertheless remains significant that -(*e*)*s* should have been present in London in the late fifteenth century. A writer's geographical roots in the -(*e*)*s* speaking area may, for example, partly account for its early appearance in the usage attested for the capital. As Chapters 4 and 5 have noted, for example, the City of London attracted vast numbers of immigrants from the north, especially apprentices, in the late Middle Ages. Our early evidence on London English also mostly comes from merchants' letters, and some of them we know had northern connections. This was, for instance, the case with Richard Cely, a member of the wool-exporting Cely family from London, and a frequent -(*e*)*s* user, as is indicated in the following extract from a letter written in 1480 to his brother George Cely. It is worth noting here that he also uses the zero form, and writes both *he prays* (as in line 2) and *he pray* (in line 4):

Syr, my Lord of Sente Jonys **commende** hym to you, and **thankys** yow for yowr tydy*ng*ys, and **prays** you of contynewans. He ys ryught glad of them, and he **prays** yow to remembyr hys sadyllys, styropys and spwrs, and clothe for hosyn. Aull tys a*t* thys Whytsuntyd he **pray** yow that hyt may be had. ([CELY] 74)

The only region of the four examined where literate writers clearly avoided -(*e*)*s* at the turn of the seventeenth century is East Anglia. This may be connected with the fact that the area was rather self-contained with Norwich as its local centre. It may also have something to do with the availability of a third alternative, the zero form, which had been attested there from the fifteenth century onwards. This suffixless form could also be used with *have*, *do*, and *say*—as in the Norfolk-based Katherine Paston's use of 'thy father **have**' (see p. 185). Elsewhere, as we have seen, these verbs preferred *-eth*. Further examples can be found, for example, in a letter written by John Mounford, a local Norfolk man, to Nathaniel Bacon in 1573:

... and also your horce shall want no shooing, to be doone allwaies at home in your stabel, for he **do** dwell within haulfe a myle of Cocthorpe. But his father **saye** that he cannot forbeare him from his occupacion to continew with yow, but I thinke if yow doo talke with his father yow shall soone intreat him ... ([BACON I] 56)

Despite this lag, the supralocal use of *-(e)s* was generalized in the East Anglian data as well in the course of the seventeenth century

-(E)TH FROM THE SOUTH

As we have seen, Figure 7.2 suggests that the southern *-(e)th* had made significant inroads into the north in the course of the late fifteenth and early sixteenth centuries, by which time it appears as the majority form in the personal correspondence of northerners. Nevertheless, there was clearly competition between the local northern form *-(e)s* and the would-be supra-local *-(e)th*, not least since the latter was supported by the printing press and administrative and legal documents, such as the *Statutes of the Realm*, which has been referred to above. Both forms were clearly known to and used by literate people in the north, although the relative proportions of this usage tend to differ depending on the person. In the Plumpton family letters, for example, *-(e)th* was more common in letters written by men than it was in letters written by women, as well as being more common in the letters of high-ranking and professional men than in letters written by men coming from lower social orders. But northerners of course never gave up their local *-(e)s* form, which regained its status as the supra-local written norm at the turn of the seventeenth century in the northern data.

The *-s* ending, with its alternative spellings *-es* and *-is*, was also the norm in Older Scots. The Helsinki Corpus of Older Scots has no instances of the southern *-(e)th* before 1500, and only a couple occur in the period 1500–1570. But there is a huge increase in the use of *-(e)th* in the HCOS in the next period, 1570–1640, and this does not diminish significantly even in the latter half of the seventeenth century. Most Scots genres at that point have at least some instances of *-(e)th*, although it is clearly favoured in travelogues, handbooks, and educational and scientific treatises. Genre-preferential patterns can also be seen in the HC data which represents southern English from the latter half of the seventeenth century; apart from the conservative verbs *do* and *have*, which commonly retain -(*e*)*th*, other verbs also take the ending in handbooks, educational treatises, sermons, and in the autobiography of George Fox, the founder of the Quaker society, although it is particularly prominent in Richard Preston's translation of Boethius's *De Consolatione Philosophiae* (1695).

Two Scots cases from the middle period are presented below. The first comes from a sermon *Upon the Preparation of the Lordis Supper* which was preached by the Church of Scotland minister Robert Bruce in Edinburgh in 1589. It has only one -*eth* form, *doeth* in line 2; all the other relevant forms end in -*es*, as in *makes* in line 2 and 3, and *hes* in lines 1 and 4. In this respect, it differs strikingly from the sermon preached by Henry Smith in London two years later (and which was discussed on p. 187) which does not contain a single instance of -(*e*)*s*:

I call it first of all, ane certaine feeling in the hart: for the Lord **hes** left sic a stamp in the hart of euery man, that he **doeth** not that turne so secretlie, nor so quietly but hee **makes** his owne heart to strike him, and to smite him: hee **makes** him to feill in his owne hart, whether hee **hes** doone weill or ill. (1590, [BRUCE] 4)

The second passage comes from a pamphlet entitled *A Counterblaste to Tobacco* which was written by King James and published in 1604. This contains an even mix of -*eth* and -*es* forms and, as such, is more anglicized than Bruce's sermon:

Medicine **hath** that vertue, that it neuer **leaueth** a man in that state wherin it **findeth** him; it **makes** a sicke / man whole, but a whole man sicke. And as Medicine **helpes** nature being taken at times of necessitie, so being euer and continually vsed, it **doth** but weaken, wearie, and weare nature. ([TOBACCO] 95)

The fact that the traditional southern -*eth* form continued well into the seventeenth century has, as the previous chapter also noted, been explained by the process of anglicization of Older Scots especially after the Union of the Crowns in 1603. A closer look at the later seventeenth-century Scots forms reveals, however, that they come from two main categories. One consists of the familiar three verbs *have*, *do*, and *say* (the first two of which also appear in the King James' extract above). These make up about half of the cases. The other group consists of verbs that end in sibilant sounds such as /s/, /z/, or /ʃ/, for example, where the suffix constitutes a syllable of its own (as in words such as *ariseth*, *causeth*, *increaseth*, *presseth*, *produceth*, etc.). Only one third of the cases are not linguistically regulated in this way.

LINGUISTIC MOTIVES FOR -(E)S

The relevance of the verb-final consonant to the choice of suffix also emerges in the southern English data. The incoming -(e)s form was favoured by verbs ending in a stop, and in particular by the presence of a final /t/ (e.g. *lasts*) and /d/ (*leads*). In contrast, and just as in the Older Scots corpus, -*eth* tended to be retained in verbs ending in a vowel and, as noted above, particularly, in verbs ending in a sibilant or sibilant-final affricate: /s/ (*compasseth*), /z/ (*causeth*), /ʃ/ (*diminisheth*), /tʃ/ (*catcheth*), and /dʒ/ (*changeth*). After a sibilant the suffix always preserves its vowel, thereby forming an additional syllable.

A means of adding an extra syllable to a verb is, of course, a very useful device in maintaining a metrical pattern in drama and poetry. The alternation between the two suffixes in the following extract from Act V of Shakespeare's *The Taming of the Shrew* can, for instance, be explained by metrical considerations. The suffix -*eth* in *oweth* is accorded a syllabic status, while a non-syllabic reading is given to -*s* in *owes*:

> Such dutie as the subiect **owes** the Prince
> Euen such a woman **oweth** to her husband.
>   (V. ii. 156–7)

But, we might ask, why could a syllabic -*es* not be used in these contexts, too? Corpora give no straightforward answer to this question, and we need to turn to contemporary Tudor commentators to see whether they could give any clues as to how to interpret this variation. After all, the spellings -*es* and -*eth* in medieval texts suggest that both these third-person endings once contained a vowel before the final consonant. Today the vowel is no longer pronounced except with sibilant-final verbs (as in *it causes*).

Vowel deletion of this kind is not restricted to third-person verbal endings but it can also be found in the plural and possessive -(e)s endings of nouns, as well as in the past tense and past participle -*ed* forms of verbs. Previous research suggests that plural and possessive nouns were the first to lose the /ə/ vowel in these positions, and this took place in all words except for those ending in sibilants. This deletion process started in the fourteenth century and was gradually completed over the course of the sixteenth. The process was slower with the past-tense and past-participle forms of verbs in which the suffix -*ed* was retained as a separate syllable in many formal styles of usage until the end of the seventeenth century. It still of course continues to be retained in adjectival forms such as *learned*, as in *a learned monograph, a learned society*.

In the third-person singular present-tense endings, the vowel loss happened earlier in the north of England than in the south. The process was faster in colloquial speech than in other registers, and was only blocked, as we have seen, by the presence of word-final sibilants. The southern -(e)th ending was, for example, the regular third-person suffix for John Hart, an early (London-based) phonetician who has already been discussed in Chapter 6. His proposals for spelling reform appeared between 1551 and 1570 and, importantly, contained detailed transcriptions of speech. In this context, Hart is, importantly, the first reliable source to distinguish between the full and contracted variants of -eth. The latter he restricts to colloquial speech, and his transcriptions only contain a few instances of /s/ (as in the words *methinks, belongs*), but none of /es/. This suggests therefore that -(e)s had lost its vowel in non-sibilant contexts by the mid-sixteenth century. Many commentators, as a result, did indeed regard -s as a contracted form of the syllabic -eth.

This contemporary evidence also indicates that the contracted forms of both -(e)th and -(e)s had become current in the course of the Tudor period, and that -s was, by this point, largely used as a contracted form. Phonologically, the contracted -s also had an advantage over the dental fricative in -th (i.e. /θ/) in that it was much easier to pronounce after verbs ending in /t/ and /d/, as in *sendeth*, for example, or *sitteth*. Although the Tudor English spelling system cannot be relied on to display vowel deletion except with writers with little formal education, the corpus evidence shows a general preference for -(e)s with verbs ending in the stops /t/ and /d/.

We are now in a better position to interpret the CEEC findings in Figure 7.2. It is probably the full and uncontracted -es form which reached London in the late fifteenth century. Like some other northern features which are also attested in London English at this time, it failed to gain wider acceptance. However, the second time -(e)s surfaced in the capital, in the sixteenth century, it involved vowel contraction, which was now common with singular third-person verb inflections in the south as well. In its short, contracted form, the originally northern suffix hence found its way into the supra-local variety used by the literate people of the time. The traditional southern form -eth had meanwhile gained a firm position in formal contexts as, for instance, in liturgical speech, but it was also retained in many regional dialects.

YOU AND THOU

Verbal endings are by no means the only linguistic systems in Tudor English which make use of the same form for both the solemn and the rural. One of the best known cases is the alternation between the second-person singular pronouns *you* and *thou*.[4] Apart from its traditional liturgical use, as in the Lord's Prayer, *thou* has continued as a regional form until the present day especially in the north and west of England. Nevertheless, and as earlier chapters in this volume have already explored, English, just like the other Germanic languages, used to have two second-person pronouns, *thou* in the singular and *you* in the plural. In Middle English (see p. 107), the use of the plural *you* started to spread as the polite form in addressing one person (cf. French *vous*, German *Sie*). Social inferiors used *you* to their superiors, who reciprocated by using *thou*. In the upper ranks *you* was established as the norm among equals. *Thou* was generally retained in the private sphere, but could also surface in public discourse. As forms of address are socially negotiable, however, no rigid rules apply, and the story of the two pronouns is rather more complex in its pragmatic details.

The Helsinki Corpus tells us that *thou* continued to recede in Tudor English. Comparing an identical set of genres and about the same amount of text, we learn that the use of the subject form *thou* dropped from nearly 500 instances in the first Early Modern English period (1500–1570), to some 350 in the second (1570–1640). It is noteworthy, however, that a full range of genres continued to use *thou* in the sixteenth century: not only sermons and the Bible but also handbooks, educational treatises, translations of Boethius, fiction, comedy, and trials. The example below, on how to 'thresshe and wynowe corne', comes from John Fitzherbert's *The Boke of Husbandry* of 1534; only the pronoun *thou* occurs in the text included in the HC.

This whete and rye that **thou** shalt sowe ought to be very clene of wede, and therfore er **thou** thresshe **thy** corne open **thy** sheues and pyke oute all maner of wedes, and than thresshe it and wynowe it clene, & so shalt **thou** haue good clene corne an other yere. ([FITZH] 41)

Thou also occurs in sermons and the Bible, as well as the Boethius translations, which are sampled from all three Early Modern English periods in the Helsinki Corpus. Henry Smith's sermon discussed on p. 187 can, for example, be used to illustrate the familiar biblical use, as in 'Loue … **thy** neighbour as **thy** selfe'.

---

[4] Unless otherwise stated, *you* here stands for the lexeme, which comprises all the case forms of the pronoun: *ye*, the traditional subject form, largely replaced by *you* in the course of the Tudor period; *you*, the form traditionally used in the object function; and the possessive forms *your* and *yours*. Similarly, *thou* stands for the subject form *thou*; the object form *thee*; and the possessive forms *thy* and *thine*.

Although the Boethius translations display widely different wordings, the use of *thou* is common to all of them, as in 'that **thou** a litel before dyddyst defyne' in the translation written by George Colville in 1556 (see further p. 207), and 'as **thou** hast defynd a lyttle afore' in that written by Queen Elizabeth herself in 1593 (both further discussed on p. 207).

The rest of the HC genres that contain *thou* suggest, however, a process of sociodialectal narrowing in its use during the seventeenth century: in comedies and fiction, for example, *thou* is commonly put in the mouths of servants and country people. To some extent, *thou* also continues to be used by social superiors addressing their inferiors. In seventeenth-century trials, for instance, the judge could still take recourse to *thou* when trying to extract information from a recalcitrant witness. The example below records part of Lord Chief Justice Jeffreys's interrogation of the baker John Dunne in the trial of Lady Alice Lisle in 1685. Note that apart from the formulaic *prithee*, the judge begins by using *you*:

L. C. J. Now **prithee** tell me truly, where came *Carpenter* unto **you**? I must know the Truth of that; remember that I gave **you** fair Warning, do not tell me a Lye, for I will be sure to treasure up every Lye that **thou** tellest me, and **thou** may'st be certain it will not be for **thy** Advantage: I would not terrify **thee** to make **thee** say any thing but the Truth: but assure **thy self** I never met with a lying, sneaking, canting Fellow, but I always treasur'd up   5 Vengeance for him: and therefore look to it, that **thou** dost not prevaricate with me, for to be sure **thou** wilt come to the worst of it in the end?
Dunne. My Lord, I will tell the Truth as near as I can. (1685, *State Trials* [LISLE IV] 114, C1)

This passage suggests that in a highly status-marked situation such as a public trial, where forms of address are derived from social identity, *thou* co-occurs with terms of abuse, threats, and other negative associations—here specifically Lord Chief Justice Jeffrey's accusations of lying. This had also been the case earlier in the Tudor period.

Moving on to private spheres of usage, in the seventeenth century *thou* can be found in letters exchanged by spouses, and parents may use it when addressing their young children. But in these cases, too, mixed usage prevails, with *you* clearly as the usual form, and *thou* often appearing in formulaic use at the beginning and end of the letter. In the following extract from a letter written in 1621 by Thomas Knyvett to his wife, *you* appears when he is discussing the choice of cloth patterns, but *thou* is used in the more intimate (if rather conventional) closing of the letter. Even there *you* intervenes in the last sentence:

I haue been to look for stufe for y^r bedde and haue sent downe paternes for **you** to choose which **you** like best. Thay are the neerest to the patourne that wee can finde. If **you** lack anything accept [except] my company **you** are to blame not to lett me knowe of it, for my selfe being only **yours** the rest doe followe. Thus in hast Intreating **the** to be merry and the more merry to think **thou** hast him in **thy** armes that had rather be with **you** then in any place vnder heaven; and so I rest

    Thy dear loving husband for ever

    Tho: Knyvett. ([KNYVETT] 56–57)

Knyvett was a Norfolk gentleman. Lady Katherine Paston, writing to her 14-year old son in 1625 to inform him that '**thy** father haue bine very ill' (see p. 185), also came from Norfolk. The writers using *thou* at all in their private letters at the time were, as these examples suggest, typically members of the country gentry. In contrast, the overwhelming majority of close family letters written by the literate social ranks only have *you* throughout the sixteenth and seventeenth centuries. As the Corpus of Early English Correspondence (CEEC) bears witness, Henry VIII always addressed his 'own sweetheart', Anne Boleyn, as *you* rather than *thou* in his love letters to her, but so did the wool merchant John Johnson, writing to his wife Sabine Johnson in the 1540s. The same is true of King Charles II, who consistently addressed his little sister, *dearest Minette*, as *you* in the 1660s. Writing to her fiancé (and later her husband) Sir William Temple in the 1650s, Dorothy Osborne used *you* well over 2,500 times. *Thou* (or rather *thee*) appears only twice, after they were married, as in the following extract from a letter of 1656:

Poor Mr Bolles brought this letter through all the rain to day. my dear dear heart make hast home, I doe soe want **thee** that I cannot imagin how I did to Endure **your** being soe long away when **your** buisnesse was in hand. good night my dearest, I am

    Yours D. T. ([DOSBORNE] 203)

LINGUISTIC CONSEQUENCES

As *you* came to be used in the singular as well as in the plural, the traditional number contrast was lost in the second-person pronoun system in supra-local uses of English. As a result, as in Modern English, it is not always clear whether *you* refers to one or more people. Different varieties of English have remedied the situation by introducing plural forms such as *youse* (see further Chapter 11), *you all*, or *you guys*. In the eighteenth century, the distinction was often made by using singular *you* with singular *is* (in the present tense) and *was* (in the past tense); in the plural *you* appeared with the corresponding *are* and *were*. This practice was, however, soon condemned as a solecism—ungrammatical and improper—by the prescriptive grammarians of the period (see further Chapter 9).

Another consequence of the loss of *thou* was an additional reduction in person marking on the English verb. As shown by the extract from Lord Chief Justice Jeffreys (discussed on p. 195), the use of *thou* as the subject of the sentence entailed the verb being marked by the -(*e*)*st* ending, as in Jeffrey's s *thou tellest*, *thou may'st*, *thou dost*. Marking the second-person singular was systematic in that it also extended to auxiliary verbs (e.g. *thou wilt*), which otherwise remained uninflected for person. It is, in fact, the second-person singular that justifies us talking about a system of person and number marking in English verbs, because it also applies to past-tense forms (as in *thou … didst define*). As we saw in the previous section, the third-person singular endings -(*e*)*th* and -(*e*)*s* only applied to present-tense forms in Tudor English, just as -(*e*)*s* does today.

Adding the second-person ending could, however, lead to some quite cumbersome structures in past-tense forms. George Colville, for instance, decided against having *thou *definedst* in his Boethius translation in 1556, opting instead for *thou didst define*. This is also the case for many other texts, such as the 1552 *Book of Common Prayer*, which preferred *didst manyfest* to **manifestedst* in the collect given below; this phonotactic use of the auxiliary was retained and even augmented in the revised version of the Prayer Book in 1662:

O God, whych by the leadinge of a starre **dyddest** manyfeste **thy** onely begotten sonne to the Gentyles; Mercyfully graunt, that we which know **thee** now by fayth, may after this lyfe haue the fruicion of **thy** glorious Godhead, through Christ our Lorde.

As we have established a connection between the second-person pronoun *thou* and the use of *do*, let us now turn to this auxiliary verb.

THE STORY OF *DO*

The rise of *do* is a grammatical development which is, in histories of the language, particularly associated with Tudor English. But even after decades of empirical work, some key issues in the history of this auxiliary continue to puzzle scholars. Where in England did it come from? Does it go back to colloquial or to literary language? And, having made its way into questions and negative statements, why did it fail, after a promising start, to spread to affirmative statements as well? The following corpus-based survey offers some answers to these questions, but will hardly provide a definitive account of this intriguing phenomenon.

If we look first at modern English, we can see an interesting asymmetry in the use of *do*. As Chapter 6 has already outlined, if there is no other auxiliary verb in the clause, *do* is required with *not*-negation (as in 'they **did** not see it'), with inversion, and especially in questions (as in '**did** they see it?'), and with emphasis (as in 'they ''**did** see it'), as well as acting as a prop-word in reduced clauses ('they saw it, and we **did** too'). But apart from the emphatic use, *do* is not required in affirmative statements ('they saw it') when no other auxiliary is present.

Present-day spoken-language corpora suggest, however, that *do* can sometimes appear in affirmative statements even when it is without emphasis. The example below comes from the London-Lund Corpus of British English conversation which was recorded in the 1970s (and which is provided with prosodic annotation). In B's contribution, the first word, *I*, is stressed, and so is the third, *know*. But no prosodic prominence is attached to *do*, which therefore appears to convey no overt semantic contrast or emphasis. In this text, it instead signposts the speaker's contribution to the discourse topic, that of smoking. Whatever its specific function, in affirmative statements *do* is more common in modern spoken-language corpora than it is in written-language corpora.

A: but ˆI !noticed that :Joseph _went :out for 'quartcr of an :h∨our# at ˆ∨onc point#ˆI'm !sure he 'went for a sm/oke# (- - laughs) - -

B: ˆI did 'know :one _Indian 'who . :i!r∨onically# -ˆlearnt to ch/ain'smoke#ˆin this !c\ountry# (*London-Lund Corpus of Spoken English* S.1.6.606–612)

Unstressed *do* is also used to mark habitual action in Welsh English and in the south-western dialects of British English from Cornwall to Somerset and Dorset. But even there *do* is not the only expression available. In Welsh English the habitual past is indicated by means of the simple past tense and the *used to* construction, as well as the past tense of *do*, as in constructions such as 'He **went/ used to go** to the cinema every week' and 'He **did go** to the cinema every week'. Examples such as these suggest that in affirmative statements the use of periphrastic *do*, as it is called in the literature, might have been quite flexible in the past as well.

ORIGINS OF *DO*

Few issues in the history of English have attracted as much interest as the rise of the *do*-periphrasis. There are some uncertain instances of it from Old English, and more certain data from the end of the thirteenth century onwards, but the periphrasis only gains ground at the end of the fifteenth century in the texts that have come down to us and in which both emphatic and non-emphatic functions are in evidence.

One of the puzzles in the history of *do* are the circumstances which give rise to the construction in the first place. As it can be seen to assume an aspectual function expressing habitual action (e.g. 'He did walk to school every day') in traditional south-western dialects (see p. 198), some scholars argue in favour of its south-western origins, probably prompted by contacts with the Celtic languages in the area. Others suggest that it may have arisen from contacts between English and Anglo-Norman French. Still others look for its origins in causative constructions of the type *the king did write a letter* that is in the sense 'the king had a letter written (by someone)/made somebody write a letter'. Because it is attested in early Middle English poetry, there are also suggestions that it started out as a metrical filler. None of these accounts is perfectly satisfactory, and not least because of problems of localization.

Let us begin by looking at some corpus evidence from the fifteenth century, the period when periphrastic *do* began to gain ground. A comparison of the regional data in the CEEC reveals the following trends. The causative construction dominates, especially at Court, in the first half of the fifteenth century but becomes very rare after 1500. Good examples can be found in the Signet Letters of Henry V, as in the following extract from a letter of 1419 (*kynwolmersh* refers to William Kynwolmersh, appointed Dean of St Martin le Grand in London in 1421): 'We wol ye **do** make a patent vnder oure greet seel vnto þe said kynwolmersh of þe Deanee of saint martin*es* grande yn London' ([SIGNET] 116). In contrast, periphrastic *do* occurs particularly in the City of London and to some extent in the west, but remains relatively infrequent throughout the fifteenth century. A typical instance appears, for example, in a letter written by Richard Cely to his brother George in 1480: 'the xxvj day of thys monthe I resauyd ij lettyrs frome you, whon to houre father, another to myselue, the qweche I **do** whell wndyrstonde, and heyr I sende yow …' ([CELY] 84).

One of the significant issues that has been debated in the history of periphrastic *do* is whether it arose in literary or colloquial contexts. Those who argue for its literary origins suggest that it grew out of the causative function (as in the example in the 1419 Signet Letter discussed above). Conversely, those who are in favour of colloquial origins refer instead to the influence of language contact or semantic weakening of the lexical verb *do*. As we have seen, causative *do* occurred frequently in official Court correspondence in the early fifteenth century. But it could also occur in private letters as something of a politeness marker, to indicate that the writer did not necessarily expect the recipient to carry out the request him- or herself, as in the following illustration from Margaret Paston's letter to her husband John in *c*1453: 'Also I pray yow þat ye woll **do** bey a loff of gode sugowr and di. j li. of holl synamun, for þer is non gode in this town' ([PASTON I] 252).

On the other hand, many instances of periphrastic *do* in fifteenth-century London merchants' letters were rather formulaic, and cannot perhaps be labelled as colloquial (cf. Richard Cely's use of *I do whell understand* on p. 199). It seems, therefore, that with periphrastic *do* the question of colloquial as opposed to literary origins, although useful in cases like *provided that*, may not be very illuminating. We will return to the issue below.

AFFIRMATIVE AND NEGATIVE *DO*

Periphrastic *do* clearly gains momentum in the sixteenth century, and interestingly affirmative statements (its least typical context today) also seem to have played a significant role in the process. In effect, it looks as though *do* had the makings of being generalized to all sentence types in Tudor English, had not something interfered with its progress in affirmative statements. Earlier research suggests that in the sixteenth century the rise of *do* was being led by interrogatives or questions, as in George Colville's 'And **doest** thou think that such thynges as suffisaunce, and power be, are to be dispysed, or contrarye wyse, that they be most worthy reuerence aboue all thinges' (from his 1556 translation of Boethius ([BOETHCO] 68–69)). This was followed by negative declaratives, and, at a somewhat slower pace, by the use of *do* in affirmative declaratives such as 'I **did** mislike the Queenes Mariage' from Sir Nicholas Throckmorton's confession of treason in 1554, which will be discussed below on p. 201–2. The non-use of *do* in interrogatives, and in negative interrogatives in particular, was already much rarer than question-forms which used *do*, although it could still be found, as the following example, from a 1521 sermon by John Fisher, Bishop of Rochester, illustrates: '**Seest** thou not his eyes, how they bee fylled with blood and bytter teares?' ([FISHER 1] 400).

However, the fact that affirmative statements are much more common in communication than negative statements, and especially questions, in fact serves to make affirmative *do* numerically the most frequent kind of periphrastic *do* in texts. We will therefore focus in the following sections on the rise of the periphrasis in affirmative and negative declaratives. Let us begin with affirmative *do* in the multigenre Helsinki Corpus. Figure 7.3 presents the average frequencies of *do* in affirmative statements between 1500 and 1710. The development clearly falls into two phases: the use of affirmative *do* first increases between the sixteenth and early seventeenth centuries, after which there is a dramatic decline in the latter half of the seventeenth century.[5]

Focusing on the usage of the sixteenth century, these findings could be interpreted to lend more support to the spoken associations of the periphrasis than to the division between colloquial and literary language. The genre with by far the highest average frequency of affirmative *do* in 1500–1570, for example, is trial records. While trials cannot of course be called colloquial, they certainly display features of interactive spoken discourse. The use of *do* is also very common in scientific and educational treatises, diaries, sermons, and comedies. By contrast, only a few instances are found in statutes, biographies, the Bible, private letters, travelogues, and histories.

The high incidence of affirmative *do* in trials in the corpus evidence is largely due to their clustering in long speeches in the 1554 trial of Sir Nicholas Throckmorton, a diplomat and MP accused of high treason. An extract from this appears on the following page; as can be seen, after the first appearance of *do* in line 1 in Throckmorton's confession that he '**did** mislike the Queenes Mariage with *Spain*', the

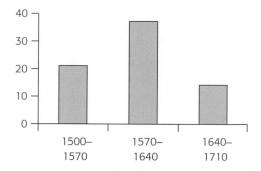

FIG. 7.3.   Periphrastic *do* in affirmative statements, 1500–1710

[5] Figs. 7.3, 7.5, and 7.6 are based on the individual genre scores normalized to 10,000 words provided by the data in Rissanen (1991: 325), Nurmi (1999*a*: 169), and Meurman-Solin (1993: 262–3), respectively. The figures show how many times *do* could, on average, be expected to appear in every 10,000 words of text in each period.

repetition of *do* is hardly emphatic or contrastive. Instead it could serve as a device to mark the relevance of the actions narrated by Throckmorton in response to the questions being put to him:

I confess I **did** mislike the Queenes Mariage with *Spain,* and also the comming of the *Spanyards* hither: and then me thought I had reason to doe so, for I **did** learne the Reasons of my misliking of you M. *Hare,* M. *Southwell,* and others in the Parliament House; there I **did** see the whole Consent of the Realm against it; and I a Hearer, but no
5   Speaker, **did** learne my misliking of those Matters, confirmed by many sundry Reasons amongst you. (1554, *State Trials* [THROCKM I] 66, C1–C2)

The other genres with high frequencies of affirmative *do* also display features of spoken interaction, such as first-person narration and references to the audience. A cluster of affirmative *do*'s can be found, for instance, in Robert Record's 1551 *First Principles of Geometrie,* in which he justifies to his readers the necessity of introducing one more category of circles:

Nowe haue you heard as touchyng circles, meetely sufficient instruction, so that it should seme nedeles to speake any more of figures in that kynde, saue that there **doeth** yet remaine ij. formes of an imperfecte circle, for it is lyke a circle that were brused, and thereby **did** runne out endelong one waie, whiche forme Geometricians **dooe** call an *egge*
5   *forme,* because it **doeth** represent the figure and shape of an egge duely proportioned (as this figure sheweth) hauyng the one ende greater then the other. ([RECORD] B2R)

Corpora again enable us to trace change through time, and in 1570–1640 the use of affirmative *do* picks up in almost all HC genres. The only exceptions are comedies and, again, trials where its usage clearly declines despite the overall rising trend. This apparent deviation has been accounted for by the greater likelihood of the record of spoken language (together with the imitation of this in drama), reflecting changes which were indeed taking place at this time in real spoken interaction. By the last period covered by the HC, 1640–1710, a rapid decline can also be seen in these patterns of usage across the rest of the genres too. Nevertheless, and despite this general pattern, non-emphatic affirmative *do* was to persist well into the eighteenth century in many written genres.

In contrast, *do* continued to advance in negative declaratives in this last HC period, but the process was not completed by the end of the seventeenth century. This is evident if we list all negative declarative sentences with *not* in the HC, and compare the number of instances which contain *do* (as in *I do not mean*) with the corresponding simple finite verb forms which are used without *do* (as in *I mean not*). Figure 7.4 presents the results, showing a steady increase in the use of *do* at the expense of the simple finite form.

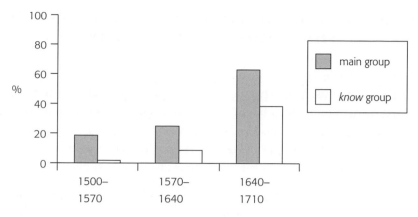

FIG. 7.4.   Periphrastic *do* in negative statements, 1500–1710
Source: Based on Nurmi (1999*a*: 146).

Just as in the earlier discussion of the shifts which can be observed over this time with reference to the singular third-person endings of verbs, the process of *do*-generalization in negative declaratives was partly one of lexical diffusion. A group of verbs called the *know*-group (including *know, doubt, mistake, trow* ('to believe'), and *wot* ('to know')) lagged behind the general development. *Do* only began to be associated with these verbs from the seventeenth century onwards. This development can also be observed in the CEEC. As a result, the *do*-less *I know not* which appears in the first extract below, taken from a 1547 letter from Queen Catherine Parr to Lord Admiral Seymour, is more typical of sixteenth-century usage than is the *I do not know* which we can see in the 1572 letter of the humanist and author of *The Arte of Rhetorique*, Thomas Wilson, to Bishop Parkhurst, and which is given in the second extract below:

My Lord where as ye charge me w*ith* apromys wryttin w*ith* myne one hand, to chaunge the two yeres into two monethes, I thynke ye have no suche playne sentence wrytten w*ith* my hand; I **knowe not** wether ye be aparaphryser or not, yf ye be lerned in that syence yt ys possyble ye may of one worde make ahole sentence … ([ORIGINAL 2] 152)

I do thinke if Mr. Mynne might haue but this moch, he wold be some what satisfied; and how your Lordship can of right denie this moch vnto hym, I **do not know.** ([PARKHURST] 107).

Overall, the correspondence evidence suggests that men generally used *do* more than women both in affirmative and negative statements in the late sixteenth century. However, the gender preference changed in both processes in the seventeenth century, as women took the lead in their divergent developments.

THE FALL OF AFFIRMATIVE DO

The correspondence corpus can also tell us more about the history of *do* in affirmative statements. More specifically, it may be used to date the time when its progress came to a halt, and a fall in its frequency began. As shown by Figure 7.3, corpus data suggest that the use of affirmative *do* reached its peak between 1570 and 1640. By contrast, earlier findings (based on a less controlled genre selection) date the beginning of its fall to the 1570s. In a case like this, diachronic comparisons will be easier to make if they are drawn from genres that can be sampled at shorter intervals. Figure 7.5 presents the development during the crucial period in the correspondence corpus. As this indicates, the CEEC evidence suggests that affirmative *do* was used very frequently in the first two decades before 1600, but that its use plummeted during the first decade of the seventeenth century. *Do* did not recover from this drop but continued to be used at this much more moderate level in the following decades.

But, importantly, there were also regional differences in the use of *do*. If we compare Nurmi's (1999) findings on London, the Royal Court, East Anglia, and the north (see the Further Reading for this chapter), we can see that in the two decades before 1600 affirmative *do* was very common among East Anglian writers and those resident at Court, or attached to it, as indeed in Queen Elizabeth's usage in the following example from 1592: 'Wel, I wyl pray for you, that God wyl unseal your yees, that to long haue bin shut, and **do** require you thinke that none shal more joy therat than myselfe' ([ROYAL 1] 70). It was also commonly attested

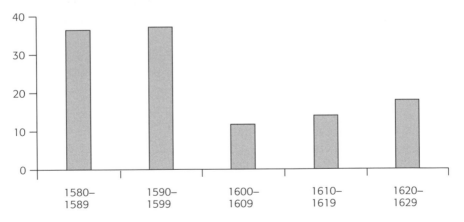

FIG. 7.5.   Periphrastic *do* in affirmative statements in personal letters, 1580–1630
Source: Based on Nurmi (1999*a*: 169; see note 5).

in the correspondence of Londoners. Philip Henslow, the London theatrical manager, can be used to provide a good illustration here, in his letter to Edward Alleyn from 1598:

ther is nothinge ther to be hade but good wordes wch trvbelles my mynd very mvche for my losse you knowe is very mvche to me J **did** move my ladey edmones in yt & she very onerabley vssed me for she weant presentley & moved the quene for me ... ([HENSLOWE] 98)

In the north, use of the periphrasis was less frequent than it was in London at this time. Nevertheless, while an upward trend continued in the north (and also especially in East Anglia) for some time after 1600, in London, and at Court this pattern of usage came to an abrupt end. A similar but more modest drop was found with negative *do*. Why should this drop have occurred in the capital after 1600? One would have expected *do* to continue to rise as it did in East Anglia. One motive might have been contact with Scots in the capital following the arrival of King James and the Scottish court in London after the death of Queen Elizabeth in 1603. The timing would match the date of change, and the new ruler and his officers must have enjoyed high prestige in the metropolis at the time. This contact hypothesis is attractive but more work is, of course, called for to confirm it.

If we turn to the evidence on northern English dialects and Older Scots, it becomes clear that affirmative *do* was indeed a latecomer in these regions. It is not attested at all in the fifteenth-century texts which are included in the Helsinki Corpus of Older Scots, but it spread through the language at a slow pace during the sixteenth and early seventeenth centuries. The process is traced in Figure 7.6. This nevertheless confirms that, by the latter half of the seventeenth century, affirmative *do* had reached the same average frequency as it had in the southern

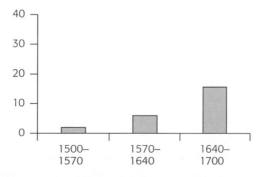

FIG. 7.6.   Periphrastic *do* in affirmative statements in Older Scots, 1500–1700
Source: Based on the data in Meurman-Solin (1993: 262–3).

British English data from the same period of time (cf. Fig. 7.3). Incidentally, the middle period, 1570–1640, shows roughly the same average level of *do*-use as does the London and the Royal Court in the English data after 1600.

In the selection of thirteen prose genres which are included in the Scots corpus, it is mid-sixteenth century pamphlets, such as William Lamb's *Ane Resonyng of ane Scottis and Inglis Merchand betuix Rowand and Lionis* of 1550 (an extract of which is given below), which first display some instances of affirmative *do*. The rise of this device in pamphlets may be connected with both Latinate rhetoric and southern influence:

Eftir the refusale to restore þe thre or four aikiris of mure, commissionaris of baith þe realmes **did** proclame þat guid ordour suld be keipit and obseruit, as wes accustummat for guid reule on þe bordouris, and siclik Lord Maxwell, Warden of þe Scottis West Merchis, **did** proclame guid ordour. ([LAMB] 47).

However, as Figure 7.6 indicates, the frequency of affirmative *do* rises slowly towards the end of the seventeenth century in Scots, becoming particularly common in trials and educational treatises. The clustering of *do* in the passage below (cited from the 1688 trial of Philip Standsfield for the murder of his father Sir James Standsfield is reminiscent of the cluster in the Throckmorton trial which was discussed on pp. 201–2:

... he **did** attempt to assassinat, and offered violence to his fathers person, and **did** chase and pursue him upon the King's high way at *Lothian-burn*, and **did** fire Pistols upon his father. And likewayes upon one or other of the dayes, of one or other of the moneth of one or other of the years of God above specified, he **did** attempt to assassinat his father
5 for his life, at *Culterallors*, and **did** fire Pistols upon him. ([STANDSFIELD] 4–5)

In general, literary evidence suggests that the *do*-periphrasis was established in Scots later than in southern English in other sentence types, too. With some dialectal exceptions, contemporary Scots follows general English usage.

LINGUISTIC MOTIVES FOR-*DO*

As affirmative *do* has attracted a great deal of scholarly interest over the years, there are numerous suggestions as to the motives which triggered its use in texts. But we should not forget that, while affirmative *do* is more frequent in texts than is *do* in the other sentence types (i.e. interrogatives and negatives), when we think of absolute numbers, it is obvious that, even in its peak period, it does not occur in the majority of affirmative finite clauses. Queen Elizabeth's use of affirmative *do*, for example, occupies the middle range with less than one *do* in every ten clauses that have no other auxiliary.

We can, for example, see that syntactic conditions motivate the introduction of *do* to negative declaratives and to clauses which involve inversion such as interrogatives: in these contexts, it provides a carrier for the tense, mood, and polarity of the clause when no other auxiliary is present. This is, of course, also true of affirmative *do*. However, many scholars argue that the appearance of *do* in affirmative declaratives in the sixteenth century was not so much to do with syntax—that is, with introducing an auxiliary to all sentence types. Instead they suggest that the influence of textual and stylistic factors which operate in response to certain structural features (constraints) in the clause could have been more important. These are related to structural complexity and ease of information flow. An adverbial separating the subject from the verb, for instance, makes the clause harder for the reader to parse. Inserting *do* into a context like this can facilitate it.

Looking at the first extract below, from George Colville's 1556 Boethius translation, structural reasons for introducing *do* are worth considering. Both instances of *do* here occur in relative clauses, and the second one in particular has several structurally marked features: the subject (*thou*) is separated from the two clause-final verbs (*defyne or detemine*) by an adverbial (*a litel before*). The clause would have become awkward to pronounce with simple past-tense forms of these verbs (**defynedst or determinedst*). In her own translation of forty years later (which appears as the second extract below), Queen Elizabeth does not use *do*-support, but neither does she relativize the second clause. She makes do with a single verb, which she puts in the perfect, and her adverbial phrase comes after the verb:

In the which I **do** iudge to inquyre fyrste, whether anye suche perfit good (as the same that thou a litel before **dyddyst** defyne or determine) myght be in the nature of thyngs, that no vayne imaginacion or shadowe deceyue vs, and put vs out of the trewth of the thynge or matter, that we be aboute to talke of. ([BOETHCO] 73)

In which first this I think to be inquyrd of, whither any such good ther be, as thou **hast defynd** a lyttle afore, among natures woorkes, leste a vayne imagination of thought deceaue us wyde from the truthe of that we talke of. ([BOETHEL] 61)

In the HC, features conducive to structural complexity were found in a large number of affirmative statements with *do*, especially in typical written genres. But this was not the case with typical spoken genres such as trials, which displayed few instances of these structurally marked uses.

In some cases, affirmative *do* could also assume an emphatic function, confirming or contradicting something. As we have seen, for example, on p. 202, Sir Nicholas Throckmorton was answering the charges made against him and admitted that some of them had not been unfounded, hence his use of *do* in 'I confess I **did** mislike the Queenes Mariage'. It may of course not always be easy to distinguish emphatic from non-emphatic instances of *do* in writing. But as suggested above when Throckmorton's trial was discussed, from these clause-level considerations it is but a short step to marking information relevant to the discourse topic. This is how the clustering of *do* in trials may be understood—just like in the modern example on smoking which was discussed on p. 198. In sum, affirmative *do* clearly proves a useful multi-purpose device in Tudor English. Comparing the seventeenth-century with present-day corpora, we also see that despite the declining numbers, there was more use for it in Stuart English than we have for it today.

IN CONCLUSION

Language change does not happen overnight or spread uniformly throughout the country across the whole social spectrum. In this chapter we have seen that even the most familiar aspects of the English language are the result of quite intricate processes of change. The modern standard variety of English largely displays features of southern (East Midland) origin, but it also contains elements that originated in the north. The verbal ending -(*e*)*s* is one of them. It first gained ground in everyday speech and informal writings, and only made its way to formal contexts with some considerable delay. The auxiliary *do*, by contrast, shows that a change need not always proceed to completion. The spread of *do* to affirmative statements was well under way in Tudor English but, unlike its continued use in questions and negative statements, the process suddenly came to a halt. Here too, dialect contact may have had a role in shaping the supra-local variety which came to be seen as the standard.

Gender differences also play a role in ongoing changes. Both today and in the past, it is usually women who more readily than men adopt incoming forms spreading across the language community. This was the case, for instance, with the third-person -(*e*)*s* ending. Many grammatical features that became the property of Tudor English were first promoted by women. Obvious exceptions to this gender advantage were changes that came from the learned and literary domains of language use. As observed in Chapter 8, the first monolingual English dictionary, Cawdrey's hard-word dictionary (1604), was compiled for the use of 'Ladies, Gentlewomen, or any other vnskilfull persons'.

When a language change is in progress, people use both old and new forms. Analysing these forms in context tells us more about the ways in which speakers and writers make use of the variants available to them. Some have linguistic constraints, such as -(e)s and do, which diffuse to certain words later than to others. Others are primarily socially determined. The spread of you at the expense of thou illustrates a deferential practice being adopted in the private sphere. As forms of address are not fixed but can be negotiated, the social status and roles of the writer and the addressee were at issue throughout this process.

In conclusion, if we wish to find out where language changes come from and how they progress through the language community, we need to compare texts from the same time period representing different genres and dialect areas, as well as texts produced by both women and men. Ideally, we should have data from all social ranks, but unfortunately this is not the case in the Tudor period. Because of their poor or, in many cases, non-existent writing skills, the voices of the lower-ranking people have only been recorded in trials and imitated in drama, and women are less well represented than men. This is one reason why we shall never know everything that happened in Tudor English. But a good deal can be learnt from the data sources that have come down to us when they are organized into corpora as structured collections of digitized texts.

References, Corpus Resources, and Further Reading

The historical corpora discussed in this chapter are available for educational and research purposes through ICAME (the International Computer Archive of Modern and Medieval English; <http://helmer.aksis.uib.no/icame.html>) and the Oxford Text Archive (<http://ota.ahds.ac.uk/>): the Helsinki Corpus of English Texts (HC), the Helsinki Corpus of Older Scots (HCOS), and a sampler version of the Corpus of Early English Correspondence (CEECS). The copyright on the texts included in the corpora is retained by their publishers or editors, and the copyright on the corpus collections by their compilers, both specified in the accompanying electronic manuals, which also give full references to the texts.

More information about the HC is given in the corpus manual, Kytö (1996), and about the Early Modern English texts in the HC by Nevalainen and Raumolin-Brunberg (1993). For the HCOS, see Meurman-Solin (1993, 1995). The CEEC is introduced by Nevalainen and Raumolin-Brunberg (2003), and its sampler version, CEECS, by Nurmi (1999*b*). Rissanen (2000*b*) and Meurman-Solin (2001) provide recent overviews of the growing number of English historical corpora.

A couple of examples from drama have been cited from the commercially available Chadwyck-Healey Literature Online database (LION), and are listed in the references, and one from the London-Lund Corpus of Spoken English (LLC), which is available through the ICAME and the Oxford Text Archive.

The story of -(e)th and -(e)s

For earlier studies on -(*e*)*s* and -(*e*)*th* variation in the history of English, see the references in Kytö (1993). LALME gives the various Middle English spellings of the two forms. A much cited early philological work is Holmqvist (1922). For a discussion of modern uses of -*eth* as pseudo archaism, see Minugh (1999: 295–7). The examples of modern regional uses of zero-inflexion on p. 184 are taken from Trudgill (1999*b*: 102).

-(e)s from the north

See Kytö (1993: 120) for further discussion of the HC genres and the patterns of -(*e*)*s* use. See Moore (2002*b*) for the language of the Plumpton family. Kytö (1993: 124) is the source of the data analysis of -(*e*)*s* use in the second HC period (1570–1640). The information on -(*e*)*s* in the CEEC data is taken from Nevalainen and Raumolin-Brunberg (2003: 220, 215). Wareing (1980) provides a good analysis of immigration patterns into London which may have influenced the fifteenth-century use of -(*e*)*s* in the capital.

-(e)th from the south

Moore (2002*b*) again provides valuable information on northern writers in this context, with specific reference to the Plumpton family; for Scots use of -*eth*, and the evidence of the HCOS, see Meurman-Solin (1993: 250–2).

Linguistic motives for -(e)s

For the metrical utility of -*eth*/ -(*e*)*s* alternation, see Taylor (1987: 350). The views of John Hart and other early commentators are discussed in Danielsson (1963, II: 174–6) and in Dobson (1968, II: 881–4).

You and thou

The second-person pronouns *you* and *thou* are discussed in most histories of English. Two recent corpus-based approaches to the topic are Busse's (2002) monograph on

Shakespeare's use of the two pronouns and Nevala's (2004) work on terms of address in personal correspondence from the fourteenth to the eighteenth century. For trials, see Nevalainen (1994), and for letter-writing formulae, see Austin (1973). For the continued regional use of *thou*, see Trudgill (1999*b*: 92–3), and also Chapter 11 in this volume. See Nevalainen (1991: 316) for the use of relevant verbal forms in liturgical prose.

The story of do

The debate on the origins of the *do*-periphrasis is summarized by Rissanen (1991: 334–8), and Denison (1993: 255–91). Denison (1993: 446–71) gives a state-of-the-art account of studies on *do* until the early 1990s; see also Stein (1990) and Nurmi (1999*a*). Ellegård (1953) is a classic in the field, based on an extensive collection of texts. See Tieken-Boon van Ostade (1987) for an examination of its use in eighteenth-century English. The examples of modern regional use on p. 198 are taken from Thomas (1994: 135).

Origins of do

See Denison (1993: 267) for further discussion of usage in the fifteenth century. The analysis of the regional data in the CEEC is based on Nurmi (1999*a*: 77–97).

Affirmative and negative do

Ellegård (1953: 162) provides an earlier examination of the diffusion of *do*. For the language of the Throckmorton trial in this context, see further Rissanen (1991: 326–7).

The fall of affirmative do

For earlier assumptions, based on a mixed database, about the decline of affirmative *do*, see Ellegård (1953: 162). Nurmi (1999*a*: 177) provides specific details of regional differences in distribution; the hypothesis that the change was influenced by contact phenomena after the Union of the Crowns in 1603 can be found in Nurmi (1999*a*: 178). McClure (1994: 72) describes modern Scots usage with reference to affirmative *do*.

Linguistic motives for do

For relevant patterns of usage in the letters of Queen Elizabeth I, see Nurmi (1999*a*: 63); for a corresponding analysis of usage in spoken genres such as trials, see Rissanen (1991: 332).

8

THE BABEL OF RENAISSANCE ENGLISH

Paula Blank

THE early modern period in England saw the first systematic attempts to create, or recreate, a universal language, a 'perfect' tongue. Significantly, the declared motive behind the numerous universal languages designed and advanced in the seventeenth century was to 'remedy Babel', to level the diversity of human vernaculars and, on a national level, to undo a perceived confusion with English itself by reconstructing or inventing a common language. Many scholarly histories of the English language have often appeared to have the same, implicit aim—pre-emptively to 'fix' the problem of linguistic diversity within early modern England. And it *was* considered a problem. Long accounted the ancient source of national, racial, and linguistic differences, the 'curse' of Babel was newly construed in the sixteenth and seventeenth centuries as a contemporary phenomenon, not just the legacy of a Biblical past, but a consequence of new, 'multicultural' developments with the vernacular. An influx of foreign words and a habit of creating new English words out of foreign elements made the early modern vernacular lexicon a 'hotch-pot' of native and alien forms. The present chapter aims to remedy the insularity of studies that focus on the rise of a standard, national language in late Renaissance England by reconstructing what Renaissance writers deemed the 'Babel' of early modern English.

This chapter will therefore survey Renaissance 'Englishes'—not the standard language of early modern vernacular writing, but the variety of regional and social dialects which came to be represented in that writing. The 'King's English' (the phrase is attributed to the reign of Henry V (1413–22)) was not yet a sovereign domain of language, establishing one, accepted 'rule' for speech or writing; rather, Renaissance English was 'broken' or divided by divergent, local forms—from southern English to northern English, elite social dialects and underworld language, to specialized terms of the trades. As thousands of foreign words, newly coined words, and revivals of obsolete words were introduced and assimilated into English in this period, writers further contested the boundaries of the native tongue.

The idea that English was 'confused' spans the period from the Middle Ages to the middle of the seventeenth century. Anxieties about English, as Chapter 4 has already discussed, preoccupied a range of writers in Middle English. And as Jeremy Smith has demonstrated in Chapter 5, these did not cease with the advent of printing. Instead, Caxton in *The Description of Britayne, & also Irlonde taken oute of Polichronicon* (1480) specifically described the difficulties he faced in attempting to choose among available varieties of spoken English as the basis for his printed texts and translations. Noting the 'diuerse englissh in the reame of englond', he observed that 'a man of kente, Southern western, & northern men speken frenssh all lyke in soune & speche, but they can not speke theyr englissh so'. As in his Prologue to the *Eneydos* of 1490 (which has already been discussed on pp. 122–3), Caxton records the way that regional diversity divided the nation into mutually unintelligible tongues. Caxton's 'good wyf', as we have seen (see p. 122–3), thus mistakes another regional English dialect as 'French'—that is, as a foreign language altogether. Alongside regionalized lexis (such as *egges* or *eyren*, both of which signified 'eggs' depending upon geographical location), Caxton includes 'curyous termes' or neologisms, and 'the olde and auncyent englysshe' (which looked to him 'more lyke to dutche than englysshe') among the 'Englishes' which he has to choose among. All provided further examples of 'strange' or alien terms within the national language.

George Puttenham's *Arte of English Poesie* (1589) reveals a similar engagement with the problem of diversity. Attempting to prescribe the 'region' of English that was suitable for formal writing, he places both northern and western speech outside the bounds of his selected norm, which is (as Chapter 5 has noted) given as 'the vsuall speach of the Court'. Socially defined varieties of English such as the 'speach of a craftes man or carter, or other of the inferiour sort, though he be inhabitant or bred in the best towne and Citie in this Realme' are, as we have seen, also deemed unacceptable in English writing, as are archaisms ('for their language is now out of vse with vs') and new coinages ('inkhorne termes so ill affected'). Despite Puttenham's strictures, however, these and other 'strange' words were in fact to proliferate in the written English of Renaissance England—even in (and sometimes especially in) literature. This 'broken English' of his contemporaries led the grammarian Alexander Gil to describe them as

'Englishmen not speaking English and not understood by English ears' in his *Logonomia Anglica*, originally written in Latin in 1619. Half-way through the seventeenth century, the lexicographer Thomas Blount declares that the 'Babel' of the vernacular made England a 'self-stranger' nation—one growing alien to itself through this diversity of available forms. He dedicates his dictionary of 1656 to the cause of having 'English Englished'. Arguably, in this context it is not the rise of a standard variety of language, but a new awareness of dialect and variability of discourse—the 'self-stranger' English of the Renaissance—that best defines the linguistic culture of early modern England.

REGIONS OF RENAISSANCE ENGLISH

Although, as previous chapters have noted, medieval authors such as Chaucer observed regional differences among speakers of English, the first programmatic accounts of the dialects of English appear in the sixteenth century. The earliest recorded use of the word *dialect*, referring to a kind of language, dates from 1577, according to the *OED*. John Bullokar's *An English Expositor* (1616) is the first vernacular dictionary to include the term:

Dialect. a difference of some words, or pronunciation in any language: as in England the *Dialect* or manner of speech in the North, is different from that in the South, and the Western Dialect differing from them both. ... So euery countrey hath commonly in diuers parts thereof some difference of language, which is called the Dialect of that place.

The poet and antiquary Richard Carew in his treatise on the *Excellencie of the English Tongue* (*c*1595) commends his native vernacular not only on the grounds that it is 'copious' in having borrowed so richly from other languages, but also because of 'the diuersitie of our Dialects, for wee haue Court and wee haue Countrey English, wee haue Northeine, and Southerne, grosse and ordinarie'. But Carew is unusual in this estimation of the 'Countrey' dialects. For most Renaissance writers, like Puttenham, the 'excellency' of English did not inhere in the variety of its dialects but—far more narrowly—in just one of them. As the historian and chorographer William Harrison, on p. 416 of his *Description of England* (1587), concurs, '[T]his excellency of the English tongue is found in one, and the south, part of this island'. For those, like Puttenham and Harrison, who favoured the centralization—and unification—of English in and around the language spoken at Court, locating 'southern', 'northern', and 'western' dialects was more than a matter of mapping the site of linguistic differences. It was about distinguishing the 'best' English from its inferiors, 'true' English from the confusion of 'Englishes' which could be heard around the nation. Although in the early seventeenth century dialect was, as in Bullokar's *Expositor*, chiefly defined in terms of regionality, notions of social 'place'—the status of speakers in relation to one another—were also implicit in these earliest linguistic geographies. In the process of demarcating the differences among the dialects of English, the Renaissance also served to establish the modern alliance between language and cultural authority.

THE 'WESTERN' DIALECT

'Southern', 'northern', and 'western' were the broad domains under which early modern writers typically distinguished the regions of Renaissance English. Renaissance writers commonly portray western English as the most foreign of English dialects, at least when seen from the standpoint of an elite social class. As Gil in 1619 writes:

Of all the dialects the Western has the most barbarous flavour, particularly if you listen to the rustic people from Somerset, for it is easily possible to doubt whether they are speaking English or some foreign language.

Although aristocrats as prominent as Sir Walter Raleigh were said to have spoken with a broad Devonshire accent (and may indeed have helped introduce westernisms into the language at court), the dialect of the south-western shires in its grammar, lexis, as well as its phonology, was generally viewed, as the poet and playwright Thomas Randolph in the fourth act of his *The Muses' Looking Glass* (1638) put it as a 'discourse [that] is all country; an extreme of [i.e. from] Urbanity'. When Ben Jonson chose the western dialect as the primary language for his last completed play, *A Tale of a Tub* (performed 1633, published 1640), he did so in order to place it at the furthest remove from the Court:

> No State-affaires, nor any politique Club,
> Pretend wee in our Tale, here, of a Tub.
> But acts of Clownes and Constables, to day
> Stuffe out the Scenes of our ridiculous Play.
> ...
> .... to shew what different things
> The Cotes of Clownes, are from the Courts of Kings.
>
> (Prologue, 1–4; 11–12)

In general, the western dialect, at least when seen from the perspective of London writers, represents the untranslatable difference—regional, social, intellectual—between courtiers and rustic 'clowns'.

As 'heard' by speakers of the 'King's English,' the signature features of western English included pronunciations which were broadly characteristic of Somerset, Devon, and Cornwall, although south-eastern elements—from Kent and its neighbouring shires—sometimes get mixed up in representations of this dialect as well. These features include the voicing of the consonants [f] and [s] to [v] and [z] respectively; the first-person pronoun *ich* (rather than *I*), and the contractions *icham, chill, chwas* ('I am', 'I will', 'I was'). Other typical markers include the prefix *i* or *y* with past participles, as in *yvound* ('found'), and the ending -*th* in the third person plural of the present indicative. Some lines from Shakespeare's *King Lear* (spoken by the exiled aristocrat Edgar in his disguise as a poor rustic) may serve to illustrate this dialect and its literary stereotyping:

Chill not let go, zir, without vurther [cagion] … Good gentlemen, go your gait, and let poor voke pass. An chud ha' bin zwagger'd out of my life, 'twould not ha' bin zo long as 'tis by a vortnight. (IV.vi. 235, 237–9)

Such forms are far removed—geographically as well as in their social implications—from those habitually used by Edgar earlier in the play. For westerners, of course, it was conversely the language of the aristocracy that could sound like a strange or foreign tongue: Columel, a simple plowman in the Tudor genealogist John Ferne's *Blazon of Gentrie* (1586), reacts to courtly diction by declaring: 'By my vathers soule … I like not this gibberishe' (2.23).

In one of *Scoggin's Jests* (*c*1565), attributed to the physician and writer Andrew Boorde, Scoggin tries to teach a poor western youth how to read and write:

The slovenly boy, almost as big as a knave, would begin to learne his A.B.C. Scogin did give him a lesson of nine of the first letters of A.B.C., and he was nine daies in learning of them; and when he had learned the nine … the good scholler said: am Ich past the worst now? … would God Ich were, for dis is able to comber any man's wits alive. Scogin then thought his scholler would never bee but a foole, and did apply him as well as he could to his learning; but he, that hath no wit, can never have learning nor wisedome.

Here the forms *ich* and *dis* mark the regional origins of Scoggin's 'scholler', as does *comber*, a contraction of *encumber*. According to Boorde, the dialect speaker can barely command an alphabet of nine letters, an abridged language that marks the limits of his intellectual powers (and which serves as a clear illustration of the growing—and stereotypical—alliance of dialect and images of cognitive deficiency). John Redford, in his mid-century play *Wit and Science*, includes, for example, a western dialect speaker among his allegorical characters who is named, simply, 'Ingnorance'. Even when asked his name, Ingnorance can only say, 'Ich cannot tell'. The anonymous *Contention between Liberality and Prodigality* (1602) makes western English the language of the labouring classes of the nation in general, whose representative in the drama announces his social role in Act II (2.4.448–9) as follows: 'Che dig, che delue, che zet, che zow,/ Che mow, che reape, che ply my flaile'—or, translated into the standard (and non-localized) variety: 'I dig, I delve, I set, I sow,/ I mow, I reap, I ply my flaile'. Nicholas Udall's court interlude *Respublica* (1553) likewise includes a character who is named, simply, 'People'. Representing, as he states, 'the poor Commontie' of the nation, People further identifies himself in Act III (III.iii.648–52) as poor, *ignoram* ('ignorant'), and oppressed:

> Lett poore volke ha zome parte,
> vor we Ignoram people, whom itche doe perzente,
> wer ner zo I-polde, zo wrong, and zo I-torment.
> Lorde Ihese Christe whan he was I-pounst & I-pilate,
> was ner zo I-trounst as we have been of yeares Late.

> ('Let poor folk have some part,
> For we ignorant people, whom I do represent,
> Were never so plundered, so wronged, and so tormented.
> Lord Jesus Christ when he was pounced upon [may alternatively
> mean 'struck' or 'perforated,' like metal or glass] and
> pilated [i.e. persecuted and scourged by Pontius Pilate]
> Was never so trounced [beaten, punished] as we have been of years late')

As 'foreign' as the western dialect seemed (or was made to seem) to southern audiences, it was, also imagined to be a kind of national *vox populi*—a 'common' language of the English 'People.'

When Boorde, on p. 123 of his *Fyrst Boke of the Introduction of Knowledge* (1542), describes the languages of Cornwall, he explains that 'In Cornwall is two speches; the one is *naughty Englyshe*, and the other is Cornyshe speche' (emphasis added). The idea that regional dialect is a kind of 'naughty' or corrupted English is implicit in most Renaissance representations of provincial language. Western speakers, for example, are often ascribed a tendency towards malapropisms—that is, to mistaking or misusing words, once again reifying the prevalent stereotypes of 'ignorance' and 'uneducatedness' which have already been discussed. Thomas Wilson in his *Arte of Rhetorique* (1553), for instance, mocks a western speaker's attempts to use Latinate diction by assuming the terms which were fashionable at the universities and court:

When I was in Cambrige, and student in the kynges College, there came a man out of the toune, with a pinte of wine in a pottle pot, to welcome the provost of that house, that lately came from the court. And because he would bestow his present like a clerke, dwellyng emong the schoolers: he made humbly his thre curtesies, and said in this maner. Cha good even my good lorde, and well might your lordship vare: Understandyng that your lordeship was come, and knowyng that you are a worshipfull Pilate, and kepes a *bominable* house ... Here the simple man beyng desirous to amende his mothers tongue, shewed hymself not to bee the wisest manne, that ever spake with tongue. (239–30) (emphasis added)

While forms such as *cha* in line 5 identify the regional origins of the 'simple man,' *bominable* in line 8 (an aphetic form of 'abominable') is just a mistake (it is not clear what he was hoping to say—perhaps something like *dominical*, with reference to the Latin, *dominus*, lord). Nevertheless, the connection that Wilson, among many others, draws between regional dialect and malapropism is an important one, for the implication is that provincial language too is an English deformed by the incapacity of its speakers.

Richard Carew, the one, true, early modern champion of regional English, whatever the region, was also the only Renaissance writer to celebrate western English as an 'antiquity' of the nation. According to Carew, the English spoken in Cornwall was actually the oldest, purest surviving descendant of an original English. Western dialect words like *pridy* ('handsome'), *scrip* ('escape'), *thew* ('threaten'), *shune* ('strange') may sound 'broad and rude', he explains, but they 'plead in their defence not only the prescription of antiquity but also the title of propriety and the benefit of significancy, for most of them take their source from the Saxon, our natural language' (1602: 127–8). But most of Carew's contemporaries were not convinced that the King's English owed anything to the provinces. Indeed, they barely recognized the people's English—however indigenous, however common—as English at all.

THE 'NORTHERN' DIALECT

Carew (1602) suggested that the western dialect might one day be restored to its former status—that its terms 'want but another Spenser to make them passable'. In invoking Spenser, Carew was making reference to the way that a Renaissance courtly poet had elevated the status of another regional dialect—the dialect of the northern shires—by incorporating its terms into the composite poetic diction of works such as *The Shepheardes Calender*. Although the northern dialect, like western English, was often set apart as marginal, both geographically and socially, to a dominant or elite culture, some sixteenth- and early seventeenth-century writers also deemed it 'passable' within the bounds of a national language.

Renaissance representations of northern English are generally more elaborate than those of the western dialect, involving a greater variety of linguistic markers. Some of the more typical features—again, as 'heard' (and duly represented) by southerners—include the use of *a* for *o* in words like *ane* ('one'), *bath* ('both'), and *fra* ('from'). This is especially common before the cluster *ng*, as in *wrang*, *amang*, and *lang*. The sound represented orthographically by *ae* or *ea* also often replaces the regionally unmarked *o*, as in *frae* ('from'), *wae* ('woe'), and *heame* ('home'). Before *n*, however, *o* usually appears instead of *a* (*ony*, *mony*). The vowel represented by *oo* in *good* or *book* occurs as *u* (*gude*, *buke*). With consonants, typical phonological markers include the metathesis (or transposition) of *r* in words like *brast* ('burst') and *brunt* ('burned'), forms such as *sic* with the velar plosive /k/, (rather than southern *such* with its final affricate); similar were *whilke* (rather than *which*), *kirk* (rather than *church*), and *carl* (rather than *churl*). Typical too was the loss of final consonants, as in *sel* for *self*. Common morphological cues include the first- and second-person singular forms of the verb *to be*, in *I is* (or *I'se*) and *thou is* (or *thou's*). Finally, the northern lexicon includes words such as *barn* ('child'), *bonny*, *deft* ('neat', 'trim'), *derne* ('dismal'), *dight* ('to prepare, arrange'), *gang* ('to go'), *gar* ('to make, cause'), *gif* ('if'), *mickle* ('much'), *mun* ('must'), and *til* ('to'). The following passage from William Warner's *Albion's England* (first part, 1586, S.24) illustrates some of these features:

> Roben hood, liell Iohn, frier Tucke,   *little*
> And Marian, deftly play,
> And lard and ladie gang till kirke
> with lads and lasses gay:
> Fra masse and eensong sa gud cheere
> And glee on ery greene.   *every*
>
>   (5.24)

Seen from the viewpoint of the capital and the court, northern English was in many ways indistinguishable, in social if not in formal linguistic terms, from the western dialect. Both were, in this sense, provincial languages, specimens of 'extreme' speech. Comedy thus often prevails in early modern representations of northern provincialism. The antiquarian Richard Verstegan in his *Restitution of Decayed Intelligence in Antiquities* (1605), for example, tells an anecdote about a London courtier who orders a northern man to 'equippe' his horse. The northerner, confounded by both the Londoner's pronunciation and his lexis, believes that the courtier desires him to 'whip' the animal. *Equip*, in the sense 'to furnish for service' is, as the *OED* records, not attested before the late sixteenth century, and the comedy here may well also turn on the incomprehension of the northern speaker in the face of a fashionable French usage which had not yet diffused throughout the country. The playwrights Thomas Heywood and Richard Brome, in *The Late Lancashire Witches* (1634), likewise chose to show their contemporaries how funny it would be—and also, perhaps, how dangerous—if northerners came to power. In the opening scene, a peasant, Lawrence, describes his new relationship with his former master:

He mainteynes me to rule him, and i'le deu't, or ma' the heart weary o' the weambe on him ... A fine World when a man cannot be whyet at heame.

(*i'le deu't*: I'll do it; *ma'*: may; *weambe*: womb; *whyet*: quiet)

The orthographic reformer John Hart, writing of those of the 'farre West, or North Countryes, which vse differing English termes from those of the Court, and London, where the flower of the English tongue is vsed', likewise expresses his fear of provincial power, especially where the language is concerned: '[I]f some such one come to any good learning ... and putteth some worke in print, his authoritie maketh many a rude English worde to be printed'. Hart's use of *rude* returns us, of course, to those negative stereotypes of dialect already discussed—its dominant sense at this time, as the *OED* confirms, signified the unlearned and ignorant, those lacking in knowledge or book-learning.

But northern England was also associated with its own, modest literary tradition, and one that potentially conferred the type of cultural and linguistic authority which Hart had denied to provincial dialects. Northern versions of certain medieval texts, like *Amis and Amiloun*, were still in circulation, and some of the poets who contributed to anthologies such as *Tottel's Miscellany* used a few northern terms in their poems. Nicholas Grimald, for example, in his verses on Latin epic, wrote of '[T]he famous woork, that Eneids hight,/The *naamkouth* Virgil hath set forth in sight' (1557: 13–14, emphasis added). In doing so, however, it is unlikely that Grimald was trying to strike a rustic note by his use of the dialect word *naamkooth* ('famous'). He probably thought such northernisms were 'old,' that is, he was confusing northern terms with archaisms or obsolete English words. By the middle of the sixteenth century, Renaissance language scholars had already hypothesized just such a relationship between old words and local expressions. In 1565, Lawrence Nowell began to compile the first Old English dictionary, the *Vocabularium Saxiconum*. Observing a resemblance between Anglo-Saxon vocabulary and terms that occurred exclusively in provincial speech, Nowell included in his dictionary 173 words from his home county, Lancashire, as well as a handful from other shires. Nowell noted northern survivals of older words as follows:

Adreoȝan.	To endure, to suffer, to abide. Lanc. to dree.
Ætwitan.	To blame, to reproache, to laye the fawte on. Lanc., to wite.
ȝeDaeft.	Clenlinesse. Lanc., deft.
Derian.	To hurt, to harme. Lanc., to deere.

As here, Nowell's pioneering work confirmed the idea that the rubble of northern English could be mined for fossils of the older language.

A careful philologist, Nowell made a significant contribution to English language study when he deduced that older elements of the language, long out of use in standard written English, sometimes survive in non-standard speech. But the enthusiasm of the earliest Saxonists generated the notion that northern English was the oldest of the regional dialects and therefore bore a privileged relation to the ancient language. While linguists such as Gil (1619) therefore continued to exclude regional language from the one, true English ('What I say here regarding the dialects ... refers only to country people, since among persons of genteel character and cultured upbringing, there is but one universal speech'), such prescriptions could at times be qualified by the possible exception of northern English. As Gil had earlier noted, 'the Northern dialect ... is the most delightful, the most ancient, the purest, and approximates most nearly to the speech of our ancestors'. In the Renaissance northern English was, as a result, regarded as a remote region of the vernacular but also, at times, as the most authentic, the most 'native' of dialects.

Towards the end of Ben Jonson's *Bartholomew Fair* (1631), a group of minor characters join together in a spirited game which they call 'vapours'. The specific object of this game, according to Jonson's stage directions, is 'Non sense. Euery man to oppose the last man that spoke: whether it concern'd him, or no.' The players include Puppy, a wrestler from southwestern England, Northern, a clothier from the northern shires, and Whit, an Irish bawd. The characters compete in their respective dialects:

Puppy:	Why, where are you, zurs? Do you vlinch, and leaue vs i' the zuds, now?
Northern:	I'le ne mare, I'is e'en as vull as a Paipers bag, by my troth, I.
Puppy:	Doe my Northerne cloth zhrinke i' the wetting? ha?
Knockem:	Why, well said, old Flea-bitten, thou'lt neuer tyre, I see.
Cutting:	No, Sir, but he may tire, if it please him.
Whit:	Who told dee sho? that he vuld neuer teer, man? (IV.iv.10–19)

Jonson recreates the urban fair as a contemporary Tower of Babel, where provincial languages cause a kind of comic oppositionality or 'confusion'. But the confrontation of regional 'Englishes' in the Renaissance was not always represented as a lot of 'nonsense'. Identifying the 'one universal speech' of the nation, and securing the site of the King's English, also depended on putting alternative Englishes in their place.

THE CLASSES OF RENAISSANCE ENGLISH

The 'new' English

The Renaissance saw the introduction some where between 10,000 and 25,000 new words into the language. Many were foreign loanwords; others were self-consciously 'invented' by writers attempting to enrich a vernacular widely held to be insufficient. Although the need for new words in early modern English was real enough, especially in fields such as medicine and law, which had previously been dominated by Latin and other foreign languages, linguistic innovation in the Renaissance generated a polemic well known as the 'inkhorn' controversy. The fundamental problem with neologisms was that, even granting their utility, they remained hard to interpret. Often derived from Latin roots and affixes, the use of 'inkhorn' terms such as *semicircle* (<Latin prefix *semi*, 'half', plus *circle*, long since nativized in English but originally from Latin *circulus*); *jurisprudence* (<Latin *jurisprudential* with anglicized suffix); or (speaking of a surplus of words) *loquacity* (<French *loquacité*—and, in turn, Latin *loquācitās*—with anglicized suffix), for example, depended on knowledge of the very language they were designed to translate and supersede. The Tudor logician Ralph Lever in his *Art of Reason, Rightly Termed Witcraft* of 1573, thus, in his section headed 'The Forespeache', compared a common man's apprehension of the Latinate term *predicate* with his own, invented 'native' equivalent, *backset*:

I wish you to aske of an english man, who vnderstandeth neither Greek nor Latin, what he conceiueth in his mind, when he heareth this word a backset, and what he doth conceiue when he heareth this terme a Predicate. And doubtlesse he must confesse, if he consider ye matter aright or haue any sharpnesse of wit at al, that by a backset, he conceiueth a thing that must be set after, and by a predicate, that he doth vnderstande nothing at all.

Ironically, however, Lever also felt it necessary to append a glossary of his 'native' coinings to his treatise, so that his readers might 'understand the meaning of

[my] newe deuised Termes'. Along with *Backsette*, Lever's glossary includes the following translations of Latin terms into native ones:

> a Foreset. Subiectum, antecedens.
> an hauing. habitus.
> a kinred. species, forma.
> a Saywhat. definitio.
> a Selfe thing, or a sole thing. Indiuiduum.
>
> a Wight. animal.
> a Yeasaye. affirmatio.

('A note to vnderstand the meaning of newe deuised Termes')

Examples of new words in early modern English which derived from Latin include *absurdity, conspicuous, contradictory, delirium, demonstrate, exotic, frivolous, insinuate, meditate*, and *obstruction*, along with a host of others that did not survive into modern English, such as *adnichilate* ('reduced to nothing'), *deruncinate* ('to weed'), *fatigate, illecebrous* ('delicate'), and *splendidious*. Inkhorn English, according to its detractors, turned the native language into a foreign tongue 'whiche the common people, for lacke of latin, do not vnderstand', as the translator Peter Ashton stated (1556 sig.vii.v)

Indeed, the new English was for many a 'counterfeit' English—that is, not really English at all. Thomas Wilson in 1553 thus indicts inkhorn language as 'outlandishe': 'Emong al other lessons, this should first be learned, that we never affect any straunge ynkehorne termes, but so speake as is commonly received ... Some seke so farre for outlandishe Englishe, that thei forget altogether their mothers language'. The court poet and playwright Samuel Daniel, in his *Defense of Rhyme* (1603), considers neologizing a form of cultural and linguistic treason (although perhaps it is also worth noting that Daniel's own usage of *audaciously* in the extract below depends on a recent coinage, a word taken from Latin and first recorded, according to the *OED*, in Shakespeare's *Love's Labour's Lost*):

We always <u>bewray</u> our selues to be both vnkinde and vnnatural to our owne natiue language, in disguising or forging strange or vnusuall wordes ... [to create] another kind of speach out of the course of our vsuall practise, displacing our wordes, or inuenting new ... And I cannot but wonder at the strange presumption of some men, that dare so audaciously aduenture to introduce any whatsoever forraine wordes, be they neuer so strange, and of themselues, as it were, without a Parliament, without any consent or allowance, establish them as Free-denizens in our language.

(*bewray*: reveal or betray)

Richard Verstegan agrees, emphasizing that Latinate terms and other foreign borrowings are 'unnatural' to English. Again (and precisely like Daniel), such 'unnatural' elements are nevertheless at times allowed into his own writing as, for instance, in his use of *derivation*, a French loanword which was recorded only from the sixteenth century in English:

For myne own parte, I hold them <u>deceaued</u> that think our speech bettered by the aboundance of our dayly borrowed woords, for they beeing of an other nature and not originally belonging to our language, do not neither can they in our toung, beare their natural and true deryuations: and therefore as wel may we fetch woords from the Ethiopians, or East or West Indians, and thrust them into our language and baptise all by the name of English, as those which wee dayly take from the Latin, or languages thereon depending: and heer-hence it cometh ... that some Englishmen discoursing together, others beeing present and of our own nation, and that naturally speak the English toung, are not able to vnderstand what the others say, notwithstanding they call it English that they speak.

(*deceaued*: deceived)

As we have already seen, new words are among several examples of 'strange' English, or dialects, whose merits are openly debated over the sixteenth and seventeenth centuries. But it is the practice of neologizing, above all, that exposes the ways in which the 'new' Englishes of the period cemented the relationship between dialect and social class or—in other words—how the distinction between 'usual' and unusual words, between those in the know and those 'unlearned' in specialized languages, served to stratify the native tongue. In the process of 'enriching' English, especially via Latin, inkhorn language advanced a 'foreign' English which was, above all, associated with an educated elite. While Latin writing was experiencing a cultural decline in the period in favour of the vernacular, the new English served to perpetuate the old class distinctions which were based, in part, on a privileged knowledge of classical languages.

That is why representations of inkhorn language throughout the Renaissance so often record the unsuccessful—and often comic—attempts of the uneducated to use it. John Hart (1570) describes the impact of neologism on his 'countrie' men:

Howbeit, I must confesse it [i.e. borrowing] beautifieth an Orators tale, which knoweth what he speaketh, and to whom: but it hindereth the vnlerned from vnderstanding of the matter, and causeth many of the Countrie men to speake chalke for cheese, and so nickname such straunge tearmes as it pleaseth many well to heare them: as to say for temperate, temporall: for surrender, sullender: for stature, statute: for abject, object.

It is of course possible that such widespread malapropism among the uneducated was a real phenomenon, a linguistic by-product of the new trade in words. Wilson (1553) observed it as well, relating the following anecdote:

[A poor man] standyng in muche nede of money, and desirous to have some helpe at a jentlemanns hand, made his complaint in this wise. I praie you sir be so good unto me, as forbeare this halfe yeres rent. For so helpe me God and halidome, we are so taken on with contrary Bishoppes, with revives, and with Southsides to the kyng, that al our money is cleane gone. These words he spake for contribucion, relief, and subsidie. And thus we see that poore simple men are muche troubled, and talke oftentymes, thei know not what, for lacke of wit and want of Latine and Frenche, wherof many of our straunge woordes full often are derived (330–1).

In Wilson's account, the poor man's 'want' is not only economic but linguistic; his malapropisms both announce and confirm his impoverishment. Wilson further cites (or composes) a letter by a 'Lincolnshireman' in search of patronage:

You knowe my literature, you knowe the pastorall promocion, I obtestate your clemencie, to invigilate thus muche for me, accordyng to my confidence, and as you know my condigne merites, for suche a compendious livyng (327–8).

It is not coincidental that neologisms are put to use by a man seeking a 'compendious livyng' from a patron. For the Lincolnshireman, new words seem to hold out the linguistic means of his social and financial gain. But it is crucial, too, that the very language of his suit advertises his failure, mocking his unworthiness to 'gain' the living he seeks. Whether this was a 'real' phenomenon or not, Renaissance malapropism—the misunderstanding of the new, Latinate English—was often a means for elite London writers to deride the social ambitions of others, to identify or (if necessary) to create distinctions of class through language.

The drama of the period, including Shakespeare's plays, is full of comic characters who cannot command the 'new' English, and who are ridiculed for their attempts to do so. Shakespeare, personally responsible (according to the evidence of the *OED*) for introducing more than 600 new words into the English language, often parodied the Renaissance fashion for neologizing. In *Love's Labour's Lost*, he pokes fun at the pedant Holofernes, the curate Nathaniel, and the pretentious Spaniard, Armado, and their penchant for 'new' Englishes. Armado is described by the court as a man who 'hath a mint of phrases in his brain', 'a man of fire-new [newly coined] words', and of 'high-borne' words (I.i.65; 178; 172). He explicitly uses neologism to distinguish himself from the unlettered classes: 'Sir, it is the King's most sweet pleasure and affection to congratulate the Princess at her pavilion in the posteriors of this day, which the rude multitude call the afternoon' (V.i.87–90). He prefers to associate himself with Holofernes: 'Arts-man, preambulate, we will be singuled from the barbarous' (V.i.81–2). Holofernes and Nathaniel, for their part, insist on distinguishing themselves, linguistically and socially, from the Spaniard, whose pretensions they critique in their own, neologistic language:

His humor is lofty, his discourse peremptory, his tongue filed, his eye ambitious, his gait majestical, and his general behavior vain, ridiculous, and thrasonical. He is too picked, too spruce, too affected, too odd as it were, too peregrinate, as I may call it ... He draweth out the thread of his verbosity finer than the staple of his argument. (V.i.9–26)

Yet while Shakespeare may have deemed some of his characters' 'fire-new words' to be inauthentic or pretentious, he uses many of them elsewhere; while *preambulate* ('walk ahead'), *peregrinate*, and *verbosity* only occur in this play, *peremptory, thrasonical* ('boastful'), *audacious, impudency, excrement,* and *eruption,* for example, all occur in contexts where no comedy is intended. Shakespeare's satire, it seems, is not directed at particular words, but at particular people—namely, those who, like Wilson's Lincolnshireman, use neologisms as a means of social promotion, to assert their own standing against that of others. The 'foreign' character of inkhorn language spoke, above all, to a new means of social ascendancy, a competition for 'place' through language.

Underclass English

If neologisms were implicitly understood to belong to a privileged, erudite dialect of early modern English, what was known as the 'canting' language was classed as a dialect of beggars and thieves. The pamphleteer Samuel Rid, in his *Martin Mark-all, Beadle of Bridewell* (1610: 58), describes how Cock Lorrell—'the most notorious knaue that euer liued'—became, in 1501, the leader of all vagrants in England, and organized them into a new society:

After a certaine time that these vp-start Lossels had got vnto a head; the two chiefe Commaunders of both these regiments met at the Diuels-arse-a-peake, there to parle and intreate of matters that might tend to the establishing of this their new found gouernment: and first of all they thinke it fit to deuise a certaine kinde of language, to the end their cousenings, knaueries and villanies might not be so easily perceiued and knowne, in places where they come.

The story of the rise of a Renaissance underworld, in its various renderings of the period, always includes the same basic elements—the creation, at the turn of the sixteenth century, of a 'society' or 'fraternity' of criminals, subject to their own laws only, who hatch and carry out their conspiracies by means, in part, of an invented language. In his account of this underworld in 1608, the dramatist (and prose pamphleteer) Thomas Dekker reminds his readers of Babel, noting that at the beginning of time, that there was one, universal language, and in those innocent days 'two could not then stand gabling with strange tongues, and conspire together, (to his owne face) how to cut a third mans throat, but he might understand them'. For Dekker, the confusion of tongues at the Tower therefore gave rise not only to nations and to foreign wars, but also to the internal 'confusion' within English boundaries—both social and linguistic. In this respect, the 'canting crew' represents the latest, hated consequences of that ancient division.

To its critics, cant, even within itself, represented a kind of Babelish confusion. Thomas Harman, the first to describe the dialect, declared cant to be 'half-mingled withe Englyshe', although he did not identify the derivation of the other half. According to Dekker (1608), many cant words (including the word *cant* itself which, as the *OED* confirms, comes from Latin *cantāre*) were Latin in origin:

As for example, they call a Cloake (in the Canting tongue) a *Togeman*, and in Latine, *toga* signifies a gowne, or an upper garment. *Pannam* is bread: and *Panis* in Lattin is likewise bread. *Cassan* is Cheese, and is a word barbarously coynde out of the substantiue *Caseus* which also signifies Cheese. And so of others.

Rid (1610) determined that cant was rather more cosmopolitan than that, and incorporated not only English and Latin, but also Dutch, Spanish, and French forms, while William Harrison (1577) noted that this 'mingled' language appeared to be augmented by a 'great number of odd words of their [the rogues'] own devising'.

Whatever the precise constitution of their dialect, the 'canting crew' was universally charged with creating an 'unlawfull language', insubordinate to English rule. Harrison describes the language as 'without all order or reason', and Dekker concurs:

as touching the Dialect or phrase it self, I see not that it is grounded upon any certaine rules; And no marvaile if it haue none, for sithence both the *Father* of this new kinde of Learning, and the *Children* that study to speake it after him, haue beene from the beginning and still are, the *Breeders* and *Norishers* of all base disorder, in their liuing and in their Manners: how is it possible, they should obserue any *Method* in their speech, and especially in such a Language, as serues but onely to utter discourses of villainies?

Gil (1619) condemned them—and their language—to death:

Regarding that venomous and disgusting ulcer of our nation I am embarrassed to say anything at all. For that destestable scum of wandering vagabonds speak no proper dialect but a cant jargon which no punishment by law will ever repress, until its proponents are crucified by the magistrates, acting under a public edict.

Wyatt had, for example, initiated a fashion for archaic language in poetry, composed perhaps, as 'V. Rubel has argued, under the influence of the Italian debates over the vernacular.[1] Archaism was certainly the most conspicuous feature of the language of the poems that appeared in *Tottel's Miscellany* (1557); Thomas Wilson's complaint (1619: 155) that 'the fine Courtier will talke nothyng but Chaucer' no doubt speaks to the prevalence of old words in courtly poetry of the period. Gil in 1619 likewise concurred that old words have a place in poetry because 'they ... bear the authority of antiquity, and because neglected, add a charm comparable to freshness'.

Spenser's language in *The Shepheardes Calender*, *The Faerie Queene*, and other works was deliberately and self-consciously archaic. Sometimes he borrowed older words from Chaucer and other medieval writers, such as *clepe* ('call'), *elde* ('age'), *iwis* ('indeed'), *sikerly* ('truly'), *swink* ('toil', 'work'), and *wone* ('dwell'); sometimes he 'invented' archaisms on their model, as in his coinings *bellibone* (to denote a 'fair maid') and *wrizzled* (meaning 'wrinkled' or 'shrivelled'). The poet's original editor, known only as 'E.K.', said that those who heard Spenser's language as 'gibbrish' ought to be ashamed 'in their own mother tonge straungers to be counted and alienes'; in the 'Epistle to Harvey' (1579), he compared Spenser's English favourably to the current idiom which is 'a gallimaufray or hodgepodge of al other [foreign] speches'. But Ben Jonson, among others, later denied that his poetic diction was English at all. 'Spencer, in affecting the Ancients, writ no Language', as Jonson famously declared in 1640. Despite E.K.'s claims that Spenser's language was 'naturall' English, literary history would have the last word, for most future readers would judge it as an example of the strangeness and artificiality of *literary* language.

Indeed, 'literary diction'—a specialized language of poetry—emerges as another, distinctive variety of English in the Renaissance. Gil in 1619 identified it as a *dialect*: 'There are six major dialects: the general, the Northern, the Southern, the Eastern, the Western, and the Poetic'. According to Gil, the 'Poetic' dialect of English, from a formal standpoint, is based on 'metaplasm': 'Metaplasm is when out of necessity, or for the sake of charm, a syllable or word is changed from its own proper form to another'. In the Renaissance, literary language, no less than provincial speech, is sometimes defined as an alteration of the 'proper' forms of current English. No doubt archaisms primarily belong, in the Renaissance and beyond, to the new 'dialect' of poetic language.

[1] See V. Rubel, *Poetic Diction in the English Renaissance: From Skelton through Spenser* (New York: Modern Language Association, 1941).

RENAISSANCE ENGLISH–ENGLISH DICTIONARIES

It is often said that the English dictionary—the prototype for our modern *Oxford English Dictionary*, among many others—was 'invented' in the early seventeenth century; up until that time, English lexicography had produced only foreign language dictionaries (Latin–English, French–English, Italian–English, etc.). But the earliest vernacular dictionaries in fact represented less of an innovation than has been imagined. They were exactly like the foreign language dictionaries that preceded them. Both provided translations of words which were largely foreign to native speakers into an English that all could understand. The first 'English–English' dictionaries did not therefore concern themselves with what Puttenham had called the 'usuall speech' of the Court; rather, they listed and defined what they called 'hard words', the foreign-sounding diction found in contemporary writing. As a result, these works are, in some ways, best understood as 'dialect' dictionaries, interpreting the new and unusual 'Englishes' of the period. Although the first actual dialect dictionary, John Ray's *A Collection of Words Not Generally Used*, did not appear until 1674, the first English dictionaries are predicated on the idea that the nation was cursed by a linguistic confusion which only translation to plain or 'usuall' English might remedy.

In fact, the original English–English dictionaries, long preceding those produced in the seventeenth century, were glossaries of the canting language. As Thomas Harman and his followers often noted, cant was otherwise known in the period as 'pedlar's French', a term which again reinforced notions of its 'foreign' nature. Harman's popular pamphlet *A Caveat or Warening for Common Cursetors* (1567) describes the underworld language as a 'leud, lousey language of these lewtering Luskes *and* lasy Lorrels … a vnknowen toung onely, but to these bold, beastly, bawdy Beggers, and vaine Vacabondes'. As a measure of social precaution, he included a glossary intended to expose the 'vnknowen toung', thereby translating the 'leud, lousey' language into 'common' English:

Nab, a head.	a pratling chete, a tounge.	quaromes, a body.
Nabchet, a hat or cap.	Crashing chetes, teeth.	prat, a buttocke.

and so on through a list that includes 120 terms.

The English dictionary that is generally recognized as the first of its kind, Robert Cawdrey's *Table Alphabeticall* (1604), advertises itself on the title page as conteyning and teaching the true writing, and vnderstanding of hard vsuall English wordes, borrowed from the Hebrew, Greeke, Latine, or French &c., with the interpretation thereof by plaine English words, gathered for the benefit & helpe of Ladies, Gentlewomen, or any other vnskilfull persons.

Cawdrey directs his work to women and to other 'unskilfull' people, promising to make 'hard words' available to all readers. But, like Harman, Cawdrey does not entirely favour the unregulated practice of neologism. He entreats his educated readers to refrain from using 'any strange ynckhorne termes, but [rather] labour to speake so as is commonly receiued, and so as the most ignorant may well vnderstand them.' In the interests of communication, 'unusually' hard words are, as he states in his opening address 'To the Reader', best avoided:

Do we not speak, because we would haue other[s] to understand vs? ... Therefore, either wee must make a difference of English, & say, some is learned English, & othersome is rude English, or the one is Court talke, the other is Country-speech, or els we must of necessitie banish all affected Rhetorique, and vse altogether one manner of language.

Cawdrey's dictionary aims to level the 'difference of English' that had arisen in the age of new words. By distributing the wealth of new words to the disadvantaged (entries under the letter *A* include *aberration, adulterate, affranchise, alienate, anarchie, anathema*, and *animaduersion*), Cawdrey hoped to advance the use of 'one manner of language' in Renaissance England.

Cawdrey's successors similarly argue for the dissolution of the language barrier as a means of social reform. Henry Cockeram thus offers the contents of his *English Dictionary* (1623) for 'the generall use'. He too remains ambivalent about the unrestricted practice of inventing words; some measure, Cockeram believed, must be introduced to curb the potential for excessive neologizing. To that end, as he explains in 'A Premonition from the Author to the Reader': 'I haue also inserted ... euen the *mocke-words* which are ridiculously vsed in our language ... by too many who study rather to bee heard speake, than to vnderstand themselues'. His contemporary, John Bullokar, also speaks out for linguistic equality in his dictionary, *An English Expositor* (1616), but expresses some concern about the reaction of the educated classes to such a project. In his dedication 'To the Courteous Reader', he writes:

I hope such learned will deeme no wrong offered to themselues or dishonour to Learning, in that I open the signification of such words, to the capacitie of the ignorant ... for considering it is familiar among best writers to vsurpe strange words ... I suppose withall their desire is that they should also be vnderstood.

Bullokar, like Harman, fears that the 'strange' words he records in his dictionary may be deliberately 'usurped' to exclude others from understanding. As this further confirms, what is at stake in early modern lexicography is, above all, access to knowledge—the 'opening up' of signification to the uninitiated, unsuspecting, or unschooled.

It is therefore no coincidence that the Renaissance also saw the rise of what we might call 'technical' dictionaries, opening the signification of words which pertained to specific fields of early modern knowledge. The proliferation of foreign loanwords and neologisms in the period owes a great deal, in fact, to the effort to translate Latin, Greek, French, Arabic, and other foreign terms in disciplines which had long been dominated by those languages. Many 'hard words' dictionaries of the seventeenth century include terms of specialized trades. Bullokar, as he indicated on the title-page of his *Expositor*, felt the necessity of translating the 'most useful terms of art, used in our Language'; other contemporary lexicographers list specific 'arts'. Blount (1656), for example, promises on his own title page to explicate 'the terms of *Divinity, Law, Physick, Mathematicks, Heraldry, Anatomy, War, Musick, Architecture*; and of several other *Arts* and *Sciences*'.

Numerous Renaissance 'English–English' dictionaries specialize in the terms of just one of these arts or sciences. Renaissance law, for example, was notorious as a discourse of 'hard words' derived from French. Abraham Fraunce, in the prefatory epistle to *The Lawiers Logike* (1588), hence complains of 'that Hotchpot French, stufft vp with such variety of borowed words, wherein our law is written', arguing that many lawyers exploit legal language to impress those who lack the education to understand it. Such men 'hauing in seauen yeares space met with six French woordes, home they ryde lyke braue Magnificoes, and dashe their poore neighboures children quyte out of countenance, with Villen in gros, Villen regardant, and Tenant per le curtesie'. John Cowell provided 'translations' of the terms of law in his *Interpreter: Or Booke Containing the Signification of Words ... requiring any Exposition or Interpretation* (1607). According to Cowell's etymologies, about half the legal terms used in Renaissance England are derived from French, another quarter are Latin, while the rest come from German, Welsh, Old English, and other languages. But though he intended his work as an aid to a specific discipline, Cowell, with a characteristic Renaissance interest in any and all new and unusual words, couldn't resist 'inserting not onely of words belonging to the art of the lawe, but of any other also, that I thought obscure, of what sort soeuer; as Fish, Cloth, Spices, Drugs, Furres, and such like' (4–5).

In the wake of the Reformation movement to translate the Bible, prayer book, and other liturgical materials into English, religion also became a discourse of hard words in the Renaissance. The debate over Englishing the Bible centered on vocabulary—the question of how to translate traditional Greek and Latin ecclesiastical terminology. At stake in this context therefore were not just 'words' but the Word of God. Catholics tended to argue for the 'faithful' preservation of original words such as *ancilla* ('handmaid'), *egenus* ('destitute', 'in need of'), *parasceve* ('preparation'), *pasche* ('Passover'), and *pontifex* ('high priest'); they believed that the foreign nature of these words lent a veil to the mysteries of scripture, a needful interposition for those too ignorant or too unworthy to receive the Word directly. At the other extreme were Puritans who felt that only words of native English derivation should be used, so that nothing would be hidden from even the most 'common' reader. The compositors of the King James Bible (1611) attempted a compromise, as they indicate in their dedication, 'The Translators to the Reader':

Wee haue on the one side auoided the scrupulositie of the Puritanes, who leaue the olde Ecclesiasticall words, and betake them to other, as when they put *washing* for *Baptisme*, and *Congregation* in stead of *Church*: as also on the other side we haue shunned the obscuritie of the Papists, in their *Azimes, Tunike, Rational Holocausts, Prapuce, Pasche* ... whereof their late Translation is full, and that of purpose to darken the sence.

Yet apparently this 'Authorized' Version did not clear up all 'obscurities', for one year later Thomas Wilson (1612) was moved to compile, as his title page affirms:

A Complete Christian dictionary: wherein the Significations and several Acceptations of All the Words mentioned in the Holy Scriptures of the Old and New Testament, are fully Opened, Expressed, Explained. Also, Very many Ambiguous Speeches, Hard and difficult Phrases therein contained, are plainly Interpreted, Cleered, and Expounded. Tending to the increase of Christian knowledge, and serving for the use of All; especially the Unlearned, who have no skill in the Original Languages, Hebrew and Greek, wherein the Scriptures were first written.

He argues that his work is needful just as 'it is necessary in Grammar Schools, that children which learn French, Latin, or Greek, have their Dictionaries & Lexicons allowed them, to interpret such hard and strange words'. Like so many Renaissance lexicographers, however, Wilson acknowledges the contemporary fear of disseminating this once privileged knowledge through translation into English:

I know that there are not a few who would not that such Books as this should be published in English, or made so common for the common people: But ... [i]f Books of all Arts and Sciences (Logick, Rhetorick, Physick, Arithmetick, Musick, Astronomy, Geometry, Alchumy, etc.) are daily translated and published in English, why not also such as this?

The publication of dictionaries of the sciences was not quite a 'daily' occurrence, but several do appear in the seventeenth century before 1660. Among early science dictionaries are Henry Manwayring's *The sea-Mans dictionary* (1644) and John Smith's *The sea-mans grammar and dictionary* (1653) which, as the former notes on its title page, contains 'an Explanation of all the Termes and Phrases used in the Practique of Navigation'. But most noteworthy, from a linguistic point of view, is the science of 'physick' or medicine. Like lawyers and religionists, physicians were often accused of deliberately keeping 'secrets'—in part, via language—from the public. Boorde, in his *Breuiary of Helthe* (1547) was among those who attempted to turn 'all such obscure [medical] wordes and names in to englyshe, that euery man openly and apartly may vnderstande them', as he indicates in his 'Preface to reders of this boke'. But the 'hard words' that continued to appear in English medical treatises prompted the compilation of works such as *A Physical dictionary, or An Interpretation of such crabbed words and termes of art, as are deriv'd from the Greek or Latin, and used in physick, anatomy, chirurgery, and chymistry* of 1657. These texts, providing translations of the terms of the trades, must be acknowledged alongside Cawdrey's or Bullokar's contributions to vernacular lexicography; they, too, are English–English dictionaries, defining the 'dialects' of the disciplines.

Although no full-scale dictionaries of the 'poetic' dialect of early modern English were produced in the period, several poets compiled glossaries of the 'hard words' that appeared in their works. Edmund Spenser supplied glosses to his *Shepheardes Calender* (1579): 'Hereunto haue I added a certain Glosse or scholion for thexposition of old wordes and harder phrases: which maner of glosing and commenting, well I wote, wil seeme straunge and rare in our tongue'(10). George Gascoigne, who acknowledged a poetic preference for old words over new ('I have more faulted in keeping the olde English wordes *quamvis iam obsoleta* [although obsolete now] than in borowing of other languages, such Epithets and Adjectives as smell of the Inkhorne'), glossed the archaisms that he used in his play *Jocasta* (1575) for reasons which are familiar from the prefaces of early modern dictionaries: 'I did begin those notes at request of a gentlewoman who understode not poëtycall words or termes', Gascoigne notes (1575: 326). Puttenham in 1589 coined new English words to replace the Latin and Greek terms of rhetoric, suggesting, for example, 'ringleader' for *prozeugma*, 'trespasser' for *hiperbaton*, and 'misnamer' for *metonimia*. The 'poetic' dialect of English too, it seems, sometimes required 'translation' or interpretation by specialists in the disciplines of literature and rhetoric.

When Thomas Wilson surveyed the state of the English language in 1553, he found a collection of sociolects, each defined by the interpenetration of a foreign language or jargon:

He that cometh lately out of France, wil talke Frenche English, and never blushe at the matter. Another choppes in with Englishe Italianated ... The lawyer wil store his stomack with the pratyng of Pedlers. The Auditour in makyng his accompt and rekenyng, cometh in with sise sould, and cater denere ... The fine Courtier wil talke nothyng but Chaucer ... The unlearned or foolishe phantasticall, that smelles but of learnyng ... will so latine their tongues, that the simple cannot but wonder at their talke ... Do we not speake, because we would have other to understand us, or is not the tongue geven for this ende, that one might know what another meaneth? And what unlearned man can tell, what [this language] ... signifieth?

The earliest English–English dictionaries answer Wilson's rhetorical question, 'Do we not speake, because we would have other[s] to understand us?', by disseminating hard words to the 'unlearned' (Cawdrey cited this passage at length in the preface to his work). But they also attempt to identify the difference between acceptable and unacceptable inclusions and innovations, to proscribe 'unEnglish' words. Puttenham in 1589, expressing his own likes and dislikes among the English dialects—including neologisms (he approved of *compendious, function, methode, numerositee,* and *harmonicall,* but would not allow *audacious, egregious, facunditie,* or *compatible*)—observed that his caveats were unnecessary to the extent that 'herein we are already ruled by th'English Dictionaries'.

But it is not so clear that Renaissance English dictionaries successfully 'ruled' the language, in the sense of establishing once and for all the bounds of English diction. The age of unified, official measures to enforce the 'standardization' of the English language was yet to come. Meanwhile, Gil in 1619 guessed correctly that the early English lexicographers were so intrigued by 'counterfeit' words that they sometimes coined them themselves: 'I grant that lexicographers collect artificial words, and even invent them, and truly disregard English ones, or even misunderstand them'. Whatever their intentions to 'rule' the native wordstock by setting *limits* on proper forms, Renaissance lexicographers, ironically, did far more to advance the expansion and diversification of the language—extending its bounds well beyond Puttenham's 'lx. myles' from 'the vsuall speach of the Court, and that of London.'

CONCLUSION

Thomas Harman, in his 1567 'caveat' against those who 'cant' rather than speak 'true' English, expresses the hope that 'by this lytle ye maye holy and fully vnderstande their vntowarde talke and pelting speache, mynglede without measure', adding that 'as they haue begonne of late to deuyse some new termes for certien thinges, so wyll they in tyme alter this, and deuyse and euyll or worsse'. He might in fact have been speaking of any of the many new and unusual dialects of the period—or even of Renaissance English itself, 'mynglede without measure'. Verstegan in 1605 complained that 'of late wee haue faln [fallen] to such borowing of woords from Latin, French and other toungs ... that it is of it self no language at all, but the scum of many languages'. Carew who, ten years earlier, had celebrated English as a 'mingled' language on the grounds that it made it more copious, acknowledged those that believed that the interpenetration of foreign and obscure elements into the language 'maketh ... [a] hotch-pot of our tongue, and in effect brings the same rather to a Babellish confusion, then any one entire language'. For many Renaissance writers and linguists, the 'multicultural' nature of Renaissance English refigured the primal Western scene of social, political, and ethnic division as a modern crisis of national identity.

It was the 'Babellish confusione' of Renaissance English that led to the call, in the middle of the seventeenth century, for a language academy to unify and rule the vernacular. In his 1665 proposals to the Royal Society of London—established, in part, for the improvement of the English language—the diarist and writer John Evelyn included a call for:

a Lexicon or collection of all the pure English words by themselves; then those which are derivative from others, with their prime, certaine, and natural signification ... all the technical words, especially those of the more generous employments ... a full catalogue of exotic words, such as are daily minted by our Logodaedalie ... and that it were resolved on what should be sufficient to render them current ... since, without restraining that same *indomitam novandi verba licentiam*, it will in time quite disguise the language.

(*Logodaedalie*: people who are cunning with words; *indomitam novandi verba licentiam*: the indomitable license of making new words)

The Royal Society also sponsored the project of creating a universal language, for all nations, that would clear up the 'confusion' of Babel altogether. The universal language movement of the seventeenth century remains the most dramatic evidence we have that linguistic diversity—whatever the prospects for unitary, early modern European languages—remained the 'curse' of the English vernacular for many writers throughout the period. Yet it is the 'Babel' of Renaissance English, in part, that gave us, among other great works in verse and prose, Shakespeare's plays and the King James Bible—which have for so long been celebrated as foundational texts for modern English language and culture. The earliest language reformers, seeking to 'remedy Babel', hoped to promote intellectual clarity and cultural cohesion, and yet, what might have been lost—even in terms of their own goals—had they found a way to rule or suppress what Thomas Sprat, on behalf of the Royal Society, condemned in 1667 as 'this vicious abundance of *Phrase* ... this volubility of *Tongue*, which makes so great a noise in the World'?

9

ENGLISH AT THE ONSET OF THE NORMATIVE TRADITION

Ingrid Tieken-Boon van Ostade

WHEN Betsy Sheridan, sister of the playwright Richard Brinsley Sheridan, came to London in 1784, one of her friends—as she later reported to her sister Alicia in Dublin—accused her 'of having some brogue which [her] Father would by no means allow'. The Sheridans came from Ireland and this was, it seems, still evident in the way Betsy spoke. Her father, Thomas Sheridan, had just published a pronouncing dictionary as part of his project to standardize English pronunciation and Betsy's elocution had already been a matter of concern (and no little parental endeavour).[1] Sheridan was, however, by no means alone in his interests in reforming language. In contrast to the 'babel' of varieties which, as the previous chapter has explored, was in many ways seen as typical of the seventeenth century, it was the desire for a standard language, in national as well as individual terms, which was to be one of the most prominent issues of the century which followed.

The beginnings of this development can already be found within the variety of discourses which typified the seventeenth century. Chapter 8 has mentioned the Royal Society which had been founded in the early 1660s, and which 'served as coordinator and clearing house for English scientific endeavours'.[2] From its very

---

[1] As part of the elocutionary training given by her father, Betsy was, for example, made to read at length from Johnson's *Rambler*, afterwards being subjected to detailed correction of the mistakes she had made. See Mugglestone (2003*a*), 147.

[2] See A. C. Baugh and T. Cable, *A History of the English Language*, 5th edn. (London: Routledge, 2002), 245.

early days, the Royal Society concerned itself with matters of language, setting up a committee in 1664 whose principal aim was to encourage the members of the Royal Society to use appropriate and correct language. This committee, however, was not to meet more than a couple of times. Subsequently, writers such as John Dryden, Daniel Defoe, and Joseph Addison, as well as Thomas Sheridan's god-father, Jonathan Swift, were each in turn to call for an English Academy to concern itself with language—and in particular to constrain what they perceived as the irregularities of usage.

Upon adapting Shakespeare's *The Tempest* and *Troilus and Cressida* in 1667 and 1679 for a contemporary audience, Dryden, for example, had discovered not only that the English language had changed since the days of Shakespeare, but that his plays contained what might be considered as grammatical 'mis-takes'. Shakespeare had used double comparatives and double negation, as in 'more softer bowels' in *Troilus and Cressida*, and 'no nearer you cannot come' in *The Tempest*; he had moreover used adjectives as adverbs, *which* with a human antecedent, for example 'The mistress which I serve' (*The Tempest* III.i.6), as well as *you* instead of *ye*, and *who* when *whom* was strictly required. Shakespeare would even end sentences with a preposition, a construction which Dryden determinedly removed from his own writing when revising his *Essay of Dramatic Poesy* in 1684. Dryden had been a member of the Royal Society language committee, and he and his fellow writers believed that an English Academy along the example of the Italian Accademia della Crusca (which had been founded in 1582) and the Académie Française (founded in 1635) might provide the solution for such irregularities in usage. An Academy would codify the language by refining and fixing it, and by laying down its rules in an authoritative grammar and dictionary. 'The Work of this Society,' Defoe argued in 1697, 'shou'd be to encourage Polite Learning, to polish and refine the *English* Tongue, and advance the so much neglected Faculty of Correct Language, to establish Purity and Propriety of Stile, and to purge it from all the Irregular Additions that Ignorance and Affectation have intro-duc'd'. English, it was felt, had no grammar, and in this it compared unfavour-ably with Latin, which it had been gradually replacing in all its important functions. 'Our Language is extremely imperfect,' Swift complained in 1712, and one of the problems noted by Addison the year before was that the language was 'clogged … with Consonants, as *mayn't, can't, sha'n't, wo'n't*, and the like, for *may not, can not, shall not, will not*, &c'. What these writers wanted to establish was a written medium that was free from contamination by the spoken language and that had enough prestige to be able to compete with Latin. This had to be brought about, as Swift put it on the title page of his famous proposal, by 'Correcting, Improving and Ascertaining [i.e. fixing] the English Tongue', and an English Academy was to take charge of the process.

But no Academy was ever founded, and the codification process was taken up instead by a series of interested individuals: clergymen, scientists, schoolmasters (and mistresses!), poets, and booksellers. And actors too, for Thomas Sheridan, although he had originally intended to become a clergyman, had felt so disgusted with the drawl of preachers that he decided to tackle the problem properly by training as an actor. Sheridan's rival John Walker, who also wrote a pronouncing dictionary (1791), likewise had his early background in acting, playing alongside the celebrated David Garrick in Drury Lane. Codifying the English language hence became the result of private enterprise, as in the case of Samuel Johnson who was invited to compile his famous *Dictionary of the English Language* (1755) because his friend, the publisher Robert Dodsley, felt he was in need of a project with which to occupy himself. The same was true of Robert Lowth, a clergyman who originally wrote his canonical *Short Introduction to English Grammar* of 1762 for his son Tom. When Dodsley, who had published Lowth's earlier work, learnt of Lowth's plans for a grammar, he decided that a grammar was just what the public needed. As in the case of Johnson's dictionary, he turned Lowth's grammar into a publishers' project. Lowth's grammar was not the first grammar of English, but the 1760s marked the beginning of a veritable explosion of English grammars, culminating during the nineteenth century in what Ian Michael characterized in 1991 as 'more than enough English grammars'.[3]

These newly published grammars and dictionaries did not, of course, have an immediate effect on the language. Instead, throughout the period, there continued to be a considerable amount of variation in spelling, grammar, and vocabulary, as well as in pronunciation. The extent of this variation has not, however, always been made visible in studies of eighteenth-century English, which have traditionally focused on the language as it appeared in print. The following excerpt from Chapter X of Sarah Fielding's novel *The Adventures of David Simple* (1744) illustrates some of the ways in which the features of printed texts can differ from equivalent forms in present-day English (indicated here in square brackets):

On these Considerations they agreed to go, and at half an Hour past Four [half past four] they were placed [took their seats] in the Pit; the Uproar was [had] begun, and they were surrounded every way [on all sides] with such a variety of Noises [noise], that it seemed as if the whole Audience was [had] met by way of Emulation [in a kind of competition], to try

---

[3] See I. Michael, 'More than Enough English Grammars', in G. Leitner (ed.), *English Traditional Grammars* (Amsterdam: Benjamins, 1991), 11–26.

who could make the greatest. *David* asked his Friend, what could be the Meaning of all this; for he supposed they could be neither *condemning, nor applauding the Play*, before it was [had] begun. Mr. *Orgueil* told him, the Author's Friends and Enemies were now shewing [showing] what Parties they had gathered together, in order to intimidate each other.

Compared to the English of today, the differences in grammar as well as vocabulary, including the capitalization of almost all nouns, can give the text an unduly formal character, while the author had merely intended to write plain narrative prose.

Private writings, such as diaries and letters, offer a very different perspective on the language from that customarily taken in histories of English, and these will be the major focus of the present chapter. The basic material for discussion will be the language of a variety of individual writers, men and women from all layers of society, ranging from those who were highly educated to those who were barely able to spell. All these people wrote letters, and many of them were socially and geographically mobile, a fact which undoubtedly exposed them to the existence (and influence) of different linguistic norms.

MOBILITY: GEOGRAPHICAL AND SOCIAL

The playwright Richard Sheridan, Thomas Sheridan's son, was a very ambitious man; he felt ashamed of his father's background as an actor, and an Irish actor at that. In her letters to her sister Alicia, which she wrote in the form of a journal, Betsy Sheridan describes Richard as 'a little *grand*'; unlike his sister, Richard shed his regional accent as soon as possible upon his arrival in London: he, too, had been the recipient of his father's speech training.[4] Regional accents were increasingly being seen as social shibboleths, although Irish seems to have been particularly stigmatized. Swift, for example, had felt embarrassed by his own Irish accent, noting that, in England, 'what we call the *Irish brogue* is no sooner discovered, than it makes the deliverer in the least degree ridiculous and despised'. In a later letter to her sister, Betsy Sheridan describes a meeting with a certain 'Irish Doctor', who 'is very civil and talks French in Public, as he says "to *hide* his Brogue"'. Of course Betsy herself may have learned to hide her brogue, too, especially when she came to live with her brother after her father's death.

Another example of someone who felt embarrassed by his regional origins is Johnson's biographer, James Boswell. Boswell recorded this embarrassment in his

---

[4] Some traces of his original accent must have remained, attracting the attention of the observant Fanny Burney (see further p. 247).

Life of Johnson, first published in 1791, writing that upon being introduced to Johnson in 1763 he

was much agitated; and recollecting his prejudice against the Scotch, ... I said to Davies [a mutual acquaintance], 'Don't tell where I come from'—'From Scotland,' cried Davies roguishly. 'Mr. Johnson, (said I) I do indeed come from Scotland, but I cannot help it'.

Boswell may not have had much of a Scottish accent because, as Frank pointed out in 1994, educated Scotsmen of the time would make every effort to avoid being caught out. Boswell had, moreover, taken private lessons in elocution with Thomas Sheridan in order to make certain that this was so.

As in previous centuries, many people at the time felt the pull of London (see the map in Fig. 9.1), attracted by the better social, economic, and cultural opportunities which the capital seemed to offer; all of them must have experienced similar anxieties and embarrassment at being confronted with a different linguistic context. John Gay, the poet and playwright, came from Barnstaple, Devonshire, and the novelist (and printer) Samuel Richardson, from Mackworth in Derbyshire; Robert Dodsley, writer and publisher, was born near Mansfield, Nottinghamshire; Henry and Sarah Fielding, both novelists, came from Dorset, though they attended school in Salisbury in Wiltshire; Samuel Johnson, the writer and lexicographer, and the actor David Garrick both came from Lichfield in Staffordshire (travelling to London together in March 1737); the grammarian Robert Lowth (later Bishop of London), was born in Winchester; Laurence Sterne, the author of *Tristram Shandy*, was born in Clonmel in Ireland, and the novelist Fanny Burney came from King's Lynn, Norfolk. William Clift, first conservator of the Hunterian Museum, originated from Bodmin in Cornwall: upon his arrival in London, his letters show that he quickly lost all traces of his local dialect. Note the speech-like quality of the first letter which he wrote home on 19 February 1792 to report his safe arrival in the capital:

I have a thousand things to write and I Can't tell where to begin first—But I think Ill begin from the time I left Fowey—Just as we was getting out of the Harbour I saw you and Cousin Polly out at St Cathrines and I look'd at you till I saw you get out at the Castle and sit down upon the Bank the other side and I look'd and look'd and look'd again till you look'd so small that I Cou'd not discern you scarcely only your red Cloak.

His later letters display considerable change; *we was*, still characteristic of southern dialects today, no longer occurs after this first letter, while other regionally-marked usages—such as *where* for *whether* and *was a week* for *a week ago*—were likewise soon shed.

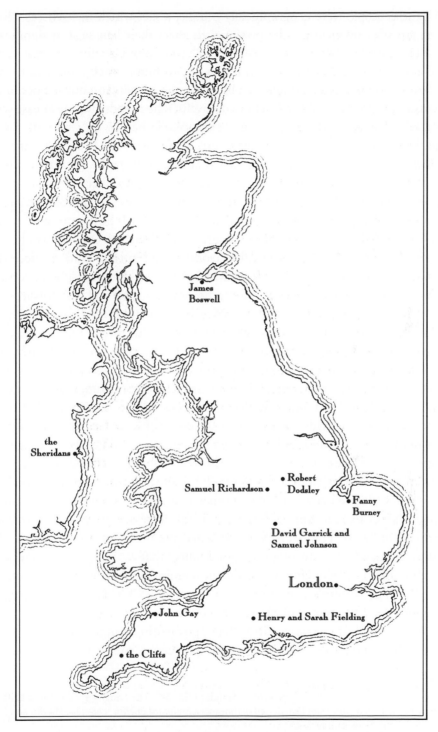

FIG. 9.1. Geographical mobility in eighteenth-century Britain

All these people were geographically mobile, a fact which in itself (as Clift's letters already confirm) had the potential to affect their language in significant ways. But some of them were socially mobile too. John Gay, for instance, came from a family of traders, and his ambition was to find himself a place at Court. Richardson's father had been a joiner, but although Richardson himself became a successful printer (as well as a celebrated novelist), he never felt quite at ease with those who had similarly made it in society. While he got on well with Sarah Fielding, one of the reasons for Richardson's rivalry with her brother Henry was his feeling of inequality due to the fact that he hadn't had a grammar school education. Robert Dodsley, who later became the publisher of most of the important writers of the period, including Johnson, Lowth, and Sterne, began his career as an apprentice to a stocking weaver; afterwards he became a footman, which is how the author Horace Walpole, fourth Earl of Orford, would still occasionally refer to him, even after Dodsley had turned into a successful bookseller. Lowth effected a social transition within a different sphere; coming from a family of clergymen, he set out to become a bishop and was, towards the end of his life, called to the highest office in the Church of England, that of Archbishop of Canterbury (although his failing health forced him to decline). Fanny Burney's father, the musical scholar and composer Charles Burney, was also a fashionable music teacher; this brought him in contact with the more highly placed in London society, and both Garrick and Sir Joshua Reynolds were frequent visitors to his home. Charles Burney saw a lifelong wish fulfilled when Fanny was appointed lady-in-waiting at the court of King George (although he must have been sadly disappointed when she became ill and asked to resign her position). The greatest social leap was, however, probably made by William Clift, who came from a very poor family indeed: his father earned a living by making sticks and setting hedges, while his mother managed to scrape together barely enough money to send him to school. William possessed great skill at drawing which, according to Frances Austin, 'attracted the notice of Nancy Gilbert, the Squire's lady, and it was through her good offices that at the age of seventeen he was apprenticed to John Hunter ... the most eminent surgeon and anatomist of his day'. [5] Upon Hunter's death in 1793, and soon after Clift arrived in London, he was appointed conservator of the Hunterian Museum.

Mobility could of course occur in the opposite direction too. Johnson's close friend, Mrs Thrale (later Piozzi), for example, came from a Welsh aristocratic

[5] See F. Austin, 'The Effect of Exposure to Standard English: The Language of William Clift', in D. Stein and I. Tieken-Boon van Ostade (eds), *Towards a Standard English 1600–1800* (Berlin and New York: Mouton de Gruyter, 1994), 287.

family but married down: her husband was Henry Thrale, a London brewer, wealthy but still middle class. The Fieldings, too, experienced a similar downward mobility; their grandparents belonged to the aristocracy but their mother married an army officer. Henry nevertheless made use of his aristocratic connections by soliciting literary patronage from his cousin, Lady Mary Wortley Montagu. His sister Sarah did not: the road to success in literature was different for women. The downward mobility of Mrs Thrale or the Fieldings may not have been sought consciously; that of Boswell, by contrast, was: he was the son of a Scottish laird, with whom he did not get along well. In search of a substitute father, he felt more attracted to Johnson and his circle. Whether upward or downward, geographical or social, any type of mobility would, as already indicated, have brought people into contact with different norms of speech, with the potential for their own language to change in response. Some, such as William Clift, may have consciously sought new linguistic models, working hard to adopt the desired norm—in this case that of his newly found patron, John Hunter. Robert Lowth similarly strove throughout his life to rise in the church hierarchy. His awareness of what was appropriate language is evident from his most formal letters, and with his *Short Introduction to English Grammar* he made this linguistic norm accessible to those who similarly wished to rise in social status.

SPOKEN ENGLISH

First-hand evidence of the way people spoke is very hard to come by. Sometimes, occasional spellings in diaries and journals indicate colloquial pronunciations, such as when Betsy Sheridan cursed her sister-in-law's father Thomas Linley with the words '*od* rot *un*' ('may God rot him'), for not allowing her the use of the family's theatre box, or Fanny Burney's mocking of Richard Sheridan's Irish accent in a letter to her sister dated 11 January 1779: 'I assure you I took it quite *koind* in him [Sheridan] to give me this advice'. On the whole, however, there is no indication in the spelling of the letters and diaries of the more educated writers to show how their words were pronounced. The letters of the uneducated members of the Clift family are a different matter. When, on 3 December 1795, Elizabeth, William's eldest sister, reported to him on their brother Robert's recovery from a recent illness, she wrote: 'whin I Left him he was abel Seet up an he Promisd me to writ to you the next day', and 'they ware All very well'. Her spelling of *whin* ('when'), *seet* ('sit'), *writ* ('write'), and *ware* ('were') suggests a different pronunciation of the vowels in question. Generally, however, her letters show a skill in spelling that did not go much beyond high-frequency words of more than one syllable (and sometimes, as the examples above indicate, not even that). But the skills she did possess were exceptional for a woman of her background, and more than enough to keep the family together by corresponding with them.

There is more evidence of the use of spoken grammar and vocabulary, and not just in the letters of the barely literate. But in looking for such evidence, not all sources can be considered equally trustworthy; the language of drama, for instance, can be a dangerous source to use. Gay's *Beggar's Opera* (1728), which features thieves and other lower-class characters, does not contain a single instance of multiple negation. This is odd, because by this time this feature was already being avoided by more highly placed people (see further p. 262). Given the stratified nature of variation within English usage, we might therefore realistically have expected some occurrences of double negation in the play. Lady Mary Wortley Montagu, in her play *Simplicity* (c1734), puts the following words into the mouth of the servant girl Lucy in Act 1: 'Says my Master, says he, 'Lucy, your mistress loves you …' 'Yes, Sir,' says I. What could a body say else?' This sounds like the authentic speech of the lower orders, but it is the only time it occurs in the play. Lucy's words function merely as an indication of her social class at the outset; the rest was presumably left to the theatrical skills of the actress in question. Better sources are the novels by writers like Tobias Smollett and Fanny Burney. In *Evelina* (1778), for instance, Fanny Burney renders the language of speech by using short sentences connected by *and* and *nor*:

'Well,' said Miss Polly, 'he's grown quite another creature to what he was, and he doesn't run away from us, nor hide himself, nor any thing; and he's as civil as can be, and he's always in the shop, and he saunters about the stairs, and he looks at every body as comes in' (Letter XLIV).

Miss Polly's use of the relative *as* instead of *that* would have called for the censure of Lowth, who proscribed the form in his grammar. Deviant spelling was not normally used at this time to indicate colloquial language or non-standard speech, as it would be in the century to come by writers such as Charles Dickens or Emily Brontë. Eighteenth-century novelists instead used different devices in attempting to render distinctive speech patterns, such as Sarah Fielding's use of the dash to indicate pauses and hesitations in Chapter 6 of her first novel *The Adventures of David Simple* (1744):

If I got any Book that gave me pleasure, and it was any thing beyond the most silly Story, it was taken from me. For *Miss must not enquire too far into things—it would turn her*

Brain—she had better mind her Needle-work—and such Things as were useful for Women—Reading and poring on Books, would never get me a Husband.—Thus was I condemned to spend my Youth ....

Although—or perhaps because—this device was also used by Richardson, the dash was obliterated from the text by her brother Henry, who got involved with the reprint that was brought out later that year. In doing so he failed to understand its function. Removing the dash was only one of the many—and often uncalled for—changes which Henry made to the text. Reflecting contemporary norms of 'good' usage, he also corrected Sarah's use of the preposition at the end of the sentence which, then as now, and in spite of Dryden's earlier strictures, remained a common pattern in usage, especially in informal language.

Plays and novels offer only fictional dialogue, but there are two eighteenth-century authors who were renowned at the time for recording the way people actually spoke. Both James Boswell and Fanny Burney carried around notebooks for noting down things worth remembering, which were later copied into their diaries. Apparently Boswell's contemporaries believed that his reported conversations in the *Life of Johnson* sounded like the real thing, while people warned each other to be careful in what they said when in Fanny Burney's presence: for all they knew they might end up as a character in one of her novels! Fanny Burney's skill in recording the spoken language of the time is evident from the large number of first recorded instances under her name in the *OED*. There are nearly three times as many of them as for Jane Austen, who is usually credited as the first to record colloquial language in her novels.

If it represents natural conversation, the following dialogue, which Fanny Burney reported as taking place between Dr Johnson, Mrs Thrale, and herself on 25 September 1778, seems rather formal, at least to speakers of modern English:

He [i.e. a Mr. Smith] stayed till Friday morning. When he was gone, 'What say you to *him*, Miss Burney? cried Mrs. Thrale, I am sure I offer you *variety*'?
'Why I like him *better* than Mr. Crutchley—but I don't think I shall *pine* for either of them'?
'Mr. Johnson, said Mrs. Thrale, don't you think Jerry Crutchley very much improved?'
Dr. J. Yes, Madam, I think he is.
Mrs. T. Shall he have Miss Burney?
Dr. J. Why—I think not;—at least, I must know more of him: I must enquire into his connections, his recreations, his employments, & his Character, from his Intimates before I trust Miss Burney with him ...

The use of titles instead of first names, of questions and negative sentences without *do* (as in Mrs Thrale's 'What say you to him?' and Johnson's 'I think not'), the presence of the interjection *why*, as well as Johnson's conspicuous wordiness ... to the modern reader all of these suggest a discrepancy between the informality of the situation and the language used. Such apparent discrepancy is also evident in the language of the letters of the period.

THE AGE OF LETTER WRITING

The eighteenth century has been called the 'great age of the personal letter'.[6] As a result of the improved postal system, which made sure that letter writers could rely on the actual arrival of their letters into the hands of their addressees, people began to communicate by letter in vast numbers. One indication of the increase in letter writing is the fact that 'by 1704 the post office was receiving 75 per cent more money per year than in 1688'.[7] Many collections of correspondence have come down to us, and a good example is the one between the Lennox sisters, which was used as material for the book *Aristocrats* published by Stella Tillyard in 1994. The letters were not only exchanged between Caroline, Emily, Louisa, and Sarah Lennox: there are, according to Tillyard in her introduction, 'thousands of ... letters—between sisters, husbands and wives, servants and employers, parents and children'. The letters themselves are unpublished, as are many other correspondences from this period that have survived: a vast amount of material is therefore still waiting to be analysed. Private letters contain important material, not only in terms of their contents (they can, for instance, provide detailed pictures of eighteenth-century society, as in the letters and diaries of genteel Georgian women which Amanda Vickery used as the basis for her book *The Gentleman's Daughter* published in 1998), but also in terms of the language of the period. Just as today's private informal communication differs from that of formal speech styles or from writing, eighteenth-century English varied depending on the formality of the situation, the topic people wrote about, and the relationship they had with their correspondents. This kind of variation is evident in spelling, grammar, as well as vocabulary, and the different styles found in eighteenth-century letters provide important evidence of this.

---

[6] See H. Anderson and I. Ehrenpreis, 'The Familiar Letter in the Eighteenth Century: Some Generalizations', in H. Anderson, P. B. Daghlian, and I. Ehrenpreis (eds), *The Familiar Letter in the Eighteenth Century* (Lawrence: University of Kansas Press, 1968), 269.

[7] Ibid., 270.

The letters, moreover, help us reconstruct social networks, the study of which is important in tracing the origins and processes of linguistic change. Based on a study of present-day speech communities carried out during the mid-1970s, the sociolinguist Lesley Milroy in 1987 described the extent to which the kind of social network one belongs to correlates with one's use of vernacular speech (as in, say, the local dialect) or, conversely, that of the standard variety. In doing so, she distinguished between closed and open networks. In closed networks, which are usually found among the working classes and in rural communities (although also within the highest social classes), everybody knows everybody else, and usually in more than one capacity at the same time (e.g. as neighbours, friends, relatives, *and* colleagues). The language of such networks serves as a means of identification to the network's members; as such, it is hostile to influence from outside so that it tends to be conservative and inhibits linguistic change. Open networks, in which people might have no more than a single loose tie with each other, are less subject to fixed linguistic norms. Such networks are typically found among the middle classes, and it is here that linguistic change may be most evident because members of open networks are usually more mobile, geographically and otherwise, than people belonging to closed networks. Their mobility brings them into contact with other social networks, and hence with different speech norms which may influence their own language and that of those around them. The social network model, therefore, has enormous potential for the analysis and description of linguistic change. In doing research on language change, it is important to try and identify people who were mobile, as these are the ones who may have carried along linguistic changes from one network to another. At the same time, many more people were probably not mobile: such people probably belonged to closed networks, and their language would therefore have been conservative compared to those people who did move about a lot.

In the eighteenth century, however, mobility (both social and geographical) was, as already indicated, an established fact for many people who—consciously or unconsciously—experienced the influence of other norms of language. If this happened on a large enough scale, we can assume that the language may have been affected accordingly. But even on a small scale the influence from other networks or from individual speakers (or writers) may have had its effect. On the other hand, as many histories of the language have stressed, the eighteenth century was also—stereotypically—the period when the English language was being codified. Codification is when the language is being submitted to rule by means of the publication of grammars and dictionaries. This is one of the final stages of the standardization process. Typical of the approach of the codifiers is that their grammars or dictionaries are normative in nature: by means of their publications, they set the norms of the language down for all to see and for all—at least potentially—to adhere to. This is indeed the function that Johnson's *Dictionary* and Lowth's grammar came to have. The latter aspect is part of the prescription stage, which completes the standardization process, although without—as other chapters have indicated—ever putting an end to it. Unlike, say, the system of weights and measures, language can never be fully fixed; if such were the case, it would no longer be functional as an instrument of communication, which has to be flexible to be able to adapt itself to changed circumstances. But the codification process did result in slowing down the rate of linguistic change: never again would the English language change as rapidly as it had done before.

All the people who have been mentioned so far within this chapter wrote letters, and some wrote diaries as well. It is nevertheless important to remember that, at least in a wider context, they do not form a representative section of society, for the majority of the population of this time did not write and hence no direct evidence of their language usage has come down to us. Tony Fairman, who has studied the language of what he calls 'unschooled people' from the early nineteenth century, calculated that 'of the one-third to 40% who could write, less than 5% could produce texts near enough to schooled English'.[8] We can assume similar—if not even lower—figures for the eighteenth century. But there is a further complication: for those who could write, the eighteenth century was also the period during which letter writing, just like spoken communication, was considered an art. Spontaneous utterances, therefore, letters were not—even if, at times, they can give the *impression* of spontaneity. Letter writing had to be learned and, as Tillyard confirms in her own account of the letters of the Lennox family, it was done so with various degrees of success. Caroline Lennox, for instance, complains about her son Ste's lack of skill at the age of 17: 'His letters are quite a schoolboy's. He is well, hopes we are, and compliments to everybody. Adieu. Yours most sincerely'. His cousin Emily, by contrast, was 'a delightful correspondent, her style quite formed'.[9] Consequently, such letters are not of interest to an analysis of the kind of unmonitored language which sociolinguists try to identify in their search for the vernacular language of the period.

    [8] T. Fairman, 'Letters of the English Labouring Classes and the English Language, 1800–34', in M. Dossena and C. Jones (eds), *Insights into Late Modern English* (Bern: Peter Lang, 2003), 265.
    [9] See S. Tillyard, *Aristocrats. Caroline, Emily, Louisa and Sarah Lennox 1740–1832* (London: Chatto & Windus, 1994), 93.

Receiving a letter was a social event and letters were usually passed around at an assembly of relatives and friends. Letter writers as a result usually knew that they did not write for the addressee alone, and their language must also have reflected this. The Lennox sisters had found a solution to this predicament: private affairs were written on separate sheets which the addressee could remove upon opening the letter and before it was made public. Such sheets contain more truly private language, and it is this kind of unmonitored writing that is interesting for sociolinguistic analysis. In other cases, spontaneous language may be found in letters to correspondents with whom the author had such a close relationship that the need to polish one's style was felt to be irrelevant. Examples are Lady Mary Wortley Montagu's letters to her husband in the days of their courtship, or those to her daughter Lady Bute later in life. Robert Lowth wrote his most intimate letters to his wife when he was in Ireland in 1755. There are sixty-four of them, and their intimacy of style is reflected in his spelling, his grammar, as well as his choice of words. Mary Lowth's letters, unfortunately, have not come down to us. Sometimes authors informed their recipients that their letters were unpremeditated, such as Betsy Sheridan who, on 19 June 1785 told her sister: 'But as I scribble a great deal I am forced to write the first word that occurs, so that of course I must write pretty nearly as I should speak'.

In eighteenth-century correspondences the relationship between writer and addressee can be determined by the form of the opening or closing formula in a letter. Opening formulas may vary in formality from, in Lowth's case, 'Dear Molly' (his wife), 'Dear Tom' (his son), 'Dear Brother' (his closest friend Sir Joseph Spence), 'Dear Sir' (friends and acquaintances), 'Sir' (acquaintances), 'Rev. Sir' (fellow clergymen), to 'My Dear Lord' (e.g. the Archbishop). Closing formulas similarly range from informality to formality: from 'Your's most Affectionately' (relatives and friends), 'Your most Obedient & most faithful humble Servt. (acquaintances), to 'Your humble Servant' (enemies). With Gay a different principle applied: the longer the formula, the greater the distance from the addressee and, hence, the more polite the letter. His shortest form, 'Adieu', is found only in a letter to his cousin. Gay is the first to use the formula 'yours sincerely', which, judging by his relationship with the people to whom he used this formula, does not indicate politeness as it does today but rather the opposite: extreme informality.

An example of how the topic of a letter can influence its style may be found in letters exchanged between Boswell and his friend John Johnston of Grange: they are often about nothing in particular, and merely serve the purpose of expressing the intimacy between them. This becomes clear from the following letter which Boswell sent to Johnston on 27 October 1762:

My dear friend: I know it will revive your spirits to see from whence this Epistle is dated, even from a Place in which the happiest moments of your life have passed. While the multitude consider it just as *the town of Edinburgh* and no more; How much more valuable is it to you, who look upon it as an ancient City—the Capital of Scotland—in which you have attended the Theatre, and there had your soul refined by gentle Music, by the noble feelings of Tragedy, by the lively flashes of comedy and by the exalted pleasure resulting from the view of a crowd assembled to be pleased, and full of happiness.

The opposite occurs in letters between Sarah Fielding and her lifelong friend James Harris, the author of *Hermes* (1751): when asking advice on her translation of Socrates, Sarah wrote to Harris as one scholar to another, adopting the kind of formal language that suits the topic. 'Dear Sir,' she began her letter of 18 August 1761:

Many Acknowledgements and thanks are due to you for your ready compliance with my Request in giving me a Translation of that hard passage about $Διαλέγεσθαι$, which I could not render into English with any Satisfaction. Where the Sense so intirely depends on the Etymology of a Word in ye Original, it requires more Knowledge than I am Mistress of, to make it clear in another language; and your friendly Kindness in doing it for me is felt most cordially and gratefully.

She had ended an earlier letter to him (from September or October 1760) with 'I should take it as a favour if you will mention to [Mr Garrott] how much I am obliged to him and his Sister. I ... beg my Compliments. I am Dear Sir with true regard your sincere and Obed[t] hum[ble] Serv[t]. S Fielding'. The use of words like *favour, obliged, sincere, obedient, humble*, and *Servant* in her letters are part of what McIntosh (1986) calls 'courtly genteel prose', the kind of language that has its origin in the language of the fifteenth-century courtier and that is characteristic of eighteenth-century letters of 'high friendship', usually exchanged between men. Sarah Fielding's letters show that women in her position were capable of such language too. In the whole of her correspondence, her use of extra initial capitals assumes its highest frequency in her letters to Harris, precisely matching the kind of patterns which we find in the printed texts of the time (see further p. 256).

LANGUAGE

According to traditional accounts of eighteenth-century English, nothing much happened to the language during the period. Spelling had been fixed since the end of the seventeenth century, and Baugh and Cable (2002), for example, discuss only the development of the passive, in particular the rise of the progressive passive (*the house is building* and *the house is being built*). On this model, English grammar would already more or less have reached its present-day state. But this perspective is based on the idea that the English language is that which appears in print (see further Chapter 10). As a result of the advent of historical sociolinguistics, which primarily looks at data derived from other sources, such as personal letters, it has, however, come to be recognized that both in the case of spelling and in that of grammar a lot more went on than was formerly given credit. There was even a large increase of new words in the period, especially during the second half of the century. Evidence for this can, of course, also be found in the *OED*, which includes considerable amounts of data from letters and journals in its second edition, a change in policy since its conception in the mid-nineteenth century.

Spelling

The first scholar who systematically studied the spelling of letters in relation to printed texts was Noel Osselton (1984), who found to his surprise that Dr Johnson's private spelling was 'downright bad'. Johnson's letters contained spellings like *chymestry, compleat, chappel, ocurrence, pamflet, stomack, stiched, Dutchess*, and *dos* ('does'), none of which were formally sanctioned in his *Dictionary*. How could such seemingly 'illiterate' spellings be reconciled with Johnson's status as the one who, in another popular eighteenth-century stereotype, was supposed to have fixed English spelling? When looking at letters by other educated eighteenth-century authors, Osselton discovered that there were at the time two standards of spelling—a public one, as found in printed documents (and duly codified in Johnson's dictionary), and a private one, found in letters. This dual spelling standard was even recognized by the schoolmasters. And, indeed, it was very widespread. People like Lowth, Sarah Fielding, and Laurence Sterne, who must all have learned to spell around the same time, likewise used very different spellings in their private writings from those which were found in printed books. Lowth's letters to his wife, for instance, contain spellings like *carryd, copys, gott*, and *immediatly*. Sarah Fielding wrote *rejoyces, intirely*, and *Characteristick*, while in the draft of Sterne's *Memoirs* we find *Birth Day, a Drift*, and *small Pox* (all were corrected in the printed version of this text). Private spelling can be called a system of its own, with different rules from those in use by the printers. And for published works the printers were responsible for correcting private spelling according to their house rules, just as in the example of Sterne's *Memoirs*. We see the same phenomenon with James Boswell, whose spelling underwent a sudden change in favour of the printed system. This change coincides with the moment when he finally gave in to his father's wishes for him to study law. Having become a serious student, he seems to have adopted the spelling of the books he read during his studies.

Osselton discovered that in printed texts there were many different spellings for the past tense and past participle endings of weak verbs. He recorded as many as seven: *sav'd, save'd, saved, sav d, lack't, lackd,* and *lackt.* The forms with the apostrophe rose steadily during the second half of the seventeenth century, reaching just over 50 per cent during the first half of the eighteenth, after which they rapidly declined. In private letters, *'d* lingered on much longer, although some, such as Johnson, abandoned *'d* very early on. Upon his arrival in London, and in his zeal to adapt to a new linguistic norm, William Clift first dropped *'d* and other contractions but later started reusing them. It is as if he were hypercorrecting, using *'d* more frequently than would be expected of him in the context of his letters, perhaps under the influence of a self-imposed reading programme. In effect, he had to learn that contractions were acceptable in private letters as part of a different spelling system. Osselton also studied the use of extra initial capitals in printed texts, which rose to nearly 100 per cent around the middle of the period, becoming almost like the pattern we find in modern German. The eighteenth-century system arose out of the practice of authors to stress particular words by capitalizing them. But in eighteenth-century manuscripts, capitals are at times very hard to distinguish from lower-case letters, and in the interest of speed of production, compositors must have decided to impose their own rules on authorial practice, hence capitalizing all nouns. Spelling was usually left to the compositors in any case, as is apparent from frequent references in the correspondence of the printer and publisher Robert Dodsley. In September 1757 Lowth, for example, instructed Dodsley as follows: 'But before you send the Book to the press, I must beg the favour of you to take the trouble of reading it over carefully yourself: & not only to alter any mistakes in writing, spelling, &c. but to give me your observations, & objections to any passages'. Five months earlier, Dodsley had commented in a letter to the printer John Baskerville that: 'In the Specimen from Melmoth [one of Dodsley's authors], I think you have us'd too many Capitals, which is generally thought to spoil the beauty of the printing: but they should never be us'd to adjective verbs or adverbs'. Sarah Fielding was also aware of the fact that her own use of capitals differed from that of published texts. In a letter to Richardson (14 December 1758) she wrote: 'I am very apt when I write to be too careless about great and small Letters and Stops, but I suppose that will naturally be set right in the printing'. Possibly she had become aware of the existence of different spelling systems by her brother's correction of the language of *David Simple.* In line with this awareness, she varied her capitalization practice in her private correspondence depending on her relationship with her addressees: the less intimate this relationship or the more formal the topic of discussion (as in her correspondence with Harris which has been discussed on p.

254), the more her use of extra initial capitals approximates that of the publishers of the time.

Spelling, therefore, had a social significance at the time, and it can be used as a marker of relative formality in a private letter. This situation would, however, begin to change towards the end of the century, as appears from William Clift's criticism of his sister Elizabeth's spelling in a letter which he wrote to her on 9 January 1798:

> I shall never be convinced to the contrary of what I now think, by you, unless you learn to mend your Orthography or spell better; because No person on earth I am very certain can understand the true meaning of what they read unless they read it right ... Now you surely do not understand the true definition and derivation of the words Lutheran, Calvinist, Methodist, &c, otherwise you could not spell them wrong.

Clift's insensitivity here may be explained by his youthful pride at being about to make it in society—he was 23 when he wrote this letter. But it seems unfair for him to expect similar spelling skills of his barely literate sister. And Elizabeth took it hard, for it would be eighteen months before she wrote to him again. She had probably never enjoyed any formal education but she did learn to spell, possibly from Nancy Gilbert, daughter of the Vicar of Bodmin and later married to the local squire (see p. 246). Her letters show that she mastered the first stages of spelling: monosyllables such as *should, thought, treat,* and *know* are generally spelled correctly. She managed some polysyllables as well (*Particular, Company, Persecuted, inherit*), while others were evidently beyond her capabilities: *upurtunity, Profshion, sevility, Grandyear* ('grandeur'). For all that, her spelling skills were more than adequate for her to communicate with her family.

For Elizabeth Clift, to be able to read and write must have meant a giant educational leap compared to her mother (who probably had had no education at all). In genteel families, the mother was responsible for teaching the children their letters. 'I am very glad,' Lowth wrote to his wife in 1755, 'to hear that the dear Tom learns his book so well'. Tom was not even two at the time. Lowth himself appears to have learnt to spell from his mother too: he had a peculiar habit of breaking off words at the end of a line, using two colons, one on each line, as in 'my Af::fairs', rather than a hyphen or a double hyphen, as was more common. A surviving letter from his mother suggests that he must have learnt this practice from her! Genteel women did not on the whole spell worse than men: as long as English was not a school subject, they would have learnt to spell alongside their brothers at home.

Grammar

As with spelling, letters contain grammatical constructions that may strike a modern reader as somewhat surprising given the social background of the writer in question. In a letter to her future husband, Lady Mary Wortley Montagu, for instance, refers to 'them admirers you speak of'; Dodsley told Garrick of his 'suspicion that you was concern'd in it on purpose'; Lowth told his wife that he had arrived safely after his journey in the following words: 'Old William, after having happily drove us to Town with great spirit, sett us down at M^r. Garnier's'; Lord Hertford informed Horace Walpole that 'Lady Mary Coke and her have conversed upon it'; Walpole, gossiping with George Montagu, wrote: 'don't it put you in mind of any thing?'; and Betsy Sheridan, commenting on the appearance of Lady Anne Lindsay, wrote that she 'should not of known her'. These kind of sentences do not occur in printed texts: they would seem more typical of the language of the lower classes (such as the servant girl Lucy in Lady Mary Wortley Montagu's play *Simplicity*), but they are found in informal letters of more highly placed writers. Even relatively educated writers had a vernacular style at their disposal, which they used in informal, private correspondence; this style was characterized by different grammatical rules from those which came to form the basis of the normative grammatical tradition. People were also familiar with the kind of grammar that befitted the style required in more formal correspondence, such as Lady Mary Wortley Montagu when she wrote to Bishop Burnet, or Lowth when corresponding with his superiors in the Church. Richard Sheridan's letters, however, show no such stylistic distinction, for they contain hardly anything remarkable grammatically speaking. In his social ambitions, he evidently took care to write by the book, irrespective of his relationship with his addressees. In doing so, he may actually have been hypercorrecting, because it seems unusual that he would not have had a vernacular style. Such behaviour is typical of people who, like Sheridan, were social climbers, who are often almost too eager to show that they fully belonged to the class of people to which they were aspiring.

Fanny Burney observed that Dr John Hawkesworth, a writer and acquaintance of her father's,

does not shine in Conversation so much superior to others, as from his writings might be expected. Papa calls his Talking Book Language—for I never heard a man speak in a style which so much resembles writing. He has an amazing flow of choice of words & expressions ... All he says is just,—proper, & better express'd than most *written* language.

What she must have meant by 'Book Language' is the kind of language prescribed by the normative grammars of the time, which was often characterized by an over-scrupulous application of rules that more frequently than not had their basis in Latin rather than in actual usage. One example is what Görlach in 1997 called the 'ablative comparationis', as in 'We have lost our good Friend D^r. Chapman, than whom no man had better pretensions to long life', a construction which Lowth used in a letter to Dodsley dated 19 June 1760. The construction as such is not very common: Görlach found only 68 instances like the above sentence in a period of 400 years. Lowth perhaps used it when he had just started on his grammar in an effort to show off his grammatical competence to Dodsley. The correct use of case was a similar point. Actual usage shows considerable variation, as with Mrs Thrale who uses both *whom* and *who* in object position in her letters to Dr. Johnson: 'who you know I haven't seen' and 'whom he was heard to call'. In a footnote on p. 127 of his *Grammar*, Lowth (1762) picks up a similar pattern of usage from the philosopher John Locke, commenting: 'It ought to be *whom*'. The correct use of *whom* in letters of the period, however, suggests an almost unnatural awareness of the grammatical stricture that was supposed to regulate usage.

Women were often blamed for breaking these rules, supposedly because they had not received as much formal and especially clerical education as men; they would therefore not know about the concept of case, and hence be able to apply it correctly—even in English which, as previous chapters have illustrated, had gradually seen the erosion of the case system it had originally possessed. Walpole wrote to a friend as follows:

You will be diverted to hear that a man who thought of nothing so much as the purity of language, I mean Lord Chesterfield, says. 'you and *me* shall not be well together,' and this not once, but on every occasion. A friend of mine says, it was certainly to avoid that female inaccuracy *they don't mind you and I*, and yet the latter is the least bad of the two.

This construction was used by women, as by Walpole's correspondent Lady Ailesbury ('by Mr Conway and I') and by Lady Hertford ('and both Mr Fitzroy and her were vastly liked here'). It was, however, also used by men, including Walpole's own friends and acquaintances such as Conway ('but what might very probably have happened to anybody but you or I') and Lord Hertford (see above). Not surprisingly perhaps, Walpole did not use it himself. This provides a good example of what Jennifer Coates in 1993 termed 'The Androcentric Rule', according to which women are blamed for whatever is perceived as wrong in the language, while men are praised for the opposite. Another example of the Androcentric Rule in eighteenth-century English is the rise of the so-called sex-indefinite *he*, as in *anyone may do as he pleases*. An alternative, then as now, is the use of *they* as a singular pronoun: *anyone may do as they please*. Such a rule would have violated the principle of number but not that of gender, as with the choice of *he*, a decision which would no doubt have been preferred by women. It is therefore odd that this rule first appears in a grammar by a woman, Ann Fisher (1745): 'The *Masculine Person* answers to the *general Name*, which comprehends both *Male* and *Female*; as, *any Person who knows what he says*' (2nd edn.

1750,[10] 117n). Did Ann Fisher record preferred practice, and by formulating it into a rule, attempted to inform her female audience of its existence, or did she draw up the rule herself? What remains clear, however, is that, despite the normative grammarians' proscriptions, both *between you and I* and singular *they* are still current today.

The grammarians were more successful in their condemnation of other items. *You was* is one of them. Usage of this construction increased considerably during the eighteenth century, and it apparently functioned as a transition in the development of *you* into a singular pronoun. There was a peak in usage during the 1760s, and this presumably caught the attention of the normative grammarians: though Lowth regularly used *you was* himself, he was the first to condemn it as 'an enormous solecism' in the first edition of his grammar. He was similarly the first to condemn the use of participles like *wrote*—as in the example he gives in his *Grammar* from the poet Matthew Prior, 'Illustrious virtues, who by turns *have rose*'—although he may have picked up the stricture from his friend James Harris. During the eighteenth century, past tense forms and participles of strong verbs regularly appeared in more than one form, such as *chose/chused* and *chose/chosen*, or *swum/swam/swimmed* and *swum/swimmed*. In their desire for regularity, the grammarians advocated the principle of one form, one function: *chose—chosen* and *wrote—written*. Again, and as illustrated above, Lowth frequently used *wrote*, *drove*, and *forgot* as past participles himself, although only in his informal letters.

In the letters of the period, grammatical forms are also attested that are not discussed in the grammars. One example is *he/she don't*, as illustrated above. It is used by Lady Mary Wortley Montagu and by Walpole and his correspondents (Montagu, Lady Dysart, Lady Suffolk), but not by Boswell, Mrs Thrale, Fanny Burney, Lowth, or Thomas Turner, who is described by Vaisey (who edited Turner's diaries) as a Sussex 'shopkeeper, undertaker, schoolmaster, tax-gatherer, churchwarden, overseer of the poor and much besides'. About a generation ago today, the use of *he/she don't* would be considered affected, and if it was typically found in the language of the higher social classes during the eighteenth century (and also the nineteenth century; see further p. 282), it may also have been considered affected in those days too. What complicates the matter is that *he/she don't* is also found in the novels of Fanny Burney and Smollett to mark non-standard speech. To social climbers, it would therefore have been a tricky form to use, as one ran the risk of being considered uneducated if one did. Stigmatized

---

[10] The first edition was probably published in 1745, although no copy is currently known to be in existence.

though the form probably was at the time, particularly to those belonging to the middle classes, we do find it in the language of Betsy Sheridan. This may therefore be taken to indicate that, despite her protestations to the contrary ('I never coveted the honor of sitting at great people's tables and every day I live I wish for it less'), that she was as much a social aspirer as her brother, though less openly so.

Another feature, not even discussed by present-day grammars of English, is found among all speakers, that is the use of *-self* pronouns instead of pronouns proper, as in 'Miss Allen & myself went to an Auction' (Fanny Burney), 'nobody is to see this letter, but yourself and ...' (Walpole), and 'myself being the bondman' (Turner). This non-reflexive use of *-self* served as an avoidance strategy, functioning as a kind of modesty device by skirting the rather more direct use of the pronoun *I* on the part of the speaker and, interestingly, even that of *you* on the part of the addressee. It is more common with modest people, such as Turner and Fanny Burney, than with men like Boswell, who was very much the opposite. Tag questions are not treated in the grammars of the period either. They do occur, even in letters (e.g. Walpole: 'is not he'), although not as frequently as today: Lowth's letters to his wife do not contain a single instance. The use of tag questions was an informal device—seeking confirmation, deferring to the addressee—that still had to become common usage.

The subjunctive has a fixed place in the grammars of the period, and it still occurred regularly, although less so in informal contexts. Lowth, for example, when writing to his wife, says 'If he writes to the Bishop in the same style', but he used the subjunctive when addressing the Duke of Newcastle, as in 'Whether the exchange were advantageous'. He also used it to William Warburton (with whom he fought what Hepworth called in his biography of Lowth, 'the greatest literary battle of the century'), just before breaking off relations with him: 'That an end be put to this Correspondence'. There was also considerable variation in the use of periphrastic *do* in negative sentences and questions depending on the style of writing, the author's background, and the degree of influence from prestigious users. Usage of *do*-less negative sentences, for example, *I question not but that ...* , in informative prose (novels, essays, history) ranges between 2 per cent (Lady Mary Wortley Montagu) and 75 per cent (Fanny Burney), that in letters between 1 per cent (Walpole) and 52 per cent (Richardson). In both styles, usage is most advanced with members of the aristocracy. Fanny Burney's exceptional status can be explained by the fact that she allowed her language to be influenced by that of Dr Johnson, who was her linguistic model. Richardson's usage is equally high in his letters as in his informative prose, which is unusual for the time: like Fanny Burney, he appears to have modelled himself on Johnson, and on the language of

Johnson's periodical the *Rambler* rather than on Johnson's other prose styles (that of his *Lives of the Poets*, for instance), which are less archaic in their use of periphrastic *do*. Another auxiliary that was changing at the time was the use of *be* with mutative intransitive verbs (*arrive, go, come*) which was increasingly replaced by *have*. It is a change which appears to be led by women. With Lowth we find the auxiliary *be* most frequently in his informal letters, as in 'I rejoice that y^e. Dear Tom is gott so well again' (to his wife Molly, 1755). This suggests that by the middle of the eighteenth century the construction with *have* had already become the predominant one.

Lowth himself did not use double negation, nor did his correspondents; this probably explains why there is no stricture against it in the first edition of his grammar. One of his critical readers must have brought this oversight to his attention, and Lowth made up for it in the second edition of 1763: 'Two Negatives in English destroy one another, or are equivalent to an Affirmative'. According to Baugh and Cable, 'the eighteenth century is responsible for the condemnation of the double negative'; double negation was indeed for the first time formally proscribed, but it was already on the way out. Well before Lowth's grammar appeared, the physicist Benjamin Martin had set out the argument which lay behind the condemnation of the double negative:

But the two negatives as used by the Saxons and French must be understood by way of apposition ... which way of speaking is still in use among us; and in this case the two negatives answer to the addition of two negative quantities in Algebra, the sum of which is negative. But our ordinary use of two negatives (in which the force of the first is much more than merely destroyed by the latter) corresponds to the multiplication of two negative quantities in Algebra, the product of which is always affirmative; as mathematicians very well know.

Martin's explanation—which appears on p. 93 of his *Institutions of Language* of 1748—is interesting because it indicates that double negation was no longer considered quite acceptable ('our ordinary use of two negatives'), but that it was common in speech ('which way of speaking is still in use among us'). It still occurred in drama and in novels, but also in letters, as by Sir Richard Steele, Lady Mary Wortley Montagu, Walpole ('I told them that I did not neither') and his correspondents (Montagu, Lord Hertford, Lady Hertford, the writer Hannah More), by Boswell ('I am troubled with no dirty sheets nor no jostling chairmen'), and by Mrs Thrale ('nor I see no Call'). But from the absence of any double negatives in the *Beggars' Opera*, commented on above, it appears that double negation was becoming stigmatized even in the spoken language—hence its presence in Lowth's grammar.

When he arrived in the capital, William Clift had to adapt his grammar to London practice and, because he was socially ambitious, he modelled himself on the language of the middle classes to which he aspired. He thus got rid of *he don't* and *you was*, as well as a range of dialectal features such as *where* for *whether* and time adverbials as in 'the Footman left us last monday was Sennight', that is 'Monday, a week ago'. The adverbial *sennight*, grammaticalized from the Old English phrase *seofon* + *niht* (literally 'seven' + 'night', meaning 'week'), also occurs once in a letter by Lowth addressed to his friend and co-executor of the anecdotist Sir Joseph Spence's will, Gloster Ridley: 'I propose being in Town ab^t. nex[t] Wednesday Sennight'. Lowth had been born in Winchester, and this instance suggests that in informal letters—Ridley was one of his closest friends—regionally marked usages might show up occasionally. But he and his social peers would avoid them in their more formal letters, upon the risk of being considered uneducated by betraying their local origins.

Vocabulary

In an age in which many new words arose, it is interesting to see that almost all authors discussed in this chapter, including those of the first half of the century, are represented in the *OED* with first occurrences of new words. This need not imply that they had actually invented these words; in many instances they were simply the first to record common usage. Some writers appear more frequently in the *OED* than others, which probably merely means that their writings were better studied by the dictionary's volunteer readers who tracked down citations and evidence of usage for the *OED*. For all that, it is illuminating to see with what kind of words their names found their way into the *OED* as first users; it could be argued, for example, that the kind of words they supposedly coined are probably representative of the kinds of social and cultural developments that were going on at the time. In order of frequency, the following authors are listed in the *OED* online edition at the time this research was carried out: Richardson (245), Walpole (214), Fanny Burney (160), Henry Fielding (108), Sterne (100), Johnson (72), Gay (43), Lady Mary Wortley Montagu (35), Richard Sheridan (31), Boswell (25), Martin (18), Mrs Thrale (18), Garrick (16), Dodsley (8), Lowth (8), Thomas Sheridan (8), Sarah Fielding (4), and Betsy Sheridan (4). Except for—not surprisingly—Elizabeth Clift, all of the others occur in the *OED* as well, although William Clift and Thomas Turner do not have any first recorded words to their name, and only very few instances of other usages, such as *bumbo* ('a liquor composed or rum, sugar, water, and nutmeg') which was used by Turner in his diary in 1756, and the palaeontological term *megatherium* (referring to an 'extinct

10

ENGLISH IN THE NINETEENTH CENTURY

Lynda Mugglestone

TRANSITIONS

'EVERY age may be called an age of transition', the novelist and statesman Edward Bulwer Lytton stated in 1833. Transitions have of course emerged as a significant topic in many chapters in this volume; as Lytton noted, 'the passing-on, as it were, from one state to another never ceases'. Nevertheless, he made one important distinction for the nineteenth century alone. 'In our age', he added, 'the transition is *visible*'.

For those who lived in the nineteenth century, this 'visibility' of change could hardly be denied. Industrialization and new patterns of transport transformed the British landscape at an unprecedented rate while, both directly and indirectly, language mapped and consolidated the advances being made. *Industrialism*, according to the *OED* (itself one of the great achievements of the age) was first used in 1833; *industrialize* as a verb appeared in 1882. *Urbanization* was later still, first being recorded in 1888, although its processes were widely apparently throughout the century; Manchester almost quadrupled in size between 1801 and 1871, Birmingham expanded by 73 per cent, and Leeds by 99 per cent. Countless acts of individual migration moreover underpinned these patterns of change, bringing a whole range of regional speakers into new (and unexpected) proximities as a result. Meanwhile, *urbanize* lost dominant eighteenth-century senses in which it had signified 'To render urbane or civil; to make more refined or polished'. Instead, by association, it gradually assumed meanings with which modern speakers are more familiar: 'The Government will ... then appeal to the urbanised counties', as the *Western Morning Chronicle* noted in 1884.

The currency of new verbs such as *to train* reflected further transformative shifts in both landscape and mobility. 'I trained up to town for the Committee of Privileges', a letter from Lord Granville stated in 1856. *Railway* demonstrated conspicuous fertility. *Railway-guides, -passes, -rugs,* and *-sickness* all exist as part of a new catalogue of combinatory forms (along with *railway spine*: 'an affection of the spine produced by concussion in a railway accident', as the *OED* noted); idioms such as *to let off steam* likewise became part of accepted verbal currency. *Macadam, cab, omnibus, bicycle,* and the earlier *velocipede*—defined in the *OED* as 'a travelling-machine having wheels turned by the pressure of one's feet upon pedals' and ridden enthusiastically around Oxford by Charles Dodgson (otherwise known as Lewis Carroll), as well as by James Murray, the *OED*'s editor-in chief—can all be used to demonstrate further intersections of linguistic and technical spheres. As Alice Mann stressed in her *General Expositor* (1862): 'Our language, as well as our arts, science, and manufacture, has partaken of the general progress, improvement, and enlargement, which have marked the surprising movements of the present century'.

The legacies of progress in the nineteenth century can therefore result in a scale—and scope—of language data which was inconceivable in earlier periods. The production of printed texts was, for example, transformed by the steam press. Whereas some 250 impressions an hour had been produced by the earlier hand-presses, the advent of steam meant that production quadrupled by 1814. By 1848, 12,000 sheets an hour could be printed. The elimination in the 1850s and 1860s of taxes on paper and newspapers likewise contributed to the increased presence of the printed word. Access to education in a diversity of forms, whether dame schools which provided a rudimentary education in the first principles of letters and numbers, night classes such as those attended three times a week (at 1^d per session) by the 18-year-old engineer George Stephenson (inventor of the first workable railway locomotive), elite public schools such as Shrewsbury, attended by Charles Darwin, as well as private schools—and Sunday Schools which also often aimed to foster language skills—also served to bring familiarity with the written word to a far broader spectrum of society. The Elementary Education Act of 1870 institutionalized the principle (and practice) of mass education but, even before this, it was clear that literacy was in the ascendant. The testimony of a wide range of working-class autobiographies and diaries (see further pp. 296–7) offers compelling evidence of the variety of linguistic experiences which await the historian of language in the nineteenth century. The 'Penny Post' which, from

January 1840, established a national and standard price of 1^d for letters (paid by the sender rather than, as previously, by the recipient according to the distance sent), brought a similarly unparalleled rise in private written communication. Some 75 million letters were sent in 1839; by 1849 the corresponding figure was 347 million. New modes of communication, both written and spoken, also came into being. Only face-to-face conversation had hitherto offered the directness— and speed—of the telegraph (introduced in 1837), and particularly the telephone (first demonstrated by Alexander Graham Bell in Glasgow in 1876). By 1872 around 15 million telegrams were being sent each year.

This image of progress is, of course, only one side of the story. While it might be tempting to construct the nineteenth century as one dominated by transcend- ent innovation and advance, then it is also salutary to remember the various images of divisiveness which also came to mark the age. Here too language played a part. The introduction of the telegraph raised fears for linguistic decline ('We shall gradually give up English in favour of Telegraphese, and Electric Telegraph- ese is as short and spare as Daily Telegraphese is longwinded and redundant', the *Pall Mall Gazette* conjectured in 1885). Advances in print culture meanwhile served to foreground linguistic difference—not least since if 'the great majority of working people spoke some form of dialect; in general they read and wrote in standard English'.[1] Conflicts of 'masters and men' isolated a language of class which had also been absent in previous centuries. As the *OED* records, here a newly extensive terminology offered the potential for self-definition (and for the definition of others). '*Higher* (*upper*), *middle, lower classes, working classes* ... appear to be of modern introduction', James Murray wrote, carefully defining *class* in 1889; *class-antagonism* and *class-barrier, class-bias,* and *class-consciousness,* all have their roots in the nineteenth century. In popular stereotypes of language practice, it was moreover not just vocabulary which implemented such divisions. As the previous chapter has indicated, accent (in the work of Thomas Sheridan and others) came to participate in increasingly normative constructions by which the 'received' and the regional were increasingly placed at odds. A range of shibboleths of pronunciation (not least the perceived stigma of [h]-dropping) were duly consolidated as the nineteenth century advanced. Contemporary images of self-help—another important image of the age—often assumed dis- tinctive linguistic resonances in response. 'The perusal and profit of the ledger should be preceded, accompanied, or at least followed, by a little study of grammar', stated *P's and Q's. Grammatical Hints for the Million* in the 1850s. The same author—an anthropomorphized Hon. Henry H.—satirized the aspir-

---

[1] See further L. James (ed.). *Print and the People 1819–1851* (London: James Allen, 1976), 22.

ations (and aspirates) of the *parvenu* (another new word, first documented in 1802) in *Poor Letter H*: 'We must, however, protest against the barbarity of a rich nobody, who having ... more money than wit, built himself a large mansion, and dubbed it his *habbey* ... he would persist in saying that the *habbey* was his '*obby*'. In a real-life correlate, the self-made 'railway king' George Hudson was widely stigmatized in the popular press for linguistic infelicities of precisely this kind (and in spite of his own purchase of the 12,000-acre Londesborough Park in Yorkshire where he had planned to build a family seat).

A variety of prescriptive agendas for reform and control hence came to exist uneasily alongside newer linguistic approaches whereby, as for the *OED*, the study of language was intentionally objective rather than subjective. Philology, dismissed as 'barren' by Johnson in the eighteenth century, assumed a new fertility in the nineteenth. It was of course under the auspices of the London Philological Society (founded in 1842) that the *OED* had its own beginnings. Language scholars such as Frederick Furnivall, W. W. Skeat, the phoneticians Alexander Ellis and Henry Sweet, and the lexicographer James Murray insisted on the salience of scientific principle in linguistic investigation. 'The sounds of language are very fleeting ... all are altered by combination, expression, pitch, intonation, emotion, age, sex', as Ellis stressed in 1869, setting out principles which bear no little resemblance to the underlying ideas of modern socio-linguistic study.

Linguistic division was manifest in other ways too. The forces of nationalism and standardization assumed, for instance, an uneven co-existence in terms of the continuing multilingualism of the United Kingdom. The use of Welsh was 'a vast drawback to Wales', concluded a special committee which investigated the state of Welsh education in 1846. Wales gained its own national anthem ten years later but the number of Welsh speakers continued to decline. In 1800 *circa* 80 per cent of the population of Wales had used Welsh in their daily lives; by 1900 the same could be said of only 50 per cent (a figure partly affected by the forces of immigration). The 1870 Education Act made English compulsory in all schools throughout the kingdom. While societies such as the Gaelic Society of Inverness (founded in 1871) and the Society for Utilising the Welsh Language (founded in 1885), as well as the Gaelic Union of Ireland (founded in 1880), attest considerable interest in distinct language varieties, the educational impetus was firmly placed on acquiring the 'proper' forms of English alone. It was essential that the person appointed as English master 'shall have a pure English accent' proclaimed the Statement by the Directors of the Edinburgh Academy in 1824. Colonial discourses, and the missionary drive to foster standard English within the Empire, presented still other facets of the divisiveness which language could serve to enact.

This range of conflicting voices means that it is in some ways virtually impossible to characterize the language of the nineteenth century within a single chapter. Even the definition of the nation changes signally over this time; by its political union with Ireland, the Britain of 1800 became the United Kingdom of 1801 ('The said Kingdoms of Great Britain and Ireland shall ... be united into one Kingdom, by the name of The United Kingdom of Great Britain and Ireland' as the Act of 1800 had declared). Definitions of the monarchy manifest other aspects of change. The century began with George III (1738–1830). It ended with Victoria, born in 1819, crowned Queen in 1837, and proclaimed Empress of India in 1877. Meanwhile English (and Englishes) expanded abroad, becoming a lingua franca for a wide range of international settings (see further Chapters 12 and 13). Describing 'English' is, as a result, fraught with complexity. Indeed, if one form of English came to be widely institutionalized in education and the printed text, it is also clear that nineteenth-century English (and its manifold varieties) were, in reality, to remain open to considerable shift and flux.

MYTHS OF STASIS

Given the insistence by historians on the nineteenth century as a period of particularly dramatic shift, it can seem ironic that, in histories of the language, it is the *absence* of significant linguistic change which instead comes to the fore. The English of the present day differs from that of 1800 'only in relatively minor ways', writes Fennell; Gerry Knowles similarly allows only 'little subsequent change [since 1800] in the forms of the standard language', even if he simultan-eously admits 'substantial change in non-standard spoken English'.[2] It is of course undeniable that the wide-scale systemic changes which characterized some of the earlier periods discussed in this volume are absent. On the other hand, to assume a situation of near stasis is clearly somewhat reductive, especially when one takes into account the linguistic variability which accompanied private writings of a variety of kinds. Moreover, while public printed texts manifest greater stability, even these are not devoid of change. 'She was not less pleased another day with the manner in which he seconded another wish of her's', states Jane Austen's *Emma* (1816), displaying principles of genitive marking which were later proscribed. '*Hers, its, ours, yours, theirs,* should never be written, *her's, it's,*

---

[2] See Fennell (2001: 168) and G. Knowles, *A Cultural History of the English Language* (London: Arnold, 1997), 136.

our's, your's, their's, as Lennie's *Principles of English Grammar* (1864) affirmed. Forms such as *chuse* and *chace*, *doat* and *chearful*, common in printed texts in the early nineteenth century, likewise gradually disappear. Print is, however, merely one domain of usage, not the language in entirety. In this sense, it often served as an inadequate reflection of the underlying realities of language in use, especially in matters of orthography and morphology. 'Except in extremely rare cases where the author is opinionated and insists on the compositor "following copy," no printed copy represents the orthography and punctuation of the man of education who writes, but only of the man of education who prints', wrote Ellis. Indeed, he added, 'the literal exhibition of the greater part of "the copy for the press," and still more of the correspondence of even esteemed men of letters, would show that our present orthography, including the use of capitals and punctuation, is by no means as settled as printed books … would lead us to suppose'.

As Ellis indicates, print culture fostered a set of norms which rationalized the variable realities of the underlying text. Correctors and printers' readers continued to act in markedly interventionist ways. 'Most Authors expect the Printer to spell, point, and digest their Copy, that it may be intelligible and significant to the Reader', Caleb Stower noted in his *Printer's Grammar* (1808). Given the nineteenth-century emphasis on the importance of standardization, it was a practice which became increasingly entrenched, consolidating a public image of a norm from which private usage—throughout the social spectrum—often conspicuously diverged. This observable gap between public and private usage indeed often prompts emendation in modern editions of nineteenth-century texts. 'Certain Dickensian peculiarities of spelling, e.g. 'Recal', 'pannel' ' are hence corrected in Michael Slater's edition of *A Christmas Carol* (2003); House and Storey similarly remark on what they term 'life-long mis-spellings'—such as *poney* and *trowsers*—in Dickens's letters. Editing the European diaries of the politician Richard Cobden, Miles Taylor isolates Cobden's 'arcane' spellings; 'much of it [is] American English … "labor", instead of "labour"', he adds. Hutchinson's (1904) edition of Shelley displayed a similar bias; 'irregular or antiquated forms such as … "sacrifize," "tyger," "gulph," "desart," "falshood," and the like' were all corrected on the grounds that they would 'only serve to distract the reader's attention, and mar his enjoyment of the verse'.

Such patterns were, however, entirely characteristic of the realities of nineteenth-century spelling practice. Both *trowsers* and *poney*, for example, appear as habitual forms in the diaries of Lady Katherine Clarendon: 'George and I dined together at 4 o'clock and drove down the Grove afterwards in the Poney Carriage', as her entry for 12 August 1840 states; *gulph* appears in the letters of Effie Ruskin (and of Ruskin himself), while spellings such as *novellist, untill, porcellain*, and *beautifull* confirm common variabilities of consonant doubling in a range of writers. The variation of *s/z* underpins a whole set of different forms. *Surprize* rather than *surprise* was used by George Eliot and Walter Scott; Michael Faraday (the pioneering English chemist and physicist) selected *fuze* rather than *fuse*. Darwin embarked on a *cruize* rather than *cruise* in his voyage on the *Beagle*. *Cozy* was the preferred form of Queen Victoria and of the novelist (and politician) Benjamin Disraeli ('the concomitant delights of cozy luncheons and confidential chats', he wrote in a letter of 17 April 1838 to his future wife). Dorothy Wordsworth preferred *cozie* while Dickens used *cosey*. These are by no means isolated examples but represent a level of systemic variability even within so-called 'educated' writers. Contemporary variation of *or/our* offers a further case in point. *Favor, favorite, honor, harbor, splendor,* and *color* (among others) are all common nineteenth-century forms. Their dominant connotations were not those of incipient Americanization (as Taylor suggests of Cobden), but instead those of modernity and advance. As Dickens explained to the philanthropist Angela Burdett Coutts on 11 July 1856, 'I spell Harbor without the letter u, because the modern spelling of such words as "Harbor, arbor, parlor" &c. (modern within the last quarter of a century) discards that vowel, as belonging in that connexion to another sound—such as hour and sour'.

Millward's contention in 1996 that 'by the end of the seventeenth century the principle of a fixed spelling for every word was firmly established for printed works, and, over the course of the following century, "personal" spelling followed suit' can hence underestimate the true situation.[3] Instead, the sense of a norm was seemingly far more flexible, allowing variants such as *poney* to appear even in printed texts until mid-century ('Clive … much preferred poneys to ride', as Thackeray's *The Newcomes* states in 1855) and permitting, as indicated above, a still wider range within the domains of private communication. Nineteenth-century punctuation practices attest, if anything, still greater diversity, and informal usage in private texts (especially in the preference for dashes above stops) can contrast sharply with the heavy punctuation which commonly attended print. Typical too is Darwin's hesitancy over the placing of apostrophes. 'Do you know *it's* name?' Darwin enquired of William Darwin Fox, on 12 June 1828. 'I am myself going to collect *pigs jaws*', he wrote on 31 August 1856 to T. C. Eyton; 'I want to know whether on a wet muddy day, whether *birds feet* are dirty' [emphases added]. Michael Faraday, Mrs Gaskell, and Sir Henry Lennox ('I am so determined, that you shall not write a second letter like your last, that, at the

---

[3] See C. Millward. *A Biography of the English Language* (2nd edn.) (Orlando, Florida: Harcourt Brace, 1996), 261.

risk of *it's* being quite illegible, I have commenced an Epistle, in the Railway Carriage', as the latter wrote to Disraeli), provide other examples of such patterns. While *it's* had undoubted legitimacy as an early possessive form, assumptions that such usage had declined by the beginning of the nineteenth century are again open to reappraisal. Public and private conventions diverge, just as they do over the retention or otherwise of long-tailed *ſ* in the representation of words such as *happineſs* and *gentleneſs* (disappearing in printed texts around 1800, it can be found in private documents throughout the century). Similar was the retention of *ye* as a scribal abbreviation for *the* ('We can stay a day or two at ye Ile of Man if either of us feel inclined to give up the ghost', writes Darwin's elder brother Erasmus in June 1825; 'Rogers hates me. I can hardly believe, as he gives out, that V[ivian] G[rey] is ye cause', Disraeli fumed in his diary in 1834).

Other aspects of language in use also displayed features which, at times, have little in common with the rhetoric of standardization which dominates popular language comment at this time. As the opening page of *Ledsham's Sure Guide to English Grammar* (1879) confirms, prescriptive traditions here maintained a healthy continuity with their eighteenth-century predecessors: '**Grammar** is the **science** of **language**, and it therefore teaches us how to **speak** and **write** correctly', it stated. Principle and practice were, however, often to be at odds. Duncan's patriotic insistence in 1890 that English was 'undoubtedly the noblest of modern tongues' hence sits uneasily alongside his admission that 'no other language of a civilized people is so badly spoken and written'. Indeed, he continued, 'errors and inelegancies of the most glaring character abound in the speaking and writing of even our best orators'. The sociolinguist Peter Trudgill's axiom that 'Standard English is not a set of prescriptive rules' necessarily lay in the future (as indeed did his emphasis on the fact that a standard is not restricted to the most formal styles alone).[4] In popular thinking in the nineteenth century, it was instead by the specification of a set of (often highly conservative) desiderata that 'good' English was to be acquired. Usage was in turn depicted as in need of stringent reform, especially when it revealed a change in progress or the influence of regional marking. 'It is an error, very common to the district between Rotherham and Barnsley, to use wrong verbs, &c. Such expressions as the following are very common:—"I *were* running," "We *was* running," "We'm running," meaning "We *am* running," "*Was* you there?"', dictated Pearson in *The Self-Help Grammar of the English Language* (1865). Standard grammar was national not local. As a result, 'the Teacher should point out to his pupils the erroneous expressions of their own locality, and endeavour to eradicate them' (see further pp. 292–5).

---

[4] See further P. Trudgill, 'Standard English. What It Isn't', in T. Bex and R. J. Watts (eds), *Standard English. The Widening Debate* (Routledge: London and New York, 1999), 117–28.

Verbal forms in fact reveal a number of significant shifts over the nineteenth century, not least perhaps in the continued diffusion of the progressive passive. Although examples of the earlier construction could still be found ('Chintz-room preparing for Mr. Sawyer', noted Harriet Acworth, the well-educated wife of an Evangelical minister in Leicestershire, in her diary in 1838), the newer form—as in 'The house was being built'—was well established by the 1830s, even if it continued to attract prescriptive censure. The escalation in other expanded tense structures elicited further condemnation, revealing another divide between linguistic practice and prescriptive principle. Constructions such as 'I intended *to have returned* on Monday' (corrected to 'to return'), 'I happened *to have been* present' (corrected to 'to be'), and 'I hoped never *to have met* him again' (corrected to 'to meet') are all given as prevalent errors on p. 14 of Ladell's *How to Spell and Speak English* (in its third edition by 1897). Traditional prescriptive considerations of logic and reason underpinned formal resistance to their use, as Duncan (1890) again illustrates: 'Some persons—we might perhaps say a majority of those who professedly speak the English language—often use the past tense and the perfect tense together, in such sentences as the following: "I intended to *have called* on him last night." "I meant to *have purchased* one yesterday," or a pluperfect tense and a perfect tense together as, "You should *have written* to *have told* her." These expressions are illogical, because, as the *intention* to perform the act *must* be *prior* to the act contemplated, the act itself cannot with propriety be expressed by a tense indicating a period of time *previous* to the intention'. The ubiquity of such constructions reveals, of course, the real situation: 'I fully expected to have seen you', wrote Fanny Owen to Darwin in the late 1820s; 'How I wish you had been able to have stayed up here', Darwin wrote to his cousin William Fox in 1829.

Changes in progress (with all their underlying variability) predictably attracted a normative response. Nineteenth-century vacillations over the subjunctive provide a further useful example. This remained obligatory (at least in theory) in the traditional environments of verbs following the expression of a wish, desire, or command, or in hypothetical constructions governed by *whether, though,* or *if.* Bulwer Lytton illustrates its formal proprieties well in a letter written on 5 October 1836: 'the English find it so bad a thing to have a wife, that they suppose it quite natural to murder her, even though *she bring him* £1000 a year' (emphasis added). Its variability, especially in informal contexts, is nevertheless clear. 'If she is in a state [i.e. pregnant], she don't shew it', Katharine Clarendon conjectured on 29 May 1840 about the newly-married Queen Victoria, deploying indicative *is* rather than subjunctive *be* (as well as the frequently proscribed *she don't*).

Seventeen years later, the artist John Millais displayed conspicuous uncertainty, even in parallel constructions within the same letter (written on 8 June 1861): 'I wd work splendidly if I was beside you. I am *perfectly certain* I could finish both pictures in less than half the time if I were with you'. In the face of this apparently fading linguistic nuance, many writers conversely attempted to comply with popular doctrines of correctness by hypercorrect uses of the subjunctive—even when strictly inappropriate. This too met with short shrift. The anonymous author of *Fashion in Language* (1906) condemned it as 'a growing tendency' which rendered it almost impossible to 'state any fixed rule at all' on the matter for the late nineteenth century. Even by 1848, as Harrison confirmed, it was clear that subjunctive usage was both 'indiscriminate' and 'promiscuous': 'a part of English grammar, in which we shall look in vain for any thing bordering upon a principle, even in authors of the highest authority'.

While Harrison recommended remedial measures for this situation, supplying a set of exercises in 'false syntax' (specimen 'incorrect' sentences to be emended by the reader/pupil) in the interests of re-establishing the 'proper' norms, the direction of change was clear. Normative exercises of this kind were common in grammatical instruction, and their dictates often readily reveal the tensions between prescriptive precepts and language in use. Common targets for correction by the reader were the 'flat adverb' ('John writes pretty'), the 'improper' use of relatives ('James was one of those boys that was kept in at school for bad behaviour'), the imperfect discrimination of *who/ whom* ('Who did you buy your grammar from?'), as well as the complex proprieties of *shall* and *will, may* and *might,* which often served as convenient touchstones of correctness in contemporary language attitudes. Real English was, as ever, often at some remove. Adverbial variation remained common, especially in private and informal writing in the first half of the century. 'They both ran down *so quick*', wrote Clarendon in her diary, describing Victoria and Albert on their wedding day on 10 February 1840; 'they went down to Windsor *very slowly*'. 'I do not believe that they *sleep separate*', she added [emphases added]. The diaries of Anne Lister, a member of the Northern gentry, provide similar examples ('our train having *gone slow* for the last 1/4 hour' (2 November 1834); 'I did not wish to *influence anyone unfairly*' (19 January 1835); 'very *civilly complained*' (23 January 1835); 'She dared *scarce speak*' (17 September 1835)), as do the letters of Charlotte Brontë ('Her lively spirits and bright colour might delude you into a belief that all was well, but she *breathes short*', she wrote in evident anxiety on 9 June 1838 [emphases added]). Variation in Darwin's letters follows the same patterns ('I am very glad to hear, the four casks arrived safe', he wrote on 24 July 1834).

thou knowest best things of another sort, such as belong to the manly heart'. The use of *thou/thee*, and the possessive *thy*, remained stylistically marked forms, regularly drawn on in private letters as well as public usage, as in Disraeli's 1833 promise to send Helen Blackwood the first bound copy of his novel *The Wondrous Tale of Alroy* 'wherein I will venture to inscribe thy fair & adored name'.

Pronouns such as *everybody* posed further problems, again trapping a variety of writers between opposing discourses of correctness and usage. The formal position was that given by Duncan in 1890 under the heading 'False Inflection and Construction'. ' "Everybody has a right to *their* opinions;" but we have no right to use a plural pronoun in construction with a singular antecedent', he declared, pointing out the 'proper' form to be employed: 'Everybody [a singular noun] has a right to *his* opinions. The error indicated here is a very common one. Even our best speakers and writers fall into it'. It is rulings of this kind which Mary Ward observes in her own letters ('Everybody did the best he could') and which Henry Bradley, editing this word in the *OED* four years later, carefully endorsed. The fact that, in the accompanying illustrative citations for this entry in the dictionary, it was the notionally 'incorrect' plural which dominated did not escape the notice of reviewers, especially given the stated intentions of the *OED* to provide a descriptive engagement with the facts of language. 'Every body does and says what they please', Byron had written in 1820; 'Everybody seems to recover their spirits', Ruskin noted in 1866. Earlier instances traced usage into the sixteenth century, rendering Bradley's comment visibly awry.

Real English again retained considerable variation on these and related matters. Mary Ward's vigilance on matters of concord can, for example, be relaxed in informal constructions such as '*three or four volumes* of these books a week *is* about all that I can do' (from a letter of 1882 [emphasis added]). 'Everybody are enthusiastic' wrote Millais in 1856, displaying a further level of variability which accords well with, say, Queen Victoria's habitual use of *news* as a plural ('These news are dreadful', she wrote in a telegram to Gladstone after the siege of Khartoum in 1885) or the nurse Elizabeth Wheeler's use of *health* as a count noun in December 1854 as she made her statement to the Parliamentary Commissioners concerning hospital conditions in the Crimea ('I think that perhaps 50 men may have had their healths injured by the want of the restoratives I desired to give them'). Other nouns such as *scissors* and *drawers* could conversely appear in the singular. 'Flan[ne]l drawers is not enough when you go out of y^r. warm room', Mary Anne Disraeli informed her husband in 1869.

The cumulative effect of such patterns, perhaps relatively minor in isolation, hence attests a range of differences between nineteenth-century English and our own. Pleonastic *be* could still be found ('Poor vulgar Mrs W—was beginning to bore me on my sister's being going to be married', as Anne Lister wrote on 1 February 1836); gerundial constructions such as 'Nothing remains but to trust *the having children* or not in His hands', as Mary Lyttelton stated in her diary on 3 December 1855, continued to flourish. 'Today has seen one of our greatest family events—*the starting of Papa* and Spencer to New Zealand', states a diary entry by her sister Lavinia on 2 December 1867; '*The sitting tight* for his arrival was terribly sad and nervous work', confessed Lucy Lyttelton Cavendish in a letter written on 28 April 1876 [emphases added]. Darwin too made use of similar forms ('the unfitting me to settle down as a clergyman', he wrote in a letter on 30 August 1831). Preterites also display considerable variability. Alternatives such as 'dug, *or* digged', 'rang, *or* rung', 'sank, *or* sunk', 'sang, *or* sung' and 'spat, *or* spit' are countenanced in Lennie's *Grammar* (1864), and duly reflected in usage; *lighted* for *lit* was also common, as was *waked* for *woke*. Weak preterites meanwhile often appeared in forms such as *clapt, stopt, drest, whipt*, and *prest*; '[I] slipt off my heels in the powdered snow by the garden door', the politician William Gladstone recorded in his diary in 1881. Past participles also failed to show the regularization formally expected in the nineteenth century (even if such variation was formally condemned in many grammars). 'The health of Prince A[lbert] was drank', Katharine Clarendon noted in her diary in 1840. *Swelled* regularly appeared alongside *swollen*, *waked* alongside *woken*.

Proclaimed standards of 'good' English, throughout the social spectrum, could therefore reveal considerable latitude when placed in the context of ordinary usage. Informal syntax, for example, regularly operated outside the strait-jacket of prescriptive rules, as in the evocative description by the scientist Humphry Davy of walking on Vesuvius as it erupted in 1819 ('I should have completed [my experiments] but for a severe indisposition owing to my having remained too long in that magnificent but dangerous situation the crater within 5 or six feet of a stream of red hot matter fluid as water of nearly three feet in diameter & falling as a cataract of fire'). While the political speeches recorded in Hansard were usually corrected by their respective speakers before publication ('I will not got down to posterity talking bad grammar', as Disraeli declared, duly correcting proofs in 1881), some qualities of oral syntax can illuminatingly be glimpsed in other public documents, allowing us perhaps to get behind the 'observer's paradox' of the nineteenth century which confines us almost exclusively to the written language. Early phonographic recordings—as of Tennyson and Gladstone—have a formality which is absent from, for example, the following extracts from two transcribed statements given in March 1855 to the Select Committee of the House of Commons Enquiry into War in the Crimea by (respectively) the Honourable Sidney Godolphin Osborne, and Archibold McNicol, a Private in the 55th Regiment:

Nothing could be more dreadful than the dysentery and cholera wards ... The thin stuffed sacking that they laid upon floors, perfectly rotten and full of vermin; and as I have kneeled by the side of the men, they crawled over my hand onto my book; in fact the place was alive with them. I have asked the orderlies why were these floors not cleaned; and the answer was, and Dr McGregor told me so, that the wood was so rotten, that if it were properly washed it could not be got dry again.

It was very close—bad smell, very—the smell of wounds and filth ... There was both salt and fresh—that is, preserved meat. There was also sago. No porter or wine. Those who acted as orderlies got grog, nobody else ... I was only six days in hospital. I then became an orderly, caught the fever and went into hospital ... It was the 9th of the month. I got every thing comfortable.

PRONOUNCED DISTINCTIONS

This is, of course, not to suggest that we do not know anything about the spoken voices of the time. Even if the ephemerality of calls made on the recently-introduced telephone ensured that no direct evidence of this kind remains, indirect evidence, from a range of sources, is plentiful. Informal spelling patterns in private texts can reveal otherwise hidden phonetic nuances, as in Anne Lister's rendering of *dreamed* as *dreampt* (with its intrusive [p]) in a diary entry from January 1835. Similarly, the Northumbrian engineer George Stephenson's letters reveal not only his laboriously (and imperfectly) acquired literacy, but also regionalities of accent in forms such as *geather* ('gather') and *gretter* ('greater'); spellings of *sute* ('suit')—presumably with [s] rather than the [sj] commended in manuals of 'correct' articulation—and of *shore* ('sure'), *yore* ('your') indicate other pronunciations which gradually established themselves as co-existing variants in nineteenth-century speech. Other private documents provide further illuminating evidence of spoken usage. As the Darwin correspondence indicates, young William Darwin's (b. 1839) habit of referring to himself as 'Villie Darvin' displayed his ready assimilation of the London accents of the servants. While this caused no little amusement in the Darwin household, from a linguistic point of view it gives incontrovertible evidence of the continued alternation of [v] and [w] into the mid-nineteenth century (often regarded as an anachronism deployed, as by Dickens, for comic effect in literary approximations of low-status speech).

Works which (on a variety of levels) explicitly focused on the spoken language also provide considerable amounts of information. Alexander Ellis's concern for phonetic exactitude makes, for example, a welcome contrast to the prescriptive appeals which featured in many manuals of linguistic etiquette. While the latter draw attention to a range of spoken shibboleths, the nature of prescriptive rhetoric can, however, make it difficult to discern the true linguistic situation. If the presence of post-vocalic [r] in words such as *car* was, for instance, frequently commended as essential in 'standard' speech, other comments make it clear that, as in modern English, its loss instead characterized a range of speakers, in upper- as well as under-class. Retained in Scotland, Ireland, and the accents of the south-west of England, its vocalization was complete by the early/mid-nineteenth century in London and the south-east. Images of literacy (and literate speech) can nevertheless, as here, influence the variants which are formally accepted. Visual proprieties undoubtedly underpinned not only the rise of spelling pronunciations for words such as *waistcoat* (earlier [wɛskɪt]), but also the increasing insistence on [h] as a marker of educatedness, leading to its presence in words such as *hospital, herb, humble,* and *humour* in which it had hitherto been silent (older or more conservative speakers nevertheless retained [juːmə] for the latter, even in the late nineteenth century). In contrast, *herb* remained [h]-less in American English. The number of books dedicated to the pronunciation of [h] alone serves to indicate the salience which accent gradually assumed during this period. Smith's *Mind Your H's and Take Care of Your R's* was published in 1866; *Harry Hawkins' H Book* by Ellen Eccles appeared in 1879, *The Letter H. Past, Present, and Future* by Alfred Leach followed in 1880, while over 43,000 copies of *Poor Letter H. Its Use and Abuse* were sold by the mid-1860s. As the Oxford scholar Thomas Kington-Oliphant declared, as he sought to define the standard English of the late nineteenth century, the pronunciation of [h] was indeed 'the fatal letter'. Even the moderate Ellis felt bound to confess that its omission where it should be present was tantamount to social suicide.

Social feelings about accent ran high, reflected even in such consummate works of reference as *Chambers's Encyclopaedia* and the *OED*. The *OED* entry for *accent*, written in fact by Ellis, reveals its changed significance in the nineteenth century. 'This utterance consists mainly in a prevailing quality of tone, or in a peculiar alteration of pitch, but may include mispronunciation of vowels or consonants, misplacing of stress, and misinflection of a sentence. The locality of a speaker is generally clearly marked by this kind of accent'. While, as here, *accent* had come to signify the localized above the non-localized (often in ways, as in Ellis's use of *mispronunciation*, which deliberately connote the non-standard), it was the accentless—that is a 'colourless' form of speech devoid of localized markers—which was popularly used to define 'educated' and 'standard' speech. 'It is the business of educated people to speak so that no-one may be able to tell in what county their childhood was passed', as the elocutionist Alexander Burrell averred in 1891. It was this which provided a core element of the 'received pronunciation' or RP which Ellis formally specified in 1869 ('In the present day we may ... recognise a received pronunciation all over the country, not widely differing in any particular locality, and admitting a certain degree of variety').

The extent to which 'standard speech' was indeed used is, on the other hand, debatable. While the rhetoric of standardization seized on accent as a further strand by which the 'best' speakers might be defined, the realities of usage were, as always, far more complex. As Ellis repeatedly stressed, received pronunciation had to be seen as highly variable. Age-grading led to the co-existence of older and newer variants. Queen Victoria recalled hearing forms such as *goold* (for *gold*) and *ooman* (for *woman*) from older speakers in the early nineteenth century. Dickens likewise manipulated awareness of the down-shifting of variants earlier praised for their refinement. His representation of words such as *kiend* and *kiender* (for *kind* and *kind of*) for the Yarmouth fisherman Mr Peggotty in *David Copperfield* ('I'm kiender muddled', 'My niece was kiender daughter-like') hence represents the outmoded (and increasingly non-standard) presence of a palatal glide /kj-/. Given as a marker of indisputable vocal elegance by John Walker in his *Rhetorical Grammar* (1781; 3rd edn, 1801), it was confined to the 'antiquated' and 'old-fashioned' by Ellis in 1869. The lengthened [ɑ:] in words such as *last*, *past*, and *path* (a marker of non-localized speech in modern English) also remained variable, both in realization and framing language attitudes. While the shipping magnate Charles Booth was condemned in the 1840s by his prospective in-laws for his 'flat northern a', realizations with the fully lengthened [ɑ:] could conversely be proscribed for their 'Cockney' associations. Compromise or 'middle' sounds, praised for their 'delicacy', were recommended for speakers worried about the precise nuances of social identity which might otherwise be revealed. 'Avoid a too broad or too slender pronunciation of the vowel *a* in words such as *glass* ... Some persons vulgarly pronounce the *a* in such words, as if written *ar*, and others mince it so as to rhyme with *stand*', as Smith's *Mind Your H's* (1866) dictated. Pronunciation of words such as *off* as [ɔ:f] shared the same evaluative patterns, being linked with under- as much as upper-class for much of the century. A specific set of non-localized pronunciation features (the presence of [h] in words such as *hand*, [ɪŋ] rather than [ɪn] in words such as *running*, the vocalization of [r] in words such as *bird*, and the use of /ʌ/ (rather than /ʊ/) in words such as *butter* and *cut*)) repeatedly surfaced in definition of the 'best' speakers in the second half of the nineteenth century.

Pressures to acquire a non-regionally marked accent could be prominent, especially in educational terms. The use of the regionally-marked [ʊ] instead of [ʌ] in words such as *cut* was, for instance, explicitly condemned as a feature of 'Defective Intelligence' (alongside the omission of [h]) by the educational writer John Gill. His popular *Introductory Text-Book to School Management* (1857) was a set text in many of the training colleges for teachers which were established after 1850. Teachers were exhorted to eradicate their own regional accents as incompatible with the educational status they sought to attain. As *The Teacher's Manual of the Science and Art of Teaching* (1874) affirmed, the good teacher had 'to guard himself' against provincialisms since 'if his intercourse with others accustom him to erroneous modes of pronunciation and speech, he will be in danger of setting these up as standards'. Inspectors of schools endorsed these objectives. 'A master ... should read frequently with [the children] during a lesson, and take pains to correct their incorrect pronunciation, e.g. the prevalent provincialisms of a district', stated H. W. Bellairs in his General Report for 1848–9; 'Attempts are made, with considerable success, to combat the peculiarities of the Lancashire pronunciation', T. Marshall commended in the same year. The favoured meta-language of such reports ('incorrectness', 'peculiarity', 'provinciality') readily participated in prescriptive notions of norm and deviation. Regional accents were 'depraved', the language scholar Thomas Batchelor had affirmed of Bedfordshire speech in 1809. Charlotte Brontë shed her Irish accent (acquired from her father) while at Roe Head School in Mirfield (being awarded a silver badge for 'correctness of speech' in recognition of her endeavours); George Eliot lost her rustic Midlands accent while at the Miss Franklins' school in Coventry. Michael Faraday attended Benjamin Smart's lectures on elocution in London in the early nineteenth century as part of his own processes of linguistic self-education.

Nevertheless, as the phonetician Henry Sweet emphasized in 1881, the 'correct speaker' remained elusive in the realities of everyday English. He compared his own quest for this phenomenon to 'going after the great sea-serpent', concluding that such a creature 'is not only extraordinarily shy and difficult of capture, but ... he may be put in the same category as the "rigid moralist" and "every schoolboy"'. In other words, 'he is an abstraction, a figment of the brain'. Instead, as Ellis observed, register, gender, age, and status all operated to influence the variants which might be deployed in any one instance. The transcriptions of speech which Ellis made while at the theatre or public lectures confirmed him in this view. Many prominent nineteenth-century speakers were self-evidently immune to popular prescriptive exhortations to shed regionalized features of speech. Gladstone retained his Liverpool articulations and Robert Peel's Lancashire accent was equally unmistakable. Thomas Hardy (his own voice marked by the 'thick, western utterance', as the novelist George Gissing disparagingly observed) was gratified in 1884 to note the 'broad Devon accent' of his host Lord Portsmouth. As such examples confirm, regionality was not, in fact, incompatible with educatedness or with status. Popular notions of an absolute norm once again foundered on the complexities of co-variation, just as they did on the pluralism of actual language practice. The spoken English of the nineteenth century remained mutable, attesting the rise of new features such as the glottal stop and the rise of intrusive [r] (as in constructions such as *idea of* /aɪdɪər əv/), or the presence of new homophones such as *pore* and *pour* which, although castigated for their 'slovenliness', came to constitute an undeniable part of the informal speech patterns of the day.

DIALECTS AND DIFFERENCE

Regionality, as we have seen, served as a popular nineteenth-century image of the non-standard, able to localize speakers in ways which prescriptive writers decried. 'Proper' pronunciation was 'maltreated ... by the natives of Somersetshire, Devonshire, Staffordshire, Lancashire, and Yorkshire', as *P's and Q's* (1855) averred. Speakers within these areas would not necessarily have agreed. William Barnes defended the expressive potential of dialect against what he termed 'book-speech'. To prove his point, he translated Queen Victoria's speech, made on opening Parliament in 1863, into Dorset (see Fig. 10.1). Barnes determinedly rejected the connotations of inferiority which regional speech could attract, noting, for example, the absence in the standard variety of pronominal distinctions which were present in Dorsetshire: 'Whereas Dorset men are laughed at for what is taken as their misuse of pronouns, ... the pronouns of true Dorset, are fitted to one of the finest outplannings of speech that I have found'. Throughout the century there was a vigorous interest in dialect writing, particularly after the foundation of the English Dialect Society (see Chapter 11), but also before. Much of this, as James Milroy has stressed, sought to 'historicize the rural dialects of English—to give them histories side by side with the standard language and, in some cases, to codify them'.[6] Just as nineteenth-century scientists strove to investigate variation within the history of forms, so did contemporary dialectologists locate the value of research into the geographical variabilities of English. Indeed, as Holloway suggested in his *Dictionary of Provincialisms* (1839), in future

---

[6] See J. Milroy, 'The Legitimate Language. Giving a History to English', in R. Watts and P. Trudgill (eds), *Alternative Histories of English* (London: Routledge, 2002), 14.

The following piece of Dorset is added to show that matter which is usually given in the language of hard words, as the poor call them, can be given them even in their own homely speech, and therefore could be given them in plain English.

HER MAJESTY'S SPEECH TO THE HOUSES ON OPENING THE PARLIAMENT, 1863.

(In Dorset.)

My Lords an' Gentlemen!

We be a-bid by Her Majesty to tell you, that, vor-all the hwome war in North America, is a-holdèn on, the common treäde o' the land, vor the last year, dont seem to be a-vell off.

The treäden bargain that Her Majesty have a-meäde wi' the Emperor o' the French, have, in this little time, yielded fruits that be much to the good o' bwoth o' the lands that it do work upon, and the maïn steäte o' the income, vor all there be many things ageänst us, ha'n't a-been at all hopeless.

Her Majesty do trust that theäse fruits mid be a-took, as proofs that the wealth-springs o' the land ben't aweakened.

'T have a-been a happiness to Her Majesty to zee the law-heedèn mind, that happily do show itself all drough Her dominions, and that is so needvul a thing in the well-beën and well-doen ov steätes.

A vew plans, that wull be handy vor betterèn o' things, wull be a-laid down vor your overthinkèn, and Her Majesty do eärnestly praÿ that in all o' your meetèns to waïgh things over, the blessèns ov Almighty God mid guide your plans, zoo as to zet vorward the welfeäre an' happiness ov Her People.

FIG. 10.1. Queen Victoria's Speech to the Houses on Opening Parliament in 1863, translated into the Dorset dialect
Source: From W. Barnes, *A Grammar and Glossary of the Dorset Dialect with the History, Outspreading, and Bearings of South-Western English* (London: Trübner & Co, 1864), 10.

years 'antiquaries may feel the same delight in poring over these remains of a by-gone age, as Cuvier did in putting together the bones of the antediluvian animals which he discovered'. Endeavours to record the regional were spurred by common fears that, like the *dinosaur* (a word coined by the scientist Richard Owen in 1841), its forms were in danger of extinction. 'Railways, telegraph, and School Boards—steam, electricity, and education—are surely killing dialects', Nicholson wrote in the *Folk Speech of East Yorkshire* (1889). He carefully noted the idiomatic force of words such as *fire-fanged* (used for a cake that has been left in the oven for too long) and *dowly* ('a lowly, gruesome spot is a *dowly* spot'). Empirical investigation was presented as important; the Committee on Devonshire Verbal Provincialisms, chaired by Fred Elworthy (a subeditor and frequent contributor to the *OED*), closely paralleled the *OED* in its emphasis on the dating and use of each form ('state, if possible, the sex, occupation, birth-place, residence, and age of the person using each recorded provincialism ... give the meaning of each recorded provincialism, ... illustrate that meaning by embodying the word or phrase in a sentence, if possible the very sentence in which it was used'). Resulting evidence presented a clear documentary record, as in the following entries:

FLEECHES = large flakes (rhymes with 'breeches'). A servant girl, native of Pawle, South Devon, residing at Torquay, and about twenty-three years of age, stated in March, 1877, that the snow was 'falling in fleeches,' meaning in large flakes. She added that the small flakes were not fleeches. 19 March, 1877.

BEDLAYER = one who is bedridden of confined to bed. Mrs. W——, aged 65, labourer's wife, of Woodford Ham, often used the word 'bedlayer'. April, 1885.

Urban dialects also attracted interest, as in Bywater's *The Sheffield Dialect, in Conversations* (1834) or *Tum o' Dick o' Bobs's Lankisher Dickshonary* by Joseph Baron (n.d.), with its opening poem in celebration of the regional forms of Lancashire (see Fig. 10.2). A common pattern was nevertheless to see these as the negative counterpart of 'purer', rural varieties. Robinson's *Dialect of Leeds* (1862) hence contrasts the 'bright 'side of dialects—'teeming with ancient word relics ... replete with the sturdiness, forcefulness, and wisdom of times when words were fewer, and had more of a meaning than they have now'—with their 'dark side', evident in 'towns and cities'. The latter was merely 'barbarous English' and 'the result of vicious habits'. As here, the fertility of nineteenth-century urban dialects, especially as a result of the immigration of workers from other areas, was regarded as corruption, lacking the legitimacy of the past. Migrants from Cornwall, Ireland, East Anglia, the Yorkshire Dales, and Scotland gravitated to towns such as Nelson and Briarfield, near Burnley; as Jill Liddington has noted, 'Cornish accents were soon mingling with East Anglian ones, Rossendale folk settling down next door to Scots or Irish families'.[7] So many Cornish families moved north that part of Lancashire was colloquially

[7] See J. Liddington, *The Life and Times of a Respectable Rebel: Selina Cooper, (1864–1946)* (London: Virago, 1984), 11.

TH' DICKSHONARY.

———o———

INTRODUCTION.

" Hyt semeth a gret wondur hough Englysch that ys the burth-tonge of
Englyschemen and here oune longage and tonge ys so dyvers of soun in this yland."

HIGDEN'S " Polychronicon"; 1387.

There's fine folk twits eaur Lanky talk an' says it's low an' foul,
That it may have a stomach an' sich, but hasn't geet a sowl,
An' so they cock their noses up, an' keeps their front door sneckt,
An' winnot a let a word come eaut that's Lanky dialect.

   *   *   *   *

Neaw Lanky dialect's rough but straight, no lappin' up o' nowt,
Swift fro' th' heart to t' lip it runs, not hauve-a-mile reaund t' fowt;
We ha' not time to waste i' words; we speik an' get it done;
An' Lancashire folk an' their dialect are as feyther an' as son.

   *   *   *   *

There may be sweeter talk that has a hurdy-gurdy chink,
But eaurs is sweet enoof for us, it's like eaur meit an' drink;
It's jannock, an' it's home-brewed; it con louf, cry, ay, or cuss,
As much as any gab in't world; an' it's good enoof for us.

   *   *   *   *

Eaur dialect's stout an' strung i' sport; it glories in a game;
It can wrostle an' run an' swim an' shoot, an' hey! for its footba' fame!
An' it's tender enoof for courtin' wi'! up chap's an' chink yore glasses!
For that mun be a bonny talk that'll win eaur bonny lasses!

   *   *   *   *

So give us th' good owd dialect, that warms eaur hearts an' whums,
That sawders us together, an' that cheeans us to eaur chums;
It may be rough an' ready an' noan so fal-lal smart,
But it's full o' goo an' gumption, an' it's gradely good at th' heart."

TEDDY ASHTON.

FIG. 10.2. 'Th' Dickshonary', by Teddy Ashton
Source: From J. Baron, *Tum o' Dick o' Bobs's Lankisher Dickshonary* (Manchester: John
Heywood, n.d.).

designated 'Little Cornwall'. Around 50,000 Irish were in Liverpool in 1841;
over 68,000 in Glasgow by 1871.

While this relationship between 'national' and 'local' foregrounds one image
of division in nineteenth-century English, further images are located in the
marginalized voices of the working classes. Often used in contemporary writings as a stereotype of linguistic infelicity, especially where urban speech forms
were concerned, such voices are often forgotten in histories of the language,
many of which present a seamless equation of 'educatedness' and 'Englishness'.
It was, however, the working classes (rather than the middle or upper sections
of society) who, at least in numerical terms, dominated Victorian Britain. The
English of the working classes hence remains an important resource for
establishing the real range and diversity of language practices at this time.

Working-class diaries, journals, and letters exist in abundance. The Lancashire weaver John O'Neil (b. 1810 in Carlisle) hence combines regional grammar with an astute understanding of the wider political situation which underpinned the cotton crisis of the early 1860s ('All the mills in Clitheroe commenced work this morning. At Low Moor there is a great many off. There is above a hundred looms standing ... Civil War has broke out in the United States ... another battle was fought in Missouri when the rebels was routed with the loss of 1500 men'); variabilities of grammar and spelling feature liberally in the journal of William Tayler, a footman born in Grafton in Oxfordshire in 1807. As in his expanded tenses and use of *do*, Tayler's words often usefully illustrate developments which are proscribed within the standard variety:

I did intend to have gon out but here are two more people has just called on me ... Had one gentleman and a lady to dinner and two old maids viseting in the kitchen—they has been servants but being unsucessfull in getting places they took a bublic house They say, when in service, they always heared servants very much run down and dispised but since they have been keeping a bublic house they have had an opertunity of seeing the goings on amongst the tradespeople [.] they consider them a most drunken disepated swareing set of people. Servants, they say, are very much more respectable.

Working-class diaries of this kind moreover exhibit an idiomatic quality of syntax which can be lost in printed texts. 'I think I was about seventeen, about 1803, when on a Sabbath day, walking out with a young man to whom I was much attached, a person put a track [i.e. tract] in my hand, which I took care off and read afterward,—but I don't recollect the exact effect [.] but this was partly owing to my friends dog running down a fowl, which my companion put in his pocket and took and eat at a house which he and I used to go to— but after this I never went more, no, not to partake of it', as the dissenter Thomas Swan recorded in the first entry in his journal in 1841. Individual examples can of course be multiplied, whether in the extensive memoirs of James Hutchinson (a Victorian cabinet-maker), or the recollections of the mining butty, Emanuel Lovekin (born in 1820 in Staffordshire), who presents a narrative characterized by its compelling orality of syntax and style ('[Edna] as ad two children, But as buried one Emanuel, is liveing at Wigan he as one child a Boy ... But every year make a change, and especially in some families. But I hope they will all do well and live happy together and honner God'). As a collective voice, records of this kind serve to challenge the patronizing stereotypes which could surround the lower classes of the nineteenth century when seen from the standpoint of those higher in the social order. The inarticulacy of Dickens's fictional weaver Stephen Blackpool in *Hard Times*

(1854), with his iterated lament of 'It's aw a muddle', in this respect bears little relationship to the clarity of comprehension and expression effected by writers such as O'Neil through (and not in spite of) their command of regional grammar.

WORLD OF WORDS

'Verily a wonderful world, when we survey it ... is the *World of Words*, but how impossible its exact census, how laborious the work of its exploration', wrote James Murray as he contemplated the editing of the *New English Dictionary* (later to be known as the *OED*). Nineteenth-century lexis was wide-ranging, and the account given in this chapter is necessarily selective. Even the *OED* would be incomplete, in spite of its intended status as an 'inventory' of English. 'The word was *spoken* before it was *written*', Murray stressed; some words might be used for some twenty or thirty years before a record of their use was found. Others would never emerge into what he termed 'the dignity of print'. It remains easy to find examples to prove his point. *Smatter* ('To dabble in (a subject)'), was used (according to the *OED*) from 1883 yet it can be antedated by half a century in Darwin's private usage. 'I ... smattered in biology', he wrote in 1838. Still more striking is the gap between the *OED*'s entry for *dolting* (< *dolt*, 'To act like a dolt, to play the fool') and the evidence available in George Eliot's private correspondence. Two sixteenth-century citations provide the substance of the *OED* entry—yet *dolting* was clearly still in use. 'The effect is dolting and feeble', Eliot wrote on 4 December 1877. The inventory of the *OED* inevitably remains open to revision and reassessment. Nevertheless, in its commitment to empirical investigation, its painstaking documentation of the history and use of words, and its scholarly regard for sources, it represents a supreme linguistic achievement. Six million citations (many collected through the endeavours of volunteers) provided the underlying corpus of evidence; over two million entries (and 178 miles of type) would make up the text of the first edition, publication of which spanned 1884–1928.

The existence of the *OED* therefore provides an unparalleled resource for nineteenth-century English (as well as that of earlier periods). The lexical range of English at this time was striking. New words from India, Africa, and the Caribbean confirmed the colonial present (as did associated connotative meanings); here might be listed such importations as *amah* ('A name given in the south of India, and elsewhere in the East, to a wet-nurse'), *dhobi* ('A native washerman in India'), *purdah*, or *laager* (S. African Du. *lager*) meaning 'a camp, encampment' which made its appearance in 1850. Africaans *kop* ('a hill') took on currency from the 1830s; *biltong* ('strips of lean meat ... dried in the sun') was recorded from 1815. Hundreds of West Indian genus types are likewise given in the *OED*, along with terms such as *jumby*, defined as a 'ghost or evil spirit among American and West Indian Blacks', a word first attested—at least in the written sources used by the dictionary—in Charles Kingsley's *At Last* (1871): ('Out of the mud comes up—not jumbies, but—a multitude of small stones'). American readers, as Murray noted, were among the most enthusiastic in sending in evidence of the new uses they had found, providing a rich resource for English in a variety of geographical settings. The writer and diplomat George Perkins Marsh co-ordinated the American contributions for the early part of the dictionary, often comparing British English and American English in his own work. While he noted that the latter does not 'discriminate so precisely in the meanings of words nor ... employ so classic a diction', a growing sense of linguistic nationalism is nevertheless evident, building on images of a triumphantly American English such as those earlier set forth by the American lexicographer Noah Webster, as in his two-volume *American Dictionary of the English Language* of 1828. As Marsh affirmed, 'In the tenses of the verbs, I am inclined to think that well-educated Americans conform more closely to grammatical propriety than the corresponding class in England'; likewise 'gross departures from idiomatic propriety, such as *different to*, for *different from* are common in England, which none but very ignorant persons would be guilty of in America'.

As in previous eras, nineteenth-century language imaged forth the history of conflict. Nelson coined the *Nelson touch* ('a stroke, action, or manner characteristic of Nelson') in 1805; *Napoleon* became a term of marked productivity, gaining at least six transferred senses. Words such as *balaclava* and *cardigan* later provided an enduring lexical record of the Crimea. A 'woollen covering for the head and neck worn esp. by soldiers on active service; named after the Crimean village of Balaclava near Sebastopol', as the *OED* states. *Cardigan* was 'named from the Earl of Cardigan, distinguished in the Crimean war'. *Raglan* was similar; taken from the name of Lord Raglan, the British commander in the Crimean War, it denoted 'an overcoat without shoulder seams', and with distinctive sleeves. *Jingoism* (and a range of derivative words) attests other aspects of war. 'We don't want to fight, yet by Jingo! if we do, We've got the ships, we've got the men, and got the money too', as the popular music hall song by G. W. Hunt affirmed in 1878 in a form of words which became the rallying cry of those who wanted to enter into conflict with Russia.

A productive mingling of Englishes from a range of sources is attested in words such as Australian *leather-jacket* ('a kind of pancake') and *barney* (first attested in the New Zealand *Evening Post* in 1880 with the sense 'to argue'), or *shout* ('To stand drinks, to treat a crowd of persons to refreshments'), a common colloquialism in mid-nineteenth century Australia and New Zealand. Canadian terms for the 'The master of a fur-trading post' (*postmaster*) and 'The filling of cracks in the walls of a house or log-cabin with mud' (*mudding*) likewise make their appearance at this time. French meanwhile continued to confirm its dominance in fashionable discourse. The politician Robert Peel (in spite of his Staffordshire accent) spoke 'with a foreign *tournure de phrases* which I delight in', as Lady Sheely noted in her diary in January 1819. That she was not alone in these preferences is amply attested by the linguistic practices of countless nineteenth-century writers. Mary Ponsonby, lady-in-waiting to the Queen, commends Osborne on the Isle of Wight for 'a certain kind of *luxe* which exists nowhere else'; she describes Victoria herself as '*dorletède*' ('spoiled'). *Betise* (favoured by Disraeli) and *dérangé* (used by Victoria) provide other examples of this trend, as does Lord Alexander Lennox's use of *engouement* ('unreasoning fondness') in a letter to Disraeli in January 1853. The latter was much in vogue, as in Thackeray's *Vanity Fair* (1848): 'She repaid Miss Crawley's *engoument* by artless sweetness and friendship'. Condemned as a species of linguistic affectation by Kington-Oliphant, such forms were essentially 'aliens', as the *OED* confirmed. 'Not in habitual use', they lacked full assimilation into the language. Other loans meanwhile could assume the more permanent occupation denoted by the *OED*'s category of 'denizens'—those 'fully naturalized as to use, but not as to *form*, *inflexion*, or *pronunciation*' (although even these might, with continued use, pass into the category of 'naturals'). Here might be included words such as *debacle*, originally borrowed from French in the specialized sense, 'A breaking up of ice in a river; in *Geol.* a sudden deluge or violent rush of water, which breaks down opposing barriers, and carries before it blocks of stone and other debris'. 'They could have been transported by no other force than that of a tremendous deluge or debacle of water', William Buckland, the Oxford Professor of Minerology, wrote in 1823. Later transferred uses demonstrate continuing processes of assimilation ('In the nightly *débâcle* [he] is often content to stand aside', as an article in the *Graphic* stated in 1887).

New forms from closer to home demonstrate the unremitting fertility of lexis. Words such as *Banting* (and its associated verb *to bant*) and *blueism* provide evidence of changing preoccupations and social roles. The former, as the *OED* records, was the 'name of a London cabinet-maker, whose method of reducing corpulence by avoiding fat, starch, and sugar in food, was published and much discussed in the year 1864'. The latter designated 'the characteristics of a "blue" or "blue-stocking"; feminine learning or pedantry' and was in use from 1822. Lexical items such as *telegram* and *photo, entomologize* and *phonograph* confirm other advances. Even if not all of these met with approval, their presence was indisputable, duly being recorded by the *OED*. Scientific terms represented an area of conspicuous growth with -*ology* emerging as particularly popular suffix. *Biology* (1819), *embryology* (dated to 1859 in the *OED* in Darwin's *Origin of Species*, although in fact used by him—and others—some time earlier), *vulcanology* ('The science or scientific study of volcanoes'), and *petrology* (among scores of others) all owe their beginnings to this time. Similar was -*itis*, as in *appendicitis*, a word first used in 1886 (and hence omitted from the *OED*'s second fascicle *Ant-Batten* which had been published one year previously). *Bronchitis* (1814), *conjunctivitis* (1835), *dermatitis* (1876), and *gastritis* (1806) attest further examples (*tartanitis*—not in the *OED*—was used to describe Victoria's Scottish enthusiasms after her acquisition of Balmoral in 1847). These too could meet popular resistance. 'Surely you will not attempt to enter all the crack-jaw medical and surgical terms', the surgeon James Dixon (a frequent contributor to the *OED*) wrote to Murray, vainly urging their exclusion from the dictionary.

Charles Dodgson's inventions of *chortle* (from *chuckle* and *snort*) and *slithy* (from *slimy* and *lithe*) meanwhile presented examples of what he christened 'portmanteau words' (since they contained two meanings within the same unit which, just like a nineteenth-century portmanteau case, could be opened up to reveal two parts). Elsewhere, however, word-formation processes could evolve into highly partisan affairs. Samuel Taylor Coleridge condemned *talented* as a 'vile and barbarous vocable', decreeing that 'the formulation of a participle passive from a noun is a licence that nothing but a very peculiar felicity can excuse'. In common with a number of other writers, he blamed America as a source of linguistic decline ('Most of these pieces of slang come from America'). The *OED* meanwhile presented the rise of *talented* with impeccable objectivity, providing corroboratory evidence from a range of writers including Southey, Herschel, and Pusey. The *OED*'s entry for *enthuse* ('An ignorant back-formation from ENTHUSIASM') could, on the other hand, reveal a problematic slippage into subjectivity. Back-formations were by no means indicative of ignorance, as can be confirmed by other nineteenth-century coinages such as *adsorb, demarcate*, and *extradite*.

Resistance to on-going semantic shifts—occasionally glimpsed even in the *OED*, as in the entries in the first edition of the dictionary for *enormity, avocation*, and *transpire*—was conspicuous in popular language comment. *Prestige* was a particular target, and the neglect of its etymological meaning ('An illusion; a conjuring trick; a deception, an imposture') in favour of transferred senses by which it came to mean 'Blinding or dazzling influence; 'magic', glamour; influence or reputation' was often decried. Similar was the continuing demise of *decimate* in its etymological sense of 'to reduce by a tenth'. Instances in which it signified 'to destroy', as in a letter from 'A Perthshire Farmer' which appeared in the *Scotsman* in 1859 ('Next morning a severe frost set in which lasted ten days, and my field of turnips was absolutely *decimated; scarce a root was left untouched*') were singled out for public condemnation, as in Hodgson's *Errors of English* (1881). Countless new senses nevertheless managed to appear in nineteenth-century English without prompting prescriptive censure, as in the changed values which *adaptation*, *variation*, and *evolution* all came to have in a post-Darwinian era.

While other notions of propriety led to the exclusion of words such as *condom* and *cunt* (as well as some slang terms such as *bounder*) from the first edition of the *OED*, the dictionary nevertheless gives a compelling picture of the idiomatic vigour of nineteenth-century English. Outside strait-laced stereotypes by which forms such as *trousers* might be referred to as *unmentionables* (a euphemistic practice deftly satirized by Dickens in his *Sketches by Boz*) and in which designations such as *breeches* were likewise to be avoided, constructions such as *a fat lot* and *a fit of the clevers, a put-up job*, and *to get it in the neck*, proliferated. In the nineteenth century, one could be *as boiled as an owl* (i.e. drunk) or *a shingle short* (an Australian colloquialism which co-existed alongside 'a tile loose'); here too can be found figurative phrases such as *a bad taste in the mouth* and *a bolt out of the blue*, the latter used by Carlyle in 1837, or—in another new type of word creation—the initialisms of *P.D.Q.* (recorded in the *OED*, originally in America, from 1878) and *O.K.*, another form of American origin which spread rapidly on both sides of the Atlantic. Such forms take us far closer to the colloquial texture of nineteenth-century usage, confronting us once again with a dynamism which is impossible to ignore.

References and Suggestions for Further Reading

Transitions

The opening quotation is taken from Lytton (1833: I, 163). Excellent introductions to nineteenth-century history can be found in Black and Macraild (2003) and Newsome (1997); see also Matthew (2000*a*). As in other chapters, biographies and collections of personal correspondence (as well as private diaries) have been used to give insights not only into the socio-historical context, but also into features of language in use in domains outside those of public printed texts. See especially Smith (1995–2000) for the letters of Charlotte Brontë; see Burkhardt (1996), Burkhardt and Smith (1985–), and also Browne (2003) for Charles Darwin; see House and Storey (1965) for Dickens, see Mitchell (2003) for Disraeli; Haight (1954–78) for George Eliot's letters; see James (1993) for Faraday's letters; for Anne Lister, see Liddington (1998); for the engineer George Stephenson, see Skeat (1973). The diaries of Katherine Clarendon and Harriet Acworth can be found in the Bodleian Library, Oxford. For other accounts of nineteenth-century English, see especially Bailey (1996) and Görlach (1999) and the relevant volume of *The Cambridge History of the English Language,* ed. Romaine (1998). Phillipps (1994) offers a nuanced discussion of the social sensibilities which often surrounded nineteenth-century usage (especially in terms of lexis and semantics).

The history of the *OED*—and its original foundation as the *New English Dictionary*—is discussed in Mugglestone (2002*b*) and also, in more detail, in Mugglestone (2004); see also the biography of James Murray by his granddaughter (Murray 1977). The data and citations of the *OED*—as for earlier chapters in this volume—provide a valuable linguistic resource for documenting language—and language change—at this time. The opening page of Mann (1862) is the source of the quotation on p. 275.

For transformations of print culture and literacy, see James (1976), Klancher (1987), and Altick (1998). Education and language is discussed in Mugglestone (2003*a*). Details of the impact of the telegraph and telephone can be found in Matthew (2000*b*). For nineteenth-century shifts in the use of *class,* see Mugglestone (2003*a*), especially chapter 2, and also Corfield (1987), Joyce (1991); for changes in pronunciation (and its significance) over this time, see McMahon (1998) and Mugglestone (2003*a*). Hon. Henry H. is discussed in the latter (see especially pp. 108–11). Lambert (1964) provides a useful biography of the rise and fall of George Hudson. For nineteenth-century philology, see Aarsleff (1983). Ellis's comments on variability can be found in Ellis (1869–89: vol. IV, 1089). For the other languages of nineteenth-century Britain, see Pittock (1999) and also Black and Macraild (2003).

Myths of stasis

Chapter 1 of Bailey (1996) discusses of the traditional neglect of nineteenth-century English. Lennie (1864: 15) is the source of the quotation on p. 278–9 which confirms changing criteria of acceptability for spelling. Ellis (1869: 591) analyses the public/private discrepancy in spelling practices; for the responsibilities of the nineteenth-century printer, see Stower (1808). The editorial comments on the perceived deficiencies of nineteenth-century writers in their use of language can be found respectively in Slater (2003: xxxvi–ii), House and Storey (1965: xxvi), Taylor (1994: 40), and Hutchinson (1904: iv).

For nineteenth-century grammar (and grammars) see Michael (1987); those discussed in the chapter, for example Harrison (1848) and Duncan (1890), represent a small fraction of those published, although their concerns can often be seen as representative. See Dekeyser (1996) for a good account of nineteenth-century prescriptivism; Hodgson (1881) provides an extensive list of perceived errors in usage, as does Ladell (1897); Duncan's criticisms of English in use can be found in Duncan (1890: 47–8). Pearson's criticisms of regional grammar are taken from Pearson (1865: 32). Hall (1873) is a good example of a writer who forcefully resisted the rise of the progressive passive; for a similar position, see *Live and Learn* (1872: 52). The citations from the Darwin correspondence on p. 282 are taken (respectively) from Burkhardt and Smith (1985–, I: 109); and Browne (2003, I: 155). See Denison (1998) for a good analysis of the range of constructions covered here. The subjunctive is discussed by S. L. I, *Fashion in Language* (1906: 28); Harrison (1848: 279) gives an earlier analysis. Evidence of Millais's variability is taken from Fleming (1998: 196). The nineteenth-century fondness for exercises in 'false syntax' is discussed by Görlach (2003).

Live and Learn (1872: 62) supplies a range of good examples of resistance to change in progress; the examples of variability given on p. 284 are taken from Burkhardt's (1996) edition of Darwin's letters and, for the Davy/ Faraday/ Phillips correspondence, from James (1993, I: 178, I: 219), although other examples could easily be found. For Shelley, see Seymour (2000: 446). Bradley (1904: 71) is the source of the criticism of on-going change (and Americanisms) given on p. 284. For the treatment of case in nineteenth-century English, see Dekeyser (1975). For Ward's usage, see Sutherland (1990: 172), and for the Martineau/ Lytton correspondence discussed on p., see Mitchell (2003: 116). For pronouns in Barnes, see Barnes (1864: 20), and Austin and Jones (2002, chapter 4).

For prescriptivism and the first edition of the *OED*, see Mugglestone (2002c). For nineteenth-century concerns with concord and number, see Dekeyser (1975). The transcript of Elizabeth Wheeler's speech, given on 22 December 1854, can be found in *Florence Nightingale and the Crimea* (2000: 130). For Mary Anne Disraeli's letter, see the (unpublished) Hughendon Papers (HP/A/I/A/509). For the usage of the Lyttelton sisters, see Fletcher (1997).

For nineteenth-century syntax, see Denison (1998) and Görlach (1999); Davy's letter to Faraday is taken from James (1993, I: 187). For Disraeli's correction of his speeches, see Bradford (1982: 388). For the transcripts given on p. 288, see *Florence Nightingale and the Crimea* (2000, 148 and 69–70).

Pronounced distinctions

Evidence of William Darwin's pronunciation can be found in Healey (2001: 176). For Ellis's concern to describe rather than prescribe usage, see further Mugglestone (1996). For nineteenth-century prescriptivism in this context, see Mugglestone (2003a); /r/ and /h/ are discussed on pp. 86–128. Elocution was a popular pastime and Burrell's concerns on p. 290 (1891: 24) can be taken as typical of late nineteenth-century attitudes in this context; see also Benzie (1972). Ellis's formative discussion of RP can be found in Ellis (1869: 23) (although see further Mugglestone (1997)). Variability in nineteenth-century speech is well-attested in a range of sources; see especially MacMahon (1998). For Victoria's comments on language, see Hibbert (2000: 358); for Booth's use of the 'flat' *a*, see Mugglestone (2003*a*: 65–6). Smith (1866) can be used to exemplify prescriptive concerns on 'good' pronunciation in this category of words, see further Mugglestone (2003*a*: 77–85) and Lass (2000). Chapter 6 of the former examines educational concerns with the acquisition of a 'good' accent; the quotations from inspectors' reports and educational textbooks are taken from p. 213; for Brontë's move away from her original regional accent, see Gordon (1994: 40); for Eliot, see Karl (1995: 25). For Faraday's endeavours to improve his English, see Pearce Williams (1965: 20 ff). Henry Sweet's sceptical discussion of the 'correct speaker' can be found in Sweet (1881: 5–6). Ellis's transcriptions of 'real speech' are given in Ellis (1869–89: 1210–14).

Dialects and difference

Wales (2002) offers a welcome shift from the traditional concentration on the standard variety alone; see also Milroy (2002). *P's and Q's* (1855: 25) exemplifies prescriptive and negative attitudes to regionality; for a very different view, see Barnes (1864), and also Austin and Jones (2002). Holloway's analogies between dialects and palaeontological research can be found in Holloway (1839: v). Fears for the future of rural dialects are discussed in Nicholson (1889: vi). The reports of the Committee on Devonshire Verbal Provincialisms were presented in 1885 and 1910. Robinson's characterization of urban dialects can be found in Robinson (1862: xx).

A collection of working-class autobiographies (including those by John O'Neil, William Tayler, and Emanuel Lovekin) can be found in Burnett (1994); Burnett (1982) is also a useful resource, as is Burnett *et al.* (1984). For the diary of Thomas Swan, see Swan (1970). For Hopkinson's journal, see Goodman (1968).

World of words

The main resource for nineteenth-century lexis and semantics remains the *OED*, though Bailey (1996), Görlach (1999), and Hughes (2000) all provide useful accounts of lexical change and innovation over this time. Murray's comments on the world of words are taken from his (unpublished) lectures in the Murray papers in the Bodleian Library; for the *OED* and opposition to words of science, see Mugglestone (2004, chapter4). For prescriptivism and the *OED*, see Mugglestone (2002*c*), chapter 5 of Mugglestone (2004), and Ward-Gilman (1990). Marsh (1860) provides a range of useful perspectives on English and American usage in the nineteenth century. For criticisms on innovation in nineteenth-century lexis, see especially Hodgson (1881). On the lexis of taboo and the *OED*, see Mugglestone (2002: 10–11), and also Mugglestone (2004), (2006, forthcoming), as well as Burchfield (1973).

11

MODERN REGIONAL ENGLISH IN THE BRITISH ISLES

Clive Upton

THE BEGINNINGS OF DIALECTOLOGY

There can be no doubt that pure dialect speech is rapidly disappearing even in country districts, owing to the spread of education, and to modern facilities for intercommunication. The writing of this grammar was begun none too soon, for had it been delayed another twenty years I believe it would by then be quite impossible to get together sufficient pure dialect material to enable any one to give even a mere outline of the phonology of our dialects as they existed at the close of the nineteenth century.

WITH these words, written in 1905, Joseph Wright, the most famous English dialectologist of the nineteenth century, sought to draw a line under the formal study of vernacular speech that had occupied many academic linguists such as himself, and many other expert amateur enthusiasts such as 'the Dorset poet' William Barnes, for more than half a century. The movement of which Wright was a part, and of which his *English Dialect Dictionary* and *English Dialect Grammar* of 1898–1905 were a high point, had been driven by a realization that the regional speech of the then largely immobile (and little-educated) majority preserved forms of language with real pedigree, the study of which put linguists in touch with those older forms of language that were the real object of their attention as philologists.

In 1876 the famous German dialectologist Georg Wenker had begun to use the German dialects as a test-bed for the theory that sound changes, an object of especial interest for philologists, occurred regularly across all the words with that sound, and across all communities which used those words (the so-called 'Neogrammarian Hypothesis'). Meanwhile, his contemporary in Britain, the gentleman-scholar Alexander Ellis, mentioned in the previous chapter, was himself embarking on a country-wide survey of existing dialects which would inform his *On Early English Pronunciation*. Ellis had made his first attempt at writing dialectal pronunciation in 1848, and published his intention systematic-ally to enquire into the subject in 1871, thereby putting him in the forefront internationally of those using non-standard speech to inform scholarly language study. The fifth (and final) volume of his great work on early pronunciation, which is wholly devoted to this issue, is a monument to this pioneer of data collection and presentation (including the devising of 'Palaeotype', an early form of phonetic notation), and of its interpretation.

Ellis's work, of course, concentrated on pronunciation, the 'accent' compon-ent of dialect and, in mobilizing a small army of enthusiasts to provide information from around the country, he showed that others shared his interest and, in varying measures, were able to understand and use his notation system. In the contemporary drive to create a *New English Dictionary* (later known as the *OED*), we can see a parallel passion of the age for the study of words, again with a focus on the diachronic, the career of the language in an historical dimension. Although the new great dictionary was to contain some current non-standard vocabulary such as *bike* ('A nest of wasps, hornets, or wild bees'), labelled 'north. dial.', and *rock* ('U.S. slang' for 'To throw stones at'), an early decision was taken that, in concert with the *OED*, an *English Dialect Dictionary* should be compiled, and in 1873 an English Dialect Society (the EDS) was created to undertake the task of gathering and ordering the material for this separate work. Under the leadership, amongst others, of W. W. Skeat, Professor of Anglo-Saxon at Cambridge University and a prominent nineteenth-century philologist, and with such people as Ellis and Barnes within its ranks, the Society created an impressively wide-ranging set of glossaries and other publi-cations which, whilst contributing in large measure to the final *Dictionary*, are in themselves a continuing source of knowledge for the linguist concerned with variation.

We might profitably consider here an item of information that has only very recently come to light in a rather neglected EDS glossary, but that is particularly relevant to a very modern dialectological concern. The pronunciation of *think* as *fink* and *brother* as *bruvver*, that is of [θ] and [ð] as [f] and [v], is termed by linguists TH-Fronting (because the substitute pronunciations are produced with the tongue advanced in the mouth). A common supposition is that this is a feature which has been moving northwards from the south, and more precisely from the south-east, of England, beginning only in the very late nineteenth century. However, C. Clough Robinson's glossary and grammar for mid-Yorkshire, published by the EDS in 1876, has, in its description of dialect sounds, the following for F:

There is a strong disposition to sound this consonant in the place of initial *th*, initially, in certain words, as in *thratch* (to quarrel sharply), *through*, *thrust* [fruost·], *thimble* [fim·u'l], *throstle*, *throng*, and in *thought*, as habitually pronounced by individuals [faowt·]. (Note the early phonetic notation here, following Ellis.)

It is apparent from this that, far from being unknown in the area, TH-Fronting was sufficiently established as a feature of Yorkshire speech in the nineteenth century to attract linguistic comment: one suspects that closer systematic study of the EDS publications would shed further light on such current linguistic controversies.

Symptomatic of the mind-set that gave rise to the quotation heading this chapter is the fact that, having handed its materials to Joseph Wright in his role as editor of the *English Dialect Dictionary*, the EDS disbanded in 1896. The Society thought its job was done. Its members had gathered together the written record on vernacular speech from the previous 200 years, and had compiled glossaries and commentaries on current dialect words. It was felt that vocabularies of local vernaculars which had been little touched by other varieties—or indeed by the standard variety itself (as a result of geographical mobility and universal education)—had been collected, and not a moment too soon. According to this thinking, no one at a later date could have access to real 'dialectal' speech.

There is an element of truth in this. The nineteenth-century scholarly impetus for dialect study was, as we have noted, historical: if one's focus is on the language of earlier times, the purer and the less cluttered with external influences the present-day object of study is, the better. Seen from a twenty-first-century perspective, however, as we remain aware of considerable regional differences in speech and when, as we shall see, impulses other than the philological are driving the desire to study speech varieties, the late nineteenth-century view of the future of the discipline appears remarkably pessimistic. And even from an historical linguist's standpoint, in fact, an announcement of the death of dialectology proved premature, as much of the best work in this area remained to be done.

THE MODERN DIALECT SURVEYS

Much scholarly dialectology in the first half of the twentieth century in fact continued the focus on the historical dimension of non-standard speech, and was the province of medievalists who knew that they would understand more about the English of the Middle Ages by looking at modern conservative dialects. While Wright turned his attention from dialect study to other aspects of historical linguistics after 1905, other linguists maintained or developed an interest in dialect. Two such were the Swiss Eugen Dieth and the Englishman Harold Orton, whose respective studies of Buchan in Fife, Scotland, and of Byers Green in County Durham, England, continued in the philological tradition. It was these two linguists who, spurred on in no small measure by the innovative large-scale linguistic surveys initiated by members of the American Dialect Society in the 1930s, founded the Survey of English Dialects (SED) at Leeds in 1948. This, and the Linguistic Survey of Scotland (LSS) which began in Edinburgh one year later, provide our first data which can realistically be thought of as wholly relevant to the modern period. Their emphasis, and that of the later SED-inspired Survey of Anglo-Welsh Dialects (SAWD) and Tape-Recorded Survey of Hiberno-English Speech, is in essence rural, being deliberately intended to tap into that reservoir of non-mobile speakers who were likely to preserve regional speech-forms in an historical continuum. Nevertheless, their data are collected according to modern principles as regards speaker documentation and comparability of questioning, and are presented to the standards expected of modern linguistic studies. It is from these large-scale surveys, and from very many more localized studies too, that our knowledge of the speech varieties of the present and the recent past stems. And one of the most singular points that the collected evidence makes is the ancient pedigree of much of that which modern speakers have often been trained to be apologetic about or even ashamed of.

SED especially is drawn upon heavily by commentators on regional difference in speech, since no other detailed geographical survey of speech-variation in England has yet been undertaken, and it is the speech of England in particular that excites most comment and criticism. The two best-known markers of the English northerner or southerner are their pronunciation of *a* in *grass* and *u* in *sun*, which shows northerners strong in their continuing support for the old historical [a] and [u] in place of seventeenth-century innovations by which, as Chapter 6 has discussed, pronunciations such as [grɑ:s] and [sʌn] gradually came into being. SED's maps for these two features are repeatedly used to illustrate mid-twentieth-century distributions: a line running east–west through Birmingham separating short northern [a] from southern [ɑ:] for *grass*; another boundary dipping further south into the south Midlands separating northern [u] from southern [ʌ] for *sun*. Clearly, in southern accents these sounds are similar to or the same as those in RP, whereas in the north they are markedly different. But whereas the 'short northern [a]', whilst being considered a giveaway of a person's northernness, is often regarded benignly in modern English (and indeed is used by many RP speakers), [u] in place of [ʌ] in *sun* tends to attract adverse judgements concerning education and sophistication. This fact has put northern [u] under some pressure in a way that northern [a] is not. Nevertheless, widespread support for both [a] and [u] remains.

THE 'DIALECT AREA'

It is worth looking in a little detail at the SED map for *thunder*, given in Figure 11.1, since not only does it show us the very large area over which the 'northern' form was supported in the local accents of the mid-twentieth century but it helps us to understand a most important fact that must always be remembered when dialects are being discussed, namely that even individual features do not occur within tidily defined boundaries.

What does this map tell us? The basic fact is clearly that, at the time of the SED fieldwork in the 1950s, northerners and most Midlanders used [u] (as many of course still do) and southerners used [ʌ] in *sun* and similar words. We must note too, however, that the line or 'isogloss' shown on the map does not demarcate limits within which only the form indicated is to be found. Rather, it is very approximately at the centre of a transition zone between the two pronunciations, within which both are to be found in mixed, and sometimes quite large, proportions: symbols relating to the southern sound are, for example, found in areas labelled for the northern one, indicating the presence of 'outliers' there. Furthermore, close examination of the SED evidence shows that an intermediate sound, a kind of compromise or 'fudge' between the two extremes (not in fact represented on the map, where it is largely subsumed in the [ʌ] area), is to be heard in and around the zone. In other words, when we talk of geographical dialect distributions we are not talking of neat boundaries, even for one feature mapped at one time for one type of speaker. If we were to superimpose another feature, such as the north–south short–long 'BATH vowel', onto Figure 11.1, we would introduce

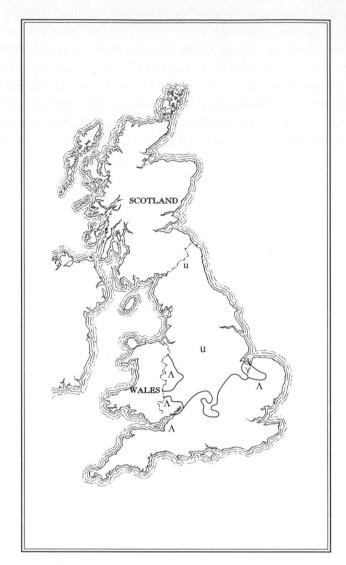

FIG. 11.1.   SED map for stressed vowel in *thunder*
Source: From H. Orton, S. Sanderson, and J. Widdowson (eds), *The Linguistic Atlas of England* (London: Croom Helm, 1978).

further isoglosses, which would cut across those already in place, blurring the picture. Factoring in matters of different speaker types, and of the vital matter of constant language change, quickly makes a nonsense of taking conventional dialect mapping far.

This is simply to say that the idea of a 'dialect area' is, in reality, a fiction. It is not possible to identify even quite loose boundaries within which speakers share a well-defined set of features to the exclusion of others, comforting though it would be to try to do so. We might, for example, take pleasure in the tidy notion of 'the dialects of England'. However, drawing together data for SED and the very-closely related SAWD permits the creation of a map such as Figure 11.2, which illustrates what we all intuitively know, that language has no frontiers. Were we to present a different SAWD/SED map, of course, the isoglosses would not coincide with those on the map shown, reinforcing the futility of trying to define dialect boundaries.

Because tightly-drawn dialect boundaries are illusory, this chapter discusses features, and their distributions and implications, without attempting that definition of dialect types which can only safely be done using a small set of items. To some limited extent, the focus is on the clues of language which people might commonly use to place other speakers in geographical or social terms: it is, of course, typically by considering a *range* of such features as clues that we can 'narrow down' a speaker's likely origins, sometimes to a very restricted region. But whilst we can perform such a locating exercise for an individual, who will be seen to share certain features with others, the territory occupied by the full range of that speaker's spoken features will be diffuse, and the picture for whole populations will always be far too complex for us to embark on the restrictive exercise of 'dialect counting'. Furthermore, an essay of this size attempting wide geographical coverage cannot hope to summarize the linguistic diversity of the British Isles. For both these reasons, the focus is on *issues* relating to variation, rather than on the *details* of that variation, although it is intended that the examples chosen to illustrate those issues will necessarily have some representative merit.

TYPES OF VARIATION

Language shows variation in three essential dimensions: pronunciation, vocabulary, and grammar. This three-fold hierarchy of variability provides a useful structure for the detailing of dialectal features. But it is a singular fact that public and official acceptance of variability is not uniform across the three dimensions. Accent, the area of variability most reliably used to locate a speaker geographically, tends not to be regarded as incorrect in modern English, although it is an undoubted fact that some urban accents are widely judged unfavourably on various aesthetic grounds. The use of localized words to express oneself, at least

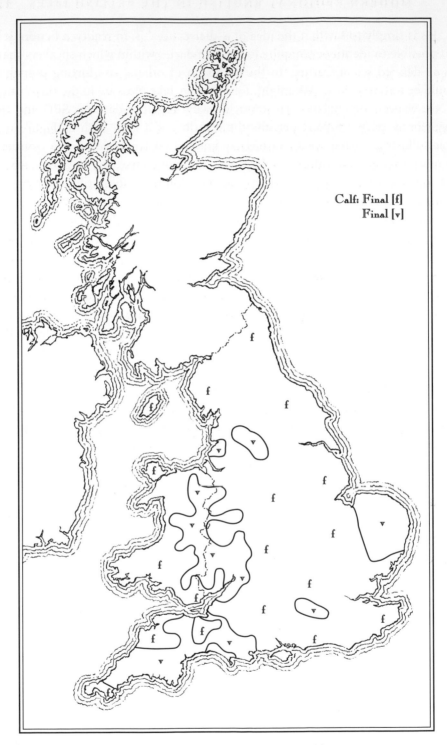

Fig. 11.2. Combined SAWD/SED map for the final consonant in *calf*
Source: From D. Parry (ed.), *A Grammar and Glossary of the Conservative Anglo-Welsh Dialects of Rural Wales* (Sheffield: National Centre for English Cultural Tradition, 1999), 244.

in speech and within the limits of comprehension, is often greeted warmly as evidence of the richness of the language and the vibrancy of local communities, even if the judgement might be combined with one of a certain lack of sophistication. Variations in grammar, however, have typically been received much less tolerantly in all circles: some differences are understood to exist within the confines of standard English, but anything which is felt to be outside the quite narrow limits of that variety is readily judged 'wrong'. But whether regarded negatively or not, over and over again one finds that those features which are well-established as characteristic of speakers from particular places are also historically authenticated. This fact of the undoubted pedigree of much non-standard speech should make those who judge its grammar or vocabulary less worthy of serious consideration than that of standard English, or its pronunciations less sophisticated than those of RP, less ready to pass comment. When we factor in the enthusiasm of speakers for their own linguistic identity, and consider the importance of such identity to our social fabric, we would do well to avoid criticism or mockery. Put simply, non-standard is not sub-standard.

Pronunciation

'Invariant /u/', which sees *put* and *putt* as northern homophones and *put* and *but* as northern rhymes, is one of two very significant pronunciation markers that have already been mentioned. The other, more enduring in terms of speaker support amid social change, is the use of short or long *a* before following /s/, /f/, or /θ/. The boundary separating these two sounds in England runs just south of Birmingham, with the older, historical [a] characterizing the north and north Midlands and [aː~ɑː] (a southern innovation which, as already noted, began in the seventeenth century) characterizing the south and south Midlands. This boundary appears stable, no doubt at least in part because [a] is also widely supported in the English accents of Wales and Scotland. In the southern zone, [ɑː] is traditionally only a feature of the extreme south-east around London, whilst the remainder of the area has had, and still largely keeps, [aː].

Two very powerful accent features then, 'northern short /a/' and 'invariant /u/', characterize the accents of northern England as a group as different from those of the south. But both the distribution and perception of these two features are different. Traditionally, the north–south boundary for the /u/ feature dips further south through the Midlands than does that for /a/. Since it attracts a certain stigma, however, probably because it involves the absence of a sound that is present in southern accents (and in RP) and can therefore be seen as 'deficient', many speakers in 'invariant /u/' areas are now either adopting /ʌ/ as used by southerners or, more usually, adopting a hybrid sound, a blending of [ʌ] and [u], that has in fact traditionally been a feature of much of the south and Midlands. No such compromise strategies seem to be needed for [a].

Some historically authenticated features are of course so widespread and so strongly supported that no one can question their viability or even their general acceptability. One such feature, that is without doubt a most striking and easily recognized marker of variation around the British Isles, is the pronouncing of /r/ after a vowel where it is present in the written word. This 'rhoticity' is characteristic of much Scottish and Irish speech, as it is of the vast majority of the accents of North America, where it has become the prestige variant. It is a curious fact, however, that although most English people would not remark on Scots, Irish, or American /r/-use, they might well judge the same feature to be unsophisticated or risible when used by a speaker from England: a recent report in the *London Evening Standard* on an interview with a rhotic Lancashire woman who had suffered a life-threatening accident glossed a quotation with the gratuitous observation 'her broad Lancashire accent making the episode sound bizarrely entertaining'. Historically, however, post-vowel or 'post-vocalic' /r/ was pronounced throughout the country, which is why it is present in spellings. Only in the last 50 years has the sound retreated from the outskirts of London, with the result that young speakers in Reading—some 60 kilometres (38 miles) from the capital—are now reported to think recordings of elderly fellow-townspeople were made by people from much further west. Today, although RP influence is such that fewer accents within England and Wales are rhotic than they once were, pockets of post-vocalic /r/ remain in the South-west, the culturally linked south-west of Wales and the southern England/Wales border country (a large area, but with the feature more strongly exhibited by older than by younger speakers), variably amongst people in Welsh-speaking areas elsewhere in Wales (since *r* is invariably pronounced in Welsh itself), in parts of south Lancashire and Greater Manchester, and (if one searches closely and listens carefully) in the north-east above Newcastle.

Speakers of rhotic accents do not all use the same /r/, however, so they are not easily to be confused even on this single feature. In Ireland, southern accents traditionally have a light-sounding post-alveolar approximant [ɹ] i.e. articulated just after the alveolar ridge in the mouth but without enough friction to cause turbulence (see the diagram on p.*** which illustrates place of articulation), while in the North /r/ tends to be a deeper, retroflex [ɻ], which is produced with the tip of the tongue curled back. (This broad distinction is complicated by the development of a retroflex /r/ in fashionable Dublin English, and its spread outside the city in a development quite unconnected to the north and led, some experts believe, by younger female speakers.) The Irish north–south distinction is a reversal of that in the parts of England where rhoticity is found, with the south-west featuring the retroflex and Lancashire/Manchester the alveolar variety. Still in England, where /r/ can still be heard, the Northumbrian version (the 'North-umbrian burr') is a throaty uvular [ʁ]. A range of /r/-types (post-alveolar, retro-flex, and a tap-sound, i.e. produced by a brief moment of contact in the mouth) is also to be found in Scotland, with the latter also being heard in northern England. Recent studies indicate that taps of this kind are more working-class and retroflex /r/s more middle-class, and that rhoticity is, as a whole, declining in Scottish urban areas. In Wales, a flapped /r/, influenced by the sound in Welsh, is widely heard, especially in the English of Welsh-speaking areas.

Such is the power of rhoticity that its presence or absence has had ramifica-tions for regional accents beyond the sounding of /r/ itself. Scottish accents, being rhotic, do not have diphthongs ending in [ə] as in *near* [nɪə], *poor* [pʊə], which in most (non-rhotic) English accents represent spellings in *-r*. So many Scottish speakers will, for example, have forms such as [nir] for *near* and [pur] for *poor*, and indeed might find [ə], as in the respective southern realizations of these words, to be an alien sound. Non-rhotic accents have final /ə/ to represent *-er*, as in *father* ['fɑːðə]. When new or exotic words requiring final [ə], such as *trivia* (deriving from Latin *trivium*, and first used in the early twentieth century), have arrived, these have been happily pronounced in such accents, but rhotic accents have had to develop ways of reconciling such words with their lack of word-final [ə]. So in Scotland one might hear final /a/, whilst in much of the English West Country these words might exhibit /-ər/ just as if they did indeed have an *-er* spelling.

Pronounced post-vocalic /r/ is just one of very many ancient pronunciations signalled by our spellings. Like rhoticity, another sure marker of Irish and Scottish speech (and also of the border country of northern England), is *wh-* pronounced [hw], giving forms such as [hwɛn] *when*. This is, of course, a mannered spelling pronunciation adopted by some RP speakers as well as being regional, but it has historical and linguistic foundations, going back to Old English. For modern Irish English [hw] can, however, be seen as doubly justified, with the imported English feature being reinforced by a similar sound from Irish.

Whilst the use of a sound that is signalled by spelling might be seen by some as especially desirable, as we have already seen in Chapter 10, the absence of a sound whose presence is supported by spelling is likely to be stigmatized. Such is certainly the case with the dropping of word-initial /h/ (see further pp. 276–7), resulting, for example, in *house* being pronounced [aʊs]. This /h/-dropping is characteristic of modern regional pronunciation in Wales and in most of

England, although it is not a feature typical of the north-east of England around and above Tyneside, of rural East Anglia, or of Scotland or Ireland. That the feature, where present, has social significance is readily apparent in Bradford, where usage varies between 12 per cent and 93 per cent depending on the social class of speakers. Like /h/-dropping, the tendency for non-RP speakers to have [n] (rather than the velar nasal [ŋ]) at the end of words spelt -*ing* can also attract criticism on the same grounds, but it is even more widespread, being quite usual throughout the whole of the British Isles. It is also a feature which exhibits very considerable social variation within communities, with figures ranging from 3 per cent to 98 per cent across social classes in Norwich, for example. Although common sense suggests that speakers might try to avoid such high-profile stigmatized forms in careful speech, it has only become fully apparent through the insights of modern social dialectology quite how predictably such features are tied to the contexts in which they are used: measurements of how such features are produced by speakers of different social profiles, and consideration of the stimuli which prompt them to make their selections, are used in the study of the mechanisms that give rise to change in language use over time.

A further -*ing* feature, although one which is characteristic of a very confined area and so an ideal indicator of English regionality, is the inclusion of the alveolar stop [g] following the velar nasal [ŋ] in non-*ing* words containing [ŋ]. This is very typical of the English north-west Midlands, an area stretching from Birmingham northwards and westwards to Manchester and Liverpool. A native of Birmingham itself will typically pronounce the name of the city ['bə:mɪŋgəm] instead of the more widely-heard ['bə:mɪŋəm], with such a pronunciation being something of a shibboleth for the true 'Brummie'. Speakers with this 'velar nasal plus' feature will pronounce *wrong* and *sing* as [rɒŋg] and [sɪŋg]; likewise *finger* and *singer*, instead of being near-rhymes as ['fɪŋgə] and ['sɪŋə] respectively, will rhyme completely, as ['fɪŋgə], ['sɪŋgə]. Speakers who have this feature might also be inclined to carry it into the -*ing* ending of other words too on occasions, thus giving ['kʊmɪŋg] alongside ['kʊmɪn] or ['kʊmɪŋ] *coming*.

Every region has such dialectal features which, if they are present in an individual's speech, at least strongly suggest that they have close local affiliation. For example, there is, extending widely in East Anglia and the English East Midlands, a characteristic dropping of /j/ wherever it occurs before /u:/, this being a continuation of the tendency which has elsewhere made it increasingly unlikely in modern English that one will hear ['sju:pə] *super*, [sə'lju:ʃn] *solution*. As these last examples suggest, this general /j/-dropping in the area might be a sign of things to come in other British accents: it is, after all, much more widespread in North America than in Britain in such words as *news* and *studio*.

For the present at least, however, it remains an especially localized symbol. It is therefore not surprising that a major food-producer in the region has long described its products as *bootiful*. Nor is it surprising to hear reports that younger speakers in Norwich adopt the feature deliberately when playfully asserting their local identity, even though they might never use it in everyday speech.

This issue of identity is crucial to the persistence of non-standard dialectal features. Strongly identifying speakers as Scottish and north-eastern English is the use of [uː] in /au/ words such as *house, about*. This [uː] is the sound from before the onset of the Great Vowel Shift: Scotland, as Chapter 6 has already discussed, is one of several places where the Shift did not fully take place, and pronunciations such as [huːs] and [əˈbuːt] are today well-known characteristics of Scots pronunciation. Traditionally, the feature is typical of the area immediately south of the Scottish border too. Today it is little heard as the norm, especially in the urban areas around Newcastle upon Tyne, but it remains emblematic of local 'Geordie' identity, occurring, for example, in such expressions as *doon toon* ('down town') to refer to Newcastle city centre, *The Toon* (Newcastle United Football Club), and *broon* in relation to Newcastle Brown Ale.

Altogether, there are too many distinguishing accent features to list in a short chapter, but we might single out also as especially localized and identifiable the [ɑː] of *time, miner* in the north-east Midlands, the [ɛː] of Merseyside and [øː] of South Walian *bird, heard*, as well as *mother* with TH-dropping in Northern Ireland (and corresponding [d] in the South). Some features that have become increasingly the focus of dialectological scrutiny and debate are, however, far from localizable. One such feature that is currently much discussed, probably because, like *h* and *ng* it is highlighted by spelling, is the presence of a glottal stop, [ʔ], in place of the stopped voiceless consonants /p, t, k/ (and especially noticeable with /t/). A very definite feature of the London accent, glottaling has nevertheless been noted in Scotland and northern England for many decades, and it is now a feature of urban accents generally. It is most frequently to be heard before a consonant (it would now be most usual to hear it in the middle of *Gatwick, Luton*), where its presence would probably pass unnoticed. More stigmatized is its use between vowels and before syllabic /l/: [ˈlɛʔə] *letter* and [ˈlɪʔl̩] *little*. The feature is less likely to be heard in Wales than elsewhere, and especially in north-east England it is likely to take the form of what is known as 'glottal reinforcement' or 'glottalization', where both the glottal and voiceless stops are heard, giving for example [ˈpeɪʔpə] *paper*. Tending to suppress the glottaling or glottalization of plosives in Liverpool is that city's particularly characteristic feature of heavily aspirated /p, t, k/ or even, especially word-finally, the rendering of them as the corresponding fricatives [Φ, t̪, x].

The quality of /l/ is a matter of considerable variation in regional accents, and one of its manifestations in particular attracts almost the same level of stigma as does /t/-glottalization. The essential difference is between a light, 'thin' or 'clear' [l] to be expected frequently in Ireland, usually in south and mid-Wales, and in England especially in the north-east, and a heavier, 'thick' or 'dark' [ɫ] characteristic of north Wales and increasing in frequency as one moves south through England. The situation is complicated by the phonetic environment in which the sound occurs (between vowels it is more likely to be 'thin', before and after vowels 'thick'), and by historical and modern processes of language change: a recent very detailed study of /l/ in Glasgow concentrates on the phenomenon of 'L-vocalization', by which /l/ becomes [ʊ], an old process that has given rise to a limited set of Scots lexical items such as *aw* 'all', and a quite separate modern process that is apparently spreading widely through British English. This latter, modern L-vocalization as in words such as *real* and *final,* has been traditionally regarded as having its roots in the immediate area of London, and some commentators suggest that London influence might be an important factor in the spread of the feature generally.

Because, like L-vocalization, it is a notable feature of the London accent, the presence of glottalization and other such features in English pronunciation elsewhere within Britain is often advanced as evidence of a so-called 'Estuary English', said by some to be spreading from the capital to other regions. The weight of the influence of London—and of other major metropolitan areas too— on areas some distance away should not be underestimated: it has been shown that linguistic features often do diffuse from larger to smaller urban areas, subsequently 'filling in' the intervening spaces once they have become firmly transplanted. But care must be taken not to assume too much from slim evidence. We have seen that TH-Fronting, itself sometimes held to be a quite modern London-influenced feature, was noted by a linguist in Yorkshire in 1876. So too, glottalization is by no means new to places far removed from the southeast of England, and it is not certain that London speech is an especially significant factor in the undoubted spread of this feature.

Furthermore, major urban features can be supplanted, or subtly changed, under the influence of pressures other than those of mere weight of population or assumed cultural dominance. Over most of the British Isles outside south-eastern and Midland England (which in this case includes an area extending north to Liverpool), where RP-like diphthongs occur in such words as *game* and *home* [geɪm], [həʊm], older, more traditional long monophthongs persist quite strongly, giving [geːm], [hoːm]. However, in what is a complex picture, exceptions do occur, a particular case being that of north-east England, where the centring diphthongs [ɪə] and [ʊə] have been typical. There is now evidence that these north-eastern forms are declining in popularity, even though they have long been typical of the speech of residents of the very large and culturally dominant city of Newcastle upon Tyne. Crucially, though, the change is not in the direction of the sounds of what some might consider the culturally (and certainly numerically) still more dominant city of London, and of RP. Rather, the 'pan-northern' [eː] and [oː] are being espoused, especially by younger and middle-class north-eastern speakers: seemingly, they are simultaneously drawing away from sounds which are regarded as expressive of old-fashioned working-class roots, whilst firmly identifying themselves as northerners by assimilating to the wider northern norm.

The pan-northern long monophthongs are not remaining static, however. In a move which signals both adherence to northern identity *and*, it has been controversially argued, a possible move towards RP, a new trend in northern /oː/ has been observed as emerging. Quite widely heard among younger speakers in Yorkshire and north-east England is a fronted version of the vowel which results in *go home* being rendered as [gøː ˈhøːm]. Here we might perhaps detect a move towards the initial vowel of the RP diphthong [gəʊ, həʊm], but it is even more apparent that there is a determined retention of the northern tendency to a monophthong: as with the north-eastern adoption of [eː] and [oː], identification with a region remains a strong factor for speakers, even in a situation of language change.

It has been observed that much of the variation that occurs in regional accents persists and changes as a result of a concept of regional identity, and is used by outsiders as a way of placing speakers geographically in a quite non-judgemental way. It is true, however, that it is this aspect of speech which, when questioned, native British and Irish residents seem most ready to comment on, sometimes quite critically. In one of several recent studies in this area, which asked respondents to rate accents as they perceived them in the abstract on a rising scale of from 1 to 7, the Liverpool accent scored 3 for educatedness, whilst RP was rated highest at 5.7. Conversely, however, when asked to judge the speakers of the accents for friendliness, the same assessors returned 3.6 for RP, and placed southern Irish highest at 5.3. Scores for honesty ranged from 2.2 for Liverpool to 4.9, again for southern Ireland. The reasons for such scores are a matter of no little debate, especially since every similar study produces somewhat different rankings, albeit with observable trends. It is undoubtedly the case that the accents of most major urban areas are held in lower esteem than those of rural areas, doubtless because the latter have pleasant associations of tranquillity and are, perhaps, holiday destinations. Places with which most assessors are likely to be unfamiliar tend also to rate well. Fashion might play a part too—the Scouse (Liverpool) accent is said to have been highly rated during the Beatles era of the 1960s. Understandably RP, which is often used for important functions such as broadcast news-reading, is likely to rate high in terms of education, but it is significant that a high rating on one scale does not imply a high rating on all. It should also be made clear that women do not accord with men in their judgements: on the attractiveness of the speakers of various accents, for example, another recent study of ten accents saw men placing West Country speakers in sixth place, whilst women placed them eighth. Also, understandably, assessors drawn from different places record different judgements as regards accents from their own and other regions. This fascinating and readily-quantifiable area of accent study, then, raises many questions and answers few: however it does, most interestingly, point to the readiness of assessors to make comments on such abstract concepts as honesty or level of education.

Vocabulary

Less contentious than variation in pronunciation, although just as likely to excite comment, is variation in vocabulary. But whereas a speaker might use their own characteristic pronunciations when speaking to someone from a different community, it is comparatively unusual for word differences to play a prominent part in communication across today's socially- and geographically-mobile society, because of the likelihood of misunderstandings arising. This is in part the reason why we know comparatively little about modern word-variation: researchers have observed that there has been some considerable erosion in the differences in vocabulary that once characterized communities, and so seem to have thought this area of language study less important than pronunciation and grammar. There have been two other causes of the neglect of vocabulary in modern dialect research, however. First, words do not occur in the readily-quantifiable systems that today's dialectologists require if they are to make empirical observations based on statistical evidence. Second, it is undoubtedly the case that it is hard to obtain detailed evidence of word-use across communities without undertaking lengthy and elaborate fieldwork, something which is hard to contemplate specifically for lexis when surveying a rich social mix of speakers. So, while we know that there is considerable variation across the UK relating to words denoting a narrow passage between buildings (*alley, ginnel, gully, jennel, jigger, jitty, snicket, gully, ten-foot, twitten*, and others), our information on the distribution of these words in terms of geographical spread or types of speakers, or indeed their precise meanings for those who use them, is no more than anecdotal. A little more is known of some words that were not covered by the older surveys with their wide geographical sweeps: for example, words for soft games-shoes include *daps* around Bristol and in South Wales, *pumps* in the Midlands and much of northern England, *sandshoes* in the north-east, *gollies* on Merseyside, and *gutties* in Scotland, but even here we have no knowledge of precise distributions. Nevertheless, although there is a shortage of information on the regional use of many words which intrigue us, it is still possible to address important issues.

One such issue is the link, and the very observable difference, between the vocabularies of English and Scots (both of Scotland and Ireland). In this we are immediately confronted with a basic issue in lexicology: what is a word? The following pairs might be considered versions of the same 'word', but it makes equally good sense for them to be considered as related, cognate words instead (the Scottish word is given first in each case): *hame/home, hale/whole* (note the survival in the English fixed expression *hale and hearty*), *mare/more, auld/old, cauld/cold, hoose/house, dee/die, deed/dead, twae/two, kirk/church, brig/bridge*. These and many more signal a close, parallel development of Old English-derived language in Scotland and England. Other pairs, however, indicate a more marked separation into two different, although intimately related, languages: *bairn/child, wean/child, brae/slope, ken/know, cuit/ankle, kenspeckle/conspicuous, birl/spin, girn/whine, mind/remember, ay/always, gey/very, gaed/went,* and so on. Whilst some words from this second list suggest a clear-cut difference between the varieties found in Scotland and England, others from both lists illustrate the point already made, that political borders are not linguistic borders. They also support the frequently-made observation that there are degrees of Scottishness in the speech of the Scots: whilst *wean* is a term of Scotland, *bairn* is widely used in north-east England by young and old alike (so that *wean* and *bairn* cannot be considered entirely synonymous, having rather different regional attachments); *birl* is a term used technically in the textile industries of northern England; *brig* and *kirk*, descended from Old Norse, have been much used in northern England until comparatively recently, and survive widely today in place-names (*Brighouse, Ormskirk*, and the like). A recent survey of various studies carried out between 1977 and 1998 into the loss of specifically Scots words strongly suggests that these are eroding quite rapidly, with passive knowledge taking over from active use, and Scots words coming often to be reserved for specialist application such as for storytelling and in songs. Scots and English words can also be kept productively apart by Scottish speakers for reasons of semantics: it has been reported from Glasgow, for example, that whilst *hame* might be used in a domestic sense, *home* is more to be expected in an institutional sense when referring to care-homes for children. In such a way, speakers can be expected to make use of a range of word-variants available to them, finely grading the distinctions which they see as significant.

An example both of lexical erosion and of the lexical 'recycling' that gives a non-standard word a new meaning is provided by the notion of 'left-handedness'. A question concerning this concept elicited no fewer than 84 different words from across the SED network of 313 localities: today, approximately half a century after that Survey's fieldwork took place, it would be hard to find as many as ten variants, and a recent survey of fifty young people drawn from a wide geographical area discovered only five, with a further five describing a left-handed person. Loss of variety in this case is probably due largely to the more liberal and less superstitious attitude of contemporary society to differences, especially to physical differences (SED records eight variants for 'bow-legged', twenty-one for 'knock-kneed', and no fewer than fifty for 'pigeon-toed'). One 'left-handed' variant, *cack-handed*, however, has acquired a well-known alternative meaning of 'clumsy' and 'incompetent': with its pejorative connotation carried by *cack* ('excrement'), the term is a less than pleasant reminder of a more judgemental time in an overwhelmingly right-handed society, whilst we can see an old word put to new work in our more sensitive age. It is likely, however, that many of those who use *cack-handed* to describe clumsiness are quite unaware of either its left-handed or lavatorial connections.

It is equally likely that the young people who use *charver* or *pikey* to identify a contemporary whose style of dress and general demeanour suggests an aimless 'street' lifestyle are unaware of the Romany origin of the first or of the original connotation 'gypsy' of the second. *Pikey*, formed from the 'turnpike' roads, has, along with *pikee* and *piker*, been used in the south-east especially since at least the mid-nineteenth century with reference to itinerant people of various kinds, and has been used by travelling people themselves insultingly to refer to travellers of lower caste. *Scally*, a corresponding label originating in the north-west of England, was taken up widely by the media and by several internet websites devoted to the phenomenon, only to be superseded by *chav*. Notwithstanding the emergence of a generic term, a very recent enquiry has unearthed 127 synonyms, with *ned* favoured in Scotland, *charver* in north-east England, and *pikey* across the south. Important to note here is the fact that existing terms are re-used to suit new needs that arise as a result of social change and that, although the media are influential in fostering support for words, there is a strong suggestion of regional variation in the new usage of a sector of the population who might be expected to be more geographically mobile than their predecessors.

The Uniformitarian Principle that informs much of modern 'social' dialectology offers as a working assumption the notion that, since human interaction is, at bottom, the same from generation to generation, what we observe happening to language now is much the same as what happened to language in former times. Traditionally, the cultural importance of the potato in Ireland resulted in a complex of terms: for size (*marley, taw, chat, crachan*); for seed (*cutling, poureen, shaleen, spachan*); uncooked (*potato, pritty, taty, spud*); cooked (*brudgy, champ, prockus*). Young people, wanting to describe a group they identify as different from (and, it would be fair to say, inferior to) themselves, adapt existing words, and where necessary invent new ones, and in doing so they declare their identity in both generation *and* place. Such needs might be expected to have arisen in every community and in every generation in all former times too.

In the influence of other indigenous (Celtic) languages can be seen another example of English drawing on an available resource, most clearly to be seen in regional vocabulary, although it can of course be observed at other levels of variation too. Frequently, the borrowing will be so heavily anglicized, and so widely understood, that its origin will be obscure even to its users. Irish Gaelic, as well as having had an important—if limited—impact on the English standard lexicon (for example, *bannock, bog, cairn, ceilidh, creel, galore*), has been observed to have been still more widely influential in Irish English, especially in the areas of social contact, as in *alanna* ('child'), *asthore* ('darling'), or *shannach* ('gossip'), and in traditional domestic life, as in *dullice* ('edible seaweed'), *boxty* ('reheated leftovers'), *caulcannon* ('cabbage and butter'), and *bonnyclobber* ('curds'). *Bannock and ceilidh* are, of course, as closely associated with Scottish Gaelic as with Irish, and Scots has received a wealth of words from that language as one might expect as, for example, *sonsie* ('lucky'), *knock* ('hill'), *claymore, sporran, clan*. Similarly, the English vocabulary of Wales has been significantly affected by Welsh: as in Ireland and Scotland, non-Celtic speakers use Celtic-derived non-standard words as a matter of course, as in *cwtch* for 'to stoop down', or 'a storage place', and *twmp* for 'hill', for example. Even in south-west Wales, an English-speaking area for more than 800 years and so dubbed 'Little England Beyond Wales', Welsh words are by no means uncommon, although pronunciation might be very heavily disguised, so that Welsh *pistyll* ('spring') becomes English *pissle* and the south Pembrokeshire village name Llangwm is pronounced as if it were spelt 'Langham'.

Other historical language contact is enshrined in lexical variation to a still more significant degree. The Old Norse ancestry of *brig* and *kirk* has already been mentioned, and to these can be added very many words characteristic of those areas settled by Viking invaders from Scandinavia. A stream throughout the Norse-settled areas of England is almost invariably a *beck*, although in Scotland it is likely to be a *burn* and quite widely in England, although with a heartland in the Midlands, a *brook*, both of which terms, like *stream* itself, are Old English-derived. A restrictively northern English, and especially Yorkshire, word which could owe its existence to either Old English or Old Norse, and which in truth exists as a result of its presence in both of these, is *laik* meaning to 'play'. The fact of its distribution across the Norse-settled regions of northern England suggests that it is Norse derivation which is the more significant, although with the dual effect of both languages making the non-standard survival more likely than it might otherwise have been. It is interesting to note, however, that the coincidence of *laik* and *play* is only partial: whilst both relate to taking recreational exercise, the former has connotations of taking time away from work whilst the latter, exhibiting still more versatility, can relate to performing on a musical instrument, making fun of someone, taking part in a game, and so on. Synonymy is likely to be only partial between non-standard and standard words.

External historical influence on non-standard English is not limited to that of Old Norse, of course, and French in particular has had its effect, often in surprising ways. French being the language of the early medieval court and administration, as Chapters 3 and 4 have discussed, we might expect its influence to be found especially in the standard dialect and in the speech of the English regions around London. Whilst this is indeed the case to some considerable extent, there are many exceptions which probe the rule. Most significantly, the presence of French-derived words in Scots is, in considerable measure, the result of the 'Auld Alliance' which saw close links between Scotland and France in long opposition to England. We might cite *corbie* ('crow') which derives from Old French *corb*, and *fash* ('to worry') which derives from Old French *fascher*, as instances of this. Within England itself, French-derived words have often gained a strong grip on the standard dialect: for example, *autumn* predominates over especially northern *back-end*, and over *fall*, which until recently has been most favoured in the Midlands and south as well as being the norm in North America. But the standard dialect has upon occasions retained an English word while it is the French word that has taken root in the non-standard. A remarkable if now very recessive example is *urchin* ('hedgehog'), a descendent of Old French *herichon*, recorded widely in the north and the West Midlands in the mid-twentieth century while the English, Germanically-compounded standard dialect *hedge* + *hog* was firmly rooted elsewhere. Somewhat similarly, though of greater significance for the modern standard dialect, is the dominance of English *adder* (and, on the Scottish and Welsh borders, its related *ether*) over French-derived *viper*, which seems only to have had a weak hold in the south and East Anglia. Old Norse is a further influence in this case, with *hagworm* recorded in the north-west and in the north-east below Teesside. Again we have typically Germanic compounding: *hag*, from Old Norse, is connected either with wet moorland or woodland, and *worm*, with cognates in both Old English and Norse, once meant 'snake, serpent, dragon'. (It is in this sense that it is found in the coastal-feature names Great and Little Orm at Llandudno and Worms Head on Gower, both on that Welsh coast along which the Vikings once raided from their Irish settlements.)

Some of the words mentioned above as examples of regional variation have been specifically referred to as recessive. As a result of greater contacts between people, the influence of the broadcast media, advertising and the like, either their geographical coverage or their speaker-base within their region of use is decreasing, or both. The fact that some words of long standing remain in use as indicators of regional identity, and that others are adapted to new use, or still others are coined afresh, suggests that lexical diversity will continue to some marked degree into the future. Even when a form retreats to a far smaller area than that which it is known to have once occupied, its eventual death is not necessarily signalled. Such seems to be the case with *while* ('until'). In quite general use when Bunyan in *The Heavenly Footman* (1688) wrote 'Run ... while thou art weary, and then I will take thee up and carry thee', this sense was still to be found as far south as his native Bedfordshire in the mid-twentieth century. *While* in the sense 'until' now seems largely to have retreated within the boundaries of Yorkshire, but there is no sign of it losing its popularity amongst even adolescent speakers there. Especially if a word comes to be seen as in any sense a badge of regional affiliation, its indefinite retention can be expected.

Grammar

There are also distinctions to be found at the interface of vocabulary and grammar, that is 'word grammar' or morphology. Within England and Wales especially, since deviations from standard grammar are most likely to be proscribed in education and employment circles, and a standard English model is very influential, the extent to which features in this category persist among the adult population is limited. But persist they do, at least in part as a result of their being employed sporadically by speakers intent on asserting their regional identity or class roots. So a Yorkshire speaker who uses *while* for 'until' might well use the personal pronouns *thou/thee* (often in a contracted form *tha*) when speaking to close friends. So might other speakers of the most distinctive regional dialects over much of northern and north-Midland England outside the north-east, and also in the south-west and south-west Midlands. Retention of this 'T/V system' (so called from its paralleling of the French *tu/vous* familiar/polite pronoun system), albeit in a diluted form where there is no clear distinction between the original subject case *thou* and object case *thee*, provides its users with a valuable social resource. It is likely to go hand-in-hand with older verb-forms too, creating quite distinctive regionalisms: *H'art tha doin'?* ('How art thou [are you] doing?', i.e. 'How are you?'), this from a young Yorkshire speaker, somewhat formulaically, to a friend. Further south, in Staffordshire, one might hear *ast?* for 'have you?' ('hast thou?') and further south still, in the English West Country, *cassn't?* ('can't you', literally 'canst thee not').

Pronouns are, in fact, a very fertile area for variation generally. The following are just some of the other pronoun phenomena which mark out non-standard from standard, and in some cases from place to place. More than simply illustrating dialectal diversity, however, they can be seen to demonstrate that diversity as a resource too.

In *youse*, many Irish English speakers have a plural form of *you* with which to address more than one person. (Irish Gaelic, like very many other languages, makes a singular–plural distinction in the second person personal pronouns, so its speakers might have been expected to create one when adopting English.) Through migration of speakers from its Irish base, this plural form has spread to become associated with, amongst others, Liverpool and Middlesbrough speech and, because a distinct plural pronoun might be seen as a useful addition to the pronominal system, it has been suggested that this is becoming more widely current in English generally. Only time will tell whether *youse* will become an accepted element in the standard English paradigm.

Variety in both the use and the forms of the reflexive pronouns shows the non-standard dialects exhibiting possibilities in advance of those available to speakers of the standard variety. Found in Ireland, for example, is a special situation which can see a reflexive used on its own without reference to another noun or pronoun: *It was himself who did it.* Although there is some evidence of such forms more generally in earlier English, the existence of parallels in Gaelic, and the uniqueness of this feature to modern Irish English, support the interpretation that foreign-language influence is largely responsible for the usage persisting. Whatever the origin, the availability of an emphatic device that does not rely solely on stress is a resource denied to the standard-dialect speaker.

We can remain with the system of reflexives to illustrate the marked level of simplification which can occur in the non-standard, arguably a sign of an enhanced level of linguistic sophistication. Whilst standard *myself, ourselves,* and the like comprise possessive pronoun + *self/selves,* standard *himself, themselves* are anomalous in being constructed using the object personal pronoun: many non-standard dialects introduce consistency in their use of *hisself, their-*

selves, which feature the possessives. (All is not consistency and simplicity, of course: broader speakers especially in the English east Midlands and Yorkshire still make extensive use of forms ending in *-sen/-sens*: *missen* ('myself'), *theirsens* ('themselves').) Where, in standard English, the use of the reflexive *myself* as a substitute for *I* or *me* tends to be regarded as an error or affectation (*give it to my colleague or myself*), this is quite usual practice in modern Scots, which should be a warning to anyone disposed to be too readily judgemental in matters of language use.

It is regularization too that produced *hisn, hern, ourn, yourn, theirn*, analogous to *mine* and *thine*, in a medieval system that remained common among dialect speakers in the south Midlands of England into the mid-twentieth century and is still to be heard today from some. But although superficially such matters might seem only to involve simplification, this is not so with the phenomenon of 'pronoun exchange' which, like Irish English *himself*, provides opportunities for signalling meaning very precisely. This phenomenon, associated espe-cially—although not exclusively—with the English south-west and south-west Midlands, sees standard subject pronouns *he, she, we, they* doing duty also for the object pronouns *him, her, us, them*: conversely, the object pronouns might serve for the subject. One can therefore hear *I gave it to she*, or *her did it*, *give it we*, or *him's the one as* [i.e. who] *said it*. Although this might seem simply to relieve a speaker of the necessity of learning both subject and object pronouns, usage can often be seen to be rule-governed, with, for example, subject pronouns especially used to make an utterance emphatic.

A tendency towards prescriptivism that particularly relates to grammar has already been mentioned. Whilst it would be wrong simply to insist in the face of this that any grammatical variant is as useful as any other in any circumstance, it is as easy to point to language history in the defence of many non-standard grammatical features as it is to use that history in defence of dialectal pronun-ciations or words: those levelling criticism at today's non-standard too often simply display their ignorance of historical fact. In what is no more than a remarkable historical survival, but which might be seen as a subtle extra element in the range of personal pronouns too, some speakers preserve the Old English masculine singular object pronoun *hine* as *un* in unstressed positions, giving, for example, *I told un so*: no doubt few people who use this form realize that they are doing more than pronouncing 'him' in a rather unusual local way, and few others who regard it as a quaint localism can have any awareness of its historicity.

Linguistic streamlining and historical pedigree are nowhere more evident than in the matter of the non-standard formation of the past tense and past participle (used to create the present perfect, *I have...* etc.) of irregular verbs. Whilst regular ('weak') verbs form their past tense and past participles in -ed (*walk-walked-walked*), irregular ('strong') verbs do so in a variety of ways which can see quite radical differences in two or all three of these positions (*find-found-found, come-came-come, write-wrote-written*, and so on). The regularization tendency of the non-standard is such that some of the complexity can be avoided, either through the transforming of normally irregular verbs into regular ones or by uniting past tense and past participle (*show-showed-showed* illustrates both possibilities). But not all is blunt regularization. It might at first sight appear that it is the former of these strategies, the change from irregular to regular, that creates *catched* as the non-standard variant of *caught*. (*Catched* has traditionally been found over most of England, with standard *caught* being found dominant in the south-east around London and significantly in some coastal areas—such as east Yorkshire, Lincolnshire, Norfolk, south Devon, the Severn Estuary—which are readily connected to the capital by sea, a fact which incidentally provides an insight into how linguistic forms can be spread.) However, although there is complicating vowel-change here, *caught*, with its [t] ending, is clearly irregular like *catched*: in fact, these two past-tense forms have existed side by side in the language for a very long time, and neither seems more historically valid than the other. And just as *catched* might attract criticism as childish, so the falling together of the past tense and past participle of *to come*, which allows for such usage as *She come to town last week*, is likely to attract judgements of ignorance. However, this is similarly not merely a matter of simplification: although they will be quite oblivious of the fact, the very many people who use *come* in this way have an Old English past-tense form, and so have pedigree on their side.

Syntax is also heavily subject to the normalizing effect of the standard dialect, and non-standard variation in this area of grammar is as stigmatized as is that in word-grammar. It is to be expected that such variation *will* exist, of course, most strongly supported by those who do not feel themselves to be subject to social pressures. And variation at this level can be expected to have a social rather than a narrowly regional base, with widespread social implications as a consequence. Doubtless the best known feature of this kind is multiple negation, which sees the negative signalled twice or more within a construction: *he didn't never have none* and the like. There is only small variation in the kinds of multiple negative constructions which are likely to be encountered from place to place, and no English-speaking region where none are found at all. Yet whilst the phenomenon is widespread geographically, and the writings of Chaucer and Shakespeare, amongst others, testify to its historicity, the taboo on breaking the rule that 'two negatives make a positive' which has been discussed in Chapter 9 remains strong, and such negation can have important social consequences for its users.

The same is true, as regards both widespread use and social stigmatization, for *ain't/ent/int* as negatives of the auxiliaries *be* and *have* (*I ain't ready*; *He ain't got one*), and the use of *never* with reference to one specific event (*I saw you do it! You never!*). And whilst some types of negation are widespread, others are more localizable. Scots in both Scotland and Ireland has the markers *nae/no*, standing alone or attached particularly to the words *can, do*, and *will*: *he'll no do it, it cannae be done*. And an as yet little-studied area of variation concerns the form *anyone doesn't know* in place of the expected *no one knows*: this appears to be a low-level but significant feature of Irish English and Scots and also of English in the north-east of England, for which Gaelic is thought to be the origin.

Not all syntactic variation is tied to social variation therefore: we can occasionally observe surprising regional variation, although it can be hard to account for this when it occurs. No better example exists of a syntactic puzzle than the quite definite regional preferences for the standard *give me it* in northern and eastern England, a non-standard *give it me* in the West Midlands, and an expanded *give it to me* in the south-west, as recorded by SED. Although the standard is where one might expect it to be, that is in area around London, its strong support in the north, and that for the other varieties elsewhere, is curious. But whilst some grammatical differences are puzzling, others have both socio-political and linguistic bases: constructions involving past and perfect, for example, are areas of grammar where Scots, Irish English, and the standard variety of English show marked differences of some complexity. To take one matter of particular note, we can observe that the three varieties have markedly different ways of indicating an event that is immediately past. The standard method is to use the present perfect, thus: *I have (just) seen him*. In contrast, a Scots speaker might be expected to use the simple past tense with *just*: *I just saw him*. In a construction that is one of the best known, even stereotypical features of Irish English, an Irish speaker can say *I'm after seeing him*, a construction which is heavily influenced by Irish Gaelic, as are many others in Irish English.

CONCLUSION

The non-standard dialects, retaining as they do a lot of the history of the language, have much to recommend them in linguistic terms. Amongst the older forms preserved are some which can be seen to have present-day utility:

whilst permitting their speakers fine-tuning of meaning which is not available to standard dialect users, they offer notable consistency where the standard is irregular; and they offer to the communities who use them a very ready means by which to express individual and collective identity. Why, then, is so little credit afforded to the non-standard? The answer seems in large part to rest with social, and with it regional, separation, at the level of which people are quite readily disposed to pass judgement on the speech of others, providing the kind of statistics presented above on attitudes to accents. Women in the Belfast community of Ballymacarrett, aware of the more acceptable pronunciation, are only half as likely to pronounce *look* as [lʌk] as their male counterparts. A peripheral member of an adolescent gang in Reading, England, is reportedly one-third as likely to say *I goes* than is a core member, and will not use *what* as a relative pronoun when the leaders use it almost without fail.

Variants, then, far from being in free variation, available to be chosen at will, have social meaning, and the society we have inherited places store by what speakers select from the available forms. Social and economic progress in mainstream society is undeniably easier for those who consistently use the variants of grammar and vocabulary belonging to what, at the present time, we have agreed to recognize as the standard dialect, so-called 'standard English'. And the nearer a speaker approaches to pronunciations of prestige, which in England are those of Received Pronunciation, the more acceptable their accent. Changing fashion over time ensures that the goalposts at which people aim will move, and indeed it is not hard to imagine that, as more people achieve mastery of particularly desirable language forms, those previously in possession of them will find ways of moving the target to maintain their exclusivity. It has been suggested by some commentators, furthermore, that it is this desire to remain exclusive that has not only brought about past innovations but has hindered the acceptance into the standard of those regularizations which we have seen to be a feature of the non-standard: if the standard dialect is kept irregular, and so difficult to attain, fewer people might be expected to achieve it than might otherwise be the case.

Whether or not one accepts this 'conspiracy theory' view of the tension between varieties of the language, it is clear that tension does exist, with the members of social groups within one locality, and the collective memberships of different regional communities, interacting to share, or to emphasize as distinct, their own especial variants. Studying that variation today, we are provided with both a window on the past and a means by which we might better understand what has spurred English on to change over the centuries.

REFERENCES AND SUGGESTIONS FOR FURTHER READING

Introductory books on regional dialectal variation in Great Britain include Trudgill *et al.* (2005), Upton and Widdowson (1996), and Trudgill (1999*b*): these illustrate many of the preoccupations and insights of dialectology and explain concepts, terms, and techniques used in the study of dialects, whilst analysing dialect data collected from a variety of practical investigations. The chapter on dialects and accents in O'Donnell and Todd (1992) also provides valuable information and insights whilst remaining very accessible to the early enquirer into the subject. For a more technical overview of the principles behind the study of variation in English speech, the reader can do no better than to consult Chambers and Trudgill (1998), which discusses materials and methods associated with the study of variation in both regional and social dimensions. Also valuable as technical handbooks, with varying degrees of concentration on the British regional dimension and the historical perspective, are Wakelin (1977), Davis (1983), and Francis (1983).

The beginnings of formal dialectology

Indispensable to anyone going on to venture deeply into traditional British English speech is access to the findings of the major regional dialect surveys of the nineteenth century. Wright's *Dialect Dictionary* of 1898–1905, and the appended *Grammar* of 1905, from the Preface of which the opening quotation of this chapter is taken, remain sources of much reliable information not only for England but also for parts of Scotland, Wales, and Ireland, even though it is now a century old and focuses on speech current from the early eighteenth century onwards. The publications of the English Dialect Society, which provided the essential source material for Wright, and of which Robinson (1876) is a particular example, provide additional material, of variable quality but ultimately of undoubted value to those concerned with the historical development of the language in the various regions: they also provide insights into the enthusiasms of members of the Society, and show what can be accomplished by committed amateurs in the field. Although less accessible than Wright, by virtue of its compilation in an age before the advent of the International Phonetic Alphabet, the pioneering pronunciation work of Ellis (1889) rewards the intrepid student with very many essential insights into nineteenth-century regional phonology. Important monographs from the earlier part of the twentieth century, since they can be seen as directly sowing the seeds of the Survey of English Dialects, are Dieth (1932) and Orton (1933). Wakelin (1977) provides an accessible yet scholarly introduction to this formative period in dialect enquiry, as does Chambers and Trudgill (1998) in more general terms.

Modern dialect surveys

Original and more modern fieldwork data collected on a large scale are now available for all the national regions of the British Isles. Mather and Spietel (1975–86) provide very detailed survey-derived data for Scotland from the middle of the twentieth century. Fieldwork data, with accompanying analysis, is provided for English in Wales by Parry (n.d. [1977], 1979, 1999). Dieth and Orton (1962) and Orton *et al.* (1962–71) give access to the very detailed raw data of the Survey of English Dialects, which covers the English counties and a small part of south-east Wales, whilst Upton *et al.* (1994), in drawing together its diffuse lexical and grammatical information, provides a digest and also acts as a thesaurus to the larger work. Extracts of recordings from the Survey, set alongside others from the Millennium Memory Bank project to afford the possibility of real-time comparison of local speech at the mid- and end-points of the twentieth century, can be heard in the English Accents and Dialects collection of the British Library's Collect Britain website <**http://www.collectbritain.co.uk/collections/dialects/**>, where accompanying notes are also provided. The website for the BBC's Voices 2005 project may also be of interest: see <**http://www.bbc.co.uk/voices/**>. Some survey material for Ireland is available in Barry (1981, 1982), although this is brief and restricted in geographical range: Hickey (2004) gives the user access to very detailed and up-to-date information on Irish English.

The 'dialect area'

A wide variety of atlases present the findings of the Survey of English Dialects cartographically: Orton and Wright (1974) and Orton *et al.* (1978) interpret much of the Survey's data in map form; further SED mapping, using a wide range of techniques to highlight various issues of geographical distribution of features in England, and doing so with varying degrees of technical complexity, is available in Kolb (1979), Anderson (1987), Upton *et al.* (1987), Viereck with Ramisch (1991, 1997), and Upton and Widdowson (1996). Parry (1999) contains Survey of Anglo Welsh Dialects maps directly in the tradition of Orton *et al.* (1978), and, since the SAWD data are directly comparable with those of SED, permits the mapping of features across the Wales–England border. It should be noted, however, that although a number of these atlases are isoglossic, the lines which they contain do not imply the existence of areas within which features are contained. Trudgill (1999) does use the concept of the 'dialect area' in order usefully to discuss basic feature distributions in an elementary book, and the impression might be gained that such areas are a reality. That this is not so is manifest from the 'mixing and fudging' discussions in Chambers and Trudgill (1998) and Upton (1995). A critique of the whole dialect area concept is to be found in Davis *et al.* (1997). There are a few specialized isoglossic dialect maps relating to Irish English variation in Barry (1981). However, the Linguistic Survey of Scotland (Mather and Spietel 1975–86), which, as well as covering Scotland takes in Northern Ireland features and those in the extreme north of England, makes use of overlaying hachuring as a technique, and in doing so demonstrates the fuzziness of boundaries.

Types of variation: pronunciation, vocabulary, and grammar

General overviews of aspects of modern speech variation are available at different scholarly levels. Trudgill (1984) ranges especially widely in the essays of a variety of authorities, while Trudgill *et al.* (2005), which has an accompanying audio cassette, provides a most accessible summary of salient features of a wide range of vernacular dialects. For pronunciation only, a core text for information is the second volume of Wells (1982), in which all the British regions are treated in some detail. Foulkes and Docherty (1999), in addition to detailed descriptions of the accents of very many major urban centres of Britain, contains an exploration of a wide range of sociolinguistic issues attendant on modern dialectological preoccupations. Trudgill and Chambers (1991) provides papers by major practitioners on aspects of non-standard dialect grammar within Britain and beyond. Concentrating on both phonology and grammar, Kortmann *et al.* (2004) contains chapters on all regions; these are accompanied by a CD-Rom and website and form part of a series detailing accents and grammar of English world-wide. Also very wide-ranging globally is Cheshire (1991). Milroy and Gordon (2003) contains a wealth of instruction on the principles and practices of the discipline of sociolinguistics.

Additional to the material of the regionally-conceived Linguistic Survey of Scotland, many aspects of present-day and older Scots are detailed in papers in Corbett *et al.* (2003), where those by Macafee, Miller, and Stuart-Smith concentrate respectively on the vocabulary, grammar, and pronunciation of modern Scots. Other authoritative works on Scots and Scottish English include Romaine (1982), Görlach (1985), and Fenton and MacDonald (1994). *The Scottish National Dictionary* (Grant and Murison 1931–76) is an essential tool for the student of the Scottish lexicon, for which see also Macafee (1994). Wide-ranging essays on Irish English are available in Ó Baoill (1985) and Kallen (1997), while Todd (1999) gives a most accessible overview of northern and southern varieties in the round. Filppula (1999) provides a quite comprehensive grammar of the varieties to be found in Ireland. Detailed study of the interaction of speech and social networks in Belfast, carried out in the 1970s by J. and L. Milroy, along with much else concerning social variation in English, is reported on most accessibly in Chambers (2003). Besides the work of Parry, also closely associated with the Survey of Anglo-Welsh Dialects is Penhallurick (1991); Coupland (1988) provides social dialectological insight into a very major variety of Welsh English. A wide range of such sociolinguistic commentary is available for varieties in England: among the most recent of these furnishing material for this chapter can be cited Kerswill and Williams (1999), Beal (2000), Watt and Tillotson (2001), and Watt (2002). The phenomenon dubbed 'Estuary English' (see further Chapter 13) is much discussed both in the media and some more serious forums: one of the most useful critiques among the latter is that of Przedlacka (2002). Information on the most modern form of Received Pronunciation, the social accent which is inevitably to be used as a touchstone from time to time in the description of other accents, is to be found in Upton *et al.* (2001).

12

ENGLISH AMONG THE LANGUAGES

Richard W. Bailey

MULTILINGUALISM is, and has been, a normal part of social life for most people, both now and in the past. Modern multilinguals look with surprise on those who believe that a single language will serve them better than several, and they can hardly imagine so isolated an existence as implied by one language or barely believe that monolinguals can be satisfied by talking to people identical, more or less, to themselves.

English is (and has been) one language among many, and this chapter introduces readers to some of the interactions between English and other languages, focusing on the period between the later Renaissance and modern English (although earlier aspects of this pattern of interaction will also be examined too). The ebb and flow of enthusiasm for other languages within the anglophone community is a tale of profound cultural importance for this history of English. Yet both sides of the linguistic divide are important. In Britain, *abroad* has been seen as sometimes repugnant, sometimes frightening—'that beastly abroad', wrote one nineteenth-century novelist quoted by the *OED*. Mistrust and suspicion is not the exclusive property of English-speakers, however. English, as seen by those who did not acquire it as a mother tongue, has been characterized in an astonishing variety of ways: *unimportant, invasive, empowering, destructive* are among the words used to describe it.

HOW MANY LANGUAGES DO YOU NEED?

In the past, heightened social value accrued around the possession of more languages than one. The Bible, for example, relates a linguistic miracle that took place in the first century AD when the followers of Jesus suddenly became fluent in languages of the many visitors to (and residents of) Jerusalem. This involved no fewer than fifteen languages. The surprise, as reported in Acts 2:4–12, was the clarity of the speech of those miraculously made fluent, a startling improvement on the halting approximations or pidgin contact languages which had been usual in that multilingual city. Even if this story is regarded as metaphorical rather than historical, it presumes a culture in which a diversity of languages is entirely normal. As Stephen of Hungary counselled his successor in the eleventh century, 'The utility of foreigners and guests is so great that they can be given a place of sixth importance among the royal ornaments'. Moreover, he added, 'a country unified in language and customs is fragile and weak'.[1] Stephen's view seems to have been commonplace in political thinking at the time that English emerged as a distinct language within the cluster of West Germanic dialects. As Matthew Townend has reminded us in Chapter 3 of this volume (see p. 62), Bede began his *Ecclesiastical History of the English Peoples* by describing the linguistic riches of eighth-century Britain and celebrating the fact that five languages were in use. Until quite recently, the prevailing opinion has been the more languages, the better.

Old-fashioned language histories have often endeavoured to look at a 'national' language as if it were a single (and triumphant) result of some Darwinian process of selection. This view ignores the abundance of languages and language varieties except insofar as they were swept up and carried forward by the inevitable rise of the national 'standard.' More recently, approaches to the 'ecology' of communities have instead demonstrated the value of describing the facts of language life for all people living in earlier times and places. People at the interface of two (or more) languages 'accommodate' to each other and thus create new linguistic identities. Twenty-first-century society is not so different to those of earlier times; the many languages of Manchester or Miami, Cape Town or Canberra, can easily be matched in the much smaller settlements of medieval

---

[1] See O. Jászi, *The Dissolution of the Habsburg Monarchy* (Chicago: The University of Chicago Press, 1929), 39.

Colchester or renaissance Cardiff. In all of these communities, a dynamic inter-action among languages (and dialects) produced new forms of expression. In recognizing that the past is often like the present, we need to search backwards for evidence of this process of accommodation.

TRAVERSING LANGUAGE BOUNDARIES

Before written records became common, it is difficult to discern just what balance among languages might have been struck in the early history of the British Isles. Place-names, as already indicated (see p. 325), can still attest the kinds of linguistic layering which often took place. *London*, for example, traces its own history into English from the Latin *Londoninium*, which is itself supposed to be based on a Celtic personal or tribal name, *Londinos*. The name of *Weston super Mare* on the Somerset coast reveals that the Latin-speakers who came there wanted to distinguish among *Westons*. This one overlooks the sea (and its final element derives from Latin *mare*); *Weston-under-Penyard* in nearby Hereford-shire lies under a hill (which bears a Welsh name). Chapters 2 and 3 have addressed the complex multilingualism of Anglo-Saxon England. Old English already had a word for the crucial social role of the translator—*wealhstod*—who stood at the interface of two languages; in Ælfric's *Life of King Oswold*, King Oswold of Northumbria (bilingual in Gaelic and Northumbrian) is hence the *wealhstod* for the Gaelic-speaking Bishop Aidan of Scotland who was to convert the Northumbrians to Christianity (aided by the linguistic skills of the king himself). In Middle English too, as Chapters 3 and 4 have stressed, multilingual-ism remained a significant fact about language use in Britain (even though, following the Norman Conquest, the individual language components of such multilingualism had decisively changed). Different languages also clearly took on different social values, and the linguistic situation was evidently far more com-plex than that later articulated in Sir Walter Scott's *Ivanhoe* (1819). In that novel, the 'boors and serfs' use Germanic terms for the animals they tend (like *deer*, *pig*, and *sheep*), while the swaggering French use Romance words for the meat they ate after the slaughter (*venison*, *pork*, and *mutton*). In post-Conquest Britain, new words also emerged for those who mediated across the boundaries which languages could create: *latimer* (first used in Laȝamon's *Brut* in the early thirteenth century), followed by *translator* (a1392), and later by *drugeman* (c1400 >*dragoman*). In early modern English still other terms were introduced for the bilingual facilitator: *truchman* (1485) and *linguister* (a1649).

Fourteenth-century texts can often reveal a complex interface of languages. English, for example, could be directly embedded in Latin texts, particularly those prepared for the use of persons in religious orders who were fluent in both languages. In many of these, the English selections included proverbs, asides, and expansive metaphors, as in the following example:

Iam dierum nesciunt quid et quomodo vellent habere formam vestimentorum suorum in eo quod habent vestimenta sua contra naturam, **for-qwy it is a meruell to se a catt with two tallys, bot now a man or a woman will haue two talles, and yt is more meruell, for a woman wyll haue a tayll a-fore off her scho and anoder byhynd off hyr gone. A man wyll haue two qwellbarowys off hys schowdyrs.** Set certe Deus non sic creavit hominem set   5 adymaginem suam, et ipse not habet talia, scio.

('Nowadays they don't know what and how they want to have the shape of their clothes, because they have clothes against [the law of] nature. For it is a marvel to see a cat with two tails, but now a man or woman will have two tails, and it is an even greater marvel, for a woman will have a tail in front of her shoe and another behind her gown. A man will have two wheelbarrows off his shoulders. But surely God did not create man thus but rather in his own image, and he does not have such things as far as I know'.)

Here the rant about fashion—*tails* and *barrows* in lines 3, 4, and 5 are methods of cutting and piecing fabric—has a 'low' element which is, in fact, typical of these mixed-language texts. English is the 'slangy' language; Latin is the vehicle for serious business. Two other English insertions in this sermon quote a tapster and a glutton. In both cases, English is the language of silliness and sin.

Fifteenth-century account books kept for London Bridge similarly show a fully integrated mixture of English, Latin, and French. Business records of this sort were often composed in this way.

It 'Thome Mede Pyle dryver opant' in quadrando scindendo & dirigendo lez pyles hoc a° infix in opibz aquaticis pro defensione fluxus & refluxus aquae ab opibz lapideis tam circa peram noui turris lapidei versus finem australem pontis' hoc anno circūlus' cum piles qᵃm in diu's alijs locis ...

('And to Thomas Mede piledriver working in squaring cutting and guiding the piles this year fixed in the water works for defence of the stone work from the ebb and flow of the water both around the pier of the new stone tower towards the southern end of the bridge encircled this year with piles and in diverse other places'.)

This entry, made in 1471–2, invites speculation that its three languages were in use along the Thames, not just by clerks who kept the accounts but also by mariners and other workers who communicated with each other across linguistic boundaries.

LINGUISTIC ENCOUNTERS

Away from south-east England, the ecology of languages had taken different forms. Dutch merchants, for example, settled in the east of Scotland, from Edinburgh north to Aberdeen, and traded with Antwerp, Ghent, and Bruges. In 1475, Flemish weavers formed a corporation in Edinburgh, and earlier Dutch military engineers had designed a catapult for use by the Scots against the English. Most of the words that were borrowed by the Scots from Dutch had, however, little currency outside Scotland; the great exception to this generalization is *golf* (<Middle Dutch *kolf*). Farther north, in Shetland, another kind of multilingual community emerged, involving Norn (the variety of Norwegian spoken in Orkney, Shetland, and northern Scotland), English, and Dutch after the construction of a naval base by the Dutch to protect their herring fleet. Multilingualism could, of course, be met with resistance. As English military and political power increased, efforts were made to put down the use of other 'national' languages within Britain. In 1366, the statutes of Kilkenny required that in Ireland, descendants of English migrants should abandon the use of Gaelic on penalty of forfeiture of their property. (This law also forbade 'fostering of children, concubinage or amour' between English men and Irish women.) In Wales, in 1536, Welsh speakers were expelled from positions of power: 'from hence forth no person or persons that use the Welsh speech or language shall have or enjoy any manner office or fees ... unless he or they use and exercise the *English* speech or language' (27 Henry VIII 20). In Cornwall, in 1549, Cornish people were compelled to become Protestants but denied liturgy in their own language; proponents of the law asserted that the Cornish should not complain since they had not understood services in Latin and so should be content not to understand them in English. In Scotland, through the 'Statutes of Iona' in 1609, the London parliament required inhabitants of the Western Isles worth the value of sixty cattle to put their sons (or, lacking sons, daughters) to school in English until they should be able to speak, read, and write the language 'sufficientlie'. Efforts like these reflect an emerging intolerance for multilingualism, but none of these laws had an immediate and radically transforming effect on the language ecology of Ireland, Wales, Cornwall, and Scotland. Over the long-term, however, English overwhelmed these other languages, as Chapter 13 will further discuss.

Early modern English, as the examples above suggest, rested on a complex foundation of both multilingual practice and attitude. Many of the books which Caxton printed in the late fifteenth-century were, for instance, translations of Latin, Dutch, and French texts so that readers not adept in these languages could have access to them. Because he was eager for commercial success, Caxton printed the works he believed would be most popular, and he printed them in a form of English that he thought would reach the widest audience. Thus, as Chapter 5 has noted, printing became a force for uniformity, privileging not just English *per se* but certain kinds of English. On the other hand, such an account leaves out the importance of languages other than English in the early book trade. Caxton imported books in foreign languages from abroad to sell in Britain, and, of some ninety that he published in London, sixteen were in languages other than English. Commercially, Caxton and his immediate successors had a good sense of what would sell, and they did not limit their productions to English. Technically, these printers were not innovators, however, and they lagged behind their continental competitors. Not until 1519 were Greek types employed. Hebrew and Arabic faces followed much later in 1592 and 1617 respectively. But England was not wholly indifferent to innovation. With a revived interest in the national past, antiquarians commissioned Anglo-Saxon types in 1567, and in 1571 Elizabeth I ordered the creation of an Irish face which was sent to Dublin so that a catechism could be printed in Gaelic. All of this activity is good evidence that there was a demand for books published in languages other than English.

In commercial and legal writing, French and Latin remained essential languages for practitioners even if none of the litigants or lawyers used these languages in speech. As a result, mixed-language texts continued to be composed in early modern English, as in the following examples of depositions from (respectively) 1514 and 1570:

1514. unus egipcius sibi publice dixit tuam fortunam congoscis for he that stantith by the schold jape the iii tymes er thou goo to thy bedd to thi husband. Et hoc allegat probare.

('A gypsy said publicly to her, You know your fortune, for he that stands beside you should fuck you three times before you go to your bed to your husband. And she offers to prove this'.)

1570. Margaria nicolson singlewoma*n* cont*r*a agnete blenkinsop vx*or* Robert in *caus*a diffama*cinois* vi*delicet* hyte hoore a whipe and a ~~era~~ cart/ and a franc hoode/ waies me fo*ᵣ* yᵉ my lasse wenst haue a halpeny halter fo*ᵣ* yᵉ to goo vp gallygait & be hanged/

('Margaret Nicolson, spinster, against Agnete Blenkinsop, wife of Robert, in a case of defamation, namely that she should be whipped behind a cart and [she was] a 'French hood.' 'Woe is me, my lass, do you want a halfpenny noose for you to go up to the Gallowgate and be hanged'.)

Scriveners who recorded these statements faced a demanding task of balancing the (increasingly conventional) Latin frame of the proceeding with the literal transcript (in English) of what had been said.

In the early modern period, London continued to be a magnet for migration, and many migrants spoke languages other than English. Interpreters must have had plenty to do on the interfaces of these languages—even though they seldom come to the foreground in the written records. Diplomatic and royal visits from abroad brought crowds of foreigners—especially from France and Spain—and these occasions too required translators. Trade with Germany, the Baltic nations, and Russia increased, and these contacts in turn left marks on the vocabulary of English—for instance, *beluga* ('whale'), *severuga* ('sturgeon'), and *tsar* ('ruler'), all words borrowed from Russian in the sixteenth century.

ENGLISH OUT AND ABOUT

One of the great 'facts' about English in the early modern period is that the language was used in exploration and conquest, and it is usual in histories of the language to display for admiration and wonder the exotic borrowings into the native tongue from languages spoken at a great distance from Britain. What is seldom made prominent in these conventional histories is that these explorings first took place nearly a century after the beginning of European expansionism; in this respect, the English followed the Spanish and the Portuguese (for instance) with a series of freebooting raids on the principle that it was easier to steal from the riches looted from the new world after they had been accumulated by other Europeans rather than competing for treasures on the ground. Precisely the same idea illuminates the empire of words. It was far easier for English people to pluck new (and exotic) vocabulary from Latin, Spanish, or Portuguese books once the sharp edges of its foreignness had, in a sense, already been rubbed off. Nearly all the famously 'American' words come into English from one of these languages—for example, *chocolate, maize, potato,* and *tomato.*

GO-BETWEENS

A representative figure in this late-coming expansion of English is the mariner John Hawkins whose exploits were celebrated and generously rewarded in his lifetime (Figure 12.1). On his first voyage in 1562–63, he sailed to the west coast of Africa where he captured two Portuguese vessels and their cargo of human beings. These captives he transported to Hispaniola and sold as slaves to the Spanish; he returned to England with goods which were sold for a great profit. His subsequent voyages were similarly successful (and unscrupulous), and they

FIG. 12.1. The crest of John Hawkins (1532–1595), who pioneered the triangular trade that connected England, Africa, and the Americas. In 1562–63, he kidnapped some Africans who had been enslaved by the Portuguese, sold them to the Spanish in the New World, and returned to England flush with profit. After a second, and similarly successful, voyage, he was granted the coat of arms reproduced above. It shows the British lion bestriding the waves, and the crest, above, a 'demi-Moor, or negro' chained. Freebooting by Hawkins and those who followed in the slave trade profoundly changed the mixture of languages into which England had become immersed.
Source: Reproduced by permission of the College of Arms, MS Miscellaneous Grants 1, f.148.

occurred both before and after the defeat of the Spanish armada in 1588, a naval action in which he was celebrated for serving. From the viewpoint of multilingualism, however, Hawkins is perhaps not so interesting a figure as those who accompanied him on his travels and who could speak the Portuguese, Spanish, and other European languages required for the success of the expeditions. Even more interesting are those who bridged the gap between the Europeans and these newly encountered African people.

One such gap-bridger—although a man not celebrated for truthfulness—is David Ingram, a sailor from Essex who accompanied Hawkins on his third voyage of 1567. On this occasion, Hawkins' vessels were surprised by a Spanish force near Veracruz in Mexico, and only two small ships of Hawkins' flotilla remained to bring the survivors back to England. Given the crowding and lack of provisions, a hundred men were set on shore and left to fend for themselves. Most went south. Ingram and two companions went north. The three of them claimed to have walked through the heart of North America, arriving one year later at Cape Breton (in what is modern-day Canada) where they found a French vessel to bring them back to Europe. While there seems to have been some scepticism about this tale at the time—the British geographer Richard Hakluyt published Ingram's *Relation* of his journey in his own anthology of travel writings, *The Principal Navigations, Voyages and Discoveries of the English Nation* (1589), and then dropped it from the 1599 edition—much of what Ingram wrote was plausible and even convincing. (His references to abundant silver, crystal, and rubies may have been invented to foster investment in further travel to the new lands.) Attention to language in Ingram's report reveals what a late sixteenth-century audience would expect to hear on the subject. Like most of his contemporaries, Ingram supposed that only one language was spoken by the inhabitants of this vast (and richly multilingual) territory. If he had actually been there, he would have known better. Six sample words are listed and glossed to represent 'the language of some of the Countreis': *gwando* ('a word of salutation'), *caricona* ('a king'), *caraccona* ('a lord'), *fona* ('bread'), *carmugnar* ('the privities'), *kerucca* ('the sun'). These seem hardly sufficient to have facilitated the long walk, and they provide no definite impression of the nature of the cultural encounter. In fact, these six 'Welsh-sounding "Indian" words' were intended to give authenticity to Ingram's tale—among the theories of origin of the North Americans was that they were a lost tribe of Welsh. But Ingram's story almost immediately struck many readers as bogus.[2] These 'Indian' words were, however, plausible to his readers.

[2] See D. B. Quinn, *Explorers and Colonies: America, 1500–1625* (London: The Hambleton Press, 1990), 404.

One European word Ingram uses is authentically connected with the new world—*cannibal*:

The people in those Countreys are professed enemies to the *Canibals* or men eaters: The *Canibals* do most inhabite betweene *Norumbega*, & *Bariniah*, they haue teeth like dogs teeth, and thereby you may know them.

Cannibal was a word introduced into colonial discourse by Columbus himself, and its origin is squarely American since it is a borrowing into Spanish of the Arawak word *caniba* ('person'). As an etymologist with a cause, Columbus connected *caniba* with *khan* and declared that the Caribs were none other than 'la gente del Gran Can,' that is, the people of the Grand Khan, whose rich palaces and mines lay just over the horizon.

Thus Ingram's *Relation* offers an example of a meandering route by which many expressions from the Americas entered English. Reported by Columbus, *caniba* gained a Spanish form, *Canibales*, and then a neo-Latin one: *Canibalis*. The word arrived in English in 1553 in a translation into English of travel writings composed by a German and published in Latin.

Scientific study of American languages began at the same time that Ingram's *Relation* became known. Thomas Harriot, an Elizabethan genius, was assigned as 'geographer' in an expedition to Roanoke (in present-day North Carolina). Harriot had already learned some Algonquian from two Amerindian men who had been brought to England for a short visit in 1584, and he went to Roanoke equipped, according to a note he jotted down later, with the sentence: *Kecow hit tamen* or 'What is this?'. After a year in America during 1585–6, Harriot had devised a sophisticated orthography and become fluent in the language. On his return, he composed *A Briefe and True Report of the New Found Land of Virginia* which was published separately and then incorporated into Hakluyt's anthology of *Navigations*. This work printed two words that are attested in the *OED* as first used in the *Report*: *cushaw* ('a kind of squash') and *werowance* ('a chief').

Evidence of this kind gives a very misleading picture of the multilingual world of English and the key figures in it: the bilinguals. English empire building in the sixteenth century was often hasty and opportunistic. On the continent, the empire builders took a longer view. The Portuguese, for example, exiled men to West Africa where they were expected to father bilingual children who, as grown-ups, could be employed as translators. Before his 1517 expedition to the Yucatan peninsula in search of the Mayan civilization, the Spanish conquistador Hernan Cortés (Captain-General of the Armada) similarly sought out Spanish castaways who had been abandoned in the Yucatan long enough to become fluent in Maya. In 1536, the French Explorer of the St Lawrence, Jacques Cartier, left two boys behind; if they survived, they would be turned into translators. English colonists benefited from such persons, though not in so calculated a way. In 1613, an East India Company vessel kidnapped two 'Souldanians' from the Cape of Good Hope for training as intermediaries. Cory, the one who survived, flourished as a translator from his return to southern Africa in 1614 until his death in 1627. One nearly contemporary report characterized Cory's pitiful homesickness during his residence in London: 'For when he had learned a little of our Language, he would daily lie upon the ground, and cry very often thus in broken English: *Cooree home go, Souldania go, home go*'.

Usually, however, the appearance of translators was the result of accident rather than policy. In 1621, three months after their arrival in what is now Massachusetts, a man emerged from the forest speaking fluent English and offering assistance to the Pilgrims. He was Tisquantum, a native of the area who had earlier been kidnapped by the English, sold into slavery in Spain, emancipated to London, and returned to New England.

As traffic increased, so did the number of bilinguals. Describing his travels to the east, another adventurer, Peter Mundy, gave currency to words associated with China. Unlike many travellers, he described the translators who had helped him and his companions:

The aforesaid interpreter was a Chincheo, runaway From the Portugalls att our beeing att Macao, who spake a little bad language. There is another Named Antonio, A Capher Eathiopian Abissin, or Curled head, thatt came to and Froe aboutt Messages as interpreter, little better then the other, runawaie allsoe From the Portugalls to the Chinois, it being an ordinary Matter For slaves on some Discontent or other to run away From their Masters; and beeing among the Chinois they are saffe, who make use of their service.

This report—describing events in 1637—does not make it clear just where the linguistic shortcomings of these translators lay, whether in their Portuguese or their Cantonese (the language of Macao). What is significant, however, is that both men were out of place. The first was from Fukien province ('Cincheo') which had suffered an imperial decree closing its maritime trade with the consequence that its ambitious people were dispersed all over south-east Asia. The second translator was, if anything, even farther from home since he was a sub-Saharan African and thus both racially and linguistically isolated. People like these two, living on the cultural divide, lubricate the surfaces of the languages in contact and help them rub off on each other. Without the misplaced Chinese translator and the multilingual helper from southern Africa, the English would have been almost entirely helpless.

Not all these expeditions were commercial or political. The early modern era witnessed vigorous efforts to convert native peoples to Christian practices. One such missionary, Roger Williams, the founder of Rhode Island, had arrived in New England in 1631. Almost immediately he set out to learn the local language and in 1643 he published (in London) his *Key into the Language of America*. Full of information about cultural contact, this little book shows the influence of an ardent Puritan on a willing convert. Using the familiar trope of the death-bed confession, Williams described the last days of his friend Wequash, a Pequot: 'He replyed in broken English: *Me so big naughty Heart, me heart all one stone!* ... I had many discourses with him on his Life, but this was the summe of our last parting untill our generall meeting'. Throughout his book, Williams shows deep respect for native peoples and even upbraids the English for lacking the generosity he sometimes found among them.

Another of the remarkable early efforts at Christian evangelism was the hard work of John Eliot, a Puritan minister, who learned the Algonquian language of Massachusetts Bay, and, with the help of a convert, translated the entire Bible (from Genesis to Revelation), publishing it in 1663. Eliot faced enormous difficulties in making the cultural context accessible, and to do so he relied frequently on inserting English loanwords into Algonquian:

Kah Saboth paumushaumoouk, Mary Magdelene, kah Mary okasoh James kah Salome, taphumwog weetemunge spicesash, onk peyaog, kah wuilissequnouh.

('And when the sabbath was past, Mary Magdalene, and Mary the mother of James, and Salome, had bought sweet spices, that they might come and anoint him' Mark 16:1.)

The names in this selection make it look more 'English' than it really is, but the borrowings of *sabbath* and *spices* are clearly apparent, and the paratactic style of the English source (with linkages using *kah* 'and') is exported to the translation. While only a handful of Native Americans became deeply literate in their own language, many preachers—both English and Native—became fluent in preaching and reading aloud. Even the most casual encounters with this kind of language introduced ideas about literacy and the value of written documents where they had not been known before.

These efforts took place at a time when the prevailing opinion among the English was that they were especially skilful at learning new languages and eager to bring home the linguistic 'treasures' found abroad. Writing at the very beginning of English expansionism outside Europe, Richard Carew, a poet and antiquarian whose work has already been discussed in Chapter 8, celebrated this genius for acquiring languages: '... turne an Englishman at any time of his age into what countrie soever allowing him due respite, and you shall see him profit so well that the imitation of his utterance, will in nothing differ from the patterne of that native language'. Williams, Eliot, and many other migrants deserved the praise that Carew offered them.

ENGLISH EXPANDS

The boundary between *early* and *late* modern English is not marked by any event as memorable as the Conquest in 1066 by the Norman French or the introduction of printing in 1476. In most histories of the language, the boundary of 1700 has been chosen partly because of the roundness of the number, and partly because historians discern in the death of the poet John Dryden (who died in that year) the end of the copiousness of the English renaissance and the commencement of plain-spoken modernity as represented by a next-generation writer like Joseph Addison. It is also an era in which the optimism of a Carew about learning foreign languages sank into the background to be replaced by the notion that English was spreading around the world and hence was sufficient by itself. As one anonymous writer wrote in 1766 as he reviewed (and refuted) allegations against the language:

The last objection that occurs to me at present, is, that our tongue wants universality, which seems to be an argument against its merit. This is owing to the affectation of Englishmen, who prefer any language to their own, and is not to be imputed to a defect in their native tongue. But the objection, if such it be, is vanishing daily; for I have been assured, by several ingenious foreigners, that in many places abroad, Italy in particular, it is become the fashion to study the English Tongue.

It would not be long before the old idea that English people were adept at foreign languages had been stood on its head. The new idea, emergent in the middle of the eighteenth century, was that English was destined to be a 'world language' and that those who did not gain it as a birthright would learn it as a necessity. Not until the middle of the nineteenth century, however, was this idea widely embraced as part of the orthodoxy of English. Then it developed into a stubborn resistance to multilingualism that continues, to a lessening extent, down to the present.

Other conventional ideas were changing too. Adventurers no longer expected, as the earlier narratives of Ingram and his contemporaries had promised, that gold, silver, and rubies could be plucked from the ground (or pilfered from the Spanish). Adventurers became far less common. It was instead merchants who came to the centre of the ideas of the multilingual world. And then the bureaucrats.

Borrowed words from this period tended to become less venturesome and more commercial. This development can be seen through the perspective of the market for woven goods, a principal source of export wealth before the mid-nineteenth century. Early names came from places in England associated with the production of these weaves: *worsted*, for instance, from a place in Norfolk, or *kersey* from a village in Suffolk. Cultural history can be seen through the growing internationalization of these names. Here is a selection with the dates of first occurrence as found in the *OED*: *arras* (< *Arras* 'a town in northern France', 1397), *holland* (1427), *calico* (< Calicut in India, 1505), *brocade* (< Spanish, 1556), *mohair* (< Arabic, 1570), *jersey* (< *jersey worsted*, 1583 <from the Channel Island), *muslin* (< Mosul, Iraq, 1609), *vicuna* (< Spanish, 1622), *seersucker* (< Persian, 1622), *denim* (< *serge de Nîmes*, < *Nîmes* 'a town in southern France', 1695), *chenille* (< French, 1738), *astrakhan* (<Russian, 1766), *cashmere* (< Kashmir, 1822), *chine* (< *China* through French, 1852), *khaki* (< Urdu, 1879).

Commerce embedded in colonialism produced yet more influence of other languages on English. In south Asia, the East India Company became *John Company*, and the great lexicographers of this part of the empire—Henry Yule and A. C. Burnell—provided a suitably local etymology for it in their celebrated *Hobson-Jobson: A Glossary of Colloquial Anglo-Indian Words and Phrases*, first published in 1886:

> ... It has been suggested, but apparently without real reason, that the phrase is a corruption of **Company Jahān**, "which as a fine sounding smack about it, recalling Shāh Jehānn and Jehānagīr, and the golden age of the Moghuls" .... And Sir G. Birdwood writes: "The earliest coins minted by the English in India were of copper, stamped with a figure of the irradiated *lingam*, the phallic 'Roi Soleil.' " The mintage of this coin is unknown (? Madras), but without doubt it must have served to ingratiate us with the natives of the country, and may have given origin to their personification of the Company under the potent title of **Kumpani Jehan**, which, in English mouths, became 'John Company'.

The relevant entry in the dictionary concedes that these etymological speculations are 'without real reason', but these fantastic ideas do connect an obvious English phrase with the Moguls and, by the puissant symbol of the lingam on the coin, with the sexual potency of John Company.

COMMERCE IN (AND ABOUT) ENGLISH

As multilingualism became more specialized, borrowing from other languages increased. An entry in a minute book prepared in India in 1761 shows that bilingual clerks had integrated many borrowings into English: 'Abuses of dustucks by Company's gomasthas and banians noticed. To prevent it, all dustucks to be registered and returned after specific time' ('Abuses of passes by Company's native agents and Hindu traders noticed. To prevent it, all passes to be registered and returned after specific time'). In addition to ephemeral loanwords like those found in this passage, the bureaucratic style had evolved the near total omission of articles and other 'small' grammatical markers and had embraced the passive voice (in which the grammatical agents become as invisible as John Company's). Documents of British India abound with grammatical shortcuts and loanwords of this kind, and this special 'insider English' appeared with nearly equal frequency in legal papers or commercial transactions among both anglophones and *compradors* or 'native agents' (< Portuguese *comprador* 'buyer' [1615]).

Social roles assigned to native peoples in south Asia produced borrowed words that gained some enduring usage in the wider community of English: *coolie* ('labourer'), *lascar* ('sailor'), *nabob* ('person of great wealth and influence'), *sepoy* ('soldier'), *subahdar* ('officer in command of sepoys').

The technology of international trade also abetted change in English. With the introduction of the telegram and cablegram, abbreviated commercial communication gained a new reason for brevity: messages were charged by the number of words they contained. A solution to this problem was found by the Anglo-American Code and Cypher Company and published in a dictionary at the end of the nineteenth century. It contained such entries as *Anes* ('Must have answer immediately'). One four-letter word thus stood for the four ordinary words, producing a 75 per cent reduction in the cost of sending this message. Such a saving could only arise in a culture already bent on the idea of brevity and abbreviation and that had already reduced the eight-word sentence upon which the four-word version is built: '*I* must have *an* answer *from you* immediately'.[3]

SCIENCE AND ENGLISH

As 'natural philosophy' turned into science, English changed in response to new impulses. A 'plain' style emphasizing nouns expressed the doctrines of the Royal Society (see p. 240–1), and new thoughts required new terms. On the intersection of the old and the new ways of expression appeared *An Historical Relation of the*

---

[3] See further R. W. Bailey, *Nineteenth-Century English* (Ann Arbor, MI: The University of Michigan Press, 1996), 59.

Island Ceylon in the East Indies, published in 1681 under the name of Robert Knox but strongly influenced by the ideas of Robert Hooke, secretary of the Royal Society. Knox had suffered a 'Detainment of 19 years 6 months & 14 days' in Ceylon, much of it spent in the fastness of Kandy, a city high in the central mountains which would resist outside colonial influence into the nineteenth century. Knox became fluent in Sinhalese and acquainted with the customs, flora, and fauna of the island. When he was finally released from 'detainment', he returned to England with a collection of biological specimens, some of them preserved in British collections today. As a scientifically-minded adventurer, Knox was a wonderful informant for Hooke who was discouraged by the abysmal state of systematic knowledge of the natural world, even that which might easily 'be obtain'd from divers knowing Planters now Residing in London'.

Knox was thus a source of precious knowledge. He himself saw his experience in terms of religion: exile and estrangement. But Hooke saw the pages of Knox's story as opening a world of science: anthropology, geography, plants and animals, government, religious beliefs. And in helping Knox prepare his story for publication, Hooke did his best to use the 'native' words for the exotic novelties reported in it: *perahera* ('a celebratory procession'), *dissava* ('a district governor'). Knox's book is cited 93 times in the *OED*, and most of the borrowed words from Sinhalese appear there for the first time: *Kittul* and *talipot* ('kinds of palm'), *wanderoo* ('a kind of monkey'). What is intriguing about this case is that the new science wanted to use borrowed words to give authenticity to these new exotica, a far cry from the impulse that had earlier led to the North American *robin* having only the slightest resemblance to the European one. (The English *robin* is a small linnet; the American one a large thrush.) Having two quite different birds named with the same word was bad science, and Hooke wanted to avoid it.

The influence of science on the English vocabulary can be traced by an examination of the elements in the periodic table. The ones known and valued before the dawn of chemistry have English names (even if they are borrowed at some early time): *gold, silver, lead.* The new chemistry produced exotic novelties influenced by Germany and France. Thus *cobalt* first appears from German in 1683; *oxygen* from French in 1789; and then, through the principles leading to the 'International Scientific Vocabulary' based on 'new' Latin, to *potassium* and *sodium* coined in 1807 by Humphrey Davy on the foundation of English *potash* and *soda.* As the periodic table filled up through discovery or synthesis, word formation became even more creative—for instance, *uranium* (1805) from the name of the planet; *lawrencium* (1961) from the name of the scientist Ernest O. Lawrence.

What makes these 'scientific' words of special importance is that their users abhorred ambiguity and were willing to suffer the jeers of etymologists or the scorn of the lay public as they used exotic vocabulary. A paraphrase of the slogan of the founders of the Royal Society shows just how much this kind of English was (and is) set apart from the usual fortunes of language change—so many meanings; just so many words.

A VARIOUS LANGUAGE

On both sides of the anglophone Atlantic, from the mid-eighteenth century forward, there was, as Chapter 9 has explored, an unprecedented interest in 'propriety' and 'correctness'. Of the 187 books concerned with linguistic etiquette published in the anglophone world in the eighteenth century, 32 were published before 1750 and 155 after. This flood of new publications, beginning at mid-century, supported finely nuanced judgements about the 'genius' of English and what properly belonged to it. Most attention was devoted to varieties within the community of English speakers, but commentators were also fascinated by the 'otherness' of the English influenced by foreign languages.

In Jamaica, the African-descended part of the population was of particular interest, as Edward Long reported in his *History of Jamaica* in 1774:

The Negroes seem very fond of reduplications, to express a greater or less quantity of anything; as *walky-walky, talky-talky, washy-washy, nappy-nappy, tie-tie, lilly-lilly, fum-fum*; so *bug-a-bugs* (wood ants); *dab-a-dab* (an olio made with maize, herrings, and pepper), *bra-bra* (another of their dishes), *grande-grande* (augmentative size, or grandeur), and so forth. In their conversations they confound all the moods, tenses, cases, and conjunctions, without mercy: for example, *I surprize* (for I am surprised), *me glad for see you* (*pro,* I am glad to see you; *how you do* (for how d'ye do?), *me tank you; me ver well*; etc.

Linguistic analysis is not sophisticated here. For instance, *fum-fum* means a 'flogging' and, like *dab-a-dab*, is thought by subsequent observers to have been influenced by an African language. Yet the writer recognizes that this is English 'larded with the Guinea dialect', and he identifies particular West African languages from which some borrowings come.

When usages like these crossed a cultural divide, they became even more a matter of interest. Here is another observation about Jamaica, this one—by Lady Nugent—recorded in 1802:

The Creole language is not confined to the negroes. Many of the ladies, who have not been educated in England, speak a sort of broken English, with an indolent drawling out of their words, that is very tiresome if not disgusting. I stood next to a lady one night, near a window, and, by way of saying something, remarked that the air was much cooler than usual; to which she answered, 'Yes, ma-am, him *rail-ly too fra-ish*'.

In this example, readers are presumed to know how 'creole' sounds: *him* for *it* and a diphthong rather than a simple vowel in *really* and *fresh*.

Increased travel and exposure to new voices led to different ideas about what constituted 'foreign' English. So Benjamin Silliman, a young American, toured Britain in 1805–6, and encountered a youth, the son of an English 'planter' in Tobago, who was on his way to school to be 'finished'. Silliman described the youth's English as 'broken' and his narrative reveals just how innocent many English people were about their language as used abroad. A high-table of Cambridge dons could not be persuaded that Silliman had grown up in New England since his speech seemed, to them, indistinguishable from that of young men brought up in south-east England. While 'creole' might be recognizable, most other varieties of English seemed not to rise to cultivated attention.

In the manifesto for romanticism published by William Wordsworth and Samuel Taylor Coleridge in 1798, there was a declaration that poetic language ought to be the 'real language' of humble people. Though these two poets did not indulge in dialect verse or draw upon the resources of 'foreign' English, others did so enthusiastically. Maria Edgeworth in Ireland, Walter Scott in Scotland, and Thomas Chandler Halliburton in Canada all became prolific and imaginative writers employing the vernacular. Halliburton is of particular interest because his cast of characters, performing in New England and Atlantic Canada, was poly-glot: Dutch, Germans, French, African-Americans, Native Americans. These voices were assigned to comedy and satire; characters who spoke in 'accented' English were often 'low' or 'rustic'. But they were also made articulate in new ways, and treated as fully human (in comparison to the notions of 'barbarism' that had weighed down views of 'exotic' foreign languages in earlier times). Such innovations in literature arose from the romantic idea that language and culture were intricately linked, and, even if the characters were 'low', they might be wise.

In Trinidad in 1844 appeared a vernacular text purporting to be 'an overheard conversation' between 'a creole of the colony' and a gentleman who was 'one of the Immigrants from North America':

She—Me Gaad, dis da really big building far true—he big more dan two church—three chapel and one meeting house put together. What he far, me wonder—St. James Barracks fool to he. Wha' go lib dere me want for know.

He—Why Marm, I guess as how them Government Folks as are very deceptious in every country, Britishers as Americans, give out that is intended for a new Government House and Court House—that may do very well for you, *natives*—but I reckon I have'nt been reared in one of the principal Cities of the United States and visited all the other worth seeing, to be taken in that sort of way. No, I guess this child knows a trick worth two of that any day, catch a 'coon asleep and then you'll find me rather obliverous about the eye lids—but not afore that I guess.

(The building under discussion turns out to be a penitentiary 'where they lock up all the people as is too good to put in a goal, but too bad to be allowed to be at large in the streets'.) Both of these characters are African-descended, and 'Eavesdropper'—the pseudonym employed by the reporter of this conversation—is condescending to them. Yet the American visitor to Trinidad, however much his pompous speech is characterized by malapropisms, is still the spokesperson for satire on the 'deceptious' nature of governments. And the woman to whom he speaks is herself capable of wise and sceptical observation: 'dese 'Merican people rally speak very droll English, but dey clever people, clever for true'. In short, there seems to be enough linguistic snobbery to go round.

This mid-nineteenth-century example represents a broad movement within the English-speaking community for writers to adopt 'foreign' accents and dialects for satiric purposes. Fools and clowns in earlier times had been allowed considerable liberty for poking oral fun (and even criticizing) the powerful and their literary descendents began to do the same in print. In the United States 'Davy Crockett', a wild frontiersman based on a real person, was developed in the 1830s as a way for the uneducated to mock the pretence of the learned, for the 'westerners' to assert themselves against the patricians of the Atlantic-coastal cities, and for the exuberant to shame those who were hidebound by their own gentility. Most of these voices were presented in newspapers, and most of them are now forgotten—except, perhaps, for their extraordinary pseudonyms: Josiah Allen's Wife, Bill Arp, Josh Billings, Hans Breitmann, Sut Lovingood, Petroleum Vesuvius Nasby, Carl Pretzel, Seba Smith. Except for just one of these subversive humorists, Mark Twain, none are commonly read nowadays, but the American example of this work inspired imitation elsewhere, particularly in late nineteenth-century Scotland where newspaper humour in the vernacular was also the mouthpiece for a variety of causes—anti-Imperial critiques, advocacy of the working class, anti-clericalism, and various progressive causes: 'Oor mere men buddies in their wise stupidity hae declared that weemen shall hae nae vote ...').[4]

---

[4] See further W. Donaldson, *Popular Literature in Victorian Scotland: Language, Fiction, and the Press* (Aberdeen: Aberdeen University Press, 1986), 183.

Here the satirist, a woman, uses the vernacular (and an oxymoron) to denounce the pig-headedness of men. In the twentieth century, this use of the distinctive Scots vernacular became part of a nationalist programme to celebrate Scotland and decry the influence of south-eastern English culture on it.

Of course the voices of the 'foreign' could also be held up for ridicule, as in, for instance, Charles G. Leland's *Pidgin-English Sing-Song* (1900) or Arnold Wright's *Babu English as 'tis Writ* (1891). Publications like these are deeply stained with the taint of racial superiority, but nowadays they seem less offensive than quixotic in their belief that only some forms of English were worthy of respect. At the same time, there was a developing taste for dialect humour in the music halls and vaudeville theatres, and guides appeared so that amateurs could also join in the fun, as in *The Dime Dialect Speaker: A 'Talking' Collection of Irish, German-English, Cockney, Negro, Yankee, and Western Vernacular Speeches* (1879). As never before, the copious variety of voices became the vehicle for humour and satire.

ENGLISH INTERNATIONAL, LTD.

As for the view of English beyond Britain, the tentative optimism of the eighteenth century gave way to a new view of 'global English', an outlook in which confidence turned into triumphalism. A turning-point in this emergent idea occurred in January 1851 when the great philologist Jacob Grimm declared to the Royal Academy in Berlin that English 'may be called justly a LANGUAGE OF THE WORLD: and seems, like the English nation, to be destined to reign in future with still more extensive sway over all parts of the globe'. Soon translated from German to English, Grimm's opinion became a commonplace and the mathematically-minded computed the increase, both biological and cultural, that would lead English to sweep around the world. Dozens of comments expressed this wisdom: 'The English tongue has become a rank polyglot, and is spreading over the earth like some hardy plant whose seed is sown by the wind', as Ralcy Husted Bell wrote in 1909.[5] Such views led to a new perspective on multilingualism: those who did not know English should set promptly about learning it! As later chapters in this volume further explore, English-speakers did not need to find a niche in the multilingual world; they could, instead, bestride it.

---

[5] R. H. Bell, *The Changing Values of English Speech* (New York: Hinds, Noble and Eldredge, 1909), 35.

One linguistic consequence of this ideological change was to reduce the import-ation of borrowed words into English. Various factors make it difficult to be precise about this development since there are difficult questions when some words enter the language, find few users, and survive only in dictionaries. But one can gain an impression of what happened by consulting the enduring new words introduced into English decade by decade. In the first ten years of the twentieth century, such words as these appeared: *adrenaline* (like *television*, representing the nomenclature of science), *aileron* (like much of the terminology of aviation—*fuselage*, for instance—introduced from French), *okapi* (like *panda* introduced from languages where the creatures were found), and various political terms that would resonate over the next century (like *lebensraum* from German or *pogrom* from Russian). Words from the 1990s are very rarely borrowed from other languages; instead, the most common practice is to form words from existing English elements: *babelicious* (< *babe* + de*licious*), *cybercafé* (< *cyber* netics + *café*), *website*. Borrowings from foreign languages quickly yielded to home-grown synonyms: *tamagotchi* (< Japanese 'lovable egg') almost immedi-ately became *cyberpet*.

Lexicographers associated with the *Oxford English Dictionary* have declared that 90,000 'new words' were introduced in the twentieth century. Only 4,500 of these 'new words' were foreign borrowings. In the twentieth century, while there came to be far more speakers of English than ever before (see further Chapters 13 and 14), far more of them were multilingual, and far more people were likely to have their neologisms recorded in a way that would be accessible to lexicog-raphers. Yet, paradoxically, there were far fewer borrowed words than in any century since the Norman Conquest. On the other hand, exportation of English words penetrated languages everywhere. Here are words that appear in nearly all the major languages of Europe; in many of them, they are fully integrated to the grammar and pronunciation of the recipient language: *biker, carpool, fairness* ('justice'), *gimmick, high* ('intoxicated'), *OK, second-hand, shredder, wild card*. Beyond Europe, only the most puristic (or isolated) language communities show resistance to English. *Okay* is an expression found hundreds of times in websites written in Arabic, Chinese, Indonesian, Japanese, Korean, and Turkish.

Before the mid-twentieth century, it was unusual to find code switching and language mixture in works of fiction or drama, a decision doubtless made on the grounds that too many demands made on monolingual readers would reduce sales. A common method for giving a taste of foreign language was, for instance, used by Hemingway, as in his *For Whom the Bell Tolls* (1940): '"*No es nada*," she said. "A bridge is nothing".' Here, simultaneous translation or paraphrase pro-vided sufficient flavour to the text.

In the post-colonial world, creative writing for multilingual audiences flourished where readers (or viewers) could appreciate it. In Anglophone communities where many languages are in widespread use, dramatic performances for stage or television have achieved sophisticated effects through the use of several languages. Some plays offer the option of scenes not in English (for instance, Kee Thuan Chye's Malaysian play, *We Could **** You, Mr. Birch*). Others employ scripts with a mixture of languages (for instance, Stella Kon's monologue for a Singaporean audience, *Emily of Emerald Hill*, employs fragments in Hokkien, Cantonese, Malay, Hindi, and even African-American English of the American south). Such works make local use of global English.

As the concluding chapter in this volume will further explore, in the twenty-first century, the membrane separating English from the other languages is ever more permeable. Consider the following extract from a resume of a Hong Kong actor:

編·導·演　　*tomcatt*

tomcatt，又名鬆毛妃。九五年加入商台廣告創作部，後轉往商業二台叱咤903當節目主持，主動創作及策劃多元性取向議題節目《男男女女》；曾任idclub.com及crhk.com.hk
創作總監。現全天候自由工作，於《Pepper》月刊定期刊載情色文字作品，並憑《姊妹》中的文字作品「我們都是這樣搞基的...」獲Media Graphics Award 2002 Book/ Editorial Magazine組別Inside Page (Series) 的 Certificate of Excellence；此外，tomcatt
亦致力參與及發展「一人一故事劇場」（Playback Theater），與青少年、婦女及家長分享，現爲「一人一故事劇場國際網絡」（International Playback Theatre Network）香港區會員秘書、國際演藝評論家協會（香港）專業會員。

Tomcatt　　Playwright/ Director/ Performer
Tomcatt, aka Luen Mo Fay, joined Hong Kong Commercial Broadcasting Company Limited in 1995 as copywriter. She was transferred to CR2 as program host in 1997. She initiated and hosted the first Gay, Lesbian, Bisexual and Transgender Radio Program "Boys and Gals." She was also involved in the creative process of idclub.com and

crhk.com.hk as Creative Director. She is a freelancer for 2 years now. She owns an erotic column in "Pepper", the monthly magazine. Her work in "Sister" has been awarded the Certificate of Excellence in the Media Graphics Award 2002, Category Book/ Editorial Magazine—Inside Page (Series). Other than writing, she is also involved in a lot of theatre productions and playback theatre. She is the membership secretary in Hong Kong of the International Playback Theatre Network (IPTN) and professional member of International Association of Theatre Critics (Hong Kong). (Tomcatt, 2004)

To a person unable to read the Chinese version, the text above the translation is bewildering. Yet in many respects it resembles those mixed-language texts we examined early in this chapter. There is no apparent reason why some portions occur in English and others do not. It is simply another form of the hybridity that has impacted English (and languages in contact with it) from the earliest times.

REFERENCES AND SUGGESTIONS FOR FURTHER READING

How many languages do you need?

Wright (2002) and Schneider (2003) discuss in detail the patterns and consequences of linguistic accommodation across language barriers.

Traversing language boundaries

The origins of English place names are treated in fascinating essays which introduce the dictionaries compiled by Ekwall (1960) and Mills (1998). Aelfric's *Life of St. Oswald*, with its account of Oswold's rolc as 'wcalhstod', can be found in Skeat (1890). Unfortunately the documentary record is so fragmentary that it is difficult to state with certainty the role and impact of multilingualism in Old English times. Toon (1983), however, offers interesting ideas about the role of group identity in the ecology of English. The best account of bilingualism in Old English times is provided by Kastovsky (1992: 299–338); after a minute review of the evidence (and the scholarship) he reaches a cautious position: 'Thus it seems reasonable to conclude that there was a certain amount of bilingualism, notably with the offspring of mixed marriages or second- and third-generation settlers ...' (p. 330). Middle English multilingualism has come in for renewed scrutiny, and Short (1979) is particularly useful.

Apart from the sources cited above, the most comprehensive recent account of borrowings from foreign languages in the period is provided by Burnley (1992a). Texts with language mixture are anthologized (among other places) in Harding and Wright (1995), and Cusack (1998); the extract on p. 337 is taken from Wenzel (1994: 70), while

Wright (1996: 183) is the source of the mixed-language extracts from the London Bridge account books on the same page.

Linguistic encounters

Murison (1971) examines Dutch-Scots contact, and its lexical consequences. Policies to encourage the spread of English through the British Isles are documented by Blank (1996), especially pp. 126–68, and by Bailey (1985). Moore (2002*a*: 404–5) is the source of the mixed-language texts cited here.

English out and about

Early modern English and the expansion of English beyond Europe is the subject of innumerable articles and monographs. The North American experience is described authoritatively by Karttunen (2000) and by Kupperman (2000).

Go-betweens

Quinn (1990) provides a thorough account of the voyages described here. Ingram's discussion of *cannibals* can be found in the facsimile edition of Ingram's *Relation* (1966: 558). Salmon (1996) discusses the linguistic significance of Thomas Harriot; Harriot's specifically linguistic writings, including his orthography, unfortunately remained virtually unknown until the last quarter of the twentieth century. See also Quinn (1985) for an account of Harriot's *Briefe and True Report*. The tale of South African Cory echoed through the English imagination for more than two centuries; it appears in Maria Edgeworth's novel *Leonora* (1806). A thorough account of this man in fact and fable is found in Merians (2001: 87–117), which is also (p. 94) the source of the quotation on p. 344 . The history of Tisquantum is given in Karttunen (2000). Bolton (2003) gives fascinating details about the contact between the English and the Chinese from 1637 forward; it is to him that I owe the story of Peter Mundy. The quotation on p. 344 is taken from the edition by Temple (1919: 192). The (1997) facsimile edition of Williams (1643: A7^r) is the source of the quotation which, on p. 345 of this chapter, describes the last days of Wequash. Carew's comments on the English talent for acquiring new languages can be found in Camden (1984: 40).

English expands

The anonymous writer with whom this chapter begins published *Some Thoughts on the English Language* in 1766; the cited extract is taken from p. 95. Bureaucratic and legal English is mostly neglected once historians of English get beyond the scribes of the late medieval Court of Chancery.

Commerce in (and about) English

The citation from the Indian minute book is taken from Islam (1978: 33). Despite archives bursting with commercial documents, the English of business has received only scant attention.

Science and English

Paulusz's greatly enhanced (1989) edition of Knox's *Historical Relation of the Island Ceylon in the East Indies* is the source of the quotations on p. 349 (see, respectively, Paulusz 1989, 2: 515, and 2: xxxi). For the history of the Royal Society, see further p. 240–1 of this volume. Like the English of commerce, the English of scientific writing has not been given much detailed attention. See, however, Taavitsainen and Pahta (2004) and Huddleston (1971).

A various language

Long's account of Jamaican English can be found in Long (1774: 427); Lady Nugent's opinions on Jamaican English can be found in Nugent (1907: 132). Silliman describes his encounter with the Tobagan youth in Silliman (1812, 2: 237). Recognition of American English in Britain is fully documented by Read (2002). Ideologies of English, more broadly, are treated historically in Bailey (1991), particularly the emergence of the idea of 'world English'. Literary representations of the post-colonial anglophone world are discussed in the influential book by Ashcroft *et al.* (1989). Important programmatic statements are found in Ngũgĩ (1986) and Jussawalla and Dasenbrock (1992).

In general, writers of vernacular humour are only slightly represented in histories of English, despite their evident value as indicators of both values and behaviour. A collection of the American humourists of the nineteenth century whose taste ran to dialect was compiled by Blair and McDavid (1983). Winer (1997: 75) is the source of the cited conversation on pp. 351–2 . The satirists of Victorian Scotland are ably discussed by Donaldson (1986) (who has also published an anthology of this ephemeral work (1989)); the quotation on p. 352 is taken from Donaldson (1989: 183). McCulloch (2004) discusses twentieth-century developments within this tradition. Both the journalists and the higher-browed writers of late nineteenth-century America are discussed by Jones (1999). The impact of American varieties of English on the world scene is the subject of Bailey (2001).

English International, Ltd.

There is an increasingly vast scholarship devoted to the spread of English around the world; see Hickey (2004) for an up-to-date collection of essays and a substantial bibliography of this work. The role of English and its impact on some of the other languages of Europe is discussed in Görlach (2002). For the role of the British Council in spreading the language abroad, see Coombs (1988), and the following chapter in this volume. Ayto (1999) provides a useful foundation for studying lexical change in modern English.

13

ENGLISH WORLD-WIDE IN THE TWENTIETH CENTURY

Tom McArthur

IN 1992, in the preface to *Events: A Chronicle of the Twentieth Century*, the British historian Philip L. Cottrell noted: 'The twentieth century has proved to be a turbulent period for humankind. The tempo of change has been unprecedented.'

In 1996, in the preface to *Timelines of the 20th Century*, the American historians David Brownstone and Irene Franck observed: 'Our century has been the century of blood and tears, and at the same time a century of scientific breakthroughs that have vastly changed human experience and possibilities.'

In 2003, in *World Englishes: An Introduction*, the linguists Gunnel Melchers and Philip Shaw, wrote: 'The worldwide expansion of English ... did not truly escalate until after the Second World War'.[1]

Also in 2003, the British linguist David Crystal noted, in *English as a Global Language*, that 'There has never been a language so widely spread or spoken by so many people as English'.[2]

ENGLISH, ENGLISHES, ENGLISH LANGUAGES

These citations say a great deal in little space about the period in which English grew from prominence to virtual dominance world-wide, in the process acquir-

---
[1] G. Melchers and P. Shaw, *World Englishes: An Introduction* (London: Arnold, 2003), 6.
[2] D. Crystal, *English as a Global Language* (Cambridge: Cambridge University Press, 2003), 189.

ing some novel names. In 1900, for most people, English was simply *English* or, more fully, either *the English language* or *the English tongue*, much as it had been for centuries. By the 1990s, however, a great deal had changed and several new labels had come into wide use, most notably *world English*, whose earliest *OED* citation is 1927 ('1927 K. MALONE in *Amer. Speech* II. 323/2: "He ... warns against a slavish conformity to the dictionary, i.e., to the prescriptions of standard English, or world-English, as some people call it"') but which was in fact in occasional, limited use several decades earlier. Thus, in the 1880s, the phonetician Alexander Melville Bell published a booklet with the title 'World-English, The Universal Language'. However, the phrase remained rare until the 1980s, by which time it was being used to mean either all varieties of English world-wide or a more or less standard international variety. Also in the 1980s there emerged two radical plural forms, *the Englishes* and *world Englishes*, and in the 1990s the phrase *the English languages* took a novel place alongside such long-established 'family' names as *the Romance languages* and the *Germanic languages*. The closing years of the twentieth century were therefore, at least in the study of this language/these languages, a time of radical terminological innovation.

The English language (to continue with the traditional usage) has, as Chapter 11 has explored, long been known for its dialects, such as *West Country* and *Yorkshire*. Until the sixteenth century, such dialects were to be found only in Britain and Ireland but, by the eighteenth century, comparable social and regional variations had begun to emerge in Britain's North American colonies and, in due course, American and other commentators applied the same distinguishing label to them. Prior to the nineteenth century, as other chapters have noted, language scholars—at least in conventional histories of the language—paid relatively little attention to such regional variation, often being more interested in 'refined' usage and the dissemination of a 'standard' variety of the language. Nevertheless, in that century, in addition to becoming fashionable in the dialogue of novels, kinds of dialect also became the focus of language surveys and related studies which crystallized into a novel scholarly discipline, *dialectology*, first used in the Presidential Address given by James Murray to the London Philological Society in 1879. This, along with *philology*, was one of the ancestral forms of present-day linguistics.

Until about 1970, however, there was a lack of organized knowledge about, and relatively little scholarly interest in, what had been happening, and what was continuing to happen, to English (and varieties of English) beyond Britain, Ireland, North America, and, to some degree, Australia. When such an interest did develop, it was most notably under the aegis of Randolph Quirk at University College, London, first in the form of the *Grammar of Contemporary English*

(1972), written with his colleagues Sidney Greenbaum, Geoffrey Leech, and Jan Svartvik. This was followed, in 1985, by their *Comprehensive Grammar of the English Language*, which drew upon the work of scholars of English world-wide as well as on the evidence of text corpora. However, whereas Quirk *et al.* were primarily concerned with the 'standard' language world-wide, Kachru and other non-Western scholars were already concerned with discussing and describing a fuller range of uses and styles, especially in territories where English was widely used but not indigenous. As a consequence of both areas of research, and others like them, the traditional term 'dialect' proved increasingly less relevant in the context of this kind of analysis.

As a result, many twentieth-century investigators took up the more neutral, flexible, and safely vaguer term *variety* and, when talking about varieties of English world-wide, found the plural form *Englishes* useful—in large part because it lacked any immediate implication of superordination, subordination, hierarchy, or sociocultural primacy. However, in a mundane but real sense, in promoting this radical usage Kachru was fortunate in the name of the entity he was studying. Pluralizing *English* (while in the opinion of many people an eccentric and disreputable thing to do) did not create the kind of confusion that would have arisen with such pluralizations as **Frenches*, **Germans*, and **Chineses* (if such languages had been the object of the same kind of attention at that time). Fortunately, from Kachru's point of view, the word *English* was pluralizable and the idea of such plurality world-wide at least plausible. Yet the issues on which he focused at that time have been just as true for other large languages as, for example, with Quebec French (as opposed to, say, Mauritian French, and the less digestible French French), Austrian German (as opposed to Swiss German and German in Germany), and Singaporean Chinese (as opposed to Chinese in China). His radical approach prompted a great deal of discussion not only of variety in English but also in relation to other large languages. As regards English, however, the five following terminological areas at least proved to be of interest to scholars of linguistic variation, all of which have developed their own sets of labels:

1 Geographical location, prompting such terms as *African English*, *American English*, *Asian English*, *British English*, *Indian English*, *Irish English*, *London English*, *Hong Kong English*, *New York English*, *New Zealand English*.
2 Linguistic and ethnic association, prompting such terms as *Bengali English*, *Chinese English*, *Maori English*.
3 Activities such as commerce, technology, education, culture, and social life, prompting such terms as *airline English*, *legal English*, *medical English*, *Public*

School English (in the UK), and *standard/Standard English* generally [cf. also such parallel terms as *Policespeak* and *Seaspeak*].

4 Combinations of location and activity, as with *American legal English* and *British medical English*, and including a large set containing the word *standard*, located either medially, as in *Australian Standard English* (where *Standard English* is primary and *Australian* secondary) or initially, as in *Standard Canadian English* (where *Canadian English* is primary and *Standard* secondary).

5 Usually informal and often tongue-in-cheek fusions of *English* with the names of other languages, providing names for what were in effect Anglo-hybrids, as with: French-based *franglais* and English-based *Frenglish*; *Hindlish* and *Hinglish* as names for a mix of Hindi and English; *Chinglish* as the label for an informal hybrid of Chinese and English; and *Japlish, Japalish*, and *Janglish* as a range of mixes of Japanese and English (the third implying also a kind of chaos).

The wry humour that underpins the fifth category of labels has tended to mask the social significance, scale of use, and range of linguistic mixing which is highlighted in this informal way. It should come as no surprise, however, that terms of this kind have been adopted only reluctantly for scholarly purposes, although quite often there is no easy way round them: they are, indeed, part of the phenomenon itself. Hybridization of this kind has in fact been common for centuries, and has operated at various sociocultural levels. It occurred, for example, when, many centuries ago, Greek technical terms became fashionable in Latin, as with *geographia* ('world writing/description') and *geologia* ('earth study'), which duly passed into French as *géographie* and *géologie* and then into English as *geography* and *geology*. As regards English itself, an initial wave of hybridization took place in the early Middle Ages between Anglo-Saxon and Danish that included, among many other items, that apparently most English of words: *the*. A second process began after the Norman Conquest in 1066, as Chapters 3 and 4 have illustrated, when English mixed with French, and began to draw, both through French as well as directly, on Latin and Greek for a wide range of cultural and technical vocabulary. Indeed, rather than being an exception, or an affront to native culture, such hybridization is a normal and even at times predictable process, and in the twentieth century a range of such flows of material has been commonplace. Indeed, they have often run both ways (as with English into Hindi, and Hindi into English in northern India), and have been not only useful for everyday purposes but also creative and productive.

A DEBATE AT THE START OF THE CENTURY

By and large, users of English who thought about 'good English' around 1900–1920 tended to suppose that it was much the same wherever it was used, despite such institutionalized differences as British and American spelling, and regardless of the casual hybridization at work in the world. They also tended to assume, notably in Great Britain and its empire, that 'good English' was a birthright of the upper reaches of society, whose children increasingly attended 'good schools'. However, this expression did not refer to the greater efficiency with which some schools might be run, but only to the *public schools*—private fee-paying boarding schools, entirely unconnected with what came to be known as *state schools*: tax-supported institutions for the general population. As a consequence, the 'good' speech of young people in such private schools was a mutually reinforcing process undergone at a non-regional level, despite the fact that such speech ultimately derived from upper-class usage in the Home Counties (the counties around London). Such public school usage was *ipso facto* 'correct' in pronunciation and grammar, was lexically rich for social rather than educational reasons, and 'standard' for its social group (and by projection also for 'the best' speakers and writers in 'society', a sense of the word which, in use from 1823, did not mean the whole of British society, but 'high society' alone: 'The aggregate of leisured, cultured, or fashionable persons regarded as forming a distinct class or body in a community', as the *OED* confirms).

Henry Cecil Wyld, professor of English first at Liverpool University from 1904 and then, from 1920, at the University of Oxford, was one of the leading scholars of English in England over the first three decades of the century. In his view, the adult speakers *par excellence* of 'good English' were army officers: holders of the king's commission who spoke the King's English in ways which, in terms of accent, revealed no trace of geographical origin. For this kind of usage he coined two terms: first, *Received Standard English*, or simply *Received Standard*, then, for the institutions in which these officers acquired their speech style, *Public School English* (*PSE*). Wyld's contemporary, the phonetician Daniel Jones, called the accent he chose for his model of British speech *Public School Pronunciation* (*PSP*), a title which, after discussion with Wyld, he changed to *Received Pronunciation* (*RP*), a term which had, as we have seen in Chapter 10, already been employed by Alexander Ellis in the late nineteenth century. Jones's system, with only minor modifications, survives to the present day as the accent at which foreign learners of British English have generally been expected to aim, which their teachers ought therefore to be able to speak (whatever their backgrounds), and which has in recent decades been used (via representation by phonetic symbols) to represent British English pronunciation in most ELT dictionaries. In effect, therefore, Wyld and Jones set the standard for the use and learning of spoken British English throughout the century.

A further significant development took place in 1922 when a national radio service, the *British Broadcasting Company* (BBC), later *British Broadcasting Corporation*, was launched, and for some years both Wyld and Jones served as its language advisers. As a result of their views and recommendations, Jones's RP model came in due course to be known widely as both *BBC English* and a *BBC accent*, gaining prestige nationally and internationally as the BBC itself acquired a reputation for both a clear, measured style and dispassionate, authoritative broadcasting.

In the UK, such factors as class, education, and socio-economic confidence continued to be invoked with regard to 'good' or 'the best' usage (much indeed as they had in the nineteenth century; see Chapter 10), until the mood of the nation began to change, particularly in the 1960s—a decade in which many received attitudes were challenged. Public commentators in print and on radio and TV had tended until then to sustain the tradition of Wyld and Jones, although both men had been largely forgotten (at least outside those university departments which engaged with the history, and historiography, of English). During and after the 1960s (the golden age of the Beatles, four working-class Liverpool pop singers who represented the speech style of another England altogether), language attitudes tended to become more 'democratic' and less judgemental. As a result, the linguistic touchstones of the early decades of the century tended to be forgotten or marginalized. However, the following quotations from Henry Wyld and the philologist Henry Sweet (who had in fact been Wyld's tutor at Oxford) can still be seen as representative of views widely held by middle-class England throughout the first half of the twentieth century:

Henry Cecil Wyld (1907): 'It is believed that from these two great types of speech—that of London, the centre of Law, Government, and Commerce, and that of Oxford, the centre of learning and culture—the Standard English which we all write, and which we all try, at any rate, to speak, has grown up.'[3]

Henry Sweet (1908): 'Standard English, like Standard French, is now a class-dialect more than a local dialect: it is the language of the educated all over Great Britain. ... The best

---

[3] H. C. Wyld, *The Growth of English* (London: John Murray, 1907), 121.

speakers of Standard English are those whose pronunciation, and language generally, least betray their locality'.[4]

We may note here the word *betray*. The following comments, which derive from two leading American language specialists a few years later, indicate, however, that the New World was already disinclined to toe such an Old World line.

Fred Newton Scott (1917): 'In fine, the idea that somewhere, in some linguistic utopia, there exists a standard English, which all cultural Englishmen use alike and cannot help using and to which distracted Americans may resort for chastening and absolution, is a pleasing hallucination'.[5]

H. L. Mencken (1919): 'I think I have offered sufficient evidence ... that the American of today is much more honestly English ... than the so-called Standard English of England .... Standard English must always strike an American as a bit stilted and precious.' [6]

Scott's and Mencken's rejection of England's class-centred norms and impositions has been a US theme since Noah Webster in the late eighteenth and early nineteenth centuries. Nevertheless (and despite their strongly expressed feelings), their identification of the term *Standard English* solely with stilted and precious class accents and attitudes in England did not catch on, in the USA or anywhere else. A majority of commentators later in the century, in the USA, the UK, and elsewhere, has instead tended to keep the concept 'standardness' distinct from any single pronunciation model, whether as the possession of a securely elevated social class or something achievable through elocution and phonetics, as in George Bernard Shaw's play *Pygmalion* (1912) and Alan Jay Lerner's *My Fair Lady*, the later *movie* [in AmE] or *film* [in traditional BrE] which was based on it. Shaw's energetic and idiosyncratic phonetician, Professor Henry Higgins, it will be noted, shares a first name with both Sweet and Wyld and, for an upmarket character, had as down-market a surname as Jones.

In 1919, the US phonetician George P. Krapp brought out a work *titled* [AmE]/ *entitled* [BrE] *The Pronunciation of Standard English in America*, which argued for independence in language as in all other things. He followed it in 1925 with *The English Language in America*, in which he introduced the term *General American* (*GA, GenAm*), which offers an alternative and American-based norm

---

    [4] H. Sweet, *The Sounds of English, an Introduction to Phonetics* (Oxford: Clarendon Press, 1908), 7–8.
    [5] F. N. Scott, 'The Standard of American Speech,' *The English Journal* 6 (1917). Cited in T. McArthur, *The English Languages* (Cambridge: Cambridge University Press, 1988), 123.
    [6] H. L. Mencken, *The American Language* (New York: Alfred A. Knopf, 1919). Cited in McArthur (1988), 123.

for natives and learners: a common-denominator accent from which distinctive regionalisms were excluded. Like RP, GA is an idealization, not a direct reflection of real-life speech although, paradoxically, it is intended to reflect standard, educated speech which is, however, by no means *homogenous* [AmE]/ *homogeneous* [BrE]. By mid-century, GA had become the model for many ESL/EFL [English as a second/foreign language] users and communities around the world. In such different ways, representations of idealized accents were thereby formulated in both nations, becoming in due course the teaching norms for millions of upwardly mobile native speakers, immigrants, and foreign learners over at least the rest of the century.

Although an idealized 'educated' or 'middle-class' version of British or American pronunciation and spoken style has its place as a model for learners, there can, alas, be no guarantee that the usage of the next native speaker a learner meets will reflect it. As regards the transatlantic debate, however, two years after Mencken's *The American Language* was published, Henry Bradley, one of the editors of the *OED*, made his own observations in the *Literary Review*:

The wiser sort among us will not dispute that Americans have acquired the right to frame their own standards of correct English on the usage of their best writers and speakers. . . . But is it too much to hope that one day this vast community of nations will possess a common "standard English", tolerant of minor local varieties?.[7]

We may, however, note two things here: first, Bradley's early use of the term *varieties*, where *dialects* (in either a social or a regional sense) would clearly have been inadequate and, secondly, that, by the end of the century, his hope was more or less realized, almost in passing. Consider the ease with which, for example, Americans may read *The Guardian* and Britons *The International Herald Tribune*, and (by and large) the lack of difficulty each side has had throughout much of the century in following the sound tracks of one another's cinematic products. The same also applied on a wider front, in the deliberations of, first, the League of Nations and then the United Nations Organization, of the North Atlantic Treaty Organization and, farther afield, of the Organization of African Unity, the Association of South East Asian Nations, and the like, among all of which English has served as a mediating language. When the twentieth century came to a close, world-wide views on what might be considered 'educated' spoken English covered a far broader social range than they had done in the early decades of the century, accommodating a range of accents (including foreign accents) in a continuum of intelligibility and

---

[7] H. Bradley, *The Literary Review*, 3 December 1921: 224. Cited in McArthur (1988), 123.

negotiability—all of which was made easier by a shared involvement with radio, television, cinema, computers, email, the Internet, and the World Wide Web.

TECHNOLOGY, COMMUNICATION, WAR, AND REALPOLITIK

At the end of the nineteenth century, many people had high hopes for the twentieth and, in terms of scientific, technological, and social breakthroughs, such hopes were more than fulfilled. By the end of the twentieth century, their grand-children were enjoying (if that is the right word) two remarkable facilities: on one side, a more-or-less standard variety (or set of varieties) of English which served an unprecedented number of people as both a home language and a global *lingua franca*, as well as fulfilling many personal, social, and professional needs at local, national, and international levels. On the other side, many millions had desk-top computers with which they could create, manipulate, transmit, and receive text, pictures, and other kinds of data predominantly—but not only—in English. The world-wide technological framework within which this took place was beyond the conception of typesetters, printers, and postal and telegraphic systems not just in 1900 but also in 1950. The key end-product, however, was not beyond anyone's conception. A printed page is a printed page, however produced, and print on screen looks much the same as it does on a modern printed page.

Embedding scores of other linguistic transformations in both lexis and meaning, the textual and other information which those millions of computer users could transmit varied in scale from a single-line *email* to a *file* containing data that can be *attached* to such an email, which could be sent without leaving one's own desk to an *email address* in another machine anywhere on the planet (where both file and *attachment* could be *down-loaded*). As the italicized words in the former sentence confirm, the discourse of computing has, in itself, been a significant development of the twentieth century—not least perhaps in its familiarity to an increasingly wide range of users. Indeed, by the closing decade of the century, the writing of such messages, in English or any other appropriately developed language, had its own range of usages: from traditional publishing-quality prose with tidy headings, sentences, and paragraphs at one extreme to what might be termed e-anarchy at the other. Such email text may include *emoticons* ('emotive icons') intended to express feelings not normally expressed or exposed in text. Indeed, in ten years of the twentieth century (and five of the twenty-first), this new communicative mode became commonplace more rapidly and pervasively than any earlier twentieth-century technical marvels had done, such as *radio* (originally AmE), *wireless* (BrE, especially c1950), *TV* (AmE and BrE) *telly* (BrE, although often with social marking, as in the citation from Muriel Spark's *The Go-Away Bird* (1958) which accompanies this entry in the *OED*: 'He said, "What do you do in the evenings, Lorna? Do you watch Telly?" I did take this as an insult, because we call it TV, and his remark made me out to be uneducated'), and the *telephone* (fixed or mobile), with no transatlantic linguistic contrasts. As a result of all of which, English (especially in its US guise) became ever more securely the world's primary language.

By 1900, English had been in wide use around the world for over two centuries, but no one could have imagined the communicative and techno-logical support available to it (and to other 'advanced' languages) by 1999. Such developments were in large part the outcome of three sets of events that affected many languages in many ways, and English more than most. These were:

1 Two World Wars (1914–18, 1939–45) in which the key victorious nations were English-speaking. Especially in *World War II* [AmE and BrE] the *Second World War* [BrE], the use of English for military, political, economic, and other purposes expanded greatly in the various war zones. In Europe, Africa, Asia, and the Pacific millions of people came into regular contact with English who would not otherwise have had much (or anything) to do with it. And where English arrived it tended to stay on after the hostilities ended, for a variety of reasons that included reconstruction, trade, and education.

2 A political and economic Cold War (1945–89) between a capitalist West and a communist East. In this long and often tense struggle for territorial and ideological influence, the USA was the foremost Western contestant. However, after the Soviet Union collapsed in 1989, the USA became the world's sole 'super-power', the perceived prestige of which impelled many people in ex-Soviet satellites, such as Czechoslovakia, Hungary, and Poland, to switch from Russian to English as their language of wider communica-tion, having already regarded it for years as a—if not indeed *the*—language of freedom. Inevitably, Russians also began to find it useful to know some English, especially in trying to catch up on a West that was now both technologically and economically far ahead of them.

3 Globalization, the name of a process, set in train after the Soviet collapse, of world-wide social, cultural, and commercial expansion (and exploitation), in which the USA was the *center* [AmE] or *centre* [BrE] of socio-economic, political, cultural, and linguistic interest. In the closing quarter of the century, English was not only a key socio-cultural language but also the communicative linchpin of both international capitalism and the world's media. By this point, the American variety had also become the main influence not only on other languages but on other Englishes (including the British variety). In its standard spoken form, AmE was now also the primary model for teaching English as a second or foreign language. For many years, key publishers in the UK's 'English language industry' had resisted this tide but when it became clear that the tide was becoming ever stronger, they began to publish courses in US usage from offices in New York, alongside their continuing operations at home and elsewhere. In this, they profited from both Englishes (and, if BrE ever did decline beyond a certain unwished-for point, they would be well placed to transfer more resources to selling the US variety).

Closely associated with the World Wars, the Cold War, and globalization were two 'tides' in the affairs of the language, one internal, the other external. The internal tide was a growing awareness of two issues: first, the major and the minor (but often subtle) differences between US and UK usage, despite their high level of mutual intelligibility and a relative lack of friction; second, the growing global significance of US usage and the ease with which, and the extent to which, Americanisms were passing into British English, into other Englishes, and into other languages. The external tide, on the other hand, was a precipitous loss of competition from other once powerful languages of European origin.

THE INTERNAL TIDE: FROM THE UK TO THE US

In both the UK and the USA, as already noted, an 'educated' accent (whatever, precisely, that might be said to be) had, since at least 1900, been widely considered desirable and useful. Rural and urban accents which might for any reason be considered uncouth could be modified through contact with the 'right' people and/or as a result of elocution and personal effort, avowedly making life smoother for their owners. By and large, accents from lower social levels and especially un-prestigious urban-industrial areas were seen as drawbacks as, for example, those of Liverpool, Manchester, and Glasgow in the UK, and those of New York, Chicago, and Detroit in the USA. Again, by and large, and unaffected by universal education, such views of how the language was spoken (or should be spoken) continued well past mid-century, remaining—especially in the UK—a key social issue. In addition, however, a marked element of counter-prestige prevailed, as where the non-establishment speech styles of pop stars and other role models had a powerful impact, including a trending down or linguistic downshifting among young people who already possessed enviable speech styles.

Although pop stars' accents did not serve widely as models, they may have contributed in the UK to accent levelling between RP and some local kinds of usage. Such levelling occurred, for example, in the Greater London area, as first reported in the early 1980s, generating a relaxed but confident speech style to which the phonetician David Rosewarne gave the name *Estuary English*—referring to the estuary of the river Thames. This compromise younger-generation style emerged out of a levelling 'up' towards RP among speakers of lower-middle and working-class London accents (notably Cockney), together with a levelling 'down' from RP and near-RP towards, with a concomitant relaxation of inter-class barriers.

Also by the 1980s, linguists, language teachers, and members of the media had become more aware of how varied the language was world-wide, and in ways that could not necessarily be described (or 'explained') in terms simply of *standard*, *dialect*, *accent*, and *class*. However, regardless of the general success of the language world-wide, the kind and quality of English that anyone might use had, during the twentieth century, been of increasing interest, including the often-stated desire to improve the language or rescue it from various dangers:

1 Concern for both the prestige and proper use of the language and the reduction of abuses of various kinds, individual or collective: a particular concern of the Queen's English Society in the UK.

2 Concern for clarity of usage and the welfare of people who might be misled or baffled by bureaucratic and other 'jargon': the key concern of the initially British grass-roots group the Plain English Campaign.

3 Concern about preserving the key position of English against inroads of any kind, for example, the organization US English that seeks a constitutional amendment that would make it the official language of the United States and therefore protect it from a rapid increase in the use of Spanish.

4 Awareness of the importance of using the standard language well in terms of both lifestyle and career opportunities, regardless of past conceptions of class and more in terms of business values associated in the 1990s with the term *globalization*.

In the seventeenth century, the norms of upper-class England were, in general, sufficient to serve the language at large as a broadly-defined reference model, despite the fact that most people would never achieve them and indeed seldom came into direct contact with them. In eighteenth-century Great Britain, upper- and middle-class people in Edinburgh and Dublin developed their own styles and usage while still acknowledging polite ('socially refined') London views and usages. Thus, while the Edinburgh and Dublin élite generally deferred to the prestige usage of London, they developed 'polite' usages of their own, notably in terms of pronunciation (although these too, as Chapter 9 has shown, could also be discarded in favour of London norms). Just as such usages gained in prestige at home and in due course elsewhere, and just as the USA by the later nineteenth century acquired the sense of linguistic autonomy noted above, so—especially in the later twentieth century—the usage of Canada, Australia, New Zealand, and South Africa gained in autonomy, as manifested in, for example, the creation of dictionaries of their national Englishes. By mid-century, however, in such places, the term that replaced such expressions as *polite*, *good*, the *best*, and *received* was *standard*, and the 'standard' in this sense was increasingly located at home: that is, to use a term usually reserved for the constitution of Canada, it had been *patriated* ('brought home'). In the course of the last two decades of the twentieth century it therefore became possible for both the world at large and, more importantly, the citizens of such nations to believe in (and, more significantly, to be comfortable about) such entities as *Standard Australian*, *Standard Canadian*, *Standard New Zealand*, and *Standard South African English*, all of which were backed by national dictionaries of their own.

The traditional approach to such matters as language, nation, capital, and provinces, and whether kinds of usage are 'better', 'worse', or simply 'different', appears as a result to have led over the course of the seventeenth to the twentieth centuries to a situation which can be summarized as follows:

1 A nation has, or should have, a state of its own, and be the home and focus of the language of that nation, as with Portuguese in Portugal. On this basis, French is the national language of the French, and the citizens of France are assumed to have a prior or greater claim to it than Belgians, Cameroonians, Canadians, Swiss, or any others who use it.

2 A nation-state is seen as having a primary, perhaps even exclusive role in using and standardizing its language whether or not that language is used elsewhere. Thus, Hungary is the land of the Hungarians, who speak Hungarian, and any ethnic Hungarians elsewhere should consider the usage of Hungary the norm.

3 All nation-states have, or should have, national languages, and, if a new nation-state is created, it should have a constitutionally established national language: a position taken up after the Second World War as various territories in the British Empire became independent, regardless of the complex relationships of communities and languages within any such new state.

4 If there is more than one language in a state, the majority language, especially if its name echoes the name of the state or the major ethnic group in the state, should be selected, and may have its name adapted, as with Bahasa Malaysia ('the Malaysian language'), the form of Malay which is, for example, deemed official in Malaysia.

It is, however, uncommon for one language to fit neatly and to the exclusion of all others within the boundaries of one nation-state. In the case of France, for example, Basque, Breton, Occitan/Provençal, as well as German have all long been in everyday regional use. The situation of English in England in particular, and in Britain at large, may therefore serve as a 'national' starting point for considering what happened to the language elsewhere in the world during the twentieth century. In England, there has for many centuries been no rival to English. On its own, therefore, England meets the ideal of a nation with a single tongue, and this is true regardless of how many hundreds of imported tongues are currently in use there among specific communities.

However, when one steps beyond England into the rest of Britain, this US-like condition ceases to apply. In Wales, English continues to co-occur with Welsh (in spite of the various disincentives evident throughout the history of these language varieties; see further p. 338). In Scotland, English co-occurs with Gaelic and with Scots, a Germanic vernacular which, like English, emerged from Anglo-Saxon. Both are recognized as minority languages of the European Union but, like English, have no legally-established status in the UK: there is, for instance, no written constitution and the law does not officially recognize any language. In Ireland, matters are equally complex. In Northern Ireland (part of the UK), a local variety of English co-habits with both Irish Gaelic and Ulster Scots (these being equivalent to Scottish Gaelic and Scots); all are non-official, as in England, Wales, and Scotland, but English is the only language used officially. In the Irish Republic, Irish (Gaelic) is the official language and is taught universally in school, but is not in wide constant use, while *Irish English* (sometimes called *Hiberno-English*), although it is used everywhere by everyone, is constitutionally second to Irish Gaelic. Few people speak Gaelic on a consistent, regular basis, but it appears above English on the bilingual road signs (if in smaller letters). As such real-life illustrations demonstrate, there is in fact usually nothing simple about the relationships between languages and nation-states.

In the world at large, the following statements were, for example, largely true at the end of the twentieth century. Many people in the USA, the UK, Nigeria, India, and other English-using nation-states spoke more than one language, as did many mainland Europeans, Arabs, and others. Indeed, as Chapter 12 has stressed, multilingualism has been *at least* as normal in the world as monolingualism and is as common in the English-speaking world as elsewhere. Moreover, although the people of England are now famously monolingual (although see further pp. 334–5), a significant minority both here and in Great Britain at large do in fact use other languages, many on a daily basis. Such variety is equally true of other English-speaking nation-states. At the turn of the twentieth/twenty-first centuries, the USA is widely polyglot, notably in such cosmopolitan cities as New York and Los Angeles and, because of a large Spanish-speaking minority, this is especially so in the western states. At the same time, however, the USA is massively English-speaking, and many of its citizens (as in the UK) have little knowledge of any other language. Canada, on the other hand, has had a major French-speaking minority for centuries as well as many smaller communities with indigenous languages, such as Kwakiutl (spoken on northern Vancouver Island and the adjacent mainland), as well as immigrant languages, such as Cantonese. In addition, Australia has both its aboriginal languages and the ethnic languages of immigrants, while New Zealand has Maori, other Polynesian languages, and immigrant languages from further afield. South Africa is a large-scale multilingual ('rainbow') nation, as is Singapore on a small scale, with four official languages: English, Chinese, Malay, and Tamil. Furthermore, in mainland western Europe, particularly in the Netherlands, Switzerland, Denmark, Norway, Sweden, and Finland, English is not an official language but is successfully used as a high-level lingua franca in, for example, academic teaching, publishing, and business. It is therefore probably safe to say that in the twentieth century (and the early twenty-first), English in the world is as often used alongside other languages as it is used on its own, even in massively Anglophone countries.

Although many commentators have emphasized a reluctance among native English speakers to learn and use other languages, a more likely reason in the modern era is a lack of need and opportunity, a lack that can be seen in part as the result of traditional geographical isolation at home, and more perhaps as a consequence of the enormous success of the language abroad. By the end of the twentieth century, if someone were a reasonably competent speaker, reader, and writer of English, in many situations and locations world-wide there might be no pressing need for anything else, especially as non-native speakers are often more than willing to practise their English with anyone who happens to come by.

What is perhaps the most significant shift in the role of English world-wide in the twentieth century—that from UK to US predominance—began slowly, then accelerated with *World War II* [AmE and BrE] or the *Second World War* [BrE] and the subsequent dismantling of empire. The independence of Jordan in 1946 was the first step in a process that ended thirty-seven years later in 1984 with the independence of Brunei (for the entire process, see the timeline 424 ff). In addition, vast numbers of people were on the move both during and after the Second World War, initially in armies and as refugees, then as migrants, business travellers, and (as the world recovered) as tourists. The presence of US soldiers in Europe was part of what, for the British, was the *defénce* of the free world (stress on second syllable) and, in the US, its *défénse* (stress on both syllables). An awareness of US/UK language differences in fact tended to become stronger after the 1930s, when the *movies* [AmE] or the *pictures*/the *cinema* [BrE] became more enticing than the *radio* [AmE] and what the British were, by the 1950s, learning not to call the *wireless*. Both nations, however, had the same word and acronym for *television/TV*, although the British also reduced it to the *telly*—something neither did to the *telephone*, both sides *favoring* [AmE] or *favouring* [BrE] the short form *phone*. As trade and travel increased, so did *mail* [more AmE] or *post* [which remains more BrE], both of which were increasingly carried over longer distances as *airmail* (although never **airpost*) in *airplanes* [AmE] and *aeroplanes* [BrE], or, by both, in *planes* and *aircraft*.

In the second half of the century, foreign learners of English, wherever they lived, increasingly needed to pay attention to both varieties, if not productively then receptively. If a choice had to be made regarding their target, many *favored* [AmE] or *favoured* [BrE] US over UK usage, only adopting such other varieties if they had associations with, or became immigrants to, for example, Australia, Canada, and New Zealand. By the century's end, many teachers and more conservative users of English in mainland Europe and elsewhere still favoured the BBC as their model (although this too was becoming increasingly diverse), but others, especially if they were younger speakers, tended to prefer the racier idiom evident in *programs* and *movies* [AmE] rather than the traditional *programmes* and *films* [BrE]. Indeed, a transatlantic *coup de grace* came in the 1980s when the US spelling *program* was adopted in computing everywhere. Even so, however, the Brits have kept *programmes* for use in *theaters* [AmE] or *theatres* [BrE], on the *telly*, and on the *radio* (seldom called the *wireless* in the later decades of the century).

Although the trend towards the dominance of US usage among foreign- and second-language learners has therefore undeniably gained strength, by 1999 BBC-style English had kept much of its social gloss, including among admiring middle-class Americans (who might consider it 'cute' but would never think of adopting it). Equally, in the UK and other parts of the world, US usage and slang had become so easy to adopt and so familiar that no one any longer recalled their origins, and US accents had little influence among native-speakers anywhere else, although they did increasingly influence foreign learners, especially in mainland Europe and East Asia. Not even the English of the net and the Web tipped the scales. Computer-literate people beyond the USA continued to manage US usage without difficulty, on the whole keeping their own styles, even if they logged on with America Online (AOL).

THE EXTERNAL TIDE: LOSS OF COMPETITION

Perhaps the most significant factor that affected the English language increasingly through the twentieth century was loss of (linguistic) competition. Many situations and institutions could in fact be highlighted as important in this regard, but one in particular needs attention, not least because it is often overlooked. Out of the Cold War between a capitalist West and a communist East emerged the North Atlantic Treaty Organization (NATO), probably the most powerful military bloc ever known, the bulk of whose members are Western European nation-states. The working language of NATO has, from the start, been English; this pre-eminence as a NATO-associated language has in turn helped to promote its use in mainland Europe (notably in Germany, where US troops have been stationed since the end of the Second World War).

In terms of NATO, the United Nations (UN), the British Commonwealth, world business, and many national and international institutions and activities, English became, in the closing quarter of the century, (to borrow a phrase from computing) the world's *default mode.* That is, given no compelling reason or need to use any other medium, those not born to English straightforwardly opted for it, both for themselves and their children. Among the many situations in which the primacy of English became manifest, one of the most patent at the century's end was international conferences. Even where simultaneous translation was provided, participants from many backgrounds preferred to listen 'straight' to deliveries in English. Partly for this reason, and partly because of the ways in which modern communicative and information-storage systems

developed, English had the serial publications (such as print and online journals), the libraries, and the databases to handle them. Closely comparable was the
use of English by the world's media, not only directly for journalism, radio, and
television, but as a behind-the-scenes source for output in languages other than
English. Routinely, material gathered in English by such agencies as Reuters and
the Associated Press was, every day, round the clock, translated into and then
transmitted in other languages.

Significantly (and for many, ominously), the external tide included a weakening in competition, notably from other European languages. German fared
particularly badly. Although in the early twentieth century it was a significant
medium for science and scholarship, it suffered as a consequence of being the
medium of Germany and Austria, nations defeated in two world wars. This
happened, moreover, despite the economic resurgence in West Germany after
the war and its reunification with East Germany in 1990. Comparably, after the
dissolution of the Soviet Union, Russian lost its international clout not only in
the Third (Non-Aligned) World, but also in the vanishing Second World of
communism: in both, former Eastern European satellites such as Poland and
Hungary, and former Asian Soviet republics such as Turkmenistan and Uzbeki-
stan, took a new interest in English as the language of both the USA and
capitalism.

The retreat of German and the displacement of Russian contrast strongly with
the twentieth-century vigour of both Spanish and Portuguese whose users in
Iberia, Latin America, and elsewhere escaped many of the effects of the World
Wars and the Cold War. Because they have secure roles in Europe and the
Americas, both remain strong, a situation different, therefore, not only from
that of German and Russian, but also from that of French. In the first decades of
the century, for example, the influence of French in Europe changed little from its
role in the nineteenth century as the language of diplomacy and high culture.
Nevertheless, its world role declined greatly as a consequence not only of the
World Wars (in the second of which it was partly occupied and fully controlled by
Germany), but also because of events within its empire after 1945, especially its
protracted wars to keep control of Algeria and Vietnam. Even so, however, there
emerged a loose post-imperial league of French-speaking nations known as *La
Francophonie* ('The French-speaking Community'), a considerable success
through which, as a counter-force to a far less formal community of world
English, they were able to promote their shared language as *le français mondial*
('world French').

The post-war fate of the British Empire was complex. As a consequence of at
least four factors (pressure from the USA, great economic loss, considerable

social hardship at home, and the election of a Labour government in 1945), a retreat from empire was inevitable. The government was not only ideologically opposed to imperialism, but realized that it simply could not afford the empire much longer (and in particular the Indian Empire). Independence was therefore granted to the nationalists in 1947, but to two countries, not one: a new primarily Hindu India and predominantly Muslim Pakistan. Immediately upon independence and the departure of British forces, sectarian conflict broke out during a massive exchange of populations. Although the two countries were at odds for decades afterwards, each continued to sustain English as a key administrative and legal language, making the subcontinent of South Asia one of the key English-using areas in the world.

In the decades that followed, many newly independent nations decided to sustain a link with the UK through what was at first known as the British Commonwealth of Nations, then the Commonwealth of Nations, then simply the Commonwealth, whose head was not the British state but its monarch, whose interests and role were considered wider and more neutral than those of any politician. Apart from the vast suffering in India and Pakistan, and later troubles in Malaya, Cyprus, Rhodesia/Zimbabwe, and Northern Ireland, the disassembly of empire was relatively bloodless. The Commonwealth grew as Empire shrank, and the new states generally had solid diplomatic and economic reasons for staying loosely (and non-politically) together. Currently, the Commonwealth not only sustains economic and cultural ties among its members but demonstrates how a linguistic default mode works, in a range of nation-states in which English is either the primary or a key secondary language. Even so, however, although English has remained one of the ties that bind, the Commonwealth as an institution did not directly serve as a means of promoting or sustaining English. Rather, English helped sustain the Commonwealth.

Although it might be supposed a close link exists in London between the Commonwealth Office and the British Council (on the analogy of *La Francophonie*), the British Council is an entirely distinct organization, set up in 1934 not to strengthen empire but to counter Nazi and Fascist propaganda in Europe, as well as to promote a wider awareness (both there and elsewhere) of the UK, its culture, and of British English. Its first overseas offices were in Europe, Latin America, and West Asia, and only in the 1950s did it become involved in the Commonwealth, as the agent of what came to be known as the British Overseas Development Administration. In 1985, a specific statement was made that the Council did not 'actively propagate British English as a commodity or as the proper model for foreign users ... and has no tradition or policy of preferring or propagating any one accent over another'. However, the Council has generally been aware of the economic significance of ELT. In 1989, for example, the then director general, Sir Richard Francis, noted that 'Britain's real black gold is not oil, but the English language' (as quoted by William Greaves in *The Times* on 24 October 1989). By the century's end, the British Council had offices in over eighty countries and over fifty teaching centres in thirty-five countries.

The British Council's interest in mainland Europe proved entirely justified. One of the more remarkable linguistic developments in the decades after 1945 was the expansion of the English language 'on the continent', where it had never previously been significant. This expansion was due both to the development of NATO and the world-wide export of US popular culture through Hollywood movies and popular music and dance, an output which greatly affected younger generations in Europe and elsewhere, including those in the UK. Both the British Council and the BBC sustained a mainland European cultural presence, notably in such Anglophile nations as the Netherlands, Denmark, Norway, Sweden, and Portugal, but also behind the Iron Curtain. As a consequence, however, of the closeness of the two major varieties of English was a rueful post-war re-conception in France of its American and British allies as a single often suspect entity, *les Anglo-Saxons*, a phrase that gave a novel twist to an ancient name.

It was left to German, however, to provide the word that best fitted the conditions affecting English throughout the century: *realpolitik*. The *New Oxford Dictionary of English* of 1988 defines this word as 'a system of politics or principles based on practical rather than moral or ideological considerations'. What shaped and strengthened English in the twentieth century (and led, by the end of the century, to such soubriquets as the *global* or *world lingua franca*) was not so much a cluster of cultural, literary, social, or educational attitudes and policies (however significant these may have been), but a combination of war, economics, politics, and pragmatism. Although such matters have sometimes been couched in terms of high culture, Shakespeare did not in any serious sense triumph over Molière or Goethe, Cervantes, or Tolstoy.

ENGLISH AND THE WESTERN HEMISPHERE

It is, as the previous chapter has already indicated, entirely the case that the activities of the UK in the eighteenth and nineteenth centuries spread English world-wide in commercial and imperial terms, and that those of the USA in the twentieth consolidated its global role culturally, technologically, and militarily. It is, however, at least as important to note that the foundation stones of the English edifice at the century's end were laid not in the UK or the USA as such, but in terms of the perceived *Europeanness*, or indeed the *Westernness*, of the language.

English was only one of eight European languages that, at much the same time, and in varying degrees, became world languages. The others were Dutch, French, German, Italian, Portuguese, and Spanish in the west, and Russian in the east. Any one of these, if the circumstances had been right, could have become *the* global lingua franca. They have all had comparable educational, literary, legal, administrative, and military dimensions, and the communities in which they emerged have generally had strong convictions regarding their ethnic, literary, and academic worth, if not indeed their outright superiority as well. There was, especially in the nineteenth and twentieth centuries, no shortage of ethnic and nationalist chutzpah associated with each of them which, by and large, serves to confirm that they are all from the same cultural matrix. As a result, with the exception of Russian (on geo-political grounds, and because it expanded by land rather than sea), these languages have been key elements in an evolving ethnic, social, and cultural complex that, in the course of the twentieth century, came to be called *the Western world*, or simply *the West*.

A common assumption about language labels like *English* and *French* is that they relate first to geography and ethnicity, and only then to culture, economics, and politics, as a result of which one may overlook the evolution of (and the senses inherent in) the labels themselves. In this regard, we can consider the apparently specific and stable meanings of three key place-related words: *America, Europe, English*. Technically (some would say 'properly'), *America* refers to a continent. More often, however, it serves as an incomplete, informal, but potent label for one nation that occupies only the middle reaches of the northern part of the Americas. It was only in the later twentieth century that the term *Europe* took on a similar ambiguous duality. Formerly, the word *Europe* referred only to a continent, and not a particularly big one at that. In the later twentieth century, however, *Europe* acquired an additional sense that brought it into line with *America*: it now meant not only the whole continent, but served as shorthand for the *European Union* (EU), a politico-economic federation, which occupies only part of that continent. As a result, the world's peoples can say *America* when they mean only the USA and *Europe* when they mean only the EU, and be understood: regardless of how the Canadians or the Swiss may feel about it. The word *English* is comparably polysemic. When used with a definite article, it designates the people of England ('the English' and not, say, the Scots or the French), but without the article (and used as an adjective) it may refer to England, its attributes and aspects ('an English rose'), to the people of England

('The English are a nation of gardeners'), and, importantly for our purposes, a language originating in England but extensively used elsewhere ('the English-Speaking Union').

It can also be ambiguous. *English literature*, for example, can mean the literature of England alone, or of Britain, or of the many countries where the language is used, as in *Indian English literature*. However, many people world-wide who have grown up in English (as the language of their families and/or schooling, in, say, Newfoundland or Singapore) do not, and indeed cannot, in their daily lives give much thought to the Englishness of what they say and write in terms of England, which they may never have visited. The unyielding proof in this regard is that English could survive even if it ceased (an unlikely prospect, however) to be used between the Channel and Hadrian's Wall, or indeed between Canada and Mexico.

The way in which the word *West* behaves is comparable, and like *English* it has close links with Europe. The language called English has long been a world language, but it is also the primary language of a psycho-cultural *West*, as opposed in particular to an *East*. Images of a geographical, cultural, and political West can be traced back over two thousand years to where the sun went down if you lived in Greece. After many centuries as an indivisible mass around the Mediterranean, the Roman Empire was divided into a Western Empire ruled from Rome and an Eastern Empire ruled from Constantinople. In this West the imperial language was Latin, while in the East it was Greek. However, as centuries passed, the Western empire shrank at the same time as its focus shifted north until it became, in the Middle Ages, the Holy Roman Empire and later the Austrian or Austro-Hungarian Empire, by which time it was Central European and no longer Western at all. By then the *West* had become Atlantic Europe, from Scandinavia to Spain. In the sixteenth century, however, a larger West emerged through the discoveries of Columbus.

The Spanish and Portuguese, restricted in a Mediterranean largely controlled by Muslims, looked elsewhere for expansion, the Portuguese finding a sea route to a *Far East* beyond the *Near East* of Islam, while both Spanish and Portuguese vessels explored a 'new' far western continent that, because of the languages they spoke, became known in due course as *Latin America*, an ethno-linguistic transplant of the Iberian peninsula. Other Europeans followed, with speakers of Spanish, Danish, Dutch, English, and French exploring and exploiting the Caribbean and what lay beyond and to the north.

To this mélange was added, in 1776, a sixth, entirely transplanted power: the United States, a group of thirteen ex-British colonies that saw themselves as *American* (and as potential defenders-cum-masters of the Americas). The British, however, controlled British North America (Canada), where they imposed their rule on French settlers already there, developed an English-speaking Ontario, and pushed towards the Pacific, where Russians from Siberia were already establishing themselves in Alaska. In successive stages, the USA gained Louisiana from the French, Florida from Spain, and took from Mexico a vast territory they informally called the *Wild West*. At that point, Spanish became a secondary European language in Western North America, which was being steadily integrated, state by state, into the USA. And when the Americans bought Alaska from them, the Russians and their language were removed as potential competitors.

As a consequence of the enlargement of the USA and the consolidation of Canada, English became the most powerful language in North America, with Spanish second (in the USA, in Mexico, and the Caribbean), and French third (in Canada, Louisiana, and the Caribbean), followed by a host of European settler languages that include Danish, Dutch, German, Yiddish, Italian, Norwegian, Swedish, Russian, and Ukrainian, all of which co-habit with a dwindling range of Amerindian languages. Apparently, the currents of multilingualism were strong, but in terms of dominance and prospects the only language on a par with English in the western hemisphere was Spanish, in its Mexican, Puerto Rican, Central American, and South American forms. Inevitably, over decades, there arose between the two (notably in the twentieth century) kinds of Hispanicized English and Anglicized Spanish, in a continuum from *español* through *englañol* and *Spanglish* to English proper. The English in this hybridizing cline includes not only the more-or-less standard language of the US schoolroom and media but also what is widely known as both *Black English* and *Black English Vernacular* (BEV), the usage of the large African-American minority that (together with Afro-Caribbean people in the USA and the Caribbean) descends from Africans transported in times past into New World slavery. Such complexity has endowed nineteenth- and twentieth-century American and Caribbean English with an immense range, variety, and vitality, much of it informal, slangy, and inventive.

As a national language, American may well be more *heterogenous* [AmE] or *heterogeneous* [BrE] than British which, because of the range of its rural and urban dialects (as well as big-city varieties influenced by immigrant languages), has tended to be regarded as the most varied English anywhere. However that may be, by the end of the twentieth century the sum total of kinds of English, and the numbers using them in the USA, Canada, and the Caribbean, made the Western Hemisphere the primary focus of the language, much as had been happening with Spanish in Central and South America and Portuguese in Brazil. All of this has, in effect, served to make the Americas the *primary* world focus of three *European* languages.

In this respect, it is therefore worthy of note that the USA, often portrayed as the most monolithic English-speaking country on Earth (and a place where learning other languages has low priority), has a foot in both linguistic camps, which in fact makes it both the most significant English-speaking nation at the same time as it is a significant Spanish-speaking nation. Thus, of the three largest language complexes in the world—Chinese, English, and Spanish—two have their centres of gravity in the Americas, one in East Asia, and none in Europe. At the same time, while English has always been dominant in the USA, Spanish became increasingly significant there as the twentieth century advanced, especially because of migrations north from Latin America, while English made further headway as a language of business in Latin America. In consequence, Europe, which at the beginning of the century had been so significant politically, culturally, and linguistically, had by the century's end lost a great deal of linguistic, as well as economic and military, ground to the New World.

Each of the Western European languages considered in this review has a profile and place, as it were, in a world-wide *peck order* [AmE] or *pecking order* [BrE] of languages. Western European languages have, over the last five centuries, had their sea-borne diasporas, through colonies established by their speakers (English, French, Spanish, Portuguese, Dutch) or by emigration from other European territories to those colonies. In addition, although many emigrants established homes in non-English-speaking territories, such as Quebec (French), Venezuela (Spanish), and Brazil (Portuguese), many settled in the USA and English Canada, and (while some sustained communities in which the mother tongue continued to be used) most were assimilated into North American English, in the process often losing what came to be thought of as their heritage languages. The ultimate outcome for the Americas as a whole has, however, been two-fold:

1 The extinction, decimation, and displacement of the aboriginal languages of the hemisphere, notably Quechua in Peru (still relatively strong in relation to Spanish), Maya in Guatemala (sustaining itself), Sioux and Cherokee in the USA (weak, but stronger than many others), and Mohawk and Kwakiutl in Canada (marginal).
2 The *chequerboard* [BrE] or *checkerboard* [AmE] establishment of various European languages, at the top of whose hierarchy have been English in North America and the Caribbean, Spanish in South, Central, and North America, Portuguese in Brazil, and French in Quebec, Louisiana, and the Caribbean. Although this pattern is unique to the New World, comparable

clusters exist elsewhere, such as English and French in West Africa, and English, Portuguese, and Afrikaans (from Dutch) in southern Africa, as well as Spanish and English in the Philippines.

Asian languages may now be following. Arabic has long been widespread as both a religious and a national language from the Gulf west to Morocco and, as a religious language, east as far as the Philippines. In the second half of the twentieth century, however, its presence in both Western Europe and North America was greatly increased by emigration from North Africa, the Middle East, and South Asia. Chinese has been significant in and beyond China for centuries and in diasporas around the world in the nineteenth and twentieth centuries, notably including the USA and Canada. Large numbers of speakers of Hindi-Urdu in northern India and Pakistan emigrated in the later nineteenth and throughout the twentieth century, initially as indentured labourers in many parts of the British Empire, later often in such middle-class roles as doctors and shop-keepers in Europe and North America. In a serious sense, the Americas in general and North America in particular have become a socio-cultural and linguistic melting pot for not only Europeans but the entire world, with English and Spanish in the key positions.

ENGLISH AND 'THE GLOBAL WEST'

While the *West* is primarily a direction and a point of the compass, in the twentieth century it also served to label a culture that was noted, among many other things, for science, technology, mass-marketing, hi-tech modes of communication, modernity and post-modernity, and for such languages as French, Spanish, Portuguese, German, Dutch, and ever-increasingly English. Yet, the twentieth-century range of English went so much farther than the *West* (properly so called) that by the 1990s it could only be discussed on planet-wide terms. Indeed, as the opening sections of this chapter have already indicated, by this point, no fewer than three labels were available to scholars, journalists, and others when describing and discussing the language at its most comprehensive: *English as a world language* or, more succinctly, *world English*; *English as an international language* or *international English*; and *English as a global language* or *global English* (see further Fig. 13.1).

All three labels are currently used (at times confusingly) either for all varieties of English, wherever used, or for the standard variety as used and understood

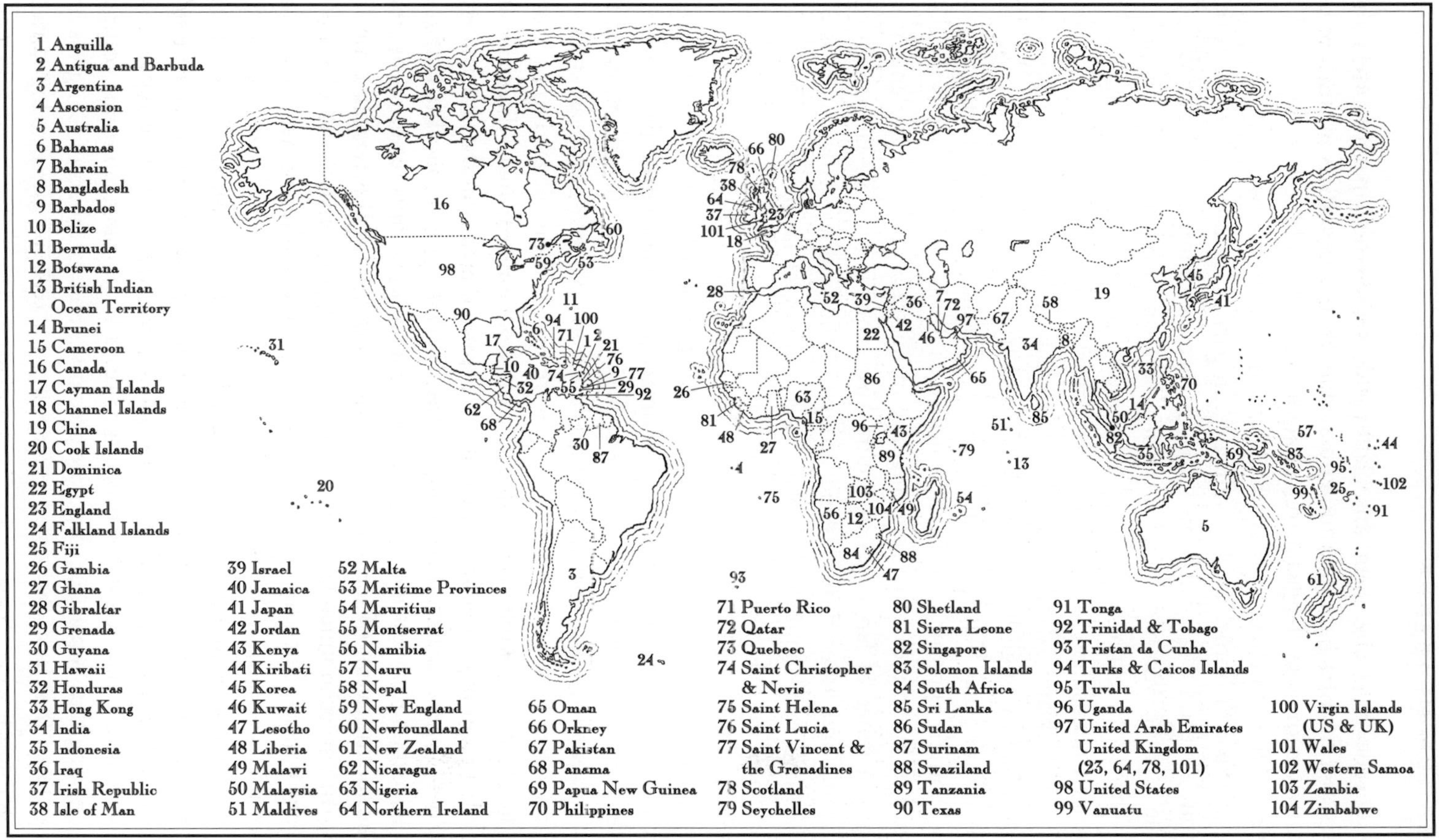

1 Anguilla
2 Antigua and Barbuda
3 Argentina
4 Ascension
5 Australia
6 Bahamas
7 Bahrain
8 Bangladesh
9 Barbados
10 Belize
11 Bermuda
12 Botswana
13 British Indian Ocean Territory
14 Brunei
15 Cameroon
16 Canada
17 Cayman Islands
18 Channel Islands
19 China
20 Cook Islands
21 Dominica
22 Egypt
23 England
24 Falkland Islands
25 Fiji
26 Gambia
27 Ghana
28 Gibraltar
29 Grenada
30 Guyana
31 Hawaii
32 Honduras
33 Hong Kong
34 India
35 Indonesia
36 Iraq
37 Irish Republic
38 Isle of Man
39 Israel
40 Jamaica
41 Japan
42 Jordan
43 Kenya
44 Kiribati
45 Korea
46 Kuwait
47 Lesotho
48 Liberia
49 Malawi
50 Malaysia
51 Maldives
52 Malta
53 Maritime Provinces
54 Mauritius
55 Montserrat
56 Namibia
57 Nauru
58 Nepal
59 New England
60 Newfoundland
61 New Zealand
62 Nicaragua
63 Nigeria
64 Northern Ireland
65 Oman
66 Orkney
67 Pakistan
68 Panama
69 Papua New Guinea
70 Philippines
71 Puerto Rico
72 Qatar
73 Quebec
74 Saint Christopher & Nevis
75 Saint Helena
76 Saint Lucia
77 Saint Vincent & the Grenadines
78 Scotland
79 Seychelles
80 Shetland
81 Sierra Leone
82 Singapore
83 Solomon Islands
84 South Africa
85 Sri Lanka
86 Sudan
87 Surinam
88 Swaziland
89 Tanzania
90 Texas
91 Tonga
92 Trinidad & Tobago
93 Tristan da Cunha
94 Turks & Caicos Islands
95 Tuvalu
96 Uganda
97 United Arab Emirates
United Kingdom (25, 64, 78, 101)
98 United States
99 Vanuatu
100 Virgin Islands (US & UK)
101 Wales
102 Western Samoa
103 Zambia
104 Zimbabwe

FIG. 13.1.   World English

world-wide. It is *English* in this planet-wide sense which parents everywhere (whatever their backgrounds and circumstances, and regardless of whether they themselves know the language well or at all) seek, or would seek if they could, for their children. In effect then, by the fourth quarter of the twentieth century (in part because of immediate US influence, in part as an aftermath of the British Empire) a 'third West' had come into existence, extending the Atlantic West just as the Atlantic West had extended the original Greco-Roman and Medieval West. This time, the extension was, incongruously but logically enough, into the southern hemisphere: most notably to Australia, New Zealand, South Africa, and the Falkland Islands. The first European settlers in these regions were predominantly English, Scottish, Welsh, and Irish, and English was predominantly the language they took with them. In Australia in particular such migrants have, entirely appropriately, been identified as *Anglo-Celtic.* English is the dominant but by no means the sole language in Australia and New Zealand, is one among a range of languages in South Africa, but is the sole language of the Falklands and other British island groups in the southern Atlantic. It is also, incidentally but significantly, a key inter-communal language in the various nationally-controlled segments of Antarctica.

In effect, the *West* had by the last quarter of the century become the name, not simply of a particular region of the world, but of a Western European core together with other areas massively colonized in two sea-borne diasporas, first to the Americas, then to the southern hemisphere. The identification of this vastly expanded space relates to both colonists of Western European stock and the languages they used, some of which were widely acknowledged to be 'world' languages (as with French and Spanish), while one in particular—English—had by the closing decades of the twentieth century become *the* world or international or global language, even though it remains far from being a *universal* language.

This expanded West inevitably has its anomalies, the most unusual of which is the identification of Japan as a *Western* rather than a *Westernized* nation, at least in an economic, industrial, and technological sense—and despite its ancient epithet, 'the land of the rising sun'. Remarkably, and with little fuss, Japan has been cited in Western news media as *Western.* Thus, a 1987 editorial in the British daily newspaper the *Independent* (24 August 1987) noted that '[d]espite its Asian roots, Japan has become suspended in the Western world'. In a similar way, in the US *International Herald Tribune* (1 June 1990) David Sanger wrote about 'tension between the West's two biggest economic competitors', noting that 'American corporate executives and members of Congress have complained that Japan has acted as a sponge for technologies developed in the United States'.

In the earlier twentieth century, the Westernizing acculturation of Japan was towards Britain and British English, but after *World War II* [AmE and BrE] the *Second World War* [BrE], as the result of military occupation, it shifted towards the USA and American English, although a strong interest in the UK and British usage survives. The Japanese have absorbed, re-created, and exported the products of Western-style technology and art, and have adopted into everyday Japanese expressions primarily from English and other Western languages, virtually on an industrial scale, as with *takushi* ('taxi'), *purutoniumu* ('plutonium'), and *seku hara* (an abbreviated version of 'sexual harassment'). However, although the Japanese have given the English language a key role in their national curriculum, they have not become widely fluent or even comfortable in the language. Yet, even so, from time to time home-grown proposals are made that Japan adopt English as a second national language.

No other non-Occidental country has opted so unreservedly to 'join the West', at least in socio-technological terms. There is, however, a range of comparable territories whose contact with the West was first commercial (principally in the nineteenth century), then through absorption into one or other European empire, then (in the later twentieth century) by on-going contact, in varying degrees of closeness, with their former imperial state, as independent nations. This was the case, for example, with both India and the Malay states (now Malaysia and Brunei) in relation to Britain; Indo-China (Vietnam, Cambodia, and Laos) with France; Venezuela with Spain; the Philippines with Spain then the USA; East Timor and Macau with Portugal; and the East Indies (now Indonesia) with the Dutch.

Singapore, a small island nation with four official languages (English, Mandarin Chinese, Malay, and Tamil), occupies a category all its own. English is the most used, the government in fact intending that its citizens should speak and write 'internationally acceptable English'. The Lion City is highly Westernized along mainly British lines, but has neither an Australian-style sense of 'kith and kin' with Britain (and Ireland) nor social, commercial, or military closeness to the USA, nor a Japanese approach to out-doing the West on its own terms—even though Singapore is materially and in business terms highly Western (and not simply 'Westernized'). The city-state may yet, however, succeed, in the process showing others how to create a long enough spoon to sup with the devil. Certainly, and uniquely, by the end of the twentieth century Singapore had become an English-speaking country in its own right, but without (as in the case of South Africa) an indigenous native-speaking minority to serve as a template. A kind of Britishness remains evident in Singapore, but there are not enough Brits or indeed Americans, Canadians, Australians, and New Zealanders to have a serious impact on Singaporean socio-political style or private inclination. The dominant role of English in Singapore is therefore home-grown, and to prove it there is a widespread younger-generation patois called *Singlish* which, while distressing the Lion City's elders, offers a vivid, home-grown, multi-ethnic sense of being safe in one's in-group, while at the same time facing the older local generation and the wider world, while also—and simultaneously— drawing on the resources of all of Singapore's native languages.

Also close to the *global West* is a range of territories variously associated with Europe or the USA or both. All are Westernized and fully aware of it, many use English for external and often internal purposes, but none has any particular wish or need to be regarded as 'Western' in the sense that Australia or indeed Japan is Western (despite their Asia-Pacific locations) or that Singapore is Westernized. These include: India, Pakistan, Bangladesh, Sri Lanka, Malaysia, and Fiji (all formerly British Asian 'possessions' with strongly indigenous cultures); the Gulf States (formerly British protectorates every bit as Arabic and Islamic as their neighbours); Ghana, Kenya, Nigeria, Sierra Leone, and Uganda (all former British colonies in which there was, apart from Kenya, no large-scale permanent British settlement, but where there has been a strong British presence and considerable acculturation). These Westernizing territories form a penumbra to the global West, and proof of their close ties to that West is the long-term, often permanent residence of large groups of their own citizens in such Western territories as the UK, the USA, Canada, Australia, and New Zealand. All such countries have substantial diasporas in the preceding five 'Anglo-Celtic' nations (as the Australians might put it), and the likelihood that such diasporas will simply fade into the local populations in the early twenty-first century, in the process forgetting their roots, is low.

However, the use of English in the global West and the greater circle of Westernization is by no means tidy. Other languages than English are used there, just as in the earlier Wests, a range of Anglo-hybrids exist, and English is also being put to work in places that could never be reckoned 'Western' or traditionally 'Westernized' as, for example, Kyrgyzstan and China. Three points are, however, worth noting in this connection:

1 English and the global West share a vast area, but are not co-terminous: English is used beyond this West as, for example, in India, and there are areas of the global West where English is not (yet) massively present as, for example, in France and Mexico.

2 By and large, within the global West, there is a shared although non-uniform and sometimes uneven standardness of English usage, particularly in education and the media. Thus, while Americans spell and punctuate differently

from the British, Canadians may be caught between the two; US and UK dictionaries of English differ considerably on many points of usage, style, and presentation; and works of language reference often, necessarily, provide different representations of the pronunciation of the 'same' words in British and American English.

3 Beyond this area, varieties of English tend to be more divergent, notably, say, where West African Pidgin English (WAPE) is in wide use, or in South Asia, where a range of highly distinctive Indian Englishes can be found alongside the normative usage of, say, *The Times of India* and All India Radio (AIR). One is, for instance, unlikely to hear someone who works as an announcer or continuity person on AIR saying to a friend in the street, regarding some colleagues, that 'They are working hard, no?', although this is an otherwise fairly common construction in which the non-standard question specifically relates to habitual (not current and continuing) activity. Although this is therefore a widespread construction in everyday Indian English, AIR professionals would say, to indicate habituality, 'They work hard, don't they?', as would their equivalents elsewhere. In this they use an internationally viable professional Indian English which is comparable to professional British or American English, and their local accent will, as it were, be set in an equivalent social position to the accents of media people in the rest of the English-using world.

It can be argued that such differences in India and elsewhere are no more remarkable than dialect and social-class differences in the UK and the USA. Whenever lines are drawn (as I have drawn them over the course of this chapter in the image of a *global West* and a range of English-using and non-English-using territories), we cannot assume that in the process anything absolute and final has been described. Models of this kind are only models, and such a complex reality as English world-wide will never quite be pinned down, especially when we consider how mobile populations became in the course of the century.

Finally, it is a curiosity of English world-wide that, while it is used on an enormous scale in such non-Western (though varyingly Westernized) regions as India and indeed China (including the special case of Hong Kong, with its own distinctly institutionalized English), the language itself continues to be identified as fundamentally Western. The ancient West knew nothing of English; a later Atlantic West was the incubator for the language as we know it; and much of the global West now uses it, along with much of the rest of the world, in a wide spectrum of ways. Indeed, the notion 'the rest of the world' poses the question of whether there will, at some point, be an Alice-in-Wonderland *universalized West* (although presumably not called by that name) in which English and other very large languages co-occur with a range of medium to large regional languages that are in no danger of extinction and may be expanding in their own right. In such a world, the word cluster *West, Western, Westernize, Westernization* might, in relation to the use of English and other matters, become a term whose original directional meaning no longer has any relevance. At that point, English would beyond any doubt be a world or international or global language.

At that point, of course, the issue of *modernity* returns, in as much as the term *Westernization* has tended to flirt with both *modernization* and *modernity*. A non-Western society engaged in *Westernization* is *ipso facto* also engaged in *modernization*—and a modernization in which English, especially in its US form, is profoundly involved. In many parts of the world, children of the financially secure may not be sent to conventional local schools but to private and fee-paying *international schools* instead (reminding us of the public schools in England). A key subject in such schools (if not indeed their sole or primary medium of instruction) is English. When children leave such schools, in India, Hong Kong, Singapore, or elsewhere, they may proceed to local English-medium universities or to universities in the global West whose sole medium may be English or (as in parts of mainland Western Europe, such as the Netherlands) where English can be used as the medium of instruction and discussion, if by so doing foreign students are likely to be attracted in greater numbers, and if no local students object. An example is the Netherlands, now virtually an English-using country in which Dutch has to date lost no significant ground.

In such situations, English (already perceived and received as the *global lingua franca*) has become in effect, and paradoxically, a 'second first language', a phenomenon that seems likely to spread in the twenty-first century. Traditionalists and protectionists in many parts of the world, including people of good will and wide experience, who also know English, may fear for the health and integrity of their national traditions and object, at times strongly. But the tide, for good or ill or something else, seems to be running against them, and within their own communities. The unarguable utility of English may win out globally as it won out (amid pain) in Ireland, Scotland, and Wales in the eighteenth century. There may be regrets, but the medium will be used by some (with manifest gain), and as a result cannot fairly be denied to others. In this, in the early years of the twenty-first century, access to English comes (perilously?) close to a human right.

Schools that offer such global qualifications as the International Baccalaureate tend to have strong local reputations for quality of education, and not only in English. This inevitably strengthens parents' hopes for a strong and safe education for their children, at the same time as such a system leads to, or expands, an élite whose aim is to ensure (through endowments, prizes, and other means) that such schools achieve even more in future. For some, this is a virtuous circle, creating the best of futures; for others it is vicious, because it may sap the strength of indigenous languages, cultures, and traditions; for others still it is simply there, to be used if possible, or to become a source of envy and resentment if not. In the meantime, however, such schools thrive like the green bay tree, and, in their own right, are a significant element in the socio-economic process known world-wide, in English of course, as *globalization*.

References and Suggestions for Further Reading

English, Englishes, English languages

Useful introductory works are Elmes (1999–2000) whose *Routes of English* provides a set of four books (each with a foreword by Melvyn Bragg) relating to a BBC Radio 4 series of the same name (see also <**http://www.bbc.co.uk/radio4/routesofenglish**>), illustrated and with eight CDs (non-academic in style and focusing strongly on English as the world's lingua franca); Jenkins (2003), a relaxed and wide-ranging source book, with many examples, specimens and quotations, and Trudgill and Hannah (1994), now in its third edition and a virtual classic on the subject of international English. McArthur (1998a) and McArthur (2002a) are also useful. The first views English as a family of languages or a 'language complex' rather than taking a traditional 'one language' view, while the second offers a detailed survey of the language, both continent by continent and in global terms. Relevant journals are *English Today: The International Review of the English Language* (edited by Tom McArthur, Cambridge University Press), *World Englishes, Journal of English as an International and Intranational Language* (edited by Braj B. Kachru and Larry E. Smith, Oxford: Blackwell) and *English World-Wide* (John Benjamins: Amsterdam & Philadelphia), edited by Edgar Schneider.

A debate at the start of the century

For images of 'good English' at the start of the century, especially in terms of the public schools and education, see Mugglestone (2003a), Chapter 7, and Honey (1988). Beal (2004) provides a good overview of modern English (up to 1945) and changes within it. For recent changes in RP (and dialect levelling), see, for example, Trudgill (2002). An excellent biography of Daniel Jones can be found in Collins and Rees (1999); his *English Pronouncing Dictionary*, first published in 1917, is now in its 16th edition (2003, edited by Roach, Hartman, and Setter). For Henry Cecil Wyld, see Milroy (1998). For the BBC and its influence on spoken language, see Mugglestone (2003a), Chapter 8. For the changing cultural dynamics of popular broadcasting in the later twentieth century, see MacCabe (1999).

For American English, see Krapp (1919, 1925) and the now classic Bailey and Görlach (1984). For African American English, see Mufwene *et al.* (1998).

Technology, communication, war, and realpolitik

Brutt-Griffler (2002) gives significant coverage of the nature and use of English in the later British Empire, while the sixteen international articles in Burns and Coffin (2001) provide, as the title indicates, a useful reader in the changing roles of English in a global context. See also Crystal (2003*b*). For language and technology, see Baron (2000), and the discussion (and references) given in the following chapter in this volume. For a general historical background to the twentieth century, see Cottrell (1992).

The internal tide: from the UK to the US

Rosewarne's initial discussion of Estuary English can be found in Rosewarne (1984); see also Rosewarne (1994*a*, 1994*b*). The subject has provoked a range of responses and articles (a number of them critical); many of these are gathered at <**www.phon.ucl.ac.uk/home/estuary**>. The website of the Queen's English Society <**http://www.queens-english-society.com**> provides information about its linguistic aims and objectives, as does that of the Plain English Society <**http://www.plainenglish.co.uk/**>.

See Kachru (1992, 1990, 1983) and McArthur (2002*a*) for discussion of national Englishes around the world and their development. Varieties of English (and their history) are illuminatingly discussed in many of the articles in Watts and Trudgill (2002). For multilingualism in the modern world, see Cronin (2003). For the influence of American English, see relevant entries in McArthur (2002*a*).

The external tide: loss of competition

For further information on relevant factors (and consequences) here, see McArthur (2002*a*), especially Parts 1 (Introduction) and 8 (Conclusion). For the British Council, see Coombs (1988) and also the website of the British Council: <**http://www.britishcouncil.org/**>.

English and the western hemisphere

Huntington (1996) gives a concise review of the situation of English and other major world languages, in which English is presented as the world's lingua franca.

English and 'the global West'

See Melchers and Shaw (2003) for an overview of global variation in vocabulary, grammar, phonology, and usage (with recordings on an accompanying CD). Maurais and Morris (2003) provide a useful survey, discussing 'a new global linguistic order', English hegemony, and the current condition of the world's (especially larger) languages. McArthur (1998b) offers a collection of papers on language teaching, reference materials, the possibility of a global library-cum-database, and the lexicography of a universalizing English, while Graddol (1997) looks at the recent situation of, and possible futures for, English as a world language.

14

INTO THE TWENTY-FIRST CENTURY

David Crystal

IT is a widespread literary trope to anthropomorphize English—to talk about its 'remorseless advance' (around the world) or its 'insatiable appetite' (for new words). If we were to continue this trope at the beginning of the twenty-first century, we would have to select much less assertive metaphors. For, as a result of the unprecedented trends which affected the language during the twentieth century, and especially during its final decade, we would need to talk of 'tentative steps' and 'uncertain directions'. We can see these new perspectives chiefly in relation to three themes: globalization, the Internet, and education.

THE LONG-TERM CONSEQUENCES OF GLOBALIZATION

As the preceding chapter has stressed, the impact of globalization brought a widespread acknowledgement during the 1990s that English had achieved a genuine world presence, receiving special status in the usage or educational systems of every country. Books and journals whose titles described English as a 'world language' or a 'global language' became ubiquitous. But because there has never been a language of such global reach and magnitude, it is unclear what happens to one in the long term when it achieves this status, or what happens to other languages as a consequence. Certainly, we saw during that decade an increase in the number of concerned reactions from other-language communities which were anxious to preserve the functional standing or formal character of their language in the face of the growing dominance of English. Anxiety over reduced functionality related chiefly to such domains as science and higher education, where English was widely used; issues of linguistic character were chiefly focused on the amount of English lexical borrowing which was taking place—words such as *email, shop,* and *AIDS*—which were entering several European languages.[1] At the same time, within English itself, the first effects of global spread were beginning to be analysed.

The immediate linguistic consequences of English becoming a global language have been reviewed in Chapter 13. The recurring pattern is one of language spread resulting in language change. As new communities adopt English, and give it an increasingly central place in their lives, so they adapt it to reflect their circumstances and needs. As it accretes functions within their society, there is a growing sense of local identity articulated through its use, in addition to whatever other languages may be available. In due course, regional literatures emerge which not only express themselves through English but also—via their themes and characters—comment upon it, and upon the linguistic situation which the communities are experiencing.

The countries of the world are at varying stages in relation to this course of development. Those which reflect a long history of divergence, such as Britain and the USA, show the emergence of distinct regional standards and a highly diverse and mature literature manifested by writing in every genre. But it is important to appreciate that all countries—even those whose separate political identities are relatively recent, such as Singapore and Nigeria (the so-called 'New Englishes')—display a use of the language which is sociolinguistically highly varied. Regional dialects reflect the often extensive geographical spread of English throughout a country. Social dialects reflect the ethnic diversity of the population, a diversity which is often reinforced by the use of separate or mixed languages (such as the Chinese and English mixing which comprises Singaporean English, or 'Singlish'). New pidgins and creoles emerge. Whatever 'Nigerian English' is, for example, it could never be a homogeneous entity, given the great size and population of Nigeria and the fact that it contains over 400 languages, each of which influences the form of English in individual ways through the use of local loanwords, pronunciations, and grammatical patterns. In addition, any New English soon evolves a set of formality levels, which depend largely on the closeness of the relationship between a variety and standard English.

---

[1] See, for example, M. Görlach, *A Dictionary of European Anglicisms: A Usage Dictionary of Anglicisms in Sixteen European Languages* (Oxford; New York: Oxford University Press, 2001).

Although futurologists have varied opinions about the very-long-term role of English as a global lingua franca, we are unlikely to see a reversal of current trends in the course of the present century. All the evidence at present points to a steady growth in the number of New Englishes, and—within these—an increase in new forms, new functions, and new literatures. There is one main reason for this, which has been acknowledged in Chapter 13: the increasing global presence of non-native speakers, now outnumbering native speakers in a ratio of three to one. But the nature of the non-native speaker bias is changing. Whereas fifty years ago most non-native speakers of English belonged to 'second-language' nations, where the British Empire had left a legacy of official language use, today most belong to countries which have had no political relationship with Britain or any other English-speaking nation. This seems to be the pattern for the future. Because there are more of these nations, we must therefore anticipate a considerable increase in the kind of inter-linguistic effects which have been repeatedly observed in earlier contact situations. Just as South African English displays large numbers of words borrowed from Afrikaans, Xhosa, Zulu, and other local languages—such as Afrikaans *agterkamer* ('back-room'), Zulu *ngoma* ('type of drum'), and a distinctive range of pronunciations which reflect the syllable-timed pattern of those languages (the name *South Africa*, for example, being pronounced by many speakers as four equally stressed syllables)—so we must expect to find an evolving linguistic distinctiveness in China, Egypt, Sweden, and the other 120 or so countries where English has status only as a 'foreign language' ('EFL countries').

At a colloquial level, this influence, seen in lexical borrowing or more extensive code-mixing, has already been institutionalized through the use of such names as 'Spanglish' and 'Japlish'. These labels, however, have to be used with caution because they have been applied to a variety of different language situations on the ground, and they are often used stereotypically. The term 'Spanglish', for example, has been used in four main senses: for a balanced mixing at all levels between Spanish and English; for the use of a large number of Spanish loan words in English; for the use of a large number of English loan words in Spanish; and for a situation where any kind of mutual influence, no matter how small, generates a public outcry from purists. For the present chapter, it is the first two senses that are relevant, such labels drawing attention to the way English vocabulary, grammar, pronunciation, or patterns of discourse have altered under the influence of other languages. Once upon a time, such variations would have been dismissed out-of-hand as 'interference errors' produced by people whose command of the standard language was imperfect. Today, as increasing numbers of highly educated people accommodate to each other in the use of such features, these 'errors' gradually take on the character of regional spoken standards. For example, in

Egypt, the universal greeting 'Welcome in Egypt' was once perceived to be an error, displaying the influence of Arabic. Today, it is in universal use, produced by native English speakers living in Egypt as well as by native Arabic speakers. Its status has even been sanctioned by its appearance in some English-language textbooks written for the Egyptian market. This process is no different, of course, from the emergence of *quarter of* instead of *quarter to* in American time-telling, or any other distinctive local use, such as *toward* vs. *towards*, which has achieved status as a regional standard.

However, the fact that such a usage has emerged in Egypt, an EFL country, and has moreover crossed the native/non-native divide, is highly significant. It is, I believe, a sign of things to come. The driving force is probably the need for linguistic accommodation. The language of people in rapport with each other readily converges. It is only natural for native speakers of English, living as a (less powerful) minority in a non-native community, and wishing to integrate within that community, to accommodate in the direction of the linguistic norms which they hear around them. And it is only a matter of time before features of this integration—vocabulary, most obviously, but also subtle features of grammar and even pronunciation—begin to be institutionalized, written down by those who listen most carefully: the novelists, poets, dramatists, and short-story writers. While at the outset these writers produce styles which are personal and idiosyncratic, over the course of time shared features inevitably emerge, and these then become models for other kinds of written language use. The similarities in vocabulary and grammar are often obscured by the diversity of spelling practices—as in the case of contemporary Scots or Caribbean writing—but we might expect a gradual standardization of spelling to emerge in the course of time.

'New Literatures' do not develop overnight. The evidence from earlier Commonwealth manifestations is that fresh literary voices take a considerable while to mature. Authors are always at first somewhat uncertain about the way to handle the non-standard or innovative varieties of English evolving in the community about which they are writing. But over time the writing gains in confidence. In relation to the presentation of non-standard varieties, there seem to be four stages:

1 All characters express themselves in standard English, whatever their linguistic background; the author makes no comment. Example:
   'How long do you intend to stay with us,' said the Colonel.
   'As long as you will have me, sir,' replied Manuel.
2 Characters express themselves in standard English; the author tells the reader what variety or language they are really using. Example:
   'I'll leave as soon as I can,' said Manuel in pidgin.

3 Characters express themselves in a local variety; the author additionally tells the reader what the variety is. Example:

'Me go quick-quick,' said Manuel in pidgin.

4 Characters express themselves in a local variety; the author makes no comment. Example:

'Me go quick-quick,' said Manuel.

It is this last stage, a stage of 'showing', not 'telling', which is a sign of real literary confidence. We can see it emerging early on (as far as the history of New Englishes is concerned) in Milton Murayama's novel *All I asking for is my body* (1959), which tells a story from the viewpoint of Kiyoshi, a young Japanese boy growing up on a sugar plantation in Hawaii. It used standard English and varieties of Hawaiian pidgin and creole English, as well as pidgin and code-mixed Japanese.[2] The extract below displays features both of showing and of telling. Standard English is used (with occasional deviations) for the main narrative as well as to express the thoughts of older people speaking in Japanese—the latter including some code-mixing, as in the last sentence of the extract.

'Kiyoshi, you understand, you're not to eat anymore at Makoto's home,' Father said evenly, now his anger gone.

I was going to ask 'Why?' again but I was afraid. 'Yes,' I said.

Then Tosh said across the table in pidgin English, which the old folks couldn't understand, 'You know why, Kyo?' I never liked the guy, he couldn't even pronounce my name right. 'Because his father no work and his mother do all the work, thass why! Ha-ha-ha-ha.'

Father told him to shut up and not to joke at the table and he shut up and grinned.

Then Tosh said again in pidgin English, his mouth full of food; he always talked with his mouth full. 'Go tell that kodomo taisho to go play with guys his own age, not small shrimps like you. You know why he doan play with us? Because he scared, thass why. He too wahine. We bust um up.'

'Wahine' was the Hawaiian word for woman. When we called anybody wahine it meant she was a girl or he was a sissy.

... 'Mama, you better tell Kyo not to go outside the breakers. By-'n'-by he drown. By-'n'-by the shark eat 'um up.'

'Oh, Kiyo-chan, did you go outside the breakers?', she said in Japanese.

'Yeah,' Tosh answered for me. 'Makoto Sasaki been take him go.'

'Not dangerous,' I said in pidgin Japanese; 'Makato-san was with me all the time.'

'Why shouldn't Makoto-san play with people his own age, ne?,' Mother said.

---

[2] This is discussed in more detail in S. Romaine, 'Hawai'i Creole English as a Literary Language', *Language in Society* 23 (1994), 536.

As the number of English-language speakers in EFL countries increases, and as their confidence to use the language in distinctive ways grows, we must surely anticipate a major growth in the expressive range of English arising out of new literary uses. There is no reason why the Hawaiian or West African novel (in English) should not have its equivalent one day in the Scandinavian novel (in English) or the Oriental novel (in English), or Caribbean poetry eventually be matched by Russian poetry (in English) or Chinese poetry (in English). An indication of the correspondingly wider linguistic and cultural perspectives needed to interpret them can already be seen in the English-language newspapers from any of the EFL countries that produce one, for example, Egypt, Japan, or Greece. A wide range of topic areas has generated an extensive local vocabulary of common nouns and proper names which have acquired local overtones (the equivalent of such forms as *Whitehall*, *Soho*, and *West End* in British English). I do not know what the equivalent of *West End* and *East End* is in the English-language description of its corresponding locations in Tokyo, Bangkok, or Berlin, but every city has names which reflect social realities, and the English which is used in these areas will include those resonances. We would need to know what they were if we were to interpret correctly any English-language novel or newspaper in Japan, Thailand, or Germany which incorporated them.

As with the literary example above, English-language newspapers uncertain of the level of awareness of their readership take pains to 'tell' their readers what they are talking about by translating potentially obscure vocabulary, especially in relation to proper names. Here is an example from a Russian English-language publication:

Russia's Ded Moroz (Grandfather Frost) whose official residence is in Veliky Ustyug [a town in Russia's northwest], Santa Claus from Lapland's village of Rovaniemi and their Yakutian counterpart Ekhee Dyyl are meeting this Saturday in the Yakutian village of Tomtor in the Oimyakon district (the Far Eastern Federal District) on the last day of the first Cold Pole-2002 festival. (*Pravda*, 2003)

This is a very high level of 'telling'. At a more mature stage of expression, there is no 'telling', only 'showing':

Wakonahana, facing one of the few rikishi smaller than himself, had little trouble with No. 6 maegashire Mainoumi, who could use none of his tricks against the technically-sound sekiwake. (*The Daily Yomiuri*, 1993)

This is confident writing, assuming an aware readership which does not have to be written down to. Those who understand Japanese sumo wrestling of course find such sentences transparent. They are no more difficult, in essence, than is a baseball or cricket report to enthusiasts of either sport, as in these American and British examples:

Brown was hit in the helmet by a Jim Taylor pitch in the top of the eighth inning and was down at home plate for three minutes.

Hussein has placed two slips and a gully and a backward short-leg for the occasional ball zipping in off the seam.

Newspapers, creative literature, and printed ephemera (such as restaurant menus) involve a very wide range of subject matter, reflecting the physical environment, history, society, and life style of the host country. As a result, the number of culturally distinctive lexical items which accumulate is extensive, as demonstrated by the 'New English' dictionaries—of South African English, Jamaican English, Australian English, and so on—which, as mentioned in Chapter 13, have already been compiled. These usually include well in excess of 10,000 entries—and this figure does not take into account encyclopaedic data, such as the names of people, places, and events, which most modern dictionaries tend to exclude. To come to terms with all this, a rapprochement between linguistic and cultural studies, at a comparative and global level, is likely to be one of the major intellectual developments in twenty-first-century English-language studies.

Linguistic terminology can hardly fail to be influenced by these new perspectives. The kinds of issue presented by code-mixed and culturally-induced lexical variation raise serious questions for the distinction between 'native' and 'non-native' English, and for the relevance of such notions as 'EFL'. Quite plainly, the experience of a Japanese speaker learning English as a foreign language in Japan is very different from that of someone learning French as a foreign language in that country. The fact that English is part of the Japanese environment in a way that French is not means that the learning experience is very different. Young children cannot avoid being exposed to English in such domains as advertising, television, the Internet, and pop music, and inevitably develop a considerable passive knowledge of (some domains of) English. There is an increased awareness of English vocabulary through the assimilation of loanwords into Japanese. And the popular appeal of English motivates a degree of spontaneous active (albeit often non-standard) use, both in speech and writing, as when children (or adults) imitate discourse exchanges they have encountered in English-language films or make use of idiomatic expressions they have seen in Internet interactions. And for 'Japanese' here, read 'people from any EFL country'. We need a term for the state of a language which arises out of its status as a lingua franca in a community. 'Nativized

English' is one which has been suggested, as by Prcic in 2003.[3] Other terms, describing the varying types of situation in different communities, must follow.

THE LONG-TERM CONSEQUENCES OF THE INTERNET

The trend towards electronic communication in the second half of the twentieth century also made its public impact during the 1990s, when the world wide web and mobile telephony arrived, and interaction through email and chatroom became routine. As earlier chapters in this volume have illustrated, a new technology always has a significant effect on the character and use of language, but when a technology produces a medium that is so different from anything we have experienced hitherto, the linguistic consequences are likely to be dramatic, involving all areas of English structure and use, and introducing new considerations into the methodology of its study.

The impact of technology has been evident at every stage in English linguistic history, from the arrival of pen and ink onwards. Writing introduced a graphological dimension to English, with all that this involved in terms of spelling, punctuation, and styles of handwriting. Printing added another dimension to written language, in the form of typography and graphic design, of further developments in the orthographic system, and of a huge expansion of language varieties through books, magazines, newspapers, advertisements, and printed ephemera. The telephone introduced new techniques of spoken discourse, and the telegraph added new written styles, such as 'telegramese' (see further p. 276). Radio broadcasting did analogously for the spoken language what print had done for the written, extending phonological expression, and introducing several fresh varieties such as announcements, sports commentaries, and news broadcasts. Over the twentieth century, film and television continued this process, adding cinematic or televisual speech varieties and also such forms of written expression as programme titles, screen credits, and commercials. In the late twentieth century, the mobile phone (or cell-

---

[3] See T. Prcic, 'Is English Still a Foreign Language?', *The European English Messenger* 12 (2003), 35–7.

phone), with its space-restricted screen, motivated the development of a further written variety, based on linguistic abbreviation, in the form of text-messaging. And the Internet has taken this process even further, with emails, synchronous (real-time) chatrooms, asynchronous discussion groups, and the many types of Web-based text showing English moving in new stylistic direc-tions, partly in response to the personalities and group dynamics of the participants, and partly because of the constraints introduced by the control-ling hardware and software.

But the Internet has done more than earlier technologies in altering our perception of what language is and how it is used. There are plainly consid-erable differences between the kind of language used on the Internet—*Net-speak*, as I have elsewhere called it[4]—and those used in traditional forms of speech and writing. Indeed, the extent of the difference is so great that it amounts to the arrival of a new medium, often called *computer-mediated communication*, which blends properties of traditional written and spoken language. Netspeak is not like traditional writing. It permits people to do things routinely to the written language which were not possible before, such as to interpolate responses into a message (as in emails) or to cut and paste from one document to another without the results clashing graphically. And it offers new dimensions of contrast which were not previously available, notably in animated graphic presentation. Nor is Netspeak like traditional speech. It lacks the simultaneous feedback which is an essential part of face-to-face conversation. It permits the carrying on of several conversations simultaneously in chatrooms, where it is possible to attend to many inter-locutors at once, and to respond to as many as taste and typing speed permit. And it allows people to participate in several totally different speech situations simultaneously—a computer may have a number of windows open at the same time, allowing the user to participate in a multi-user chatroom, engage in a one-to-one conversation using Instant Messenger, role-play an imaginary character in an Internet game, and much more. Participants are well aware of what they are doing, as the following conversation shows. It took place in 2003 between a group of established adult members of a chatroom and a newcomer (a 'newbie', Artman), puzzled about how to behave. (Nicknames have been changed, but the text is otherwise exactly as it appeared.)

---

[4] See D. Crystal, *Language and the Internet* (Cambridge: Cambridge University Press, 2nd edn 2006).

Artman:	how can you listen and chat at the same time? it boggles the mind.
Toots:	for now anyway
Mo:	add chewing gum and you can try for Mensa
Deedee:	It takes skill artman
Toots:	HEy, we love Boggle
Artman:	heheh
Pluto:	you're a mere newbie. You'll get the hang of it. Just realign both halves of the brain and stuff
Hop:	I've been chatting/listening/watching tv shows at the same time for long time
Artman:	well, I'm impressed. :)
Deedee:	Sometimes I listen, chat, AND play Bejeweled
Benj:	Throw in fic writing, and I hear ya.
Hop:	it's kinda overwhelming at first
TKD:	after a couple of go-arounds, you find that having 7 conversations at once is perfectly normal
Artman:	sure
Benj:	Not necessarily 7 perfectly normal conversations
DIY:	you will often write in the wrong window
DIY:	but we don't care
TKD:	well, its when you start having them without the computer that people start to stare
Artman:	oh yeah, that happens all the time
Artman:	lol [= 'laughing out loud']
Mo:	It makes the conversation more interesting

It is linguistically interesting too, for the practices break most of the traditionally understood conventions governing how successful conversations are supposed to proceed. The general concept of the conversational exchange, for example (as discussed by Stubbs in his 1983 analysis of the structure of discourse), or the more specific notion of the 'adjacency pair' (i.e. a privileged sequence of sentences, such as question + response), has to be fundamentally revised to cope with such material.

Just as radical a development is the way the Internet is altering our conception of what the written language is for. The vast majority of traditional writing has represented the language of public record and debate, as manifested in administrative, academic, and expository material (e.g. newspapers, ephemera). It is formal in style, for the most part constructed with care, and expressed in standard English (in one of its regional incarnations). Creative literature, displaying a wider range of styles, forms only a small part of the written output over the centuries, as the relative proportions of texts in any modern corpus show.[5] Informal writing (as seen in letters) forms an even smaller part although, as Chapters 7 and 9 have shown, its linguistic importance is great. All kinds of imbalances exist. Texts written by men far outnumber texts written by women, at all stages in the history of the language. Texts written by young children or teenagers hardly ever achieve a public presence; nor do texts written by handicapped people or marginalized groups. It is difficult to find public examples of unedited regional or dialect writing after standard English is established. Likewise, the written language of many social groups, such as ethnic minorities, rarely achieves an outside audience. At any stage in the history of English, if I wanted to find out what an in-group was saying, or how it used the language, as an outsider the task would be virtually impossible. The Internet has changed all this.

Probably the most important linguistic effect of the Internet is the way it offers an unprecedented degree of written public presence to small-scale regional and social groups, and thus a vast potential for representing local identities. At the level of regional dialect, developments have taken place both intranationally and internationally, corresponding to the way the Internet has—since the late 1990s—become increasingly multilingual, offering opportunities for self-expression to all languages, including many that are seriously endangered. At the level of the social group, every conceivable interest group now has an Internet presence, fostering new styles of linguistic interaction and giving rise to a range of fresh social concerns (see below). The opportunities are unlimited even at the level of the individual: anyone with access to the medium can now present a personal diary-type statement to the world, of unlimited length, in the form of a *blog* or 'Web log'—one of the most proliferating functions of the Web in the early 2000s.

The representation of dialect was an early manifestation. Any intranational regional dialect which has a history of enthusiastic support will now have its web pages. In the UK alone, there are hundreds of sites devoted to the local English of Scotland, Wales, or Northern Ireland, as well as dialect sites focusing on Yorkshire, Lancashire, Newcastle, London, and elsewhere. A major BBC-inspired web-based project, 'Voices 2005', a nationwide interactive survey of regional variation, and including transcriptions of dialect usage and sound recordings, began in January 2005 (and was aired on BBC Radio 4 in August 2005). And at an international level, many of the New Englishes now have available a written electronic identity which previously could be achieved only through conventional creative literature. Because the Internet is uncontrolled by the hierarchy of grammarians, lexicographers, publishers, printers, copy editors, and proof-readers who have traditionally established,

---

[5] See D. Crystal, *The Cambridge Encyclopedia of the English Language*, 2nd edn. (Cambridge: Cambridge University Press, 2003), 451.

disseminated, and controlled standard English (see Chapters 9 and 10 for earlier manifestations of this particular domain of language activity), it seems likely that we will see a much greater presence of informal written interaction than at any previous stage in the history of the language, and thus the rapid emergence and consolidation of local group norms of usage—several of which will privilege non-standard forms. These new varieties are bound to achieve a more developed written representation than would ever have been possible before, and through the global reach of the Internet they may well extend their influence beyond their locality or country of origin. A whole new range of Internet-mediated regional written standards is the likely outcome. And as the amount of written language on the Internet will eventually far exceed that available in traditional print form, a new type of relationship between non-standard varieties and standard English will one day emerge.

What is especially interesting, from a linguistic point of view, is that most of this material will be unedited. Editorial involvement represents the biggest difference between speech and writing. By 'editing' I mean the presence of an intermediate stage of adaptation (usually by a professional) of a speaker/writer's output before it is received by a listener/reader. Most of the spoken language around us is unedited, in this sense, the only real exception being certain kinds of broadcast and cinematic material where producers, directors, or recording specialists may be heavily involved. By contrast, most of the written language around us is edited, often several times over. The exceptions include only informal letter-writing, graffiti, and a few other manuscript phenomena, which in modern times comprise a very small proportion of written English. The Internet is changing this balance—not so much on the web, where a great deal of editing takes place, but in email, chatroom, and instant messenger interaction, and especially in blogging, where the most 'naked' forms of writing appear. There is no single style. Even in the short extract above, we can see different principles at work in the use of capitalization, punctuation, abbreviations, and non-standard spellings. These personality-influenced variations will certainly increase, as the population-base of the Internet grows, and the present generation of Internet-literate individuals grows old. But in all genres, from web diaries to fantasy games, we will expect to find writing which reflects the speech rhythms, regional and class backgrounds, ages, personalities, and education levels of the participants. There has been nothing like it since the manuscript era of Middle English. And the renewal of connection with medieval times may in due course be complete, for digital representations of handwriting already exist, and may well become routine—assuming of course that, at this point in the future, people are still being taught handwriting!

At the same time, the long-term linguistic character of the Internet remains unclear. This is partly because the technological revolution is in its earliest phase. Given the changes that have taken place in the last decade or so (the web itself is a creation from as recently as 1991, and mobile phone technology more recent still), we must expect there to be further innovative developments, especially of an interactive kind, which will push the language in unexpected directions. A spoken dimension of Internet use, supplementing the present graphic dimension, is in prospect. It is never possible to predict language outcomes. Text-messaging, with its array of idiosyncratic abbreviations such as *lol*, used on p. 403, or *c u l8r* ('see you later'), was a totally unexpected linguistic innovation in the UK in the late 1990s. And since 2000 we have seen even more esoteric forms of usage arising out of the way in which the Internet is being used in unpredictable ways. In relation to emails, for example, the early years of the new millennium have seen most email users suddenly having to cope with the arrival in their inboxes of large numbers of unwanted messages ('spam') which have been distributed in huge quantities from a single source. Efforts to prevent such messages through automatic filtering of their subject lines have resulted in ingenious efforts on the part of spammers to evade the filters. A whole new genre of English has been the consequence, chiefly seen in the subject-line of emails, and illustrated by such usages as:

supr vi-agra online now znwygghsxp
VI @ GRA 75% off regular xxp wybzz lusfg
fully stocked online pharmac^y
Great deals, prescription d[rugs

Many of the bizarre graphological expressions have been generated randomly, in itself an unprecedented procedure in everyday written communication.

Chatrooms provide another domain of innovation which has led to unexpected linguistic outcomes. I am not here referring to the distinctive use of rebuses and colloquial abbreviations which characterize 'textspeak'. It was perhaps not surprising to see the emergence of such forms in the technically constrained environment of a mobile phone, where there was a limit of 160 characters per screen, and space was at a premium. Nor was it surprising to see such abbreviations taken up universally in teenage interaction, where they are widely used as an economical and 'cool' style of communication. Much more unexpected was the way users adapted so quickly to the communicative potential of the medium and exploited it as part of a newfound virtual identity in which anonymity is the norm and the choice of personality (as expressed through a nickname or an on-screen character, or 'avatar') is limited only by imagination.

The uncontrolled nature of many sites (especially teenage chat sites) has motivated their participants to indulge in every kind of fantasy, regularly resulting in written representations of language which previously would have been confined to maximally informal speech, and which would never have been included in traditional publishing outlets in the interests of public decency.

Obscene or aggressive exchanges have presumably been part of youngster communication since the invention of the teenager, and have been given some study. For example, sociolinguists have long known about the kind of ritual street confrontations described under the heading of 'verbal duelling',[6] in which participants try to outdo each other in flights of linguistic fancy exploiting taboo language to the full. Competitive joke rituals similarly have an ancient history. What is unusual is to see such rituals carried on, at great length and often with great verbal skill, in the written language—especially when such material is spelled and punctuated according to the conventions of standard English, as happens in a surprising number of cases. It is a new genre of English writing—and one which will be very difficult to research, as many of the interactions are accompanied by the exchange of webcam images which, if downloaded to a researcher's computer, would bring obvious risks. There is, understandably, immense concern over the opportunities presented by chatrooms to paedophiles, who simulate the language found there as a preliminary to gaining the trust of the participants. It is perhaps the first time in the history of linguistics that a domain of language has become off-limits (especially to male researchers) without a sophisticated system of protective legal safeguards being first put in place. And it may well be that several domains of Internet use will eventually be incapable of unimpeded investigation.

This, then, is a necessary qualification about the linguistic character of future Internet English. Editing, in the traditional sense, there may not be. But moderating, in the modern sense, there certainly will be. Many chatrooms are now moderated—watched over by a person whose role is to exclude unacceptable submissions to a site being seen by other participants. The notion of acceptability is very wide-ranging: it includes people who send in messages which are irrelevant ('off-topic'), aggressive ('flaming'), misleading ('trolling'), blasphemous, or obscene. It focuses on content, rather than linguistic structure (although doubtless there is a punctuation chatroom site somewhere where a moderator is sanctioning apostrophes), and usually takes the form of the deletion of a whole message rather than an editing of it. But the natural evolution of the discourse is inevitably

---

[6] See, for example, A. Dundes, J. W Leach, and B. Özkök, 'The Strategy of Turkish Boys' Verbal Duelling Rhymes', in J. J. Gumperz and D. Hymes (eds), *Directions in Sociolinguistics* (New York: Holt, Rinehart and Winston, 1972), 130–60.

affected by such activity. How much, it is difficult to say. It is practically and economically impossible to moderate everything and, even in moderated sites, the attention-span of the moderator has its limitations—especially when dozens of messages are arriving simultaneously from many members, and being displayed at various locations on screen. The degree of sanitization varies greatly across the records of chatroom interactions, and also depends greatly on the personality of the moderators, whose censorship reflects to a degree their individual beliefs and tastes. Many sites publish logs of what their participants have said. However, many of these logs are a remove or two away from what actually went on in the session. Coping with this kind of material will be a new challenge for corpus linguistics.

THE LONG-TERM CONSEQUENCES OF EDUCATIONAL CHANGE

During the latter part of the twentieth century, a noticeable trend towards a more egalitarian society began to reduce the severity of social-class distinctions, recognize the value of diversity, safeguard the rights of minorities, and revitalize demotic values. The immediate linguistic effect was a move away from the prescriptive ethos of the past 250 years which has been described in Chapters 9 and 10, and it brought the introduction of new educational paradigms of language study. But in an age when the prescriptive tradition is still very much part of the language consciousness of older members of society, the transition between old and new paradigms presents the new generation (and their teachers) with an uncertain linguistic climate whose character is still evolving.

The new climate has particularly called for a reassessment of the relationship between standard and non-standard language and for a fresh and realistic appraisal of just what a 'standard' language involves. We seem to be at a transitional point between two worlds. The 'old world' is one where a tiny number of rules, selected and defined by prescriptive grammarians, totally conditioned our sense of acceptable 'standard' usage, so that all other usages were considered to be inferior or corrupt, and excluded from serious consideration. The 'new world' is one where non-standard regional usage is achieving a new presence and respectability within society, reminiscent of that found in Middle English when, as we have seen in Chapter 4, dialect variation in literature was widespread and uncontentious. It is not a question, in this new climate, of non-standard in any sense replacing standard. Rather, the two dimensions of language use are being brought into a new relationship, in which the essential role of the standard language (as a means of guaranteeing intelligibility and continuity among educated people) is seen to complement the essential role of the non-standard language (as a means of giving expression to local identities). It is a move away from the confrontational situation which has had so many traumatic consequences for individual language users, most of whom have been brought up to believe that there is something seriously wrong with their demotic speech.

Eliminating such feelings from public consciousness will nevertheless take some time. As Chapter 13 has pointed out, once people have been given an inferiority complex about the way they speak or write, they find it difficult to be rid of it. But it is only a matter of time. In the later decades of the twentieth century there were clear signs that institutionalized prescriptivism was already beginning to come to an end. The most important area of change was in educational practice—especially significant because it was only through the school system that prescriptivism had been able to propagate itself. In the UK, from the 1970s, changes in school syllabuses and examination systems introduced a new dispensation. The unthinking adherence to mechanical sentence analysis and old-style canons of correctness began to be replaced by a broad-based investigation of the functions of language in all their social manifestations—a 'language in use' era of linguistic pedagogy. By the end of the 1990s, in the new National Curriculum, as well as in the syllabuses which were being devised for higher examinations, the study of linguistic forms had been added to functions, with a complete change in emphasis. Similar educational changes took place in other parts of the English-speaking world.

The new emphasis integrated the insights of the 'language in use' approach with aspects of the earlier tradition of structural analysis, now seen through linguistic spectacles. Classes and exam papers no longer asked students to parse sentences or to make decisions about correctness in relation to such issues as split infinitives. Instead, the questions began to make students *explain* what happens when language is used—to go beyond the mere 'spotting' of a linguistic feature (a passive, a simile, a piece of alliteration) to a mode of inquiry in which they explored the reasons lying behind the linguistic choices being made by language users. It was no longer enough to say, 'I see an unusual adjective order in that poem'. The interesting answer—and the one which gained the marks in an exam—was to be able to say why it was there. Only in that way, it was reasoned, would students be able to develop a sense of the consequences of choosing one kind of language rather than another (such as formal vs. informal), when it came to using language themselves or evaluating the effect of a language choice upon other people. The aim, in short, was to promote a more responsive and responsible approach to language, in which students would come to understand why people use language in the way they do, and would put this knowledge to active use to become more able to control language for themselves.

This change in emphasis is now being realized in the form of textbooks and teaching materials,[7] but the new approach does not yet have an agreed name. It is not a matter of a 'prescriptive' approach being replaced by a 'descriptive' one, as has sometimes been suggested, for this pedagogy goes well beyond description into a world of explanation and evaluation. A better term would be 'pragmatic' (as opposed to 'dogmatic'), with all that this implies—an ability to adapt knowledge to meet the needs of differing circumstances and a readiness to judge cases on their merits. The pragmatic approach instils an awareness that variation and change are normal features of linguistic life, demanding recognition and respect. And it carries with it the corollary that those who make use of this variation must themselves be recognized and respected. In its strongest and most positive manifestation, the pragmatic approach replaces the concept of 'eternal vigilance' (beloved of prescriptivists and purists) by one of 'eternal tolerance'.

Although an educational perspective is crucial, in moving away from an institutionalized prescriptivism towards a more egalitarian linguistic era, it cannot operate alone. Other social institutions need to be involved. Indeed, without a sense of linguistic disquiet within society as a whole, it is unlikely that any change in educational practice would have taken place at all. What is interesting about the later decades of the twentieth century is the way that different social trends began to reinforce pragmatic educational linguistic thinking. In the UK, for example, leading media organizations such as the BBC opened their doors to regional speech, partly as a reaction to the emergence of independent local radio and television stations. A fine radio presenter, Susan Rae, had to stand down from Radio 4 in the early 1980s because of antagonism towards her Scots accent, but she was back reading the news on Radio 4 at the end of 2003. Business management recognized the importance of speech variation in interacting with clients: the regional accents of a new linguistic order (international as well as intranational) may be heard now at the end of a telephone at many a call centre. Organizations such as the Plain English Campaign focused attention on the linguistic responsibilities of organizations towards the needs of the individual. Political correctness, in the

---

[7] See, for example, D. Crystal, *Making Sense of English Grammar* (London: Pearson Education, 2004).

best sense, fostered notions of gender and racial equality. And there was a fresh awareness of the nature of regional and ethnic identity, which led to a greater valuing of linguistic diversity. These trends had their parallels in other English-speaking countries.

But changes in linguistic attitudes and practices are not accepted overnight, or even over a decade. The cumulative effects of ten generations of prescriptive teaching are still around us. Organizations which were set up to 'safeguard' the English language, with their founding ideals in the prescriptive era, continue to exist and to attract members. Usage manuals presenting an idealized vision of standard English as a uniform, unchanging, and universal norm of correctness continue to be published. And senior managers today, whether in government, law, medicine, business, education, or the media, cannot rid themselves entirely of prescriptive thinking, because they are the last generation to have experienced this approach in their schooling. Their influence is considerable, because they unconsciously pass on their linguistic anxieties and preoccupations, often half-remembered and poorly understood, to subordinates who, in the absence of linguistic knowledge of their own, accept their opinions as dictates. In a few years time, the new generation of schoolchildren, well-grounded in pragmatic principles, will be out there in society, able to counter unthinking prescriptive attitudes; and once they are in senior positions, the confrontation will be over. But in the meantime, innumerable schoolchildren and adults have developed feelings of inadequacy and inferiority about their natural way of speaking, or about certain features of their writing, being led to believe that their practice is in some way 'ugly' or 'incorrect'. We are coming towards the close of a linguistically intolerant era, but—as happens in last-ditch situations—conservative reaction can be especially strong as seen in the Trussian promulgation of 'zero tolerance' in *Eats, Shoots & Leaves* (2003).[8]

The intellectual achievement of the prescriptive writers of the eighteenth century was to give definition to the future character of the standard; but their emotional legacy was to instil in everyone guilt about everyday usage and a fear of 'breaking the rules' which can reach paranoid proportions. It was they alone who chose which features of grammar were to be the sign of an educated writer, and their prescriptions were sufficiently powerful to persuade generations of writers how to behave, right up to the present. The main contribution of linguistics to this debacle has been to develop a fresh conception of standard English—one which gets away from prescriptive preoccupations, occupying as they do only a

[8] See L. Truss, *Eats, Shoots & Leaves. The Zero Tolerance Approach to Punctuation* (London: Profile Books, 2003).

tiny proportion of grammatical 'space', and allows us to concentrate on the core areas of grammatical structure that actually do govern the way we express and respond to meaning and style. In a typical reference grammar of 1,500 pages, only a dozen or so pages will be taken up with the issues that so worried the prescriptive grammarians. What linguistics has done is underline the importance of the topics covered by the remaining pages—topics which turn out to be much more closely bound up with questions of intelligibility, clarity, precision, and elegance of expression than could ever be found in the pages of a prescriptive grammar.

A transition between linguistic eras is not a comfortable stage. It takes time for people to adjust their mindsets to assimilate new ways of thinking, and for teachers to be prepared to cope with this thinking. It took half a century for the prescriptive era to become firmly established, and it will probably take a similar period to be fully weaned away from it. In 2005 we are perhaps half-way through this period. But a new social climate has emerged, in which new linguistic mores are being formed by the impact of globalization and technology. It is a world where intranational preoccupations have been firmly put in their place by an international presence of unprecedented proportions—with the population of world English-language users approaching two billion. No one nation can any longer be said to 'own' English, and no one nation's anxieties over local norms of usage will make much impact in a world where diverse regional standards are the norm, and where the Internet provides these varieties with new levels of public display. A new intellectual sociolinguistic climate is slowly but surely being formed, to which the present volume will no doubt make a significant contribution.

REFERENCES AND SUGGESTIONS FOR FURTHER READING

The long-term consequences of globalization

There is little as yet published on linguistic trends in the new century, as the period has hardly begun; but the globalization and technological trends noted in this chapter were repeatedly anticipated in the 1990s. I have discussed these trends in some detail in Crystal (2001, 2004c) and the literary trends in Crystal (2004a). On the changing role of English, see McArthur (1998a), Graddol and Meinhof (1999), and Burns and Coffin (2001), as well as Chapter 13 in this volume. On the evolution of standard English, see the papers in Wright (2000). The position of English in Europe is discussed in a series of essays edited by Görlach (2002), and overseas in several papers in Volume 5 of the *Cambridge History of the English Language* (Burchfield 1994).

The long-term consequences of the Internet

On computer-mediated communication, see the collection of essays edited by Herring (1996) and the volume by Baron (2000); for its impact on general English usage, see especially Crystal (2006) and also Crystal (2004*d*).

The long-term consequences of educational change

Doughty *et al.* (1971) provide a useful example of the 'language in use' era of linguistic pedagogy. Recent educational trends are discussed in Crystal (2004*a*), which is a development of the position adopted by the papers in Watts and Trudgill (2002).

A Chronology of English

*c*1500 BC	First evidence for some languages of the Indo-European group.
*c*1000–500 BC	Emergence of Proto-Germanic.
*c*300–200 BC	Break-up of Proto-Germanic.
*c*45–*c*410	Britain becomes part of the Roman Empire, forming the Roman colony 'Britannia'.
*c*410	Collapse of Roman Empire; Romans leave Britain.
449	Traditional date for the invasion of Britain by the Angles, Saxons, and Jutes.
597	Arrival of Roman mission in England and introduction of Christianity.
601	Augustine becomes the first Archbishop of Canterbury.
664	Synod of Whitby.
670s	Presumed date of composition of Cædmon's *Hymn*.
*c*700	First surviving written evidence of Old English.
*c*700–20	Lindisfarne Gospels written (in Latin).
731	Bede completes his *Ecclesiastical History of the English People* (in Latin).
735	Death of Bede.
757 (–96)	Reign of Offa as King of Mercia.
780s	Period of Scandinavian invasion begins.
793	Sacking of the monastery at Lindisfarne by Scandinavian invaders.
849	Alfred born in Wantage, Oxfordshire.
870s	Scandinavian settlement in England.

871(–99)	1	Reign of Alfred as King of Wessex.
	2	Production of translations of, for example, Bede's *Ecclesiastical History*, Boethius's *Consolation of Philosophy*, Gregory's *Pastoral Care*.
878		Battle of Edington, in which Alfred triumphs over Vikings and agrees on areas of Scandinavian settlement (later to be known as the 'Dane-law').
from *c*890		Production of *Anglo-Saxon Chronicle*.
899		Death of Alfred.
937		Battle of Brunanburh.
from *c*950		Benedictine Reform.
*c*950 (–970)		Glosses to Lindisfarne Gospel added (in Old English) by Aldred, Provost of Chester-le-Street in Northumbria.
*c*955		Birth of Ælfric.
*c*970s		Exeter Book and Vercelli Book copied.
990s		Ælfric writes his *Catholic Homilies*.
991		Battle of Maldon.
*c*1000		Copying of Junius (or Cædmon) manuscript and *Beowulf* manuscript.
1005		Ælfric becomes Abbot of Eynsham in Oxfordshire.
*c*1010		Death of Ælfric.
1016(–35)		Reign of the Danish king Cnut over England.
1066		Battle of Hastings; William I (the Conqueror) reigns over England (until 1087).
1086–7		Compilation of the Domesday Book, the first survey of the nation's land resources.
*c*1122		The Peterborough Chronicle is copied, and the First Continuation begins.
1154		Peterborough Chronicle ends.
*c*1170s		The *Ormulum*.
1172		Henry II becomes King of Ireland.

1204	Loss of Normandy; England becomes the sole remaining home of Norman English.
1215	Magna Carta.
c1225	*Ancrene Wisse.*
1258	Proclamation of Henry III: first Royal Proclamation issued in English since the Norman Conquest.
1284	Annexation of Wales.
c1300	*Cursor Mundi.*
1330–80	Evidence of East Midland influence on language of London; evidence of limited standardization in manuscripts written in London.
1337(–1454)	Hundred Years War with France.
1340	Dan Michel's *Ayenbite of Inwyt* completed.
c1343	Birth of Geoffrey Chaucer.
1348	First outbreak of the Black Death.
1362	Statute of Pleading; English becomes the official language of the law courts.
1380s	Wycliffite Bible (first complete Bible in English).
1381	The Peasants' Revolt.
1387	John Trevisa completes English translation of Ranulph Higden's *Polychronicon* (1327).
c1395	Second version of the Wycliffite Bible in English.
1400	Death of Geoffrey Chaucer.
1417	Signet Office begins issuing the king's letters in English.
1422	Brewers' Guild of London decides to switch to English as language of proceedings and accounts.
1425	First surviving Paston letter.
1430	Chancery adopts East Midland *koiné* as its written form.
c1450	Death of John Lydgate.
c1470	Death of Thomas Malory.

1475	Printing of *The Recuyell of the Historyes of Troye* by William Caxton in Bruges—the first book to be printed in English.
1476	William Caxton sets up his printing press in Westminster and publishes the first printed books in England.
1485	Henry VII becomes the first Tudor King after Richard III is killed at the Battle of Bosworth.
1489	French no longer used as the language of Parliament.
1490	Caxton's *Eneydos* published (with prologue remarking on variability of English).
1491	Death of Caxton; succeeded by Wynkyn de Worde, who moves his printing press to Fleet Street.
1492	Christopher Columbus arrives in West Indies.
1497	John Cabot reaches Newfoundland, providing the first English contact with Canada.
1525–6	Publication of William Tyndale's New Testament in English.
1534	English Reformation (Henry VIII breaks with the Catholic Church).
1535	Publication of Miles Coverdale's Bible (the first complete Bible to be printed in English).
1536	First act of union between England and Wales.
1542	Andrew Boorde, *Fyrst Boke of the Introduction of Knowledge*, illustrates regional dialects.
1549	Book of Common Prayer.
1562	John Hawkins starts British slave trade.
1564	Birth of Shakespeare.
1565	Lawrence Nowell, *Vocabularium Saxiconum*, first Old English glossary; included northern English words.
1567	Thomas Harman, *A Caveat or Warening for Common Cursetors*, first glossary of the 'canting language' or dialect of the underworld.
1577(–80)	Francis Drake circumnavigates the world.
1585	Thomas Herriot, a scientist, visits Roanoke in America to gather information on the flora, fauna, resources, people, and languages.

1586	Publication of William Bullokar's *Pamphlet for Grammar*, the first grammar of English.
1600	Founding of the East India Company.
1600(−)	English begins to be used in records of legal proceedings.
1603	Union of the Crowns; James VI of Scotland succeeds to the English throne, as James I, after death of Elizabeth I.
1604	Robert Cawdrey, *A Table Alphabeticall*, the first English–English dictionary, translates 'hard words' and inkhorn terms into 'common' English.
1607	Jamestown in Chesapeake Bay founded in North America—the first successful British colony.
1611	The Authorized Version of the English Bible (the 'King James' Bible), attempts to resolve questions about Englishing the Word of God.
1616	Death of Shakespeare.
1619	Alexander Gil, *Logonomia Anglica*, first vernacular grammar to treat English dialects systematically.
1623	Publication of the First Folio edition of Sheakespeare's plays.
1653	Publication of John Wallis's *Grammatica linguae Anglicanae*.
1655	Britain ousts the Spanish from Jamaica and extends its influence and language into the Caribbean and to West Africa.
1660	1 Restoration of the monarchy.
	2 Royal Society of London founded, in part, as the first English language academy.
1670	Hudson's Bay Company formed.
1710	Copyright Act.
1711	Publication of Greenwood's *Essay towards a practical English Grammar*.
1712	Publication (anonymously) of *A Proposal for Correcting, Improving and Ascertaining the English Tongue; in a Letter* by Jonathan Swift, which proposes the foundation of an Academy to regulate English usage.
1713	Having defeated the French, the British exile French-speakers from Atlantic Canada. A later attempt by France to maintain colonies in

present-day Illinois failed, and their defeat at Battle of Quebec in 1759 ensures dominance by English speakers in the west.

1714   Death of Queen Anne: all chances of setting up an English Academy lost.

1715   Elisabeth Elstob published the first grammar of Old English.

c1745   Publication of Ann Fisher's *New Grammar* (Newcastle upon Tyne), the first grammar to be published by a woman.

1747   Samuel Johnson published the Plan for his Dictionary.

1752   Britain (and its colonies) move from the Julian to the Gregorian calendar, losing 11 days between 2 and 14 September.

1755   Publication of Samuel Johnson's two-volume *Dictionary of the English Language*.

1757   In India, the British military victory at Plassy institutes English dominance in South Asia that will last until 1947. In the hands of expatriate and native soldiers and bureaucrats, English becomes the language of government.

1762   Publication of Robert Lowth's *Short Introduction to English Grammar*.

1770   Botany Bay, Australia, discovered by James Cook.

1775   War of American Independence begins.

1776   Declaration of American Independence.

1780   Publication of Thomas Sheridan's *General Dictionary of the English Language. One main object of which, is, to establish a plain and permanent standard of pronunciation.*

1783   US Declaration of Independence formally recognized by the British.

1783   Noah Webster's *American Spelling Book* (the 'Blue-backed Speller') published.

1787   Abolitionists in Britain establish Sierra Leone in West Africa and settle 2000 freed slaves there. They employ English in governing themselves and the indigenous peoples.

1788   Establishment of a penal colony near present-day Sydney begins to form the distinctive English of Australia.

1789   Publication of Noah Webster's *Dissertations on the English Language*, which advocated the institution of a national American standard of usage.

1791	Publication of John Walker's *Critical Pronouncing Dictionary and Expositor of the English Language.*
1793	A delegation from Britain arrives in China to open trade relations. 'Pidgin English' begins to emerge as a trade language.
1795	Publication of Lindley Murray's *English Grammar, adapted to the different classes of learners.* Over 1.5 million copies would be sold by 1850.
1800	Act of Union with Ireland.
1801	Union with Ireland begins.
1803	Purchasing the huge central portion of what is now the USA, the US government ensured the extension of English throughout much of the American west.
1806	British establish control of South Africa (English becomes the official language in 1822).
1810	William Hazlitt publishes *A New and Improved Grammar of the English Tongue.*
1821	Liberia is supported by the USA as a place of re-settlement for freed slaves. All who arrive in Monrovia as part of this 'colonization' effort are English speakers.
1825	Opening of the Stockton to Darlington Railway.
1828	Publication of Noah Webster's *American Dictionary of the English Language.*
1830	Opening of the Liverpool to Manchester Railway.
1832	Passing of the First Reform Bill.
1837	Death of William IV; accession of Queen Victoria.
1840	1 In England, introduction of the Penny Post on 10 January; by the end of the year 168 million letters have been posted (compared to 76 million in 1839).
	2 The Treaty of Waitangi was the foundation document in the establishment of exclusive British sovereignty in New Zealand.
1842	Foundation of the London Philological Society.
1844	First telegraph line established between Baltimore and Washington.

1845–48	The annexation of Texas and the defeat of the Mexican army extends the USA westward to California. Vast numbers of migrants to the west, especially after the gold rush of 1848, overwhelm the institutions of Spanish culture.
1850	Public Libraries Act.
1854–6	Crimean War.
1858	Proposal for *A New English Dictionary* (later known as *The Oxford English Dictionary*) made by the London Philological Society.
1866	Atlantic Cable completed, linking Valencia, Ireland and Trinity Bay, Newfoundland by submarine cable.
1867	1 Second Reform Bill (extending franchise to all those who could demonstrate ownership of property worth £7).
	2 Canada given self-government.
1869	Alexander Ellis publishes the first volume of his *On Early English Pronunciation* in which he defined 'received pronunciation' for the first time.
1870	In England and Wales, Elementary Education Act passed, providing compulsory elementary education for all children.
1872	Education in Scotland made compulsory until the age of 14.
1873	Founding of the English Dialect Society.
1876	Introduction of the telephone by Alexander Graham Bell.
1877	Invention of the phonograph by Thomas Edison.
1881	Education in England and Wales becomes compulsory until the age of 10.
1884	First fascicle of *A New English Dictionary on Historical Principles* (later *OED*) published, covering the words *A-Ant*.
1888	The British East Africa Company is established to oversee the development of British interests in Kenya, Zanzibar, and Uganda.
1889	Publication of fifth volume of A. J. Ellis's *On Early English Pronunciation: The Existing Phonology of English Dialects*.
1892	Publication of Joseph Wright's *Grammar of the Dialect of Windhill*.
1896	The English Dialect Society disbanded.

1897	Founding of the first regional dialect organization, The Yorkshire Dialect Society.

1898(–1905) 1 The Spanish–American War extends US dominance from the continent of North America and into Puerto Rico and the Philippines.

2 In England, publication of *The English Dialect Dictionary* and *English Dialect Grammar*, edited by Joseph Wright.

1899(–1902) 1 The South African War (Boer War) concludes with the British in control of present-day South Africa.

2 First magnetic sound recordings.

1901 1 Guglielmo Marconi received the first transatlantic radio signals, sent between Poldhu, Cornwall and Signal Hill in New-foundland.

2 Australia is transformed from a colony to a commonwealth. Among the first laws passed was the Immigration Restriction Act which required all prospective immigrants 'to write out at dictation and sign in the presence of the [custom's] officer a passage of fifty words in length in a European language directed by the officer.' This language incorporated the 'dictation test' used in Natal in 1897 to exclude most Indians from South Africa.

3 Death of Queen Victoria.

1906 First public radio broadcast.

1907 New Zealand becomes a dominion of the British Empire.

1910 The Union of South Africa becomes a dominion of the British Empire.

1914(–18) The *First World War* (UK), *World War I* (US).

1918 The Englishman Sir Evelyn Wrench and the American Alexander Smith Cochran found the English-Speaking Union, to encourage partnership between the UK, its dominions, and the USA. [There is currently an English-Speaking Union of the Commonwealth (HQ: London) and of the United States (HQ: New York).]

1919 The German colony of Tanganyika in East Africa is ceded to Britain, and Kamerun in West Central Africa is divided between France (Cameroun) and Britain (Cameroon).

1920 Kenya becomes a British colony.

1921	Ireland achieves Home Rule and is separated from Great Britain. Gaelic is made an 'official' language in addition to English.
1922	Foundation of British Broadcasting Company (BBC).
1925	The Afrikaans language gains official status alongside English in South Africa.
1928	Completion of the first edition of the *Oxford English Dictionary*.
1931	The British Commonwealth is formed, and South Africa becomes a dominion of the British Empire.
1934	The British Council is founded, with its headquarters in London, as a vehicle for British cultural diplomacy and teaching English as a foreign or second language.
1935	The Philippines becomes a self-governing Commonwealth in association with the USA.
1936	The Republic of Ireland severs all constitutional links with Great Britain.
1937	In Wales, a new constitution for the festival the National Eisteddfod makes Welsh its official language.
1939–45	The *Second World War* (UK), *World War II* (US).
1945	Signing of the United Nations Charter and the decision to make the headquarters of the UN in the USA gives English an unprecedented importance as a language of diplomacy.
1946	1 The Philippines gains its independence from the USA.
	2 Transjordan gains its independence from the UK as Jordan.
1947	1 India is partitioned into Pakistan and India and is freed from British control. The constitution provides that English remain the language of national government for only fifteen years. The approach of that date results in riots led by those fearing the dominance of Hindi and the loss of power for their own language communities. English remains as the most important of India's 'national languages' even though few learn it as a mother tongue.
	2 New Zealand gains its independence from the UK, and joins the Commonwealth.
1948	1 In England, the Survey of English Dialects is founded.

2 Burma gains its independence from the UK, and declines membership of the Commonwealth.

3 Ceylon gains its independence from the UK as Sri Lanka, and joins the Commonwealth.

1949   1 The Linguistic Survey of Scotland founded.

2 Newfoundland becomes a province of Canada.

3 Two New Guinea territories are combined by the United Nations as an Australian mandate, the UN Trust Territory of Papua and New Guinea.

1952   Puerto Rico (see 1898) becomes a Commonwealth in association with the US, with Spanish as its first and English its second language.

1953   The creation of the United States Information Agency (USIA) and its overseas arm, the United States Information Service (USIS).

1955   About this time, the number of speakers using English as an additional language surpassed the number who had learned it as a first language.

1957   1 The New Zealand-born lexicographer Robert W. Burchfield becomes the editor of a *Supplement* to the *Oxford English Dictionary* (eventually published in four volumes 1972–86).

2 The Gold Coast (as Ghana) and Malaya gain their independence from the UK.

1960   Nigeria becomes independent from the British and Somalia from the British and Italians.

1961   1 South Africa becomes a republic, leaves the Commonwealth, and adopts Afrikaans and English as its official languages.

2 The British colony of Cameroon divides, part joining Nigeria, part joining the ex-French colony of Cameroun, to become the Republic of Cameroon, with French and English as its official languages.

3 Sierra Leone, Kuwait, and Cyprus gain their independence from the UK.

4 In England, 1961–72, publication of the *Basic Material* of the Survey of English Dialects.

1962   1 Jamaica, Trinidad and Tobago, and Uganda gain their independence from the UK.

2   Caribbean English becomes the vehicle for popular culture, especially calypso, Rastafarianism, and reggae.

1963   1   Nigeria becomes independent as part of the wave of 'decolonizing' that took place throughout the former British colonies. West African Pidgin English emerges as a major and widely spoken regional language.

2   Kenya gains its independence from the UK.

3   Malaya unites with the newly independent colony of Borneo to become Malaysia.

4   In Wales, the first public protests by the Cyndeithas yr Iaith Gymraeg (the Welsh Language Society) take place, seeking a fuller use of Welsh in the Principality.

1964   1   Malta gains its independence from the UK.

2   Tanganyika and Zanzibar (as Tanzania), Nyasaland (as Malawi), and Northern Rhodesia (as Zambia) gain their independence from the UK.

1965   Gambia, the Maldives, and Singapore gain their independence from the UK.

1966   Barbados, Basutoland (as Lesotho), Bechuanaland (as Botswana), and British Guiana (as Guyana) gain their independence from the UK.

1967   1   In the UK, the Welsh Language Act gives the Welsh language equal validity with English in Wales, and the Principality is no longer deemed to be part of England.

2   Aden gains its independence from the UK as South Yemen.

1968   1   The Survey of Anglo-Welsh Dialects is founded.

2   Swaziland, Mauritius, and Nauru gain their independence from the UK.

1969   English and French become the official languages of Canada.

1970   Fiji and Tonga gain their independence from the UK.

1971   Bahrain, Qatar, and the Trucial States (as the United Arab Emirates) gain their independence from the UK.

1972   1   Martin Cooper makes the first public call on a personal, portable cell phone.

2   East Pakistan secedes and becomes Bangladesh.

1973	The Bahamas gain their independence from the UK.
1974	1 The Cyngor Yr Iaith Gymraeg/Council for the Welsh Language is set up to advise the Secretary of State for Wales on matters concerning the Welsh language.
	2 Grenada gains its independence from the UK.
1975	Papua New Guinea gains its independence from Australia.
1976	The Seychelles gains its independence from the UK.
1977	In Quebec, Loi/Bill 101 is passed, making French the sole official language of the province and banning public signs in other languages.
1978	1 In England, publication of *The Linguistic Atlas of England*.
	2 Dominica, the Solomon Islands, and Tuvalu gain their independence from the UK.
1979	St Lucia, St Vincent and the Grenadines, and the Gilbert and Ellice Islands (as Kiribati) gain their independence from the UK.
1980	The UK government averts a fast to the death by Gwynfor Evans, leader of Plaid Cymru (the Welsh National Party), by honouring election pledges to provide a fourth television channel broadcasting in both Welsh and English.
1981	Antigua (as Antigua and Barbuda) and British Honduras (as Belize) gain their independence from the UK.
1982	Canada's constitution, until then kept in London, is 'patriated' to Ottawa.
1983	St Kitts and Nevis gains its independence from the UK.
1984	1 Brunei gains its independence from the UK.
	2 David Rosewarne identifies 'Estuary English'.
1990	South West Africa gains its independence from South Africa as Namibia.
1991	1 Tim Berners-Lee launches the World Wide Web.
	2 The Marshall Islands and Micronesia gain their independence from the USA.
1994	Text messaging introduced.

1996   South Africa ratifies a constitution in which English becomes one of
                eleven 'official' languages.

1997   Hong Kong is returned to China and becomes the last of the colonies
                in Asia to be freed from British sovereignty.

1999   A Survey of Regional English proposed.

2000   The European Union fosters bilingualism as a goal. In 2000, the largest
                of the then fifteen member states were estimated to have the following
                mother tongues: German (24%), French (16%), English (16%), Italian
                (16%), Spanish (11%). Once the population speaking these languages
                in addition to the mother tongue were added in, the figures show:
                English (47%), German (32%), French (28%), Italian (18%), and
                Spanish (15%).

2003   Text messages sent in the UK pass 20 billion.

2004   The British Library 'Collect Britain: English Accents and Dialects'
                website launched.

2005   The British Broadcasting Corporation 'Voices' project launched on 17
                January.

NOTES ON CONTRIBUTORS

RICHARD W. BAILEY is Fred Newton Scott Collegiate Professor of English at the University of Michigan, Ann Arbor. He is past president of both the American Dialect Society and the Dictionary Society of North America. His books include *Images of English* (1991), *Nineteenth-Century English* (1996), and a biography of a philological murderer, *Rogue Scholar: the Sinister Career and Celebrated Death of Edward H. Rulloff* (2003).

PAULA BLANK is Associate Professor of English at the College of William and Mary in Virginia. She is the author of *Broken English: Dialects and the Politics of Language in Renaissance Writings* (1996), and articles on the language and rhetoric of Spenser, Shakespeare, Donne, and Jonson. She is currently working on a book on the rhetoric of 'equality' in the Renaissance.

MARILYN CORRIE is a lecturer in the Department of English Language and Literature at University College London. She is the author of a forthcoming study of Sir Thomas Malory's *Le Morte D'Arthur* and the editor of *A Concise Companion to Middle English Literature*, forthcoming from Blackwell.

DAVID CRYSTAL was Professor of Linguistics at the University of Reading for several years, and is currently Honorary Professor of Linguistics at the University of Wales, Bangor. His authored works are mainly in applied linguistics and English language studies, and he is editor of a series of general reference encyclopedias, first for Cambridge University Press and now for Penguin Books, along with their online incarnations.

TERRY HOAD is a Fellow of St Peter's College, Oxford, and Tutor in English Language and Medieval Literature. He is also a lecturer in the English Faculty at Oxford University, and previously taught at Queen Mary College, London, and at the University of Arizona. His publications include the second (revised) edition (1978) of Henry Sweet's *Second Anglo-Saxon Reader*, and *The Concise Oxford Dictionary of English Etymology* (1986).

SUSAN IRVINE is Professor of English Language and Literature in the Department of English at University College London. She is the author of *Old English Homilies from MS Bodley 343* (1993) and *The Anglo-Saxon Chronicle MS E* (2004), and co-author (with Bruce Mitchell) of *Beowulf Repunctuated* (2000). She has also published articles on writings of the transitional period between Old and Middle English, on rhetoric and meaning in Old English poems, and on King Alfred's translation of Boethius's

Consolation of Philosophy. She is currently working (with Malcolm Godden) on a critical edition of Alfred's *Boethius.*

TOM MCARTHUR is an Honorary Fellow of the Institute of Linguists, London. He has, among other posts and activities, been Head of English, Cathedral School, Bombay/Mumbai, India, an Associate Professor of English at the Université du Québec in Canada, an Honorary Fellow at the University of Exeter (in the Dictionary Research Centre), and a Distinguished Visiting Professor at both the Chinese University of Hong Kong and Xiamen University, Fujian, China. He is founding editor of the quarterly journal *English Today: The International Review of the English Language* (Cambridge, 1985–) and the *Oxford Companion to the English Language* (1992), and is the author, among other works, of *The Longman Lexicon of Contemporary English* (1981), *The English Languages* (Cambridge, 1998), and *The Oxford Guide to World English* (2002).

APRIL MCMAHON is Forbes Professor of English Language at the University of Edinburgh. She has research interests in English phonology, past and present; in language classification; phonological theory; and evolutionary linguistics. Her publications include *Understanding Language Change* (Cambridge University Press, 1994), *Change, Chance, and Optimality* (Oxford University Press, 2000), *Lexical Phonology and the History of English* (Cambridge University Press, 2000), and *Language Classification by Numbers* (with Rob McMahon; Oxford University Press, forthcoming).

LYNDA MUGGLESTONE is a Fellow in English Language at Pembroke College, Oxford, and News International Lecturer at the University of Oxford. She has published widely on language in the late eighteenth and nineteenth centuries. Recent work includes *Lexicography and the OED. Pioneers in the Untrodden Forest* (Oxford University Press, 2002), *'Talking Proper'. The Rise of Accent as Social Symbol,* 2nd edn. (Oxford University Press, 2003), and *Lost for Words. The Hidden History of the Oxford English Dictionary* (Yale University Press, 2004).

TERTTU NEVALAINEN is Professor of English Philology at the University of Helsinki and the Director of the Research Unit for Variation and Change in English. Her research focuses on historical sociolinguistics, language change, and early modern English. Her publications include 'Early Modern English Lexis and Semantics', in R. Lass (ed.), *The Cambridge History of the English Language,* Vol. 3 (Cambridge University Press, 1999); *Historical Sociolinguistics; Language Change in Tudor and Stuart England* (Longman 2003; with H. Raumolin-Brunberg); and *An Introduction to Early Modern English* (Edinburgh University Press, forthcoming). She is also the director of the research project 'Sociolinguistics and Language History', which has produced the *Corpus of Early English Correspondence.*

JEREMY J. SMITH is Professor of English Philology in the University of Glasgow. His publications include *An Historical study of English* (1996), *Essentials of Early English* (1999) and *An Introduction to Middle English* (with S. Horobin, 2002). He is currently working on a new survey of Middle English transmission (with S. Horobin and M. Stenroos), and a study of the actuation of sound-change in the history of English.

INGRID TIEKEN-BOON VAN OSTADE is senior lecturer in the English department of the University of Leiden. She has written a study of periphrastic *do* in eighteenth-century English (1987) as well as a book on the use of multiple negation in Malory's *Morte D'Arthur* (1995). In addition, she has edited a variety of international collections of articles. Her research interests include social network analysis in the history of English and the standardization process (especially codification and prescription), on which subjects she has widely published. She edits an internet journal called *Historical Socio-linguistics and Sociohistorical Linguistics.*

MATTHEW TOWNEND is Lecturer in English at the University of York. He is the author of *English Place-Names in Skaldic Verse* (1998) and *Language and History in Viking Age England* (2002), and is the editor of *Wulfstan, Archbishop of York* (2004). He has also published many articles on Old Norse poetry and Anglo-Norse contact, and is currently editing the Old Norse poems in honour of King Cnut.

CLIVE UPTON is Professor of Modern English Language in the School of English at the University of Leeds. He was formerly a teacher in universities in Africa and Papua New Guinea, and a researcher in the Universities of Leeds and Birmingham and at the National Centre for English Cultural Tradition at the University of Sheffield. His research specialisms are in English dialectology and pronunciation: he has been associated with the Surveys of English Dialects and Anglo-Welsh Dialects for more than thirty years, and is currently developing a new dialect survey, the Survey of Regional English. He is also pronunciation consultant to Oxford University Press, where he is responsible for the description of Received Pronunciation carried by the larger native-speaker Oxford English Dictionaries.

ACKNOWLEDGEMENTS

The author would like to thank the following for permission to reproduce material: the British Library Board for permission to reproduce the manuscript image of lines 2677–87 from the Beowulf Manuscript (taken from the *Electronic Beowulf*, ed. K. Kiernan (London: The British Library Board, 2004); the English Place-Name Society for permission to reproduce Map 10 from A. H. Smith, *English Place-Name Elements* (Cambridge: Cambridge University Press, 1956); the Corpus of Anglo-Saxon Stone Sculpture for permission to reproduce the photograph of the inscribed sundial at Aldbrough; the Department of Special Collections, Glasgow University Library, for permission to reproduce the passage illustrating Caxton's use of English from *The Myrrour of the World* (Westminster: *c* 1490; A4v, Sp Coll Hunterian Bv.2.30); the Bodleian Library for permission to reproduce William Barnes's Dorset translation of Queen Victoria's speech on opening Parliament in 1863 (from W. Barnes, *A Grammar and Glossary of the Dorset Dialect with the History, Outspreading, and Bearings of South-Western English* (London: Trübner & Co, 1864)), and for permission to reproduce 'Th' Dickshonary', by Teddy Ashton, from J. Baron, *Tum o' Dick o' Bobs's Lankisher Dickshonary* (Manchester: John Heywood, n.d.); I would also like to thank the College of Arms for permission to reproduce the manuscript drawing of the Arms of Sir John Hawkins; David Parry for permission to reproduce the SAWD/SED map for *calf* from *A Grammar and Glossary of the Conservative Anglo-Welsh Dialects of Rural Wales* (Sheffield: National Centre for English Cultural Tradition, 1999: 244). I would also like to thank Lucinda Rumsey for her many helpful suggestions on the text, and April Warman for her assiduous checking of quotations and references throughout the volume.

References

Primary sources

Manuscript sources

Acworth Papers: Diaries of Harriet Garland Acworth 1833–46. Bodleian Library MSS. Eng. misc. e. 1571–83.

Lady Clarendon Papers: Diaries of Lady Katharine Clarendon, 1840–50. Bodleian Library MSS. Eng. d. 2048.

Murray Papers: Uncatalogued papers of James A. H. Murray. Bodleian Library, Oxford.

Published sources

ALLEN, R. (ed.) (1992). *Lawman: Brut*. London: J. M. Dent & Sons Ltd.

ANDERSON, P. (1987). *A Structural Atlas of the English Dialects*. London: Croom Helm.

ASHTON, P. (trans.) (1546). *A shorte treatise vpon the Turkes chronicles*. London: E. Whitchurch.

AUSTEN, J. (1816). *Emma: A Novel in Three Volumes*. London: John Murray.

AUSTIN, F. (ed.) (1991). *The Clift Family Correspondence*. Sheffield: CECTAL.

BABINGTON, C. and LUMBY, J. R. (eds) (1865–86). *Polychronicon Ranulphi Higden Monachi Cestrensis; together with the English Translations of John Trevisa and of an Unknown Writer of the Fifteenth Century*. 9 vols. London: Longman, Green, Longman, Roberts, and Green.

BAKER, F. (1980). *The Works of John Wesley*, vol. 25. *Letters* I. 1721–39. Oxford: Clarendon Press.

BARNES, W. (1864). *A Grammar and Glossary of the Dorset Dialect with the History, Outspreading, and Bearings of South-Western English*. London: Trübner & Co.

BARON, J. (n.d.). *Tum o' Dick o' Bobs's Lankisher Dickshonary*. Manchester: John Heywood.

BATCHELOR, T. (1809). *An Orthoëpical Analysis of the English Language . . . to which is added, a Minute and Copious Analysis of the Dialect of Bedfordshire*. London: Didier and Tebbitt.

BATELY, J. (ed.) (1986). *The Anglo-Saxon Chronicle MS A*. The Anglo-Saxon Chronicle: A Collaborative Edition. Cambridge: D. S. Brewer.

BATTESTIN, M. C. and PROBYN, C. T. (eds) (1993). *The Correspondence of Henry and Sarah Fielding.* Oxford: Clarendon Press.

BENNETT, J. A. W. and SMITHERS, G. V. (eds) (1968). *Early Middle English Verse and Prose* (2nd edn.). Oxford: Clarendon Press.

BENSON, L. D. *et al.* (eds) (1988). *The Riverside Chaucer.* Oxford: Oxford University Press.

BERTHELETTE, T. (trans.) (1532). *Jo. Gower de Confessione Amantis.* London: T. Berthelette.

BIBBESWORTH, WALTER DE. (1990). *Le Tretiz.* London: Anglo-Norman Text Society. Electronic edition: <**http://and4.anglo-norman.net/texts/bibbes-contents.html**>.

BIRCH, W. DE G. (ed.) (1885–93). *Cartularium Saxonicum: A Collection of Charters relating to Anglo-Saxon History.* 3 vols. London: Whiting [vols I–II]/ Clark [vol. III].

BLAKE, N. F. (ed.) (1973). *Selections from William Caxton.* Oxford: Clarendon Press.

BLAKEMORE EVANS, G. (ed.) (1974). *The Riverside Shakespeare.* Boston, MA: Houghton Mifflin.

BLOOM, E. A. and BLOOM, L. D. (eds) (1982). Fanny Burney, *Evelina.* Oxford: Oxford University Press.

BLOUNT, T. (1656). *Glossographia. Anglistica & Americana* 32. New York: Georg Olms Verlag, 1972.

BOLTON, W. (ed.) (1966). *The English Language: Essays by English and American Men of Letters 1490–1839.* Cambridge: Cambridge University Press.

BOORDE, A. (1542). *Fyrst Boke of the Introduction of Knowledge,* ed. F. J. Furnivall. London: Early English Text Society, 1871.

—— (1547). *The Breviary of Helthe.* London: W. Middleton.

—— (*c*1565). *The First and Best Part of Scoggins Jests,* in W. Carew Hazlitt (ed.), *Old English Jest Books.* London: Willis & Sotheran, 1866.

BROOK, G. L. and LESLIE, R. F. (eds) (1963, 1978). Layamon. *Brut,* Early English Text Society o.s. 250, 277. London: Published for the Early English Text Society by Oxford University Press.

BULLOKAR, J. (1616). *An English Expositor: Teaching the Interpretation of the Hardest Words Used in our Language.* London: J. Leggatt.

BURKHARDT, F. (ed.) (1996). *Charles Darwin's Letters. A Selection 1825–1859.* Cambridge: Cambridge University Press.

—— and S. SMITH (eds) (1985–). *The Correspondence of Charles Darwin.* 13 vols. Cambridge: Cambridge: University Press.

BURNETT, J. (ed.) (1982). *Destiny Obscure: Autobiographies of Childhood, Education, and Family from the 1820s to the 1920s.* London: Allen Lane.

—— (ed.) (1994). *Useful Toil. Autobiographies of Working People from the 1820s to the 1920s.* London and New York: Routledge.

BURNLEY, D. (ed.) (1992*a*). *The History of the English Language: A Source Book.* London: Longman.

BURRELL, A. (1891). *Recitation. A Handbook for Teachers in Public Elementary Schools.* London: Griffith Farran Okeden & Welsh.

BURROW, J. A. and TURVILLE-PETRE, T. (eds) (2005). *A Book of Middle English* (3rd edn). Oxford: Blackwell.

BUTLER, H. E. (ed.) (1949). *The Chronicle of Jocelin of Brakelond.* London: Nelson.

BYWATER, A. (1834). *The Sheffield Dialect, in Conversations 'Uppa are Hull Arston'. By A Shevvild Chap.* Sheffield: A. Whitaker and Co.

CAMDEN, W. (1616/1984). *Remains Concerning Britain*, ed. R. D. Dunn. Toronto: University of Toronto Press.

CAREW, R. (*c*1595). 'The Excellencie of the English Tongue', in W. Camden, *Remaines Concerning Britaine: But Especially Englande, and the Inhabitants thereof.* London: Iohn Leggatt, 1614, 36–44.

—— (1602). *Survey of Cornwall*, in F. E. Halliday (ed.), *Richard Carew of Antony.* London: Andrew Melrose, 1953, 73–237.

CARTLIDGE, N. (ed.) (2001). *The Owl and the Nightingale: Text and Translation.* Exeter: University of Exeter Press.

CAWDREY, R. (1604). *A Table Alphabeticall.* London: E. Weaver.

CAWLEY, A. (ed.) (1958). *The Wakefield Pageants in the Towneley Cycle.* Manchester: Manchester University Press.

CAXTON, W. (trans.) (1480). *The Description of Britayne, & also Irlonde taken oute of Polichronicon.* Westminster: W. Caxton.

CHAMBERS, R. W. and DAUNT, M. (eds) (1931). *A Book of London English 1384–1425.* Oxford: Clarendon Press.

CHAPMAN, R. W. (ed.) (1952). *The Letters of Samuel Johnson: with Mrs. Thrale's Genuine Letters to Him.* 3 vols. Oxford: Oxford University Press.

—— (ed.) (1980). James Boswell, *Life of Johnson.* rev. by J. D. Fleeman. Oxford: Oxford University Press.

CLARK, C. (ed.) (1970). The Peterborough Chronicle (2nd edn.). Oxford: Oxford University Press.

CLEMOES, P. (ed.) (1997). *Ælfric's Catholic Homilies: The First Series: Text.* Early English Text Society, Supplementary Series, 17. Oxford: Published for the Early English Text Society by Oxford University Press.

COLGRAVE, B. and MYNORS, R. A. G. (eds) (1969). *Bede's Ecclesiastical History of the English People.* Oxford: Clarendon Press.

Contention Between Liberality and Prodigality, The (1602). Oxford: Malone Society Reprints, 1913.

COWELL, J. (1607). *Interpreter.* Facsimile edn. Union, NJ: The Lawbook Exchange, 2002.

CRAIGIE, W. A. and ONIONS, C. T. (eds) (1933). *A New English Dictionary on Historical Principles; Founded on the Materials Collected by the Philological Society. Edited by James*

A. H. Murray, Henry Bradley, William A. Craigie, C. T. Onions. Introduction, Supplement, and Bibliography. Oxford: Clarendon Press.

CROTCH, W. J. B. (ed.) (1928). *The Prologues and Epilogues of William Caxton.* Early English Text Society o.s. 176. London: Published for the Early English Text Society by H. Milford, Oxford University Press.

CUSACK, B. (ed.) (1998). *Everyday English 1500–1700.* Edinburgh: Edinburgh University Press.

DANIEL, S. (1603). *Defense of Ryme,* in G. Gregory Smith (ed.), *Elizabethan Critical Essays,* vol. 2. Oxford: Oxford University Press, 1904, 356–84.

DARWIN, F. (ed.) (1888). *The Life and Letters of Charles Darwin* (rev. edn.), 3 vols. London: John Murray.

DAVIS, N. (ed.) (1971). *Paston Letters and Papers of the Fifteenth Century: Part I.* Oxford: Clarendon Press.

DEKKER, T. (1608). *Lanthorne and Candle-light: or The Bell-man's Second Nights Walke.* London: J. Bushie.

—— (1612). *O per se O. Or, a new Cryer of Lanthorne and Candle-light.* London: John Bushie.

DICKENS, C. (1850). *The Personal History of David Copperfield.* London: Bradbury & Evans.

—— (1854). *Hard Times, for these Times.* London: Bradbury & Evans.

DICKINS, B. and ROSS, A. S. C. (eds) (1954). *The Dream of the Rood* (4th edn.). London: Methuen.

—— and WILSON, R. M. (eds) (1956). *Early Middle English Texts* (3rd edn.). London: Bowes and Bowes.

Dime Dialect Speaker, The ([1879]). New York: Beadle and Adams.

DOBBIE, E. V. K. (ed.) (1942). *The Anglo-Saxon Minor Poems.* Anglo-Saxon Poetic Records VI. New York: Columbia University Press.

DONALDSON, W. (ed.) (1989). *The Language of the People: Scots Prose from the Victorian Revival.* Aberdeen: Aberdeen University Press.

DUNCAN, A. (ed.) (1997). *John Barbour: The Bruce.* Edinburgh: Canongate.

DUNCAN, P. (1890). *How to Talk Correctly: A Pocket Manual to Promote Polite and Accurate Conversation, Writing, and Reading … with more than 500 errors in Speaking and Writing Corrected.* London: William Nicholson and Sons.

ECCLES, E. (1879). *Harry Hawkins' H Book. Shewing How He Learned to Aspirate his H's.* London: Griffith and Farran.

ECCLES, M. (ed.) (1969). *The Macro Plays.* Early English Text Society o.s. 262. London; New York: published for the Early English Text Society by Oxford University Press.

EKWALL, E. (ed.) (1960). *The Concise Oxford Dictionary of English Place-Names.* Oxford: Clarendon Press.

ELIASON, N. and CLEMOES, P. (eds) (1966). *Ælfric's First Series of Catholic Homilies (British Museum Royal 7 C. xii, fols 4–218)*. Early English Manuscripts in Facsimile, 13. Copenhagen: Rosenkilde and Bagger.

ELIOT, J. (trans.) (1663). *Mamusse wunneetupanatamwe Up-Biblium God*. Boston: Samuel Green and Marmaduke Johnson. Electronic edition: <http://wwwlib.umi.com/eebo/image/45378> (accessed January 21, 2004).

ELLIS, A. J. (1869–89). *On Early English Pronunciation*. 5 vols. London: Trübner & Co.

EVELYN, J. (1665). 'Letter to Sir Peter Wyche', in J. I. Spingarn (ed.), *Critical Essays of the Seventeenth Century*, 3 vols. Oxford: Clarendon Press, 1908–9, vol. 2, 310–13.

FERNE, J. (1586). *The Blazon of Gentrie*. London: A. Maunsell/T. Cooke.

FISHER, J. H., RICHARDSON, M., and FISHER, J. L. (eds) (1984). *An Anthology of Chancery English*. Knoxville: University of Tennessee Press.

Florence Nightingale and the Crimea, 1854–55 (2000). London: Stationery Office.

FRAUNCE, A. (1588). *The Lawiers Logike*. London: T. Gubbin and T. Newman.

FREEBORN, D. (ed.) (1998). *From Old English to Standard English: A Course Book in Language Variation across Time* (2nd edn.). Houndmills: Macmillan.

GASCOIGNE, G. (1575a). 'Certayne Notes of Instruction Concerning the Making of Verse', in J. W. Cunliffe (ed.), *The Posies*. Cambridge: Cambridge University Press, 1907, 465–73.

—— (1575b). 'Jocasta', in J. W. Cunliffe (ed.), *The Posies*. Cambridge: Cambridge University Press, 1907, 244–326.

GIL, A. (1619). *Logonomia Anglica*, part 2, trans. R. C. Alston, ed. B. Danielsson and A. Gabrielson, *Stockholm Studies in English* 27 and 28. Stockholm: Almquist & Wiksell, 1972.

GILL, J. (1857). *Introductory Text-Book to School Management*. London: Longman & Co.

GOODMAN, J. B. (ed.) (1968). *Victorian Cabinet-Maker: The Memoirs of James Hopkinson 1819–1894*. London; Routledge & Kegan Paul.

GÖRLACH, M. (2001). *A Dictionary of European Anglicisms*. Oxford: Oxford University Press.

GRANT, W. and MURISON, D. (eds) (1931–76). *The Scottish National Dictionary*. Edinburgh: The Scottish National Dictionary Association.

GRAY, D. (ed.) (1985). *The Oxford Book of Late Medieval Verse and Prose*. Oxford: Oxford University Press.

GREENE, R. (1591). 'The Art of Conny-Catching', in A. B. Grosart (ed.), *The Life and Complete Works in Prose and Verse of Robert Greene*, vol. 10. New York: Russell & Russell, 1964, 15 vols, 1–61.

GRIMALD, N. (1557). 'Concerning Virgils Eneids,' in E. Rollins (ed.), *Tottel's Miscellany*, vol. 1. Cambridge, MA: Harvard University Press, 1929, 2 vols, 99.

H., HON. HENRY. (1854). *Poor Letter H: Its Use and Abuse*. London: John F. Shaw and Co.

—— (1855). *P's and Q's. Grammatical Hints for the Million* (2nd edn.). London: Seeley, Jackson, and Halliday.

HAIGHT, G. S. (1854–78). *The George Eliot Letters*. 9 vols. New Haven: Yale University Press.

HALL, F. (1873). *Modern English*. London and New York: Scribner, Armstrong.

HALSBAND, R. (1965). *The Complete Letters of Lady Mary Wortley Montagu*, vol. I. Oxford: Clarendon Press.

—— and GRUNDY, I. (eds) (1977). Lady Mary Wortley Montagu. *Essays and Poems* and *Simplicity, a Comedy*. Oxford: Clarendon Press.

HARDING, V. and WRIGHT, L. (eds) (1995). *London Bridge: Selected Accounts and Rentals, 1381–1538*. London: London Record Society.

HARMAN, T. (1567). *A Caveat or Warening, for Commen Cursetors*, ed. E. Viles and F. J. Furnivall. Oxford: Oxford University Press, 1869.

HARRISON, M. (1848). *The Rise, Progress, and Present Structure of the English Language*. London: Longman, Brown, Green, and Longmans.

HARRISON, W. (1577). *The Description of England*, ed. G. Edelen. Ithaca, NY: Cornell University Press, 1968.

HART, J. (1569). *An Orthographie, conteyning the due Order and Reason, howe to Write or Paint Thimage of Mannes Voice, most like to the Life or Nature*. London: no publisher. Reprinted in facsimile Menston: The Scolar Press, 1969.

—— (1570). *A Methode or Comfortable Beginning*. London: H. Denham.

HEMINGWAY, E. (1940). *For Whom the Bell Tolls*. New York: Charles Scribner's Sons.

HEYWOOD, T. and BROME, R. (1634). *The Late Lanchashire Witches*, in *The Dramatic Works of Thomas Heywood*, vol. 4. New York: Russell & Russell, 1964, 6 vols, 167–262.

HICKEY, R. (2003). *Corpus Presenter. Processing Software for Language Analysis*. Including *A Corpus of Irish English*. Amsterdam: John Benjamins.

HODGES, R. (1644). *The English Primrose*. London: Richard Cotes.

HODGSON, W. B. (1881). *Errors in the Use of English*. Edinburgh: David Douglas.

HOLLOWAY, W. (1839). *A General Dictionary of Provincialisms, Written with a View to Rescue from Oblivion the Fast fading Relics of By-Gone Days*. Sussex, Lewes: Baxter and Son.

HOLT, R. and WHITE, R. M. (eds) (1878). *The Ormulum*. Oxford: Oxford University Press.

HOLY BIBLE. (1611). Facsimile edn. of the Authorised Version. Oxford: Oxford University Press, 1911.

HOUSE, M. and STOREY, G. (eds) (1965). *The Letters of Charles Dickens*, vol. I. Oxford: Clarendon Press.

HUTCHINSON, T. (ed.) (1904). *The Complete Poetical Works of Shelley*. Oxford: Clarendon Press.

INGRAM, D. (1966). *The Relation of David Ingram* [1589]. March of America Facsimile Series, 14. Ann Arbor: University Microfilms.

IRVINE, S. (ed.) (1993). *Old English Homilies from MS Bodley 343*. Early English Text Society, Original Series, 302. Oxford: published for the Early English Text Society by Oxford University Press.

IRVINE, S. (ed.) (2004). *The Anglo-Saxon Chronicle MS E.* The Anglo-Saxon Chronicle: A Collaborative Edition. Cambridge: D. S. Brewer.

ISLAM, S. (ed.) (1978). *Bangladesh District Records: Chittagong, 1760–1787.* Dhaka: University of Dhaka.

'Jacob Grimm on the Genius and Vocation of the English Language' (1853). *Notes and Queries* (February 5), 125–6.

JAMES, A. (ed.) (1993). *The Correspondence of Michael Faraday.* 2 vols. London: The Institution of Electrical Engineers.

JONSON, B. (1616). *EPICOENE, Or The Silent Woman.* London 1616. *English Drama (1280–1915).* Department of English, University of Helsinki. 8 Aug. 2003. <**http://collections.chadwyck.com/**>.

—— (1618–19). 'Conversations with Drummond,' in C. H. Herford, P. Simpson, and E. Simpson (eds), *Ben Jonson*, vol. 1. Oxford: Clarendon Press, 1966, 11 vols, 128–78.

—— (1631). 'Bartholomew Fair', in C. H. Herford, P. Simpson, and E. Simpson (eds), *Ben Jonson*, vol. 6. Oxford: Clarendon Press, 1966, 11 vols, 1–141.

—— (1640). *Discoveries,* in C. H. Herford, P. Simpson, and E. Simpson (eds), *Ben Jonson*, vol. 8. Oxford: Clarendon Press, 1966, 11 vols, 555–649.

—— (1633–40). 'A Tale of a Tub', in C. H. Herford, P. Simpson, and E. Simpson (eds), *Ben Jonson*, vol. 3. Oxford: Clarendon Press, 1966, 11 vols, 1–92.

JOHNSON, S. (1755). *A Dictionary of the English Language.* 2 vols. London: W. Strahan. Repr. in facs. Hildesheim: Georg Olms Verlagsbuchhandlung, 1968.

JUSSAWALLA, F. and DASENBROCK, R. W. (1992). *Interviews with Writers of the Post-Colonial World.* Jackson: University Press of Mississippi.

KEE, T. C. (1995). *We Could **** You, Mr. Birch.* Petaling Jaya: Published by the author.

KELSALL, M. (ed.) (1969). Sarah Fielding, *The Adventures of David Simple.* Oxford: Oxford University Press.

KINGTON-OLIPHANT, T. L. (1873). *The Sources of Standard English.* 2 vols. London: Macmillan & Co.

KINSMAN, R. (ed.) (1969). *John Skelton: Poems.* Oxford: Clarendon Press.

KLAEBER, F. (ed.) (1950). *Beowulf and the Fight at Finnsburg* (3rd edn.). Boston: D. C. Heath.

KOLB, E. (1979). *Atlas of English Sounds.* Bern: Francke.

KON, S. (1989). *Emily of Emerald Hill.* London: Macmillan.

KORTMANN, B., SCHNEIDER, E., BURRIDGE, K., MESTHRIE, R., and UPTON, C. (eds) (2004). *A Handbook of Varieties of English: A Multimedia Reference Tool.* 2 vols plus CD-Rom. Berlin: Mouton de Gruyter.

KRAPP, G. P. (ed.) (1932). *The Anglo-Saxon Poetic Records, V: The Paris Psalter and the Meters of Boethius.* London: Routledge, Kegan Paul; New York: Columbia University Press.

—— and DOBBIE, E. V. K. (eds) (1936). *The Anglo-Saxon Poetic Records, III: The Exeter Book.* London: Routledge, Kegan Paul.

L., I. S. (1906). *Fashion in Language*. London: H. M. Pollett and Co.

LADELL, H. R. (1897). *How to Spell and Speak English* (3rd edn.). London: Relfe Brothers.

LEACH, A. (1880). *The Letter H. Past, Present, and Future. A Treatise*. London: Griffith & Farran.

Ledsham's Sure Guide to English Grammar (1879). Manchester: J. B. Ledsham.

LEFANU, W. (ed.) (1960). *Betsy Sheridan's Journal. Letters from Sheridan's Sister* [repr. 1986]. Oxford and New York: Oxford University Press.

LELAND, C. G. (1900). *Pidgin-English Sing-Song*. London: K. Paul, Trench, Trübner & Co.

LENNIE, W. (1864). *The Principles of English Grammar* (58th edn. 'with alterations'). London: William Tegg.

LEVER, R. (1573). *The Arte of Reason, rightly termed, Witcraft*. London: H. Bynneman.

LEWIS, W. S. *et al.* (eds) (1937–83). *The Yale Edition of Horace Walpole's Correspondence*, 9 vols. New Haven: Yale University Press.

Live and Learn: A Guide for All who Wish to Speak and Write Correctly (1872) (28th edn.). London: John F. Shaw & Co.

LONG, E. (1774). *The History of Jamaica*. London: T. Lowndes.

LOWTH, R. (1762). *A Short Introduction to English Grammar: with critical notes* (2nd edn., 1763), London: printed for A. Millar; and R. and J. Dodsley.

MANN, A. (1862). *Mann's Modern Expositor; Containing Alphabetical Collections of the Most Usual and Expressive Words in the English Language: Carefully Divided, and Properly Accented, and the Meanings Given According to the Best and Most Recent Authorities*. London: Thomas W. Grattan.

MANWAYRING, H. (1644). *The Sea-Mans Dictionary*. London: J. Bellamy.

MARSH, G. P. (1860). *Lectures on the English Language*. New York: C. Scribner's Sons.

MARTIN, B. (1748). *Institutions of Language*. London. Repr. in facs. by R. C. Alston, Menston: The Scolar Press, 1974.

—— (1749). *Lingua Britannica Reformata*. London: printed for J. Hodges; S. Austen; J. Newbery; J. Ward.

MATHER, J. Y. and SPIETEL, H. H. (1975, 1977, 1986). *The Linguistic Atlas of Scotland*. 3 vols. London: Croom Helm.

MILLER, T. (ed.) (1890–8). *The Old English Version of Bede's Ecclesiastical History*. 2 vols. Early English Text Society, Original Series, 95–6, 110–11. London: Published for the Early English Text Society, by N. Trübner.

MILLS, A. D. (1998). *A Dictionary of English Place-Names*. Oxford: Oxford University Press.

MITCHELL, B. and ROBINSON, F. C. (eds) (2001). *A Guide to Old English* (6th edn.). Oxford: Blackwell.

NICHOLSON, J. (1889). *The Folk Speech of East Yorkshire*. London: Simpkin, Marshall and Co.

NORTON-SMITH, J. (ed.) (1966). *John Lydgate: Poems*. Oxford: Clarendon Press.

NOWELL, L. (1595). *Vocabularium Saxiconum*, ed. A. H. Marckwardt. Ann Arbor, MI: Michigan University Press, 1952.

NUGENT, M. (1907). *Lady Nugent's Journal* [1801–1815]. London: Institute of Jamaica.

—— and WRIGHT, N. (1974). *A Word Geography of England*. London: Seminar Press.

ORTON, H. (1962). *Survey of English Dialects (A): Introduction*. Leeds: E. J. Arnold.

—— HALLIDAY, W. J., BARRY, M. V., TILLING, P. M., and WAKELIN, M. F. (eds) (1962–1971). *Survey of English Dialects (B): The Basic Material*. 4 vols, each of 3 parts. Leeds: E. J. Arnold.

—— SANDERSON, S., and WIDDOWSON, J., (eds) (1978). *The Linguistic Atlas of England*. London: Croom Helm.

PARRY, D. (ed.) (n.d. [1977]). *The Survey of Anglo-Welsh Dialects: Volume 1, The South-East*. n.p.: privately mimeographed.

—— (ed.) (1979). *The Survey of Anglo-Welsh Dialects: Volume 2, The South-West*. Swansea: University College of Swansea, privately mimeographed.

PAULUSZ, J. H. O. (ed.) (1989). *An Historical Relation of the Island Ceylon in the East Indies*, by Robert Knox (1681). 2 vols. Dehiwala: Ceylon Historical Journal Monograph Series, 14.

PEARSALL, J. (ed.) (2001). *The New Oxford Dictionary of English*. Oxford: Oxford University Press.

PEARSON, W. (1865). *The Self-Help Grammar of the English Language*. London: Hamilton, Adams & Co.

A Physical Dictionary (1657). London: J. Garfield.

PUTTENHAM, G. (1589). *Arte of English Poesie*, ed G. Doidge Willcock and A. Walker. Cambridge: Cambridge University Press, 1970.

QUINN, D. B. (ed.) (1985). *The Roanoke Voyages, 1584–1590*. 2 vols. London: Hakluyt Society.

QUINTILIAN, *The Institutione Oratoria*, trans. H. E. Butler. London: Loeb Classical Library, 1921.

RANDOLPH, T. (1638). *The Muses' Looking Glass*, in W. Carew Hazlitt (ed.), *Poetical and Dramatic Works of Thomas Randolph*, vol. 1. London: Reeves & Turner, 1875, 2 vols, 173–266.

RAY, J. (1674). *A Collection of English Words Not Generally Used*. London: T. Burrell.

REDFORD, J. (c1550). *Wit and Science*. Malone Society reprints. Oxford. Oxford University Press, 1951.

R[ID], S. (1610). *Martin Mark-all, Beadle of Bridewell; his Defence and Answere to the Belman of London*. London: J. Budge and R. Bonian.

ROBINSON, C. C. (1862). *The Dialect of Leeds and its Neighbourhood*. London: John Russell Smith.

—— (1876). *A Glossary of Mid-Yorkshire Words Pertaining to the Dialect of Mid-Yorkshire: With Others Peculiar to Lower Nidderdale: to which is prefixed an Outline Grammar of the Mid-Yorkshire Dialect*. London: Trübner and Co., for The English Dialect Society.

ROBINSON, R. (1619). *The Art of Pronuntiation,* ed. E. J. Dobson (1957), *The Phonetic Writings of Robert Robinson.* Early English Text Society o.s. 238. London: Published for the Early English Text Society by Oxford University Press.

ROWLANDS, S. (1610). *Martin Markall, Beadle of Bridewell,* in *The Complete Works of Samuel Rowlands,* vol. 2. New York: Johnston Reprints, 1966, 3 vols.

SCRAGG, D. G. (ed.) (1981). *The Battle of Maldon.* Manchester: Manchester University Press.

—— (ed.) (1992*a*). *The Vercelli Homilies.* Early English Text Society, o.s. 300. Oxford: published for the Early English Text Society by Oxford University Press.

SEDGEFIELD, W. J. (ed.) (1899). *King Alfred's Old English Version of Boethius De Consolatione Philosophiae.* Oxford: Clarendon Press.

SHADWELL, T. (1688). *The Squire of Alsatia. A Comedy.* London: J. Knapton.

SHAKESPEARE, W. (1623). *The Taming of the Shrew.* London 1623. *English Drama (1280–1915).* Department of English, University of Helsinki. 8 Aug. 2003. <**http://collections.chadwyck.com/**>.

—— (1623). *The Two Gentlemen of Verona.* London 1623. *English Drama (1280–1915).* Department of English, University of Helsinki. 8 Aug. 2003. <**http://collections.chadwyck.com/**>.

SHEPHERD, G. (ed.) (1991). *Ancrene Wisse Parts Six and Seven* (rev. edn.). Exeter: University of Exeter Press.

SHERIDAN, T. (1780*). A General Dictionary of the English Language, one main object of which is to establish a plain and permanent standard pronunciation, to which is prefixed a rhetorical grammar.* 2 vols. London: printed for J. Dodsley, C. Dilly, and J. Wilkie.

SIDNEY, Sir P. (1595). *Defense of Poesie,* in A. Feuillerat (ed.), *The Prose Works of Sir Philip Sidney,* vol. 3. Cambridge: Cambridge University Press, 1968, 4 vols, 1–46.

SILLIMAN, B. (1812). *A Journal of Travels in England Holland, and Scotland, and of Two Passages over the Atlantic, in the Years 1805 and 1806.* 2 vols. Boston: T. B. Watt and Company.

SIMPSON, J. A. and WEINER, E. S. C. (eds) 1989. *The Oxford English Dictionary First Edited by James A. H. Murray, Henry Bradley, W. A. Craigie, and C. T. Onions combined with A Supplement to the Oxford English Dictionary edited by R. W. Burchfield and Reset with Corrections, Revisions, and Additional Vocabulary.* 20 vols. Oxford: Clarendon Press.

SISAM, K. (ed.) (1921). *Fourteenth Century Verse and Prose.* Oxford: Clarendon Press.

SKEAT, W. W. (1890 [1966]). *Ælfric's Lives of Saints.* Early English Text Society, o.s. 94. London: published for the Early English Text Society by Oxford University Press.

SLATER, M. (ed.) (2003). *A Christmas Carol and Other Christmas Writings.* London: Penguin.

SMITH, C. W. (1866). *Mind Your H's and Take Care of Your R's.* London: Lockwood & Co.

SMITH, J. (1653). *The Sea-mans grammar and dictionary.* London: A. Kemb.

SMITH, M. (ed.) (1995–2004). *The Letters of Charlotte Brontë: with a Selection of Letters by Family and Friends.* Oxford: Clarendon Press.

'Some Thoughts on the English Language' (1766). *Annual Review,* 194–7.

SPENSER, E. (1579). *The Shepheardes Calender,* in E. Greenlaw *et al.* (eds.), *The Works of Edmund Spenser,* vol. 7, part 1. Baltimore, MD: Johns Hopkins University Press, 1932–57, 11 vols.

SPINGARN, J. I. (1908–9). *Critical Essays of the Seventeenth Century.* Oxford: Clarendon Press, 3 vols.

SPRAT, T. (1667). *The History of the Royal-Society of London.* London: J. Martyn.

STANLEY, E. G. (ed.) (1960). *The Owl and the Nightingale.* London: Nelson.

STOWER, C. (1808). *The Printer's Grammar; or, Introduction to the Art of Printing . . . With the Improvements in the Practice of Printing.* London: L. Wayland.

SWAN, W. T. (ed.) (1970). *The Journals of Two Poor Dissenters, 1786–1880.* London: Routledge & Kegan Paul.

SWANTON, M. (ed.) (1987). *The Dream of the Rood* (rev. edn.). Exeter: University of Exeter Press.

SWEET, H. (ed.) (1871–2). *King Alfred's West-Saxon Version of Gregory's Pastoral Care.* Early English Text Society, Original Series, 45 and 50. London: published for the Early English Text Society by Oxford University Press.

—— (1881). *The Elementary Sounds of English: a paper read before the Spelling Reform Association on 22 November, 1881.* London: John Street.

[SWIFT, J.] (1712). *A Proposal for Correcting, Improving and Ascertaining the English Tongue; in a Letter.* London: Printed for Benj. Tooke.

TAYLOR, M. (ed.) (1994). *The European Diaries of Richard Cobden 1846–1849.* Aldershot: Scolar Press.

The Teacher's Manual of the Science and Art of Teaching (1874). London: Spottiswoode & Co.

TEMPLE, R. C. (ed.) (1919). *The Travels of Peter Mundy in Europe and Asia, 1608–1667.* London: The Hakluyt Society.

TIERNEY, J. E. (ed.) (1988). *The Correspondence of Robert Dodsley 1733–1764.* Cambridge: Cambridge University Press.

TOLKIEN, J. R. R. (ed.) (1962). *The English Text of the Ancrene Riwle: Ancrene Wisse, Edited from MS. Corpus Christi College Cambridge 402,* with an introduction by N. R. Ker. Early English Text Society, 249. London: published for the Early English Text Society by Oxford University Press.

TOMCATT, (2004). **<http://hk.geocities.com/catttom/gap_team.html>** (Accessed August 18, 2004).

TREHARNE, E. (ed.) (2004). *Old and Middle English c. 890–c. 1400: An Anthology* (2nd edn.). Oxford: Blackwell.

TRENCH, R. C. (1860). *On Some Deficiencies in Our English Dictionaries* (2nd rev. edn.). London: John W. Parker & Sons.

TROIDE, L. E., *et al.* (1988–). *The Early Journals and Letters of Fanny Burney.* Oxford: Clarendon Press.

UDALL, N. (1553). *Respublica*, ed. L. A. Magnus. London: Kegan Paul, 1905.

—— and WIDDOWSON, J. D. A. (1996). *An Atlas of English Dialects.* Oxford: Oxford University Press.

UPTON, C., KRETZSCHMAR W. A., Jr., and KONOPKA, R. (2001). *The Oxford Dictionary of Pronunciation for Current English.* Oxford: Oxford University Press.

—— SANDERSON, S., and WIDDOWSON, J. (1987). *Word Maps: A Dialect Atlas of England.* London: Croom Helm.

—— PARRY, D., and WIDDOWSON, J. D. A. (1994). *Survey of English Dialects: The Dictionary and Grammar.* London: Routledge.

VAISEY, D. (1984). *The Diary of Thomas Turner 1754–1765* [repr. 1985]. Oxford and New York: Oxford University Press.

VERSTEGAN, R. (1605). *A Restitution of Decayed Intelligence.* London: J. Norton and J. Bill.

VIERECK, W., with RAMSICH, H. (1991). *The Computer Developed Linguistic Atlas of England: Volume 1.* Tübingen: Niemeyer.

—— (1997). *The Computer Developed Linguistic Atlas of England: Volume 2.* Tübingen: Niemeyer.

WALKER, J. (1791). *A Critical Pronouncing Dictionary and Expositor of the English Language.* London: G. and D. J. Robinson.

—— (1801). *A Rhetorical Grammar or Course of Lessons in Elocution* (3rd edn.). London: G. Robinson and T. Cadell.

WALKER, R. S. (ed.) (1966). *The Correspondence of Boswell and John Johnston.* London: Heinemann.

WARNER, W. (1586; 1612). *Albion's England*, in A. Chalmers (ed.), *The Works of the English Poets from Chaucer to Cowper*, vol. 4. London: J. Johnson *et al.*, 1810, 21 vols, 509–658.

WEISS, J. (ed. and trans.) (2002). *Wace's Roman de Brut: A History of the British.* Exeter: The University of Exeter Press.

WELLS, J. E. (ed.) (1907). *The Owl and the Nightingale.* Boston: D. C. Heath.

WILCOX, J. (ed.) (1994). *Ælfric's Prefaces.* Durham: Durham Medieval Texts.

WILLIAMS, R. ([1997].) *A Key into the Language of America* [1643] (Facsimile edn.). Bedford, MA: Applewood Books.

WILSON, T. (1553). *The Arte of Rhetorique*, ed. T. J. Derrick. New York: Garland Publishing, 1982.

WILSON, T. (1612). *A Complete Christian Dictionary.* London: W. Jaggard.

WOGAN-BROWNE, J., WATSON, N., TAYLOR, A., and EVANS, R. (eds) (1999). *The Idea of the Vernacular: An Anthology of Middle English Literary Theory 1280–1520.* Exeter: University of Exeter Press.

WRIGHT, A. (1891). *Baboo English as 'tis Writ.* London: T. F. Unwin.

WRIGHT, J. (ed.) (1898–1905). *The English Dialect Dictionary: being the complete vocabulary of all dialect words still in use, or known to have been in use during the last two hundred years*. 6 vols. London: Henry Frowde.

—— (1905). *The English Dialect Grammar*: *comprising the dialects of England, of the Shetland and Orkney islands, and of those parts of Scotland, Ireland & Wales where English is habitually spoken*. Oxford: Henry Frowde.

YULE, H. and BURNELL, A. C. ([1976]). *Hobson-Jobson: A Glossary of Colloquial Anglo-Indian Words and Phrases* (1886, 1903). New York: Humanities Press.

SECONDARY SOURCES

AARSLEFF, H. (1983). *The Study of Language in England, 1780–1860*. London: The Athlone Press.

AITCHISON, J. (1981). *Language Change: Progress or Decay?* London: Fontana.

AITKEN, A. J. (1981). 'The Scottish Vowel-length Rule', in M. Benskin and M. L. Samuels (eds), *So Meny People, Longages and Tonges*. Edinburgh: Edinburgh University Press, 131–57.

ALBROW, M. (1996). *The Global Age: State and Society Beyond Modernity*. Cambridge: Polity Press.

ALLEN, C. L. (1997). 'Middle English Case Loss and the "Creolization" Question', *English Language and Linguistics*, 1: 63–89.

ALLERTON, D. J., SKANDERA, P., and TSCHICHOLD, C. (eds) (2002). *Perspectives on English as a World Language*. Basel: Schwab Verlag.

ALLMAND, C. (1992). *Henry V*. London: Methuen.

ALTICK, R. D. (1998). *The English Common Reader. A Social History of the Mass Reading Public, 1800–1900* (2nd edn). Ohio: Ohio State University Press.

AMOS, F. R. (1920). *Early Theories of Translation*. New York: Columbia University Press.

ANDERSON, H. and EHRENPREIS, I. (1968). 'The Familiar Letter in the Eighteenth Century: Some Generalizations', in H. Anderson, P. B. Daghlian, and I. Ehrenpreis (eds), *The Familiar Letter in the Eighteenth Century*. Lawrence: University of Kansas Press, 269–82.

ARNOLD. J. (2000). *History. A Very Short Introduction*. Oxford: Oxford University Press.

ASHCROFT, B., GRIFFITHS, G., and TIFFIN, H. (1989). *The Empire Writes Back: Theory and Practice in Post-Colonial Literatures*. London: Routledge.

AUSTIN, F. (1973). 'Epistolary Conventions in the Clift Correspondence', *English Studies*, 54: 9–22, 129–40.

AUSTIN, F. (1994). 'The Effect of Exposure to Standard English: The Language of William Clift', in D. Stein and I. Tieken-Boon van Ostade (eds), *Towards a Standard English 1600–1800*. Berlin and New York: Mouton de Gruyter, 285–313.

—— and JONES, B. (2002). *The Language and Craft of William Barnes, English Poet and Philologist (1801–1886)*. Lewiston: The Edwin Mellen Press.

AYTO, J. (1999). *Twentieth Century Words*. Oxford: Oxford University Press.

BAILEY, R. W. (1985). 'The Conquests of English,' in S. Greenbaum (ed.), *The English Language Today*. Oxford: Pergamon, 9–19.

—— (1991). *Images of English: A Cultural History of the Language*. Ann Arbor, MI: The University of Michigan Press.

—— (1996). *Nineteenth-Century English*. Ann Arbor, MI: The University of Michigan Press.

—— (2001). 'American English Abroad,' in J. Algeo (ed.), *The Cambridge History of the English Language*. Vol. VI: *English in North America*. Cambridge: Cambridge University Press.

BAILEY, R. W. and Görlach, M. (eds) (1984). *English as a World Language*. Cambridge: Cambridge University Press.

BAKER, P. S. (2003). *Introduction to Old English*. Oxford: Blackwell.

BALDI, P. (1983). *An Introduction to the Indo-European Languages*. Carbondale: Southern Illinois University Press.

BAMMESBERGER, A. (1992). 'The place of English in Germanic and Indo-European', in R. M. Hogg (ed.), *The Cambridge History of the English Language*. Vol. 1: *The Beginnings to 1066*. Cambridge: Cambridge University Press, 26–66.

BARBER, C. (1993). *The English Language: A Historical Introduction*. Cambridge: Cambridge University Press.

—— (1997). *Early Modern English* (2nd edn.). Edinburgh: Edinburgh University Press.

BARCHAS, J. (1996). 'Sarah Fielding's Dashing Style and Eighteenth-Century Print Culture', *ELH*, 63: 633–56.

BARON, N. S. (2000). *Alphabet to Email. How Written English Evolved and Where It's Heading*. London: Routledge.

BARRY, M. V. (1981). *Aspects of English Dialects in Ireland*. Vol. 1: *Papers arising from the Tape-recorded Survey of Hiberno-English Speech*. Belfast: Institute of Irish Studies.

—— (1982). 'The English Language in Ireland', in R. W. Bailey and M. Görlach (eds), *English as a World Language*. Ann Arbor, MI: University of Michigan Press, 84–133.

BATELY, J. M. (1988). 'Old English Prose Before and During the Reign of Alfred', *Anglo-Saxon England* 17: 93–138.

BAUGH, A. and CABLE, T. (2002). *A History of the English Language* (5th edn.). London: Routledge.

BEADLE, R. (1994). 'Middle English Texts and their Transmission, 1350–1500: Some Geographical Criteria', in M. Laing and K. Williamson (eds), *Speaking in Our Tongues: Proceedings of a Colloquium on Medieval Dialectology and Related Disciplines*. Cambridge: D. S. Brewer, 69–91.

BEAL, J. (2000). 'From Geordie Ridley to Viz: Popular Literature in Tyneside English', *Language and Literature*, 9/4: 359–75.

—— (2004). *English in Modern Times: 1700–1945*. London: Arnold.

BELL, R. H. (1909). *The Changing Values of English Speech*. New York: Hinds, Noble and Eldredge.

BENNETT, M. J. (1983). *Community, Class, and Careerism: Cheshire and Lancashire Society in the Age of Sir Gawain and the Green Knight*. Cambridge: Cambridge University Press.

BENSKIN, M. (1992). 'Some New Perspectives on the Origins of Standard Written English', in J. A. van Leuvensteijn and J. B. Berns (eds), *Dialect and Standard Language in the English, Dutch, German and Norwegian Language Areas: 17 Studies in English or German*. Amsterdam: Netherlands Academy of Arts and Science, 71–105.

—— (2004). '"Chancery Standard"', in C. Kay, C. Hough, and I. Wotherspoon (eds), *New Perspectives on English Historical Linguistics: Selected Papers from 12 ICEHL, Glasgow, 21–26 August 2002*. Vol. II: Lexis and Transmission. Amsterdam Studies in the Theory and History of Linguistic Science, 252. Amsterdam: John Benjamins, 1–40.

—— and LAING, M. (1981). 'Translations and *Mischsprachen* in Middle English Manuscripts', in M. Benskin and M. L. Samuels (eds), *So Meny People, Longages and Tonges: Philological Essays in Scots and Mediaeval English Presented to Angus McIntosh*. Edinburgh: Middle English Dialect Project, 55–106.

BENVENISTE, E. (1973). *Indo-European Language and Society*, trans. E. Palmer. London: Faber.

BENZIE, W. (1972). *The Dublin Orator: Thomas Sheridan's Influence on Eighteenth-Century Rhetoric and Belles Letters*. Leeds: University of Leeds.

BIJKERK, A. (2004). '*Yours Sincerely* and *Yours Affectionately*: On the Origin and Development of Two Positive Politeness Formulas', in T. Nevalainen and S.-K. Tanskanen (eds), *Letter Writing*. Special issue of *Journal of Historical Pragmatics*, 5/2: 297–311.

BJÖRKMAN, E. (1900–02). *Scandinavian Loan-Words in Middle English*. Halle: Niemeyer.

BLACK, J. and MACRAILD, D. M. (2003). *Nineteenth-Century Britain*. Basingstoke: Palgrave Macmillan.

BLAIR, W. and McDAVID, I. R., Jr. (eds) (1983). *The Mirth of a Nation: America's Great Dialect Humor*. Minneapolis: University of Minnesota Press.

BLAKE, N. F. (1981). *Non-standard Language in English Literature*. London: Deutsch.

—— (ed.) (1992). *The Cambridge History of the English Language*. Vol. II: *1066–1476*. Cambridge: Cambridge University Press.

—— (1996). *A History of the English Language*. Houndmills: Macmillan.

BLANK, P. (1996). *Broken English: Dialects and the Politics of Language in Renaissance Writings*. London and New York: Routledge.

BLOOMFIELD, L. (1933). *Language*. London: Unwin.

BOLTON, K. (2003). *Chinese Englishes: A Sociolinguistic History*. Cambridge: Cambridge University Press.

BRADFORD, S. (1982). *Disraeli*. London: Weidenfield and Nicholson.

BREE, L. (1996). *Sarah Fielding*. New York: Twayne Publishers/London: Prentice Hall International.

BROWNE, J. (2003). *Charles Darwin*. 2 vols. London: Pimlico.

BROWNSTONE, D. and FRANCK, I. (eds) (1996). *Timelines of the 20th Century: A Chronology of 7,500 Key Events, Discoveries, and People that Shaped Our Century*. Boston: Little, Brown & Co.

BRUTT-GRIFFLER, J. (2002). *World English: A Study of its Development*. Clevedon: Multilingual Matters.

BURCHFIELD, R. W. (1973). 'The Treatment of Controversial Vocabulary in the *OED*', *Transactions of the Philological Society*, 1–28.

—— (ed.) (1994). *The Cambridge History of the English Language*. Vol. V: *English in Britain and Overseas*. Cambridge: Cambridge University Press.

BURNETT, J., VINCENT, D., and MAYAL, D. (eds) (1984). *The Autobiography of the Working Class: An Annotated, Critical Bibliography*. Brighton: Harvester.

BURNLEY, D. (1983). *The Language of Chaucer*. Houndmills: Macmillan.

—— (1992*b*). 'Lexis and Semantics', in N. F. Blake (ed.), *The Cambridge History of the English Language*. Vol. II: *1066–1476*. Cambridge: Cambridge University Press, 409–99.

BURNS, A. and COFFIN, C. (eds) (2001). *Analysing English in a Global Context: A Reader*. London: Routledge.

BUSSE, U. (2002). *Linguistic Variation in the Shakespeare Corpus: Morpho-Syntactic Variability of Second Person Pronouns*. Amsterdam and Philadelphia: Benjamins.

CAMPBELL, A. (1959). *Old English Grammar*. Oxford: Oxford University Press.

CAMPBELL, L. (2001). 'What's Wrong with Grammaticalization?', *Language Sciences* 23: 113–61.

CANNON, C. (1998). *The Making of Chaucer's English: A Study of Words*. Cambridge: Cambridge University Press.

CARR, P. (1999). *English Phonetics and Phonology: An Introduction*. Oxford: Blackwell.

CARRUTHERS, M. J. (1990). *The Book of Memory: A Study of Memory in Medieval Culture*. Cambridge: Cambridge University Press.

CHAMBERS, J. K. (2003). *Sociolinguistic Theory* (2nd edn.). Oxford: Blackwell.

—— and TRUDGILL, P. (1998). *Dialectology* (2nd edn.). Cambridge: Cambridge University Press.

CHESHIRE, J. (ed.) (1991). *English around the World: Sociolinguistic Perspectives*. Cambridge: Cambridge University Press.

CHOMSKY, N. and HALLE, M. (1968). *The Sound Pattern of English*. New York: Harper & Row.

CHRISTIANSON, C. P. (1989). 'Evidence for the Study of London's Late Medieval Manuscript-Book Trade', in J. Griffiths and D. Pearsall (eds), *Book Production and Publishing in Britain 1375–1475*. Cambridge: Cambridge University Press, 87–108.

CLANCHY, M. T. (1993). *From Memory to Written Record: England 1066–1307* (2nd edn.). Oxford: Blackwell.

COATES, J. (1993). *Women, Men and Language* (2nd edn.). London: Longman.

COCKBURN, J. S. (1975). 'Early Modern Assize Records as Historical Evidence', *Journal of Society of Archivists*, 5: 215–31.

COCKERAM, H. (1623). *The English Dictionarie*. London: E. Weaver.

COLEMAN, J. (1995). 'The Chronology of French and Latin Loan Words in English,' *Transactions of the Philological Society*, 93: 95–124.

—— (2004). *A History of Cant and Slang Dictionaries*. Vol. 1: *1567–1784*. Oxford: Oxford University Press.

COLLINS, B. and REES, I. M. (1999). *The Real Professor Higgins: the Life and Career of Daniel Jones*. Berlin: Gruyter.

COLMAN, F. (1983). 'Vocalization as Nucleation', *Studia Linguistica* 37: 30–49.

COOMBS, D. (1988). *Spreading the Word: the Library Work of the British Council*. London: Mansell.

CORBETT, J., McCLURE, J. D., and STUART-SMITH, J. (2003). *The Edinburgh Companion to Scots*. Edinburgh: Edinburgh University Press.

CORFIELD, P. (1987). 'Class by Name and Number in Eighteenth-Century Britain', *History*, 72: 39–61.

COTTRELL, P. L. (ed.) (1992). *Events: A Chronicle of the Twentieth Century*. Oxford: Oxford University Press.

COUPLAND, N. (1988). *Dialect in Use: Sociolinguistic Variation in Cardiff English*. Cardiff: University of Wales Press.

CRANE, S. (1997). 'Social Aspects of Bilingualism in the Thirteenth Century', in M. Prestwich, R. H. Britnell, and R. Frame (eds), *Thirteenth Century England VI: Proceedings of the Durham Conference 1995*. Woodbridge: Boydell, 103–15.

—— (1999). 'Anglo-Norman Cultures in England, 1066–1460', in D. Wallace (ed.), *The Cambridge History of Medieval English Literature*. Cambridge: Cambridge University Press, 35–60.

CRONIN, M. (2003). *Translation and Globalization*. London & New York: Routledge.

CRYSTAL, D. (2000). *Language Death*. Cambridge: Cambridge University Press.

—— (2003a). *The Cambridge Encyclopedia of the English Language* (2nd edn.). Cambridge: Cambridge University Press.

—— (2003b). *English as a Global Language* (2nd edn.). Cambridge: Cambridge University Press.

—— (2004a). *The Stories of English*. London: Penguin/Allen Lane.

—— (2004b). *Making Sense of English Grammar*. London: Pearson Education.

—— (2004c). *The Language Revolution*. Cambridge: Polity.

CRYSTAL, D. (2004*d*). *A Glossary of Netspeak and Textspeak*. Edinburgh: Edinburgh University Press.

—— (2006). *Language and the Internet*. 2nd edn. Cambridge: Cambridge University Press.

DANCE, R. (2003). *Words Derived from Old Norse in Early Middle English: Studies in the Vocabulary of the South-West Midland Texts*. Tempe: Medieval and Renaissance Texts and Studies.

DANIELSSON, B. (1963). *John Hart's Works on English Orthography and Pronunciation (1551, 1569, 1570)*, Part 2, *Phonology*. Stockholm: Almqvist and Wiksell.

DAVIS, L. M. (1983). *English Dialectology: An Introduction*. Alabama: University of Alabama Press.

DAVIS, L., HOUCK, C., and UPTON, C. (1997). 'The Question of Dialect Boundaries: The *SED* and the American Atlases', in A. Thomas (ed.), *Current Methods in Dialectology: Proceedings of the Methods IX International Conference on Dialectology, Bangor, 1996*. Bangor: University of Wales Bangor, 271–283.

DAVIS, N. (1972). 'Margaret Paston's Uses of *Do*', *Neuphilologische Mitteilungen*, 73: 55–62.

—— (1983). 'The Language of Two Brothers in the Fifteenth Century', in E. G. Stanley and D. Gray (eds), *Five Hundred Years of Words and Sounds: A Festschrift for Eric Dobson*, Cambridge: D. S. Brewer, 23–28.

DEES, A. (1971). *Etude sur l'evolution des demonstratifs en ancien et en moyen francais*. Groningen: Walters-Noordhoff.

DEKEYSER, X. (1975). *Number and Case Relation in 19th Century British English. A Comparative Study of Grammar and Usage*. Amsterdam: De Nederlandske Boekhandel.

—— (1996). 'Concord of Number in Lindley Murray's *Grammar*: The Dialectics between Prescription and Usage', in I. Tieken-Boon van Ostade (ed.), *Two Hundred Years of Lindley Murray*. Münster: Nodus Publikationen, 193–206.

DENISON, D. (1993). *English Historical Linguistics: Verbal Constructions*. London: Longman.

—— (1998). 'Syntax', in S. Romaine, *The Cambridge History of the English Language*. Cambridge: Cambridge University Press, 92–329.

DEVITT, A. (1989). *Standardizing Written English*. Cambridge: Cambridge University Press.

DIETH, E. (1932). *A Grammar of the Buchan Dialect (Aberdeenshire): Descriptive and Historical*. Cambridge: W. Heffer.

DOBSON, E. J. (1955). 'Early Modern Standard English', *Transactions of the Philological Society*, 25–54; reprinted in R. Lass (ed.), *Approaches to English Historical Linguistics*. New York: Holt, Rinehart and Winston (1969), 419–39.

—— (1968). *English Pronunciation 1500–1700* (2nd edn.), 2 vols. Oxford: Clarendon Press.

—— (1976). *The Origins of Ancrene Wisse*. Oxford: Clarendon Press.

DONALDSON, W. (1986). *Popular Literature in Victorian Scotland: Language, Fiction, and the Press*. Aberdeen: Aberdeen University Press.

DOUGHTY, P., PEARCE, J., and THORNTON, G. (1971). *Language in Use*. London: Edward Arnold.

DUNDES, A., LEACH, J. W., and ÖZKÖK, B. (1972). 'The Strategy of Turkish Boys' Verbal Duelling Rhymes', in J. J. Gumperz and D. Hymes (eds), *Directions in Sociolinguistics*. New York: Holt, Rinehart and Winston, 130–60.

DUNNING, J. H. (ed.) (2003). *Making Globalization Good: The Moral Challenges of Global Capitalism*. Oxford: University Press.

ECO, U. (1995). *The Search for the Perfect Language*, trans. J. Fentress. Oxford: Blackwell.

'Eighth Report of the Committee on Devonshire Verbal Provincialisms' (1885). *Transactions of the Devonshire Association for the Advancement of Science, Literature, and Art*, 77–117.

ELLEGÅRD, A. (1953). *The Auxiliary 'Do': The Establishment and Regulation of its Use in English*. Stockholm: Almqvist and Wiksell.

ELLIOTT, R. W. V. (1989). *Runes: an Introduction*. Manchester: Manchester University Press.

ELMES, S. (1999–2000). *The Routes of English*. 4 vols + 8 CD Roms. London: BBC Education.

FAIRMAN, T. (2003). 'Letters of the English Labouring Classes and the English Language, 1800–34', in M. Dossena and C. Jones (eds), *Insights into Late Modern English*. Bern: Peter Lang, 265–81.

FEBVRE, L. and MARTIN, H.-J. (1976). *The Coming of the Book: the Impact of Printing 1450–1800* trans. D. Gerard; ed. G. Nowell-Smith and D. Wootton. London: N.L.B.

FENNELL, B. A. (2001). *A History of English. A Sociolinguistic Approach*. Oxford: Blackwell.

FENTON, A. and. MACDONALD, D. A. (eds) (1994). *Studies in Scots and Gaelic: Proceedings of the Third International Conference on the Languages of Scotland*. Edinburgh: Canongate Academic and The Linguistic Survey of Scotland.

FILPPULA, M. (1999). *The Grammar of Irish English: Language in Hibernian Style*. London: Routledge.

FINEGAN, E. (1992). 'Style and Standardization in England: 1700–1900', in T. Machan and C. T. Scott (eds), *England in its Social Contexts. Essays in Historical Sociolinguistics*. Oxford and New York: Oxford University Press.

FISHER, J. (1977). 'Chancery and the Emergence of Standard Written English in the Fifteenth Century', *Speculum*, 52: 870–99.

FLEMING, G. (1998). *John Everett Millais: A Biography*. London: Constable.

FLETCHER, S. (1997). *Victorian Girls. Lord Lyttelton's Daughters*. London: The Hambledon Press.

FOULKES, P. and DOCHERTY, G. J. (eds) (1999). *Urban Voices: Accent Studies in the British Isles*. London: Arnold.

FRANCIS, N. M. (1983). *Dialectology: An Introduction*. London: Longman.

FRANK, R. (1994). 'King Cnut in the Verse of his Skalds', in A. Rumble (ed.), *The Reign of Cnut: King of England, Denmark and Norway*. London: Leicester University Press, 106–24.

FRANK, T. (1994), 'Language Standardization in Eighteenth-Century Scotland', in D. Stein and I. Tieken-Boon van Ostade (eds), *Towards a Standard English 1600–1800*. Berlin and New York: Mouton de Gruyter, 51–62.

FRANZEN, C. (1991). *The Tremulous Hand of Worcester: A Study of Old English in the Thirteenth Century*. Oxford: Clarendon Press.

GASH, N. (1985). *Mr. Secretary Peel: the Life of Sir Robert Peel to 1830* (2nd edn.). London: Longman.

GERNER, J. (1996). *Untersuchungen zur Funktion des emphatischen* do *im Englischen*. Frankfurt am Main: Peter Lang.

GNEUSS, H. (1972). 'The Origin of Standard Old English and Æthelwold's School at Winchester', *Anglo-Saxon England* 1: 63–83.

—— (1993). *Language and History in Early England*, Aldershot: Variorum.

GODDEN, M. R. (2002). 'Ælfric as Grammarian: the Evidence of his Catholic Homilies', in E. Treharne and S. Rosser (eds), *Early Medieval English Texts and Interpretations: Studies Presented to Donald G. Scragg*. Tempe, AZ: Arizona Center for Medieval and Renaissance Studies, 13–29.

GODRÍGUEZ-GIL, M. (2002). 'Ann Fisher: First Female Grammarian'. *Historical Sociolinguistics and Sociohistorical Linguistics* 2 <http://www.let.leidenuniv.nl/hsl_shl/> (→Contents→Articles).

GOMEZ SOLINO, J. (1984). *Variacion y Estandarizacion en el Ingles Moderno Temprano 1470–1540*. Unpublished PhD thesis, University of Oviedo.

GORDON, E. V. (1957). *An Introduction to Old Norse* (2nd edn.), rev. A. R. Taylor. Oxford: Clarendon Press.

GORDON, L. (1994). *Charlotte Brontë. A Passionate Life*. London: Chatto and Windus.

GÖRLACH, M. (ed.) (1985). *Focus on Scotland*. Amsterdam: John Benjamins.

—— (1986). 'Middle English—a Creole?', in D. Kastovsky and A. Szwedek (eds), *Linguistics Across Historical and Geographical Boundaries in Honour of Jacek Fisiak on the Occasion of His Fiftieth Birthday*. 2 vols. Berlin: Mouton de Gruyter, i: 329–44.

—— (1991). *Introduction to Early Modern English*. Cambridge: Cambridge University Press.

—— (1997). '. . . A Construction than which None is More Difficult', in T. Nevalainen and L. Kahlas-Tarkka (eds), *To Explain the Present. Studies in the Changing English Language in Honour of Matti Rissanen*. Helsinki: Société Néophilologique, 277–301.

—— (1999). *English in Nineteenth-Century England: An Introduction*. Cambridge: Cambridge University Press.

—— (2001*a*). *Eighteenth-Century English*. Heidelberg: Universitätsverlag C. Winter.

—— (2001*b*). *A Dictionary of European Anglicisms*. Oxford: Oxford University Press.

—— (ed.) (2002). *English in Europe*. Oxford: Oxford University Press.

—— (2003). 'A New Text Type: Exercises in Bad English', in F. Austin and C. Stray (eds), *The Teaching of English in the Eighteenth and Nineteenth Centuries. Essays for Ian Michael on his 88th Birthday, Paradigm* 2: 5–14.

GRADDOL, D. (1997). *The Future of English?* London: The British Council.

—— and MEINHOF, U. H. (eds) (1999). *English in a Changing World. AILA Review* 13.

—— LEITH, D., and SWANN, J. (eds) (1996). *English: History, Diversity and Change.* London: Routledge.

GREEN, D. H. (1998). *Language and History in the Early Germanic World.* Cambridge: Cambridge University Press.

GRETSCH, M. (1999). *The Intellectual Foundations of the English Benedictine Reform.* Cambridge Studies in Anglo-Saxon England 25. Cambridge: Cambridge University Press.

HANDS, R. (ed.) (1975). *English Hawking and Hunting in The Boke of St Albans.* London: Oxford University Press.

HAUGEN, E. (1966). 'Dialect, Language, Nation', *American Anthropologist,* 68: 922–35.

—— (ed.) (1972). *First Grammatical Treatise.* London: Harlow.

—— (1976). *The Scandinavian Languages.* London: Faber.

HEALEY, E. (2001). *Emma Darwin: The Inspirational Wife of a Genius.* London: Headline.

HELLINGA, L. (1997). 'Nicholas Love in Print', in S. Oguro, R. Beadle, and M. Sargent (eds), *Nicholas Love at Waseda.* Cambridge: D. S. Brewer, 143–62.

HEPWORTH, B. (1978). *Robert Lowth.* Boston: Twayne Publishers.

HERRING, S. C. (ed.) (1996). *Computer-mediated Communication.* Amsterdam: Benjamins.

HIBBERT, C. (2000). *Queen Victoria. A Personal History.* London: HarperCollins.

HICKEY, R. (ed.) (2004). *Legacies of Colonial English: Studies in Transported Dialects.* Cambridge: Cambridge University Press.

HIGHAM, N. J. (1997). *The Death of Anglo-Saxon England.* Stroud, Glos.: Sutton.

HOFSTETTER, W. (1988). 'Winchester and the Standardization of Old English Vocabulary', *Anglo-Saxon England* 17: 139–61.

HOGG, R. M. (ed.) (1992*a*). *The Cambridge History of the English Language.* Vol. I: *The Beginnings to 1066.* Cambridge: Cambridge University Press.

—— (1992*b*). *A Grammar of Old English.* Vol. 1: *Phonology.* Oxford: Blackwell.

HOLMAN, K. (1996). *Scandinavian Runic Inscriptions in the British Isles: Their Historical Context.* Trondheim: Tapir.

HOLMQVIST, B. (1922). *On the History of the English Present Inflections, Particularly* -th *and* -s. Heidelberg: Carl Winter.

HOLT, D. E. (ed.) (2003). *Optimality Theory and Language Change.* Dordrecht: Kluwer.

HONEY, J. (1988). '"Talking Proper": Schooling and the Establishment of English "Received Pronunciation"', in G. Nixon and J. Honey (eds), *An Historic Tongue: Studies in English Linguistics in Memory of Barbara Strang.* London: Routledge, 209–27.

HOPPER, P. and TRAUGOTT, E. C. (1993). *Grammaticalisation*. Cambridge: Cambridge University Press.

HOROBIN, S. (2003). *The Language of the Chaucer Tradition*. Chaucer Studies 32. Cambridge: D. S. Brewer.

—— and SMITH, J. J. (2002). *An Introduction to Middle English*. Edinburgh: Edinburgh University Press.

HOWARD, M. and LEWIS, W. R. (1998). *The Oxford History of the Twentieth Century*. Oxford: Oxford University Press.

HOWE, N. (1989). *Migration and Mythmaking in Anglo-Saxon England*. New Haven and London: Yale University Press.

HUDDLESTON, R. D. (1971). *The Sentence in Written English: A Syntactic Study based on an Analysis of Scientific Texts*. Cambridge: Cambridge University Press.

HUDSON, R. (1980). *Sociolinguistics*. Cambridge: Cambridge University Press.

HUGHES, A., and TRUDGILL, P. (1996). *English Accents and Dialects: An Introduction to Social and Regional Varieties of British English* (3rd edn.). London: Edward Arnold.

HUGHES, G. (2000). *A History of English Words*. Oxford: Blackwell.

HUNTINGTON, S. P. (1996). *The Clash of Civilizations and the Remaking of World Order*. New York: Simon & Schuster.

ILMBERGER, F. and ROBINSON, A. (2002). *Globalisation*. Tübingen: Gunter Narr Verlag.

IRVINE, S. (2000*a*). 'The Compilation and Use of Manuscripts Containing Old English in the Twelfth Century', in M. Swan and E. M. Treharne (eds), *Rewriting Old English in the Twelfth Century*. Cambridge Studies in Anglo-Saxon England 26. Cambridge: Cambridge University Press, 41–61.

—— (2000*b*) 'Linguistic Peculiarities in Late Copies of Ælfric and their Editorial Implications', in J. Roberts and J. Nelson (eds), *Essays on Anglo-Saxon and Related Themes in Memory of Lynne Grundy*. King's College London: Centre for Late Antique and Medieval Studies, 237–57.

JACOB, E. (1961). *The Fifteenth Century*. Oxford: Clarendon Press.

JAMES, L. (ed.) (1976). *Print and the People 1819–1851*. London: James Allen.

JANDA, R. (2001). 'Beyond "Pathways" and "Unidirectionality": On the discontinuity of language transmission and the counterability of grammaticalization', *Language Sciences*, 23: 265–340.

JASANOFF, J. H. (1997). 'Germanic (Le germanique)' (in English), in F. Bader (ed.), *Langues indo-européennes*. Paris: CNRS Editions, 253–82.

JÁSZI, O. (1929). *The Dissolution of the Habsburg Monarchy*. Chicago: The University of Chicago Press.

JENKINS, J. (2003). *World Englishes: A Resource Book for Students*. London and New York: Routledge.

JENKINS, R. (1995). *Gladstone*. London: Macmillan.

JESCH, J. (2001). 'Skaldic Verse in Scandinavian England', in J. Graham-Campbell, R. Hall, J. Jesch, and D. N. Parsons (eds), *Vikings and the Danelaw: Select Papers from the*

Proceedings of the Thirteenth Viking Congress, Nottingham and York, 21–30 August 1997. Oxford: Oxbow, 313–25.

JESPERSEN, O. (1909). *A Modern English Grammar on Historical Principles*. Vol. 1: *Sounds and Spellings*. Copenhagen: Munksgaard.

—— (1956). *The Growth and Structure of the English Language* (9th edn.). Oxford: Blackwell.

JOHNSTON, P. (1997). 'Older Scots Phonology and its Regional Variation', in C. Jones (ed.), *The Edinburgh History of the Scots Language*. Edinburgh: Edinburgh University Press, 47–111.

JONES, C. (1988). *Grammatical Gender in English: 950–1250*. London: Croom Helm.

—— (ed.) (1997). *The Edinburgh History of the Scots Language*, Edinburgh: Edinburgh University Press.

JONES, G. (1999). *Strange Talk: The Politics of Dialect Literature in Gilded Age America*. Berkeley and Los Angeles: The University of California Press.

JONES, R. F. (1953). *The Triumph of the English Language: A Survey of Opinions Concerning the Vernacular from the Introduction of Printing to the Restoration*. Stanford, CA: Stanford University Press.

JORDAN, R. (1974). *Handbook of Middle English Grammar: Phonology*. Trans. and rev. E. J. Crook. Janua Linguarum, Series Practica, 218. The Hague: Mouton.

JOYCE, P. (1991). 'The People's English: Language and Class in England *c*.1840–1920', in BURKE P. and R. PORTER (eds.), *Language, Self, and Society. A Social History of Language*. Cambridge: Polity Press.

KACHRU, B. B. (1983). *The Indianization of English: the English Language in India*. Delhi and Oxford: Oxford University Press.

—— (1990). *The Alchemy of English: the Spread, Functions, and Models of Non-native Englishes*. Urbana: University of Illinois Press.

—— (ed.) (1992). *The Other Tongue: English across Cultures* (2nd edn.). Urbana: University of Illinois Press.

KAGER, R. (1999). *Optimality Theory*. Cambridge: Cambridge University Press.

KALLEN, J. L. (ed.) (1997). *Focus on Ireland*. Amsterdam: John Benjamins.

KARL, F. (1995). *George Eliot. A Biography*. London: HarperCollins.

KARTTUNEN, F. (2000). 'Interpreters Snatched from the Shore: The Successful and the Others,' in E. G. Gray and N. Fiering (eds), *The Language Encounter in the Americas, 1492–1800*. New York: Berghahn Books, 215–29.

KASTOVSKY, D. (1992). 'Semantics and Vocabulary,' in R. Hogg (ed.), *The Cambridge History of the English Language*. Vol. 1: *The Beginnings to 1066*. Cambridge: Cambridge University Press, 290–408.

KEAST, W. R. (1957). 'The two Clarissas in Johnson's *Dictionary*', *Studies in Philology*, 54: 429–39.

KELLER, R. E. (1978). *The German Language*. London: Faber.

KERSWILL, P. and WILLIAMS, A. (1999). 'Dialect Recognition and Speech Community Focusing in New and old Towns in England: the Effects of Dialect Levelling, Demography, and Social Networks', in C. Upton and K. Wales (eds), *Dialectal Variation in English: Proceedings of the Harold Orton Centenary Conference 1998*. Leeds: Leeds Studies in English XXX, 205–41.

KEYNES, S. (1998). 'King Alfred and the Mercians', in M. A. S. Blackburn and D. N. Dumville (eds), *Kings, Currency and Alliances: History and Coinage of Southern England in the Ninth Century*. Woodbridge: The Boydell Press, 1–45.

KIBBEE, D. A. (1991). *For To Speke Frenche Trewely. The French Language in England, 1000–1600: Its Status, Description and Instruction*. Amsterdam: Benjamins.

KING, A. (1997). 'The Inflectional Morphology of Older Scots', in C. Jones (ed.), *The Edinburgh History of the Scots Language*. Edinburgh: Edinburgh University Press, 156–81.

KITSON, P. R. (1992). 'Old English Dialects and the Stages of the Transition to Middle English', *Folia Linguistica Historica*, 11 [for 1990]: 27–87.

—— (1993). 'Geographical Variation in Old English Prepositions and the Location of Ælfric's and Other Literary Dialects', *English Studies*, 74: 1–50.

KLANCHER, J. P. (1987). *The Making of English Reading Audiences 1790–1832*. Madison and London: University of Wisconsin Press.

KNOWLES, G. (1997). *A Cultural History of the English Language*. London: Arnold.

KNOWLSON, J. (1975). *Universal Language Schemes in England and France 1600–1800*. Buffalo and Toronto: University of Toronto Press.

KRAPP, G. P. (1919). *The Pronunciation of Standard English in America*. New York: Oxford University Press.

—— (1925). *The English Language in America*. 2 vols. New York: Frederick Ungar.

KUHN, W. M. (2002). *William and Mary Ponsonby. Life at the Court of Queen Victoria*. London: Duckworth.

KUPPERMAN, K. O. (2000). *Indians and English: Facing Off in Early America*. Ithac, NY: Cornell University Press.

KYTÖ, M. (1993). 'Third-person Present Singular Verb Inflection in Early British and American English', *Language Variation and Change*, 5: 113–39.

—— (ed.) (1996). *Manual to the Diachronic Part of the Helsinki Corpus of English Texts* (3rd edn.). Helsinki: Department of English, University of Helsinki.

LAING, M. (1991). 'Anchor Texts and Literary Manuscripts in Early Middle English', in F. Riddy (ed.), *Regionalism in Late Medieval Manuscripts and Texts: Essays Celebrating the Publication of a Linguistic Atlas of Late Mediaeval English*. Cambridge: D. S. Brewer, 27–52.

—— (1993). *Catalogue of Sources for a Linguistic Atlas of Early Medieval English*. Cambridge: D. S. Brewer.

—— and WILLIAMSON, K. (eds) (1994). *Speaking in our Tongues: Medieval Dialectology and Related Disciplines*. Cambridge: D. S. Brewer.

LAMBERT, R. S. (1964). *The Railway King. 1800–1871. A Study of George Hudson and the Business Morals of his Time*. London: George Allen & Unwin.

LAPIDGE, M. (1993). *Anglo-Latin Literature 900–1066*. London: Hambledon.

—— (1996). *Anglo-Latin Literature 600–899*. London: Hambledon.

LASS, R. (1976). *English Phonology and Phonological Theory*. Cambridge: Cambridge University Press.

—— (1987). *The Shape of English*. London: Dent.

—— (1988). 'Vowel Shifts, great and otherwise: Remarks on Stockwell and Minkova', in D. Kastovsky and G. Bauer (eds), *Luick Revisited*. Tübingen: Gunter Narr Verlag, 395–410.

—— (1992). 'What, If Anything, was the Great Vowel Shift?', in M. Rissanen, O. Ihalainen, T. Nevalainen, and I. Taavitsainen (eds), *History of Englishes: New Methods and Interpretations in Historical Linguistics*. Berlin: Mouton de Gruyter, 144–55.

—— (1994*a*). *Old English: a Historical Linguistic Companion*. Cambridge: Cambridge University Press.

—— (1994*b*). 'Proliferation and Option-Cutting: The Strong Verb in the Fifteenth to Eighteenth Centuries', in D. Stein and I. Tieken-Boon van Ostade (eds), *Towards a Standard English 1600–1800*. Berlin and New York: Mouton de Gruyter, 81–113.

—— (1999*a*). 'Phonology and Morphology', in R. Lass (ed.), *The Cambridge History of the English Language*. Vol. III: *1476–1776*. Cambridge: Cambridge University Press, 56–186.

—— (ed.) (1999*b*). *The Cambridge History of the English Language*. Vol. III: *1476–1776*. Cambridge: Cambridge University Press.

—— (2000). 'A Branching *path*: Low vowel lengthening and its friends in the emerging standard', in L. Wright (ed.), *The Development of Standard English 1300–1800*. Cambridge: Cambridge University Press, 219–29.

LEONARD, S. A. (1929). *The Doctrine of Correctness in English Usage, 1700–1800*. Madison: University of Wisconsin.

LERER, S. (1993). *Chaucer and His Readers: Imagining the Author in Late-Medieval England*. Princeton: Princeton University Press.

LIDDINGTON, J. (1984). *The Life and Times of a Respectable Rebel: Selina Cooper (1864–1946)*. London: Virago.

—— (1998). *Female Fortune: Land, Gender, and Authority: The Anne Lister Diaries and Other Writings, 1833–36*. London: Rivers Oram Press.

LOCKWOOD, W. B. (1972). *A Panorama of Indo-European Languages*. London: Hutchinson.

LONSDALE, R. (1965). *Dr. Charles Burney. A Literary Biography* [repr. 1986]. Oxford: Clarendon Press.

LUICK, K. (1920–40). *Historische Grammatik der englischen Sprache*. 2 vols. Leipzig: Tauchnitz; reprinted (1964) Oxford: Blackwell.

LUTEIJN, M. (2004). 'Lowth's Letters to his Wife: Reconstructing the Life of an Eight-eenth-Century Wife and Mother'. MA thesis, English Department, University of Leiden.

LYTTON, E. BULWER (1833). *England and the English.* 2 vols. London: Richard Bentley.

MACAFEE, C. (1994). *Traditional Dialects in the Modern World: A Glasgow Case Study.* Frankfurt am Main: Peter Lang.

MACAFEE, C. (2003). 'Studying Scots Vocabulary', in J. Corbett *et al.* (eds), *The Edinburgh Companion to Scots.* Edinburgh: Edinburgh University Press, 50–71.

MCARTHUR, T. (ed.) (1992). *The Oxford Companion to the English Language.* Oxford: Oxford University Press.

—— (1998*a*). *The English Languages.* Cambridge: Cambridge University Press.

—— (1998*b*). *Living Words: Language, Lexicography and the Knowledge Revolution.* Exeter: University of Exeter Press.

—— (2002*a*). *The Oxford Guide to World English.* Oxford: Oxford University Press.

—— (2002*b*). 'World English: Unity and diversity, profit and loss', in F. Ilmberger and A. Robinson (eds), *Globalisation.* Tübingen: Gunter Narr Verlag, 113–25.

—— (2004). 'Is it World or International or Global English, and Does it Matter?', *English Today,* 79 (20/3): 3–15.

MACCABE, C. (1999). *The Eloquence of the Vulgar. Language, Cinema, and the Politics of Popular Culture.* London: BFI Publishing.

MCCLURE, J. D. (1994). 'English in Scotland', in R. Burchfield (ed.), *The Cambridge History of the English Language,* vol. v, *English in Britain and Overseas.* Cambridge: Cambridge University Press, 23–93.

MCCONCHIE, R. W. (1997). *Lexicography and Physicke: the Record of Sixteenth-Century Medical Terminology.* Oxford: Clarendon Press.

MCCULLOCH, M. P. (ed.) (2004). *Modernism and Nationalism: Literature and Society in Scoitland, 1918–1939 (Source Documents for the Scottish Renaissance).* Glasgow: Associ-ation for Scottish Literary Studies.

MCELDERRY, B. R., Jr., 'Archaism and Innovation in Spenser's Poetic Diction,' *PMLA* 47/1 (1932): 144–70.

MACHAN, T. W. (2003). *English in the Middle Ages.* Oxford: Oxford University Press.

MCINTOSH, A. (1967). 'The Textual Transmission of the Alliterative *Morte Arthure*', in N. Davis and C. L. Wrenn (eds), *English and Medieval Studies Presented to J. R. R. Tolkien.* London: Allen and Unwin, 231–40.

—— (1973). 'Word Geography in the Lexicography of Mediaeval English', *Annals of the New York Academy of Sciences,* 211: 55–66.

—— , SAMUELS, M. L, and BENSKIN, M., with LAING, M., and WILLIAMSON, K. (1986). *A Linguistic Atlas of Late Mediaeval English.* 4 vols. Aberdeen: Aberdeen University Press.

MCINTOSH, C. (1986). *Common and Courtly Language. The Stylistics of Social Class in 18th-Century British Literature.* Philadelphia: University of Pennsylvania Press.

McMahon, A. (1994). *Understanding Language Change*. Cambridge: Cambridge University Press.

—— (2000). *Lexical Phonology and the History of English*. Cambridge: Cambridge University Press.

—— (2001). *An Introduction to English Phonology*. Edinburgh: Edinburgh University Press.

MacMahon, M. K. C. (1998). 'Phonology', in S. Romaine (ed.), *The Cambridge History of the English Language*. Vol. IV: *1776–1997*. Cambridge: Cambridge University Press, 373–535.

Mair, C. (ed.) (2003). *The Politics of English as a World Language*. ASNEL Papers 7. Amsterdam: Rodopi.

Martinet, A. (1955). *Economie des changements phonétiques*. Bern: Francke.

Matthew, C. (ed.) (2000a). *The Nineteenth Century: The British Isles: 1815–1901*. Oxford: Oxford University Press.

—— (2000b). 'Public Life and Politics', in C. Matthew, *The Nineteenth Century: the British Isles: 1815–1901*. Oxford: Oxford University Press, 85–133.

Matthews, W. (1937). 'The Vulgar Speech of London in the Fifteenth to Seventeenth Centuries', *Notes and Queries*, 172: 2–5.

Maurais, J. and Morris, M. A. (2003). *Languages in a Globalising World*. Cambridge: Cambridge University Press.

Melchers, G. and Shaw, P. (2003). *World Englishes*. London: Arnold.

Mencken, H. L. (1919). *The American Language*. New York: Alfred A. Knopf.

Merians, L. E. (2001). *Envisioning the Worst: Representations of 'Hottentots' in Early-Modern England*. Newark: University of Delaware Press.

Meurman-Solin, A. (1993). *Variation and Change in Early Scottish Prose; Studies Based on the Helsinki Corpus of Older Scots*. Helsinki: Academia Scientiarum Fennica.

—— (1995). 'A New Tool: The Helsinki Corpus of Older Scots (1450–1700)', *ICAME Journal*, 19: 49–62.

—— (2001). 'Structured Text Corpora in the Study of Language Variation and Change', *Literary and Linguistic Computing*, 16: 5–27.

Michael, I. (1987). *The Teaching of English: from the Sixteenth Century to 1870*. Cambridge: Cambridge University Press.

—— (1991). 'More than Enough English Grammars', in G. Leitner (ed.), *English Traditional Grammars*. Amsterdam: Benjamins, 11–26.

Millburn, J. R. (1976). *Benjamin Martin. Author, Instrument-Maker, and 'Country Showman'*. Leyden: Noordhoff International Publishing.

Miller, J. (2003). 'Syntax and Discourse in Modern Scots', in J. Corbett *et al.* (eds), *The Edinburgh Companion to Scots*. Edinburgh: Edinburgh University Press, 72–109.

Millward, C. M. (1996). *A Biography of the English Language* (2nd edn.). Orlando, Florida: Harcourt Brace.

MILROY, J. (1997). 'Internal vs External Motivations for Linguistic Change', *Multilingua*, 16: 311–23.

—— (2002). 'The Legitimate Language: Giving a history to English', in R. J. Watts and P. Trudgill (eds), *Alternative Histories of English*. London: Routledge, 7–26.

—— and MILROY, L. (1997). *Authority in Language: Investigating Standard English* (3rd edn.). London: Routledge.

MILROY, L. (1987). *Language and Social Networks* (2nd edn.). Oxford: Blackwell.

MILROY, L. and GORDON, M. (2003). *Sociolinguistics: Method and Interpretation*. Oxford: Blackwell.

MINUGH, D. C. (1999). '*What Aileth Thee, to Print So Curiously?* Archaic Forms and Contemporary Newspaper Language', in I. Taavitsainen, G. Melchers, and P. Pahta (eds), *Writing in Nonstandard English*. Amsterdam and Philadelphia: Benjamins, 285–304.

MINKOVA, D. (1999). Review of Roger Lass (ed.) (1999), *The Cambridge History of the English Language*. Vol. III: *1476–1776*, *Journal of English Linguistics*, 29: 83–92.

—— and STOCKWELL, R. (2003). 'English Vowel Shifts and "Optimal" Diphthongs: Is there a logical link?', in D. E. Holt (ed.), *Optimality Theory and Language Change*. Amsterdam: Kluwer, 169–90.

MITCHELL, B. (1980). 'The Dangers of Disguise: Old English Texts in Modern Punctuation', *Review of English Studies*, 31: 385–413; reprinted in B. Mitchell (ed.), *On Old English: Selected Papers* (Oxford: Basil Blackwell, 1988), 172–202.

—— (1985). *Old English Syntax*. Oxford: Oxford University Press.

—— (1991). 'The Englishness of Old English', in M. Godden, D. Gray, and T. Hoad (eds), *From Anglo-Saxon to Early Middle English: Studies Presented to E. G. Stanley*. Oxford: Clarendon Press, 163–81.

—— (1995). *An Invitation to Old English and Anglo-Saxon England*. Oxford: Blackwell.

MOORE, C. (2002a). 'Reporting Direct Speech in Early Modern Slander Depositions,' in D. Minkova and R. Stockwell (eds), *Studies in the History of the English Language: Millennial Perspectives*. Topics in English Linguistics, 39. Berlin: Mouton de Gruyter, 399–415.

—— (2002b). 'Writing Good Southerne: Local and Supralocal Norms in the Plumpton Letter Collection', *Language Variation and Change*, 14: 1–17.

MUFWENE, S., RICKFORD, J. R., BAILEY, G., and BAUGH, J. (eds) (1998). *African-American English: Structure, History, and Use*. London: Routledge.

MUGGLESTONE, L. C. (1996). ' "A Subject so Curious and Useful": Lindley Murray and Pronunciation', in I. Tieken-Boon van Ostade (ed.), *Two Hundred Years of Lindley Murray*. Munster, Germany: Nodus Publikationen, 145–63.

—— (1997). 'John Walker and Alexander Ellis: Antedating RP'. *Notes and Queries*, n.s. 44: 103–7.

—— (ed.) (2002a). *Lexicography and the OED. Pioneers in the Untrodden Forest*. Oxford: Oxford University Press.

—— (2002*b*). ' "Pioneers in the Untrodden Forest": The *New* English Dictionary', in L. C. Mugglestone (ed.), *Lexicography and the OED. Pioneers in the Untrodden Forest.* Oxford: Oxford University Press, 1–21.

—— (2002*c*) ' "An Historian and not a Critic": The Standard of Usage in the *OED*', in L. C. Mugglestone (ed.), *Lexicography and the OED. Pioneers in the Untrodden Forest.* Oxford: Oxford University Press, 189–206.

—— (2003*a*). *Talking Proper: The Rise of Accent as Social Symbol* (2nd edn.). Oxford: Oxford University Press.

—— (2003*b*). 'Sheridan in the Schoolroom', in F. Austin and C. Stray (eds), *The Teaching of English in the Eighteenth and Nineteenth Centuries. Essays for Ian Michael on his 88th Birthday.* Special issue of *Paradigm,* 2: 22–28.

—— (2004). *Lost for Words. The Hidden History of the Oxford English Dictionary.* London and New York: Yale University Press.

—— (2006, forthcoming). 'The Indefinable Something: Taboo and the English Diction-ary', in M. Gorji (ed.), *Rude Britannia* (London: Routledge).

MURISON, D. (1971). 'The Dutch Element in the Vocabulary of Scots, in A. J. Aitken, A. McIntosh, and H. Pálsson (eds), *Edinburgh Studies in English and Scots.* London: Longman, 159–76.

MURRAY, J. A. H., BRADLEY, H., CRAIGIE, W. A., and ONIONS, C. T. (eds) (1884–1928). *A New English Dictionary on Historical Principles.* Oxford: Clarendon Press.

[MURRAY, J. A. H and MURRAY, H. M. R.] (1910). 'English Language', in *Encyclopedia Britannica* (11th edn.). Cambridge: Cambridge University Press, 9: 587–600.

MURRAY, K. M. E. (1977). *Caught in the Web of Words. James A. H. Murray and the Oxford English Dictionary.* New Haven and London: Yale University Press.

NEVALA, M. (2004). *Address in Early English Correspondence; Its Forms and Socio-pragmatic Functions* (Mémoires de la Société Néophilologique de Helsinki, 64). Helsinki: Société Néophilologique.

NEVALAINEN, T. (1991). 'Motivated Archaism: The Use of Affirmative Periphrastic *Do* in Early Modern English Liturgical Prose', in D. Kastovsky (ed.), *Historical English Syntax.* Berlin and New York: Mouton de Gruyter, 303–20.

—— (1994). 'Ladies and Gentlemen: The Generalization of Titles in Early Modern English', in F. Fernández, M. Fuster, and J. J. Calvo (eds), *English Historical Linguistics 1992.* Amsterdam and Philadelphia: Benjamins, 317–27.

—— (forthcoming). *An Introduction to Early Modern English.* Edinburgh: Edinburgh University Press.

—— and RAUMOLIN-BRUNBERG, H. (1993). 'Early Modern British English', in M. Rissa-nen, M. Kytö, and M. Palander-Collin (eds), *Early English in the Computer Age.* Berlin and New York: Mouton de Gruyter, 53–73.

—— and RAUMOLIN-BRUNBERG, H. (2003). *Historical Sociolinguistics; Language Change in Tudor and Stuart England.* London: Longman.

—— , RAUMOLIN-BRUNBERG, H., and TRUDGILL, P. (2001). 'Chapters in the Social History of East Anglian English: The Case of Third Person Singular', in J. Fisiak and P. Trudgill (eds), *East Anglian English.* Cambridge: D. S. Brewer: 187–204.

NEWMEYER, F. J. (2001). 'Deconstructing grammaticalization', *Language Sciences*, 23: 93–340.

NEWSOME, D. (1997). *The Victorian World Picture: Perceptions and Introspections in an Age of Change*. London: J. Murray.

NIELSEN, H. F. (1981). *Old English and the Continental Germanic Languages*. Innsbruck: Institut für Sprachwissenschaft der Universität Innsbruck; Innsbrucker Beiträge zur Sprachwissenschaft, 33.

—— (1989). *The Germanic Languages: Origins and Early Dialectal Interrelations*. Tuscaloosa: University of Alabama Press.

—— (1998). *The Continental Backgrounds of English and its Insular Development Until 1154*. Odense: Odense University Press; A Journey through the History of the English Language in England and America, vol. 1; North-Western European Language Evolution, Supplement 19.

NÖJD, T. (1978). *Richard Hodges's The English Primrose (1644): A study of the strong-stressed vowels and diphthongs with some regard to A special help to ortographie (1643), The plainest directions (1649), Most plain directions for true-writing (1653)*. Stockholm: Almqvist & Wiksell International.

NOKES, D. (1995). *John Gay. A Profession of Friendship. A Critical Biography*. Oxford: Oxford University Press.

NURMI, A. (1999a). *A Social History of Periphrastic DO*. Helsinki: Société Néophilologique.

—— (1999b). 'The Corpus of Early English Correspondence Sampler (CEECS)', *ICAME Journal*, 23: 53–64.

Ó BAOILL, D. P (ed.) (1985). *Papers in Irish English*. Dublin: Irish Association for Applied Linguistics.

O'BRIEN O'KEEFFE, K. (1990). *Visible Song: Transitional Literacy in Old English Verse*. Cambridge: Cambridge University Press.

O'DONNELL, W. R. and TODD, L. (1992). *Variety in Contemporary English* (2nd edn.). London: Routledge.

OKASHA, E. (1971). *Hand-List of Anglo-Saxon Non-Runic Inscriptions*. Cambridge: Cambridge University Press.

—— (1992). 'The English Language in the Eleventh Century: The Evidence from Inscriptions,' in C. Hicks (ed.), *England in the Eleventh Century*. Stamford, Lincs.: Paul Watkins, 333–43.

ORTON, H. (1933). *The Phonology of a South Durham Dialect*. London: Kegan Paul, Trench, Trübner and Co.

OSSELTON, N. E. (1984). 'Informal Spelling Systems in Early Modern English: 1500–1800', in N. F. Blake and C. Jones (eds), *English Historical Linguistics: Studies in Development*. Sheffield: CECTAL, 123–37. Repr. in: M. Rydén, I. Tieken-Boon van Ostade, and M. Kytö (eds), *A Reader in Early Modern English*. Frankfurt: Peter Lang, 33–45.

PAGE, R. I. (1971). 'How Long did the Scandinavian Language Survive in England? The epigraphical evidence', in P. Clemoes and K. Hughes (eds), *England Before the Con-*

quest: Studies in Primary Sources Presented to Dorothy Whitelock. Cambridge: Cambridge University Press, 165–81.

—— (1987). *Runes*. London: British Museum Press.

—— (1999). *An Introduction to English Runes* (2nd edn.). Woodbridge: The Boydell Press.

PARKES, M. B. (1992). *Pause and Effect, an Introduction to the History of Punctuation in the West*. Aldershot: Scolar Press.

PARRY, D. (ed.) (1999). *A Grammar and Glossary of the Conservative Anglo-Welsh Dialects of Rural Wales*. Sheffield: National Centre for English Cultural Tradition.

PEARCE WILLIAMS, L. (1965). *Michael Faraday. A Biography*. London: Chapman and Hall.

PENHALLURICK, R. (1991). *The Anglo-Welsh Dialects of North Wales*. Frankfurt am Main: Peter Lang (University of Bamberg Studies in English Linguistics, vol. 27).

—— and WILLMOTT, A. (2000). 'Dialect/"England's Dreaming"', in R. Penhallurick (ed.), *Debating Dialect: Essays on the Philosophy of Dialect Study*. Cardiff: University of Wales Press, 5–45.

PHILLIPPS, K. C. (1984). *Language and Class in Victorian England*. Oxford: Basil Blackwell.

PHILLIPSON, R. (2003). *English-Only Europe? Challenging Language Policy*. London: Routledge.

PINKER, S. (1994). *The Language Instinct*. Harmondsworth: Penguin.

PITTOCK, M. (1999). *Celtic Identity and the British Image*. Manchester: Manchester University Press.

PRCIC, T. (2003). 'Is English Still a Foreign Language?', *The European English Messenger*, 12: 35–7.

PRZEDLACKA, J. (2002). *Estuary English?: A sociophonetic study of teenage speech in the Home Counties*. Frankfurt: Peter Lang.

PUTTER, A. (1995). *Sir Gawain and the Green Knight and French Arthurian Romance*. Oxford: Clarendon Press.

QUINN, D. B. (1990). *Explorers and Colonies: America, 1500–1625*. London: The Hambleton Press.

QUIRK, R. (1985). *A Comprehensive Grammar of the English Language*. London: Longman.

—— and WIDDOWSON, H. (eds.) (1985). *English in the World: Teaching and Learning the Language and Literatures*. Cambridge and New York: Cambridge University Press for the British Council.

QUIRK, R., GREENBAUM, S., LEECH, G., and SVARTVIK, J. (1972). A *Grammar of Contemporary English*. Longman: Harlow.

QVIST, G. (1981). *John Hunter*. London: William Heinemann Medical Books Ltd.

RAW, B. C. (1978). *The Art and Background of Old English Poetry*. London: Edward Arnold.

READ, A. W. (2002). 'British Recognition of American Speech in the Eighteenth Century' (1933), in R. W. Bailey (ed.), *Milestones in the History of English in America*. Durham: Duke University Press for the American Dialect Society.

REANEY, P. H. (1925). 'On Certain Phonological Features of the Dialect of London in the Twelfth Century', *Englische Studien*, 59: 321–45.

REDDICK, A. (1990). *The Making of Johnson's Dictionary 1746–1773* [rev. edn. 1996]. Cambridge: University Press.

RIGG, A. G. (1992). *A History of Anglo-Latin Literature 1066–1422*. Cambridge: Cambridge University Press.

RISSANEN, M. (1991). 'Spoken Language and the History of *Do*-periphrasis', in D. Kastovsky (ed.), *Historical English Syntax*. Berlin and New York: Mouton de Gruyter, 321–342.

—— (2000*a*). 'Standardization and the Language of Early Statutes', in L. Wright (ed.), *The Development of Standard English, 1300–1800: Theories, Descriptions, Conflicts*. Cambridge: Cambridge University Press, 117–30.

—— (2000*b*). 'The World of English Historical Corpora: From Cædmon to the Computer Age', *Journal of English Linguistics*, 28: 7–20.

ROACH, P., HARTMAN, J., and SETTER, J. (2003). *English Pronouncing Dictionary*. Cambridge: Cambridge University Press.

ROBINSON, O. W. (1992). *Old English and its Closest Relatives: A Survey of the Earliest Germanic Languages*. London: Routledge.

ROMAINE, S. (1982). 'The English Language in Scotland', in R. W. Bailey and M. Görlach (eds), *English as a World Language*. Ann Arbor: University of Michigan Press, 56–83.

—— (1994). 'Hawai'i Creole English as a Literary Language', *Language in Society*, 23: 527–54.

—— (ed.) (1998). *The Cambridge History of the English Language*. Vol. IV: *1776–1997*. Cambridge: Cambridge University Press.

ROSEWARNE, D. (1984). 'Estuary English', *Times Educational Supplement*, 19 October 1984: 29.

—— (1994*a*). 'Estuary English—Tomorrow's RP ?', *English Today*, 10/1: 3–9.

—— (1994*b*). 'Pronouncing Estuary English', *English Today*, 10/4: 3–9.

ROTHWELL, W. (1968). 'The Teaching of French in Medieval England', *Modern Language Review*, 63: 37–46.

—— (1976). 'The Role of French in Thirteenth-Century England', *Bulletin of the John Rylands University Library of Manchester*, 58: 445–66.

—— (1991). 'The Missing Link in English Etymology: Anglo-French', *Medium Aevum*, 60: 173–96.

—— (1998). 'Arrivals and Departures: The Adoption of French Terminology in Middle English', *English Studies*, 79: 144–65.

RUBEL, V. (1941). *Poetic Diction in the English Renaissance: From Skelton through Spenser*. New York: Modern Language Association.

RYDÉN, M. and BRORSTRÖM, S. (1987). *The Be/Have Variation with Intransitives in English*. Stockholm: Almqvist & Wiksell.

SALMON, V. (1996). 'Thomas Harriot (1650–1621) and the Origins of Algonkian Linguistics' (1994), in K. Koerner (ed.), *Language and Society in Early Modern England: Selected Essays, 1981–1994*. Amsterdam: John Benjamins, 143–72.

SAMUELS, M. L. (1963). 'Some Applications of Middle English Dialectology', *English Studies*, 44: 81–94.

—— (1972). *Linguistic Evolution, with Special Reference to English*. Cambridge: Cambridge University Press.

—— (1981). 'Spelling and Dialect in the Late and Post-Middle English Periods', in M. Benskin and M. Samuels (eds), *So meny people, longages and tonges: philological essays in Scots and mediaeval English presented to Angus McIntosh*. Edinburgh: Middle English Dialect Project, 43–54.

—— (1985). 'The Great Scandinavian Belt', in R. Eaton *et al.* (eds), *Papers from the Fourth International Conference on English Historical Linguistics*. Current Issues in Linguistic Theory 41. Amsterdam: John Benjamins, 269–81.

SCHÄFER, J. (1980). *Documentation in the OED: Shakespeare and Nashe as Test Cases*. Oxford: Clarendon Press.

SCHNEIDER, E. (2003). 'The Dynamics of New Englishes: From Identity Construction to Dialect Birth,' *Language*, 79: 233–81.

SCOTT, F. N. (1917). 'The Standard of American Speech,' *The English Journal*, 6 (January): 1–15.

SCRAGG, D. G. (1974). *A History of English Spelling*. Manchester: Manchester University Press.

—— (ed.) (1991). *The Battle of Maldon, AD 991*. Oxford: Basil Blackwell in Association with the Manchester Centre for Anglo-Saxon Studies.

—— (1992b). 'Spelling Variations in Eleventh-Century English', in C. Hicks (ed.), *England in the Eleventh Century: Proceedings of the 1990 Harlaxton Symposium*. Stamford: Paul Watkins, 347–54.

SEIDLHOFER, B. (2003). *Controversies in Applied Linguistics: Section 1. The global spread of English*. Oxford: Oxford University Press.

SERJEANTSON, M. S. (1935). *A History of Foreign Words in English*. London: Kegan Paul.

SEYMOUR, M. (2000). *Mary Shelley*. London: John Murray.

SHARPE, R. (1997). *A Handlist of the Latin Writers of Great Britain and Ireland before 1540*. Turnhout: Brepols.

SHELSTON, D. and A. (1990). *The Industrial City, 1820–1870*. London: Macmillan.

SHORT, I. (1979–80). 'On Bilingualism in Anglo-Norman England', *Romance Philology*, 33: 467–79.

—— (1992). 'Patrons and Polyglots: French Literature in Twelfth-Century England', *Anglo-Norman Studies* 14: 229–49.

SISAM, K. (1953). *Studies in the History of Old English Literature*. Oxford: Oxford University Press.

SKEAT, W. O. (ed.) (1973). *George Stephenson: The Engineer and his Letters*. London: The Institution of Mechanical Engineers.

SMITH, A. H. (1956). *English Place-Name Elements*. 2 vols. English Place-Name Society 25–26. Cambridge: Cambridge University Press.

SMITH, J. J. (1988a). 'The Trinity Gower D-Scribe and his Work on Two Early *Canterbury Tales* Manuscripts', in J. J. Smith (ed.), *The English of Chaucer and his Contemporaries: Essays by M. L. Samuels and J. J. Smith*. Aberdeen: Aberdeen University Press, 51–69.

—— (1988b). 'Spelling and Tradition in Fifteenth-century Copies of Gower's *Confessio Amantis*', in M. L. Samuels and J. J. Smith (eds), *The English of Chaucer*. Aberdeen: Aberdeen University Press, 96–113.

—— (1991). 'Tradition and Innovation in South-West-Midland Middle English', in F. Riddy (ed.), *Regionalism in Late Medieval Manuscripts and Texts: Essays Celebrating the Publication of a Linguistic Atlas of Late Mediaeval English*. Cambridge: D. S. Brewer, 53–65.

—— (1995). 'The Great Vowel Shift in the North of England, and Some Spellings in Manuscripts of Chaucer's *Reeve's Tale*', *Neuphilologische Mitteilungen*, 94: 259–77.

—— (1996a). *An Historical Study of English: Function, Form and Change*. London: Routledge.

—— (1996b). 'Language and Style in Malory', in A. Edwards and E. Archibald (eds), *A Companion to Malory*. Woodbridge: Boydell and Brewer, 97–113.

—— (1999). *Essentials of Early English*. London: Routledge.

—— (2000). 'Scots', in G. Price (ed.), *Languages in Britain and Ireland*. Oxford: Blackwell, 159–70.

SOLOMON, H. M. (1996). *The Rise of Robert Dodsley*. Carbondale and Edwardsville: Southern Illinois University Press.

STARNES, D. T. and NOYES, G. E. 1991. *The English Dictionary from Cawdrey to Johnson, 1604–1755* (with an introduction and a select bibliography by G. Stein). Amsterdam: John Benjamins.

Statement by the Directors of the Edinburgh Academy Explanatory of the Scheme of that Institution. (1824). Edinburgh: John Hutchinson.

STEIN, D. (1990). *The Semantics of Syntactic Change; Aspects of the Evolution of DO in English*. Berlin and New York: Mouton de Gruyter.

STENROOS, M. (forthcoming). 'A Variationist Approach to Middle English Dialects', *Studia Anglica Posnaniensia*.

STOCKWELL, R. P. (1961). 'The Middle English "long close" and "long open" mid vowels', *Texas Studies in Literature and Language*, 2: 259–69.

—— (1975). 'Problems in the interpretation of the Great English Vowel Shift', in D. L. Goyvaerts and G. K. Pullum (eds), *Essays on the Sound Pattern of English*. Ghent: E. Story-Scientia, 331–53.

—— and MINKOVA, D. (1988*a*). 'The English Vowel Shift: Problems of coherence and explanation', in D. Kastovsky and G. Bauer (eds), *Luick Revisited*. Tübingen: Gunter Narr Verlag, 355–94.

—— and—— (1988*b*). 'A Rejoinder to Lass', in D. Kastovsky and G. Bauer (eds), *Luick Revisited*. Tübingen: Gunter Narr Verlag, 411–17.

—— and—— (1990). 'The Early Modern English vowels, more O'Lass', *Diachronica* VII: 199–214.

—— and—— (1997). 'On Drifts and Shifts', *Studia Anglica Posnaniensia*, XXXI: 283–303.

—— and—— (1999). 'Explanations of Sound Change: Contradictions between dialect data and theories of chain shifting', *Leeds Studies in English* (*New Series*), 30: 83–101.

STRANG, B. M. H. (1970). *A History of English*. London: Methuen.

STUART-SMITH, J. (2003). 'The Phonology of Modern Urban Scots', in J. Corbett *et al.* (eds), *The Edinburgh Companion to Scots*. Edinburgh: Edinburgh University Press, 110–37.

STUBBS, M. (1983). *Discourse Analysis*. Oxford: Blackwell.

SUTHERLAND, J. (1990). *Mrs Humphry Ward: Eminent Victorian, Pre-eminent Edwardian*. Oxford: Clarendon Press.

SVARTVIK, J. (ed.) (1990). *The London-Lund Corpus of Spoken English: Description and Research*. Lund: Lund University Press.

SWEET, H. (1908). *The Sounds of English, an Introduction to Phonetics*. Oxford: Clarendon Press.

SZEMERÉNYI, O. J. L. (1996). *Introduction to Indo-European Linguistics*. Oxford: Oxford University Press.

TAAVITSAINEN, I. and PAIVI, P. (eds) (2004). *Medical and Scientific Writing in Late Medieval English*. Cambridge: Cambridge University Press.

TAYLOR, E. (1987). 'Shakespeare's Use of *eth* and *es* Endings of Verbs in the First Folio', in V. Salmon and E. Burness (eds), *A Reader in the Language of Shakespearean Drama*. Amsterdam and Philadelphia: Benjamins, 349–69.

THOMAS, A. R. (1994). 'English in Wales', in R. Burchfield (ed.), *The Cambridge History of the English Language*. Vol. v: *English in Britain and Overseas*. Cambridge: Cambridge University Press, 94–147.

THOMAS, D. (1990). *Henry Fielding*. London: Weidenfeld and Nicolson.

THOMASON, S. G. (2001). *Language Contact: An Introduction*. Edinburgh: Edinburgh University Press.

—— and KAUFFMAN, T. (1988). *Language Contact, Creolization, and Genetic Linguistics*. Berkeley: University of California Press.

TIEKEN-BOON VAN OSTADE, I. (1987). *The Auxiliary Do in Eighteenth Century English: A Sociohistorical-Linguistic Approach*. Dordrecht: Foris.

Tieken-Boon van Ostade, I. (1990). 'Drydens versies van The tempest en Troilus and Cressida: De bewerker als purist', in *Traditie & Progressie. Handelingen van het 40ste Nederlands Filologencongres.* 's Gravenhage: SDU Uitgeverij, 161–9.

—— (1994). 'Standard and Non-Standard Pronominal Usage in English, with Special Reference to the Eighteenth Century', in D. Stein and I. Tieken-Boon van Ostade (eds), *Towards a Standard Language 1600–1800.* Berlin/New York: Mouton de Gruyter, 217–42.

—— (1998). 'Standardization of English Spelling: The Eighteenth-Century Printers' Contribution', in J. Fisiak and M. Krygier (eds), *English Historical Linguistics 1996.* Berlin: Mouton de Gruyter, 457–70.

—— (1999). 'Of Formulas and Friends: Expressions of Politeness in John Gay's Letters', in G. A. J. Tops, B. Devriendt, and S. Geukens (eds), *Thinking English Grammar. To Honour Xavier Dekeyser, Professor Emeritus.* Leuven/Paris: Peeters, 99–112.

—— (2000a). 'Sociohistorical Linguistics and the Observer's Paradox', in D. Kastovsky and A. Mettinger (eds), *The History of English in a Social Context.* Berlin/New York: Mouton de Gruyter, 441–61.

—— (2000b). 'Social Network Analysis and the Language of Sarah Fielding', in I. Tieken-Boon van Ostade, T. Nevalainen, and L. Caon (eds), *Social Network Analysis and the History of English,* special issue of *EJES* 4.3: 291–301.

—— (2000c). 'Normative Studies in England', in S. Auroux, E. F. K. Koerner, H.-J. Niederehe, and K. Versteegh (eds), *History of the Language Sciences/Geschichte der Sprachwissenschaften/ Histoire des Sciences du Langage.* Berlin/New York: Walter de Gruyter, 876–87.

—— (2000d). 'Female Grammarians of the Eighteenth Century'. *Historical Socio-linguistics and Sociohistorical Linguistics* 1. <http://www.let.leidenuniv.nl/hsl_shl/> (→Contents→Articles).

—— (2002a). '*You Was* and Eighteenth-Century Normative Grammar', in K. Lenz and R. Möhlig (eds), *Of Dyuersite & Chaunge of Langage: Essays Presented to Manfred Görlach on the Occasion of his 65th Birthday.* Heidelberg: C. Winter Universitätsverlag, 88–102.

—— (2002b). 'Robert Lowth and the Strong Verb System', *Language Sciences* 24: 459–69.

—— (2003a). '"Tom's grammar": The Genesis of Lowth's *Short Introduction to English Grammar* Revisited', in F. Austin and C. Stray (eds), *The Teaching of English in the Eighteenth and Nineteenth Centuries. Essays for Ian Michael on his 88th Birthday.* Special issue of *Paradigm,* 2: 36–45.

—— (2003b). 'Lowth's Language', in M. Dossena and C. Jones (eds), *Insights into Late Modern English.* Bern etc.: Peter Lang, 241–64.

—— and Bax, R. (2002). 'Of Dodsley's Projects and Linguistic Influence: The Language of Johnson and Lowth', *Historical Sociolinguistics and Sociohistorical Linguistics* 2. <http://www.let.leidenuniv.nl/hsl_shl/> (→Contents→Articles).

—— Nevalainen, T., and Caon, L. (eds) (2000). *Social Network Analysis and the History of English,* special issue of *European Journal of English Studies* 4/3.

TILLYARD, S. (1994). *Aristocrats. Caroline, Emily, Louisa and Sarah Lennox 1740–1832.* London: Chatto & Windus.

TODD, L. (1999). *Green English: Ireland's Influence on the English Language.* Dublin: O'Brien Press.

TOLKIEN, J. (1934). 'Chaucer as a Philologist: *The Reeve's Tale*', *Transactions of the Philological Society*, 1–70.

TOON, T. E. (1983). *The Politics of Early Old English Sound Change.* New York: Academic Press.

TOWNEND, M. (2000). 'Viking Age England as a Bilingual Society', in D. M. Hadley and J. D. Richards (eds), *Cultures in Contact: Scandinavian Settlement in England in the Ninth and Tenth Centuries.* Turnhout: Brepols, 89–105.

—— (2001). 'Contextualizing the *Knútsdrápur*: Skaldic Praise-Poetry at the Court of Cnut', *Anglo-Saxon England*, 30: 145–79.

—— (2002). *Language and History in Viking Age England: Linguistic Relations between Speakers of Old Norse and Old English.* Turnhout: Brepols.

TROTTER, D. A. (ed.) (2000). *Multilingualism in Later Medieval Britain.* Cambridge: D. S. Brewer.

TRUDGILL, P. (ed.) (1984). *Language in the British Isles.* Cambridge: Cambridge University Press.

—— (1986). *Dialects in Contact.* Oxford: Blackwell.

—— (1990). *The Dialects of England.* Oxford: Blackwell.

—— (1999a). 'Standard English. What It Isn't', in T. Bex and R. J. Watts (eds), *Standard English. The Widening Debate.* London: Routledge, 117–28.

—— (1999b). *The Dialects of England.* (2nd edn.). Oxford: Blackwell.

—— and CHAMBERS, J. K. (1991). *Dialects of English: Studies in Grammatical Variation.* London: Longman.

—— and HANNAH, J. (1994). *International English: A Guide to the Varieties of Standard English* (3rd edn.). London and New York: Edward Arnold.

——, PETER, ARTHUR HUGHES, and DOMINIC WATT (2005). *English Accents and Dialects.* 4th edn. London: Hodder Education.

TRUSS, L. (2003). *Eats, Shoots & Leaves. The Zero Tolerance Approach to Punctuation.* London: Profile Books.

'Twenty-Second Report of the Committee on Devonshire Verbal Provincialisms' (1910). *Transactions of the Devonshire Association for the Advancement of Science, Literature, and Art*, 64–92.

TURVILLE-PETRE, T. (1996). *England the Nation: Language, Literature, and National Identity, 1290–1340.* Oxford: Clarendon Press.

TWEDDLE, D., BIDDLE, M., and KJØLBYE-BIDDLE, B. (1995). *Corpus of Anglo-Saxon Stone Sculpture Volume IV: South-East England.* Oxford: The British Academy.

UPTON, C. (1995). 'Mixing and Fudging in Midland and Southern Dialects of England: the *cup* and *foot* vowels', in J. W. Lewis (ed.), *Studies in General and English Phonetics: Essays in Honour of Professor J. D. O'Connor*. London: Routledge, 385–94.

UPTON, C. and WIDDOWSON, J. D. A. (1999). *Lexical Erosion in English Regional Dialects*. Sheffield: National Centre for English Cultural Tradition.

—— and WALES, K. (eds) (1999). *Dialectal Variation in English: Proceedings of the Harold Orton Centenary Conference 1998*. Leeds: Leeds Studies in English New Series XXX.

VAN COETSEM, F. (1988). *Loan Phonology and the Two Transfer Types in Language Contact*. Dordrecht: Foris.

VICKERY, A. (1998). *The Gentleman's Daughter. Women's Lives in Georgian England*. New Haven and London: Yale University Press.

WAKELIN, M. (1977). *English Dialects: An Introduction* (rev. edn.). London: Athlone Press.

WALDRON, R. (1979). *Sense and Sense Development*. London: Deutsch.

WALES, K. (2002). "North of Watford gap": A cultural history of Northern English (from 1700)', in R. J. Watts and P. Trudgill (eds), *Alternative Histories of English*. London: Routledge, 45–66.

WALKER CHAMBERS, W. and WILKIE, J. (1970). *A Short History of the German Language*. London: Methuen.

WARD-GILMAN, E. (1990). 'Dictionaries as a Source of Usage Controversy', *Dictionaries*, 12: 75–84.

WAREING, J. (1980). 'Changes in the Geographical Distribution of the Recruitment of Apprentices to the London Companies 1486–1750', *Journal of Historical Geography*, 6: 241–49.

WA THIONG'O, N. (1986). *Decolonising the Mind: The Politics of Language in African Literature*. London: James Currey.

WATT, D. and TILLOTSON, J. (2001). 'A Spectrographic analysis of Vowel Fronting in Bradford English', *English World-Wide* 22/2, 269–302.

WATT, D. (2002). '"I don't speak with a Geordie accent, I speak, like, the Northern accent": Contact-induced levelling in the Tyneside vowel system', *Journal of Sociolinguistics*, 6, 44–63.

WATTS, R. J. and TRUDGILL, P. (eds) (2002). *Alternative Histories of English*. London: Routledge.

WEINREICH, U. (1953). *Languages in Contact: Findings and Problems*. New York: Linguistic Circle of New York.

WELLS, J. C. (1982). *Accents of English 2: The British Isles*. Cambridge: Cambridge University Press.

WENZEL, S. (1994). *Macaronic Sermons: Bilingualism and Preaching in Late-Medieval England*. Ann Arbor, MI: The University of Michigan Press.

WILLIAM CANDEN, *Remains Concerning Britain*. Yorkshire: EP Publishign, 1974.

WILSON, R. M. (1943). 'English and French in England: 1100–1300', *History*, 28: 37–60.

WINER, L. (1997). 'Six Vernacular Texts from Trinidad, 1838–1851,' in E. W. Schneider (ed.), *Englishes around the World: Studies in Honour of Manfred Görlach*. 2 vols. Amsterdam: John Benjamins, 2: 69–83.

WOLFE, P. (1973). *Linguistic Change and the Great Vowel Shift in English*. Berkeley, CA: University of California Press.

WOLLMANN, A. (1993). 'Early Latin Loan-words in Old English', *Anglo-Saxon England*, 22: 1–26.

—— (1996). 'Scandinavian Loanwords in Old English', in H. F. Nielsen and L. Schøsler (eds), *The Origins and Developments of Emigrant Languages*. Odense: Odense University Press, 215–42.

WRIGHT, J. (ed.) (1905). *The English Dialect Grammar*. Oxford: Frowde.

—— (1914). *Old English Grammar* (2nd edn.). London: Oxford University Press.

WRIGHT, L. (1996). *Sources of London English: Medieval Thames Vocabulary*. Oxford: Clarendon Press.

—— (ed.) (2000). *The Development of Standard English 1300–1800*. Cambridge: Cambridge University Press.

—— (2002). 'Code-intermediate Phenomena in Medieval Mixed-Language Business Texts,' *Language Sciences*, 24: 471–89.

WRIGHT, S. (1994). 'The Critic and the Grammarians: Joseph Addison and the Prescriptivists', in D. Stein and I. Tieken-Boon van Ostade (eds), *Towards a Standard Language 1600–1800*. Berlin/New York: Mouton de Gruyter, 243–84.

WYLD, H. C. (1907). *The Growth of English*. London: John Murray.

—— (1936). *A History of Modern Colloquial English* (3rd edn.). Oxford: Blackwell.

WEBSITES

http://www.bbc.co.uk/radio4/routesofenglish

http://www.collectbritain.co.uk/collections/dialects/

http://www.bbc.co.uk/voices/

http://www.phon.ucl.ac.uk/home/estuary

http://www.plainenglish.co.uk/

http://ets.umdl.umich.edu/m/mec/

http://dictionary.oed.com/

http://www.queens-english-society.com/

INDEX